MW01148719

# GAMEMASTERS
## *of the* WORLD

*"The essence of life is discovering what is on the other side of the mountain. We start out with a dream, and are propelled by the challenge of the unknown, the lure and the mystery of faraway places.*
*Upon reaching the destination, we realize that there is no end. Distant mountains lie before us; it is time to meditate and give thanks.*
*Most of all, we must share with others the delight of God's creation."*

**—Chris R. Klineburger**

# GAMEMASTERS
## *of the* WORLD

A CHRONICLE OF SPORT HUNTING AND CONSERVATION

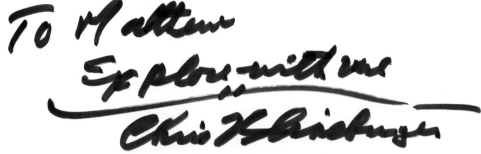

*To Matthew*
*Explore with me*
*Chris Klineburger*

AN AUTOBIOGRAPHY OF THE PIONEER OF
ASIAN HUNTING & CONSERVATION

## Chris R. Klineburger

EDITED BY

**Stan Skinner**

COORDINATED BY

**Grace Mathis**

*and Gene Klineburger*

Skyhorse Publishing

Skyhorse Publishing books may be purchased in bulk at special discounts for sales promotion, corporate gifts, fund-raising, or educational purposes. Special editions can also be created to specifications. For details, contact the Special Sales Department, Skyhorse Publishing, 555 Eighth Avenue, Suite 903, New York, NY 10018 or info@skyhorsepublishing.com.

www.skyhorsepublishing.com

10 9 8 7 6 5 4 3 2 1

Library of Congress Cataloging-in-Publication Data

Klineburger, Chris R.
  Gamemasters of the world : the chronicle of sport hunting and conservation : an autobiography of the pioneer of Asian hunting & conservation / Chris R. Klineburger.
      p. cm.
  Includes bibliographical references and index.
  ISBN 978-1-61608-157-7 (alk. paper)
  1. Klineburger, Chris R. 2. Hunters--United States--Biographpy. 3. Taxidermists--United States--Biographpy. 4. Hunting--United States. I. Title.
  SK17.K55A3 2010
  799.292--dc22
  [B]
                              2010022553

Printed in China

## DEDICATION

### GOD

—the great Creator of this wonderful world and everything in it. He has provided magnificent terrain of mountains, plains, deserts, tundra, and ice; He created lakes and streams and seas; He created countless vegetations from giant trees to lichen; He created fish, mammals, insects, and birds of countless varieties; He created man and gave him stewardship over it all.

*GENESIS 1:26*
*"Let us make man in our image and likeness, and let them rule over the fish of the sea and the birds of the air, over all the earth, and over all creatures that move along the ground."*

There are many theories of evolution, but if one opens his eyes to the millions of living things, he would see they could not start from amoebas without a profound Divine guidance—a Creator. Man evolved late in the process as a predator of sorts. He developed skills and weapons for hunting and fishing and even learned how to domesticate living things. He became the most important player in the Balance of Nature. If removed, there is no "Balance." Sport hunting and fishing is a continuance of man's inbred heritage from his primitive ancestors and is an important modern role in the dominion over the earth that God gave us.

*My prayer to God is that people be good stewards over all wildlife and the habitation, which is the earth itself. And to give guidance and knowledge to our forestry and wildlife officials to do proper management of these renewable resources. And for activist groups to begin to work for true and honest conservation. To continue to guide and direct the hunting-conservation organizations in their enhancement programs of propagating wildlife. And thank God for providing us with such great outdoors and all living things. Amen.*

It is said that everyone has a purpose in life. It took me a long time to realize it, as I look behind and put all the pieces together, I can see perhaps my direction was shaped by a Divine guidance. Alone, this little boy from a small Arizona town could certainly not have followed the path seen in this document.

—*Chris R. Klineburger*

# Contents

# Contents

# Acknowledgments

Neither this historical document nor my accomplishments would have been possible without the help of others. From my early childhood to the present, others made it all possible through upbringing, faith, understanding, teachings, patience, camaraderie, toil, and encouragement.

My folks taught me life's values, responsibility, to work hard, and to respect the environment. My brothers partnered with me when growing up, throughout our life's occupation and closeness in our waning years. Our firm was a "family" business and I had continuous support from Bert and Gene, as well as their wives. My own family, Colleene and Kent, made it possible for me to be absent during those long trips away from the office.

I must also acknowledge those many guides and outfitters all over the world who provided knowledge and opportunity, as well as the numerous hunting companions, whose expertise and camaraderie contributed to the fulfillments. I owe the deepest gratitude to the government officials in charge of wildlife in those Third World countries for their understanding and encouragement that allowed me to go forward with the sportsmen-financed wildlife programs. I humbly recognize the many hunting and conservation organizations that afforded support.

I honor those countless individuals who kept after me to write a book, while pointing out that these priceless records may become lost forever.

Once inspired to start writing, I relied totally on my beloved companion, Grace Mathis, to tackle the difficult job of structuring it into a readable format, while correcting my grade-school level of writing. Her high-tech knowledge of the computer allowed her to format it into just what the publisher wanted. And I must honor the person that took it to the next level of perfection, Stan Skinner, the genius who edited the copy after putting in long hours after his regular job as editor of *Safari* magazine and the *Safari Times* tabloid.

# Prologue

The Klineburgers' father, Chris Sr., took his sons, Chris, Bert, and Gene hunting for rabbits, rattlesnakes, and other small game in Sulphur Springs Valley near their hometown of Warren, Arizona, just three miles from the Mexican border. Chris, born in 1927, was nine when his dad passed away, so during the Great Depression, cottontail and even jackrabbit—along with the occasional delicacy of rattlesnake—were an important part of the menu.

Hunting and the lonely trapline gave Chris time to study nature and wildlife and gain respect for their balance. As time went by he saw how people utilized wildlife for food and clothing as well as man's inherent desire to hunt. He also observed some cases of waste and lack of concern for the wildlife and environment. As a result, it became Chris's mission to educate all concerned about proper utilization of the earth's natural and renewable resources.

After high school, toward the end of World War II, Chris got a job as hiking counselor for the YMCA Camp in Washington at Spirit Lake by Mount St. Helens. He then proceeded into the Navy for three years where his ship took him to exciting destinations like Bikini Atoll for the atomic bomb tests, China, and the South Pacific, all of which added to his desire to travel and explore. His ship also got him to Seattle, where the famed Jonas Brothers Taxidermy Studio was located.

After the Navy, Chris went to the University of Arizona in Tucson and worked his way through college doing taxidermy in his own studio in the basement of a sporting goods store. During this time, he collected most of the Southwest and Sonora big game, including desert sheep, Coues deer, javelina, desert mule deer, Kaibab mule deer, antelope, and White Mountain elk. He was one of the early members of the Arizona Game Protective Association. Summer vacations found him in Seattle working for Guy Jonas, where Bert was already employed full time as a taxidermist.

After receiving a degree in mechanical engineering, Chris got a job with Boeing Airplane Company as an engineer in Seattle. By 1952, it was goodbye to engineering and hello to the outdoor world for good. Brother Gene joined Bert and Chris in taking over Jonas Brothers of Seattle and building it into an outdoor empire that included not only the world's leading taxidermy chain, but also retail stores and taxidermy receiving stations in Anchorage, Fairbanks, and Nome, as well as Seattle, featuring Alaskan arts and crafts and fur garments. They had their own fur manufacturing company, tannery, and fur skin trading business. They literally "introduced" fur parkas to Alaska and the rest of the world through a wholesale fur business.

Post World War II was effectively an era that was the beginning of sport hunting, as we know it today. It was a time when people had money and leisure time, as well as the availability of air travel making distant travel a reality. It was also the time that the Klineburgers were involved in the ground floor of most all that happened in sport hunting.

The Klineburgers' foresight and ambitious drive, for the first time in hunting history, brought the hunting and outfitting fraternity closer together, as well as opening new hunting opportunities at affordable prices. They became involved with guides and outfitters the world over, encouraging and advising them of the need for quality hunting arrangements, and to conserve their renewable resource and the habitat. In those postwar years, the Seattle taxidermy operation became the most important link between sportsmen and hunting operations. The Klineburgers became involved in the formation of hunting clubs for the purpose of bringing together those with common interests as well as conserving the wildlife that they loved.

Chris, being the single brother with no home ties in those early days, spent much of his time away from Seattle managing the stores. There was always time for hunting so he collected specimens of most North American game. In the late '50s, he spent considerable time with the Alaska Eskimos hunting by dog team and skin boat in an attempt to develop a fair chase sport for marine mammals and other game.

In 1960, the Klineburgers had just purchased an Eskimo arts and crafts store in Nome, so Chris invited Colleene, a lady friend from Seattle, to join him in the takeover and they decided to get married on the spot...an occasion not known to happen before in Nome! Chris even flew to St. Lawrence Island on the wedding day to pick up some muktuk from a freshly killed whale to serve at the reception. Chris and Colleene were married on May 7, 1960 to the delight of their new Eskimo friends and surprise to their families. Thus was Colleene's introduction to the Company—taking inventory before and after the ceremony. After 42 years of adventurous marriage, Colleene succumbed to cancer in 2002.

In the winter of 1961–62 Chris spent a few months in Kampala, Uganda, training taxidermists after setting up Jonas Brothers of Africa. The Ugandan connection, which the Klineburger brothers were partners in from the start, led to actual booking of hunts along with airline and hotel arrangements. Thus, instead of a "guide referral" business, Jonas Brothers Worldwide Travel was formed.

Before that, Africa safaris were in their infancy, with only a few of the relatively elite going there. The Klineburgers' involvement brought the first "affordable" safaris to the public. It was here also that much of their dealings were at government levels, showing them, with proper utilization of wildlife, there could be many benefits to the country, the people, and the game. Therefore, the Klineburger firm made their mark throughout Africa and in doing so they explored and collected specimens from all corners of the continent. In most areas, they trained in proper field care of trophies and even established trophy forwarding depots and procedures for proper shipping and documentation.

North America and Africa were mere steppingstones for the Klineburgers, as the rest of the world, especially Asia, was a challenge. India Shikars were the only thing going in that fourth of the world's land mass.

Chris had studied the writings of the early explorers of Inner Asia, which era ended in the mid-1920s. Since then most of Asia was closed to travel until after WW II when the doors were slowly opened one by one. In many instances, hunting was among the first, if not the first, tourism.

Knowing that most all these countries had either no game department or wildlife program, Chris developed the sportsmen-financed wildlife program effort, which included the introduction of wildlife management, game reserves, and proper utilization of renewable resources. His program included opportunities for foreign sportsmen to collect specimens and bringing in an influx of hard currency, part of which must go into management of all wildlife, whether hunted or not. The program also included training of hunting staff for proper outfitting, guiding, field care of animals, safety, and all other attributes of handling clients and their specimens.

Through the Klineburgers' friendship with officials in Iran, as well as training two Persian taxidermists for the country's museum work, in 1965 permission was granted for Chris and Colleene to hunt various sheep species and start a private hunting operation, opening the doors for foreign sportsmen to follow. On the same trip, the couple continued on to India to collect a tiger, panther, sambar, axis deer, and muntjac.

Asia then became a major focus of attention for the Klineburgers. In the late '60s the program was introduced into Afghanistan and Mongolia. While Bert was still focused mainly on African programs, Chris's prime focus was on Asia. In 1970, Chris led the first expedition into the U.S.S.R. opening the world's largest nation to hunting by foreigners. Other nations that followed were Nepal in 1974 and China in 1984.

When the South Pacific surfaced as a hunting destination back in the '60s, Chris worked with those first operators in Australia and New Zealand to establish their tariffs and hunting conditions.

Most of the hunting programs in Asia that existed had the Klineburger signature on them. Chris himself negotiated or led most all the maiden exploratory trips for setting up hunting programs all over Asia.

By the late '70s, Chris's brothers Bert and Gene left the organization. Bert went to Central African Republic to manage a safari company established by the government and foreign partners, while Gene retired. In the meantime, the company name was changed to Klineburger Brothers to prevent confusion with Jonas facilities in Colorado and New York. Chris, Colleene, and their son Kent continued the business, while closing down branches and nonrelated enterprises, concentrating on taxidermy and the hunting travel business.

In 1996, Chris turned the reins over to his son Chris Kent, and in the name Klineburger Enterprises, streamlined the business to specialized taxidermy, including museum and trophy room design, trophy appraisals and sales, trophy room restoration, and museum donations.

Not wanting Chris's pioneering of hunting & conservation and lifetime achievements to be unnoticed, various organizations, including Safari Club International, the Weatherby Foundation and the Water for Wildlife Foundation honored him at a banquet in January of 2007 in Seattle.

Chris's other achievements include a Weatherby Award of Special Recognition and being inducted into the Hunting Hall of Fame and also the Mountain Hunter Hall of Fame.

# The Renewable Resource of Wildlife

Editor's note: This article may appear somewhat premature in this chronicle of historical events of hunting and wildlife conservation, but as one progresses deeper into the book the CIC sustainable principles are reflected throughout by the author. Therefore, the contents should be taken open-mindedly to embrace the fact that hunting is an essential part of the balance of nature.

The role of hunting as an important part of wildlife conservation is encompassed in an article appearing in a publication "African Indaba" (indaba meaning gathering place) resulting from the 55th General Assembly of CIC in April 2008. CIC is the International Council for Game and Wildlife Conservation. The Assembly was widely attended by international governments including organizations like FAO, CITES, CMS, AEWA, as well as many hunting organizations from the Americas, Europe, Asia, and Africa. Gerhard Damm and Rolf Baldus of Indaba and CIC wrote the resulting article, and I quote, "That the renewable resource wildlife can be utilized forever provided the use is sustainable. We stressed that wildlife use takes place on land, which is nearly everywhere a scarce commodity. It consequently competes with all other forms of land use. Many well-meant efforts advocating the total protection of wildlife do not consider the social and economic consequences for the people living with or close to wildlife. Total protectionism as well as emotional blackmail by some animal rights organizations makes wildlife lose most of its economic and sociopolitical value. Consequently wildlife comes out second best and often last in the competition for the most appropriate land use, although international agreements, like the "Convention on Biological Diversity" and the "Addis Ababa Principles and Guidelines for the Sustainable Use of Biodiversity," confirm the right and the need for the sustainable use of natural resources. It is well understood that uses and human interventions, particularly in national parks, need to be minimized. However, wildlife populations have to be managed to balance their impact on other species and on vegetation, even in the most protected national parks— the elephant culling issue in South Africa is a case in point. Management processes should include a combination of hunting, culling, live game sales, and ecotourism to maximize economic, ecological, and sociopolitical benefits.

The public needs to be made aware that sustainable use and long-term protection of wildlife do not exclude, but complement each other. They are two sides of the same coin. Together they are called "conservation," although this particular meaning is all too often overlooked, sidelined, or intentionally misinterpreted.

Regulated hunting is recognized internationally as a legitimate and essential part of conservation, but we must not overlook the fact that a small but vociferous faction actively tries to undermine this. They replenish their ammunition from many forms of unsustainable and unethical hunting. Consequently, hunters have a dire necessity to look at and act upon such abuses. Sustainable use of nature is not only a recognized principle, which underlines our right to hunt; it is at the same time a binding obligation and lifelong commitment for all hunters.

Hunting tourism has a special significance. Of all wildlife uses, trophy-hunting tourism is of particular economic relevance. It has the potential to generate extraordinarily high revenues with a minimal take-off of individual game animals—usually older male specimens. The "ecological footprint" of hunters is considerably smaller than any other form of ecotourism. Hunting tourism can therefore develop into an economic and social force of significant impact in underdeveloped rural, remote, and agriculturally marginal areas, underpinning the ecological, economical, and sociopolitical pillars of sustainability.

At the same time, there is significant potential for abuse and malpractices inherent in hunting tourism: corruption, fraud, bad governance, overshooting of quotas, bad management, and consequently the loss of wildlife numbers and biological diversity. Examples of bad practices exist on all continents. On the other hand, there are many best practices, showing the opposite as proof of the positive hunting tourism on game and nongame species alike, their habitats, and the people who live with wildlife and manage it.

Hunting tourism is indeed widely accepted as an integral part of rural development. However, every effort has to be made that hunting and hunting tourism are practiced in proper, ethical, and sustainable ways. Only then will hunting tourism be a positive management tool and powerful incentive, generate revenue for conservation and at the same time provide economic and social benefits for the rural populations who usually bear the direct and indirect costs of wildlife on their land.

The discussion and development of best practices in hunting tourism are a special and important responsibility of the global hunting community and the CIC has taken up this challenge. Hunters have to demonstrate that they are conscious of the consequences hunting engenders and that they accept responsibility for the wild resources they are using.

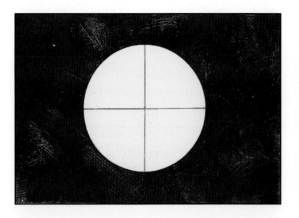

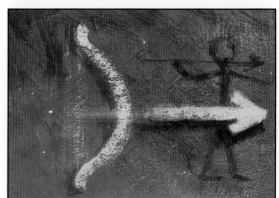
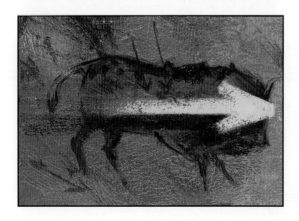

Story Board of Man the Hunter.

# Man the Hunter

Amazing wildlife has come, gone, and come again over a span of millions of years on this fragile planet of ours. Signs of man's presence on earth only appear relatively recent. Studies show that he has always been a hunter as well as a gatherer. He became a rather sophisticated predator, using projectiles like rocks and pointed objects in his pursuit of mammals, which sometimes were big and dangerous. He also got crafty making covered pits and using snares and traps. As time went by some animals were domesticated and killed more conveniently.

Nevertheless, man has always been a hunter. Our more recent pioneering ancestors were hunters by necessity. Sport hunting is modern man's heritage and tradition, while sport hunters have been the salvation for wildlife and its increase by donating time, knowledge, energy, and funds so that all can enjoy our wilderness and wildlife.

# GAMEMASTERS *of the* WORLD

# THE NURTURING OF THE AUTHOR INTO HIS LIFE'S WORK

One might call this part Chris' baby steps in his adventurous life. There was not one dull moment of the Klineburger brothers' lives, from their childhood to partnering in a business, that made them the pre-eminent leaders in their field of endeavor, which is briefly outlined herein. Although you might think some of these events are unrelated to Chris's most prominent notoriety, but the lean times, hard work, and diversity of interests and activities gave him a broad worldly vision and nurtured him for his ultimate accomplishments. The "Chapters" reflect phases of the brothers' lives and business endeavors, while the "Reflections," sidebars as such, tell of humorous or serious subjects, entertaining, and sometimes educating, occurring during an important and historic era.

You will see that, by his mid-20s, Chris had hunted, trapped, climbed snowcapped mountains, traveled the Pacific, fought forest fires, was an auto mechanic and machinist, served his country, ran his own business, received a college degree in engineering, and worked on the development of the B-52 bombers—probably more than most people experience in a lifetime. The text then tells how the brothers helped bring the world hunting fraternity together.

PART I

# THE NURTURING OF THE AUTHOR
# INTO HIS LIFE'S WORK

# CHAPTER 1

# Growing Up in Arizona

There are three towns in the Mule Mountains in southeastern Arizona: Bisbee, Lowell, and Warren. These towns are all connected in a canyon that starts very steep from the top, which is Bisbee; as the canyon widens out it is called Lowell; then at a basin at the bottom is Warren. Bisbee and Lowell were copper mining towns, while Warren was a residential area at the bottom of the canyon. Bisbee was known as the city with one dimension—length. It was in the bottom of the canyon with hillsides too steep to build on. In the other direction is Tombstone, 25 miles to the west, out on the flats.

It was said that none of the desperadoes hung around Tombstone, where they would be spotted and gunned down. They all headed for the hills, which were the Mule Mountains. Brewery Gulch in Bisbee was infamous in the town's history—a source of a lot of the Old West's history. Regardless, the area was a great place for the Klineburger brothers to grow up in the 1920s.

Brother Eugene (Gene) was born in Tucson in 1919, Albert (Bert) born in Bisbee in 1926, and Chris born in 1927, also in Bisbee. Gene was named after a well-known political figure of the time, Eugene Debs. Bert was named after one of the leaders of Phelps Dodge

🐾 **Warren, Arizona, as seen from an early Klineburger residence.**
**Lowell and Bisbee are up the canyon in upper right.**

Corporation of copper mining fame, Albert Reifsnider, while I was named Chris, a shortened version of Chrisman, which was Dad's name. Once the folks saw me, they figured they'd better call it quits!

In those days, nicknames were the style. I was "Junior," of course. Gene's best pal was Emmet Claunch, who was dubbed "Bluke," so Dad called Gene "Luke." Thus the two friends were Bluke and Luke. When Gene got out of hand, Dad would call him Luke McGook. You'll hear about Bert's nickname later. The nicknames stuck until each kid developed some sort of maturity—kind of like becoming an intelligent being!

My dad Chrisman and mom Reba migrated west around World War I from Pennsylvania—they called themselves Pennsylvania Dutch. Little is known of Dad's lineage, while Mom's maiden name was Erb, originally from Holland. There are a number of Erb spin-offs scattered from Pennsylvania to California, besides the Klineburger boys.

Dad was a machinist by trade and worked for the mines. He was fond of the outdoors and hunting. He would take us into the desert, usually hunting for rabbits, but he always was on the lookout for rattlesnakes. He liked to catch them for their skins, meat, and bones—yes, bones.

Mom could hold her own in the Wild West, even though she was a polished lady.

The Indians used to boil the bones, paint them different colors and string them for a necklace—so that's what Dad did. The meat was good eating. It was mild. I remember it tasting like chicken. We always had snakeskins around, some of which went into hatbands and belts. Dad also tried his luck at prospecting and placer mining for gold, but not with enough luck to cover expenses.

We used to go down to the Sulphur Springs Valley to visit our farmer friends, Frank and Ann Murphy. There were a lot of rabbits, both cottontails and jackrabbits. Among my fondest memories was driving around at night, sitting on the front fender and shooting jacks. One time while down there, brother Bert caught a rattlesnake and put it in the car to bring it home for a pet. Frank dubbed Bert the nickname "Rattlesnake," which stuck throughout his growing-up years. While down on the farm, we all pitched in doing a little farm work. Our family was rewarded with all the potatoes and onions we could use, besides an unlimited supply of rabbit meat.

Dad hunted deer every year, but had to pack up the Model T and pitch camp in either the Pedregosa or Huachuca Mountains. Gene got to go sometimes, but Bert and I were too young. I must have had a craving to go on the deer hunts. Mom told the story of one fall when Dad loaded everything for the hunt in

**Our father trying his luck for gold.**

the Model T. It really wasn't "in" the car, but in the luggage racks on the running boards, then covered with canvas.

It was time to say goodbye, so Mom called us kids. "Junior, Junior—so where's Junior?" Soon someone spotted some rustling under the canvas on the running board. There was Junior, stowed away, and determined to go on the deer hunt.

I always felt the reason I hunted so much in later life was because I was deprived of hunting when I was young. The one thing Dad told me that stuck throughout life was that your eyes were the most important part of survival in the wilderness and success in hunting. Watch for rattlers. Know what is ahead of you and side-to-side. I didn't always remember that, until almost stepping on a rattlesnake or walking too fast and spooking the game in front of me. So, later I developed the theory "you hunt with your eyes, not with your feet."

Dad was a Mason, Mom in the Eastern Star, and Gene got into the DeMolay International. Dad was into everything that happened in little old Bisbee. If a circus came to town, Dad seemed to volunteer himself as the reception committee. He would introduce them around and tell them everything they needed to do. Yes, we got free circus tickets. One of the major league baseball clubs did their spring training at the "Warren Park," our local baseball field. Again, Dad was right there getting involved.

The tri-city conglomerate also had their own ball club, the Bisbee Bees. Dad started his own concession at the park. One was

Little Chris with his first gun—a toy.

renting cushions. I remember his slogan "soft seats, five cents." We kids had to go around picking them up after the game and loading them into the car. At times he had us handling the refreshment stand, selling pop, lemonade, and Mom's homemade cookies. The pitcher for the Bees was a man named Mule Washburn, dubbed Mule because of his big ears. Every once in a while at a very critical pitch Dad would call out "look at the ears on 'im!"

The question might be asked, why do something like this for extra money? We kids grew up during the Great Depression. Dad had a heart attack early on, and he had to quit the heavy work as a machinist. So, he

# REFLECTION
# Mine Water

**B**isbee, Arizona, was rich in copper ore, so there were a lot of open-pit mines and mine shafts. Although the area was quite arid, the shafts and pits would fill up with water. So they had to pump the water out and into a reservoir. They made use of the water by running water lines to the residential area to be used for watering the lawns and trees. It was dirty and full of minerals, so it was no good to drink. They simply called it "mine water."

The water for drinking and other household use was from a well down by the little town of Naco, on the Mexican border. A separate water system was piped to the homes to use this water source. They called the fresh water "Naco water." So most homes had two water systems, mine water and Naco water. Most of the outdoor spigots were for mine water, but often there would be Naco water also outside and, of course, the spigots all looked the same. We were taught to know the difference. We kids always preferred drinking water from a garden hose, as it was a great inconvenience to go inside the house for a glass of water, besides Mom didn't want us tracking dirt in the house. She did always remind us, "Don't drink the mine water."

One time when I was very young, the folks loaded up the Model A and took a long trip—a hundred miles to Tucson. We stayed in a "cabin"—they hadn't come up with the name "motel" yet. I was outside wandering around and got thirsty. There was a man sunning himself in a lounge chair at a neighboring cabin and the garden hose was on. I asked him, "Is this mine water?" He looked kind of puzzled, as if he were talking to some idiot, but said, "Sure, it's yours, you can have all you want!"

only did watchman jobs in pumphouses for the mines. I guess his pay might have been a dollar a day.

We were poor, but didn't know it. We always ate well, didn't require many clothes and didn't have the worry of expensive toys. For bicycles, we would inherit some one else's derelict, get some discarded rubber air hose, run a wire through it and cinch it down on the rim, and away we would go. It had no brakes, but who needs a luxury like that? A lot of our shopping was across the border in Mexico, where we could buy beef for five cents a pound and get gasoline for five cents a gallon.

# CHAPTER 2

# Pets and Hobbies

Gene, being 7 and 8 years older than Bert and I were, had his own friends and hobbies. His biggest fascination was tinkering with cars. His first endeavor was to take a 1926 Model T Ford, remove the body, and make what we called a "strip down"—the forerunner of a hot rod. He then inherited a burned-out 1928 Model A Ford and completely restored it to new condition. Before that, Dad got a '28 Model A, so father and son had matching cars.

Bert and I liked animals, and animals seemed to like us. Anything with legs or wings seemed to find a home at the Klineburgers'. Of course, we always had dogs—useless, but loveable. Anyone in town who wanted to get rid of a hobby gone bad, such as raising pigeons, knew where to unload them. We scrounged up enough scrap to build pens and nesting boxes. After maybe a year at that, we ended up eating the whole lot. I had found out a far cheaper way to get pigeon meat. There was an office building downtown called The Warren Company building. The pigeons would nest under the eaves. I would sit down below and pick off the nesting birds with my .22. It seemed to be great entertainment for the office workers watching me out the windows, as they applauded whenever I got one. No one seemed to care about me shooting into the overhang of their roof.

We had geese and chickens running around the yard. Mom hated the geese, as they would chase her when she went out to hang up the wash, so we ended up eating them. Turtles weren't a problem. We would drill a hole in the edge of the shell and tie a long string to it, so it could find its own food. We would paint each geometric design on its shell a different color, making them a sight to behold. Later, it was a donkey and horses. The donkey's name was Nelly. We were popular with the neighbor kids, as they all got a chance to ride Nelly. Even getting bucked off was a thrill for them.

My horse was a retired racehorse named Lucky. He was fine for covering distance, but oh, how hard it was to stop him! I had seen movies of Tom Mix shooting while chasing desperadoes. I thought it would be neat to

**Chris (with head in front of saddle horn) and Bert over the top of Nelly's saddle, and the Drummond family waiting their turn to ride.**

## REFLECTION
# Bullets Not Ballots

**I** was only two years old at the time my big brother Gene, age 10, remembered the excitement just across the border in Sonora, Mexico, just three miles from Warren, where we lived. There was a war going on. Gene remembers Dad driving us down to the border (a barbed wire fence) and watching the fighting. The war was between the two political parties. Instead of ballots, they used bullets! This was in the year 1929, and the victorious party stayed in power to the end of the 20th century.

They hired American bush pilots with single engine biplanes to fly over and drop bombs, by throwing them out the rear cockpit of the plane. The bombardier was a Mexican from across the border. At first they tried a suitcase full of dynamite, the fuse of which was lighted by the cigar in the Mexican's mouth. They didn't work too well, so they got some real bombs. The bombs were about three feet long, fins on the back and a percussion cap on the nose, probably loaded with a shotgun shell, which exploded the charge. We had a couple of those bombs as yard decorations. Gene finally gave them away before moving to Seattle in the mid-'50s. This kind of entertainment was better than kids get watching TV today.

chase a jackrabbit and shoot it. Lucky didn't think much of me shooting a shotgun over his head while on a dead run. Oh well, I've had worse spills than that.

Bert and I had a paper route—the *Tucson Citizen*, for the whole town of Warren. We split the town in half, each having our own customers. Walking took entirely too long out of my busy schedule, so I decided to use Lucky to cover my route. We rolled the papers; rubber-banded them, used the "paper bag" like a saddlebag over the horse's neck, and swished through the route in no time flat. I think some of the papers ended up in the wrong yard, as my galloping trajectory was sometimes miscalculated. After a while, we found out the paper route was not that profitable. We charged 65 cents per month to the customer, but we had to pay 60 cents to the *Citizen*. We had to collect the money too, and I heard every excuse in the world why they couldn't pay—another lesson in entrepreneurship.

One hobby that Bert had, in which he took great pride, was his egg collection. We were always fascinated by the beautiful colors of wild bird eggs, compared to the familiar chicken eggs. Bert decided to start his egg collection. You'd be surprised at how many different birds abided in the Bisbee area 'til you start robbing nests. Actually, we were very careful not to disturb a nest by carefully taking one egg, without leaving human odor.

Birds rarely nest in easy-to-get-to places. I recall Bert crawling far out on a flimsy branch, while I thought about how was I going to get his crushed body back home after the fall. But he made it. The only bone I ever broke was my wrist, when I fell out of a mulberry tree seeking a nest. To preserve the eggs, Bert merely removed the contents by making a small hole in the end and sucking the liquids out with an eyedropper.

# CHAPTER 3

# A Change in Our Lives

Our lives changed in 1936 when Dad passed away. He died of pneumonia. I was nine years old, and I remember a circus had just come to town and Dad took me there while they were setting up, which I felt was more exciting than the circus itself. I remember Dad having a very bad cough—a few days later he was gone.

After the funeral, which I think was put on by the Masons, Mom had a meeting with us and informed us she was going to have to get a job to support us. We were all shocked to think Mom would not be home to do the housewife bit. Gene started out by saying "No, I'll get a job." He was 17 at the time. Bert and I joined in and said we'll get jobs, too. Can you imagine two kids 10 and 9 saying that? Well, we all did, and kept Mom at home, doing what she did best.

Gene got a job right away working at the Standard service station in Warren after school and on weekends. After he graduated, he got a job in the mines. I think Bert and I still had the paper route, the profits from which probably just barely kept us supplied with ammunition. I started doing yard work at 10 cents an hour. I think Bert did the same.

**REFLECTION**
# Eating—Life's Great Pleasure

Eating has always been one of my great pleasures in life. I've been an "adventurous eater," trying every ethnic food around the world. My mom had a favorite tale about my appetite. She said that when I was about four years old, the folks took me to dinner at a friend's home. Trying to teach me to say "Thanks" after the meal, she said, "What do you say, Junior?"

My response? "More!"

That kind of set the pace for food the rest of my life. It's a good thing I've always been extremely active, to burn off those calories, otherwise I would be the original 5x5.

Mom was an exceptional cook and very frugal. We lived just a few miles from the Mexican border, near Bisbee, Arizona. Every Saturday, it was down to Naco, Sonora, to buy the weekly meat supply. The butcher knew Mom and anticipated her order. After looking over the beef supply, she would have him cut off a section of the top round. Then she pointed out what fat to cut off, before the routine of having him grind it up—*true* ground round, and not that concoction called hamburger.

Mrs. Mathewson, just across the street, had a big garden, growing flowers and vegetables. Weeds grew good there too, so I got quite a bit of work there. I also remember bringing home some vegetables, but I don't remember whether I stole them or she gave them to me. There was always yard work available around town. What I hated most was hoeing weeds in that hard, dry ground Arizona is known for. I always had to be careful in my "landscaping" work. Under every rock or board there would be a scorpion, centipede, or vinegarone—or all three. Sometimes a rattlesnake would be lurking in piles of trash.

When we got bigger, Bert and I got a job on a garbage truck. It was a small dump truck, and we had to be able to lift the cans and dump them over the side into the bed. In the back, where the gate was, it was a little lower, so they let me dump my cans there. Later on, I got a job as the janitor for the Hillcrest Apartments. If I went around the roadways it was about two miles away, but if I ran across the desert, it was probably only one mile. My job was to sweep all the hallways and entranceway and empty the cigarette stands. The work had to be finished around 6 AM, so that worked out fine for before school.

Then she'd select a roast—a rib roast, again trimmed and boned—all before weighing. This was a time during the Depression of the '30s. The meat was probably a nickel a pound.

Now came the cooking. Sunday was always roast day, along with the potatoes and vegetables. It was a big roast, so there were lots of leftovers. We could count on hash one night with potatoes, onions, and veggies thrown in.

Another of her favorites was "pasties." She rolled out freshly made dough; put in a handful of leftover, chopped-up beef, potatoes, and veggies; folded them in half; sealed the edges, and baked them. This made a fine meal, cold or heated. The ground round ended up in a meatloaf one would die for. Another of her favorites for the ground round was tacos. She would put the raw meat in a folded corn tortilla, then fry it that way, getting the juices of the meat cooked right into the tortillas. Then she would add onions, cheese, and so on, after they were done. Here's a joke on Mom. We would often get tacos in Mexico and it was known that the meat was reconstituted jerky. She asked the lady making them how she made the meat tender. In her broken English, she said, "chaw it." Not understanding the process of chewing, Mom asked for a demonstration. She put the jerky in her mouth and started chewing—no more tacos in Naco!

Bert quit school when he turned 16, and went to work as a machinist apprentice at Phelps Dodge Corporation, but quit before he turned 18 when he joined the Navy.

When I started high school, I got a job with the bakery in Lowell. I can't remember the name of it. A family of Bohemians ran it. They were tough bosses, which was OK by me because I figured I could do more than was asked of me.

Again, this was an early morning job. Lowell was two miles from Warren, and it was another two miles to Bisbee. So I had to go four miles to high school. No, there were no school buses. About 5 AM, I was running to work. If a car came by, I would "thumb" a ride—people would always pick up hitchhikers if they had room. My job was to load the delivery trucks with the bread and pastries. I would then ride the truck that serviced Bisbee, and my further function was to service the stores along with the driver, right up until the time school started. After school I would go back down to Lowell to grease the bread pans, having them ready for the night shift to bake for the next day. Somehow, we always had bread at home while I had that job.

My next job, when I was about 15 years old, was at Bledsoe Ford Co. in Lowell, as a mechanic's helper. When I was younger, Gene let me tinker with cars and he would show me the workings of engines, so I knew the basics.

I was assigned to a mechanic who was more than willing to let someone do all his work. Engines were quite simple in those days, not the impenetrable mysteries of today. We would pull the engines, and depending on the scope of the job, tie into whatever needed to be done. My boss taught me everything, and readily turned over the function to me after showing me one time. This included overhauling carburetors, grinding valves, replacing piston rings, reboring cylinders, changing main bearings and rod bearings— everything. One time, I was happily grinding valves when the big boss came around and saw me—he blew his top, and chewed out the mechanic. It took a while to convince management that I was capable, "but only under the mechanic's supervision."

My next job was 3½ years in the U.S. Navy, starting at age 17. More on that later.

# CHAPTER 4

# The YMCA and a Caring Person

After Dad died, I started wandering into the YMCA in Bisbee. I don't know why I did, as I do not remember any other kids doing that. A man started visiting with me, and befriended me—he was in charge of the "Y." He called himself the "Secretary." He said I could do anything I wanted there—swim, work out in the gym, or just sit around and read. His name was Joe Tibbetts. I don't know what his family background was, but he was single, and treated me like a son. He learned of my interests and the status of my family and knew that I liked the outdoors. One of the lodging guests at the "Y" who was passing through ended up leaving two shotguns there and never reclaimed them, so Joe gave them to me. One was a Browning automatic and the other a side-by-side double, both 12-gauges. Was I in heaven?!

The "Y" had a summer camp at Chiricahua Monument in the Pedregosa Mountains. Knowing I couldn't afford the camp, Joe arranged for me to go free. Wow, my first time ever to see pine trees, and streams with fish! It was actually the first time out of the desert for me. I was absolutely amazed at the forest—I never realized there could be so many big trees. I even saw a deer. It must have been a Coues deer. It was also my first experience in camping. I learned

## REFLECTION
# Bisbee Kids Were Lean and Mean

In the mid-1990s I went back to Bisbee for the "War Years" high school reunion. I was surprised to see that most of the "kids" were in pretty fit condition, as they approached the 70-year-old mark, as most of my acquaintances elsewhere nearing that age were really old looking. Upon thinking about it, I decided that the kids growing up in the steep Mule Mountains of Bisbee, with its tough lifestyle, got the right start in life to live healthy and long lives.

There, kids had to go long distances to school on foot or bicycle, and there was no such thing as flat country. Bisbee High School went down in *Ripley's Believe It or Not* as having four floors with a ground entrance on every floor. Is that steep, or what?

There was no such thing as junk food back then. In fact, I don't ever remember seeing a restaurant all the time I was growing up. In high school, I do remember a little café that did serve hamburgers and hot dogs. Also, one time Joe Tibbetts took me to a place in Brewery Gulch where we had a meal. They served it family style, with everyone sitting at one table. There were no grain-fed beef or chicken farms—everything you got was lean.

There were a lot of fruit trees—peaches, apricots, pomegranates, figs, and mulberries. Nothing went to waste. Ice cream we made at home in the old hand cranker—usually with peaches or some other fruit in it. We frequently had wild game to eat. Also, I don't remember anyone being fat, like a high percentage of the kids now, as we go into the 21st century. Everyone was lean and mean. We ate right and worked hard. Another thing we had little of were soft drinks. I know Pepsi-Cola and root beer were available. I don't think we ever had any in our home. Lemonade and Kool-Aid was about it.

to make a "mattress" from pine boughs and how to build a lean-to over the bed, which stuck with me throughout life. It was knowledge I used many, many times in my backpacking days. I learned how to catch trout by looking for a submerged overhanging rock where fish like to rest. By very slowly sliding my hand along the bottom 'til I felt the belly of the fish, I would grab the fish, and he would be mine!

In the mountain area, a new government program called WPA (Works Progress Administration) impressed me. They were building roads into those areas, making parks and campgrounds. The purpose of the program was to create jobs for people during the Great Depression.

I had another adventure in growing up. Joe took me on a trip to New Mexico (first time out of Arizona). First we went to Elephant Butte Dam, which I believe is the headwaters of the Rio Grande River, then to White Sands Desert, and then to Carlsbad Caverns. I never realized such interesting places existed.

Joe was then transferred to Portland, Oregon, as the manager of the YMCA there. We had kept in touch by mail. As I matured somewhat and developed my hiking and outdoor skills, Joe got me a job as hiking counselor at the YMCA summer camp in Washington, at Mount St. Helens. It was on Spirit Lake, called Camp Meehan right at the northern base of the Mountain. He also got Mom a job as assistant cook for the summer. So off we were to Portland on the Greyhound bus. I had always dreamt of the "North

Woods" and certainly I was blessed by a dream come true. Before the campers were scheduled to arrive, we were transported up the Toutle River to do preparatory work. I remember the first job us counselors did was to dig a cesspool for the sewage. It was nothing more than a six-foot deep, square hole that we lined with tree limbs to prevent the sides from caving in, then covered with logs and covered with dirt. I always wondered what happened when the logs rotted and someone fell through.

The camp, and my work there, provided one of the most educational experiences I ever had in developing my skills for my life to come. I led kids to the top of Mount St. Helens twice, and around the base of it once. Around the base was a 40-mile trek, that took us five days to accomplish—of course, backpacking all the way. I saw my first elk on that trip, a huge and magnificent bull. Then we saw small herds of cows and calves and plenty of blacktail deer.

Another fine experience from the camp, as the summer went on and got drier, was a lightning storm, which started forest fires. We counselors were all drafted to fight fires. They provided us with a pack that had "all the comforts of home," along with axes and picks. Then away they took us, to remote areas where I believe no man had ever walked. Our main job was making a firebreak, to keep the fire from spreading, which we did by cutting trees, removing brush, and putting out flare-ups. It was not a major fire, and was limited mainly to a ground fire.

Seeing and knowing Mount St. Helens and Spirit Lake in all its beauty at that time was a wonderful experience. I knew "Harry Truman"—not the President of the U.S., but the owner of the Spirit Lake Lodge. His lodge was maybe a mile from Camp Meehan, so we frequented his store for goodies on occasion— Harry was always happy to chat with us.

The mountain, Spirit Lake, and the entire northern landscape changed forever when three cubic miles of the mountain blew out, and was strewn everywhere. The blast was so terrific that it mowed down forests of huge Douglas fir trees for miles in its path, and of course, Harry Truman and his lodge.

Almost 60 years later, I finally nerved going to Johnson's Observatory some 10 miles from the mountain, to observe the new, recovering landscape. Tears came to my eyes, remembering those sweet yesteryears—and remembering Joe Tibbetts, and his contribution to my growing up.

# CHAPTER 5

# Out on My Own in the Wild

One goes around a lot of curves on the highway of life, and for me one of the big bends in the road happened when I was at the ripe old age of nine. Dad died, and I started working, taking on responsibility at home and beginning to see what is outside the safety zone of family life.

I played some with neighbor kids, but I didn't have a lot of time for it. Also, my interests and ideas of fun were a lot different from most, and I was a little bit of a loner—maybe one would consider me shy. Bert, being 1½ years older, had his own pals, and Gene, being 8 years older, seemed like adults.

We lived at 711 Cole Avenue, in Warren, Arizona, and about 30 of my short paces behind the house was a barbed wire fence, beyond which was totally remote, and alluring, hilly desert. Just over the rise, probably not a hundred yards away, I could be out of sight and sound of civilization. I just enjoyed solitude. Who knows what went through my little mind, but for sure, I was wondering what was beyond the next hill.

Mom would always say, "Don't go too far, and watch out for rattlesnakes." There were rattlers around, and one of my early remembrances was when we found a rattlesnake in the bathtub. The drain of the tub went out into a ditch—a good way to get rid of "the gray water." Well, there was nothing to stop that rattler from likewise coming up through the pipe, into the tub.

While out in the hills, I remember seeing wildlife, usually rabbits, dove, and quail, but also rodents, lots of reptiles, lizards, horned toads, and an occasional Gila monster. I even saw a fox one time, chasing a mouse. There were a lot of tracks of various sizes in the sand, from small dog size, on up, as well as deer tracks. As time went by, I ventured farther, taking the family .22 Remington pump and returning with an occasional cottontail. Mom liked that, giving us a little variety in our diet. I wanted to save the skins, but at first it was total failure. I didn't know about curing skins

with salt. First, the maggots got into a rabbit skin, so I decided I would put it in water to drown the critters. By the time I took it out of the water, the hair all slipped off, and it stank something terrible—my first lesson in taxidermy.

In thumbing through the Sears and Roebuck catalog, I spotted steel traps. That was it—I would become a trapper and fur trader. So I sent away for a variety of sizes, one for skunk, and another for fox, and still another for the big game—coyote and bobcat.

Upon receiving the traps, I had the feeling if I never got another thing in life, it was OK—I had it all, guns and traps. Daniel Boone had nothing on me! My first warning

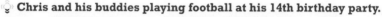

**Chris and his buddies playing football at his 14th birthday party.**

from Mom was "Don't go catching any of the neighbors' cats and dogs—or your fingers!" No problem; I figured I would set my trap line out so far away that—but wait, maybe those Apaches would have dogs, too!

The trap line did start taking me farther and farther into the wilderness—alone. I found that solitude sharpened my senses and awareness. Besides improving my alertness, I feel it also enhanced my reaction time—to be ready for whatever may come. By not having my .22 in readiness, I missed chances at many a rabbit. They may give you two seconds before darting away. I imagine I even thought of what to do if coming face to face with a puma—shoot him right between the eyes, as he made that final lunge to get me?

Trapping was slow, but certainly a learning experience about the cunning ways of wildlife. I did catch the occasional kit fox (a small version of the grey fox), coyote, and bobcat (more rabbits, than any of the above). I caught a barn owl once. I kept it alive thinking it would be a nice pet, 'til he clutched my hand with his needle-like claws.

I feel that trapping lent more to my naturalist abilities than anything else. I tried mounting a rabbit once—you never saw such an atrocious-looking creature in all your life! I knew absolutely nothing about taxidermy procedures.

During all this time of my wandering off alone, when not doing odd jobs to make money, the other kids started wondering about my not associating with them. The word got around that I was a little strange. One time I was out in the flats and was hungry. I had a cottontail in my game bag, so I built a fire in the shade of a mesquite tree, skewered the skinned bunny, and barbequed it over the glowing coals. This desert was flat, and accessible by cars. Sure enough, a family came chugging along in their Model A, and saw this dirty old Klineburger kid gnawing on a rabbit carcass. Back in town, the word spread that surely I was a "wild boy."

# CHAPTER 6

# Sweet 16—Driver's License

In the early 1940s, the war was in full swing. Everyone was patriotic and joined in all the war efforts. We saved tin foil, rubber bands, and copper wire—everything that could be recycled. No new cars were made. Gas was rationed, along with food. The speed limit was 35 mph, for optimum fuel efficiency. We could always get gas and food from Mexico, just a few miles away. A lot of people garaged their cars, as there really wasn't anyplace to go. This made a buying opportunity for me.

The day I turned 16, I got my driver's license and went out and bought two cars. One was a classic 1930 Buick coupe with a rumble seat, wood spoke wheels, and in mint condition. The other was a 1916 Model T Ford touring car. It was also a classic, but I didn't know this.

The first thing I did was remove the body from the Ford, to make a strip-down. I did save the kerosene headlights, and gave them to Gene. The seats and all went with the body, so I had to sit on the gas tank to drive it. We had a steep driveway to get out on the road.

The steering on the Model T was very abrupt. You'd turn the steering wheel a short way, and the front wheels would be turned *all* the way. Well, I went down that driveway, made the turn, but I went flying off the side of that gas tank. Another thing about the Model T; when you let

## REFLECTION
# A Near Death Experience

Only one road ran from downtown Bisbee up to Bisbee High School, and it was steep. Everyone going to school either walked, or drove up that road. If they had a bike, they had to push it—too steep to pedal. If a car came up, everyone possible would jump on the running board to hitch a ride up the hill. Any reader here not at least 60 years old probably doesn't know about running boards. Every early car had a step that went from the front fender to the back fender (oh, hell, you probably don't know what a fender is either).

Anyway, when I was a junior in high school, I jumped on the running board of a car going up, but the inconsiderate driver didn't have his windows down, so I didn't have anything to grab onto. So I fell off and went under the car, and it ran over me. No big deal—I got up, and continued up to school. The little episode kind of hurt my left thumb. As time went by, the thumb got to hurt more and more. One friend said, "I bet you have a bone felon." (I learned later that was an infection inside the bone.) I went to a doctor at the Copper Queen Hospital and told the doctor, "I'll bet I have a bone felon." He looked it over and, wanting to get me out of his office, he put some Mercurochrome on it (the skin wasn't even open, so why the Mercurochrome?) and gave me some aspirin.

Some time went by, and the thumb was really hurting and swelling. I was losing ambition, eating less, and losing weight. Someone told me about a good doctor down in Douglas, about 25 miles away. So I drove there, and he said, "I'll bet you have a bone felon." He lanced it and doctored it up and told me to soak it in Epsom salts. I did what the doctor said, but I was getting much worse, really sick, losing more weight, almost immobile. I couldn't drive, and Mom *didn't* drive.

Finally a good doctor in Bisbee was found, who arranged to have me taken to the hospital. He said he was going to try to get some penicillin sent in (a word none of us ever heard before). By now I had gone from 135 pounds down to 90 pounds—skin and bones.

The first thing he did at the end of my rotting thumb was to pull the end joint out, like pulling a tooth. My right leg and the left side of my abdomen were swollen. X-rays showed there were large pockets of pus. Those areas were opened, and rubber tubes were put in for draining. In the meantime, penicillin had just been located, and was sent in by Greyhound bus.

That miracle drug saved my life. It was about March, so I missed several months of school, and didn't go back till the beginning of school the next fall. Within six months, I went from the 90 pounds up to 160 pounds, which was a good weight for me. I do have my scars as a reminder—a stubby left thumb, and deep scars on my right leg and left side.

your foot off the low gear pedal, it goes into high gear. Guess what? There went my car down Cole Avenue, without me! Fortunately, it took off across a vacant lot and was stopped by a mesquite tree. That's part of growing up and learning the hard way.

The Buick was another story, as fine an automobile as was ever made. I soon found out that I was one of the only kids in high school that had a car. Boy, did I get popular all of a sudden. Even the rich kids didn't have a car. But they soon found I didn't use my car to pick up girls—it was my hunting car.

I could now go anywhere I wanted, to hunt. A shotgun and .22 were always in the car. With any spare time on my hands, it was not "Shall I go hunting?" but "Where will I go?" The trap line was now a thing of the past, but it was perfect for me before I had wheels.

# CHAPTER 7

# World War II

**B**ack to the war. Every boy turning 18 was drafted in the Army. Gene was drafted in 1942. At first, he was rejected. When Gene was young, a kid shot him in the face with snake shot from a .22. It blinded him in one eye, so now the Army didn't want him. Gene's patriotism flared up. His insistence got him in, but he was restricted from front line duty. He became an Expert Marksman and got a medal for it. He served primarily as a military police escort guard, managing German and Italian prisoners of war. Gene met this fine woman, Betty Thurman, who worked at an Army camp in Ogden, Utah, and soon married her.

Bert became of age, but to beat the draft, before turning 18 he could join any branch of the service he chose, so it was the Navy, for him. In those days, boot camp in San Diego was short, but not sweet. They wanted to get everyone on the front line as quickly as possible, so off to the Pacific it was, on the USS Kittson, an attack transport.

When I was 17, I wanted to go into the Marines. I thought I was kind of tough. Everyone was against

## REFLECTION
# My First Knowledge of the Great Beyond

As a kid, the only books I can remember are funny books and Big Little Books that other kids gave me after they were finished with them. Someone gave me a book and suggested I read it, knowing my interest in the outdoors. The book was *Call of the Wild* by Jack London. Wow, was I ever impressed at the time, by that book. Now, 70 years later, I do not recall the story, but what I do remember is the fascination instilled in me about The Great Northwest. I can truly say that, within me, there was always a dream, a yearning, maybe a focus—on tall trees, snow, alpine meadows, snow-capped peaks, wilderness lakes, and trappers' cabins. I do not remember at the time whether I had a determination to fulfill my dream, or to face the reality that I might be a fixture in the desert lifestyle of southern Arizona for the rest of my life.

it, knowing how high the casualties had been, and the expectations of the inevitable landing in Japan. Mom put her foot down, so I agreed to the Navy, which welcomed me with open arms.

Since shortly after turning 16, I was supporting Mom, as Gene had his own family to support and Bert was overseas earning $30 a month, including sea pay. Betty also came and lived with us for quite a while. Until now, I was able to keep up with the expenses, but how Mom was going to make it was a big concern. I had some savings from my jobs (and frugality) and from selling my cars and a few other assets. Also, I arranged for 50 percent of my Navy pay to go to Mom, and the government matched that, giving her $30 a month net income. Knowing how frugal mom was, she probably had money left over. One thing I remember, she would use a tea bag about four times—I imagine a tea bag cost about one cent, in those days.

# CHAPTER 8

# Serving My Country

My next big job was in the Navy. Being 17, I signed up for the Kiddy Cruise, which meant they had to let me out when I turned 21. Boot camp was tough for a lot of the recruits, but it didn't bother me one bit. Into six weeks, they crammed in a grueling endurance test that either made you or broke you. They taught discipline, respect, responsibility, survival, fighting skills, marksmanship, firefighting, and more. It was seven days a week, without leave. To some spoiled kids, it was a real shock. One of the first things to do right out of Boot Camp was to have your I.D. card fixed. San Diego print shops specialized in changing your birth date, to make you of legal age to go into bars.

I was immediately sent to Treasure Island in the San Francisco Bay, where I was assigned to a ship that was being "upgraded" into what I later found was intended to accommodate a lot of "high brass," that is, military officers and other dignitaries. Everyone without special skills ended up in the deck force. I didn't want that, so I told them I was a machinist, having just worked as an auto mechanic. They promptly put me in the M division, and into the machine shop under Chief Setorus. It was only the Chief and me, to maintain this whole ship. I soon found out that chief petty officers didn't like to work, as they had a lot of

**Chris visiting Mom in Tucson while on leave.**

social functions to take care of in the chief's quarters. He taught me the workings of the lathes and milling machines, so I readily took care of the ship's maintenance.

My special sea detail, while on watch, was operating the throttle. I was the guy maintaining the exact amount of steam going through the turbines, to travel at the proper speed fore or aft. When at sea, which was most all the time, I stood watch four on and eight off, otherwise, I worked in the shop daily from 8 AM to 4 PM. This meant if I was on the 4 to 8 watch they got me up at 3:30 AM, reporting on watch at 3:45, then getting off at 7:45, maybe enough time to grab a quick breakfast before working in the shop from 8 AM to 4 PM, but reporting again on the throttle at 3:45 PM and getting off at 7:45 in the evening.

That made a long 16-hour day. If on the "mid watch," 12 midnight to 4 AM, it was up at 11:30 at night, getting off at 3:45 AM, getting a couple hours sleep before reveille. We got so hungry at times that we stole the C-rations from the life rafts, to have a snack during those long nights. We would take the lagging off a steam coupling to fry the spam. After a time, the commissary figured they better do something, so they made us a sandwich for the midnight watch.

The best news of the war came when we learned of the atomic bombs dropped on Hiroshima and Nagasaki, and making the Japanese "cry uncle." That changed the whole course of things—so now what? Our first postwar mission as a command ship was overseeing the atomic bomb tests at Bikini Atoll. We were among the first ships to Bikini, as well as to Eniwetok and Kwajalein, where the control operations were being put into place. We watched them bring in all sorts of ships, some our own surplus, but also many Japanese and German ships. They were placed in a convoy pattern inside the huge atoll. An atoll is a circular reef, which actually is a volcano rim that forms from underwater. Bikini was ideal, as it was a deep crater, besides having a high rim 50 feet or so above sea level, stopping a tidal wave.

The first bomb test was from above the fleet. Our ship's position was upwind, maybe 10 miles from the blast. They had everyone possible topside and gave us a piece of smoked glass to hold over our eyes to prevent blindness from the glare. It was quite a sight, but the ships were blanketed by the cloud, which soon formed the signature "mushroom."

There was no tidal wave. In fact, when we hurried in to assess the damage, the ocean was smoother than I had ever seen it.

Chris, #24, played guard on the ship's team that played other teams in Tsingtao, China.

Once inside the atoll, we saw some ships were sinking while others were listing. Most were still afloat, a few burning, but most badly singed, blackened with peeled paint.

In a real life situation, most ships may survive, but not likely the crews. We left the atoll while a number of special units were studying the effects of the blast. Then we spent considerable time in parts of the Marshall Islands. The surviving ships were repositioned, and I believe more ships were added to the fleet.

During the second test, which was the underwater test, we were again positioned outside, but more in readiness for a tidal wave. No smoked glass this time. This blast was more spectacular, as a giant plume of water, maybe a quarter mile across, shot straight into the air. One huge ship was visible going straight up in the air along the edge of the waterspout.

Again we set sail immediately into the atoll to review the aftermath. Ships were scattered because their anchors could not withstand the horrific force, while many other ships were sinking and listing.

Before long we headed straight for the Bremerton Shipyards near Seattle for an overhaul, to get rid of the radioactivity which penetrated all our systems. A love affair began between the Seattle area and me during this time. I often visited Jonas Brothers of Seattle

 **I was fascinated with the many cultures around the Pacific Rim.**

taxidermy studios, which my brothers and I eventually took over.

Once (apparently) free of radioactivity, it was across the Pacific again, this time to China. With brief stops in Shanghai, our destination was Tsingtao (now called Qingdao) where our command ship was overseeing the evacuation of the Chinese Nationalists. The Tsingtao area was the last stronghold of the Nationalists as they fled the communist onslaught. We did spend a lot of time there enjoying the area, including playing football against other ships' teams. They called us "the big red team" as most were really big—I was the littlest guy on the team. I played guard, and did pretty well. There were only enough uniforms for one string.

In those days, teams played both offense and defense—no such thing as substitutes.

Before our job was finished in China, our ship was called to go all the way down to the South Pacific, to Indonesia. The Indonesians and the Dutch were having problems. One of the early United Nations Conferences was held on our ship, "the Renville Conference"—our ship was the USS Renville. We were at the island of Java in the city of Batavia, which is now called Jakarta. Apparently negotiations were slow, as we spent a lot of time there. The whole Navy experience was wonderful for me, traveling the entire Pacific. It no doubt set the pace for my curiosity about faraway places and love for world travel.

# CHAPTER 9

# After the War

After 3½ years on a wild ride all around the Pacific, I was now 21 years old and could legally drink. Actually, I felt like I had lived a mature life for the last decade, and had everything I wanted along the way. Gene and Bert had both been out of the service for some time now.

Gene and his family had settled in Tucson, and he was working for the power company. Gene and Betty started raising a family just before the end of the war, with Dianna born in March of 1945. Then along came Judy and Lloyd. Once they had a son, they called it quits.

Bert went to work for the mines in Bisbee right after his Navy days, as a machinist apprentice, worked for two years until he received his Journeyman Machinist papers, worked for one day, and then moved to Seattle in 1948. While still in Bisbee he had married a high school girl-friend, Vivian Ramsauer. He had a job awaiting him working for Guy Jonas of Jonas Bros. of Seattle taxidermy—again an apprentice, at 85 cents an hour. He caught on quick, and soon became a favored taxidermist for the firm. Bert had three daughters, Jody, Jan, and Barbara—all born in Seattle.

Mom had moved to Tucson after Gene relocated there, so I lived with her in a small house not far from the University of Arizona where I promptly enrolled to study mechanical engineering. The first semester was making up some high school credits that I needed before advancing to the college courses.

My favorite hunting car. The model A coupe was perfect for the desert near Tucson.

The GI Bill paid my tuition. Otherwise I could not have done it. They said four years of college credits were required for a Bachelor of Science degree, but I felt that I didn't have that much time, and needed to get on with life. So I crowded all the courses into 3½ years, including the first half-year making up for high school.

I did get a job right away in a service station. I worked long hours at the station and studied long hours Monday through Saturday, went partying every Saturday night, and went hunting all day Sunday. That was my routine every week until the summer break of 1949.

Bert had arranged a summer job for me at the taxidermy studio, so I went up to Seattle and stayed with him. Finally I learned the artistry and the technology of the trade, and even mounted a few specimens of my own with Bert's help. Taxidermy came very naturally for both Bert and me.

You might say we were born naturalists, having taken a real interest in wildlife through hunting and trapping. Throughout,

we constantly studied anatomy of our own or other people's specimens.

Upon returning to Tucson, I was confident I could start my own taxidermy business. I talked to my friend and owner of Carmichaels Sporting Goods Store, Chet Carmichael, about taking over the unused basement of his store. He agreed, and Klineburger Taxidermy suddenly was born!

I was the only taxidermy studio south of Phoenix, as well as the only taxidermist that had no customers or trophies to mount. This soon changed. I was a member of the Arizona Game Protective Association, which was the local sportsman's club.

As word of my taxidermy studio spread and the fall hunting season starting, the deer, javelina, and elk starting flowing in. I was up 'til midnight every night, skinning and salting trophies. I had full-time work throughout my college days. In fact, I had too much work and took in a helper and hunting buddy, John Doyle, and taught him the trade. The business flourished until after the summer semester of 1951 at the U of A. At that point I gave the business to John, who later moved to a larger location of his own, and successfully continued in his own name.

During these hard-working and hard-studying years, I still had time to do the summer jaunts to Seattle working for Jonas. Bert and I always hunted or fished every weekend in Washington. There was always something to do—bear season (which was open year-round), rabbit hunting on San Juan Island (there were thousands of domestic rabbits gone wild), salmon fishing on the coast

⚲ **During my summer jaunts to Seattle, Bert and I always hunted and fished while off the job. I caught this 44-pound salmon off Grays Harbor, Washington.**

⊙ **My first bear taken near Darrington, Washington.**

and in rivers, freshwater fishing for trout and sea-run steelheads, and seal hunting on the Stanwood Flats, where we could chase them with our outboard and shoot them with buckshot when they surfaced. It was great sport, and a way to eliminate a few of the world's worst predators. Seals would seal off the mouths of rivers and take a bite out of every salmon coming to spawn.

While in Arizona, I managed to go on many a trip, some to Sonora, Mexico, to hunt desert mule deer and desert sheep— also to Cholla Bay (Puerto Penasco) or Guaymas for deep-sea fishing in the Sea of Cortez. I collected pronghorn antelope from the south rim of the Grand Canyon, mule deer from the north rim, elk from the Apache Indian Reservation in the White Mountains and plenty of Coues deer and javelinas in the Tucson area.

Javelina hunting was a sport in my early years in Arizona.

A running shot—and the coyote was running too!

## REFLECTION
# Arizona & the Guns

Guns were part of life in Arizona. In the late '40s around Tucson, where I was at the time, no one thought anything of seeing someone walking around town with a six-gun on his side. Stop and think: Arizona was the last of the states admitted in the "South 48," only 36 years before. Keep in mind during that time there were two World Wars and the Great Depression. Cars were just really coming into their own, airplanes were not significant, and roads were still mainly wagon trails smoothed over. Horses were still an important means of transport. Things had not actually changed that much. The one big change was the cowboys and Indians finally called a truce, and it was mighty peaceful. But that didn't mean they hung up their guns or even checked them at the door. Guns are an American heritage, and sort of a freedom of speech.

At the sporting goods store, we had the opportunity to buy a case of 10 Winchester rifles that were crated in the year 1900. They were the model 92 (1892) caliber .44-40. They were heavily coated with grease and in mint condition. Ten of us got together to buy them, each taking one. The workmanship of those rifles is far superior to the similar models made today. That rifle in that caliber, in its day, was known as "the gun that won the West." After getting that rifle, I had the opportunity to get a Colt .44-40 revolver so I could have the pair—same ammunition for rifle and pistol. I really enjoyed both, and they were part of me when hunting.

Coming back to town after hunting, we kept pistols on our side, going into a café, bar, or even a store. People were used to it and thought nothing of it. On a couple of occasions, we would put blanks in the pistols, and in a bar, a buddy of mine, Bruce Wyant, and I would have a fake argument, then a "shoot out." They saw right away it was for fun and the people were entertained.

# CHAPTER 10

# Romance

I suppose everyone is curious about all the romances I had with the opposite sex during those years of growing up? I could leave this page blank and that would pretty well sum it up. In racking my brain about those early romantic days, I am certain that the entire community was completely devoid of girls. Perhaps they were all sold off as slaves. Well, maybe it was because not too many of them frequented the most important destinations of those times, i.e., trap lines, abandoned mine shafts, stalking jackrabbits, catching rattlesnakes, breaking donkeys, or just wandering around the desert. I do recall girls in the classrooms at school, but what happened after school is a mystery. I remember them as being kind of silly.

Once I was in high school, girl presence was more noticeable. Incidentally high school grades were 9 to 12, while grade school was 1 to 8, with no kindergarten. There was only one high school and that was Bisbee High. The teachers were really old. The same teachers who taught us also taught most of the kids' folks and some of their grandfolks. Maybe part of the reason was we had just been through the Great Depression and now we were in the middle of World War II.

Getting back to chasing girls—did I say, "chasing"? I guess that pretty well sums it up. It certainly didn't turn out to be "catching" girls. I guess I was lucky, not catching any. Once I got my Buick coupe, suddenly girls discovered that I existed. They really loved to ride in the rumble seat. That's not where I was—I was driving.

## REFLECTION
# Dead or Crazy

One of the renowned western artists made his mark in southern Arizona, the late Ted DeGrazia, was a resident of Tucson. I first met Ted in Bisbee, Arizona, where he was doing a special lighting effect for the Lyric Theatre. I was still a kid going to high school, but he was very friendly with me while I perched on top of a ladder and handed strings of lights to him.

Several years later, during my college days in Tucson, I passed an art studio on the west side of Campbell Avenue north of Speedway, with the name DeGrazia on it. I stopped by and, sure enough, there was Ted painting away. He actually remembered me from Bisbee. I was fascinated by his paintings, especially the characterizations of Indian children. I visited with Ted off and on until I left Arizona for the Northwest. I think in those early days, Ted could be called a "starving artist," just getting by.

One time in passing his studio, I noticed a wild colored change on the outside, with bright colors and a little art thrown in. I stopped and commented to Ted, "What's with this crazy exterior? It shouts a daring message!"

His answer was, "I've concluded that to become famous, one has to be dead or crazy. I've got a lot of living to do, so I'm getting a little crazy!" His wild approach apparently was what it took to get people's attention, as he became extremely popular from then on. Somehow, I ended up with a print of a young Indian girl that I have to this day. I don't recall if Ted gave it to me or I bought it, but I cherish it. A good friend in Las Vegas gave another print to me, "Apache Mother"—DeGrazia Studio in the Sun.

I did have one female friend whom I liked. Her name was Wanda Edge. I liked her family also. In fact, I would go to their home a lot and play rummy (a card game). I also took her dancing a couple of times down in the Sulphur Springs Valley where there was a hall. They often had a dance when they could get enough guys with instruments together and call themselves a band. I didn't know much about dancing. I did what they called the two-step.

While going to the University in Tucson I organized an occasioned social event—usually on a Saturday night (my only night out). Sometimes it was just a cookout in a nice cool riverbed that we could drive to. We would have a fire, cook some hot dogs and marshmallows, then lie around and neck.

One time when I was out hunting in the desert, I came across an old abandoned house. Actually the house was gone, but there was a large concrete slab, which was the floor. The only thing still standing was a fine stone fireplace. So I would throw a party there with a cozy fire in the fireplace and have dancing.

I always took my wind-up victrola with my collection of exotic records to set a romantic mood, while enjoying some fine cuisine. It wasn't always hot dogs and marsh-mallows. One of my favorites was kebob, skewers with game meat and veggies.

I guess you could sum up my early romances with the gals as pretty low on my priorities. I worked hard, studied hard, and spent all spare time possible out in the desert enjoying God's creation. I only allowed myself one night a week to party, and that was Saturday night. If girls fit into anything I did, they were welcome company, but it was usually always my way. There would be plenty of time later for romance, but I was busy honing my future while growing up.

# CHAPTER 11

# Fast Forward into My Life's Work

Toward the end of my engineering education at U of A I realized that engineering was probably not for me, as my love was the outdoors. I already had a permanent job offer, working with Bert at Jonas Bros., but I figured I would give engineering a try. I applied for a job with Boeing Airplane Co., which just happened to be in Seattle—imagine that, right where Bert and Jonas Bros. were located.

I got the job, and they paid moving expenses. I had a Chevy carryall. That's what they called them before someone came up with "van." Mom and I loaded all our earthly possessions and moved to Seattle. Sadly, we left behind a lot we wished we had room for. I worked for Boeing for exactly one year, which is what I promised myself to do.

I was put in the Weights and Balances Division and the project of the time was building the two experimental models of the B-52 bombers. These planes were named the X & Y B-52s. Our job was to determine the weight of everything in each section, from wire bundles to rivets to skin. I guess we did alright, because those aircraft are still flying good right into the 21st century, well over 55 years later.

It was goodbye to engineering. One might think the engineer schooling and job with Boeing was a waste of time, but going through

# REFLECTION
# The Call of the Wild

While hunting in the deserts around Tucson I was always fascinated when hearing the loud squeals of a jackrabbit when confronted by a coyote. Many a time, usually around daybreak, the silence of the desert was shattered by that shrill cry of the rabbit. I am sure the main food source for the coyote was the rabbit. I got to thinking if I could imitate that sound, I could have fun with the coyotes.

My first attempt was with a blade of grass between my thumbs that I blew through. I did get coyotes to come in, but it was awkward, and not quite the sound I wanted. I kept experimenting with different things, but what I finally came up with was as close to perfection as one could expect. I took an old duck call apart and just used the reed part in my mouth to blow and vary the sound however I desired. I could get the coyotes coming in on a dead run. There were a lot of coyotes at the time—this was in the late '40s.

Factory reps were always calling on Carmichael's Sporting Goods, where I had my taxidermy studio. They would have time on their hands and often wanted to go hunting. I was more than happy to guide them. I took one rep out that was with one of the big manufacturers. I put him in a blind of bushes where the wind was right, and good visibility in the direction I figured the coyote would come.

I got further back in the bushes and started to call. Coyotes came from every direction! Very often a pack will scatter to try to stir up the rabbits, which probably was the case in this instance. They came in on a dead run. My hunter panicked, and didn't get a single coyote. I have to admit, I was a little concerned myself—it was a little scary.

Anyway, it wasn't long after that when predator calls started coming on the market. I have always wondered whether this representative went back to his company and got them to make the calls—could I have invented the predator call?!

« » **I skinned many coyotes taken with the use of my makeshift coyote call.**

all that was an excellent mental exercise. Engineering was tough, and it put my brain to the maximum test. It taught me how to think, how to figure things out, and how to solve problems. Life before me was a problem waiting to be solved—not really problems, just challenges.

A job was waiting for me, being a taxidermist at Jonas Bros., but was this a step forward—or backward? The one thing I did know is that my future had to be associated with the outdoors. I loved nature and I loved wildlife. Taxidermy was the only thing I knew that connected me to the outdoors. So that was it. I joined the company with Bert, and I gave it all I had. It was the same with Bert. We both gave the job 110 percent, which was the way it was with us in every endeavor in life.

Guy Jonas was ailing from a heart condition and needed good and honest help, and he had it in Bert and me. Bert started taking over some of the office responsibilities from Guy. Wanting to retire, he agreed to sell the business to us, but not for two more years, when he reached 65 and would be on Social Security. We basically ran the company for him for those two years. We got to know the customers and the hunting guides.

On July 1, 1954, we bought the company. We promoted it every way we could, especially with the hunting outfitters in Alaska, Canada, Africa, and India. We got to know them all. Strategically, Seattle was well located for hunters heading north and guides coming south. We encouraged them all to stop by for a visit. Anytime anyone came to Seattle, we offered to pick them up at the airport, give them a tour of our studios, and take them out to dinner or cater to their needs.

One thing we planned right away was to give fast service. Historically, taxidermists were slow in getting trophies back to the customers. One of their problems was getting the skins tanned. To do a high-quality mount, the skins had to be tanned, and fur dressers were slow in getting them back to the taxidermist. How do you solve that problem? Start your own tannery. There was a fur-dressing company in town by the name of S. Johnson Company. We bought them, and brother Gene moved to Seattle to run our fur-dressing company. It worked out great, and for the first time in taxidermy history, hunters got their trophies back while the hunt was still fresh in their minds.

# CHAPTER 12

# New Technology for Taxidermy

Taxidermy is certainly one of the fine arts. But it wasn't always that way. Who knows what the earliest form of taxidermy was? It wasn't mentioned in the Bible, but one can be sure that somewhere back in history, feeble attempts were made.

One ancient form of taxidermy was shrunken heads. Actually the heads were not shrunken as such. The heads were skinned from the skull, eyelids and mouth sewn shut. Then they were cured somehow, stuffed with hot sand, and allowed to dry. Once the head was hard, the sand was removed, and a perfect specimen was ready for display! Preserving skins for leather and fur garments certainly goes back to the beginning of recorded history.

Existing specimens of animals from recent history were "stuffed" by various means, but "mounting" of a skin on a mannequin was the basic principal still used today. The early mannequins were built by using bones, wood, or metal frames, then adding the "flesh" by using wood, excelsior, burlap, plaster, clay, or whatever, to get the desired form. The quality left a lot to be desired, and they were certainly extremely heavy.

In more recent history, up to the mid 20th century, taxidermists used an actual form. First a sculpture was made on an armature and finished off with modeling clay. Then a plaster cast was made. This plaster cast was used to mold a form, sometimes with plaster and burlap, or by using laminated paper maché. Removed from the mold, the hollow form would be used for mounting the skin.

Always looking for a better product, and with plastics coming onto the market, we began experimenting. Finally, we settled on laminated fiberglass as the ideal form. The forms were super-strong and really lightweight. Our first use of these forms was a life-size polar bear standing on its hind legs. We rushed it through to ship to Fairbanks, Alaska, for a special outdoor show.

The bear was a central attraction on a covered speakers platform. A strong wind

**A young hunter in the Klineburgers' taxidermy showroom dreaming of when it will be his time.**

**Chris sculpting a giant bear with clay before it is cast in fiberglass.**

came up and took the canopy like a sail. Everything with it, including the bear, scattered all over the fairgrounds. The bear survived unscathed. Had it been on what was then a conventional form, the bear would have been flattened.

From then on, it was fiberglass forms, which was our contribution of modern technology to the taxidermy industry. It wasn't long before supply houses took notice and offered plastic in various types. Today, all taxidermists use plastic of some sort under the skins of mounted animals.

Chris & Bert looking over the 20,000–pound killer whale completed with the use of fiberglass.

It was not uncommon for a visitor to observe a dozen or more leopards from Africa and India in process at one time at the Klineburgers' studios.

## REFLECTION
# The Story of Jonas Bros.Taxidermy

**T**here were five brothers in the Jonas family in Hungary. Most of them had some taxidermy experience. They had the opportunity to migrate to the U.S.A., so they decided they would come and set up a taxidermy business. They chose Denver, Colorado, being in the Rocky Mountains and the center of the Wild West. The time was between the two World Wars, so it was a good time to get established.

The older brother, Coleman, came first, and set up the business in his own name. Once the business was established, he called for Guy, John, Louis, and Leslie to come join him. But the business was in Coleman's name, so they had to work for him. The business did go well, as there was little competition. The company was named Jonas Brothers.

Things did not always go well. Guy told us how hard he worked to create a perfect specimen and how Coleman would meticulously inspect the job until he could finally find some minor thing to complain about. It ended up that all four brothers left Coleman to pursue their own interests.

Leslie had an engineering background, so he left the taxidermy trade, and the other three went out and established their own companies. Guy established his studio in Seattle, as it was the stepping-off place to Alaska and Canada and also was a seaport for overseas shipments.

John started first in Montana, but his wife missed the social life, so he moved to Mt. Vernon, New York and started taxidermy there. Louis Paul Jonas also went to New York, but went strictly into museum work, not catering to sportsmen. Coleman, John, and Guy did some promotion, including catalogs, together, even though their taxidermy businesses were competitors.

In Denver, the brothers also had a fur apparel company. After the brothers left, Coleman's son Joe ran the fur business, while Coleman ran the taxidermy.

Joe had two sons. Joe Jr. was trained in taxidermy, and Jack was taught the fur trade. As the two kids started their apprenticeships, Coleman died.

Family squabbles caused Joe Jr. to leave the company, so he came to work for us in Seattle in the 1960s. Jack then moved in to help manage the Denver Jonas taxidermy studios.

Joe Jr. eventually moved back to Denver, where he started his own company, Joe Jonas Jr. Taxidermy. Joe Jr. was the only surviving family member to learn the art of taxidermy, and we were the ones to give him his final training.

In New York shortly before he died, John Jonas sold his business holdings to one of his employees, Steve Horn, who continued the business under the name Jonas Bros. of New York.

Guy Jonas started Jonas Bros. of Seattle in 1937, while the Depression was still leaving its mark. The country was soon at war, but he managed to make a go of it. Business did boom for him once the war was over, which tied right in to the era of trophy sport hunting.

We purchased the Seattle Jonas Company in 1954 and expanded it worldwide as Jonas Bros. of Seattle, Jonas Bros. of Alaska, Jonas Bros. of Africa, Jonas Bros. Outdoor Clothing & Equipment, Jonas Bros. Outdoor World, and Jonas Bros. Worldwide Travel, thus putting the name "Jonas" on the world map. To enhance recognition of the Jonas name, we were constantly in the public eye, through countless press releases, magazine articles, television coverage, exhibits at sport shows, and word of mouth.

The original Denver Jonas Company filed a lawsuit against us to the effect that only the original company had the right to the name, and we were to discontinue its use. After the attorneys got rich on both sides, the judge ruled in our favor, and the Patent Office said the Seattle based Jonas Company did far more for the name than the original Denver Company ever did.

Even though we won the case, later we felt it would be to our advantage to start using our own name, so we started by blending Klineburger in with Jonas. After a time, we eliminated Jonas altogether.

# CHAPTER 13

# Expanding to Alaska

From our involvement with the taxidermy firm in the early '50s, it was apparent Alaska had to be the most important focal point of our source of customers. After taking over Jonas Bros. in 1954, we could easily see the hunting outfitters everywhere could use more help related to trophy care. Some did a good job of field preparation of the skins, but many did not. A lot of trophies were poorly skinned and some heads not ever skinned at all when the shipments came in.

We knew that a taxidermy receiving station in Alaska would be the ideal service, and we knew that Anchorage would be the best place to have it. One of our good friends and a previous employee of ours, Lonnie Temple, had a small taxidermy studio in Anchorage. He was not interested in being our representative there, as he had all the work he could handle. Naïvely, we felt it wouldn't be right for us to set up shop in Anchorage and compete with him, so we held back. Fortunately he shut his business down in '56, so we wasted no time to start planning our Alaska operation.

Guy Jonas had gone into the fur business in a small way, so we kept our hand in, as well. We felt that just having a taxidermy receiving station in Anchorage would not be cost effective because of the seasonal nature of hunting. We thought a retail store carrying furs would be good, as well as fur products such as Eskimo-made moccasins, mukluks and mitts, walrus ivory carvings, and gold nugget jewelry—there seemed to be no limit.

Our stores became the central source of native arts and crafts in Alaska. Here is a pair of ladies' dress mukluks.

We rented a vacant store with a basement to accommodate the trophy handling. A store manager was hired in Seattle, where we put him into training. We designed a line of fur parkas, mainly of inexpensive furs such as rabbit and mouton lamb. We had all sizes from infant-size to adult, both women and men.

In the summer of 1957, we opened the doors in Anchorage. First, Bert took the manager up to get him started. Later, I went there before the hunting season started and stayed for the season.

Business went better than expected. Retail sales were excellent. It is the first time fur parkas were ever available at a reasonable

Colleene Klineburger models a natural muskrat Eskimo-style parka from their line of fur parkas.

price. Besides the manager, we had a sales lady, plus an Eskimo woman to do in-house production of native products.

The big game outfitters loved it, because they could bring trophies in for us to skin, while they could get on with their guiding. Alaska was just starting to come into its own as a tourist destination. Likewise, sport hunting was only getting under way.

After World War II, the economy began to surge, along with air transportation, making Alaska accessible. Keep in mind that before the War, the world had been in the grip of the Great Depression, which started just as people were coming out of the horse and buggy days. So it was boom time for hunting and tourism.

For me, to think of going to Alaska had been beyond my wildest expectations, but here I was boarding a Pacific Northern Airlines plane to Anchorage. To show you how naïve this little Arizona desert rat was, I had only seen military aircraft in action at war, so I started looking around for my parachute.

Once I got over the airline not taking my safety into consideration, I settled down to enjoy the beautiful coastline of the Inside Passage. The rugged, snow-covered Chugach Mountains were an awesome sight, as we approached Anchorage.

Our manager met me, and since it was Sunday, with the store closed, I asked to be shown Alaska. I wanted to see everything of interest—things Alaskan. He was stumped. He finally said, "There are a lot of good bars around." He did drive me around, and it was interesting to see there were a lot of dirt roads and wooden sidewalks. Yes, there were a lot of bars, too. Other than that, there wasn't much in the form of tourist attractions.

That bothered me. I felt perhaps we could do something for the community by supplying the city with full-sized, mounted animals of all the Alaska big game. We arranged a visit with the city officials and

 Jonas Brothers Anchorage museum, the Klineburgers' store, was visited by every tourist.

The Klineburgers made fashionable garments, hats, purses, and other accessories from Alaska furs. Here Colleene shows a set from spotted hair seal.

made that offer, emphasizing that it would be a fine attraction for their city.

We were received coldly. They had no place for such a museum, they told us—and no funds to provide one. I went to the airport and made the same offer to the Port Authority, indicating it would be a great attraction for people getting off the planes. They said they would be happy to rent the space to us to put in the display.

Well, so much for that. With our ambitions and foresight, we began looking at the possibilities to do it ourselves. After the first season, we had already outgrown our facility. We found that during the war, volunteer help built a huge log building for the servicemen

President Eisenhower being shown through our museum by the store manager, Peter Bading.

to have a place to go for recreation, sort of like a USO. The most Alaskan-looking structure imaginable, it eventually outlived its usefulness for the servicemen. It was a perfect place for our store/museum combo.

We rented it, and away we went with our plans. Bert and I had specimens of a good percentage of the Alaska wildlife that we quickly mounted and put into place. Now we needed a broader selection of merchandise for the store. We expanded the fur line with a broader selection of parkas, as well as a complete selection of fine furs. Our jewelry line expanded to include Alaska jade, hematite, ivory, gold, even fur earrings, bow ties, and so on. We had the broadest selection of stuff for tourists and residents alike than Alaska had ever seen.

Every tourist who hit Anchorage would be sure to visit the "Jonas Bros. Anchorage Museum." Hunting guides would always be sure to bring their clients to see us. When President Dwight Eisenhower was scheduled for his official Alaska visit, the military and city officials met, and concluded they would show him two things—Elmendorf Air Force Base and Jonas Bros. Museum.

We were the most Alaskan thing that there was in Anchorage. The official name of our Alaska branch was Jonas Bros. of Alaska. That was the label used in our fur garments and other products. The word spread, and there was more and more demand for our products.

## REFLECTION
# Gold Jewelry

**D**o you remember when gold was $35 an ounce prior to the year 1971? That's when we designed a line of jewelry for hunters and other animal lovers. We sculpted heads and many full-bodied replicas of a variety of mainly North American and African wildlife. We had them cast by a good friend, wholesale jeweler James L. Houston. We had a wide array of designs for men and women both.

A basic design was an oval 1¼ x 1¾ inches, which was made from a choice of Alaska jade or ivory, with or without a gold nugget trim. Or it could be made with solid gold nuggets. The animal figure would be centered on the oval, and then used for a variety of jewelry such as a ladies brooch or pendant, men's bolo tie, or a selection of them for a ladies bracelet

We had elaborate watch bands for men and women, rings, earrings, belt buckles, tie pins, cufflinks – dozens of designs.

We would also create custom design jewelry to suit. Available were about 45 different gold animal figures to decorate most any type of jewelry. A person wearing this flashy jewelry really stands out in the crowd. One of my favorites

**«** **The cover of our jewelry brochure showing Chris, Colleene, and Gene modeling many of our creations.**

is using the gold tie tacs as studs on my tuxedo – just listen to the oohs and aahs!

Our gold jewelry line set a fashion trend for hunters, as well as for anyone adoring wildlife. Bert's wife offers the jewelry line to this day, but with gold at $1,000 an ounce, it ain't what it used to be.

« **Brigitte Klineburger assembling their line of gold jewelry.**

# CHAPTER 14

# Expanding in Alaska

**B**ack in Seattle, because of the great demand for our furs, the fur department became a major part of the operation, so we hired several full-time furriers. We bought out another company, Valcauda Fur Company, which mainly dealt in raw skins. We even hired Valcauda himself to work for us. We also contracted a New York manufacturer, Vitoff and Danzer, to do the less-expensive parkas that we had designed.

Once well established in our log cabin museum store, we felt we must do the same in Fairbanks, another hub for hunting. It was a smaller town, with fewer tourists, so a smaller store was in order. We decorated that store in an Eskimo theme, with a native sled drawn by mounted huskies, mannequins with true Eskimo apparel, etc., along with mounted Arctic wildlife.

Our next expansion occurred when we were awarded the fur and gift concessions on the military bases in Alaska, including permanent stores at Fort Richardson and Elmendorf Air Force Base. For other bases, such as Big Delta and Kodiak, we had "Caravan Sales," which meant taking goods to those locations for a week or so, once or twice a year.

We were having a tough time obtaining enough authentic native arts and crafts to supply our stores. It seems as if we contracted every

## REFLECTION
# The Idea of a Snow Machine

There was a company back in the 1950s that made a high-quality garden tiller called the Merry Tiller. The same company worked with the Forest Service to make a tiller unit with a single track on it (like a miniature bulldozer track), to make mountain trails. Then the company designed a unit like a giant wheelbarrow, with a track on it for carrying supplies on a mountain trail. They felt that this "Carryall" unit might be good to use out on the tundra of Alaska.

Knowing that we dealt with hunting outfitters all over Alaska, they asked us if we would try selling the units and be their Alaska representative. We did, and they were well received. The way they worked was that, the operator would walk behind the self-powered machine, hold onto the two handles, and guide it along the desired route.

By now, I had spent considerable time with the Eskimos, mostly out of Point Hope, a point of land protruding into the Chukchi Sea north of the Arctic Circle. I became very familiar with dog teams, the only means of transportation for those fine hunters. My engineering mind started working. Why wouldn't a version of the Merry Carryall work on snow and ice?

However, the unit was too slow and cumbersome. I talked to the Merry people about designing a sort of motorized dogsled, having a higher speed rubberized track and a step where the musher (driver) could stand on the back. I got too busy with all our expansion activities to follow up on such a dumb idea. I certainly did notice in years to follow that snowmobiles started popping up.

Could I have invented the snowmobile concept?

« A. Polet Eskimo Arts & Crafts store in Nome was purchased by the Klineburgers to enhance their supply of native arts.

Eskimo in Anchorage and Fairbanks to supply us, but still we were always in short supply. Then Emily Bouchet from Nome contacted us to see whether we would be interested in buying an Eskimo trading post. Emily was the remaining heir to their family store, A. Polet Eskimo Arts & Crafts, a company that dated back to the Nome gold rush days.

We said yes and made the deal sight unseen.

Once established there, we had all the Eskimo goods we needed. We supplied the raw materials, such as tanned skins and walrus ivory to the Eskimos with a price established for them to do the labor. One real problem was actually getting some of the finished crafts from the Eskimos.

The Board of Trade Bar (the main saloon in town) was right on the way from King Island Village to our store, so we would have to buy our goods from the bar. The owner was a good friend, so he would call us when he got a supply of our goods. So we finally did get the goods from the Eskimos—indirectly.

# CHAPTER 15

# Expanding Outside Alaska

O ur fur parkas were appearing on ski slopes all over the U.S.A. They had become unique fashionable sportswear. No one could beat our price. Here's the price list—infant spotted rabbit parka with foxtail ruff $9.95; ladies' Kenai-style rabbit parka with fox ruff $19.50; ladies' Kodiak-style rabbit parka with badger ruff $29.50; ladies' Eskimo-style parka with calf trim on cuffs and bottom, with badger trim & ruff $39.50; sheared mouton lamb (looks like beaver) parkas for ladies were $10 more; men's mouton parkas ran about $10 more than ladies—no rabbit for men.

We were approached by a department store to see whether we would be interested in wholesaling our line of fur parkas. We agreed and eventually contracted a manufacturer's representative who specialized in sportswear to take on our line. Before long our Jonas Bros. of Alaska label ended up in high-end stores all over America, including I. Magnin, Macy's, Best's Apparel, and Marshall Fields.

In 1962, the Seattle World's Fair was coming, so why not put in a retail store in downtown Seattle with our Alaska product line? We did so and expanded the gift line to include all Northwest items, as well as World's Fair stuff. We also beefed up our fine fur line in the store.

Although we were expedition outfitters, we had fashionable outdoor products.

Pistol-packing Bert lets the stewardesses try on styles from our valuable cargo of fine furs, full length mink and chinchilla coats. In those early days we received permission to guard our expensive luggage.

The theme of the store was Arctic Alaska, so it was an Alaskan adventure to visit our store in Seattle.

As time marched on, we found that hunters and tourists alike who had been exposed to our furs and Alaska native goods would contact us requesting our catalog. We didn't have a catalog. So we went into the mail order business—at first in a small way, with brochures and price sheets on our gold jewelry and fur parkas.

As our overall business expanded in Seattle (we had already moved the taxidermy operation once before to a bigger space) we needed a much bigger facility. We found

the ideal location between Pike and Pine on 12th Avenue on Capitol Hill, which is "Uptown." We named the building "Seattle Fur Building," because of the diversity of what was now in it. The building was an auto dealership previously, so it had an elevator big enough to handle automobiles.

We always encouraged hunters to stop by and visit on their way to or from a hunt in Alaska or Canada. They would always get the grand tour, and most ended up buying available products off the showroom floor. These same hunters also had a hard time finding good cold-weather gear for their hunts, so we referred them to downtown stores.

Since the start of the Alaska and Canada Gold Rush days, Seattle was known for outfitting and for anything outdoors. So, we went into the outfitting business. Tied in with our furs and Alaskan gifts, we assembled the most complete line of clothing and equipment ever offered in a mail order business. I believe the only other mail order businesses at the time were Eddie Bauer (specializing in down clothing and sleeping bags only), L.L. Bean, Herter's, and Norm Thompson (a small specialty outfit in Portland, Oregon). All of the above specialized in some way or another, but none offered a complete line for hunters and campers. We stayed out of firearms and the broad variety of fishing gear, but we had the clothing and equipment for sub-zero arctic weather to scorching deserts. We included free shipping to anywhere in the U.S.A. or Canada in our already reasonable prices.

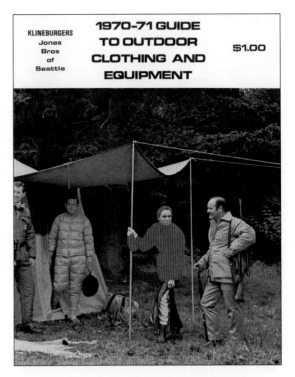

KLINEBURGERS
Jonas
Bros
of
Seattle

# 1970-71 GUIDE TO OUTDOOR CLOTHING AND EQUIPMENT

$1.00

Our fur department specialized in custom-made garments, even from customers' own furs like this zebra jacket with sheared beaver trim.

A cover of one of our catalogs in which, at the time, we offered the only complete line of outdoor clothing and equipment from sub-zero weather to scorching deserts, along with gift items for animal enthusiasts.

Gene, Chris, and Bert Klineburger model clothing and jewelry for their catalog.

## REFLECTION
# Better Service for the Guides

**H**aving taxidermy drop-off points at our stores in Anchorage, Fairbanks, and Nome was not all we offered hunting outfitters. The guides were professionals at getting the game for their clients, but it was easy to see that many of them needed more information and material to do proper field care of trophies.

Bert recalled an incident from his early days with Jonas, around 1949, when a box came in from Northern British Columbia sent by George Ball, who was one of the early outfitters. Thrown in the box, sent by surface mail, a whole steelhead trout and an unskinned mountain goat head. The fish was rotted and stinking and quickly discarded. Bert painstakingly skinned the goat, treated it with alum and salt, and managed to save it. The goat was the new world record, belonging to E.C. Haase, and it remains the world record to the day of this printing.

We offered skinning instruction diagrams, canvas shipping bags with plastic liners, salt if needed (we shipped granulated salt to Alaska by the ton—most guides thought rock salt was desirable), and we even gave out large "buck"-size knives to whoever needed them.

Polar bear hunting was becoming popular and outfitters were sending us full polar bear skins from two bases of operation, Kotzebue and Point Barrow. The skins were usually layered with fat, often with the head unskinned. Bert flew to Kotzebue during the spring season, taking fleshing and skinning knives to see how he could help. He rented a shed and started fleshing and skinning bears.

An Eskimo friend of ours, Art Fields, stopped by and said, "You shouldn't do that woman work, not good for men." So from then on, Bert, Gene and I took turns spending the seasons in both places working with guides, hunters and Eskimo women to provide better service. After the women meticulously skinned and fleshed the skins, they would make a hole in the ice, tie a rope to the bears nose and thoroughly wash the skin in the seawater, then dry clean it in the powdery snow. Bears were then tagged, rolled up, placed in shipping bags, and allowed to freeze in the sub-zero temperature before shipping direct to our tannery in Seattle.

# CHAPTER 16

# Anyone for Getting Married in Nome?

There are countless exotic places to get married, including Niagara Falls and Las Vegas—but Nome, Alaska? Even most Eskimos prefer to go to Anchorage, Fairbanks, or even Seattle to get married, but no one ever went to Nome to get married—until I did.

Well, there's a story behind it. I was a 32-year-old confirmed bachelor, spending full time working and hunting, with an occasional wild party thrown in. I had my share of lady friends, but I thought none would ever pin me down to family life. Being the only single one among three brothers, I was the one that spent most of the time on the road. Bert and Gene traveled plenty on business-related ventures, as well as other important things such as hunting, but I was dispensable for boring or lengthy ventures. (Nothing was ever boring in our company!)

I met this fine young lady, Colleene Porter, at a party in the Washington Athletic Club. A lady friend of mine, Ruth McCormick, put on the party. Bert and I usually went to the club to work out after work each day, so Ruth invited us to join her gathering. After our workout that day, we happily accepted since we planned on spending most of the night waiting for a flight scheduled well after midnight.

The flight carried Elgin Gates (world-renowned hunter) who was just returning from his Marco Polo sheep hunt in Hunza, a province of Pakistan. After Ruth's party, we invited Ruth and Colleene to join us in the Ladies' Lounge, where a nightly dance band performed. Once the dancing ended there, we took them to the Town and Country Club, an after-hours club. Bert went to pick up Elgin while I enjoyed entertaining the ladies. Bert returned with Elgin, and the party went on. Colleene obligingly gave me her phone number.

A few days went by before I called Colleene to invite her to see our taxidermy studios. She had just recently had her 20th birthday and was still living at home. She was born February 29th, a leap-year girl, and Colleene showed me an article in the Seattle paper about this "girl that just turned five."

Colleene's mom, Gladys, was in Idaho at the time visiting relatives, so I invited Colleene and her dad, John, out to dinner at a seafood restaurant. I hit it off good with father and daughter both.

When Colleene's mother returned, I took them some leftover tacos I had made. They had never had Mexican food before and didn't like my tacos. I also gave them some postcards, one of which pictured me, clothed in Eskimo gear, dragging a dead seal. They really started wondering about this weird guy that Colleene brought home.

That was early March 1960. In the weeks to follow, I was back and forth on business to New York and Alaska, taking time when in Seattle to court my new love. In late April I was in our Fairbanks store training our manager, whom I was to accompany to Nome to run our soon-to-be-acquired Eskimo trading post, A. Polet Eskimo Arts & Crafts.

Colleene called. "I need your opinion," she said. "Since I have my vacation from Boeing, where do you think I should go? Mexico City, Hawaii, or New York?"

"How about Alaska?" I offered.

"Well, I have to consult my folks," she said.

"If we can't trust you there," they replied, "we can't trust you anywhere."

"I'm coming!" she told me.

"You're going to have to work," I said.

"OK," she replied.

Shortly after her arrival in Fairbanks, we boarded a Wein Alaska flight to Nome, where Emily Bouchet, the owner of the trading post, greeted us. After settling in at the only and not very fancy hotel, we saw for the first time the new store that we had agreed to purchase sight unseen.

It had not quite been love at first sight with Colleene and me, but maybe the second or third. Being a novice at true love, I wondered *what do I do now?*

Yes, I proposed. If I recall it was, "Let's not grow old—(but) together." I left the "but" out, but she was smart enough to know what I meant.

In my whole life from when I was a little kid, after I decided to do something, the next step was to do it. Colleene made some comment like, "I can't wait to tell my folks, and have them start making arrangements."

I don't recall my exact words, but it was something like, "What's wrong with now in exotic Nome, Alaska?"

She agreed.

Making the announcement, we sent the word in short order by "mukluk telegraph" from the ice-packed shoreline to King Island Village (the Eskimo residential area, where the King Islanders stayed till break-up).

The first order of business was to get the marriage license. We figured there would be a long waiting period because of rules preventing natives from getting drunk and wanting to get married at that moment, but that was not the case.

We met with the Public Administrator, who happened to be a drinking acquaintance of mine from Anchorage. "We want to get married," I said.

He said, "I already heard."

"I understand we have to wait," I said.

"I'll issue it now," he replied.

So, the date was set—May 7, 1960.

Although little was accomplished in taking over the Trading Post, there seemed to be plenty of time for fun.

Alaska had just become a state the year before, and Nome was a very small town. It had one main street paralleling the sea front, which was still frozen over and ice-jammed, and people stopped us in the street thanking us for coming to Nome to get married. Emily, the selected bridesmaid, arranged for old, new, borrowed, blue. A Presbyterian Church had been recently constructed and the pastor was thrilled to be asked to perform the wedding ceremony. Plenty of volunteers helped with the plans, including a reception.

A jeweler made wedding bands adorned with Nome gold nuggets. A local politician took us for a joy ride in his single engine aircraft, taking great pleasure in flying into narrow box canyons, barely missing the sides in the turn.

Take note, that the young girl from Idaho had never been anywhere except from Boise to Seattle, so the whole Alaska adventure was a wild ride for her! Was her life about to change, or what!

Finally, the wedding day was here.

That morning a pilot friend said, "I hear that the Eskimos got a whale on St. Lawrence Island off the village of Gambell. I have to fly a part out there for a machine. Do you want to go?"

"Yes," was my response, thinking how wonderful it would be to get some fresh muktuk for the reception.

Muktuk is the skin and blubber cut from the whale. The skin is black and soft (not leathery) and about an inch thick. The blubber is white, so they leave about one inch of blubber to make tasty-looking snacks.

The weather was not at its best, and by the time we approached the distant coast, Gambell was clouded-in to the point the pilot had to "bird dog" his way to the landing field—that is, locate the radio signal from above the clouds, then make spiral turns down to find the ground.

The whaling crew was nearby, cutting up the beached whale. The Eskimos happily gave

**Newlyweds Colleene and Chris pose on the ice pack at Nome after the ceremony.**

me a lot of muktuk. Upon radioing Nome, we found that Nome was fogged in—we had to wait.

Wedding time was approaching, and people were standing in the street listening for the drone of our plane. Colleene recalls saying, "What am I getting into with this guy?"

Well the fog lifted and we did get in—wedding delayed, no problem. No one had anything else to do anyway.

It bears noting that no flowers or liquor were available in Nome. Upon announcing our unconventional actions and requesting the essentials to be airfreighted to us, panic hit my Anchorage manager, and we got messages ranging from, "Don't do it," "We'll get you out of it," to, "Did you lose your mind?" Lonny Temple even sent up a toy shotgun and fake ball and chain for someone to hang on our hotel room door.

Back in Seattle, Colleene's folks and my mom took it well, and a meeting was arranged so our respective parents could become acquainted. I got one call from a girl friend (that I let Colleene listen in on) who said, "You don't have to get married, and I will leave you alone!"

The wedding was a gala affair. A military friend of mine, Major Larry Flannigan, gave the bride away, while our store manager was best man and Emily the bridesmaid. Many of the townspeople attended, including Eskimos.

The reception that followed was at Emily's home. Emily did a hot pickle on the muktuk after cutting it into bite-size pieces. Other snacks such as smoked fish accompanied the muktuk, and our booze supply helped make the day an occasion to remember.

It bears noting that once back in Seattle, we had two wedding receptions—one for Colleene's family and friends, mostly non-drinking and churchgoing people. The other was for the drinking and rowdy Klineburger friends—not that we didn't go to church as well.

## REFLECTION
# Out at Daybreak

Here's another case of my naïve ways. The only sports I ever experienced up to my late 20s, even after moving to Seattle, were hunting and fishing. I was always on the spot at the break of day to surprise my prey with hook or bullet. Physical activity for me was scarce in winter times, so I decided skiing would keep my legs in shape in the slack of winter. There were a number of ski runs less than 50 miles from Seattle, so why not?

A skier friend of mine offered to show me the fundamentals and even gave me his old wood skis and boots, a deal I couldn't pass up. It was up to Snoqualmie Pass in the Cascade Mountains for my lessons. The first lesson was how to get up after falling down, which would soon be my most frequent maneuver. I caught on pretty fast, and was soon on my own on the bunny slopes.

After that, I was ready to do it alone, figuring I could get a couple hours practice first thing in the mornings before work. So there I was at daybreak, ready to get on the lift.

No one was around!

I assumed they were closed, until I saw a lonely person walking by. "Not open today?" I asked, as I stood there with my skis over my shoulder. He had a dumfounded look, checked his watch, and shook his head as if to indicate I was some kind of loony, then politely said, "Yes, we'll be running on time today at 10."

"What kind of sport is this?" I thought, "Losing hours of valuable daylight!"

# CHAPTER 17

# High Lonesome Ranch

Once back in Seattle after the wedding in Nome, Colleene and I rented an apartment not far from our business location. Bert and I had been renting an apartment together after Vivian and Bert decided their lifestyles were far too different, and agreed to go their own ways. Before that, I had a home in suburban Bellevue, where Mom lived with me. Since I traveled extensively, Gene asked Mom to live with him and Betty, since their kids were splitting off on their own, after which I sold my home.

We soon found that Colleene was pregnant, so the search was on for our family residence, both of us agreeing we didn't want city life. We had a good friend, Fred Dodd, on the east side out in the country, where he had a chicken farm and a lot of land. I asked Fred to sell us a few acres to build on. He did not want to break up his land, but he did call a while later and told us to get out there.

An adjoining 44 acres to his place had become available. A couple had been developing a horse ranch when things got bad with their marriage, causing them to have to sell to settle the estate. Fred guided us, and paused at the gate to show the beautiful landscape, accented by white fences with farm buildings up the slopes.

I said, "We'll buy it." The area was on the Sammamish Plateau, east of Lake Sammamish.

The home was being enlarged, so it was not yet livable, but there was a very nice apartment in the upper barn that we moved into upon closing the deal.

☉ **Part of the High Lonesome Ranch as seen from the air, with Allen Lake in the background.**

Colleene said we had to come up with a name for our remote paradise, and we came up with a lot of screwy ideas that didn't fit. Then one morning I woke up and said, "I dreamt we named it the High Lonesome Ranch."

So that was it. Our bottomland was close to, but not on, 12-acre Allen Lake, but 6 acres of waterfront on the lake joining our property became available, so we bought that as well, making 50 acres total. There were two large barns, nicely finished on the outside, but without internal improvements. Both barns had haylofts, and there was a dredged area behind the house that we finished off to be a small lake that we stocked with fish.

After completing the work on the ranch house, we began improving the barns by making high-quality stables, with knotty-pine facing, grain bins, overhead access to hay feeders, outdoor paddocks for each stable,

and Dutch doors inside and out. There was an individual locker for each stable with two saddle racks and tack hangers. Roy Rogers called it "a hotel for horses." We went on to build a "frontier town" from old cedar barn wood. The town included The Lavender Horse Saloon, a working blacksmith shop, a hotel (bunkhouse), a livery stable, feed store, and saddlery.

Besides getting registered quarter horses for ourselves, we bought a bunch more horses for a "dude string," which we rented out by the hour or the day. We obtained various wagons, from buckboards to freight wagons, to use for hayrides.

We took boarders—horses, that is—in the stables or just for pasture. We rented the saloon out for any occasion, mostly for parties to groups, but also for weddings, think sessions, and church parties. We had

⟨⊙⟩ **A portion of the Frontier Town on the ranch.**

no neighbors, so late and loud bands were not a bother. The ranch was the closest thing to a dude ranch in western Washington.

We started a horse club, The High Lonesome Riders, after putting in a riding ring with all the barrels, jumps, etc., and we formed our own drill team that starred in the annual Redmond Celebration parade. Our club challenged other horse clubs to "play days" (western-style horse competition).

One of the exclusives that we offered on the ranch was the "Suicide Race," an obstacle course on the steep hillsides, over logs, through deep gullies, and ending by swimming the horse through our pond. We did trail rides and campouts in the high Cascade Mountains, and we had progressive dinners on horseback. We'd start with snacks at one home on the plateau, a second for salad, third for main course, and the last house for dessert.

⟨⊙⟩ **Our brochure for the ranch.**

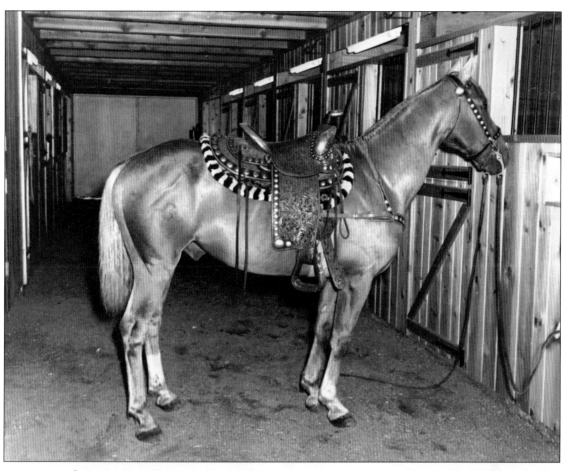

Chris's stallion inside the stables. Roy Rogers called it a hotel for horses.

The upper barn, which included the stables.

In growing up, Chris's son Kent Klineburger thought it quite ordinary to have the rich and famous as houseguests. Here Roy Rogers plays with Kent, while Colleene looks on.

We entertained many a group and individuals at the ranch. Besides horse-club meetings, we had Memorial Day parties, Christmas parties, and dance parties for our friends, besides groups like the King County Sheriff's Posse and the Seattle Sounders Soccer team. Individuals included an array of celebrities such as Roy Rogers, Chuck Connors, Joe Bowman, Astronauts Wally Schirra and Stu Roosa, Princes Abdorreza Pahlavi of Iran and Sultan Mahmud Ghazi of Afghanistan, as well as many heads of state from the Soviet Union and China. A taste of the "Old West" was always a treat for foreigners.

Astronaut Wally Schirra enjoys our hospitality on the High Lonesome Ranch. Colleene and Kent pose with him in our trophy room.

## REFLECTION
# A Wild West Warning

**W**e wrote this and burned it on buckskin, prominently displaying it in the Lavender Horse Saloon on the High Lonesome Ranch:

"Jessie James and Billy the Kid were bad galoots they say–
They also claim that Ringo was the meanest of his day.
Old Sam Bass and Miss Belle Starr rode roughshod where'er they went–
And Jack Slade's six-gun was the cause of many a man Hell sent.
There's tales they tell of the Dalton boys and how their guns caused fear–
And it seems that death would leave its mark when Holliday was near.
Wes Hardin had a lightning gun that lawmen knew too well–
For murder, Club Foot George was hung and kicked his way to Hell.
Black Bart's poems would cool the fact that he would rob and steal–
And no man crossed Cole Younger or his hot lead they would feel.
But if you think these folks were mean, you ain't seen nothin' yet–
Just try to steal from this saloon and see how mean we get."

# CHAPTER 18

# Living with the Eskimos

**P**olar bear hunting was gaining momentum as a popular sport, and it was certainly a unique specimen to have in a trophy room. The popular method devised to hunt the polar bear was to fly out over the ice pack in ski-equipped Super Cubs and locate the desired bear from the air.

By watching from a distance, the hunters would determine the route of the bear, then circle around to the direction the bear was traveling and find a place on the ice to land. There were always plenty of places to hide the aircraft, because of the many pressure ridges, caused by moving ice colliding and building ridges. Then the hunters would plan a stalk in the direction where they hoped the bear would be, climbing the pressure ridges to spot for the bear.

If a bear were taken, the pilot/guide would go back to the aircraft and bring it as close as possible to the bear. The bear would be rough-skinned on the ice, usually leaving the head and paws unskinned. The skin and as much meat as could be accommodated would be bagged and put behind the passenger seat, then they would fly back to shore.

Two planes would always fly together for safety reasons, so there was usually extra room on the second aircraft. The remaining carcass would be left for Arctic foxes that usually followed the bears. The meat was normally given to the Eskimos.

I wanted to hunt polar bear, but I typically resorted to do it the hard way. Visiting with a good friend and outfitter, Don DeHart, I discussed the matter with him, and he studied and explored the possibilities of such a hunt.

He felt that the best location was Point Hope. This point protrudes westward from Alaska's west coast, above the Arctic Circle into the Chukchi Sea. Point Hope was the chosen hunting ground for Eskimos from when they first migrated from Asia.

This location was chosen because all marine mammals, including polar bears, funnel around this point in their north-south migrations. The village we would use as a base was called Tigara. Don befriended some of the Eskimos there and arranged for an experimental hunt for March of 1958 for me and John Belcher from California. We flew from Kotzebue to Point Hope in a Wein Airline cargo bush plane—a single engine Norseman on skis.

We lived in an Eskimo's house and would go out daily by dog team onto the ice pack. During one period, conditions were not good nearby because of unusually violent movement of the ice, so we packed the sleds with tents and went up-coast toward Cape Lisburne where ice conditions were better.

During our long stay with those fine people, we joined them on a caribou hunt inland, again by dog team and camping out. The hunt was successful for bear, caribou, and many seals. Don had done a great job

in organizing the hunt and he offered this sporting hunt for years to come.

This experience rated as one of the greatest adventures of my life, and I personally gained a love and respect, as well as friendship, for these fine natives. I kept in touch with some of the Eskimos by mail, and they never failed to encourage me to come back. We started skin trading with them for their seals, polar bears, white foxes, and wolves. They even invited me to come and join them in the spring whaling season. I found this to be unusual, as I understood there was a superstition against white people being in whaling camp. Anyway, the next spring I returned at a later time to tie in with the break-up, when the sea ice begins to move out. I stayed at the home of John Oktollic, one of the more enterprising of the villagers, who was the manager of the trading post. I took my ever-present 16mm movie camera, but no gun this time, just to live with the Eskimos.

John had a wood frame house, similar to many in town. A good many of the families still lived in sod huts, the type the natives used from their earliest history, claimed by many to be superior to the modern stick homes. The sod is like a ready-made adobe block. Through eons of vegetation growth in a swamp area, much like a peat bog, the building blocks were cut to size and unearthed. The homes were built by first digging a short way down, just above the permafrost level. The walls were all made from sod block, lined with boards on the inside, as well as floor and ceiling. There was always a wind tunnel for the entranceway, a barrier from the bitter weather outside. This also served as sort of a mudroom, where wet outer garments are left, along with mukluks. There were always vents of sorts in rooms, some overhead and sometimes a window. Modern heating from oil stoves and electricity (on a limited scale from the town diesel generator) was available for old or newer homes.

The lifestyle in the '50s for these people was basically the same as that of their ancestors. Every able-bodied family had a team of about 12 dogs, usually Siberian huskies. They liked little dogs, saying, "Big dogs eat too much and don't pull harder."

The main dog food was seal meat, and it took about a seal a day to feed them. So it was seal hunting on a regular basis. The modern natives had "varmint rifles," high powered, but small caliber. While out following open

leads (where the floating and moving ice separates), they would constantly wait for surfacing seals, shoot them in the head, and retrieve them with their *ni kip owtuk* (translated "throw it hard"). It is a wood float about the size of your fist, with metal or ivory barbs, tied to a long cord that is wrapped around the short legs of a wooden stool that we all carried to have a place to sit while out on the ice.

The natives were not the only ones hunting seals. Polar bears were also looking for their main source of food. A bear's main diet was the fat from the seal. The bear would lie down facing an ice hole, a hole in the sea ice kept open by seals for a place to come up for air or to climb out for a rest on the ice.

The holes were the diameter of a seal's body, up to 1½ feet wide. If the water begins to rise in the hole, the bear knows a seal is

**Bringing in water supply. Blocks cut from nearby fresh water lake.**

🔊 **Harnessing the dogs in readiness for the hunt.**

🔊 **Life in Point Hope in the 1950s. Most Eskimos lived in sod huts and depended on dog teams. The dogs were always outside, tied up, or in harnesses.**

**Chris fishing through the ice for shee fish on Kobuk Lake.**

about to surface. Once the head clears the surface, a swipe from the bear's sharp claws is all it takes to set the table with fine cuisine. With the combination of claws and teeth, the bear skins the seal and eats the 2 to 3 inches of succulent fat, leaving the carcass for the waiting Arctic foxes that follow the bear.

Understandably, the Eskimos always had their keen eyes searching for bear, which they would also take when possible, along with foxes. Back in the village, seal carcasses were taken in whole for the women to skin. They would clean the skin and stretch it on a frame for drying. The fat was usually saved to use as cooking oil, fuel for seal oil lamps, or as lard for baking. They had their own special knife called an *ulu* or *ooluruk*, better known as a "woman's knife," similar to a non-rotating

pizza knife. The liver would be saved for consumption, as it is mild as calf's liver. The meat and innards were cut into chunks for the dogs, and frozen. If a bear were taken, the skin was removed out on the ice, meat cut into quarters for easy handling. Innards were usually left behind along with the liver, which could be deadly to humans, being so rich in vitamin A.

The village had its own trading post, which was stocked with staples such as flour, sugar, canned goods, some apparel, bolts of cloth and canvas, ammunition, and hardware. The villagers would bring the skins that they didn't use for their own needs to the post and trade them for the goods they needed.

The storekeeper would keep an ongoing account of debits and credits, but there were times when cash was used to balance an account. There was also a church ministered by a Caucasian couple that the villagers dearly loved. They had me over for a modest dinner one night, while we shared yarns of Alaska and beyond. The Oktollics introduced me to a single native lady named Tilley. They said I should stay in Point Hope and marry her. The church couple agreed saying, "She obviously would make you a good wife and mother as she already had two kids."

Whaling was soon to start and everything was to be in readiness. The umiaks (skin boats) had been stored all winter, upside down on racks made from whale jawbones. The skins of choice for the boats in this area are from ugruk (giant bearded seal). The same skins are used for the soles of mukluks because of their toughness and resistance to water.

The boats are inspected for damage and sturdiness. Rope made from raw skins of ugruk or walrus along with the sealskin floats are all checked out along with the darting guns and flensing knives. During the last whaling season, they had problems with the bombs from the darting guns not exploding. They asked for my help in analyzing the problem.

An explanation is in order to explain the workings of a complex harpoon, which is thrust at the head of a surfacing whale from the skin boat. The darting gun is mounted on the end of a heavy wood shaft. Sort of piggybacking on the main shaft is another shaft that protrudes out in front of the gun. On the end of this shaft is a harpoon head attached to the rawhide rope, which in turn is attached to the sealskin float.

Alongside the harpoon shaft is a rigid, triggering rod that strikes the whale just after the harpoon penetrates the skin. The rod hits the trigger of a gun that fires a 10-gauge shotgun charge. The shell propels the bomb into the whale, after which it is supposed to explode. This happens simultaneously as the thrust is made. The harpoon head and rawhide rope released themselves from the unit. By now the whale has sounded, but his

« Chris and Amos Lane looking over his skin boat, which had been stored all winter on the whale jawbone rack.

whereabouts is known by the sealskin float that sometimes disappears under water.

Upon dissecting a bomb to examine its workings and the source of the problem, I could see a number of things that could go wrong. Upon shooting the bomb, a cap is fired, igniting a short delay fuse, which burns long enough for the pointed projectile to penetrate deeply before exploding. I solved the problem and made good brownie points with all concerned.

Once the ice began breaking up and moving offshore, about a half dozen whaling station camps were set up 50 to 100 yards apart along the shore ice. Each camp had its umiak, a whaling crew of about six oarsmen plus the harpoonist, tentage, women, and children. It was party time, as they sat and patiently waited, played some cards, and sang chants accompanied by Eskimo drums (walrus stomach skin stretched over a round wood or ivory frame). The women often would jig for tomcod with their olasones (women's jigging rigs).

The boats, everything, and everyone were always ready. By now the days were long so it was a 24-hour watch for whales to start passing through. Every crew had a member on a vantage point, watching for the first spout from an approaching whale. Once a whale was spotted, a vocal signal put everyone into motion.

It seemed like only seconds passed as boats slipped into the icy water and paddles thrust each craft into what the whalers hoped would be the path of the whale. A lot of luck was involved for a boat to be at the exact, right spot to strike the whale's head as it surfaced. As one might guess most all the whales got through without contact, but the theory is that one whale each season would be considered a satisfactory hunt.

Sure enough, that one whale did present himself at the right time and place. The second boat out was the one that made first contact, and it appeared that the bomb had exploded so the chase was on. It is not likely the first bomb will kill the whale, so it's full speed for all boats as they follow that sealskin float. They had to follow it for quite a distance before another boat made contact, which ended the chase. According to established protocol, handed down through generations, the whale parts were specifically allocated to the boat crews in the order that they made contact with the whale. The first boat got the choicest part, while second, third, etc would get a specific cut. After the boats were awarded their share, the rest was divided up with everyone in the village.

The work began by beaching the tail end first in the selected spot. While most of the whale was still in the water, the cutting started, and a continuous caravan of dog sleds took loads to the respective deep freezers, which are holes in the permafrost ground. It took days to complete the job and break camp, before settling back in the village for a hunt celebration. And a celebration it was, with muktuk and whale meat served in a variety of ways, along with the traditional victory celebration of dancing and singing to the beat of drums.

My next stay in Point Hope with these wonderful people was my honeymoon by dog team a few years later, in the winter of 1961–62. Discussing the best time for hunting polar bear with Amos Lane, a very good native friend and my guide for many a hunt, he said, "In the dark of winter."

Amos described the habits, movement, and life of the bear. In the summer they are in the far north as the ice pack recedes toward the Pole. These bears (unlike those in the Hudson Bay region) live solely on the ice, never hibernating, except the sows. They hibernate once every three years for about a month while having their cubs.

They will find an ice cave in a pressure ridge for their den, or they may go on land to find a suitable birthplace for their one, two, or—rarely—three babies. In a month, the newborns will have sea legs enough to face the rest of their days on floating ice.

In the fall, the sea slowly starts freezing over from north to south, with the bears following hard ice, looking for the ever-present seal or an occasional pod of Beluga whales, which are white in color and the smallest of the whales. By the dead of winter, ice conditions at Point Hope are favorable for the bears that funnel around this point of land during their migration southward, a time when bears are most abundant.

When I married Colleene in Nome, May of 1960, I told her I wanted to put off our honeymoon till year-end to take her to an exotic paradise, hunting polar bear by dog team in Point Hope, where the sun will never show its bright face the whole time we are there. Colleene was soon lucky enough to become pregnant, so the ensuing adven-ture would have to be postponed, with an expected birth sometime in February. So we planned to depart right after Christmas of '61. First stop, Fairbanks, to check out things at our store where they were having near record cold, hovering around 50 degrees below zero. Next stop Kotzebue, with hopes of continuing right on to Point Hope. The cold and other weather conditions pinned us down for a few days, giving us time to visit our many friends there, the Shallabargers, Walkers, Salinases, Bakers, Fields, and many others. We stayed in Steve Salinase's hotel, and had nightly invitations to dinner.

Finally, Wein Airlines decided to make the flight, which carried their only two passengers along with much-needed supplies for that remote settlement. The ski-equipped Norseman taxied close to the village in a howling snowstorm. John Oktollic was there with a sled, and he grabbed Colleene, placing her in the sled, placed caribou robes under and over her, before mushing to "Point Hope Lodge."

Allen and Frances Rock made a facility to accommodate the rare visitor. The Lodge was about 20 feet square, with a small bedroom in the back, left corner with a small twin-size bed and a "honey bucket" (a portable potty) in the corner. We were able to shove our duffels under the bed, giving just enough room to walk around it to dress.

Our bedroom door faced the counter, behind which was the kitchen. In front of the counter and the space outside the bedroom accommodated a card table and a number of chairs, along with a small oil stove and a

Allen Rock puts on his Sunday best, while Colleene Klineburger borrows Frances Rock's dress parka to pose by Point Hope Lodge, during our "honeymoon by dog team."

jukebox. On the ceiling over our bed were great globs of ice that built up on nail heads, which was OK until the weather finally warmed to around zero, and the ice started to melt and drip on us all night.

Frances Rock always provided us with food from her very limited supplies. One thing that blew her mind is when Colleene made a sandwich from her akatuk (Eskimo ice cream) and put mustard on it. Akatuk is largely caribou tallow, whipped up with a little seal oil, then adding bits of cooked caribou meat and berries before freezing. I would say mustard would be the sauce of choice, over chocolate syrup.

The weather was not cooperative during our month of twilight, when the sun hides below the southern horizon, only giving us around five hours of daylight each day. The worst thing was almost constant east winds that kept pushing the ice pack offshore,

**Spotting for bear from a pressure ridge, caused by colliding of moving sea ice.**

making dog sledding and hunting limited to grounded ice along the shorelines.

The natives were dangerously low on dog food, (not the kind you get at Petco), so they resorted to heading inland for caribou, which they did find. The game is always skinned on the spot, boned, and cut up into the desired size before it becomes frozen. It stays frozen until final use for cooking or throwing a chunk to a dog. Once the meat is removed from the leg bones, the bones are broken, and the already frozen marrow is removed and eaten on the spot. This is a delicacy for the Eskimos.

Nonhunting time, of which there was a lot, was delightful as we enjoyed the people and their craftsmanship. They made good use of that time of year by doing all their indoor work. Once days get longer—24 hours long in summer—it is all hunting, fishing, and gathering.

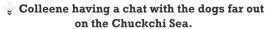

**Colleene having a chat with the dogs far out on the Chuckchi Sea.**

**Chris on the move to higher ground in search for caribou.**

The women's work was skinning, curing skins, sewing garments, slippers, and mukluks. Women's front teeth became short with age, from chewing skins. The chewing is not what you think—it is crimping raw and tough ugruk skins to form soles for footwear. The making of the needed waterproof and tough sole starts with a flat piece of the raw hide cut to shape, from which the hair has already been removed. To shape the hide to a 1½-inch-deep shell to fit the foot, by folding upward, the woman would make dozens of vertical crimps with her teeth, both toe and heel, which permanently forms the perfect mukluk sole for all who venture out to the frozen beyond.

The men were busy with many crafts besides maintaining their sleds, harnesses, and skin boats. Crafts included making baleen baskets (a rare art form, weaving fine strips of whale baleen into a tightly constructed basket), carving whalebone masks, or carving ivory for jewelry and ornaments such as billikens and animal figures.

They also brought in the water supply, which were blocks of ice carved from inland lakes. Very old sea ice was also OK, as over time it loses its salinity. The ice supply was stacked right outside the door. The women would bring chunks in to add to their ever-present water pot on the stove, being careful

**Colleene's polar bear.**

Some Eskimo friends in Point Hope were our hosts Allen and Frances Rock, guides Amos Lane and "Lincoln," trading post manager and host John Oktollic, ivory carver John Tingook, artist Eugene Killigivuk, bone mask artist Alec Frankson and baleen basket weaver George Omnik.

John Tingook using a bow drill to Carve ivory.

not to get "yellow ice" that the dogs had wet on.

Even with the ice condition the way it was, Colleene did collect a polar bear, and had great sport shooting seals, besides having an experience that could never be repeated as the native way of life quickly changed in years to follow. The honeymoon by dog team was a special time in our 42 years of marriage.

As some may not agree to my use of spelling, Eskimos never had written anything, as they had no alphabet—so spell it anyway you like, as long as it sounds right. An example: Colleene always had fun using the usik from her bear to mix drinks. A usik is the penis bone of the bear, so whether she told them she used her usik or oosik, it didn't make the drink taste any worse.

George Omnik, perhaps the last person skilled in weaving whale baleen.

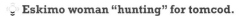

Eskimo woman "hunting" for tomcod.

⚲ **Colleene in the graveyard, fenced by whale jawbones.**

⚲ **The darting gun used for whaling contains a 10-gauge shotgun charge that propels a bomb into the whale.**

⚲ **Whaling crew with skin boat. Note sealskin floats: skinned and inflated seals.**

Both the polar
bears and I
were surprised
as I topped the
pressure ridge.

Chris jigging »
for fish off Point Hope.

Dogs resting on the sea ice,
while the hunters take time for lunch.

Chris with hair seal taken by ice hole. Note
his ni kip owtuk slung over shoulder and tok, a
pick to test ice where walking.

Chris buying furs from John Oktollic, manager of the Point Hope Trading Post.

Eskimo family in Point Hope

Alec Frankson carving whalebone masks.

# REFLECTION
# Skin Dealers

**A**t the height of our fur-manufacturing business, our company was one of the major skin dealers in Alaska. The skins of interest to us were hair seal, wolf, wolverine, and polar bear, furs needed for parkas, mukluks, and slippers. All these animals were in abundant supply, while the hair seal and wolf had a bounty because of their overpopulation and destruction of other wildlife.

We bought all the skins we could from the native trading posts that needed an outlet for polar bears, wolves and seals. However, the natives could not supply the demand, so we depended on the Seattle Fur Exchange and independent skin dealers. We got a big kick out of dealing with the independents, who were very shrewd traders.

We became very friendly with one independent, Sol Rubin, and even socialized with him on occasion. I was in his post buying skins once and observed his antics. A trapper from Alaska came in with a bundle of furs and proceeded stacking them on the sorting counter.

The skins were not a thing of beauty, but they were OK. Then Sol came over and barked "Get those things off my bench!" with a look on his face that expressed fear of total contamination of his premises. He followed this with a concerned "Well, OK." the first put-down to set the stage for a low bid. Once he'd graded the lot, Sol offered his price, which was not satisfactory. So the trapper packed up his catch and left to get a bid from the next trader.

When the trapper returned after getting a lower bid down the line, Sol hit him with his next shrewd maneuver: "You should have taken my earlier offer. I just received a telex from the New York market, showing prices had dropped." So now the bid dropped from before. The bewildered trapper knew it would be the same story down the line, so he sold to Sol.

One time I was buying skins from Sol. Both he and I knew the going rate for the skins, but he had to go through his canned sales talk, "Oh, these are superior grade, just look how well-handled they are, etc."

"No need to go through all that," I said.

"Don't stop me," he interrupted. "I'm selling now!"

When he was buying, it was "These skins are poorly handled, unprimed, singed, etc.—I'm buying now!"

# CHAPTER 19

# Art in Taxidermy

The early 1960s acclaimed our taxidermy establishment "The World's Leading Taxidermists." We were well known among the African professional hunters and the Indian shikaris, together, which comprised probably 95 percent or more of all the guided hunting outside North America. As for Alaska and Canada, we received a lion's share of the specimens in the Seattle studios. We used slogans like "On the Border of Bear Country." In fact, we were doing around a thousand bears a year; mostly in the form of rugs and life-size mounts. Besides a number of our taxidermists specializing in bears, we had one technician that did nothing but repair bears and do the preparation around the lips, eyes, and ears before handing them to the taxidermist. We had one full-time rug stretcher, who had his own special drying room to accommodate the huge boards on which the bears were stretched. Another department was rug lining, where two full-time seamstresses put on borders, interlinings, and linings. Another person in the art department put on the finishing touches around the mouth, eyes, ears, and claws.

Bert and I were hands-on with the taxidermists, doing everything possible to elevate the quality and have the trade recognized as a fine art. We were never able to go on an extensive hunt together, as one of us was in the shop daily inspecting everyone's work. Being artists ourselves, we worked with our clients to have unusual life-size mounts, not just a stiff specimen staring at the observer, but have an action mount portraying its movements in the wild. One such creation was

🐾 **Our studio's motto "On the Border of Bear Country" is exemplified in their workshop with the photo of polar bears.**

for a good client of ours, Bob Brittingham, who had sent us full-sized skins of bongo and leopard from an African safari. He allowed us to mount the leopard leaping onto the back of the frightened bongo. The leopard was fully supported by a steel rod protruding from one of the leopard's paws into a socket in the back of the bongo. To our knowledge, it was the first time in the taxidermy trade that this kind of technology was used.

Through the years, besides doing much museum work, we did numerous multiple mounts for sportsmen, who started taking a different perspective about their collections. Hunting only started on a grand scale after World War II and a time people started having the heads mounted. Trophy rooms (special rooms in the house to display the specimens)

🐾 **The Klineburgers pioneered multiple mounts and encouraged sportsmen into the next level of displays with habitat scenes in their trophy rooms. Here we sculptured a bongo that supported a leopard by a single steel rod into a socket on his back.**

◯ **Chris and Roy Rogers checking out Roy's specimens from his safari in Tanganyika.**

**18** The Seattle Times    Saturday, December 17, 1960

**AFTER HUNT:**
**Prince's Trophies Prepared**

**GOING TO IRAN:** Lee Carr Durdan, taxidermist at Jonas Brothers here, worked on a mountain goat bagged in British Columbia by Prince Abdorreza Pahlavi of Iran. Jonas Brothers is preparing 40 hunt trophies to ship to the prince, who has returned to Iran after a North American hunting trip. Some of the trophies include, from upper left, a Bighorn sheep from Wyoming, a desert sheep bagged in Nevada, a stone sheep shot in British Columbia, an Alaskan doll sheep and, at lower left, a buffalo bagged in Wyoming.

were rare, and they usually just had rows of heads lined on the wall. We encouraged hunters to save full skins of unusual animals, to consider full mounts. More and more, our ideas were accepted, and soon sportsmen were running out of space to display their specimens. So trophy rooms were popularized, with people adding onto existing homes, or selling out and building new, showcasing the hobby in which they had pride.

« ◯ **The Klineburger studios performed their services for a worldwide clientele. This clipping from *The Seattle Times* tells of 40 specimens prepared for H.I.H. Prince Abdorreza Pahlavi of Iran.**

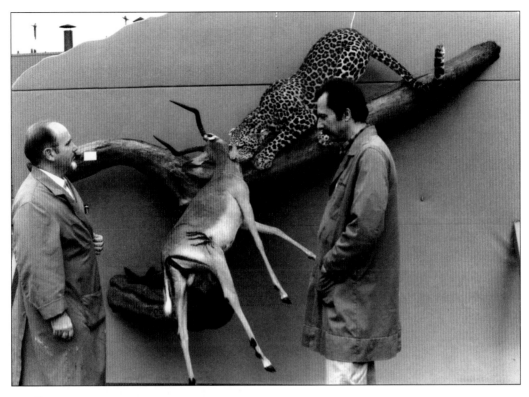

⚜ **Chris and Nouri Tadjbakhsh admire an artistic piece with a leopard and its kill.**

## REFLECTION
# Humor in Taxidermy

**H**unters are fun-loving people, and occasionally will do the bizarre. Here are a few strange requests that come to mind. A few nimrods were hunting black bears on the Olympic Peninsula adjacent to a field that had Black Angus cattle. The others picked on the novice hunter of the three, warning not to shoot one of those cows by mistake. The novice got a really big black bear, that the others claimed was a Black Angus, and wouldn't let up. Upon delivering their specimens to our studios, the two accusers instructed us on the side to get a Black Angus hide and mount it per the given instructions. Upon completion, we sent the Black Angus, open-mouth, snarling rug to the hunter. We got a heated call, and explained to the client that we had mounted the skin he gave us. After the joke surfaced, we sent the hunter his magnificent black bear.

Speaking of black bear, we had a customer who owned an eating establishment, The Black Bear Restaurant. He wanted a huge black bear to adorn his entranceway. This resulted in us taking a very large polar bear, dyeing it black, and mounting the towering beast on its hind legs, which apparently enhanced his business by curiosity seekers.

One of our good customers, John Stone, author of the book *Going For Broke,* had us create a Sasquatch (abominable snowman) for his trophy room. We sculpted the most perfect creature imaginable, covering it with a likely fake fur. While it was prominently displayed in our showroom, it created a lot of controversy, including our being investigated for mounting a possible humanoid.

Having every kind of animal skin imaginable floating around our studios, as well as a lot of mounted trophies for display, there was a demand for their use by individuals, businesses, and even for motion pictures. Sometimes I would get a little wild myself. Once I drove all over town with a fully mounted leopard in a sitting position in the passenger seat, staring out the window, almost causing collisions. Another time, Ruth McCormick and I were going to a Halloween costume party. We adorned ourselves as cave people, with leopard-skin garments and a wig I made from the long frontal hair of a bison. We did crazy things at the party, like dragging Ruth across the floor by her hair, while cameras were flashing, including mine that someone had put to use. A few days later I had the pictures back, and invited Ruth to a fancy restaurant. As we sat in our high-backed booth I noticed in one photo

that Ruth had bitten my leg while dragging. I said in a loud voice, "Hey you're biting my leg!" Heads poked around from all angles of curiosity seekers, expecting nothing less than an orgy.

« At a Halloween costume party, Chris and Ruth dressed as cave people, using the many surplus skins of the company.

We often did animations of sorts, with mounted specimens, usually for fun. We once had a full-sized moose on display at our booth at a sports show. We had the ears hinged to move, with a single thread back leading around to the attendant. While someone admired the moose, a little jerk on the thread would cause observers to snap their heads around on a double take. No more movement, until about the time the person would begin to look away—another jerk. They would go away shrugging and talking to themselves. We had a dear friend and customer, Wayne Ewing, a born kidder. He had us mount a lion with a tail that switched, and an elephant with ears that moved, both operated by remote control. Many a friend probably quit drinking from his well-stocked bar after touring his trophy room.

One of the more unusual requests we had was from a renowned prince of Saudi Arabia who sent in a full-sized hippo for mounting. Now hippos are big, just a step down from an elephant in body size. He wanted a trap door in the side, so that his kids could hide inside and when royal guests would tour his magnificent trophy room, they could jump out and scare them. We took it a step further to make it more comfortable and usable, by building in benches, carpeting the floor, putting padded lining over all of the internal fiberglass shell, and putting in a tape-deck for internal use, as well as a speaker in the hippo's mouth with a tape of hippo sounds.

# CHAPTER 20

# Hunting and Conservation Clubs

The sportsman has been making a contribution to America's outdoor landscape since the Colonial days, blazing the trail for the farsighted conservation programs he supports today. He has been in the forefront of every worthwhile conservation movement, by contributing time, hard work, and providing an ever-increasing flow of hunter-generated money. It was the sportsmen, the hunters, and anglers, who first saw the ill effects of expanding civilization on wildlife, forest, fields, and streams. They approached the problems with the same characteristic and perseverance of the hunt. In doing so, they needed strength in numbers, so clubs and organizations were the solutions.

In the late 1800s, three sportsmen, Theodore Roosevelt, Gifford Princhot, and George Grinnell, founded the first Audubon Society and the Boone and Crockett Club. (See Teddy Roosevelt, Chapter 10, Part II for details). The establishment of an international organization dealing with sustainable hunting and wildlife management was first brought up in 1910, at a hunting exhibition in Vienna. But it was only in 1928 when a special conference was held, resulting in the establishment of an international council called "Conseil International de la Chasse" (CIC). In 1930 the first general assembly was held in Paris, and it was widely

Colleene Klineburger took on the responsibility of organizing mounted animal specimens from our vast collection for sports shows and conventions. Here she narrates a style show for the Eddie Bauer Company, which at the time was the leading fashion and supply store for safaris. Between shows, she takes on tiger wrestling.

attended. CIC, like Boone & Crockett, established a measuring system for scoring all of the world's big game. The organization has grown and, to this day, has been influential in establishing wildlife conservation criteria.

The late '40s following World War II marked the dawn of international big game hunting. Prior to that, relatively few elite and adventurous individuals enjoyed African safaris and Indian shikars. Air travel, world peace, opportunity, and wealth (for some) contributed to an era of hunting never before experienced. Along with it came camaraderie among those collectors, most of whom started the first trophy rooms.

A group of mostly American hunters formed a club based in San Francisco to share their love of the outdoors and hunting. The club was named The Mzuri (pronounced similar to Missouri) Safari Club; mzuri is the word for "good" in Swahili, the predominant native language in British East Africa. At the time the club was restricted to 100 members, with certain qualifications. Fortunately, we Klineburgers were accepted in the club, where we contributed considerable knowledge with visual programs and articles in their publication, the Mzuri Drumbeat.

In 1937, a special interest group of duck hunters formed Ducks Unlimited. Realizing that the majority of all North American ducks and geese are born in Canada, nesting habitat was the focus of their efforts. Over the years, tens of millions of waterfowl hunter's dollars have gone into improving marshlands, which has increased waterfowl populations enormously in all of North and

Central America—another case of hunters initiating and paying for conservation.

In 1952, another exclusive club surfaced, the Shikar Safari Club, which limited its membership to 200. The criteria for belonging were to have at least two hunts to Africa and/or India. Realizing hunters were true conservationists, a foundation was eventually formed to raise money for conservation projects. Their earliest project was to save the almost extinct Arabian Oryx. They bought every known living Arabian Oryx, funded a compound at the Phoenix Zoo where the animals did well and multiplied, producing surplus quantities that eventually were returned to its native habitat in the Middle East, where it thrives today. Included in their many projects are helping to educate people in wildlife management worldwide. Conventions are held annually, exchanging information and raising funds for conservation. Bert Klineburger was inducted into the club early on, and has contributed greatly to their programs.

In the mid-'60s, a group of Texans, headed by Harry Tennison, and in cooperation with the Sportsmen's Clubs of Texas (SCOT), planned the first international hunting convention to be held in San Antonio. A new club was formed called Game Conservation International (Game Coin). Sportsmen and professional hunters all over the world were encouraged to join, and attend the first-ever conference of this sort.

Harry called on us in the early stages, requesting our support. We volunteered our extensive mailing list and wildlife decoration for the event. The date was set in the spring

Gathered at an early Game Conservation International Convention in San Antonio are Cotten Gordon, a hunting operator, Colleene Klineburger, Bill Jeffries and wife of jewelry fame and Thornton and Helen Snider, renowned sportsmen.

of 1966, and we loaded a Texas-bound truck container with dozens of life-size mounted animals from our Seattle studios and organized the use of specimens from the homes of San Antonio clients of ours.

The five-day event was an outstanding success, exchanging information and raising mega funds for conservation projects in various countries. Most importantly, this convention got the attention of world sportsmen and set a model of how hunters can join together and conserve wildlife everywhere. Our company had the only commercial booth at this historic convention, offering hunting expeditions outside North America, as well as our gold animal jewelry.

Game Coin planned their next conventions every second year, feeling that there was not enough new information to have the convention each year. As a result, the Mzuri Safari Club got fired up on this great concept and formed the Mzuri Safari Foundation to host a convention each odd year from the Game Coin conventions. The plan was made for Mzuri's convention in 1967 at Lake Tahoe, and our company offered the same support as we did for Game Coin the year before.

The club decided to take it one step farther by holding an auction of donated artwork, hunting trips and other outdoor-related goods. Also, we offered booth space to artists and hunting operators. Again, this added concept set a model for all future conventions to be held. Mzuri's conventions along with the alternating Game Coin conventions brought more and more attention to

the concept of hunters joining together for worldwide conservation of wildlife and their habitat.

Los Angeles was a hub for a great number of international big game hunters. We Klineburgers joined a well-established club, The Southern California Safari Club based in LA, where we attended their meetings and offered programs. We also enjoyed camaraderie with very many friends.

In 1971 the Safari Club of Los Angeles spun off and expanded rapidly under the leadership of C.J. "Mac" McElroy. We had a much broader concept of accomplishments and felt that "Los Angeles" was too restrictive,

**Conventions gave hunters the opportunity to discuss management and conservation needs with world leaders. Here at a Mzuri Safari Foundation Convention, Tom Bass presents the Governor of California, Ronald Reagan, with a Colt Sauer rifle.**

☝ **From the earliest hunters conventions in North America, the Klineburgers participated with information booths. Here, Skip Jennings of Klineburgers, left, and Colleene and hunting operator Jose Simoes, right, meet with a delegation of top wildlife officials from Sudan.**

so in 1972 changed the name to Safari Club International (SCI). Soon we moved the headquarters to Tucson, Arizona.

Yes, conventions were in our focus, as hunters everywhere were relishing the concepts established by those wonderful pioneers, Mzuri and Game Coin. So in 1973 we helped SCI launch their first convention, which took place in Las Vegas at the Riviera Hotel. Once again we had the only commercial booth.

As before, hunters came with big bucks, to support the SCI conservation efforts.

In meetings to follow, we came up with another new concept associated with clubs—establishing chapters in various locations worldwide. The first SCI chapters were Los Angeles and Chicago. I started the Northwest Chapter in 1974, which encompassed Oregon, Washington, Idaho, Canada, and Alaska. As time went by, our Northwest

RONALD REAGAN
GOVERNOR

**State of California**
GOVERNOR'S OFFICE
SACRAMENTO 95814

April 1, 1974


Mr. Chris Klineburger
Klineburger Bros.
1527 - 12th Avenue
Seattle, Washington 98122

Dear Mr. Klineburger:

Thank you for your kind remarks about my address before the
Muzuri Safari Foundation.

I appreciate your concern over irresponsible legislation.
However, we do not believe that the California Endangered
Species Act of 1970 falls in this category.  This act gave
authority to the California Fish and Game Commission to
establish rare or endangered classification for animals
native to California.

The legislation you refer to was an importation act similar
to New York's "Mason Act".  The importation into California
and sale of certain animals, including those which have been
declared "endangered" by the Secretary of the Interior, are
prohibited by Sections 653(o) and 653(p) of the State Penal
Code.  Your remarks regarding the inclusion of certain "abundant" animals in this importation act directed to endangered
species are well founded.

I can certainly appreciate your comments on big government.
I believe there is a hazardous tendency in our country to run
to government for answers to all the problems.  People have
forgotten that America's prosperity was not a gift from
government or anyone else.  Free enterprise and competition,
not government, is the source of our wealth.  Our high standard of living is based on a steady growth of the private
sector, the expansion of our technical capacity, and the
rising productivity of vast new industries.

In regard to my possible candidacy for the Presidency in
1976, I appreciate your confidence and trust, but it is too
soon to make any decisions beyond my present term as Governor
of California.  It will take single-minded concentration to
accomplish the things yet to be done in the time I have left.


In the event that we should ever decide to put together
another formal campaign, your letter will be on file.  I
am grateful for your support and hope I will continue to
merit your confidence.

Sincerely,

*Ronald Reagan*

RONALD REAGAN
Governor

**Ronald Reagan's response to an issue that Chris had discussed with the governor.**

Chapter spun off ten other chapters, which, combined, have thousands of members. Understandably, the local chapters have their own regular meetings and support local as well as international conservation efforts and also add to the interest in the National Chapter in Tucson.

SCI has grown to be the largest such club, with the broadest conservation efforts, and also having the largest convention held each winter, with more than 20,000 attendees and housing nearly two thousand exhibitors, raising funds into the seven figures for conservation efforts.

Specialty clubs of hunters with special interests have started in post war years. The first I remember was the Grand Slam Club. There are four different North American wild sheep: the dall sheep, stone sheep, Rocky Mountain bighorn sheep, and desert bighorn sheep. Whoever collected all four had the Grand Slam of sheep. Who first came up with the term, no one knows, but authors and hunting-related clubs used it from early on.

Bob Householder, a southern Arizona hunting guide started the club, which was mainly an information-sharing bulletin that Bob circulated about four times a year. The club also keeps track of those who collected the four sheep species. I contributed a lot of information for his newsletter in those early days until Bob's health failed and he turned the club over to someone else who has continued it to the time of this writing.

Once our company began opening Asia to hunting, wild sheep hunting became the

Apollo 13 Astronaut James Lovell and Colleene, at a Safari Club International Convention.

optimum specimen that collectors sought. An ardent hunter, Jay Mellon, collected 12 different sheep around the world, and wrote an article coining the name "Super Slam," describing his accomplishments.

While hunting bharal (blue sheep) in 1974 in the high Himalayas, five of us hunters met, and decided to form a Super Slam Club. Joe Quarto, Mahlon White, Bob Speegle, Ozzie Davis, and I went home and started the International Sheep Hunters Association (ISHA) as the keeper of records of the Super Slam hunters that collected 12 different species of the world's sheep. The main purpose, however, was to study and maintain records of all wild sheep outside North America including the argalis, urials, Asiatic bighorns, and pseudo sheep. The data we compiled on all the various subspecies

Conventions occasionally had taxidermy competitions.
Here, our Altai argali sheep took best of show.

has been the basis for almost all scientific data recognized today on wild sheep. One very important function of the club was to educate people worldwide about the importance of conserving this magnificent renewable resource.

Not long after we established ISHA, one of the all-time great special interest hunting clubs emerged, the Foundation For North American Wild Sheep (FNAWS). As before, the Klineburgers worked with this club from its inception. Their conventions have raised great sums of money to fund on-the-ground wild sheep enhancement projects, probably more than all other clubs combined. They work more closely with state and provincial game departments to help support their needs in conservation, disease, and transplant programs.

During 2007, FNAWS and ISHA joined together to be the preeminent organization that supports world sheep conservation and propagation. In addition to the sheep, they have also taken on the wildlife that share the same habitats—the caprinae, wild goats that include ibexes, markhors, chamois, tahr, and the like, as well as the Rocky Mountain goat. The name of the

combined clubs has changed to the Wild Sheep Foundation, which reflects its world-wide affiliation.

Many other special-interest hunting clubs have emerged, including the Mule Deer Foundation, the Elk Foundation, Ducks Unlimited, and many others that have done wonders for propagating and conserving wildlife and wildlife habitat. Books could be written about the entire range of hunting clubs and other organizations such as the Weatherby Foundation,

« The hunting and conservation conventions in America drew from around the world, including high profile people like Alexis von Goldsmidt-Rothschild of France, one of the founding fathers of the International Professional Hunters Association, who poses with Colleene.

In 1986 the World Hunting Congress was hosted by Safari Club International in Las Vegas, where countries from the world over exhibited. Klineburger Taxidermy supplied the specimens and created the booth for the U.S.A.

Raphik Kafarov, the head of the Hunting Department for the U.S.S.R., Intourist, is greeted by a host of Americans at the World Hunting Congress. Klineburger Travel supplied the booth for the U.S.S.R. From left, Chris, John & June Cotten, Raphik, Colleene, and Bob Markworth.

Water For Wildlife, The National Rifle Association, National Shooting Sports Foundation (NSSF), International Union Conservation of Nature (IUCN), National Wildlife Federation, the Izaak Walton League, local rod & gun clubs, and many more that are doing great things for wildlife conservation. The bottom line is that most all wildlife conservation existing in the world comes directly or indirectly from hunters.

## REFLECTION
# Safari Parties

In the early '70s hunting and conservation conventions were going full swing right after the first of each year, one after another, which became known as the convention season in the U.S.A. Seattle was a crossroads for guides and hunters alike, who would rarely fail to stop by and visit the Klineburgers' facilities. How do you handle so many visitors at one time on their way to the first convention in Reno or Las Vegas? Simple——throw a big party at our facility. In 1974, we had our first "Safari Party" in a big room lined with life-size mounts of every animal imaginable, including an elephant. The food was strictly exotic meats from land and sea, from cougar sausage to alligator to tapir burgers. It was too well attended by locals and out-of-towners alike——you might say, "standing room only."

So as years went by, we expanded into the taxidermy studios, a large 1,500-square-foot area. The food service was all along the small-portioned artists studios, each one with a different motif. One would display only wild boar type mounted specimens of wart hog, javelina, bush pig, giant foresthog, etc., while the meat would be sausages, kebobs, or chili verde made from hog-type wildlife. Another studio would have mounted

Lanny Wigren dips into the "Missionary Cocktail," a hit at all the Klineburger Safari Parties. The spiked concoction was in a huge iron pot, smoking with dry ice.

It appears there is standing room only, as the crowd flocks into a Klineburger Safari Party.

The seafood service area is typical of the dozen different wildlife cuisines served at the Safari Parties.

fish, king crabs, and other sea critters, while having seafood of every sort, from octopus to squaw candy. Another was supplied with deer species with venison, from moose to Coues deer, exotically prepared. The main floor was cleared of all rug-stretching and -lining equipment, and made into a fine, animal-lined restaurant.

Included in the lengthy affairs were special guest speakers like Roy Rogers and Stu Roosa (Apollo 14 astronaut). Entertainment included acts like a Filipino dance group, Bob Markworth, the famous archery act, and talks by Jack O'Conner and the like.

In years to follow it appeared our guests wanted to hang around Seattle for a while, so we expanded the party over parts of three days. Many arrived the day before the banquet, so the evening before we hosted a big cocktail party. During the day of the party we had hunting films and guest speakers in our in-house auditorium. The next morning we hosted a brunch within our studios. All in all, it ended up being a mini convention of sorts. A good friend and hunting buddy attending from the Bay Area said, "You ought to be ashamed, you have more people attending your Safari Party than Mzuri Foundation has attending their convention."

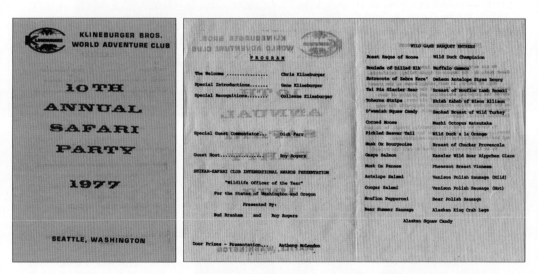

**The 10th Annual Safari Party of the Klineburgers was typical of what to expect.**

« Colonel Stuart Roosa, astronaut, takes the mike, while Bert (left) and Chris and Colleene (right) look on during the presentation at one of Klineburgers' Safari Parties.

Astronaut Wally Schirra was « » guest host at our 7th Annual Safari Party. Gene, on right and Colleene, seated, look on while I greet Wally.

« Colleene presents Roy Rogers an award at the Safari party, while brother Gene, seated, and Alaska outfitter Bud Branham, right, look on.

# CHAPTER 21

# Safari Island and the Ranches

It wasn't enough, all that expansion in North America, so we couldn't resist some fun encounters closer to home. A few tracts of irresistible land presented themselves that we felt could best be utilized as private hunting reserves. The first one was thousands of acres of land in the Quilomene Creek Canyon that extended from the Washington Cascade foothills down to the Columbia River, a few miles north of Vantage, where Interstate 90 crossed the Columbia Gorge. The area was rich in elk, mule deer, sage grouse, and chukar partridges.

We rounded up about a dozen hunter friends, who each agreed to chip in and buy it. We formed a corporation called Gamemasters Inc. Soon the word got around that we had posted it and prevented the public from using the land they thought was their own. The name "Gamemasters" echoed all the way from Yakima to Seattle, so we quickly changed the name to Quilomene Cattle Company, which seemed to ring better and help people understand why they shouldn't trespass.

There was already a cabin, but we put in a big manufactured home for the comfort of the shareholders. Some fine times were had by all, till the Washington State Game Department asked us to sell it to them to add to many more thousands of acres they had adjoining us. We

⟨⟩ **The Quilomene Cattle Company was a hunting preserve, later taken over by the Washington State Game Department. This photo shows the ranch house near the base of Quilomene creek before it flows into the Columbia River Gorge.**

did sell, and the Quilomene became a coveted reserve. Special drawings are conducted yearly for mule deer permits there because of the demand for the high-quality bucks the area produced.

Our next encounter was a tract of land in eastern Oregon bordering the Grande Ronde River, north of La Grande, in the Umatilla National Forest. Again, the area was prime elk and mule deer country, and it also had turkeys and other game birds. The ranch had a well-made, hand-hewn log lodge on it, besides a couple of well-situated cabins.

It wasn't hard to muster up a dozen outdoor enthusiasts to chip in with us to purchase what we named the Grande Ronde Ranch. We did a lot of entertaining there in that beautiful forested paradise; guests included our good friend Roy Rogers. One problem we had was that a main road went through the property, and there was no fencing to prevent trespassing. Eventually, the owners decided to sell for a profit.

The next opportunity came from a good friend and well-known big game hunter, Tony Sulak of Seattle. He had bought an island in the San Juan Islands before World War II, when owning islands was not fashionable. It was Spieden Island, a 3½-mile long island off the north tip of San Juan Island. Tony, being a pilot himself, built a runway on it and a hanger. There were a few old homes on it, but he built a huge log lodge, swimming pool, boathouse, and other structures along

The lodge at the ⟨⟩» Grand Ronde Ranch overlooked a small lake before the land gradually sloped off to the Grand Ronde River in northeastern Oregon.

with a small road system. The island has a variety of terrain with grassy, barren slopes on the south side. It is parklike on top, with oak trees and Douglas fir. On the north side are dense forests of cedar, fir, and spruce trees. He had domestic sheep and cattle on it to keep the grass down. From the lodge on top, a few hundred feet above sea level, the view is across to Roche Harbor on San Juan, to the right is Vancouver Island and right down below is small Sentinel Island, which was owned by movie star Bob Burns, whom you old timers might remember as the bazooka player.

As Tony aged, he found the island too much bother to maintain, so asked us if we wanted to buy it. We said, "Sure, give us a little time." Our idea that we presented to potential partners was to remove the cattle and sheep and stock it with exotic wildlife. About 15 people jumped on the bandwagon, and the deal went through.

I already had a surplus of fallow deer, sika deer, and mouflon sheep on the High Lonesome Ranch, which I contributed to the cause. The Seattle Zoo likewise wanted to cut their expanding herds of deer back, as did a game farm in Northern Washington. Other exotic animals were brought by stock truck from Texas where game farms abound. Before long, we had respectable herds of fallow deer, sika deer, red deer, Barbary sheep, mouflon sheep, axis deer, wild turkeys, and pheasants. We changed the name to Safari Island.

For a few years the island paradise was enjoyed by all, mainly fishing, crabbing, clamming, game viewing, and just plain enjoying the serenity of the calm, island waterways.

Washington State Ferries has one run that goes from Anacortes, Washington, to Sidney, B.C., on Vancouver Island, and it passed right by our island. They would slow down when wildlife was in view on the open slopes, and make an announcement. On their maps, they put "Safari Island" (Speident Island).

The wildlife must have enjoyed the island living, as they propagated to the point of overpopulation. We began culling by offering a limited hunting program for the older male animals. The female and young seemed to always be in view, but the wise, old guys hung out in the dense forests during the day, making it tough hunting, and often unsuccessful for a visiting sportsman.

In the late '60s it seemed American people were mentally stable and still believed in man's inborn hunting heritage. "Anti-hunting" was certainly not in the vocabulary of the American people. CBS apparently decided to launch an anti-hunting era, starting with Safari Island. Walter Cronkite approached us, saying that we had a wonderful idea of making better land use of the island and wanted to film our operation. We agreed, and they sent a film crew at a time when we were sure to have a hunter that they could feature. They followed the hunter for several days, during which he took a few specimens. They had the hunter shoot his rifle a number of times, saying they needed the shots to splice in for the sequence of the hunt.

Another call from CBS said in order to complete the story, they needed film of how we brought animals to the island. Some months later, we happened to have some new

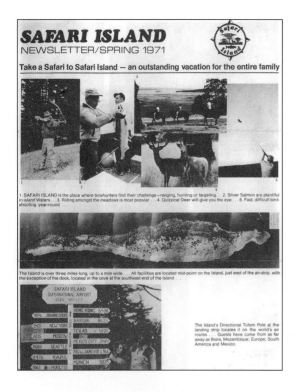

SAFARI ISLAND
NEWSLETTER/SPRING 1971

Take a Safari to Safari Island — an outstanding vacation for the entire family

1. SAFARI ISLAND is the place where bowhunters find their challenge—ranging, hunting or targeting . . . 2. Silver Salmon are plentiful in island Waters . . . 3. Riding amongst the meadows is most popular . . . 4. Quizzical Deer will give you the eye . . . 5. Fast, difficult bird-shooting year-round . . .

The Island is over three miles long, up to a mile wide . . . All facilities are located mid-point on the Island, just east of the air-strip, with the exception of the dock, located in the cove at the southeast end of the Island . . .

The Island's Directional Totem Pole at the landing strip locates it on the world's air routes . . . Guests have come from as far away as Beira, Mozambique; Europe; South America and Mexico.

**Here is the front page of a newsletter distributed by Safari Island.**

**Another Klineburger business we started, as an expansion of the Taxidermy Department, was creating wax figures for museums and special exhibits. Here Chris looks over "John Wayne" to promote the movie *True Grit*. On left is "Moses" being created for a religious exhibit; Saudi royalty on the right, and a nude Indian maiden in the back.**

breeding stock coming from Texas, so they sent a film crew to record the unloading of the stock trailer on the island. They made a number of shots of the animals exiting the trailer.

Featured on national television was a sequence of the confused animals leaving the trailer. Dubbed-in were many shots of the hunter shooting, followed by the bloodiest shot they could muster up of the man with a trophy. They obviously wanted the viewer to believe the hunter was shooting the wildlife as it exited the trailer.

Soon after, other tainted TV films came out making hunters and hunting look as bad as possible, including *Say Goodbye* and *Guns of Autumn*. This was the beginning of an era that changed American values forever. It bears noting that all this happened during the time when hunters were forming international conservation clubs and foundations to protect and propagate wildlife the world over.

## REFLECTION
# The King and Queen of Nepal

Jonas Brothers of Seattle, our taxidermy company, became the most knowledgeable source of hunting information in the world. We knew the hunting operators and kept track of where the best specimens were coming from, and which outfitters were the best.

Somehow the Nepalese Embassy had heard of us and inquired about an Alaska hunt for Their Imperial Highnesses King Mahendra and Queen Retna of Nepal, who wanted to get everything possible on a single trip. They had a short list of registered guides for us to review, and we recommended Al Burnett, an up-and-coming and versatile operator.

Once selected, the U.S. Department of State requested Al to come to Washington for instruction on the handling of foreign diplomats, indicating no holds barred. Washington even contacted the Coast Guard in Alaska to provide support for the expedition. Al arranged with other operators to assist, as hunting would be done in various locations on the Alaska Peninsula and the Alaska Range, as well as various tundra locations.

The time was set for the entourage of over a dozen staff, along with the imperial couple on Air Force One, to arrive at Elmendorf Air Force Base in Anchorage. An entire floor was secured at the Captain Cook Hotel, before chartering to one destination after another.

Coast Guard aircraft were volunteered for various segments of the hunt. Strange requests were fulfilled at Their Highnesses desires, such as fresh pineapple from Hawaii. The hunt went well, and fine shooting by the imperial couple resulted in Alaska brown bear, moose, caribou, mountain goat, and Dall sheep. My brother Bert accompanied most of the trip as an advisor and to oversee the trophy care.

All went well, and Their Highnesses were very happy with their official visit to Alaska. The only other tour of North America, aside from an official visit in Washington D.C., was a visit with the Klineburgers in Seattle.

The Seattle city fathers were more than happy to provide a motorcade to our taxidermy studios and later to the Space Needle Restaurant, which we had blocked off for our huge party.

**The King and Queen of Nepal, left with backs to camera, listen while Chris tells of his tiger hunt in India. Secret Service and police were ever-present.**

A note of interest: the Whittaker brothers, who managed the sports store Recreation Equipment Inc. (REI) and who recently climbed the summit of Mount Everest in Nepal, requested the royals to come tour their facilities just around the corner from us.

Their response was a simple, "No, we came here to visit the Klineburgers." Another interesting result of the hunt was that, after all the instruction and promised support by our country's fathers, when it came to paying up, Washington refused to have any part of it.

The Alaska Game Department filed charges of illegal flying (by the Coast Guard), all of which almost threw Al Burnett into bankruptcy, and he had his guide's license revoked.

# CHAPTER 22

# Maquiladora

By the late 1970s we had a great number of clients from Mexico having us do their taxidermy work. When the finished mounts would be shipped into Mexico it seemed that every customs official would come up with a new rule, with the idea of getting paid off to offset the rule. A few of our good Mexican friends convinced us that a branch studio south of the border would be a highly profitable business. We agreed, but at the time, government regulations required a majority ownership by Mexican citizens, so we were 49 percent owners, while our partners had 51 percent. It so happened that one partner had a facility the perfect size for our studio in the city of Monterrey, N.L., a place that had many big game hunters.

So Klineburger Taxidermia de Mexico became a reality. I took Heda Tajbakhsh to Monterrey along with a large inventory of supplies to get started. Heda was one of the two brothers that we had trained for Iran, but who were still in our employment. His function was to train the Mexicans, along with doing taxidermy himself.

At this same time Texas was overrun by big game hunters, and a new trade agreement had begun between the U.S.A. and Mexico, called Maquiladoras. These Mexican manufacturing facilities could be established, utilizing Mexican labor on products that would come to U.S.A. duty-free. So why not start a taxidermy facility as well in nearby San Antonio, Texas, to be the sister company on the U.S.A. side of the border? Klineburger Taxidermy of Texas was soon formed, where we put Nouri Tajbakhsh, who was the other Iranian brother, in charge.

All seemed to go well, as both studios were busy doing their own thing. However two major problems arose from the Mexican side. One was the fact that our Mexican partners refused to ever show us a financial statement, nor would they pay us for the great amount of supplies we kept sending them. The other major problem was that the Mexicans avoided obtaining proper documentation required by the respective Fish & Wildlife Departments. Their reasoning was that it took longer and cost much more to do things legally than illegally. They said they had to bribe the Mexican officials every step of the way. But by doing things illegally, they would get immediate action, and only pay one bribe!

We wanted no part of doing business without legal documentation, and concluded that we would never see a penny of profit, so we told our Mexican partners they could have the business free and clear, just take our name off the building. As a result, we shut down the San Antonio operation as well.

# ACCOUNTS OF NOTEWORTHY NORTH AMERICAN ADVENTURES

By the early 1960s, Chris had collected 26 different North American big game species—polar bear, glacier bear, black bear, grizzly bear, Alaska brown bear (Kodiak Island and Alaska Peninsula), bison, javelina, desert sheep, bighorn sheep, Dall sheep, Fannin sheep, Stone sheep, mountain goat, barren ground caribou, mountain caribou, Alaska moose, Canadian moose, mule deer, Coues deer, blacktail deer, desert mule deer, elk, cougar, seal, and walrus.

Multiple specimens of a number of species were taken, including two Grand Slams of North American wild sheep. To write stories of most hunting experiences, including a number of unsuccessful trips, would tax the patience of even the most ardent reader, not to mention a delay in getting into some of Chris's most challenging expeditions. However, a few North American adventures are noteworthy or out of the ordinary, and are included.

PART II

# ACCOUNTS OF NOTEWORTHY
# NORTH AMERICAN ADVENTURES

# CHAPTER 1

# The Big Bad Bull of Klavesna

One does not normally consider the American buffalo to be a tough animal to hunt, even in Alaska, but not so for Chris. Bisons were originally planted in the Big Delta area east of Fairbanks. The herd propagated very well and the state began allowing hunters to cull the herd, issuing permits on a drawing basis. The herd kept expanding and small groups started wandering farther and farther from Big Delta, in some cases hundreds of miles to the south.

The State Game Department announced they would allow a one-time season on the wandering critters. The regulation stated that anyone could hunt and they could use a moose or bear tag on their kill (if they didn't have a bison tag), and that the season would be cut off after 25 animals were taken.

I called my good friend Wayne Heimer with the Game Department in Fairbanks and one who was involved with the bison. I asked his opinion of my trying for a trophy. He said they were widely scattered, and in some tough areas to get into. He did tell me of one big, old, lone bull that hung out at the edge of the Wrangell Mountains near the Klavesna Glacier. He said on surveys they occasionally spotted the bull, and would fly low to look him over. The bull would brace himself, hook his horns at the plane, and paw the ground as if to say, "Come a little closer, and I'll get you!" Well, that was the bull for me.

I talked to a good friend Eldon Brandt, who lived at mile 123 on the Denali Highway out of Anchorage to see whether he was interested in joining me on the pursuit of "The Big Bad Bull of Klavesna," a name coined by Wayne. Eldon was a well-known outfitter and bush pilot with whom I had some fine adventures. Eldon said, "Let's do it."

We tanked up his Super Cub and away we went east till we got to the area of the Klavesna Glacier, a great ice flow exiting westward from the rugged Wrangell Mountains. Sure enough, we eventually located the notorious bull. We stayed away so as not to spook him, but he still gave us his signature I-dare-you horn hook. We found a gravel bar some distance away that Eldon landed on. We set up camp with my little pop-up two-man mountain tent. Eldon didn't care much for our muddy landing strip, saying if it rained, we might not be able to take off on that gummy surface, so we flew around to see if we could find more solid ground. A few miles into the forested lowlands, Eldon spotted what looked like an old prospector's strip, all grown over with grass, alongside a small river. As he touched down in the foot-high grass, the right wheel struck a boulder and sent us into a spin, destabilizing the plane. (See Chapter 4 "Crash Landings" for details.) Eldon radioed Jack Wilson, a bush pilot from Gakona, who flew in and landed on our well-marked runway. Jack flew me to our other campsite to dismantle and bring

the camp to my new abode. We put the bent prop, broken gear and other damaged parts into Jack's Super Cub, along with Eldon and I waved them goodbye with a departing, "I'm going hunting."

The rest of the day I used to set up camp and cooking a freeze-dried meal and hot chocolate on the Coleman stove. In surveying my hunt strategy for the next day, it was apparent I had to cross the river to pursue my quarry, so I cut a 10-foot sturdy pole to use as a third leg when crossing the small glacial river, which appeared to be about three feet deep in the channel of the fast flowing icy waters. Ice was starting to form on the banks on this October day. I readied my wood-molded army pack board with my rucksack containing my 16mm Bell & Howell 240T movie camera, Retina folding still camera, spare ammo, survival kit, knives, candy bar, and apple, as well as my spare T-shirt to be used as a towel.

Up at daybreak, after an oatmeal breakfast, I slipped on my hiking boots without socks (no hip boots) and with my pants and socks secured to my pack board, rifle slung over my head, I set out for the frigid crossing. Once to the other side, I dumped the water out of my boots and dried off with the T-shirt. Then I put on my pants and dry wool socks over legs and feet that were a fine shade of blue, before lacing up those wet boots.

I trotted for a while to get the blood into circulation, as I proceeded in a direction where the bull was the day before. Within an hour, I was at the edge of the vast alluvial plain, beyond which were the slopes of the Wrangells. No bison to be seen. Figuring he probably came to the wooded area for the night, I patrolled the forest edge for tracks. I encountered a number of huge, older tracks that could only belong to moose or bison. Upon close inspection of differences, I found some were more elongated. I decided that had to be moose, resulting from their swampy habitat.

Eventually I found fresh bison hoof impressions that led into the woods, so I began to track. Recent rains left the ground wet enough to reveal disturbance in the vegetation and an occasional hoof mark. I also saw fresh droppings.

Moving with dead silence, gun in readiness and eyes studying every object in view, I was delighted to realize my direction was somewhat toward my spike camp. It was slow moving, as each step had to be void of twig snapping and a pause after every few steps to search the everchanging horizon, knowing that the wise, old fella could be circling back to the wide-open spaces.

The thrilling moment finally came upon topping a low rise when I spotted the bulky mass, undisturbed, not more than 150 yards away. He was close enough for an offhand shot, but not to take chances, I slid the rifle onto a rest as I lay prone, and squeezed a round off into the bull's shoulder.

I didn't see more than a flinch from him, as he stood looking around and pawing the ground. He heard the rattle as I jacked another round into the chamber, after which I quickly placed another shot into his shoulder. He was still on his feet and heading my way,

so I placed a third shot into his head, and that brought him down.

With a fully loaded magazine, I approached the still breathing, but unconscious mass from the backside and placed another shot between the horns on top of the head. I put a forked stick in the ground to hang the movie camera on, started it, and walked into the view for an action shot of me approaching the trophy.

To my amazement, the bull started to get up. I quickly moved around to place a shot directly into the forehead, which put him down again. Rewinding the camera, I went through the same process as before. And yes, the bison tried to get up again. Another round into the forehead finally put him down for good.

A later study of the skull revealed why it was so difficult to finish off this great animal. I found that my first two shots into the head merely indented the skull with a slight crack, about the size of a half dollar.

I theorized that my .300 Weatherby Magnum's soft-point bullets balled up in six-inch-long, dense, wiry hair before it contacted the one-inch-thick forehead skin, which stopped the projectile completely. The third bullet probably went through parted hair, and made its way through the skull.

Have you ever heard the expression "now the hard work starts" after a successful chase? You ain't heard nothin' till you hear about this kid, all alone, skinning and packing out this ton of an animal!

After the movies and some pictures with the self-timer on the camera, the biggest-single

**"Now how am I going to get this monster skinned and packed back to the strip?"**

skinning job that I have ever encountered was about to begin, and last for the next day and a half. It was about midday, so I dove into it. Since I was saving the skin for a life-size mount, I couldn't quarter the animal with skin attached. Therefore, it took me about two hours to lay one side of the skin back, and cut the quarters of meat and back section off the skin. It would have been impossible for me alone to roll the animal, or even open the belly enough to eviscerate him, so everything had to be done piecemeal. The days were getting short, so I figured I had better start heading back to camp. I cut one section of meat, about 125 pounds, and strapped it

to the pack board and headed back to the bank of the river about a mile away. I left the meat lying there before crossing the river in the same fashion I did before. It was good to get into the tent. With the use of a Coleman stove, it got warm enough to make it quite comfortable so I could have a nice meal. The one big problem was that the heat and moisture in the tent would condense on the inside poles and then start dripping. Until things froze down real good, it got kind of wet.

The next morning I found a pair of frozen boots, which did thaw out as I walked through the water. Instead of changing at this point, however, I virtually ran to the buffalo and started a fire to thaw myself out. This was to be my routine for the next couple of days.

After I thawed out, I spent the rest of the day removing the meat from the skin instead of the skin from the meat. Then I had to get the meat into pack-sized loads before it froze. After I got the meat off the second side of the skin, it is needless to say that the first half, which I had skinned out the day before, was frozen solid. So I built a reflector fire and propped the skin up so it would thaw enough to roll it up.

Once I got the skin rolled up, with head and skull removed, I strapped it to the pack board. No matter how I tried, I could not get off the ground with that load, which was perhaps 300 pounds. A buffalo hide is unbelievably heavy, with skin up to an inch thick in places and a good 10-foot squared on the ground.

So I unrolled it and cut it in two, right behind the shoulders and, even at that, I think the front half must have weighed 175 pounds. All the meat was boned out, relayed to the river in the next couple of days, and left there with the hope in mind that Eldon would think to bring a pair of hip boots or waders.

Throughout the hunt I have been on grizzly and wolf watch, with rifle always

**A load of meat and horns on the riverbank, carried in my molded wood army pack frame.**

To give an idea of the size of a bison skin, I'm showing Bert Klineburger and Stan Burrell, guide, with Bert's wood bison taken in the Northwest Territories.

within reach. Fortunately, I had not seen any fresh bear signs. I figured they might have already migrated lower near the Copper River that has salmon runs. Still, with all this meat around, I was on a 360-degree watch.

By the end of the fourth day of strenuous work, I was ready to rest. Then, at about noon the next day, I heard the welcoming sound of Jack's Cub. Eldon had a second hand prop and the other repaired parts and, yes, hip boots. Jack agreed to wait so that he could haul all the meat and skin to Gakona,

so I donned the hip boots and ferried it all across the river, which had receded somewhat because of the cold temperatures.

Eldon and Jack were shaking their heads in amazement that I actually had ventured out on my own, found the bison, and packed-out all the meat and full skin. I was now carrying load after 100-pound-plus load through the river, with my 10-foot third leg steadying me. As Jack bid us goodbye, he patted me on the back and said, "You're some kind of guy."

# REFLECTION
# The Water Hole

**I** don't know whether it was poor airline connections or just a good place for a rest stop for hunters en route to Alaska or the Yukon. Regardless, Seattle was the crossroads where these nimrods would regroup. Early on, our taxidermy company was a must to visit—and socialize. The back office-cum-bar didn't seem to fit the bill, so a spare office was furnished for the frequent bull sessions.

No matter how spacious our entertainment center was, it seemed to outgrow itself. As our company expanded, each of the three times we moved, locations were allowed space for an ever-increasing "visitor center," which became known as the Water Hole. At our last location, circa 1975–1996, near First and Spokane Street, the Water Hole encompassed 2,000 square feet of party space. It became much more than a place to serve cocktails to transient hunters, because locals frequented it, as well as clubs and other groups needing a meeting place. The motif was African, with a rondoval bar capped with a grass-thatched roof, yet equipped for visual and audio entertainment, or as a banquet facility.

Aside from being enjoyed by "the good old boys," the Water Hole lounged celebrities of every sort—movie stars, royalty, astronauts, entrepreneurs, foreign heads of state, entertainers, politicians, and hunting outfitters who ventured out of Alaska and Canada. Once they'd winterized their bush planes and horses at season's end, many outfitters snowbirded with Seattle and Klineburgers' hospitality being the first stop. This included the Water Hole and a nice dinner at the waterfront—fresh crab, clams, and salmon—mmm.

Did I mention gangsters and the mob? One of our favorites was a New York mobster who hunted every year in Alaska or Canada (he was afraid to hunt overseas and go through immigration), who would always spend at least an extra day in Seattle to be with us. One time Joey (not his real name) stopped by, and he was very depressed. "Boit and Chrees (Bert and Chris), I am very noivous. Even tough I neva' did a thing to hoit anotha' poisson, they got me on a tiny ting, dat could put me in da Big House." He lectured us—if you want to do away with someone, don't use a car bomb, as it could kill the wife or some other innocent person. It's best to become close pals with the guy, then after a year, do away with him, and no one will suspect you. (Joey did spend time, and he was never the same after.)

Guide, gangster, or prince, they were just friends with common interests, and were treated just the same. If the walls of the Water Hole had ears and could record all the great stories told, perhaps three more books could be written.

" The Water Hole has seen visitors from around the world, including these guests from China. Miss Jao Yufen, second from left, is the Head of China Women's Travel Service that we used extensively for our clients travelling through Beijing or sightseeing anywhere in China. Ralph Williams, our agency manager, and son Kent, on the right.

# Ghost Bear

Probably the rarest and most elusive of all North American big game is the glacier bear. He's about as hard to find as a ghost, and he's treated with as much respect as a ghost by his cousins the black bear and the Alaska brown bear, which share the same, rugged country.

"Look at that black bear!" Al Burnett exclaimed.

"He must have seen a ghost," was my reply.

"There must be a brown bear up there!" Al mumbled.

We watched him until he went out of sight, over the ridge, far above us.

Black bears were no exceptional sight to us at this point, because by actual count, this was 73 bears we had looked at since the start of our hunt over a week before. I had hunted Kodiak bear with Al the year before, and he ran a fine operation.

Besides being a big game guide, he likes a little adventure and excitement, and it was through a conversation over a plate of seafood in Seattle a couple of months earlier that we started planning this hunt for the most rare of all North American big game trophies, the glacier bear. Al said he had a good friend, Pat Stearns, an Indian in Yakutat, who had a boat and knew the area where glacier bears range. Within a month's time, after Al's return to Kodiak via Yakutat, he had the hunt arranged.

The glacier bear is a smaller cousin of the black bear, and it's noted for its blue-grey color. It is sometimes called the blue bear. Its range is basically in southeastern Alaska along the glacier-laden mountain ranges that separate Alaska and British Columbia, thus being dubbed "glacier bear." Yakutat is one of the few settlements along the forbidding, rugged coast, and the heart of the glacier bear habitat.

The hunt was arranged to start around mid-May, about break-up time when the bears were just out of hibernation, but before the trees and brush were leafed out so we had better visibility. I flew to Anchorage and took a short connecting flight to Yakutat. Al met me after flying there from Kodiak in his Cessna 185. He had already set up a tent at a pre-established point among the glaciers at

the base of the towering St. Elias Mountains. Al flew my gear to the camp, while I visited with Pat and Emma Stearns on their beautiful 32-foot fiberglass cruiser, which was ready to go north around the peninsula and into Russell Fiord to rendezvous with Al and me at our camp. Soon Al was back, and as soon as he had refueled, we were airborne for camp.

We landed and taxied into the cove at our tent camp. We could see fresh brown bear tracks where the water had receded. We were lucky to have any gear or tent left, as the brownies are known for their destructiveness. Evidently the bear was working the

**Pat and Emma Stearns on their boat that we used as transport during the glacier bear hunt.**

beach for mussels and sea urchins and didn't notice our camp.

The next day Pat's boat was to rendezvous with us at camp, but did not show, so we flew up the fiord to look for him. A tremendous glacier and icebergs tumbling from it had the channel blocked, making it dangerous to come through. Pat's boat was at an anchorage outside the channel, in a place between grounded icebergs, which is where we landed.

We hashed out strategy over a cup of hot tea. After looking at the snow conditions inside the fiord, we were convinced the bears weren't quite out of hibernation for lack of feed. We decided to move into a seal-hunting cabin of Pat's on Egg Island where we could tie up the airplane and leave the bulk of our supplies, and then hunt mainly by boat and foot along the glaciers.

The town of Yakutat lies at the foot of a large peninsula along Alaska's Inside Passage. The peninsula extends some 50 miles to the north, separating the huge bay "Russell Fiord" from the passage. Egg Island lies in the glacier-laden bay at the head of the peninsula and fiord. Hubbard Glacier flows right out toward the head of the peninsula, often almost closing off Russell Fiord, which was the case now. Huge icebergs were moving in and out of the gap with tides rushing up to 30 miles an hour.

During our time with Pat Stearns I assumed that he was a Thlingit Indian and a lot of our discussions were about these interesting people peculiar to this area. When Al and I talked about our hometowns where we grew up in Arizona, Pat revealed that he was a full-blooded Apache Indian from Apache Junction, Arizona, so it was "old homecoming" for a few desert rats as we drifted among the icebergs.

Pat's wife was a full-blooded Tlingit, who had been with him for his 25 years in Alaska. Pat explained the reason why the Indians had white man's names was that the early explorers and settlers had difficulty pronouncing their names so they renamed them. He told me about a friend, Ham George, whose wife had problems when their son was born. The doctor said she could no longer bear children, so they named him "Lonesome," thereafter being Lonesome George.

For the next nine days we constantly patrolled up and down the peninsula, often staying on the boat in Chicago Bay, a protected inlet some 15 miles north of Yakutat. We moved at trolling speeds, so we frequently had lines out for salmon. Pat put crab and shrimp pots out at Egg Island and Chicago Bay and we frequently hit beaches and dug for clams—we ate well. However, no time was spent from dawn to dark without being on constant watch for gray objects. We glassed thousands of gray rocks, hoping for movement.

While we watched the black bear mentioned at the beginning of this story run out of sight, Al's voice broke out with excitement "Glacier bear!" he exclaimed. His glasses were trained on the spot where we had seen the running black bear.

He explained where it was and I took a look. "It's a rock," I said.

From dawn 'til dark, it was constant glassing of the hillsides, as Chris does here. Note Hubbard Glacier in the background, which is 6 miles across, and 400 feet high at the tide level.

"No, it's a bear" Al replied.

I had seen a thousand objects that color already in the past week, but then I saw it move. The sight left us all speechless for several moments.

"What time is it?" Pat inquired.

"8 PM," was my reply. "Maybe an hour and a half before dark."

Our hearts all sank. Without saying it, we knew it was too late to go after that bear. It was practically a mile straight up, which under normal hiking conditions would be nothing, but through the alders and devil's club, it would take three hours to get that far.

We watched that beautiful silver-blue spot on the mountain for the next several minutes, until it disappeared into the brush.

As we headed back for our anchorage, Pat told us it was believed that the brown and black bears in the area always treated the glacier bear with respect, even though he is the smallest of the North American bear species. He said that quite often he had seen other bears excited when a glacier bear was around, but has never seen a glacier bear associating with another type of bear. He also told us that when the glacier bear was first seen by the Indians they believed that it was a ghost of a black bear, but the legend eventually wore off.

Dawn revealed a storm out in the straits preventing us from going out to see whether we could once again spot the bear. It had been raining, and the clouds were very low, which meant very poor visibility for spotting. Therefore, we decided to troll the area closer to Egg Island along the beaches in toward Hubbard Glacier.

Pat had been towing an outboard-powered skiff behind his cruiser, so we used it and stayed fairly close to shore as the clouds closed down to a fog. It was a weird feeling as we cruised around the blue icebergs in the dead calm of the water and fog. In a break in the fog I was looking at, a long snow slide coming down off the mountain, and silhouetted right in the center of it was a glacier bear!

The fog passed over it, hiding it from our view. When it cleared seconds later, the bear was gone. Al had caught a glimpse of it, too; and we stood there in amazement as if there was something to this ghost bit. In actual fact, because of the steepness of the slide, the bear had just paused to catch its footing and then had run to the other side.

All the bears we had seen seemed to be on the move, so we decided we should do something to try to intercept this one. We went quite a way beyond the direction the bear had been going and beached the skiff at the base of a snow slide that extended to the mountaintop.

Al and I worked our way up the slide to get above the bear hoping to get lucky enough to catch him crossing the slide. Climbing was bad for us as the slope must have been about 60 degrees, and if we slipped we'd find ourselves sliding several hundred yards before we'd be able to stop.

We took turns kicking steps into the crusty snow. Once we were high enough we split and went to opposite sides of the slide to sit and wait. I sat on a rocky outcrop to the side, which gave me a good view of the slide below.

I watched Pat in the skiff down among the icebergs and could see why bears don't pay much attention to boats in this area. With all the ice drifting by, along with the bears' poor eyesight, they don't seem to take a second look at anything in the water. Also, there is so much noise from the glaciers, the icebergs breaking and the wind that I doubt whether sound would make any difference to them either.

There was a break in the fog, and from where I sat I had a fantastic panorama of the inlet where I could look one way and see Hubbard Glacier with its deep blue ice plunging into the bay. Straight ahead was Malaspina Glacier, which is bigger than the state of Rhode Island. Beyond that was Mount St. Elias, more than 18,000 feet high, and Mount Logan, almost 20,000 feet high, the second highest in North America.

In fact, the St. Elias Range is mostly over 10,000 feet in elevation, giving life to the hundreds of glaciers. There was constant thundering of internal breaking of ice in the glaciers and when a piece let go of "Old Mother Hubbard" the sound was deafening with hundreds of tons of ice falling several

Author and Al are mighty proud of Chris's rare specimen.
After making a life-size mount of the bear, Chris donated it to the International Wildlife Museum in Tucson, Arizona for permanent display.

hundred feet into the ocean. The "small" arm of Hubbard Glacier visible to me is six miles across the foot and 400 feet above the tide level. These awe-inspiring sights almost made me forget why I was sitting there. These bears don't know how safe they are. It would be near impossible to ever stalk a bear in this dense, brushy country—let alone see them.

Quite a bit of time had gone by when Al appeared across the slide and signaled we better start down. Every foot of my climb was well earned, so I didn't want to give it back too soon. I decided to go very slowly, and keep my eyes and ears open. The fog had lifted for a while, but an occasional patch still moved across the landscape.

Still sort of lost in a dream world, with all this excitement of the seeing of a glacier bear and the beautiful panorama of the country, I stopped momentarily while a patch of fog moved just below me across the slide. As it cleared, there—standing a couple of hundred yards below me, in the middle of the slide—was the glacier bear. It was as if it were an optical effect in a motion picture.

If I have ever believed in ghosts, spirits, fate, you name it—I did at that moment. I sat down in the snow, resting elbows on knees and placed the crosshairs just under the brisket. I had been priming myself for such a steep straight up or down shot, where there would be less bullet drop than on horizontal. The scope was sighted at 200 yards on the level, so the bullet would be several inches high at a steep angle like this.

I squeezed off, and the bear collapsed. It rolled into an outcrop of brush and stopped.

We together slid the bear on the snow down to the beach, not saying much in this emotional moment. Sometimes words are too small.

Al, Pat, and I shared the same feelings of contentment and excitement—a feeling that can only be understood by a sportsman who has experienced similar success. It was all our combined and continuous efforts that made it possible. This was one of the great experiences of my life, and certainly one of my most coveted specimens.

**Our bag for the two-week hunt was two glacier bears and five black bears. Here Al Burnett does the final skinning on my bear.**

🐾 **Chris packs out the skin of a huge black bear that he collected in the Yakutat area.**

## REFLECTION
# Northern British Columbia Guides

Like hunters, the big game outfitters began organizing in order to share common interests and present themselves as a negotiating body when dealing with game laws and other matters relating to their livelihood. One of the first such organizations was the North British Columbia Guides and Outfitters Association, which set precedent for others to follow.

One might wonder how and why these pioneers evolved to fill a vital need of opening up backcountry to adventure-seeking people and explorers alike. What came first, the horse or the cart? Those seeking outfitting were the catalyst for forming guide services, including prospectors, scientists, hunters and fishermen, and anyone wanting to see what was on the other side of the mountain. Of all these, hunters were the predominant force establishing the need. Who were the potential outfitters? Those who had access to potential destinations, including the means of transportation. The transport was usually horses or bush planes, supplemented with back-packing.

Not to get too much into detail of such a broad subject, let's take the model of Canada's Northern British Columbia to demonstrate the evolution. As said before, sport hunting in large part started only after World War II. At the same time, ranching expanded further into the wilderness, so these ranchers were the ones positioned to become outfitters, and many of them did. Those who excelled in outfitting for hunters became the leading conservationists and babied their hunting areas. As gratitude, the Provincial Game Department allocated exclusive hunt areas to each regis-tered outfitter, in order to have privacy while guiding nonresidents. (Cana-dian residents were free to hunt wherever they pleased, in their respective provinces.) Foreigners to Canada were required to hunt with a registered outfitter to prevent waste and provide safety to those not properly prepared for such adverse conditions.

The guides normally worked long hours without rest from spring to fall. At season's end, usually dictated by severe weather and shorter days, they got their horses into winter range; they were ready for a party—that's when they scheduled the annual meeting for the Outfitters Asso-ciation. It was held in November, in Fort St. John, the town furthest north that had a commercial airport, as well as being situated on the Al-Can Highway. Ready for a party ourselves, Colleene and I would fly up to join in the fun and visit with these rough-and-ready friends that we got to know through the years. Yes, they had serious meetings among themselves, and with the game officials also attending, but the real purpose was to have a three-day party and totally unwind. It was a rare couple that ever slept during the whole affair. The guides' wives were a tough bunch, most of which were part of the outfit—-cooks, wranglers, and some even guided. When the western band stopped playing at wee hours in the morning, parties resumed in the rooms of the Fort St. John Hotel, where booze kept flowing.

One always remembers where they were when President John F. Kennedy was assassinated and our good friend John Connally was seriously wounded—well, that's where Colleene and I were. A delegation of outfitters had a solemn meeting with us and asked our opinion (the only Americans there) of whether they should cancel the gathering at that point. We said Kennedy and Connally would want us all to continue on, so after some prayers, the party resumed.

Like the early Northern B.C. Associations, guides and outfitters organizations became established in most hunting areas around the world. The ultimate is the International Professional Hunters Association, in which Bert and I are life members. Little did I know, at those early times in Northern B.C., that in my involvement with future hunting programs in Asia, I would be assisting in establishing guides and outfitters and even supplying the equipment to handle foreign hunters.

# CHAPTER 3

# Exploring the Ice Floes by Skin Boat

As the 1960s arrived, walruses were not on the list of big game trophy animals for a sportsman's den. After already spending considerable time hunting marine mammals with the Eskimos, I yearned to venture into the Bering Sea for another adventure with these fine natives. Here is my story:

I'd left Nome by Wien Alaska Airlines, in clear, warm weather, flying over the broken ice of Norton Sound from Northeast Cape to Gambell at the extreme westerly tip of Saint Lawrence Island. The pilot of the C-46 flew low, trying to spot walruses for us. It was still full winter at Savoonga, but off Gambell the sea was open, heaving in ground swells that swept in from the west.

At Gambell's landing field we met Joe Slwooko, our outfitter, a cheerful and handsome Eskimo with a wonderful spread of a drooping Mongolian mustache. The town's sole "taxi," an ancient weasel, waddled up. I got aboard with my overweight load of baggage, including a week's groceries. I wanted a good walrus for our wildlife museum and store at Jonas Brothers in Anchorage. And I wanted to look over the native art products of Saint Lawrence Islanders, for distribution through our Jonas Brothers of Alaska outlets in Fairbanks, Nome, and Anchorage.

The people of Savoonga and Gambell are noted throughout Alaska for their imaginative work with walrus ivory, jet-black baleen from whales, skins, and furs.

It was evident why Joe had advised us to bring our own groceries. The native store, awaiting twice-yearly supplies brought in by ship only in July and September, was down to scouring pads, canned salmon and ham.

I dropped off my gear at Joe's pleasant home and set out with him on an escorted tour of this village of 390 people, all Eskimos with the exception of schoolteachers and minister. Joe spotted a young walrus not more than 30 feet from the beach, and ran toward it, making grunting sounds in imitation of the call of the mother.

Young walruses are in great demand, both for the superlative rope made from the hide peeled in a continuous 3/4-inch wide strip, and for sale alive to zoos in the 48 "outside" states. Baby walruses take readily to captivity, thriving on a diet of canned clams and evaporated milk—a fair substitute for the rich-in-fat mother's milk that promotes their remarkable, fast growth. This baby was wiser than most. He swam along the beach for a half-mile, his bullet-head lifted to investigate Joe's maternal grunts, but he finally turned straight out to sea.

Next morning it was overcast with intermittent fog. Sven Gillsater, professional photographer representing Scandinavian television and the magazine *WE* asked whether he could join me on the hunt to get photos of wildlife. I agreed, so we took our

time moving our gear to the beach where the boats are stored.

The Eskimo *oomiak* appeared frail, elevated, and lying upside down on its drying rack. Light shone through its translucent covering of stretched, split hides of walruses. Its graceful 20- to 30-foot frame of bent driftwood appeared little sturdier than the framework of a kite.

We looked over the double-ended craft, which was very large for an *oomiak*, with the motor well-located one-third from the stern and just to one side of the keel. Vernon and Roger, Slwooko's brothers, joined us and we all shoved the boat over gravel and snowdrifts into the surf. We headed out east toward Savoonga, against the movement of drifting ice. A large gray whale appeared, blowing and diving not 500 yards off shore. The Eskimos paid no attention, valuing only the bullhead or black whale.

On the leeward side of up-thrust, snowy hills behind Gambell, we hit calm water, weaving in and out in broken ice with no more sound than the purr of the outboard motor, and occasional thumps as floating ice struck and bounced off the boat's skin. As we went easterly toward Savoonga, the ice grew denser. An occasional pressure ridge gave us a vantage point from which we glassed for walruses. Thick ice finally forced us north and west, in a large circle. As the village of Gambell came back in view, Joe spotted a young *oogruk* sleeping on the ice. It woke, and as it started to wriggle into the water, I took it with a headshot. We pulled the bearded seal onto flat ice, skinned it out, and stripped the meat for drying, as fog settled over us like cold, wet smoke.

Joe took a compass reading and zeroed in to Gambell. We finished off the day with a luscious feed of *oogruk* liver, the most delicious liver I have tasted.

Next day we decided to switch operations to Savooga, located at the center of the north side of the island. As soon as the decision was reached, the village burst into life. A sled was hooked onto the weasel and huge piles of gear were loaded aboard. We set out for the north shore where our boat had been left the night before.

Each boat owner has at least two boat racks, widely separated for use according to wind and water conditions. Two dozen villagers of all ages served as escort while we tried to guess which among them would crew the boat. You never know until the boat actually is in the water. This time we took aboard guide Joe, his father Charlie, brother Roger, and another Eskimo Victor Campbell. Most Eskimos have white men's as well as native names—a convenience, as Eskimo names are incomprehensible to outsiders.

The ice that had turned us back the day before was gone, swept clean by tide and wind. Thus, we chose a great arc, extending far out in the Bering Sea, in a new search for ice, without which we would find no walruses. To our relief, Savoonga was still iced in. The picturesque village, set on a cliff some 50 feet above the water and backed by 3,000-foot mountains, apparently was still in the grip of winter.

Villagers ran down to the water's edge to meet us, joining in a welcoming *oooo-up* (Eskimo version of heave-ho) to lift our boat high up on the beach. We white men were the center of a large party that descended on the schoolhouse and teacher Mrs. Goranson, who graciously offered the beginners' classroom as our bivouac. As the school year had terminated the day before, there was no limit on our use of the room and the school kitchen. Members of the crew, who brought with them no bedrolls, food or personal gear of any kind, just disappeared into the sod-chinked frame homes of friends.

Our coming was a rare event in this isolated village, reason enough for a community "sing." The host's home was packed so tightly that there remained scant room for the six-man drum band seated on the floor along the far wall. Each number began sedately, chanting drummers accompanying the rhythmic beat of instruments fashioned of circular frames of bone or baleen, over which the skin of walrus stomachs had been stretched.

Suddenly the chant changed to a wild beat, voices rising in a tumult of sound. The rhythm possessed the audience. A woman leaped out before the band, keeping time with her hands and the sway of her body. When the tempo turned fast, her dance became a hula at high speed, a bewildering pattern of head, hand, and body motions, all done without moving the feet. Dances of the men were even faster, as they are allowed to move their feet in the heel-thumping pantomime that is the only history of a people without written language. The purpose of a sing is serious, rather than social—no intermissions, no refreshments, and no chattering or socializing.

Eskimo dancing looks deceptively simple. Sven was handed the gloves that must be worn by each dancer. He leaped out, sure that he could follow the strong rhythm, but gave a performance more like that of a Swedish photographer standing on a cake of ice, in the middle of a bunch of walruses, trying to take pictures with two cameras at the same time.

The people of Savoonga reported good hunting. We were up very early next morning, eager to get out to sea, but one look at the heavy, low-lying fog over the water was enough. Our Eskimo crew was nowhere to be seen. Eskimos don't consider it necessary to report changed plans owing to weather conditions.

The delay gave us time to pace the boardwalks over the boggy ground and observe the work of villagers. We set out in search of a woman named Ruth, who makes bread. Mukluk telegraph passed on the word that we were in need of food, and soon we had breakfast rolls and bread and invitations out to dinner. Nathan Noongwook, the storekeeper, had little but bare shelves in his grocery department, but he had some excellent examples of native jewelry, animal carvings, mukluks and wearing apparel.

The work of an Eskimo village is divided sharply between tasks appropriate for men—hunting, trapping, ivory carving, building houses, butchering meat and making frames of skin boats and weapons of the hunt.

Eskimo women make all the clothing and footwear, skin all animals brought in to the village whole, and flesh out all skins. Woman's work is the preparation of the skin of walruses for stretching over the frames of boats. Walrus skins run from one inch to 1-3/4 inches thick, and when dried in their natural thickness, resemble boilerplate, but too heavy for the light boats.

❝ **Upon our arrival by skin boat at Savoonga, we were met by villagers who assisted us in settling in.**

We were welcomed by the Savoonga Eskimo villagers, who performed a song and dance with the accompaniment of their walrus-stomach skin drums.

So the skins are stretched on a large wooden rack leaned against a building. Because of the height of the rack, women stand on a staging, beginning their work at the top of a skin. The hide is split edgewise, precisely in half, with an *ooluruk*, known also as an *ulu* or "woman's knife," a curved knife with the handle on the back edge. At the lower edge of the hide, the skilled worker leaves the skin joined by the last half inch so it may be spread out to exactly twice the area and half the thickness of the original.

After drying in the sun, the skin is removed from its rack, soaked and stretched again over the prepared frame of the new boat. It takes two such skins to cover a boat, which may last three to five years. The skins give a little when struck by ice and thus withstand many times the abuse of less resilient materials. The hides are strung to the frame with rope made from the hide of baby walruses—an ideal material because it does not freeze and has three times the strength of manila rope.

By 6 o'clock in the evening, the fog lifted slightly and thinned farther out to sea. Our crew materialized. We took on a heavy load of gas and set out fast. The prevailing south wind had moved much of the nearby ice out. Soon we were in open water, heading north into increasing ice. An occasional oogruk or seal was spotted, but no walruses.

Four hours and 50 miles out of Savoonga, Roger spotted four widely scattered floats of walruses from the top of a jagged pressure ridge. As excitement began to churn inside us, everyone took his position in the boat and checked his equipment.

Victor inserted the harpoon head into the spear, tying one end of a walrus hide rope to the harpoon and the other to a hair seal float made of the full skin of a seal completely skinned out through the mouth. A wooden

clamp fits the head of the sealskin, sealing it off like an air-filled balloon. The harpoon and float are employed to the wounded walrus, which otherwise will sink immediately.

I took up position in the bow. Sven spread his camera gear in the stern. Charlie's battle station was at the helm, Roger's at the 35 hp motor. Joe sketched a walrus head with a few swift pencil strokes, and on it indicated the bend in the neck just behind the skull. "You shoot here," he grunted.

Eskimos say that a bullet will bounce off the heavy skull after losing its steam, in nearly two inches of hide. So heavy and folded is the skin of walrus, attached firmly apparently

**An Eskimo woman splitting a walrus hide precisely in half with use of her oolaruk. Once she reaches the bottom, the double skin will be stretched sideways utilizing the other half of the rack.**

Eskimo men making rawhide rope from a baby walrus skin, by cutting continuously around for maximum length.

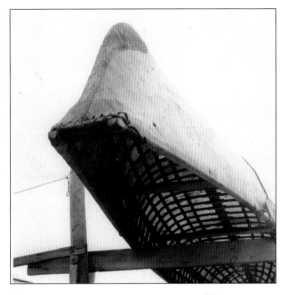

A completed skin boat, drying upside down on its rack. It takes two "double" walrus skins to cover a boat that can be up to 30 feet long.

only at the top of the skull and at the flippers, that you get the feeling the huge animal is hiding out within his own skin, and is invulnerable to any but a well-placed shot at the base of the skull.

Putting an ice cake between our prey and us, we headed for the closest bunch, drifting in quietly with engine at idle. At 20 yards the Eskimos took up paddles for the final approach. At five yards the biggest walrus woke and lifted his great head to show one tusk of outstanding size and another broken off to six inches. His companions were young ones, so we put on power as the walrus slid into the water with an indignant look.

We cruised slowly to a second float, half a mile away, cutting off power and drifting past for a close look at ivory as heads bobbed up one by one. Suddenly the sleepy scene was shattered by a terrific roaring splash, as the whole tangle took off directly toward us and surfaced around the boat.

This was the moment that taught me new respect for the Eskimos' hunting ability. As Roger gunned us away, Sven ran film through his cameras to a wild monologue in Swedish. The failing sun, now low on the horizon, rapidly dipped into a bank of black storm clouds.

With rising wind, the sea roughened in a nasty, short chop as we approached the next bunch of walruses. Of five animals on this ice block, one appeared to be a good trophy, but not the animal I wanted for the Wildlife Museum, so the Eskimos opened fire on them. I had agreed to let the guides take some, as they are allowed four walruses per day, per boat, as long as they save all the meat.

**Patrolling the ice flows by skin boat, in search for walrus.**

As we drifted alongside the ice, I saw two walruses, wounded by the Eskimos, lunge into the sea. The Eskimos grabbed paddles and pumped furiously alongside the boat, yelling at me to finish them off when they came up. One emerged so close, I could not get into position to shoot. Victor smacked the water with the boat hook and the big tusker dived with a chilling roar. When he broke surface again, I was in position and ended the attack. The harpoon scored immediately after the bullet, and the walrus was secured. The second wounded animal rolled on the surface 50 yards away. Under power, we went alongside and ended his clam-digging days.

It took an hour's hard, fast work to butcher the walruses into meat chunks small enough to throw in the boat. Skin boats have an amazing capacity. They'll take the meat of four walruses—a three- to four-ton load.

The weather worsened fast, as we appro-ached four bulls on a big, flat ice floe a mile distant. We eased up, and Joe and I sneaked

across the ice as the bulls came to attention. One of them was my trophy animal, the biggest walrus I ever hope to see! His tusks were tremendous, great yellow daggers so long, they forced his heavy head back.

My rifle shook a little as I took aim for the vital spot and flattened him. As his enor-mous weight careened down on the wet glare ice, the floe shattered, leaving the walrus on a section that barely accommodated his vast bulk, with a foot to spare at either end.

We gingerly boarded the ice, Sven holding to the painter and keeping the boat within ready reach. I looked at my watch—it was straight up midnight, as we began the long, tedious job of skinning the 12-foot monster for a full-size mount. It became more and more difficult to stand on the slippery ice, as it was now coated with blood and fat. We sank to our knees and set our knives to flying, as chunks of ice crumbled away. Just as we tackled the hind flippers, we heard an ominous crack beneath us. The ice sheared

**On an ice float barely large enough to support the walrus, the largest bull raised his head to reveal one tusk broken off at six inches.**

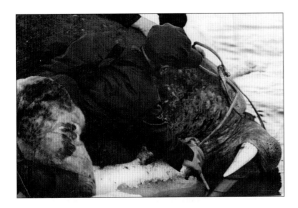

Joe Slwooko slips the rawhide noose around the neck of one of their "meat" walrus that went down on the ice flow. Note his sealskin pants.

off, and the carcass rolled into the sea. We clung desperately to the hide, cutting away the meat with flashing knives, as the carcass, buoyant with fat, bobbed like a deadhead, just under the surface. We finished as the meat finally sank out of sight, all of us now standing on the hide on the remaining bit of ice. Rolling the 600-pound mass of skin into the boat, we set our compass bearing for warmth, food, and dry clothing 50 miles away at Savoonga.

The boat sailed low in the water; its freeboard greatly reduced by the load of meat and heavy hide. The wicked chop of the shallow Bering Sea slopped over the sides, as we set our blind course for Savoonga's safety. I knew it would be nip-and-tuck, which would arrive first—the storm or us. Eskimos, who depend largely upon their quarry for the very food of life, do not jettison meat lightly.

We made out the dim outline of Savoonga's cliff looming in the mist and swept up to

the beach just as the storm broke in full fury. The villagers up and watching for us *oooo-upped* with a will, their voices drowned in the wind, pulling the boat higher with each surge of surf.

The storm pinned us down for three days, our personal food supply long since exhausted. Eskimos live by a communal plan that well might be emulated by the rest of the world. With true hospitality, the people of Savoonga took us in like members of the family. We lived contentedly, on strong tea and oogruk liver, helping with the task of cutting meat in strips for drying, until the skies cleared.

Home in Seattle, I learned that my big bull at the time was the largest Pacific walrus ever taken by a sportsman. Eskimos have taken larger animals for display in American museums, but the huge sea mammal that raised his kingly head as I crept toward him over a Bering Sea ice floe will top the current sportsmen's records.

As Joe and I stalked across the ice flow, the midnight twilight gave me just enough light to make a perfect shot.

« After a few hour's sleep in the school house, Sven and I emerged to find the weather subsided enough to get photos of my trophy, alongside the best one the Eskimos had taken.

Waiting for the seas to calm gave us time to take care of my walrus skin and enjoy the native life. An Eskimo man surveys his winter take of walrus. The tusks were a profitable trade for the natives, whether sold as raw ivory or made into crafts. A cleanup crew of husky pups enjoys flesh from a walrus skull. Eskimo children look over hair seals, brought for use as dog food and for the fur trade.

## REFLECTION
# What's That Smell?

**I**n the mid-20th century, Alaska was called the last frontier. The major cities of Anchorage, Fairbanks, and Juneau were anything but upscale, but they took pride in the old-time attributes of frontiersmen. It wasn't unusual to find a scrubby old trapper or prospector, fresh out of the bush, catching the first flight from Anchorage to Seattle. Other flight passengers enjoyed the unique experience of hearing the character's yarns of surviving the winter at 50 degrees below; that is, once they got used to the smell!

That legend probably took a turn for the worse when Chris returned to Seattle from his walrus hunt. It went like this—Wein Alaska Airlines only flew about once a week to Saint Lawrence Island. Chris's heavy-laden skin boat pulled up to the bank alongside the airstrip at Gambell, just after the plane landed. The Eskimo crew waved the plane to come over to pick up Chris and his luggage, which consisted largely of his bag with full walrus skin. The pilot obliged, and Chris was soon off to Nome, the first leg of his return trip.

The connections were almost too good, as the connecting flight to Anchorage was about to close the door. Chris—still fully clothed in his mukluks and hunting parka, splattered with blood and blubber, unbathed and unshaven for two weeks—gladly boarded the plane. Now, this kind of presentation was a little far out, even on a bush run from Nome, but still acceptable, using the word loosely.

Wouldn't you know it? Alaska Airlines had a Seattle connection within the hour. Well, I was really anxious to get home and have the walrus hide cared for, so why not? As I boarded the aircraft (the last one on) there was total silence, passenger's eyes opened wide, and jaws dropped, in an almost full flight. As I worked my way back, those with a spare seat sort of shuffled over to fill the gap. Out of dead silence, I could almost hear poet Robert Service reciting:

*"There are strange things done in the midnight sun*
*By the men who moil for gold;*
*The Arctic trails have their secret tales*
*That would make your blood run cold;*
*The Northern Lights have seen strange sights,*
*But the strangest they ever did see*
*Was that day on the plane, by a man insane*
*When they took a look at me."*

# CHAPTER 4

# Crash Landings

Every bush pilot will have tales of a narrow escape—that is, those that are still alive to tell about it. The Klineburgers and some of their hunting friends who have been passengers of those daring pilots could spend a whole evening, over a bottle of Wild Turkey, with interesting flying yarns. Here are just a few:

Eldon Brandt and I had successfully gotten a moose from a camp on a pretty good-sized lake in Alaska's Nilchina area. We broke camp and loaded everything in Eldon's L-1 Stinson, a big, single-engine workhorse on floats. There was plenty of room for takeoff, so he throttled at full power, onto the steps, faster and faster, finally off the water, but dangerously close to lake's end, with a forested hill ahead. His expert quick judgment told him to throw the plane back on the water, and aim for an open spot on shore. We ended up 30 yards or so high and dry, back in the woods, just missing trees on both sides.

After unloading meat, trophy, and camp gear, we proceeded cutting trees and log sections about three feet long with the single axe we had. This big plane, probably four times the weight of a Super Cub, had to be turned around in the direction of the water. By walking the plane's floats onto the logs, by use of full throttle, rudder, and me bouncing the plane by grasping onto the tail wheel, we maneuvered it around and back into the water on our log skids. Eldon figured on take-off, the wind was burbling down over the hills alongside the lake, pushing the plane down, preventing it from gaining altitude. The floats and plane were undamaged—a miracle—and Eldon's skill gave us a happy ending.

\* \* \*

I was flying with George Dalziel in his Super Cub on floats one time in Northern British Columbia. We spotted a small lake near a sheep mountain that might be a good campsite. So Dal, as we called him, put us down on the lake. Upon throttling down, Dal said, "Oops, I miscalculated this lake." The lake was down in a depression; he throttled up to take off by making step turns round and round the lake. This is a maneuver of speeding around, getting the craft up on the pontoon steps, ready for take off, and at the same time causing waves (or chop) on the water and picking up as much speed as possible while circling the lake. After lift off, again it was round and round above the water until we reached enough altitude to exit the area. It was the only maneuver possible, and his skill got us out safe and sound.

\* \* \*

Two of our closest friends, Bill Neimi (owner of Eddie Bauer Company at the time) and Tony Sulak, headed up to Point Barrow for a polar bear hunt. Two planes are used, usually Super Cubs on skis so that in case of emergency out on the ice, the other plane was there for the rescue.

Tony's pilot went in for a landing on the sea ice. He miscalculated by taxiing out on "young ice," which was not firm enough to support the plane, which immediately broke through some 30 yards from hard ice. The two climbed out and stood on the wing of the slowly sinking craft. The pilot, having

been taught the impossibility of surviving in seawater in sub-zero weather, went down with the plane.

Tony did not know that, so he frantically started swimming toward hard ice, breaking the young ice with his fists. The other plane had landed securely on hard ice. They tied a rope to an empty five-gallon gas can and threw it in Tony's direction. Eventually Tony reached the rope. With already frozen hands, he wrapped the rope around his arms, and by rolling on his back he was able to slide up on the ice. He was then dragged to hard ice. They continued to drag him to the plane, as he was completely immobile.

Getting him and Bill in the back of the tiny Super Cub was no easy matter. Having been radioed, the hospital's makeshift ambulance awaited their arrival. He had major frostbite, especially on his rear-end, which was exposed while he was dragged on the ice. It was a week before they could be flown to Seattle for further care. He returned to good health, and gave credit to the flotation qualities of his Eddie Bauer down clothing.

\* \* \*

Again, I brought bad luck to Eldon Brandt, when he tried landing his Super Cub on what appeared to be a fine runway. We were going bison hunting near Alaska's Wrangell Mountains and needed a campsite within hiking distance of a bull that we had located.

The strip had not recently been used, as it was covered with tall grass. Eldon made a perfect approach, and made a soft three-point landing, immediately hitting a huge rock, shearing off the right landing gear. Tipping forward, the prop dug into the ground, but Eldon reared back and prevented flipping over. We spun out, while the right wing struck the ground, bending the strut. The rock had a mate, so they were obviously tie downs for a plane.

He sent an SOS and was answered by a mutual acquaintance, Jack Wilson, who had a guide service in Gakona, on the Copper River. By the time Jack arrived, we had the Cub off to one side and propped up, and had cleared the strip of any debris. We had the bent aluminum prop removed, along with the damaged gear, and a list of things needed to repair the damaged fabric on the wing and fuselage. Jack and Eldon left me there in our spike camp for my successful bison hunt.

Several days later they returned. Jack flew my bison trophy and meat out, while Eldon and I patched up his Super Cub for our return flight. Fortunately there was no engine damage from the prop hitting the ground. Back in Anchorage, we had a week's work in getting Eldon's Super Cub back to normal.

\* \* \*

**While Chris hunted for bison, the Super Cub laid alongside the strip, supported off the right broken landing gear, awaiting Eldon and Jack to return with a new prop and other parts.**

Brother Bert had a nasty plane accident on the Alaska Peninsula, flying with veteran pilot Lynn Marshall. Lynn's Super Cub was equipped with "donut" wheels, those big balloon tires used for landing on most any terrain from muskeg to rocky gravel bars.

They were looking for a landing spot in brown bear country. Lynn located a smooth-looking place that was grassed over, and touched down for a landing. All went well until the wheels went down into a deep, unseen bear trail, flipping the plane over onto its back. Their first job was to get to the battery, turning it right side up. They radioed Eldon Brandt to airdrop a block and tackle. Within a couple of days, they had their hoist, and a big brown bear. By hooking the line to the rear wheel, running it over the balloon tire, while one person lifted the tail section, the other operated the hoist, raising the plane up and over. Without further ado, they flew away without incident.

* * *

Bert and Eldon had another accident that occurred when they landed on a frozen lake with their ski-equipped Super Cub. Apparently there had been some ice movement, causing an open crack that hadn't completely frozen over. As they stopped, the right ski went through the ice.

Quick-thinking Eldon told Bert to get out and lift the plane up by the wing tip. Once it was high enough, Eldon gunned it and got over to hard ice. Eldon joked later that his thoughts were, "I think I'll just fly off and leave Bert there—flying these Klineburgers brings me nothing but bad luck!"

"Bert and Lynn had a successful brown bear hunt while waiting for an airdrop of block and tackle to right the aircraft.

## REFLECTION
# Grand Slam of Wild Sheep

In 1947 Grancel Fitz, an official of the Boone and Crockett Club, wrote a magazine article "Grand Slam in Rams." The article related to collecting the four different species of North American wild sheep found from the Arctic to Mexico. The term "Grand Slam" has been used ever since as reference to the sheep, as well as a plateau for collectors of wildlife specimens. The evolutionists think originally there were no wild sheep in North America, but that they evolved from the Asiatic bighorn (or snow sheep), *Ovis nivicola*, that migrated from Asia during a time of a land bridge or ice bridge that connected the two continents.

At any rate, North American sheep are very different from those of Asia, by color and horn shape, so maybe the "Big Man" up there had something to do with it. Starting from the north is the pure white Dall sheep, whose habitat includes most all the mountain ranges of Alaska, the Yukon, and Northwest Territories. Coming down into Northern British Columbia, we find the Stone sheep, which sports a blue-gray color. Both the Dall and the Stone varieties are known as the "thinhorns."

Farther south are the "bighorns." In southern British Columbia, Alberta, and the northwestern United States is the Rocky Mountain bighorn, which is the largest-bodied, with the most massive horns. The pelage of a mature ram with winter coat can be a chocolate brown.

In the desert mountain ranges of the southwest U.S.A., from Texas to California, as well as northwest Mexico (including Baja California), is the desert bighorn. Its harsh habitat and sparse food supply leads to its smaller body and horn size. The hair color of the desert variety is more beige, but in some habitats, a slate gray. All rams have large, heavy horns that curl to a full circle, while the ewes have small sickle-shaped horns. The bighorns have a more rounded horn cross-section, and the thinhorns have a more triangular cross-section.

White or brown, big or thin, as a whole, wild sheep live in the "high country," encompassing beautiful and breathtaking, challenging landscapes, out of reach of most *Homo sapiens*. The adventure of sheep hunting, along with the magnificence of a trophy ram, makes the challenge of achieving the Grand Slam the apex of North American hunting adventures.

Chris took two Grand Slams by the early '60s—not to take more than his share, but mainly to add variety by collecting a Fannin sheep, which sports a pure white head and neck and a gray body, although it's still rated as a Stone sheep. He also took a California bighorn, determined by some to be a separate subspecies. He also wanted a desert bighorn from Baja California, to complement his Sonoran sheep.

# CHAPTER 5

# Tough Going for the Stone Sheep

I first met G.C.F. "Dal" Dalziel and his wife June in the fall of 1954 while en route to my first (and unsuccessful) Stone sheep hunt, in British Columbia's Cassiar Mountains. Our floatplane was forced to land on Dease Lake because of darkness. At the south tip of the lake we saw smoke rising from a house, which drew us in.

There I met the couple, which began a long relationship. During and after dinner, the talk had turned to sheep, and Dal told me about some outstanding Stone rams that he had seen in the Cassiars.

In November of 1962 I had met Dal again, who now was a full-time outfitter after years of experience as a bush pilot. Again, Stone sheep hunting was the topic of our talks, and Dal told me about an area he wanted to check out that had not been hunted before. This area was too tough for horses, and the nearest lake was too far away to be reached by foot the same day. Backpacking would be the only means to reach the sheep. That being my weakness, I asked, "When do we leave?"

In mid-October of 1963, after Dal had his horses out of the mountains and into their winter range, we flew in Dal's Super Cub from his winter home in Watson Lake, Yukon Territory, into Blue Sheep Lake

*Dal sealing the Cub's tanks before we packed out of Blue Sheep Lake.*

in the heart of the Cassiar Range. With our heavily loaded backpacks we headed north, picking a pace that would not tire us too much. We packed in for two days, pitching our lean-to over a bed of boughs at night. We camped as high as possible, but still within reach of firewood and water.

The next day Dal and I saw quite a few ewes and lambs. We also spotted a small ram that seemed to be on the move, probably toward the ewes. His horns had slightly less than a full curl, so I was content to watch him for a while, as it was too early in the hunt to take an average specimen.

By the third day, I was finally getting used to the thin air of this elevation. We took to the ridges and covered a lot of territory

*Typical Stone sheep country that provides openness and plenty of escape routes.*

studying basin after basin on both sides, never exposing ourselves until we knew what was ahead. We saw a number of ewes, lambs, and small rams, but were careful not to spook them.

One time, while resting, Dal slipped over a small hogback to glass the area ahead of us, spotting three young rams, about the size of the one we had seen before, with horns just under a full curl—a beautiful sight, but not our trophy for now. We figured on the way back later we could probably find one of these again. It was late in the day, so we dropped down below the timberline to camp. The next day we planned to come back up the same ridge that we were now on, except a few miles farther so as not to disturb the three rams and look into what we thought should be good ram country.

We continued on, stopping only long enough to glass every basin and ridge. There

seemed to be a complete lack of fresh signs on the ridge we were hunting. As we topped out, Dal was slightly in the lead. He suddenly stepped back and dropped to his knees. I joined him and we both moved forward to take a look at a ram about 500 yards away feeding among the scrub balsam at the timberline. Dal thought the horns would go 40 inches or more. We also saw another one a short distance away, a little smaller, but still a good ram. Both were working their way down into the heavier cover. We decided not to wait too long, as the big one looked good to me, and I decided to try for him.

As soon as the rams were behind trees, we worked our way toward them rapidly. Dal and I checked a basin just to our right to make sure there wasn't anything better there. It was empty. The wind was right as we moved swiftly down to an opening near where we had last seen the rams. We wanted to get below them, as they would at least hesitate before running up. If we were above

them, a few leaps would put them into the protection of the forests below.

As we moved through the timber our visibility was poor—no signs or sounds of the sheep. We dared not even whisper. We traversed a little knoll, knowing any bush might conceal my ram. We stared at one another, thinking we had waited too long, and the rams had probably passed us.

We worked our way over to a little point, for a breather. As we reached the crest, we looked up, and standing out in the open about 200 yards above us was one single ram, looking at us, I believe the bigger of the two we had seen. I was puffing and unsteady. I couldn't sit down because of the brush in front of me. I took a step over to a tree, but couldn't steady the rifle against it because it was literally covered with limbs. I had to shoot offhand. I squeezed the trigger as the reticle of my Leupold scope crossed the shoulder—a complete miss. One jump, and the ram was out of sight. I had my chance and had muffed it!

We were silent as we headed back to camp. We came to the place where Dal had spotted the three young rams the day before, and they were still there. Higher up, I saw yet another ram. We studied him. Decidedly bigger than the other three, he was equally as big as the one I shot at earlier. The ram was in the open, and three small draws away from us. Dal and I dropped back and down so that we could get past the three small rams. When

**Chris with his fine stone ram, and the packing of the trophy back to Blue Sheep Lake.**

we topped out, we were obviously as close as we would ever get to the ram still over 300 yards away. Two very steep draws separated us, but conditions were good. The ram didn't see us and he was in the open.

I set my variable scope to 9X and looked the ram over once more—a nice trophy. Only one problem—because of the curvature of the hill that I was on in relation to the ram, I could not use the sitting position. An offhand shot was out of the question because of distance, and a prone shot would put me below the crown of the hill. The only answer was to crawl to the crown and try a prone shot.

I made like a snake, trying to conceal my bulky form behind six inches of clump grass, but finally I was in position. The only way I could get a perfect, steady rest was to place the fore-end of my rifle on my clenched fist, putting the butt under my armpit. I peered through the scope, the crosshair was lying just right—about 2/3 of the way up the shoulder. I squeezed the trigger, and Dal had to tell me what happened next.

Blood trickled down from the scope cut over my right eye, obscuring my sight (a scope cut is an arc shaped gash in the skin of the forehead, over the eye, caused by the backward kick of the gun—in this case, my eye was too close to the scope, so my forehead took the full brunt of the rifle's kick). Dal reported the ram had collapsed and tumbled down out of sight.

We worked our way over to the ram. We discovered the Remington 180-grain bullet; pushed along by 82 grains of 4831 from my Improved 300 H&H Magnum, hit right in the center of the shoulder. Preliminary taping with a dollar bill (six inches long)—indicated horns about 40 inches long. I had my trophy after the disappointment of the earlier miss. Later measurements, after the necessary 60-day drying period, placed my Stone ram in the Boone and Crockett record list. That gave me a much-improved Grand Slam—three of them in the record book.

Packing the full skin and boned-out meat was a monumental chore, but little can compare to the satisfaction I received from a tough hunt and a fine specimen.

## REFLECTION
# Game Farms

There has been a lot of controversy over game farming, most all of which has started in the late 20th century. That's when most of the "Anti's" began surfacing—those naïve individuals that apparently didn't have much of anything important on their minds, so they decide that something they know nothing about is wrong. One might get tired of being anti-progress, anti-development, anti-American, anti-smoking (or just complain about everything around them), so why not anti-game farms?

Game farming has been around forever, but has become more and more popular, as population goes rampant. If you look way back, our hairy ancestors got tired of throwing rocks and spears at their prey, so they got smart and put them in enclosures and even domesticated them, so they could knock them in the head when they got hungry. (Anyone not following this, think cattle, pigs, sheep, and goats.) The Europeans were the first to see the value of keeping wildlife separate from domestic animals. It turned out to be simply better land use. Was it better to have a greater kudu, or cow? The kudu is more valuable, whether being sold to a zoo, or allowed to be hunted, or just there for game viewing. The kudu eats less, while using a greater variety of vegetation. The kudu is a better survivor in harsh conditions.

The critic may object to having wildlife in an enclosure. The fencing is as important to keep domestic animals out as much as it is to contain the wildlife. A number of diseases carried by domestic animals have endangered game animals, including anthrax, lung diseases, and mad cow disease. Barbed wire is satisfactory for a cattle farm, but a sheep-fence type of mesh is needed to contain wildlife. Most game farms are very large enclosures, usually thousands, often tens of thousands of acres. Furthermore, most of them utilize a natural habitat, with hills, valleys, running streams, dense cover, and plenty of appropriate vegetation. Many a game farm in South Africa or Texas is so large, a visitor may never see a fence in an hour's drive.

An important advantage of game farming is the propagation of wildlife. Rare species can be introduced and multiplied, and then returned to their original habitat. Examples are the Indian blackbuck and Arabian oryx, both almost extinct in their native range, propagated in southwest U.S.A., and reintroduced in India and Arabia.

As population explodes and more loss of wildlife habitat occurs, caring landowners will turn more to game farming. So get used to it and enjoy!

Chapter 6

# El Borrego

Chris Klineburger was one of the few early sportsmen to collect desert sheep, or *borrego*, as the Mexicans called it. Born and raised in Arizona, Chris established a taxidermy business in Tucson after World War II and spent all his spare time hunting in the Southwest and Mexico, where he collected his first desert bighorn in 1949, in Sonora, Mexico. He recalls hiking out from his base camp at a waterhole, shared with burros and cattle, with a quart canteen, oranges, candy bars, and a blanket for sleeping in caves or rock overhangs. When his supplies ran out and he walked into base camp, his companion looked at him as if he'd seen a ghost, for Chris was totally dehydrated and very lean. These great experiences got him started in sheep hunting, and gave him experience for his future hunting of the cunning sheep of North America and the rest of the world.

As time went by, Chris returned to Mexico on a hunt for *el borrego* on the Baja Peninsula in 1966, guided by the Belloc Brothers. They made a four-day pack trip by mules and donkeys from the end of the road out of Bahia Los Angeles to get to the Assembleya Mountains. He not only wanted to hunt a different area, but also to obtain a larger specimen and save a full skin for a life-size mount. Here is Chris' story of the adventure:

I flew from Seattle to San Diego where I connected to a Cessna 170 single-engine charter to Tijuana for clearing immigration, then on to Bahia de Los Angeles, a few hundred miles down on the shore of the Sea of Cortez. Besides an airstrip, there was one restaurant/bar, and little else except a Mexican fishing camp. José Belloc and a few Mexican helpers in a surplus army jeep met me.

Because of the language barrier, a lot of the details were difficult to find out. At one time, I spoke Spanish fairly well, being born and raised on the Mexican border of Arizona, but it has been more than twenty years since I had used the language. José knew a few words of English, and he turned out to be a good student. By the end of the hunt he was picking up quite a bit of English. We drove several hours inland on an unmaintained dirt road, through picturesque saguaro and candle tree-studded valley, to a fly camp supplied with gear and livestock.

Daybreak found all of us rustling around, getting things packed after a very skimpy breakfast and equally skimpy dinner the night before.

We were to meet a much more elaborate outfit in about four hours riding time by burros at the old abandoned San Luis Ranch, toward the Assembleya Mountains. The pack string consisted of a few mules and about ten burros. I was fitted with a saddle and given a mule. Several more Mexicans joined us there including local guides, a cook, and packers.

The heat was the worst obstacle, but there were other things that I constantly had to be aware of, such as rattlesnakes, scorpions, and vinegerones. The first day out, my memory was jogged by the dangers of rattlers when I almost stepped on one as I was backing up with the movie camera on tripod, getting

At the abandoned San Luis Ranch we met with more help and pack animals.

in position to take some trail pictures. The rattler was kind enough to give the all-familiar warning as I got too close. I instantly knew what the sound was, so changed directions without any hesitation. From then on, I didn't back up anymore, I always looked forward several paces ahead.

For four days we traveled through a most beautiful country. I say "beautiful" if you can look at it through a pair of dark glasses with a cold cerveza in your hand, in the shade of a mesquite tree.

In one place the landscape looked like a planned golf course nestled in a high valley, with huge boulders flanking it on three sides (without the grass, of course).

We arrived at our fourth campsite, which was to be our base camp at the foot of the higher Assembleyas. José chose to take one of the trackers and take a hike up into the mountains while the rest of us set up our camp and spotted for game from below. This was thoughtful and smart thinking by José, as they would have a chance to take a quick preliminary look at the country without being slowed down by this gringo.

We didn't spot anything, but a few hours later José was back with the good news that he'd spotted several sheep with a couple of rams, one of which was very possibly a suitable trophy. We were all excited about this and the next morning we were into the hills, partway by burro. After an hour, we continued on by foot to a vantage point near where José had spotted the sheep, and looked over much more area.

*El borrego* stayed only in the less rocky, steeper terrain, rather than in the picturesque boulder country below. The laymen wouldn't think too much about this, but according to José and the guides, the sheep were afraid a cougar would get them in the flatter, less open country, which had many hiding places for the cats. A sheep's best defense is its keen eyesight, so they prefer open terrain where they can observe wide areas. In fact, sheep are often not alone, with one or more in the band always on the lookout. A very old ram, whose eyesight is failing, will usually have a younger sentry ram along to keep watch.

We topped out at a point where the wind was in our favor and looked down into the draw where José had seen the sheep the night before. After carefully poking our heads over several different places, we finally spotted the sheep. The bigger ram was not what I would

consider trophy class. Therefore, we backed off, careful not to spook them, hoping for something bigger. Earlier, as we were coming up the ridge, we had seen some fairly large, fresh tracks that went down the ridge and onto an adjoining range, so by midday, one of the guides, Eliodoro, and I decided to follow the tracks.

The guides we had, similar to native trackers that I have had the pleasure of hunting with, had almost an animal-like ability to track and understand the game. We followed the tracks for a couple of hours, but they continued on down a very steep, rocky ridge that went on into the desert about 5,000 feet below. With only our two-quart canteens of water, we decided we had gone far enough. We spotted for a while longer, not seeing any signs of life. Therefore, we

**Yep, you guessed it—the cuisine was tortillas and beans, and a bean burrito for the trail.**

turned back and returned to the ridge where José and Lorenzo were.

They were all excited about having spotted several sheep on a distant ridge, and they thought a few of them were exceptional trophy rams. We were in a difficult place to look them over. We didn't have enough water with us to stay out overnight, and it was too far to get to the sheep before dark. Finally, the sheep came out more into the open, and we counted 16 in all, three or four of which would have been trophy rams. With only two hours of daylight, we returned back down to camp, except for Lorenzo, with whom I left my spotting scope and binoculars to watch until dark to see where they would bed down for the night.

Because of the lengthy time in and out of the sheep area, plans were made to pack lightly and stay in the mountains. By late morning the next day, we chose a spot up on the ridge for our fly camp. We dropped off our supplies and proceeded onto the ridge in the direction of the sheep.

Our first sighting of the sheep was about a half a mile away where one of the rams and some ewes' sky lighted themselves. From this point, we were able to determine where we would make a stalk, which would not be easy over the very steep, loose, rocky hillside. By now, the midday April sun was burning down on us. We worked our way down the ridge and below.

We saw no signs of sheep for quite a while until finally we saw a ewe and lamb about 700 yards away on the next ridge over. We were about ready to back up and circle around to that next ridge, when suddenly José's keen eyes spotted one lone ram in the middle of the basin we were in. The ram was standing broadside for a perfect shot, although the distance was around 300 yards. In getting in position, I touched against a jumping cactus (cholla), which made me very uncomfortable. Foolishly, I tried to get into a prone position, putting my rucksack under the fore piece of the rifle and carefully squeezed off, but the bullet sheared off a serio cactus (candle tree), which had partially obstructed the body of the ram. The ram turned and started running away, up over the hill before I could get up and get in position again. We quickly went back over the ridge to see whether we could cut off the ram. We went as far as possible on the ridge, seeing only a few odd sheep, including a half-curl ram.

The next morning, I was trying to grow horns on every rock in the Assembleya Mountains, although I felt that there wasn't too much use looking in this particular vicinity after we had disturbed it. However, surprisingly enough, I did spot a ram very deep in a draw about a mile away, which was actually just across and down from where I had shot the day before. My tracker and I decided to go after it on foot, with full canteens.

After following the ram for about two hours, we discovered that he was just traveling through and he, too, was heading deep into the desert below. We finished the day looking into all possible basins in the vicinity then moved on down to our previous camp.

The guide knew of one good area that was only another four hours ride to what was referred to as "*La Punta*." It was a sheep type of mountain sticking out from the rocky plateaus of the Assembleyas. I was warned that if we went there, this was the last chance to hunt sheep on this short ten-day hunt. Since we were sure it had been undisturbed, it sounded like a good plan to me.

Around the campfire, our talks turned to conservation of wildlife. I expressed my delight that for the past week we had seen sheep every day, in every part of the mountains. José said that he and his brothers work closely with the wildlife officials, educating the local people about the importance of protecting all wildlife. He informed me that the number of sheep permits issued was less than five percent of the estimated population. Furthermore, the Game Department was keeping predators under proper control.

At daybreak only Eliodoro and a packer had saddled up to go with me. We went off with very light gear that we could tie behind our saddles. We got to our destination about midday, staked out our mules, and started scouting. Soon, we saw some large sheep tracks that excited us. We carefully glassed ahead at all times while following the tracks. Eliodoro was unbelievably good at tracking, and he could climb around the mountains as well, or better, than the sheep. He was probably about 50 years old and didn't weigh more than 100 pounds, soaking wet. The sheep seemed to have gone down and around the ridge, and then in the direction

of our mules. After three hours of very hard hiking, following the tracks, Eliodoro told the packer and me to stay on a ridge, and he would follow the tracks farther. It was amazing how he could walk at top speed and follow the tracks, rarely losing sight of them. After we saw that Eliodoro started circling back to the mules, we went on back and grabbed a snack before rolling out our bedrolls for the night.

The next morning, we headed farther out on La Punta, which stuck way out toward the desert and then dropped off steeply on all sides, to the bottom several thousand feet below. The guide left with all the empty canteens, while the packer and I began traversing the ridge. After a while, Eliodoro had caught up to us with still-empty canteens after he found that the water hole had gone dry. This left us with about two quarts of water, so he sent the packer with all the canteens to another waterhole several miles away.

We continued on the ridge of La Punta, and a couple of miles out, I spotted a ram with my binoculars. After looking it over through the spotting scope, we were very excited, as it was a large ram. It must have been at least a mile and a half away and even with the 40-power eyepiece, which magnified the ever-present mirage, I couldn't really determine how big it was, but I knew the horns were massive and it was a good full curl. From the side view, the horn obscured a large portion of the neck and came down below the lower jaw. These are indications of very large horns. The ram was in a good

🔹 **Chris and his well-earned desert bighorn sheep, with a Serio cactus backdrop.**

" **I did my part by packing out the horns, full skin, and part of the meat.**

We kept going very quietly as we approached the last saddle, before we would top out and be in position for the big ram. As we rounded the hill into the saddle, eleven sheep jumped up and ran toward the end of the point where the big ram was, and I had just seconds to analyze the situation. They were about 200 yards ahead of me, and there were three rams with good horns. Looking them over through my riflescope, one appeared larger than the others. A slight hesitation of the big ram before topping out was all I needed to take my shot. One crack of my 7 mm Remington Magnum sent the running ram staggering down into the draw to the left. It was a perfect chest shot, although I didn't know until I inspected the entrance

place where we could make a satisfactory approach.

Without saying a word, we headed out onto the ridge keeping on the hidden side. Less than half a mile from where the ram was, we saw very fresh tracks and droppings of a band of sheep, both large and small, heading in our intended direction. Neither of us said anything, but we had the same thoughts. There was the possibility of jumping these sheep and if we did, they would run off the end of the point and take the big ram with them. It was the next to last day of my hunt, and I knew that if any jumped up ahead of us, I would probably have to make a fast selection from the herd.

**Curing the meat to make jerky.**

## REFLECTION
# Is That Gun Loaded?

**W**e old-timers remember the good old days when, if a hunter flew, he could take his rifle right on the airlines with him. I remember a couple of times the stewardesses asked if they could put the rifle in the flight deck with the pilot. I couldn't understand why they wanted to do that, as surely the pilot didn't have a lot of spare storage room. Anyway, that was fine by me, as a rifle in its case, soft or hard, did take up a lot of room alongside my seat.

One time, while driving back from a hunt in Mexico, my buddies and I saw some coyotes along the road. We loaded our rifles and had sport

The Belloc brothers: left is Juan, center is Gorge, and José on right, pose with my sheep horns in front of a candle tree (Serio).

hole later. We skinned it out for a full mount to complete my collection of life-size mounts of all North American sheep species. Preliminary Boone and Crockett measurements showed this head to qualify for the records at more than 165 points, by their scoring system.

The large ram that we never got to on the end of La Punta will always live in my memories. Naturally, I am disappointed that I didn't have a chance at him, but I was plenty happy with a truly interesting Mexican adventure and getting a fine life-sized specimen.

shooting at running targets. We missed, but decided to keep shells in the magazine in case of more coyotes. We crossed the border and I was delivered to the Tucson airport for my connection to Seattle, via Los Angeles. In flight, the stewardess asked if my gun was loaded. I joked, "Oh yes, I always keep it loaded, not knowing when I would need to use it." Then I got to thinking—it is loaded! During the stop in L.A., I took the rifle into the men's room and removed the ammo from the magazine.

In those days, most people were sane—that was before lunatics became jealous of freedom and democracy, thus setting out to find ways to do away with innocent and loving people. Now I can't take toothpaste, let alone my rifle, on the plane.

# CHAPTER 7

# High on the Chugach

I had already collected desert sheep from Mexico and mountain goat from southern British Columbia, as well as hunted Stone sheep and mountain caribou in north B.C.'s Cassiar Mountains and bighorn sheep in the Canadian Rockies. I had a love affair with high country. The majority of my hunts were alone—backpacking. In me was the tremendous lure of the stark and forbidding peaks, high meadows, and the openness. Most of all, I liked the feeling of being there just with myself, enjoying the stillness and wondering what was on the other side of the mountain. My mentor, Teddy Roosevelt, said that he liked to go out at night and stare at the stars until he felt small again. I think it helped me to realize how small were the problems I left behind and helped put them in their right perspective.

I had a bad case of "sheep fever," and a break came for me when, in 1957, for the first time in many years, a nonresident of Alaska was allowed to hunt Dall sheep without the requirement of a registered guide. I liked to hunt alone, especially on backpack hunts; besides, at the time I really couldn't afford to pay for a guided hunt. I called my friend, Jack Lee, who lived in Anchorage and had been guiding in Alaska since World War II. Just the year before I had heard all about Frank Cook's hunt in the Chugach Mountains, where he packed in and got the existing world record Dall ram. I asked Jack if he would fly me up in the Chugach Mountains and drop me off for my proposed hunt. He said he had been looking over areas just below the ice fields around Mount Marcus Baker, the summit of the Chugach. He found one flat spot on a glacier just below the ice fields where he might be able to land with a specially equipped plane.

That was enough for me, and on August 19, the day before the season's opening, Jack had me come to his private strip just out of Anchorage, with my spike camp equipment. The Super Cub was equipped with tandem wheels to absorb the shock for this type of landing. The "tandem" wheel equipment consisted of two wheels, one in front of the other, pivoting on each axle, instead of the usual single wheel. I had my kitchen and bedroom, along with everything else I would need, strapped to my army pack frame along with my rifle. Jack carefully went over instructions for me upon landing. He said we would be landing uphill on the ice and, once the plane was about to stop, he would turn 90 degrees, and I should hop out with my backpack and rifle and hold on to the wing strut. I was then to help turn the plane downhill for his takeoff.

We followed the highway east from Anchorage and soon headed straight over the massive Knik Glacier, while climbing higher and higher toward the summit of the mountains. Before landing, he flew over an adjoining canyon called Paradise Valley, the highest in the Chugach range. We could see a few sheep in the distance, but he informed

**Camera in readiness, I snapped a photo of the plane taking off. Note tandem wheels. Beyond is that moraine-covered glacier, the site of my first camp. Over the pass is Paradise Valley. »**

me he didn't want to fly too close and scare them out of the open areas.

Our landing worked very smoothly, and even though the landing site was very short, by approaching at an uphill angle, it allowed us to come to rest almost as soon as we touched down. I hopped out as instructed and held the strut. Fortunately, the ice was not slippery. I dragged my pack out of the way, gave the plane a turn by pushing on the uphill strut, and he was promptly out of sight and sound.

A lonely feeling came over me as I sat on my pack in the middle of the glacier, alone in the most remote area I had ever been. I had backpacked some fairly long distances into remote areas, but I knew the ground I

had walked over. In this case, being flown in over some very rugged country gave me an uncertain feeling.

I had told Jack to come back and check on me in about a week, and if he found my pack lying on the ice he was to land. Otherwise, take a pass through my routing to Paradise Valley to see if I waved him on or not—providing he could find me.

The rugged canyon I was in contained no sheep or any life of any type, according to Jack. I sat there surveying the rugged moraine-covered glacier. It completely filled the basin I had to cross to get into the adjoining valley where I was to hunt.

It was about midday and I knew I would not be able to get into Paradise Valley that day. I had everything in my pack, so any place I decided to stop was home.

As I started up the glacier, I found the going terrifically slow. Things looked a lot flatter from the air. There were boulders, mud, and water covering the broken ice, all combining to make this about the sloppiest traveling I had ever encountered.

About two-thirds of the way up, before it got really steep, I decided I had better pitch camp, but for the life of me I couldn't find a level place. I didn't have a tent, only a sheet of polyethylene, 4x8 feet.

A light, wet snow was coming down so I knew I had to make a lean-to. I found a big boulder that could support the upper side of my shelter, but I had to level the ground with rocks and mud alongside it, flat enough for my bed. Rocks held one side of the plastic sheet on top of the boulder, while the lower side was tied to rocks, making my home. Then a ground cloth, air mattress, and down bag made my bedroom complete.

Water boiled fast at this altitude (about 9,000 feet) on my little Primus stove. My total food supply was dehydrated and prepared dinners, raisins, and candy. I got into bed early to get out of the weather, now mixed rain and slushy snow.

During the night something suddenly awoke me out of a very deep sleep. It was very dark and silent, so I proceeded to fall back asleep. Later I woke up with some water oozing through my sleeping bag from the bottom. I started feeling around to find out what caused the water to run onto my air mattress.

About 6 inches from my head was a big boulder on top of the polyethylene. I then knew what had awakened me earlier. A boulder above me had rolled down the hillside and had landed just inches above my head. I pushed the rock off the plastic sheet and rerouted the stream of water. It would be dangerous to try to move camp in the black of night, so I cuddled up as close as I could to my protective boulder, and waited until daybreak.

Needless to say I didn't sleep anymore that night, as I heard continuous crashing of rocks throughout the basin, some of which sounded like the crack of a rifle. Glaciers are always on the move, and this one was taking half of the rocky mountain with it.

As I progressed on up the miserable, cliffy hillside towards the pass I looked the area over for a better base camp. As I got out of the steepest part, the slope was somewhat gentler towards the ridge. I set my pack down and headed for the ridge, taking only my gun and binoculars.

Just as I started out, I looked up on a rocky peak to my right and saw a big, lone billy goat looking down at me. He was probably 600 yards away. I felt that if I put on some speed and went straight for the ridge and not toward him, he might stay there and I could get above him.

I did want to get a good Alaskan mountain goat, and I felt this might be my chance. I turned on the steam. As soon as the goat saw my line of travel he wheeled and started heading up the same way to beat me through the pass.

The race was on. I was in top physical shape, and figured I could give this big, old billy a run for his money. Because of the rugged texture of the ground, I only got a glimpse of him every once in awhile. He had to go farther than I did, and was headed on a direction angling right across my path.

When we got close to our intersection I was only about 100 yards away, but I couldn't get a shot off because of the curvature of the hillside. By standing on my tiptoes I could just barely see the top of his back as he angled across. The next time I saw him he was a good 500 yards up the slope to my left and never looked back. He didn't want any part of being on the same hillside with me.

The next several days I spent traveling up and down the ridge above the relatively gentle slopes of Paradise Valley. At the bottom of the valley was a glacier that stretched from

My first spike camp offered a scenic view of the landing strip far below on the opposite side of the glacier. To the right and above is the summit of the Chugach Mountains, Mount Marcus Baker.

the ice fields above to many miles below, flowing towards the Knik Glacier. The other side of the valley was extremely rugged. The only hope I had for sheep was on my side of Paradise.

Periodically, I saw sheep. My biggest problem was the weather, with clouds continually closing in on me whenever I had spotted something in the distance. On many occasions, I made stalks through the clouds to get closer, never to find the sheep again. Finally on the fifth day I came to a point on the ridge and saw three rams grazing within 250 yards.

It was one of those typical blizzard days with the clouds moving across the hillside.

There was no opportunity to stalk any closer so I proceeded to get comfortable in a prone position. All three rams were good, but one ram was decidedly bigger in body size and his horns were proportionately larger. I knew that was the one I wanted.

I put the binoculars aside and trained my scope in their direction as the fog once again cut me off. The sheep were scattered and as one sheep would come into view through the fog it was impossible for me to tell whether it was the big one.

Without comparison, they all looked alike. They were all better than full curl with a slight flair. Their horns cut deep across their necks and down below the lower jaw. Any one of these would be a fine trophy, but the fact that one was decidedly bigger meant I had to wait him out. I felt the only time I could be sure would be to see at least two of them at one time. If one appeared bigger, I'd know for sure.

I waited for the most frustrating two hours of my life. They were bedded down, so luck was in my favor. The wind whistled across the mountainside at a right angle. Except for the fog and the extreme cold, everything was well.

Finally, the weather quieted down, and the fog started to lift. My ram was lying down at an estimated 250 yards. I had no claim as a sharpshooter, and I hated to take such a long shot at an animal lying down. On the other hand, I couldn't wait until he got up because of the possibility the clouds might cut me off again.

I had a 300 H&H Winchester bored out to a Weatherby magnum, which was adequate for such a shot. I rested the gun very carefully, placed the crosshairs high on the ram's back and moved them a little to the upwind side to allow for windage. I carefully squeezed off, and the rifle cracked.

Not a thing moved.

I knew I must have hit the sheep or he would have been out of there like a shot. The other two sheep just lay there, one still asleep and the other looking around.

I put another cartridge into the chamber and waited. Evidently, because of the crosswind, the sound of the rifle was muffled. In the last several days, however, I had noticed many sharp cracks of glaciers breaking, rocks falling, and the like that would make any gunshot sound like kid stuff.

Studying carefully with the binocular, I could see a red spot on the shoulder of the ram. I still waited, however, until one of the other rams finally jumped to his feet, followed immediately by the other one. They no doubt had caught wind of the blood from my specimen. The two rams inspected their leader and then slowly trotted away. I didn't expose myself until they were completely out of sight, so as not to disturb anything in the area.

I didn't have a tape measure, but the ram was obviously a very fine specimen. I didn't realize just how good he was, as I was more preoccupied with getting the horns, skin and the boned-out meat out in two trips down the

" The camera's self-timer catches Chris with his magnificent Dall ram.

rugged and dangerous mountain. Not until I had everything resting on the glacial landing strip did I break out a six-inch dollar bill and measure my ram to an amazing 45-inch curl and 15-inches around the base.

On the seventh day, the red pack was lying on the ice, as scheduled, when I heard the drone of Jack's Cub in the distance. We were lucky he was able to slip under the clouds and return me to Anchorage from one of the very most memorable hunts of my life.

Jack came in under the clouds to fetch me and my trophy. Note glacial moraine piled high on the ice.

## REFLECTION
# Say Goodbye to Eskimos' Livelihood

One theory is that the native people of the Western Hemisphere migrated from Asia, possibly during a time of a land bridge, ice bridge, or even by boat to Alaska, and then on south. Regardless of theory, the Alaska Eskimos look a lot like the Mongolians. Migrated or not, they settled all around the Arctic coast, living mainly on marine mammals for food and clothing. In fact, aside from some caribou, fish, wolf, etc., everything they used, wore, or consumed were from the marine mammals, which include whales, various kinds of seals, walrus, and polar bear. Their entire livelihood and survival centered on these mammals. That's why they lived where they did—and they had a very good life, even though it was lived under harsh and challenging conditions.

From the beginning, thousands or perhaps tens of thousands of years ago, they happily went about making all of life's necessities. From walrus teeth and ivory and sperm whale teeth they made harpoon heads, sled runners, tools, doweling, buttons, fishing jigs and sinkers, bird spears, ivory carvings, and more. From the skins of polar bears, seals, and walruses they made skin boats, seal-skin floats, mukluks, pants, parkas, robes, blankets, rope, harnesses, musical drums, mittens, and containers. From whale baleen they made twine, bowls, and baskets.

No meat from the marine mammals was wasted, utilizing their ever-present deep freezer, a hole in the permafrost ground. As the white man began appearing, trade followed, and they were encouraged to make crafts for bartering and obtaining modern supplies, a trade that the Eskimos became largely dependent upon for income, occupation, and livelihood, including a well developed fur trade. They also became guides for hunters seeking marine mammals.

Like many poorly planned and thoughtless schemes, the U.S. Fish and Wildlife Service submitted and Congress passed the Marine Mammal Act of 1972, protecting all marine mammals, including prohibiting the Eskimos (as well as anyone else) from selling or trading any marine mammal or part thereof. It instantly changed the Eskimo way of life and the traditions so dear to them. The Act did allow Native Americans to kill marine mammals, providing they consumed them all themselves. At this point, however, the food supply became much less important to them, while the trade of arts and crafts of marine mammal parts, as well as their guide services, had become a major source of income.

Besides putting the Alaska natives out of business, the Marine Mammal Act had a far-reaching effect on the lives of all North Americans. For starters, the Act threw the balance of nature out of whack. By removing man from nature's picture, there is no balance of nature, as he is the most important part.

You may not have noticed the constant decline of native "seafood" (and the increase in farm-raised seafood), but you probably noticed the accelerating price of "wild" sea products. You can thank some of the worst predators on the face of the earth, those cute, honking seals and sea lions that will take a bite out of every fish they come in contact with, whether hungry or not. Our federal government should have left game control with the wonderful state game departments. They are much more capable of handling wildlife matters than the Washington bureaucrats—those puppets dangling from the string of the "Antis."

# CHAPTER 8

# My Teacher Was the Bighorn Sheep

The Rocky Mountain bighorn sheep gets its name from its home in the Rockies, from their northern extremities in Canada well into the Northwest U.S.A. Early on, the excellent game departments of both Canada and the United States recognized encroachments by the ways of man. Sportsmen also organized, and began working with game officials to conserve wildlife. One such hunter's organization, the Foundation For North American Wild Sheep, was established to "Put Sheep on the Mountain." That organization changed its name recently to the Wild Sheep Foundation. The author was a member of this fine organization of big game hunters, which has raised millions of dollars for the preservation of wild sheep.

I had hunted the Rocky Mountain bighorn seven different times before I collected one. I hunted four times in southeastern British Columbia, including the Elk River, the Bull River, and practically every tributary to the Kootenay River. This was almost the whole bighorn sheep range, outside of Banff National Park and Kootenay National Park on the B.C. side of the Canadian Rockies.

One time I hunted with outfitter Earl McGinnes in the Elk River valley along the Alberta border. The other three times were with Ed Cretney, two of the hunts were strictly backpacking every canyon along the Bull River and headwaters of the Kootenay. I also hunted in Central B.C. for the California bighorn, on the headwaters of the Chilko River and Bridge River in familiar places such as Red Mountain, Nine Mile Ridge and Yalakom Mountain. The outfitter was the Christie brother, who did find me a nice trophy of that subspecies.

On the Alberta side of the Rockies I hunted three different times, covering the Red Deer River, Clearwater River and the Brazeau River. The guides I used in Alberta were the Sands brothers and Stan Burrell. Most of my hunting for bighorn sheep occurred in the 1950s, the last being 1962 in Alberta. Of all the North American big game animals, the bighorn sheep was by far the most challenging for me. Yes, I could have taken what I felt was an acceptable specimen in most of my earlier hunts, but true sportsmen usually hold out for a big, older animal, where life will soon end by suffering one of nature's ways.

At 12 years or so, most horned or antlered game top out their maturity. Sometime after that, the old male animals became weaker and lose their ability to reproduce, becoming useless to the herd. After that, they are susceptible to dying in a number of nature's ways, none of which are a pleasant way to go. These include starvation, freezing to death, being taken down by a predator and being eaten while still alive, all of which are slow and torturous. Any old male that can live a long life and be fortunate enough to end it quickly while giving great satisfaction to a hunter is lucky, indeed.

For a variety of reasons, the Rocky Mountain bighorn is tough to get. Without question the supply is much shorter than the demand. He has a lot going for him, however, in the way of protection. Some of the protection is man-designated sanctuaries where he can live out his life unmolested by hunters.

Outside of these sanctuaries, where he can be hunted, he becomes a smart, old fella who stays in timberline country. He likes the places with outcrops of open area, but with nearby forests where he can retreat rapidly. He has eyes equivalent to a man with a pair of 9X binoculars, but he knows how to use them better. When a band of sheep beds down to sleep, one or more scouts, or sentries, will be watching for danger.

One thing in the favor of the bighorn sheep is that they think the way the U.S. and Canadian Park Departments think—or maybe it's vice versa. At any rate, their habitat is invariably the kind of picturesque terrain that is made into national parks.

Good examples are the renowned Jasper National Park and Banff National Park on the British Columbia-Alberta border as well as Glacier National Park and Yellowstone National Park, all of which are in the Rocky Mountains where the main habitat for the bighorn sheep lies. Glacier, Jasper, and Banff Parks comprise most of the Continental Divide from central Canada well into the U.S.A. The park boundaries are just on the edge of where the mountains drop off into foothills on both sides of the range. The foothills are open areas that often allow hunting. In the winter, some sheep come out of the parks to the lower area, but that usually happens in November when the rutting season starts and the hunting season is closed.

I have often heard how abundant bighorns were down in the foothills of southern Canada during the regular hunting season back in the period just after World War II. Alberta was the most noted area for good sheep hunting, up until the early fifties. During that time, however, people started moving in on them. Oil exploration and ranching made the biggest difference, when roads were pushed through most all the areas outside the national parks. This access was probably the main cause of the sheep retreating to the parks. It is the nature of wild sheep to roam the high mountains. This is their most suitable environment, well away from people.

Alberta is just one example of the problem. On the other side of the Rockies in B.C., it was logging roads, rather than seismic roads. Over in the Chilcotin area of Central B.C., ranchers, loggers, prospectors—everyone seemed to have reason to penetrate the country with roads. The entire bighorn habitat followed the same pattern, more or less.

Thank God for the parks, which all sportsmen know are an important part of conservation. These parks do feed out some fine trophy rams into open areas, to provide sportsmen a continuing supply, assuming the park services keep the predators under proper control.

So the loss of sheep habitat is a major reason for the difficulty of obtaining a good specimen, but the wisdom of these clever animals supersedes all other reasons. First of all, they know the safety of their sanctuaries, but when they roam outside, one can be sure that they are smarter than the hunters.

Of my eight bighorn sheep hunts, about half were horseback trips, which has pros and cons. In some of the areas I went into, the only practical transport was horseback. However, once I was in sheep country, the continued use of horses, I believe, contributed greatly to my getting skunked.

There are times when you should leave those horses behind, but some of the guides were glued to them. To get them to walk up to a ridge, instead of riding those big, conspicuous horses, was close to impossible. On many occasions we spent half our time worrying about horses, trying to find pasture for them, or looking for horses that got away. Some areas had pasture only in sheep habitat. Also, a horse-pack trip required more people and the more people, the more equipment, the more equipment, the more horses, and it goes on and on.

Anyway, that's why the other half of my bighorn sheep hunts were backpacking trips. I found backpacking to be less conspicuous, which enabled us to get closer to the sheep. Our expeditions were simple. They consisted of two people—my guide and me. We carried everything we needed right on our backs. We could pitch camp very close to the sheep area, and just continue on to fresh areas as long as our stamina and ability to find food held out, sometimes two weeks nonstop.

During my bighorn sheep hunting, I learned more about their behavior because I got skunked a lot. I saw a lot of sheep that I would have been happy to have in my collection. I was faced with every possible situation imaginable, and between my guide and me, managed to make every possible mistake.

The one thing I learned more than anything else about the bighorn is that he is totally unpredictable. Just about the time I thought I knew what his next move would be, he would do just the opposite. I would look for him where I knew he must be—in the timber to protect himself from the nasty weather. Then I would look up to the windiest, coldest ridge, and there he would be—lying, chewing his cud, as if out in a warm, green pasture. When it was hot and mucky, I would look for him in the shade or in a cool breeze but find him sunning himself in the hottest place imaginable.

I will relate a few of the consistent habits I have experienced with the Bighorn. They have two favorite places that they like to bed down—on a ridge, or on an open hillside. When they bed down on a ridge they might be found almost anyplace—in small rock outcroppings where sometimes only their heads stick over the rocks, and sometimes on a peak or rounded knoll. Occasionally near a saddle. One of their favorite places is right out on the point of a ridge where it breaks off. In almost all of these cases, however, where they bed down on a ridge, they will rarely ever be sky lighted unless the viewer happens to be at a lucky angle. Most of the time they will be just below the ridge in slight depressions. Invariably, however, they will have scouts higher up, or just over the ridge, spotting the

other direction. "Scouts," sometimes called sentries, who are usually young rams or ewes, are in charge of the watch for danger. When bands of sheep are sleeping, there are always one or two that stay awake and, interestingly enough, they will be looking in opposite directions.

On an open hillside, they will usually pick out a spot where they can look long distances in all directions. They will rarely, if ever, be in a depression, but will appear more frequently on a hog's back, a ridge coming down off a main ridge, or on the face of a gently rounded hillside, where they can see from side to side as well as up and down. One of their favorite spots is in shale slides where they can easily paw out a bed. Their coloration also blends in with the shale. They will often lay around among sheep sized boulders making them look like just another rock. There have been times, however, when I was ready to come down with eye fatigue, trying to grow horns on rocks when I would glance over to a green, grassy patch and see a bunch of sheep beautifully silhouetted against the green.

Bighorn seem to always have one thing in their favor. A place where they can quickly exit out of sight. They have always got an ace in the hole where they can go—into a thicket, behind some rocks, over a ridge, or down a gulley. I have seen the south end of more sheep vanishing out of sight than I like to think about.

When spooked, and when a band of rams see their foe, they will usually go in the opposite direction and vanish out of sight as quickly as possible. If they see a distant possible danger, a long way away, they will keep the intruders in sight and watch what they do. If the intruder goes the opposite direction and goes out of sight, the sheep will probably stay put, but keep watch to see if the intruders reappear. But if the intruder stays put, a good trick that I learned in a situation like this is to leave everything possible in sight of the sheep like the horses, equipment and even the guide, and then the hunter quietly slip out of sight and circle around to make the stalk.

If rams get spooked by getting a whiff of a human but does not see his foe they will react in different ways. When the wind is in a positive direction they will usually move as fast as they can downwind to the nearest exit, and leave the mountain completely. When the wind is swirling around and not coming from a certain direction, rams will usually group tightly together as if to be talking the situation over. Any young, inexperienced rams in a band of rams will probably run off, possibly with the idea that the intruder will go for them. After carefully sniffing the wind and comparing notes, the old granddaddies would nearly always stick together and move out at a rapid but careful pace. Very often they will go straight down as long as the wind is not coming from down below. At any rate, nearly always-changing mountains, at least cross over to the other side of the valley. Another thing that seems to always be in the bighorn's favor is that the rams are not likely to be seen doing the same thing day after day,

so if you see them there today, go someplace else tomorrow.

I have had my crosshairs on plenty of rams and most of them, even though of legal size, were not quite adequate for me at the time. Most regulations require the minimum size allowable at three quarters curl, a ram of around 5 years old. Let's put it this way—the first days of the hunt, the horn size might not be adequate, but the last few days of the hunt they would have been plenty good, if I could only have found them again. On a couple of occasions I lost the draw of the straws and sat there weeping while my hunting partner fumbled around and muffed the shot. Most of the time, I refused to be with another hunter, and, I hate to say this, but many times I left the guide behind so I could do it my way.

Through all those years, I had great sport with an animal that was able to outwit me so many times. Each time I returned without success, I had greater admiration for the wise and clever old bighorn. It seems some old philosopher once said, "Failure is mere stepping stones to success." Mr. Bighorn became my teacher. Little did I know that perhaps God was grooming me for greater challenges awaiting me in the great beyond—-Asia?

Finally, in 1962, hunting with Stan Burrell, I obtained my ram. It was in the Big Horn Creek area of Alberta. We packed in with horses and did our hunting on foot. It was a lone ram on a hogsback, halfway up a mountainside. It required a three and a half hour stalk beginning at the valley floor to the

Chris's well-earned Rocky Mountain bighorn, taken on his seventh try. «

« My California bighorn was taken in south-central British Columbia, on Yalakum Mountain.

head of the valley, up to the top of the mountain, back along the ridge and then down to just above the ram. Everything went just like planned. He was a heavily broomed ram, forty and two-eights-inch horn length with sixteen-inch base. I'm glad it didn't work out like that on the first hunt, eight years before, as it no doubt made a better man of me.

My favorite backpacking guide was Ed Cretney from Ft. Steele, B.C., on left. On this Bighorn hunt, Lonnie Temple from Anchorage joined me.

In the endless bighorn habitat, horses certainly helped to cover the vast area.

" I learned early on, you hunt with your eyes, not with your feet—and so more time was spent looking than walking.

Rocky Mountain goat, elk, and mule deer shared the bighorn habitat. Sometimes we went out of our way not to spook other game, to keep an area undisturbed.

Chris donning his backpack. The luxury of cabins was sometimes enjoyed, when conveniently located.

Horses packed, Ed Cretney and I are ready to move above timberline.

The Canadian Rockies offered beauty seen by very few.

## REFLECTION
# Eddie Bauer

**W**hen I first came to Seattle in the late 1940s, I met Eddie Bauer in his modest sporting goods store on Union Street, near downtown. He found there was a need for quality goose-down products like sleeping bags and coats, which he began producing and doing very well with. As business expanded, the aging Eddie sold out to a Seattle sportsman, Bill Niemi. After establishing our taxidermy business, Bill became one of our closest friends. Bill shut down the retail sporting goods and moved the flourishing manufacturing and mail-order business to the old downtown Seattle, which became an industrial district. The goose-down product line of apparel and sleeping bags kept expanding and the mail-order business became popular with outdoorsmen all over the U.S.A., as they were the absolute top of the line. Our taxidermy studio was a regular stop for hunters going to Alaska and Canada. We suggested they get themselves outfitted at Eddie Bauer's when en route, even though the company wasn't set up for drop-in trade. Bill and his staff were delighted that we would bring our clients by, especially when they would spend like a kid in a candy store.

Bill would frequently stop by our office and have coffee on his way to work——not so much for the coffee, but more for the bull sessions. We suggested it would be a good idea to open a retail store——and he did, right down from us on Pine Street. That was the beginning of the Eddie Bauer stores and soon expanded to a full scale sporting goods store featuring hunting, fishing, skiing, and camping. Outgrowing the first store, they moved downtown to a larger location, while keeping the manufacturing of the goose down production in the same old location, as well as maintaining the mail-order business.

Our fur-manufacturing division began supplying fur ruffs for their arctic clothing and ski wear, and we designed and manufactured a special mukluk (cold weather boot) for the Bauer line. We had a very close relationship with Bill and the Bauer firm. Plans began for the expanding company to go public, prospectus prepared, more expansion, and then part of the plan was to take over our company, Jonas Brothers of Seattle and all its divisions, following the stock offering. In the meantime, Bauer encouraged our company to expand our own Outdoor Clothing and Equipment Division, with the idea in mind that we would handle more of the hunting end, in order to keep the Eddie Bauer name more pristine, with skiers and campers.

We did our part and anxiously awaited our association with Eddie Bauer. The public offering had delays and more delays. Bill Niemi had a number of excuses but was not very specific. What happened was that the food giant General Mills got wind of the proposed offering and made a takeover deal with the Bauer Company. As time progressed, the antihunting food company wanted no part of a hunting-related company like ours, but worse, stripped the Bauer operation of anything related to hunting or fishing and other sporting equipment, and shut down the goose-down product line. General Mills opened Eddie Bauer stores all across America, offering, in my opinion, mediocre lines of clothing, some of which are for the outdoorsman. I'll bet Bill turned over many times in his grave, seeing his great accomplishments dissipated in this fashion.

# CHAPTER 9

# Spreading the Money

Life had apparently been quite boring for the people of Saudi Arabia, with almost everything fun-loving being taboo. The hierarchy had a lot of money, and many of them pursued a fun-loving sport—hunting. A status symbol present among royalty was falconry. Those involved had their own falcons, and would go far and wide to compete or to hunt. I'll tell a few fond stories of my experiences with various Saudis. All of my own and my company's association with these fine people had been on the highest-level, honorable relationships. In these excerpts, I will not use names, as I feel they may want it that way.

On the subject of falconry, I was leading a hunting party in southeastern Kazakhstan, one of the Asian countries of the former U.S.S.R. I was in the process of guiding governor Tom Bolack of New Mexico for ibex, saiga antelope, and urial sheep. While there, I ran into a Saudi prince who was on an expedition, both hunting for falcons and hunting with his own falcons, for chukars and other game. (Our company already had a number of dealings with Saudi royalty, so we had much in common.) To hunt for falcons, they would use a live bird below a near-invisible net, in which the falcon would become entangled when it attacked the bait.

To say "expedition," I must explain. For starters, there was a $50,000 Kazakh government fee for the prince to fulfill his desires. The entourage arrived in the prince's private 747 aircraft on an abandoned airstrip built for emergency purposes circa World War II. His plane carried several jeeps, staff, and equipment for an elaborate signature Arabian (black) tent camp, with all the amenities of a royal palace. We had some nice visits talking, mostly centered on hunting.

One of our fine Arabian Prince clients had our taxidermy firm mount a huge Alaska brown bear life-size standing on its hind legs. His Highness liked to display it in a gazebo in the courtyard of his main residence in Riyadh, to show off during royal gatherings. The only problem was that when air conditioning was off, the bear "baked" in the glass-enclosed gazebo in the blistering Arabian sun. It became bleached and developed cracks in the skin and more, but the prince wanted it restored. After receiving photos showing the damage, I agreed to come to Riyadh and make the necessary repairs.

After I had gathered patching material, dyes, etc., a first-class airline ticket and visa arrived for my trip. The prince's English butler met me, and he cared for my needs while in Riyadh. "Why a butler?" I asked him.

He explained that during a royal visit in England, His Highness was greatly impressed with the butler's elegant performance, so thereafter his public greeter was the charming butler. I had the royal treatment, while making his trophy look like new again. Even though my labor was free, the expenses made it a costly repair job for him—but, then again, perhaps the prince just wanted to visit about past and future hunts (yes, he agreed to give his bear better quarters in the future).

One of Saudi Arabia's military leaders was perhaps the foremost big game hunter of the

country. This prince had hunted in various places around the world. King Mahendra of Nepal invited him to hunt tiger, gaur, panther, and various other forest wildlife. His Highness had a successful hunt, and asked what he could do to repay the fine hospitality. "Friendship" was the King's answer. However, during the prince's visit, it became apparent that medical facilities in Nepal were lacking. At the prince's expense, he had a huge hospital built in Katmandu. That's not the end of the story. As always, this Prince wanted the Klineburger's to do the taxidermy. The U.S. Fish and Wildlife Service refused this top military official of a close ally permission to ship his trophies into the U.S.A. The reasons being the animals were on the U.S. Endangered Species list, yet not endangered in Nepal. The solution to the idiocy of the U.S. bureaucracy was to send Gene Klineburger to Nepal to tan the skins and take measurements for the taxidermy forms. Klineburger Taxidermy was to premake all the forms and supplies and send one of their taxidermists to Saudi Arabia and do the work in a condominium cum taxidermy studio—and a nose-thumb to the U.S. officials.

One of the most prominent Saudi princes had a ski retreat in one of Colorado's notorious ski resorts. My brother Bert Klineburger escorted the prince to the Alaska Peninsula to hunt for Alaska brown bear at Warren Johnson's Bear Lake Lodge. The prince arrived with an entourage of 20, including FBI, bodyguards, and servants. He took a huge bear and brought it to us to do the taxidermy work. He asked my

# REFLECTION
# A Letter from the Teacher

The conversation among the kids at Redmond (Washington) Elementary School went something like this: "What did you do on the weekend?"

"Was bored, Aunt Amy came over from Spokane—Ma and Amy just talked a lot, but we did have hamburgers in the backyard."

Our son Kent said, "Had a great time. Roy Rogers and I took a couple of shotguns from the rack and shot trap in the back pasture. Then we caught some fish from the pond and put 'em in the smoke house . . ."

The teacher caught wind of it and sent a sealed letter home to Colleene (who happened to be the PTA president that year, she was kind of the Harper Valley type). "Dear Mrs. Klineburger, you really need to talk to your son about his fantasizing with the other kids. He actually told them that Roy Rogers stayed with you over the weekend—etc."

Colleene wrote in response, "Dear Ms. Holmes, I assure you that Kent did not fantasize in this particular case. Roy Rogers, along with Dale Evans, are close personal friends. Roy did stay with us and the boys did shoot and fish together. Incidentally, please don't jump to any conclusions of his fanatisizing in the future if he happens to bring up, but not limited to, the following . . ." and she went on to list a number of other entertainers, politicians, foreign dignitaries, astronauts, sports heroes, etc.

suggestions for position of the proposed life-size mount to be displayed at his ski retreat. I said I needed to know more about his facility in order to give my advice.

The prince flew me to the Colorado resort city at an established rendezvous time. I was met at the airport by a staff member in a fine vehicle and driven a short distance out of town and stopped at a high, solid gate in a blind fence that extended out of sight to each side. A couple sentries stopped us and inquired of this visitor, then proceeded to use long-handled mirrors to inspect the undercarriage of the vehicle in search of bombs that may have been placed there. All clear, as the motorized heavy gates opened toward us, I could see large steel columns just inside the gate lowering into the ground. I assumed the purpose was if a vehicle tried to crash through the gates, it would halt abruptly when it struck the steel columns.

A quarter of a mile into the complex brought us to a rambling building that went on and on. Upon meeting the prince in a modest den-like office, it was apparent there was no trophy room as such, nor a meeting place suitable to display trophy animals, besides lower-than-normal ceiling height. I suggested he add on a room with high ceilings, and make it a place for entertaining visitors. After some very pleasant camaraderie, he said thank you and goodbye.

Several months went by before I got a call from the prince—"Come see my new room." Another trip similar to the first took us past the main complex and up an unfinished road, leading to a massive log structure high on the hillside overlooking the valley. Construction workers were everywhere; finishing the most magnificent log lodge I've ever seen. The prince wasn't happy with the normal foot or so diameter logs, so those on this structure approached three feet across. Although it was unfinished, I could visualize a trophy house that could accommodate specimens for the rest of his hunting career. We mounted his huge bear standing on hind legs, to tower over visitors as they walked into this magnificent showplace.

# CHAPTER 10

# Teddy Roosevelt

Teddy Roosevelt was my mentor, post mortem. T.R., as he was known, was one of the most visionary leaders of American history. Growing up as a sickly child, he devoted himself to vigorous exercise, gaining physical stamina, and love for outdoor sports. When he was in his mid-20s, both his wife and mother died on the same day. He retreated to solitude for a time, in the Badlands of North Dakota, where he fine-tuned his focus on his career and the great outdoors.

By the time he was 30, Roosevelt's political career started. He began with the U.S. Civil Service Commission, and advanced to N.Y. Police Commissioner, then on to Assistant Secretary to the Navy and Governor of New York, before becoming the U.S. Vice President, then President of the United States for two terms.

The Spanish-American War punctuated his political career. He was the leading proponent of this war, and he helped organize the "Rough Riders" as a cavalry unit. Lacking horses, the Rough Riders fought as infantry. Led by Roosevelt, they charged up Kettle Hill in the battle of San Juan Hill.

T.R. was the first conservationist-minded president. He established the National Wildlife Refuge Program, the U.S. Forest Service (later changed to the National Park Service), and The Reclamation Service under his National Reclamation Act, the Antiquities Act, and formed the National Conservation Commission.

During his presidency, he withdrew 235 million acres of public timberland from sale, to set aside as national forests. He initiated water projects in all western states, including dams, beginning the task of reclaiming the desert southwest.

Roosevelt extended federal control over the West's scenic wonders, including Native American artifacts and relics. He created 16 national monuments, 51 wildlife refuges, and 5 national parks. Treasures he saved from encroachment by developers include the Grand Canyon, Crater Lake in Oregon, the Anasazi Ruins in Mesa Verde, Colorado, and many more.

Teddy Roosevelt was a renowned big game hunter, but he recognized early on that major conservation efforts would mainly be initiated by those who loved the wildlife most—the hunters themselves. He, like other hunters at the time, was a first-hand witness to the near destruction of a most valuable resource, wildlife.

In 1887, T.R. and other hunters joined together to form the first public organization to restore America's wild lands, the Boone and Crockett Club. The Club championed the passage of game laws and the designation of wild lands, which today make up our nation's conservation system. The National Park, the National Forest, and National Wildlife Refuge systems exist today in large part because of the extensive efforts of the Boone and Crockett Club and its dedicated membership of big game hunters.

Furthermore, the Boone and Crockett Club established hunting ethics, referred to as "Fair Chase," which later became the foundation for hunting and game laws in the U.S.A.

In addition, the Club established a point system devised to keep records of larger specimens of big game taken by hunters. This was done to maintain records of horn and antler size, which have a direct relationship to herd health and condition of habitat. These records are compiled and updated frequently and published under the title *Boone and Crockett Club's Records of North American Big Game.*

What did Teddy Roosevelt and I have in common? I could make a mile-long list of things we did not have in common, but if I dig deep enough, I might come up with a few similarities. I had been fascinated early on by T.R. as a man's man, an adventurer, a doer, a leader, a risk-taker, a conservationist, a hunter, a lover of nature and wildlife—in my eyes, the perfect man. What more could I want as my mentor?

A clue to our common interests might come from our one thing in common, our astrological links—we are both Scorpios. Some traits of Scorpios:

- are born to lead, pioneer, create, and venture;
- want to know, want to learn;
- are free to live their life their way;
- will realize their potential and their dreams;
- believe that in life all things are possible;
- are the most intense, profound, powerful characters in the Zodiac;

- they like truth, hidden causes, being involved, work that is meaningful;
- they dislike flattery and flattering.

These traits certainly apply to T.R., but to me?? Some things we both had in common were vision, love of wild lands and wildlife, solitude, exploring the unknown, love for the U.S.A., conservation of natural resources, authoring, and loving thy neighbor.

Here are some of Teddy Roosevelt's quotes that I hold dear to my heart:

## About Character:

- *I care not what others think of what I do, but I care very much about what I think of what I do.*
- *Character is the decisive factor in the life of an individual.*
- *The one thing I want to leave my children is an honorable name.*
- *The only man who never makes a mistake is a man who never does anything.*
- *With self-discipline, most anything is possible.*
- *Speak softly and carry a big stick; you will go far.*

## About Work and Effort:

- *No man needs sympathy because he has to work.*
- *Far and away the best prize that life offers is the chance to work hard at work worth doing.*
- *I have never in my life envied a human who led an easy life; I have envied a great many who led difficult lives and led them well.*

- *It is only through labor and painful effort, by grim energy and resolute courage that we move on to better things.*
- *When you are asked if you can do a job, tell 'em "certainly I can." Then get busy and find out how to do it.*

## About Sports and Firearms:

- *I do not in the least object to a sport because it is rough.*
- *In life, the principle to follow is—hit the line hard; don't foul and don't shirk, but hit the line hard.*
- *There is but one answer to be made to the bomb, and that can best be made with the Winchester rifle.*
- *An honest man must protect himself and until other means of securing his safety are devised, it is foolish and wicked to persuade him to surrender his arms, while men who are dangerous retain theirs.*

## Being Humble:

- *I am only an average man but, by George, I work harder at it than "the average man."*
- *If you kick the person in the pants responsible for most of your trouble, you wouldn't sit for a month.*

## About Stamina:

- *Just after an assassination attempt upon him, T.R. credited the thickness of his speech papers shot through as having prevented the bullet from entering his heart. Within five minutes of being shot, he delivered his entire speech, starting: "Friends, I shall ask you to be as quiet as possible. I don't know whether you fully understand that I have just been shot; but it takes more than that to kill a Bull Moose."*

## About Conservation:

- *The conservation of our natural resources and their proper use constitute the fundamental problem, which underlies almost every other problem of our national life.*

- *To waste, to destroy our natural resources, to skin and exhaust the land instead of using it so as to increase its usefulness, will result in undermining in the days of our children—the very prosperity which we ought to hand down to them amplified and developed.*

## About Challenges and Vision:

- *Far better it is to dare mighty things, to win glorious triumphs, even though checkered with failure, than to rank with the poor spirits who neither enjoy much nor suffer much, because they live in the grey twilight that know neither victory nor defeat.*

- *The (Panama) Canal was by far the most important action I took in foreign affairs during the time I was President. When nobody could or would exercise efficient authority, I exercised it.*

- *The credit belongs to the man who is actually in the arena; whose face is marred by the dust and sweat and blood; who strives valiantly; who at the best, knows in the end the triumph of high achievements, and who, at worst, if he fails, at least fails while daring greatly, so that his place shall never be with those cold and timid souls who know neither victory nor defeat.*

- *Do what you can, with what you have, where you are.*

- *It is hard to fail, but it is worst never to have tried to succeed.*

- *Never throughout history has a man who lived a life of ease left a name worth remembering.*

If more people would choose a man like Teddy Roosevelt as their mentor, the world would be a better place.

# REFLECTION
## Alaska

**H**ere are some unique facts about "THE GREAT LAND"

- *$^1/_5$ THE SIZE OF THE CONTINENTAL UNITED STATES*
- *Over 65% of all U.S. NATIONAL PARK and PRESERVE Lands*
- *Over 33% of all U.S. Bureau of Land Management lands*
- *The two largest National Forests in the U.S.*
- *88% of Alaska is public land*
- *Nearly 12% of Alaska is owned by Native Corporations, while less than .14% of Alaska is privately owned*
- *There are 14 species of big game, 20 species of sport fish, over 20 species of marine mammals, over 400 species of birds and species of furbearers*
- *Fifty thousand miles of saltwater shoreline and over 1,800 islands*
- *Over three million lakes, three thousand rivers, five thousand glaciers and active volcanoes*
- *Thirty-nine mountain ranges*
- *Over 130 million acres of forest and 190 million acres of rolling tundra*
- *Almost a virtual subcontinent in itself, the vast habitats of the GREAT LAND offer what many feel as the greatest outdoor opportunities in the world.*

Courtesy of Alaska Professional Hunters Association, dedicated to the conservation of wildlife.

# CHAPTER 11

# Arctic Tales

*Gene Klineburger*

I t was early April 1963, and the days were getting longer as the sun returned to the northern world. We now had sufficient light to fly out over the frozen Chukchi Sea and track the elusive polar bear. In order to eat, the bear follows open leads—cracks caused by the constant changing of tides—to hunt seal and other marine life.

After arriving in Kotzebue, (Otz) Alaska, I caught a ride to the Rotman Hotel on their supply truck. Numerous small planes, owned and used by the guide-outfitters, were already tied up on the frozen bay in front of town. Most of these were Piper Super Cubs, with an occasional Taylorcraft or Cessna.

After settling in at Rotman's, I located some of the outfitters around the village, including guides Ron Hays and Jack Lee and a game department biologist, Lee Miller, who were having breakfast at Art Field's establishment, which served as Art's home, base of operations for his guide service, and a restaurant.

Up North we didn't listen to traffic reports in the morning but to the weather reports from Russia to hear what was coming toward us from Tunetken on the Chukotsky Peninsula of Siberia. The weather was cold (minus 35 degrees) and clear and calm, so Ron said, "Hey, why waste a day, let's take Lee and Gene for a flight. Gene can shoot a bear and Lee can analyze it for the Fish & Game Department." The Game Department got a lot of free research from the hunters and guides, who often let them ride in the cover plane, if no other passenger was going along. Even when the biologists didn't go out on a hunt, they examined every hide and skull that was brought in, usually taking a tooth out of the jaw, in order to determine the age of the bear. Cutting the tooth and analyzing the growth rings could do this.

We headed northwest, passing Kivalina and Point Hope, just west of Cape Thompson, and headed for the open ice pan. If we didn't turn back in time, the next landfall would be Russia. I was in the back seat of Ron's Super Cub and Lee was flying with Jack. Ron is a big person, so I couldn't see much ahead but had a good view out of each side of the plane. We saw quite a few tracks in the snow, like a sow with two cubs and a male following. But we didn't see any large enough to induce us to pursue. By midmorning we came across a real interesting set of tracks that were obviously worth following.

We followed them for over half an hour and felt we were soon to see this huge trophy; suddenly a bloody carcass came into view at the termination of the tracks. Ron and Jack were discussing on the radios, in no uncertain terms, our misfortune when another voice cut in saying "Yea, if you guys didn't party so much in the evening and got hunting early enough, you too might find big trophies."

We knew the voice to be that of Nelson Walker, who lived in Otz and was an outstanding outfitter, guiding many hunters to trophies that earned a place in the Boone and Crocket Record Book. We landed to examine the carcass, then refueled the wing tanks with some of the gas in five-gallon cans carried in the rear of the planes, then continued on with our hunt.

It wasn't long before we came upon another track, with prints almost the same size as the previous polar bear. We got our adrenaline up, and the hunt was on! Soon we observed a big, male bear in the distance, near a pressure ridge. Fortunately there was a smooth looking pan of ice past the ridge where we could land. From there, we cautiously walked toward the ridge and were

" One of our Super Cubs being refueled on the ice pack from 5-gallon cans. Note ski-wheel combination.

ⓐ **Gene Klineburger and his record-class polar bear.**

able to see the bear within about 300 yards, which afforded a good shot.

Using the Weatherby 300 with 180-grain bullets and a Bushnell scope, it wasn't too difficult to down the bear with a shot to the right side of the rib cage. This caused nanook (polar bear) to turn swiftly and another shot on the left side put him down permanently. Upon close examination, it was evident that this was an outstanding trophy; probably close to the size of the one taken by Walker's party.

After the kill comes the hard part. Skinning this animal took four people, with difficulty, to just roll it over as the skin is removed, while being careful not to damage it because it is to be made into a life-size mount for

the Seattle Klineburger studio. Lee Miller had brought a scale, a tripod, and hooks so he could weigh the parts after it was cut up, in order to estimate the weight, adding what was determined to be blood and fluids lost during skinning. Lee figured the bear would have weighed over 1,200 pounds and my measurement of the skull assured us that it would indeed go into the record book.

When we first landed, we had covered the engines of the planes with special engine covers to keep them somewhat warm. After the hunt and skinning was completed, Ron put what gasoline was left into the tanks and brought the plane around to the bear. We put the hide and skull, which were now in a Klineburger hide bag, into the plane. This provided a seat cushion for me in the rear, elevating me so I could see more toward the front.

We took off knowing we had been out a long time. It was now late afternoon and our gas supply may not be sufficient to return to Otz. Having been up late the night before (as Nelson Walker had reminded us) I was dozing off, lulled by the drone of the engine, when all of a sudden I was jerked awake by a deathly silence—the engine had quit!

It turned out that Ron was trying to use every drop of fuel in the right wing tank before switching to the valve to the other tank. Fortunately, he had gained some altitude in anticipation of this happening and while losing altitude the prop wind milled enough to restart the engine when it sucked in some fuel. The sound of the engine running again was the best sound I ever heard, especially due to the fact that we were flying over an open lead at that moment.

We did make it back to town by sundown and as soon as we tied the planes down and turned the polar hide over to an Eskimo villager to have his wife flesh and wash it, we hurried over to Nelson Walker's cabin to see the bear his client had taken. As we got "the rest of the story" it turns out two clients, brothers named Longoria from Mexico, had booked with Nelson for a hunt. In deciding who would get to take the first trophy bear, they flipped a coin and the younger brother won the toss. A medium-sized male bear was spotted, stalked, and taken early in the day. After taking to the air, they found the large

tracks that brother, Shelby, was successful in collecting the specimen that we had observed earlier.

I was an official measurer for the Boone and Crockett Club, so I carefully measured the length and width of the huge skull, which was a total of 30 inches. This would easily make it a new world record, topping the old record taken in 1958 by Governor Tom Bolack of New Mexico.

In celebration of an outstanding day of successful hunting (three bears) and some vital Game Department research, we had a round of drinks at Walker's place before facing the night air and the beautiful aurora borealis lights. We went next door to the Rotman building (now owned by Steve Salinas, who had married one of Rotman's daughters) to have some wine and a T-bone steak dinner, which had arrived by airfreight that afternoon.

Even though the bear I took that day had almost the same size body, the skull only ranked #86 in the Boone and Crockett book—still nothing to be ashamed of. It made an excellent life-size mount, as did Longoria's.

The next day, one of the experienced Eskimo women fleshed all possible fat off the inside of our hides, finished boning out the feet, nose, etc. saving the fat to be rendered down and used by her family. After cutting a hole in the ice, she then lowered the hide into the cold, salty ocean water, securely tied with a rope, to wash as much blood and fat off as was possible. It was then placed on the snow, covered with more snow, walked on, and rubbed to further clean it, sort of a dry-cleaning process. It was next placed into one of our clean canvas shipping bags, left outside to freeze, and then shipped in the cold cargo bay of a Wein Airlines plane to our tannery in Seattle.

> *There are strange things done in*
> *the midnight sun*
> *For the men who moil for gold*
> *The Arctic trails have their secret tales*
> *That would make your blood run cold——*

Here are some of Gene's tales——-

- One time, Ron Hayes took off and one of the cables that steady his skis broke and the ski was sitting at a very odd angle, the front pointing down. I wasn't with him at that time but was there when he returned to Kotzebue. The hunter had to stick his rifle out the door and push down on the back of the ski as they landed so the ski wouldn't dig into the ice. Ron made a perfect landing, no problem.

- Another time, one of the fellows was getting ready to gas up his plane that was

Looking north from town the bear-hunting guides parked their aircraft, waiting to explore the vast ice pan beyond.

parked on the ice outside of Kotzebue. He drove to it with a truck that had gas in it and when they touched the gas nozzle to the airplane the whole thing went up in flames, evidently due to static electricity. There was nothing left but a metal skeleton; a very expensive loss.

- Another fellow built a Piper Cub out of spare parts in the living room of one of the small hotels there. He got it all together and ready to go, but of course couldn't have wings on it inside, so he pushed it outside. They had to cut the door bigger to get it out. He pushed it outside, bolted the wings on and scrounged around till he found a few gallons of gas, and by golly that thing took off. He flew around a bit and decided that it was air-worthy. He scrounged some more gas and told people that if they would give him some gas that

A pleasant April day on the main street of Kotzebue, on the waterfront of the Chukchi Sea.

he would get them some caribou meat. So he flies away and in a few hours he came back. When he landed, he quickly jumped out, hoping it wouldn't go up in flames because the gas tank, which is up in the cowl, similar to a Model A Ford, was dripping gas. There was gas and blood from the caribou sloshing all over the floor of the airplane, but there isn't much that runs on electricity in those simple Piper Cubs, so the gas didn't ignite. People just got a little gas-tasting caribou meat to eat the next week or two.

- Many adventures happened in relation to polar bear hunting. For instance, Lee Holan was over the arctic ice between Alaska and Siberia when he made a forced landing and damaged his plane so badly that he could not fly it back to shore. He did not have a second plane to help him get back, so he was on his own. He and his passenger took one of the gas tanks out of the plane to use it as a boat in case they had to cross an open lead coming back, which they did end up using across open water. Eventually, they made it to shore and lived to fly another day.

- Jack Lee, another pilot that I had hunted polar bear with, later had a serious accident that ended his career. He landed on a smooth glacier where he had a hunting camp. In landing his Super Cub on the inclined ice, he turned the plane sideways and got out. The craft started sliding, so he jumped back in, turned the plane and attempted to start the engine. It didn't take and Jack and the plane went off the end of the glacier and crashed. Jack lived, but permanently crippled.

- One of the more colorful guides that I knew who used to guide for polar bear and other game in Alaska, was named Bob. I won't mention his last name, but I remember one time he came to Barrow with a couple of girls of ill repute that he had flown up from Fairbanks to stay with him and his hunters, to add a little entertainment. He also had quite a load of booze and food. I asked him one time how long he was going to be at their camp before going back to Fairbanks, and he said, "When we run out of booze, we'll go back." Anyhow, a few years later he was flying in the interior of Alaska and he had been drinking heavily. He did fly into the ground and that was the end of Bob.

- Another one of the bush pilots that I knew well was named Jules Thibedeau and he was flying a load of drinks and food in preparation of guiding out of Barrow. He was flying a Taylor Craft, similar to the plane that I learned to fly in. He was so heavily laden that he couldn't make it over Anactuvuk Pass and he crashed and was killed.

- One time Pete Merry, Cleo McMahan, and I were flying from Point Barrow to Umiat and saw a nice wolverine and tried to land and go after it, but the snow was so deep and powdery that the plane started sinking and if we had stopped moving, we would never have gotten back off the snow. So I jumped out and helped to keep the plane moving forward till we could pick up speed, and then I jumped onto the ski and eventually managed to get back into the plane. I remember that we did shoot a red fox on that hunt, which was surprising because you see a lot of white fox in the Arctic, but seldom see a red fox.

- Another time we left Barrow in mid-morning and headed southeast, toward the Colville River. As we were flying along low and at low speed in order to read the tracks in the snow, I looked out the left side of the plane, only to see a snowy owl accompanying us and looking us over, like asking himself, "Who are you, invading my territory?" We made a landing, to relieve ourselves, and spotted a fox eyeing us from a distance. It looked like a long shot, but Pete urged me to try for it. Having the Weatherby 300, it made an interesting challenge. Much to everyone's surprise with one shot the fox flipped over. We flew on until we spotted a wolverine, so we made a landing beyond where he was heading. We stalked toward the little guy until he came into view. A sitting shot presented a good potential opportunity, so I pulled off a shot and got him. It had a prime coat. The wolverines are cherished for their beautiful, ice-resistant fur, especially good for parka ruffs around the face. (I had a parka made with that pelt for ruff and ribbon seal for the body of the parka.) As we lost track of time, shadows began forming and as we continued east,

we realized we were too far from Barrow to return and we were running low on fuel. We hadn't brought extra cans of AV gas like we did when going out over the ice for bear. At one time, oil exploration crews had set up a camp along the Colville River at a place called Umiat. We made it that far before sundown. By the time we had anchored the aircraft and found a Quonset hut that seemed to give some protection, it was almost dark. We had food and sleeping bags, so we tried to start a fire to get the chill off and cook some food. There was an oil stove, which we managed to light but soon the room was filled with smoke. We had to turn it off, eat cold snacks, and crawl into our sleeping bags on the cold floor. When we looked at the thermometer on the wing strut it said minus 32 degrees. The next morning we prepared a hasty breakfast over a Primus stove that we had and then wondered how we could return to Barrow while low on fuel. Snooping around the abandoned camp we lucked out and found four five-gallon cans of AV gas that had not been opened. Since this wasn't enough to fill the tanks, we kicked various 55-gallon drums that had been left years ago and we managed to find enough old gas to fill both planes. On the return trip to Barrow, we spotted some wolves following caribou, intent on making a kill. At that time, wolves were considered a menace since they killed young animals and the Alaska Fish & Wildlife Agency paid a bounty to kill them. We got on the trail of a big male wolf. I opened the right side of the plane (boy, was that cold!) and took him with a 12-gauge shotgun, using buckshot.

- One sunny day a pair of Super Cubs left Kotzebue (Otz) for a day of hunting. The hunter was an older man from Texas who somewhat regretted putting off the adventure of his lifetime to get a polar bear. In fact, his doctor had accompanied him just in case a problem arose. All went well and, after about one and a half hours of looking for sizable tracks, they crossed a trail, which they followed. The hunting party landed, outfitter Ray Capisella having the hunter with him. After a short stalk, the old hunter was in a good position to sit and make a successful shot, which hit home, dropping the bear. Skinning started immediately, but before the job was done the hunter swayed sideways

**Leon Shellabarger's place of business on the main drag of beautiful Kotzebue.**

and passed out. While the doctor and one guide tried to revive him, the other outfitter finished the last of the skinning and stuffed the hide into the Klineburger hide sack, which was put in the cover plane. The hunter was positioned in the rear seat of Ray's plane and they were soon airborne, headed to Otz. A call was made via the radio alerting the officials of the problem; however, he died en route. We met the planes when they came in, but had difficulty removing the hunter from the cub because by now, between the cold plane and the start of rigor mortis he was pretty well established in a sitting position. At any rate, we got him to the little hospital where he was officially pronounced dead, allowed to thaw out enough to place him in a pine box, and airfreighted back home. He died doing what he wanted, although it would have been nice if he could have enjoyed the results of his hunt.

- Leon Shellabarger had a shack in Otz that he agreed to rent to Reinholt Thiele and me for the season. Well, after getting directions, Riney and I trudged up to it only to find it half full of snow. Some Eskimo kid probably threw something through the window, causing quite a hole. With considerable effort we managed to remove the snow, get a fire going, and eventually made the place quite livable. This provided us a nice base of operation, Riney for his guide service and me for the taxidermy business. One day, Leon needed to make a flight up the Kobuk River to

deliver some supplies to the villages of Kiana and Shungnak and invited me to accompany him, and of course I jumped at the opportunity. It was a nice clear cold day, ideal for ski plane flying—the only difficulty being that no matter how hard you try, it isn't possible to keep warm in a Super Cub. Whenever a plane would arrive in a village, most of the inhabitants would turn out to see who was coming, what they were bringing, could they be of help, and probably sending messages or items "outside." Roads did not exist between villages, and distances were long. In the summer, motorboats could use the river, but in winter all was ice and snow. After unloading our deliveries and loading numerous items to go back to Otz we struggled into the air, as we

**Art Field took Gene to Kobuk Lake by dog team, where he's pulling in a pile of shee fish.  »**

**" Art Field's restaurant was one of the only gathering places in Otz. Gene in white parka hobnobs with the gang on a no-fly day.**

were somewhat overloaded. We pretty much followed the river westward and all seemed to be going well. I dozed in the rear seat when suddenly the plane started to vibrate violently, bringing me to attention. Leon yelled, "Oh, hell, I think the engine swallowed a valve!" Fortunately, we had been flying at about 5,000 feet so, using the radio, we could communicate with Otz. Leon told them we had a mechanical problem and might have to set down on the river. Well, Leon did a good job of nursing the plane along and gradually losing altitude until Otz came into view. By now, we were no longer feeling the cold but were sweating out staying airborne. The faithful little plane did safely carry us to a smooth set down on the ice off the coast and we were able to taxi to Leon's usual tie-down spot. So ended another potentially dangerous situation.

- I have flown with Leon numerous times and frequently stayed in his mini-rooming house. Roy Rogers stayed there when he hunted polar bear. Leon wasn't a very neat person and was overweight, so didn't present a good impression. One time he was out hunting bear and he asked me to meet another client at the airport and bring him to the rooming house. Leon's pickup truck, which I was to use, was pretty messy and I was a bit embarrassed to put this wealthy client in it. The cab (and truck bed) was cluttered with junk and cigarette butts, a piece of sausage hung out of the glove box, and I used a screwdriver as an ignition key. We arrived at the house ok, and the client had a successful hunt. Leon was a good pilot and guide. His Super Cub plane had papers, cigarette butts, etc. on the top of the dashboard. I told Leon he should fly upside down once in a while to dump the stuff off the dashboard—he didn't take my advice nor did he appreciate it, but we still got along fine. One evening, Leon and his wife, Marie, and I wanted some entertainment and the nearest excuse for nightlife was Stubby's Coffee House. Well, liquor was not for sale in Otz but everyone brought their own bottle and spiked the drinks that Stubby sold—coffee, canned pop, or whatever he could obtain to sell that day. I had a down jacket with big pockets, so Marie handed me her whiskey bottle when we were ready to leave their house and we walked the short distance to Stubby's (I think the

painted sign over the door said "Little Pete's"). Some patrons put money in the juke box and turned it up and we were all enjoying each other's company when in walked the state trooper (Joe Rychet) who's job it was to patrol the whole area, so when he came in and observed some bottles of booze (including Shellabargers's) he proceeded to take them outside and dump the contents into the snow. Marie almost cried to see the expensive liquor wasted like that (airfreight from Anchorage consisted largely of liquor). I heard later that Stubby was badly hurt unloading a 50-gallon drum of fuel.

- As I recall, Leon borrowed a Cub and after untying the wing tie-downs, he revved it up and took off but immediately felt he was in deep trouble as the plane was barely manageable. He circled and landed on the ice in front of Otz, only to find an oxygen bottle tied to the tailskid, intended to help tie the plane down. Many other incidents come to mind as I think of the "polar bear hunting days." Like Art Field's restaurant set up in the front part of his house. Breakfast was one of the main events—the patrons frequently arrived before Art was out of bed, but since the door didn't have a lock on it we just went in, put the coffeepot on and cooked up eggs, bacon, spuds, and toast. The commotion usually aroused the host, and he would join us. There was a painted wood door leading to the living quarters, and one day when Art didn't appear before the patrons left, we couldn't find a piece of paper to tell him we owed him for breakfast, so we wrote on the door that Gene was here, etc. Well, that door began to get a life of it's own, as everybody who was anybody wrote their name there. I remember Roy Rogers (and Trigger) had autographed it. I wonder where that door is today?

- Outfitter Ralph Marshall guided an acquaintance of mine, Bill Commack, from Johnson City, Texas on polar bear hunt. They spotted a bear 60 miles west of Point Hope and landed on the opposite side of a pressure ridge. After leaving the plane they climbed the ridge and were within 150 yards of the animal. This seemed to afford a relatively easy shot so Cammack lay prone on the ridge and pulled off a shot, followed up with three more just to make sure the bear would stay put. Well, the bear had other plans and, although badly wounded, swiftly circled behind the ridge. As Bill and Ralph cautiously pursued the trophy, they heard a sound behind them and upon turning were startled to see the bloody and wounded bear charging like a freight train: with mouth open and eyes flashing, intent on destruction. Both hunters used the bolt actions as fast as possible, hitting the bear numerous times, but to no effect. The bear finally got to Bill and as he tried to push the bear away with the rifle, he pulled off a shot, only to explode the rifle barrel, spreading it back about four inches and rendering it useless. The bear now had Bill down and was chewing and clawing furiously. It managed to chew through several layers of wool and down clothing, biting into Bill's left rib cage, while clawing into the other end of Bill, badly damaging his rump. Marshall managed to get off two more shots into the neck and shoulder, being careful not to hit Cammack. This caused the bear to relax on top of Bill. With Ralph's help, he was able to slide out from under the profusely bleeding adversary. After Ralph rough-skinned the bear, he helped Bill into the rear seat of the Cub, and flew to Point Hope. Ralph radioed ahead for help and some Eskimos were there to assist. They laid Bill on a sled and took him to a house where he could get emergency care. The next day they set out for Otz where a village medical center could give him better treatment. Unfortunately, after only a few miles out, the engine quit and an emergency landing was made on the frozen Chukchi Sea. Ralph walked back to Point Hope and borrowed a plane to fly out to rescue Bill, who was very miserable in the 30° below freezing weather. They flew back to Point Hope because by now visibility had dropped to about 500 feet. Going on to Otz was out of the question. Eventually, 2½ days after the fateful hunt, they made it to Otz where Bill was rushed to the local medical facility for treatment. Bill excitedly relayed the events to me as he waited in Otz until he felt well enough to take a flight back home, almost two weeks after his arrival. Since then, he has made a complete recovery.

- In the Arctic, as I knew it, almost anyone was more than anxious to help a fellow human in trouble or need. That is how they have survived in this hostile environment. Nothing went to waste. Meat, bones, skins, tusks—all were utilized. What few berries grew in the long summers were harvested and used year-round; same with fish, seal, etc. Wolves, wolverine, fox, ermine, and caribou skins were used largely for clothing. Eskimos originally did their own tanning of hides, using whatever supplies they could obtain, including urine. The final result was almost a raw skin, worked until it was flexible enough to use. Sometimes a tourist or hunter would buy a garment up in the Arctic, take it home, and have it in their nice home. In a day or two, everyone would be wondering what that very strong odor was; you guessed it—the Eskimo parka! Our Klineburger Company had a modern tannery, which I was primarily responsible for, that tanned the hides for our own use, but also for other people. Well, word got out, and numerous Alaska and Canadian natives started sending their raw hides to us for processing. Thomas Brower of Barrow, Alaska, used to send me his tanning jobs. His father, Charles Brower, went north on a whaling ship and stayed near Barrow, starting a community called Browerville. Charles wrote a book about his adventures

called "50 Years Below Zero." Eventually the tourist trade became large enough and the Eskimo carvers could not get enough walrus ivory to meet the demand. Well, I came to the rescue—elephant ivory was in surplus at the time.

- After World War II, I learned to fly aircraft using the G.I. Bill, and it came in handy once in a while. One day we went north out of Point Barrow—two planes and four people—and we successfully got a polar bear for the customer in the other plane. When coming back, the pilot in my plane decided to take a few nips out of the whiskey bottle that he had in the plane. It was so cold up there that even the whiskey was starting to solidify, but he managed to get a few good slugs out of the bottle and was feeling pretty good and happy about getting a polar bear, so he told me to take over and I ended up flying the plane back to Point Barrow.

Editor's note: *When the Marine Mammals Protection Act was passed in 1972 by the Department of Interior, it virtually changed Alaska's Arctic forever. Hunting was the center of livelihood in the Arctic, especially for the Eskimos, whose lives changed overnight. The Alaska Fish and Game Department no longer had jurisdiction over their marine mammals, which they had professionally managed throughout the years. Polar bear, walrus, and seal hunting were a thing of the past for everyone except Native Americans, who could kill and utilize them for their own needs, but were forbidden to sell or trade the by-products that they artistically produced and sold from their early existence. The Act also put out of business a lot of outfitters, trading posts, and other businesses.*

*The Klineburger's fur-dressing (tanning) operation, that depended greatly on the Eskimos' fur product industry as well as their own fur-manufacturing and hunting specimens, eventually closed down. Gene Klineburger, who had reached retirement age, felt it was time to leave the business and enjoy his hobby of collecting and restoring antique and classic cars.*

## REFLECTION
# Memories with Photography

Stories of hunts in the Western Hemisphere are limited in PART II of this book. Even though my expeditions overseas began in the early 1960s, I have never stopped taking every opportunity to enjoy the great outdoors of the Americas. Whether I hunt or fish for my own satisfaction, or guide others, being out there to outsmart the game or be outsmarted, the paramount reason is the enjoyment of God's gift.

Every outdoor experience is a story in itself. I realize now that the use of cameras should have been as important as the gun or rod. As I search through my skimpy records to give visual aid to this autobiography, I find that sort of material to be almost nonexistent. In my early years, I didn't own a camera, but thoughtful companions did provide a few memorable photos. Later on I had cameras, but mostly the wrong thing. I tried 35mm, 120, 620, 2¼ x 2¼ and, of course, Polaroid. I used Kodachrome, Ektachrome, color negative, black and white—the works. However, none of that mattered; the camera was in the bottom of my pack. With rifle, binoculars, spotting scope, and, yes, movie camera in hand, the still-picture taking suffered.

However, a few photos have surfaced that bring me fond memories, and I will share some of them with the readers.

☉ **Tracking desert mule deer with skilled Indian guides in Sonora ranks high in adventure.**

« » **The author with a Canadian moose from central B.C.**

☝ **From left Mary and Eldon Brandt and Colleene Klineburger loading their barren ground caribou specimens and meat into the huge LI Stinson aircraft.**

☝ **Chris with a Toklat grizzly taken above the Arctic Circle.**

☝ **My hands are dwarfed by the huge paw of my brown bear taken on the Alaska Peninsula.**

☝ **A barren ground caribou from the Alaska Peninsula. Note lack of palmation on the beams.**

" Chris's mountain caribou from Northern British Columbia bears heavy palmation.

" A Rocky Mountain goat taken by Chris during one of his bighorn sheep hunts.

" A hunting camp in Yukon's Glenlyon Mountains, from where Belle Desrosier guided Chris for Fannin sheep and other game.

Here is brother Bert's top trophy, an Alaska moose, which held the all-time world record from 1961 to 1979 and only then was dominated by a point or two. The specimen is now in a museum in Greece.

Chris with his Kodiak bear.

# FONDEST MEMORIES OF THE GREAT CONTINENT OF AFRICA

An African safari was no longer just in focus, it was reality. Our taxidermy studio, Jonas Brothers of Seattle, mounted specimens from every part of Africa—I could identify the hundred common animals at a glance—And I knew the anatomy and horn size that constitutes a good trophy. However, I did not know how well trained I was for safari from my broad hunting experiences in North America: tracking desert mule deer and sheep with Indians; being outsmarted by elusive sheep and deer; enduring the most severe weather, from 50 below to 120 above; living with natives whose lives depended on hunting; physical exertion; determination; alertness and quickness, to react instantly for a quick shot or to sidestep danger.

Africa is a different world; however, my accumulated skills carried me safely and successfully from the Red Sea Hills of Sudan to the continent's southern regions of Mozambique and South Africa. Aside from extreme cold conditions, Africa's hunting was similar in mountains, deserts, savannahs, bush country, forests, and jungles. The most prominent difference is the quantities and varieties of plainsgame, supported by vast and lush savannahs of Africa.

Reporting on my African adventures requires considerable restraint——I would like to write about it all, but in order to prevent total boredom, I am limiting the stories in this section to my fondest memories of the great continent of Africa.

PART III

# FONDEST MEMORIES OF THE GREAT CONTINENT OF AFRICA

# CHAPTER 1

# Uganda— The Pearl of Africa

**B**y the early 1960s, our company had become a world-leading taxidermy studio, as well as probably the single greatest source of hunting and wildlife information. We knew where the good trophies came from, and who the good outfitters were. Sportsmen sought our knowledge to line up their hunts, whether it was a North American hunt, an Indian shikar, or African safari.

From early on, British East Africa—Kenya, Tanganyika, and Uganda—was the major destination for safaris. Most professional hunters were British, and Nairobi, Kenya was the base and pivot point for most operators. Early safaris would start from Nairobi, with a caravan of lorries (large trucks laden with all the provisions), hunting vehicles, staff, and clients, and would strike out for several weeks or several months, being entirely independent.

Uganda was one popular destination where the safari operators would go, collecting much game, but spending little more than the cost of the inexpensive hunting licenses. Uganda and other countries were not profiting from their valuable resources.

In 1962, Uganda became independent from Great Britain. With Britain's help, an infrastructure was established to make the country self supporting, by forming Uganda Development Corporation. Under that was Uganda Wildlife Development (UWD), a company formed to operate their own exclusive hunting operation. The company was overviewed by the Uganda Game Department headed by Chief Game Warden, John Blower.

The first order of business was to confer with some professional hunters (PHs) from Nairobi. Another Englishman, Ernest Juer, acted as organizer, front man, and sales manager to get the plan started. The subject of the all-important hunting clients surfaced early in the talks. They would need a lot of customers, and need them soon. The question was, how could they get them without the long process of advertising?

The PHs said "Why not contact the Klineburgers? They send us a lot of business." Therefore, Ernest Juer arrived unannounced at our Seattle offices and told us of their plans.

The result of that historic visit was the beginning of the Klineburgers going worldwide. We were involved in the structuring of what would be the first ever "affordable" African safaris.

Not to go into the lengthy details of how, what, when and where, the bottom line was for the inclusive price of U.S. $2,350, a client would fly from New York on Alitalia Airlines, with a stopover in Rome, continue on to Entebbe, Uganda; have a nice hotel in Kampala; travel by hunting car to the first camp already set up with resident PHs; hunt for one week in each of three camps that were already set up and scouted for game.

After 21 days of hunting, in three different areas with the highest quality camps, and well-maintained Land Rover hunting vehicles, hunters would pay trophy fees at the end of the hunt for what they collected. Example: Cape buffalo $22, kob $14, lion $143, hartebeest $11, elephant $143. In addition, ivory tax was figured on a sliding scale to be paid by the pound. A 50-pounder (weight of each tusk) $300, while a hundred pounder would be around $1,000.

We assured Ernest we could send them a steady flow of clientele, so UWD quickly got the camps and equipment together while we started calling our friends and customers to be on standby. Once UWD fired the starting gun, Bert Klineburger escorted the first six clients for the adventure of their lives. Group after group followed, to hunt that beautiful and game-rich country.

The Klineburgers were suddenly in the travel business, booking airlines, arranging visas and hotels en route. Our staff was overworked, so a separate office and staff made up Jonas Brothers Worldwide Travel, an agency serving the sportsmen. This division of our company expanded rapidly for foreign outfitters. In those early years in the travel business, we refrained from representing North American outfitters, but still referred clients to them.

Paralleling the planning of the Uganda safaris, we made immediate plans for the all-important caring for trophy specimens, which require special treatment for their long steamship journey to their final destination. That job ended up on my shoulders. I took one of our willing taxidermists, Wayne Hathaway, to Uganda to assist me in establishing Jonas Brothers of Africa—Taxidermy and Forwarding Company.

Our purpose was two-fold—preparing raw skins, horns, and skulls for shipment, then packaging and crating them, as well as actually doing taxidermy work on location. North American hunters opted to have their raw trophies sent to their respective taxidermists, but European clients often preferred to have the trophies mounted before shipping to their homes.

There was much more to handling raw skins than the packing, because of disease and insect control. There was a process referred to as "dipping" that was coined from the early procedure of actually dipping the skins and other animal parts in a bath that included arsenic and other curing agents, to preserve the trophies for as long as needed.

With then-modern insecticides and our newly developed processes, we eliminated the need for dipping. Yet skins had to be properly identified, dried, and folded in such a way as to reduce the "cubic weight" to a minimum.

Ocean freight in the old days was the only practical shipping method. Steamships were concerned only with space, not weight, so our packaging was on a no-space wasted basis. Our crates were made from rough-cut hardwood, and they were heavy—there was no light lumber in East Africa. Documentation was another of our functions, including any required export or import permits. In other words, the professional hunters only had to worry about taking proper field care

of the specimens and getting them into Kampala, and we did all the rest.

Our first order of business was to hire staff and find a proper location. We hired an English taxidermist and his African "boy" from Rowland Ward Company in Nairobi. Most Europeans in Africa had their own personal African servants of sorts—their boys. As an example, a professional hunter might have a boy that would be a skilled tracker, gun bearer, or vehicle driver, while a taxidermist might have an assistant that would be skilled in the unessential tasks.

Rowland Ward of Nairobi, headquartered in London, was to my knowledge the only taxidermy company in Africa. I hired a variety of Africans with skills varying from carpenter, to skinning, to sewing, to guard.

For location, I found a fine "godown" in Kampala's industrial area. A typical godown (the common term for an industrial business location) is a walled and gated compound, with a yard and buildings for storage and workspace. We put everyone to work getting our work benches, shelving, skull boiling, and crating areas all ready for production.

In the meantime our big shipment arrived from Seattle with the head molds of every Uganda animal, specialty tools, glass animal eyes, and other supplies. It was round-the-clock work for Wayne and me until we were satisfied with well-trained staff doing their assigned work.

One snag I recognized early-on related to Africans' work hours. East Africa operated on the "siesta" pattern, i.e., work four hours, take a lengthy lunch break, then supposedly put in another four hours of work late in the day. The help would go home for their break, get an inadequate meal (if at all), usually consume some banana beer (a seemingly ever-present beverage for those folks), and return useless for the afternoon shift.

Enough of that—I gave them a one-hour lunch break, during which everyone stayed on the premises. I provided them with a good, healthy lunch, consisting of meat, *posho*, (a traditional mush made from a root), fruit, and tea or coffee. The guard was the chef in a well-equipped kitchen and dining area. At first, they strongly objected to my Americanizing them, but soon they got to liking it, as it was probably the best meal, if not the only meal, they had all day—besides having the evenings with their families.

After several weeks, business was going rather smoothly, and I was ready to start having fun—going hunting. I had bought a used Land Rover that helped greatly while getting the Jonas Brothers of Africa off and running. I had many fine meetings with John Blower, who befriended me and gave me considerable information on the known wildlife infrastructure of Uganda.

He also explained there was a number of areas in the country they knew little or nothing about. I also had gotten well-acquainted with the professional hunters of UWD when they had a break between safaris. These legendary professionals included Briane Herne, Dave Williams, Nicky Blunt, and John Northcote. In fact, Briane Herne gave me the use of his home while he was out in the field, as he preferred it occupied while out in the bush for weeks on end.

All the PHs were very open about sharing information, usually exciting yarns about interesting encounters and narrow escapes. How I would have loved to join any of them in their camps, but they were far too busy providing the ultimate pleasure to the continuous flow of our clients. Intermittently, I had time to leave the business in Wayne's hands and take off on my own.

I asked Chief Game Warden, Blower, if I could explore some of the unknown areas in Uganda, rather expecting a negative reply. But he responded with "absolutely!"

He said he would like to get a report on the area along the Tanganyika and Rwanda borders that UWD had not yet utilized. He indicated it was a short day's drive, and there were roads—a good way to get my feet wet for hunting on my own. He instructed the game warden in Mbarara, a town along the way, to issue me a permit to enter and hunt the area. (Here is your lesson in Swahili: when an N or M precedes a consonant, you say the letter, then pronounce the rest of the word. Example, em-barara; mbogo=em-bogo; nyala=en-yala.)

John also suggested a trip later to the Karamojo in the northeast and the Acholi area along the north, bordering Sudan, because they knew little about this country.

I went about gathering camping equipment, borrowed a .375 H&H Magnum rifle from UWD, and hired three Africans, one that could drive, one that could speak a little English, and a general helper. I was ready to face the African bush and whatever it might bring on. I bought my hunting license, which listed all the Uganda game except rhino, so I just assumed I had no restrictions.

I need to say a few words about the infrastructure of this most beautiful country, perhaps Africa's finest at that time. Many referred to it as "The Pearl of Africa." After Winston Churchill experienced a safari there, he called it "a fairy tale." I refer to it as the apex of Africa. After all, the major waterways flow in all directions from its elevated position near the center of Africa.

The source of the great Nile River is from Lake Victoria in Uganda's southeast. To the west, south, and east are watersheds that drain both to the Atlantic and Indian oceans. Central and South Uganda is blessed with lush, grassy savannahs that support herds of a great variety of plains

**Uganda's first safari in 1962, when Bert Klineburger led the group and the beginning of our Jonas Brothers Worldwide Travel. From left, Tony Sulak, Harold Trulin, W.T. (Yoshi) Yoshimoto, PH David Williams, Web Hilgar, Bert, Ernest Juer, (unknown), PH Briane Herne, and PH Nicky Blunt (PH meaning Professional Hunter).**

**The author standing on the central meridian of Planet Earth.** »

game. The northwest, along the Nile, has rich forests that were some of the finest elephant habitat.

The north and northeast areas are drier, yet rich, bush country and fine grazing for the Karamojang warrior tribe that inhabited the escarpment on the Kenya border. On the west along Belgian Congo (now Zaire) border are the high snow-covered Ruwenzori Mountains, the home of the mountain gorillas.

Being situated right on the Equator, Uganda does not have torrential monsoon rains. Instead there are more mild early rains around May and the late rains around November, giving ideal conditions for farming every type of crop, including some of the world's best coffee and tea. At the time, the native people were the happiest and most prosperous of all I had visited throughout Africa.

# CHAPTER 2

# Hunting Africa the Hard Way

## Hunting Cats and Plains game

**M**y first hunting safari was not like any the average sportsman is ever to take—or want to take, for that matter. Hunting big game does not vary much in essential detail from place to place. The habits of the animals vary, of course, in keeping with the environment where they must spend their lives. The same is true of the natives who inhabit the country with them.

When I hunt in an area, I like to make myself as inconspicuous as possible. For this reason, I am a loner. I enjoy the companionship of good men, but I like to slip into an area without making too much fuss about it and, to the greatest possible degree, become part of the area. I have guided some, and have accompanied others into the wilds, but most of my hunting has been alone or in the company of natives.

My first safari now became reality when I took off with my African staff to explore the Kikagati Triangle, an area in the extreme southwest of Uganda. I had obtained a seven-day permit from the Game Department to hunt in an area on the Uganda-Tanganyika border, west of Lake Victoria and east of the Congo. I had a week of hunting and getting the feel of the country, where I took a number of excellent trophies, but spent a lot of time looking for the big cats—lion and leopard.

In spite of all my efforts to meet the big cats in an eyeball-to-eyeball encounter, they cleverly eluded me until the sixth day out. Then, while driving along in the Land Rover, I spotted a leopard running ahead of us at a distance of about 150 yards. I knew that I was extremely fortunate, for the leopard is so completely nocturnal in its habits that seeing one in daylight—purely by chance—is an experience that one cannot expect to enjoy with any degree of frequency.

Upon spotting the leopard running ahead of us, I slid the Land Rover to a stop and focused my binoculars on the moving object. Actually, I was not yet aware that it was a leopard, but I knew it was a cat. Even through the binoculars, at only a hundred and fifty yards, it did not appear to have the spots that a leopard is supposed to have. Needless to relate, the cat disappeared into the bush.

I engaged my African companions in a discussion of the matter. One of them was from Sudan, where most of the men are hunters, and he had a good knowledge of African wildlife. From what I was able to learn, I began to understand that the spotted effect of the leopard's hide is not visible at a distance, as the colors all blend together, especially when the animal is moving. Actually, this cat had appeared more the color of the cougar of the Americas.

I left the Land Rover in the bushy terrain along the river where the leopard had disap-

peared. I wanted to see whether it had stopped to hide or had gone on out of the area. Obviously, the latter was the case.

It was getting along toward sundown, but I decided to hang a bait to see if I could induce the leopard to return. I suppose almost any professional hunter could have told me that it wouldn't work, but I was like a bumblebee. Any good engineer can tell you that, according to the laws of aerodynamics, the bumblebee can't fly. The weakness in this argument is that the bee doesn't know the laws of aerodynamics and just flies anyway.

I didn't know that leopards couldn't be induced to come to bait hung in an area where they recently have been spooked, so I just hung the bait up anyway. Using two hindquarters from a waterbuck, which I had been saving for just such an occasion, I tied them behind the Land Rover and dragged them in a wide arc to leave a scent trail and then to a tree near dense cover where we hung the bait. Darkness was deepening rapidly, and I didn't have time to build a blind of a specified type, but there were two anthills that could serve as a blind.

It was almost completely dark by the time we had completed our makeshift preparations so we got into the Land Rover and headed toward camp. We hadn't gone too far when the right front wheel dropped into a deep warthog hole, and we found ourselves stuck, unable to move in either direction. We had quite a time extricating ourselves, and to add to our troubles, a thundershower came up and drenched us thoroughly. In an effort to avoid further trouble, one of the natives and I walked out in front to spot any holes before the truck fell into them. It only took about 45 minutes of this—in a downpour—to convince me it would be much better just to sit it out until daybreak.

The only dry, warm place was right inside the Land Rover, so we just crowded in and sat, dozing off occasionally. The natives were miserable, unaccustomed to the cold, and thoroughly dejected. They kept mumbling to themselves most of the night, and it was almost morning before I found that they were blaming all this misfortune on the one-horned oribi I had shot the day before, being a sign of bad luck. Being from the state of Washington where it does rain, I could recall northwestern nights when I had been forced to lie out in the protection of a cedar grove.

At daybreak, we were all pretty tired out, and went back to camp for some badly needed rest before returning to the leopard bait. It was about midafternoon, and we were approaching the bait set-up, when I spotted a large reedbuck. Since I was using a

The oribi with only one horn that I had collected was a sign of bad luck, according to the natives.

.375 H&H for everything, I decided to load up with solids, thinking a soft point might damage the skin. I got off a shot at the buck. It was hit, and the sight picture retained in my memory led me to believe that it was in the hindquarter, so we started tracking it. It led us in a wide arc, heading in the general direction of the leopard bait, and we soon lost the track completely. The buck was still going strong, and I concluded that I had only grazed it.

This brought up a problem. It was getting very late in the afternoon. If we took time to go all the way back to where we had left the Land Rover, and drove to the bait area, it would be too dark to see. The best option was to go check the bait. I studied it carefully

The next morning in camp was the first chance for the game guard and me to pose with my prized specimen.

through my binoculars, and finally concluded it had not been touched. I decided to cut it down and go back to camp. Closer examination showed a few bites had been taken from the bait, and there were claw marks on the tree.

I signaled my companion to back away quietly and not to speak another word. We "snuck" back behind the anthill. In addition, I got into position. It was six o'clock in the evening, and at exactly ten minutes past six, the leopard came running out of the bush, and stopped at the base of the bait tree.

Many thoughts flashed through my mind and brought me to the conclusion that I should shoot now and not wait to see if it would climb the tree. My reasoning told me the leopard must have been watching when we stood under the tree a few minutes before and it would not now climb to the bait.

I fired at a range of no more than 50 yards, aiming the solid bullet dead center on the shoulder. It turned a flip and disappeared into thick cover. I dispatched my companion back to the Land Rover, with instructions that they were to bring it in. Meantime, I perched on top of the anthill, waiting, listening, and rather daring the leopard to come out and give me another chance. I guess I expected this leopard to be far more naïve than leopards are supposed to be.

The African made record time going back and moving the Land Rover up to the bait area. I now changed to soft-point bullets,

**My makeshift safari camp in the Kikagati Triangle, an area in the extreme southwest of Uganda where it borders Tanganyika and Rwanda.**

and started to seek out the leopard, because I would rather have its hide damaged than my own.

I inspected the spot where the cat had been standing when I fired. There was no blood, but a round hole where the bullet had entered the tree and raised a place where it had bulged the bark on the other side. I then inspected the area where the leopard had entered the bush. No blood.

I began to wonder whether I had actually hit it at all, and my imagination began to conjure up all kinds of excuses—there was quite a bit of grass between the tree and me, the light was bad, and it might have been standing on the other side of the tree, rather than the side next to me.

This presented a lot of problems. Would the leopard be more dangerous if wounded? Would it be more dangerous if it were just hanging around, hating us for molesting its evening meal?

Regardless, I felt that I had to go into the bush and find out the true state of affairs. The patch of cover where it had gone was only about 100 yards square, and dangerous game that has been wounded and left to survive becomes a menace to all men they meet thereafter. I gave myself an encouraging pat on the back, and plunged ahead. My brave Sudanese companion chose to go in with me.

With the safety catch off and ready to shoot from the hip, and followed by the Sudanese boy with his panga raised, we inched through the bush side by side, ready for instant action. The thicket consisted of heavy clumps of bushes with well-worn paths between them. The paths through thick bush were only leopard height, so we were on our hands and knees most of the time, side by side. We saw no sign of blood. There was a deafening silence. Without a word being spoken, we sensed what each of us had to do in seeking out our potentially dangerous adversary. I was ready to swing and fire at anything that moved. Minutes dragged by like hours. Occasionally we would get a whiff of the strong smell characteristic of all cats, but the wind shifted constantly, not giving us any clue as to the source.

Finally, there it was—a smear of blood under one of the clumps. Now, we knew that the die was cast. We had to find that cat, and darkness was coming on fast.

Each clump of cover might conceal a leopard waiting in ominous silence—a fact not calculated to give us complete peace of mind.

Some of the clumps were a good 10 yards across, and thicker than the hair on a dog's back. However, they were not thick enough to prevent a leopard from penetrating just far enough to reach the soft flesh of our throats with its first spring. Darkness had cut visibility to virtually nothing.

Suddenly, the strong odor of cat hit me right in the face at a moment when the breeze was holding steady from one direction. I knew exactly where it was coming from. I pointed with my rifle barrel and whispered, "Right there." The Sudanese boy nodded grimly and clutched his knife a little tighter.

Slowly and tensely, together we parted the thin wall of bush. There was our leopard, very dead, and lying quietly on a soft pillow of grass. The delay in getting the Land Rover up to the bait area had worked out just right. It had given it time to die harmlessly, whereas following it any sooner might have led to disaster out in the African bush.

The solid bullet had made a clean hole right behind the shoulder, passing entirely through the body, and then through the tree. We carried it out to the Land Rover, all of us a mass of raw nerve ends after the tension of the past hour.

We all laughed, rather foolishly, I expect, dancing around and embracing each other. In the back of my mind was a deeply satisfying, rather sober thought that brought me a feeling of humility and profound gratitude.

This was MY leopard. I had hunted it. I had offered to meet it on its own ground, and I had won. I had learned about leopards as Karamojo Bell must have learned about them. This was a treasured moment of my first week on safari in Africa.

### Hunting for Mbogo—Cape Buffalo

Before going to Africa myself, I had read and heard many stories of dangerous encounters people had had with cape buffalo. Therefore, when I started out to make the personal acquaintance of mbogo (the Swahili term for buffalo), I was not under any delusions as to what I was facing. It was rather a sobering prospect, and made more so by the knowledge that I would not be backed up by the heavy double rifle of the professional hunter.

The mbogo has keen senses in all departments—seeing, hearing, and smelling. He is stubborn, brave, and gifted with more intelligence than his phlegmatic appearance might lead you to believe. He is not afraid of anything, but he is not foolish, and does not often get caught unawares.

He will usually run at the sight or scent of man, but when he thinks his rights are being infringed on, it's a different matter. If he is wounded, or if a cow thinks her calf is being threatened, then, more often than not, a charge will be launched with all the persistence of a locomotive.

I hunted buffalo south of the Equator, and not far from Rwanda and the Belgiam Congo borders. An African game guard and an African grade-school teacher who was on his Christmas vacation accompanied me. A game guard is one who is hired by the game department to help prevent poaching. Both boys were instinctively good trackers, and the game guard could speak a little English.

During the first three days out, we saw in excess of 200 buffaloes. This was usually the result of finding tracks and tracking the herds, but there were a couple of occasions when we saw the herd before seeing their tracks. The country in this area is usually covered by dense bush in the lower areas, with the higher ground being generally given over to semi-open forest. This is excellent buffalo country, and it supplies both food and cover in abundance. Most of Uganda is lush and green, thus is able to support large herds of game.

Early one morning, in a low bushy area around a wallow, we came upon some tracks, which appeared larger than any we had seen. My trackers boosted my enthusiasm to the danger level when they assured me these were some of the largest tracks they had seen. They estimated the tracks were two days old, but assured me that the buffaloes would be within a 5-mile radius of where we stood, and were all for taking off on the track at once. I needed little urging.

I loaded my .375 H&H, with alternating bullets of soft point and solids. My reason for doing this was I had figured that, on a shoulder shot, I might be able to drive the solid clear through. This would break down the bone structure, thus rendering the big ox unable to come for me.

I knew the big soft points would not have the penetration power of the solids. They would dissipate all their energy within the animal, doing a lot more damage to tissue and bone. In other words, they would deliver a lot more shock. In the event of a charge, I figured the solids would have a chance to penetrate the skull, or give the animal enough of a headache to distract its attention, at least momentarily.

There were, my trackers informed me, eight animals in the small herd we were tracking. There was a good possibility that they were all bulls. They pointed out, however, that cows often grow to tremendous size, and that it is not always possible to distinguish between them by tracks alone.

We had followed the tracks for about an hour when some fresher tracks made by smaller buffaloes covered the ones we were following. It required real skill to unravel the converged trails, but my trackers were equal to it, and we were soon on our way again.

We came upon a newborn buffalo calf, a cute little fellow, and he just lay, motionless in the grass hoping we did not see him. I was all set to shoot a few pictures, but my trackers were adamant against it. They advised me, in no uncertain terms, that the greater distance we could put between the calf and ourselves, the safer we would be.

They explained that the mother buffalo will often go quite a distance from her young to feed, but that there was no guarantee this one had done so. She might, they explained, be watching us at that very moment, preparing to do what mother buffaloes usually do when their young are threatened. Need I say we departed the scene forthwith?

Within an hour, after carefully analyzing the tracks, the trackers advised me, that they were much fresher, probably having been made as recently as the previous night. In the event they had bedded down for the day, we could be very close. The air became tense with suppressed excitement. We were, it seemed, nearing the "moment of truth."

The game guard removed from his pocket a dainty looking handkerchief, which was tied to a pouch containing some very fine powder. I didn't inquire as to its nature, but judged it to be either flour or fine-sifted meal. He explained to me that his wife always prepared one of her handkerchiefs for him in this way before he left, believing that it would bring him good luck. Its purpose was to determine the direction of the wind. A slight jerk of the hand would cause enough powder to filter through the cloth to drift visibly downwind.

From here on, no words were spoken. We communicated only by signs, and we were all very careful to avoid making the slightest noise. The bush was thick and, in most places, visibility was limited to a maximum of 50 yards. We knew that when things started to happen, it would be too close for comfort, and fast.

It was obvious that the herd was not going anywhere in particular, just meandering along, and the tracks were growing fresher by the minute. I stopped watching the tracks, and began scanning the bush for the first sign of our quarry. One of the trackers kept his eyes glued to the tracks at all times, but the other kept a sharp lookout on the cover up ahead.

Tension began to build and the pace lessened considerably. We took each step as if we were picking our way, barefoot, through broken glass. I am sure that my native companions sensed that the buffalo were quite close. Even though the tracks did not look any different to me, they knew that the time for explosive action was drawing very near.

It is possible they relied somewhat on their sense of smell, not dulled by years of exhaust fumes and industrial air pollution. They were from hunting tribes where life depends upon being able to hunt successfully, and they have developed far keener senses than we possess.

We had been moving in single file, one of them ahead of me and the other behind, but the game guard who was in the lead motioned me to move up on his side. He knew that, once we exposed ourselves to the herd, we'd have no time to change our positions. The bush was growing denser, and visibility was lessening. A little thrill ran up my spine as I realized the significance of his invitation for me to move up by his side.

Just minutes later, we both saw, apparently at the same time, the unbelievably huge black hulk of a buffalo bedded down not more than 75 yards away. We moved slightly to one side in order to obtain a clearer view, and at just that moment, the herd became aware of our presence, and rose to their feet. At a glance, I saw that several of them were big.

There wasn't enough time to use a binocular, as they started to move as soon as they had reached their feet. The trackers pointed out two animals separated from the rest and indicated which one was the biggest. I had no trouble determining the one he meant. That one seemed to be all horn.

I had no time to do anything but shoot, and it would have to be done quickly. I let go an offhand shot to the shoulder as the bull started running full speed to my left. The soft point followed right behind. Then the whole herd was out of sight, and the only sign that they had been there was the shaking bushes and the sound of their hooves pounding away from us.

We ran to where the bull had been when I fired, hoping to find a dead buffalo or, at the very least, blood. We could see nothing but tracks leading off. We went over the area with care. I had begun to think my bullets might have hit some of the tree trunks that were quite close together where the bull had been running.

Again, we found nothing. I could not be sure whether I had hit the buffalo, but I had come to trust the sight image left in my mind when my gun is discharged. This led me to believe that both shots had been hits.

We followed the tracks of the stampeding herd for about a quarter of a mile, but found no blood sign or indication that any of the animals were beginning to slow. We started making small circles back and forth through the bush where the buffalo would have gone if it had been wounded and left the herd. There were so many tracks in the area that the only things we could look for was a dead buffalo or a blood sign.

It would have been far too dangerous for my unarmed natives to go into the bush alone, so all three of us stayed together. I was prepared to sell our lives dearly, my gun now loaded with four solids.

At least an hour must have passed while we searched back and forth through that bush. My trackers did not share my discouragement. They chose to remember all the meat I had brought to bag on previous plains-game I had taken, and showed far more confidence in my shooting ability than I felt. This is their way. They are very seldom able to make instantaneous kills with their arrows or spears, so are not disturbed by delay after a shot is fired.

Our nerves were wound as tightly as violin strings. In a situation of this kind, one dare not relax for a second. Then, at long last, the trail showed blood, already dry on the leaves.

Now, we had a track leading into the thickest part of the bush. That brought some relief, even though we were fully aware we might be facing a very grim situation. It seems that the known—though unpleasant—is easier to face than the unknown.

However, there was still a lot we didn't know. Buffalo bulls are known for their vindictive nature, which often leads them to circle back on their trail, and lie in wait for their pursuer. We did not know what we faced in that heavy cover, so the only thing to do was be prepared for anything.

Quietly, we inched our way through the bush, moving branches out of our way to look on the other side before going ahead. We were not in a hurry. In the event the bull was hard-hit, time was in our favor. Soon we spotted a dark spot in the bush ahead of us. It did not move. I looked at it through my binoculars, and it was the buffalo. I was unable to make out the whole animal, just a part of its back.

Was it down for keeps, or was it just waiting in ominous silence to charge us when we came within range? We stood motionless for about five minutes while I observed it through my glasses. So far as I was able to determine, it was motionless, not even breathing.

We started slowly edging our way in a half-circle, to be able to approach it from the side. We were only about 20 yards from where the animal lay. As we began to move in, we became confident that it was dead. It was. It had gone into the bush, circled back on its trail, cleared a small area by trampling down the bush, and died, grimly facing the direction from which it expected its enemies to come.

If we had been able to follow it directly, the story might have been different. It was a magnificent specimen, with horns measuring 42³⁄₈ inches on the curve, and 13½ inches in palm width.

## Into the Karamojo and the Unknown

The next leg of my journey would take me up into the very country where Karamojo Bell had, so successfully, plied his trade. I would be hunting lion and other game found in the more arid north, still doing it the hard way. Would Lady Luck continue to smile on me, or would she, this time, look the other way? Only time would tell.

**The wounded buffalo made a circle and came back to rest close to its original path.**

A fine roan antelope and common eland were collected on the buffalo hunt.

After hunting southern Uganda, I was looking forward to seeing the northern part to contrast the country, the people, and the game. I was to be joined by Ernest Juer, and we were to make an egg-shaped loop covering all of unexplored northern Uganda, starting at Kampala, go northeasterly to the Karamojo, then northwesterly to Sudan, and then follow the Nile upstream (southeast) back to Kampala.

Our only plan was to get what information we could from the local natives as we traveled, and to explore anything that sounded interesting. Right now, however, I am going to confine myself to Karamojo district that we took in on the first leg of our journey.

The southern part of the Karamojo district is an easy day's travel from Kampala, over a reasonably good road with pavement two-thirds of the way. We headed toward the Kenya border and then, just short of it, turned north past Mount Elgon to the town of Mbali. There, we were able to pick up a few last minute items that were lacking in our outfit.

After an hour's drive, we could see Mount Debasion where, just to the south, Uganda Wildlife had established a hunting camp. We observed a lot of game between Elgon and Debasion. We guessed the plains to be at just less than 4,000 feet. Elgon towers to 14,178 feet, while Debasion rises to 10,050 feet. Even though Uganda straddles the equator, the elevation prevents the temperature from becoming unbearably hot. This escarpment is the boundary between Uganda and Kenya.

In the few native settlements along the road, we began to observe changes in native habits. The women no longer wore long, colorful, flowing garments or the men trousers and shirts. The women were bare from the waist up, and the men's dress was confined to a skimpy piece of cloth thrown over one shoulder. We knew that the deeper we penetrated the Karamojo, the more primitive the people would become. This was, more or less, a buffer area between today and yesterday.

On our way, we paid a brief visit to the Uganda Wildlife hunting camp where two white hunters were out with clients exploring the fringes of this vast district. To the north lie hundreds of miles of country that has never been hunted systematically. Beyond that, the land is virtually unknown.

Driving into the hunting camp seemed like driving through a game preserve. We observed 11 different species without leaving the Land Rover. The camp was located on the Loporkoche River. This part of Uganda has a sort of built-in wildlife conservation program. The natives do not eat game and there are, at a guess, no more than 20 white people living in the Karamojo district, most of them being government officials who stay pretty close to headquarters. The hunting camp was immaculate, and offered all the luxury one might expect in the Waldorf.

We were treated to a tasty buffalo steak dinner, with all the "fixin's" including our choice of drinks. Two hunters came in after dark and reported that they had leopards coming to bait. One of the white hunters reported that he and his client had been in their blind, awaiting the appearance of their leopard, when they heard quite a commotion about 100 yards off, and saw a leopard kill a baboon.

Conditions did not make it possible for them to bring the leopard to bag, but they were very happy to know that leopards were staying close to their bait area. As we drifted off to sleep that night, it seemed that the sound of the jackals and the hyenas blended right into the songs of many different birds greeting us as we awoke at dawn the next morning.

We had decided to use Moroto as our jumping-off point, it being just a day's easy drive to the north on a fair gravel road at the base of Mount Moroto. With its 9,700-foot elevation, Mount Moroto is probably the highest peak on this part of the escarpment that separates Kenya and Uganda.

In Moroto, we met Captain Robson, the game warden over the entire Karamojo district. He gave us enough information to make it possible for us to formulate a rough plan for some kind of an itinerary. He put us in touch with the District Commissioner who advised us about the areas that would be comparatively safe for us to enter.

It seems that as far back as the records go, the various tribes in the Karamojo and western areas have always raided each other in quest of cattle and women. In Karamojo, there are the Dodoth, the Jie, the Matheniko, the Pian, and the Noken tribes. Just over the escarpment, in Kenya, are the Suk and the Turkana tribes. All of them lead a very simple life and, evidently, look upon raiding as sport. Not being tribes who hunt, they vent competitive their spirit on each other.

White men are generally safe, but the Commissioner did not want us in an area

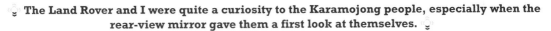

**The Land Rover and I were quite a curiosity to the Karamojong people, especially when the rear-view mirror gave them a first look at themselves.**

Karamojong men resting on a hill. Men take pride in hairdos, working clay into their hair, sculpturing a design, and coloring it. Some insert wire coils to display ostrich plumes. The "neck stool" on rock is used as a pillow to protect the hair.

We moved our base of operations to Kotido where we contacted the District Commissioner who was able to advise us concerning some extremely remote country. It was in Kotido that we got the news I had been hoping for. We were told about rumors of a cattle-killing lion back in the Kapeta River country.

Although this was terrain where the Land Rover could not go, our spirit of adventure was running high and we decided to try for it. The Commissioner gave us a guide and an interpreter who could speak English as well as his own language, which was Jie (pronounced gee-a).

Juer and I were not sufficiently acquainted with Swahili to really depend on it, but we did have one native with us who could speak both English and Swahili. Therefore, in a more or less complicated way, we were able to communicate among ourselves and with any natives we were likely to meet.

where we might get caught in the middle of tribal conflict. We were thus forced to forgo the area where we had planned to hunt greater kudu.

Out of Moroto, we probed in three different directions observing the game, and looking for a suitable campsite. I took a number of marvelous specimens, including oryx and Grant's gazelle, found in Uganda only in the Karamojo district.

We explored the Matheniko Plains, which is a sort of "no man's land." This roadless area is just a little bit too far from the tribal centers for even Africans to live. We saw hundreds of dik-diks scurrying across our paths and observed herds of hartebeests, zebras, giraffes, etc.

Oryx are found on the arid plains of the Karamojo area.

**Chris with a Roberts gazelle, which is similar to the Grant gazelle.**

The first leg of our journey took us to a Jie settlement, which we were able to reach in our Land Rover without any great difficulty. The settlement was known as Kacheri and was completely out of contact with civilization. It consisted of a number of huts separated by yards—one hut and yard being for each wife a man might have. The huts were constructed of grass, and were intended to fill the requirements of the wife and her children.

Each man has as many wives as he can afford, and the number of cattle he owns judges his wealth. He trades cattle for wives, as well as using the cattle as a source of food. Blood is drawn from the jugular vein, mixed with milk, and permitted to sour and curdle. This, supplemented with millet, occasionally makes up the menu upon which these people survive. A man's full time is devoted to caring for his cattle.

They were very shy, and they reacted to our arrival—I imagine—in about the same way we would if we looked out one morning and saw a flying saucer on our front lawn. Once we got them to understand that we were here to kill the lion that

had been raiding their herds, they immediately lost their timidity, and became very cooperative. They were willing to assist us in reaching the area where the lion was thought to be.

Although these men prove their manhood by going after lions armed only with spears, they want but little to do with cattle killers. This was almost in the nature of a superstition

**A Jie compound. Note the thornbush fence and corral area where cattle can be brought in for the night.**

These natives had Ankoli cattle, which could be the ancestors of the Texas longhorns.

Inside the Jie compound a girl grinds millet. Note millet cache on left, while a wife's hut is on the right.

Chris offering chewing gum to Jie girls.

connected with a lion so evil as to wantonly slaughter sacred cattle with impunity.

We were furnished a tribesman who guided us for a good many miles to where the Lolei and the Kapeta Rivers converge. This was as far as the Land Rover could go. We set up camp here, and were joined by four more Jie tribesmen and six women.

They were completely amazed at the amount of equipment white men seem to need when they travel. They traveled very light with virtually no clothing and no shoes, but with two spears and a shield suspended from their shoulders. Their only other piece of equipment was a "neck stool." This served a two-fold purpose. They sat on it, and when retiring, used it to hold their heads off the ground to keep from mussing their fancy hairdos. The women wore skin skirts and carried large gourds filled with their provisions—soured milk and blood. The reason for their being along was to act as porters.

We were traveling light, but felt a little embarrassed in view of what these people had. We need not have worried, however, for the next morning some of the cattle grazing in the area were driven into camp, and we watched the men pierce the jugular vein with

**A Jie man with a traditional hairdo. Note his ever present "neck stool" carried over his arm.**

a small arrow, and replenish their food supply. Afterwards, they patched the tiny puncture mark with mud.

We pared our own equipment to the bare minimum, but it was still too much for us even with the help of the women porters, so two of the men condescended to bear loads. One could tell that it was a great blow to their dignity.

We started up the Lolei River, figuring on following the riverbed as much as possible, checking water holes for sign as we went. It was the dry season, and water was flowing only sporadically, disappearing sometimes into the sand, and then reappearing again for a short distance.

Less than two miles out of camp, we came upon elephant tracks. This was something of a surprise. We knew that this had, at one time, been great elephant country but it is the general belief of most people that elephants have gone from the Karamojo district, except the extreme northern part. Even the game warden in Moroto, when we had questioned him about game, had made no mention of elephants. There were two possibilities. They may have just moved in, or the area might be so remote that only the tribesmen ever came here and were the only ones who knew that elephants were here.

The sand of the riverbed was completely covered with tracks, as if it were a wildlife freeway. Among the tracks were eland, Jackson's hartebeest, waterbuck, and giraffe. We saw one herd of giraffes that looked like a strange forest of trees. There must have been at least 50 in the herd. Waterbucks stood and watched us from the banks of the river, evidencing little fear.

We heard the trumpet of an elephant in the distance and went to investigate. We located a small herd of cows and calves and, on our way back to the river, saw an enormous bull with tusks that we estimated at least 90 pounds each. The wind was right, and I went in close enough to take pictures.

About noon, we came to the Namore River, and followed it for the rest of the day. At evening, we made camp in a beautiful setting by a water hole. As I lay on my bedroll, I had the feeling of complete freedom, which I seem to always experience only when I am unable to see machines, buildings, or any of the other scars left on the face of nature by the engineering ingenuity of man. Contentedly, I lay watching the Jie natives making themselves comfortable on their neck stools to protect their hairdos, and then it was morning.

One of the men was talking about a leopard he had heard coughing during the night, and they were discussing the roars of a lion they had heard far to the north, but they quickly decided that it was not the one we were seeking.

We had been traveling in a northeasterly direction along the Loleita, and had turned to a northwesterly direction when we reached the Namore. After much jabbering among the natives, it was decided that we should cut out across country, in a direction a little south of west, roughly paralleling the Kapeta River.

We traveled about a day and a half in that direction over rough country consisting of small hills covered with thorn bush. I shot a very nice Jackson's hartebeest and a warthog to round out my collection. On the way, we saw hundreds of heads of game. I skinned, salted, and air-dried the capes while the guides smoke-cured the meat to the consistency of jerky, called biltong. This was to carry us through the remainder of the trip. Biltong, after being boiled, is not bad fare at all.

During our travels, we saw many sets of lion tracks, but something about them convinced the herdsmen that none of them was the one we wanted. Finally, we turned straight south, giving ourselves barely enough time to make our camp on the river by nightfall.

About a mile from the river, we heard the bawling of cattle and saw, from the rising dust, that they were headed in our direction. We waited for the herdsman to reach us. He was moving his herd as far and as quick as was humanly possible. He informed us that, no more than an hour ago, he had lost a cow to the cattle-killing lion. It was about an hour's journey to where the kill was said to have taken place, and we decided unanimously that there would be little chance to take the lion that evening so we set up camp.

Next morning we were up, fed, and packed before daylight, and started to make our way up the Kapata. About two miles upstream, our Acholi guide led us off at about a 45-degree angle from the riverbed. His sense of direction never lost its fascination for me, even though I saw it at work almost constantly. He had formed a picture in his mind about just where to look

for the lion, using heaven only knows what evidence.

I would, in all probability, have headed for the highest point in the general area, and sat down to watch. I would have observed any other wildlife in an effort to determine the general position of the lion. Above all, I would have kept my eyes on the vultures coming in to share the kill. The tracker, however, was wholly unconcerned about any of these things until he felt he had reached the exact spot from which to begin observation.

We must have walked for an hour and a half without a word being spoken. An occasional bird or bushbuck would be spooked almost from under our feet. Ernest and I would have them covered with our rifles at the first flash of movement. The tracker paid not the slightest attention but proceeded straight to the place where the sign indicated that the attack on the hapless cow had been made the day before and, at this point, his manner changed abruptly and he became the very soul of caution.

We took our position with the tracker out in front, armed with only his African version of a machete. I stood behind him and Ernest behind me with chambers filled and our thumbs resting on the safety catches of our rifles. The other two Africans brought up the rear.

Everything was completely quiet, and no game was to be seen. We were traveling along a narrow ravine filled with semi-brush, while the rolling hills on either side were comparatively open. There were, however,

**A remote settlement in the area of the cattle killing lion.**

some areas with grass six to eight feet tall. This if I remembered my homework correctly, was "lion" country.

The instinct of the tracker told him that the lion would be in the bush because; due to the rising sun and resultant temperature, it would seek out shade. Therefore, we stayed about 100 yards above the bush, and traveled parallel to it.

Suddenly, our tracker "froze." We knew he had seen something since he kept moving his head from side to side, trying to focus on something. However, he slowly raised his hand and pointed to his nose, indicating that he had smelled something.

The wind was shifting around, so it was difficult to determine the direction from which the warning smell had come. We could only be sure that it came from the bush somewhere up ahead. With a palm-downward motion, the tracker indicated that we should move forward in a crouching position.

About 50 yards further on, I caught a glimpse of something red, partly hidden by the tree. I touched the tracker on the shoulder. He looked in that direction and nodded, indicating that it was the lion.

The distance was about 100 yards, so I knelt and aimed the .375 H&H in that direction, to be ready for what might come at any moment. I was using iron sights, figuring that this would call for quick close action, so I did not have the advantage of magnification. It was obvious, however, that the lion was moving around, staying behind the trees that were too close to shoot through.

A few moments later—each moment seemed like an hour—the lion turned and started running straight away. Before it came out into the open where I could chance a shot, it must have been 150 yards distant, angling off about a 45-degree angle. I had a solid rest, and didn't feel that I would be taking too much of a chance, so I let one go. The lion's only action was to sway slightly, and keep right on heading for the tall grass on the other side of the ravine. We knew that the bullet had hit, but had no indication where. We could tell that it was a massive animal from its deliberate, bounding motion.

We headed straight for the grass where we figured the lion had entered, but kept back about 20 or 30 paces and made a sort of half-circle around the area. Ernest and I kept at least 20 paces apart, increasing the chances of at least one of us getting a clear shot in case it charged out.

The African boys, except the tracker, stayed back quite a distance since there was no reason to subject them to needless danger. The tracker went in close to pelt the area with sticks and rocks to see if we might get some response. There being no sign of life, Ernest and I stood guard and had the Africans start looking for blood. They didn't find anything until they returned to where the lion had been when I fired. There they found blood and some small pieces of flesh, indicating that my shot had done some damage.

We had a wounded lion on our hands, and we knew that, if we didn't finish it off, it might no longer be satisfied with cattle killing. We steeled our nerves and took the trail. Once the tracker was on the trail, he followed it immediately into the high grass. From this point on, there was nothing to do but carry this to its conclusion.

We entered the grass, which was at least six feet tall, with the indescribably brave tracker right on the trail. I was walking right beside him with my gun barrel parting the grass ahead of us. Ernest was about four steps behind and two to one side. We knew if the showdown came, we would have about half a second to do what had to be done. None of us was laboring under any delusions about the seriousness of our situation.

We advanced for some distance, and came to a thorn tree where the sign showed that the lion had lain down and lost considerable blood. We continued on, following the zizzagging trail the lion had left. It seemed, now, that he was losing very little blood on the grass as he slipped through it.

This was a very ticklish situation for me. It would have been little different for a man whose background had prepared him for such an emergency. Animals can pass through this type of grass only to have it close behind them, leaving scarcely a trace.

We had to move deliberately, depending upon the occasional smear of blood to assure us that we were on the right trail. We came to another thorn tree that I climbed, hoping for a shot at the lion. I came back down and followed the trail off at right angles to our previous direction.

The trail led us straight ahead for about 100 yards and then circled back under the thorn tree. The blood indicated the lion had passed under the tree I was up in, going within five steps of the trunk. I think I must have shivered a little, even in the equatorial heat, knowing that we were not only the hunters but also the hunted.

Several times we came to places where the lion had lain down. Each time it had lost blood, but each time, a little less. This continued for at least three hours. The sun was straight overhead and about as hot as I have ever experienced anywhere in the world. Added to the discomfort of the heat, the unrelenting nervous strain was beginning to have its effect on all of us.

Finally, the tracks led out into an open area that had been burned off some weeks before. The ground was so dry and hard that we could hardly see our back trail, much less the soft pads of the lion.

Our tracker followed the trail straight across this open area. When he would locate a splotch of blood, he would draw a circle around it, so if we ever lost the trail, we could come back and pick it up again. The track headed for some thick bush on top of a small plateau. We headed straight into it, and it became thicker with each passing step, until we had to crawl beneath the thorn brush on hands and knees at times.

Suddenly we heard a noise. It was not a growl, nor yet a roar. It was more like a grunt, typical of a lion. We had to make a quarter-circle around this area to get the wind in our favor. It was rather steady, and from one direction, so we were deeply grateful. I felt, personally, that, except for the thick bush, we had things going our way.

We edged around a bush, and at the end of an open area about 25 yards across, the tracker spotted something—just a motion. He stepped back about four feet for a better look. There were some overhanging limbs of a tree, so I immediately sat down, aimed the .375 in that direction, and released the safety catch. Juer got to one side to back me up.

No sooner did I get into position than the lion saw us and took a lunge in our direction. I fired and the report of Ernest's rifle echoed my shot. Both were hits, but they failed to stop the cat. He kept coming, obviously crippled, but driven by a hatred that only death would subdue.

So quickly as to stagger the imagination, he closed the distance to 10 or 15 paces. I let off one more shot as it made its final lunge. As the lion came to the ground, he crashed into the tree I was under. He then turned his anger fiercely upon the tree—fighting it, tearing off branches, and sinking his teeth into the bark of the trunk in his final effort, thinking he had me.

Ernest finished the lion off with a final shot. I turned weakly to see where our Acholi tracker had gone and found him standing there, panga raised, ready to tear into the lion if it had reached us. The other two Africans had vanished and did not put in an appearance until they heard the talking around the carcass.

We looked at our watches. It was exactly four hours since we had first spotted the lion and opened hostilities. It suddenly occurred to me that I was more exhausted than I had ever been in all my life. Yet, beneath the indescribable weariness was the feeling of having satisfied a longing I had carried in my heart most of my life. As a lad, I had read stories of men like Karamojo Bell. I had met Africa as they had met her, on her terms, and as they had won, so had I.

Examination showed that my first shot had hit just about where it should, but at an angle, which enabled the ribs to deflect it from entering the chest cavity. This had allowed the lion to keep going for so long. We measured it, and found the length to be just over 10 feet. Examination of its stomach contents proved it was the cattle killer we were after.

**The tree that I was under protected me as the lion died thinking he was tearing into my limbs.**

⌃ **The cattle-killing lion that provided Chris with a hair-raising adventure.**

## REFLECTION
# A Tribal Hunt on the Uganda & Sudanese Border

**A**fter leaving the Karamojo area, Ernest Juer and I headed north to explore unknown areas in the Acholi District that borders Sudan. We came across what we found to be an annual tribal hunt at which the Acholi join with the Sudanese tribe. There were hundreds of participants, the men armed with spears and women following carrying the loads. The men spread out for miles on a game drive after setting grass fires and awaiting any game that crossed their line. Here are some photos.

**A lone Acholi hunter informed us of a tribal hunt he was to join.** ◌»

Men gather around Chris's vehicle while the laden women shyly stand away. The nearest road was at least 50 miles away, so we were an oddity.

Well-equipped Acholi hunter. Axe hung on shoulder, knife around neck, and three spears in hand.

With multiple spears, the hunters curiously gather around the Land Rover. Even though barefooted and mostly shirtless, somehow most had modern shorts.

The women bearing loads on their heads followed a ways behind the hunters.

Where the dry grass was tall, fires were set to aid in the game drive.

The game drive is on. The hunter in rear with a skimpy animal skin loincloth already killed a small gazelle.

## REFLECTION
# Wildlife Conservation at Its Best

Uganda Wildlife Development was perhaps the perfect model for a wildlife conservation program, which the Klineburgers were proud to be a part of. The country was rich in wildlife, yet the people had taken all the animals they could by hunting, trapping, and snaring. The program emphasized education of the local people that their wildlife was a valuable renewable resource. Money from the safaris was shared with the local tribes as well as providing them all the surplus meat from the hunts. When it was necessary to cull an overpopulation of a species, the locals were hired and the meat and skins were given to them. When a tribal farm was being destroyed by wildlife, the game department came to their rescue. During the hunting program, the wildlife flourished, because the game was kept in balance by a quota system, besides the natives becoming game protectors rather than poachers.

In 1971, a sad ending came, however, when Idi Amin overthrew the free Uganda government and disbanded most government agencies, including UWD and the game department, and evicted most Europeans and Asians, who were the backbone to the country's industry. The wildlife was reduced to a minimum by Amin's army for meat for the troops, and by widespread poaching in the lawless country.

Amin's rule of terror and economic madness ended in 1979 when Tanzanian forces drove him out, but the following rulers paralleled Amin's era. Unfortunately, a great many African countries followed the same pattern through ignorant and greedy dictators destroying the infrastructure that made them free, prosperous, independent, and happy before getting their independence.

Uganda Development Corporation and most all businesses such as Jonas Brothers of Africa were a thing of the past. At this writing, the situation has improved somewhat; yet political unrest still exists. Who knows when or if Uganda will ever be a pearl of Africa or a fairy tale?

# The Early Days of Sudan

Even though Sudan had been hunted intermittently by early expeditions, it wasn't until the late 1970s safari operators received permission to hunt in game rich southern Sudan on a regular basis. On this trip, we were to explore three different areas—a savannah area east of the Nile, a forest area on the Zaire border (formerly the Belgium Congo) and a swamp area west of the Nile.

I had actually hunted Sudan in January 1963 when I was exploring the Acholi area of Uganda. My little outfit consisted of my Land Rover, three black helpers, and traveling companion, Ernest Juer. We joined up with a band of Acholi hunters who were on their way to meet Sudanese tribal hunters across the unmarked border for a traditional tribal hunt they did annually with their bows and spears.

It was a huge game drive that lasted a full day with the natives lining up as far as the eye could see, burning grass as they went and followed by the load-bearing women—what an exciting time. After that, we continued northwesterly till we neared the Nile and followed it back into Uganda.

The following is a copy of excerpts from my journal of the Sudan trip of February 1979.

*30 January 1979*

*After flying from Seattle to New York, I was scheduled to rendezvous with Bob Chisholm, Arnold Minks, and Jack Shelton—all of the Pizza Hut chain. They are flying in from Wichita. We're all scheduled on TWA flight 840 at 2100 to Rome—an all night flight arriving at 1055. Then we were to connect with Alitalia flight 894 at 1335 to Khartoum, Sudan, to arrive at 2050. We have a short stay at the Khartoum Hilton, and then off at 0600 on Sudan Airways flight 308 to Juba in southern Sudan—48 hours of flying, at or to and from airports, except for an estimated five hours sleep in Khartoum.*

TIME LAPSE

*The Gemmeiza Savannah Area*
*East of the Nile River*

*01 February*

*Arrived in Juba on time and met by Juan (Joao) Cardoso, Zeca Carvallo, and Luis Mena—all professional hunters. They informed us all licenses and details were worked out and everything ready for the hunt. I knew Luis Mena from Safrique in Mozambique. He guided Curtiss Scarritt while Colleene, Kent, and I hunted in 1973, at which time we got pretty well acquainted.*

*We claimed our bags and went to the headquarters of José Simoes's company, Nimerico Safaris. We changed to our bush clothes, had a couple of drinks, while hunt plans and other business were discussed. José had brought a new generator down from Europe, and after we got power, they talked on the radio to the Gemmeiza Camp where we were first to hunt.*

*Had a nice lunch of tiang steaks (a topi-like antelope), rice, and fresh mango.*

*Juba is Sudan's second largest city. There is such a fuel shortage here that the electric power is turned on only from 5 to 9 PM—so here right in the city, they had to install their own generator. The safari company hauled their own fuel up by truck from Nairobi, Kenya—also their main food supply.*

*It was around 5:30 PM before we started driving in our four-wheel-drive Land Rover hunting cars to Gemmeiza Camp—some four hours and 120 kilometers north on the east bank of the Nile River. We crossed the bridge, crossing the Nile at Juba. Probably the only bridge on the Nile south of Khartoum—some 900 miles (1,400 kilometers) to the north.*

*The bridge was steel construction with wooden cross runners. It is a low bridge that would not allow a boat of any size up the Nile beyond this point—maybe a low barge, but a thoughtless piece of construction.*

**The Gemmeiza camp in a beautiful setting.**

The road up the east bank is the main road to Khartoum. For about 50 km it is an improved dirt road—from then on, it is one of the worst roads I have ever seen. Every rainy season (May to November), it gets completely washed out. Now it is just drying out.

It was soon dark and our trip on the rough part of the road took three more hours—less than 20 km per hour. We passed several trucks that were carrying cargo from Kenya to Khartoum—one of which was a truck/trailer.

The trucks could not last more than a few trips with such torturous treatment. On the other hand, the Nile River would be the very best means of freight hauling. They do haul some by sternwheelers. It takes ten days by river, including stops, from Juba north (downstream), and about fourteen days from Khartoum south.

We traveled through Dinka villages and occasionally saw some of the stark naked men, covered with ash and carrying spears, on our way to the Gemmeiza Camp. We arrived about 10 PM The staff were all awaiting us with drinks, snacks and later, dinner.

The lodge was a multi-room rondoval, thatch roof, native styled building. It had a bar/lounge area with comfortable furniture—a very relaxing atmosphere. There was also a large dining room with grass thatch chandeliers and all rooms had the overhead rotating fans.

There are 10 individual rondoval sleeping huts—grass-thatched rooms, some of which have air conditioning. All have plumbing—toilets and showers for our comfort, luxury that I am sure is not even available in Juba for the public. To bed by midnight—after a much needed shower.

02 February

Up at 5:30. After a quick continental-type breakfast, our cars were awaiting us shortly after daybreak. Bob and I teamed up and went out with Duri Simoes, José's son, who was already in the camp. We drive north on the "highway" then turned east. There are next to no tracks (roads) so we were driving across the open savannah. The area had been well burned. They burn the grass after it dries out to get rid of the old tall grass so that the young grass can have a chance to provide good feed for the game.

We only saw an occasional oribi and duiker until we got a few miles from the river. The Dinkas (natives) live all along the river. They have their cattle herds, and they hunt (they all

**A Dinka boy helping to watch over a herd of Ankoli cattle. The people sleep in the extinguished embers of their fires to keep warm and it is said the ash is a bug repellent.**

carry spears), keeping the game moved back. Once we got a distance from civilization, game started appearing everywhere. First, we saw a herd of Mongalla gazelles (very similar to the Thompson's gazelle of east Africa). Then a herd of tiang (a topi-like animal)—then a few reedbucks.

Our tracker spotted a roan antelope. Bob wanted one, so we took off after it. A closer look revealed it to be nice, but not quite big enough for Bob. There was not a period in the next few hours that we were out of sight of game. At one point, we saw some vultures flying and some roosting in a spot.

We all thought lion—so proceeded in the car over to check it out. When we got within 50 yards of them, they all dived down into the grass. I'm sure the same thing went through our minds—a lion had been on something there that the vultures went in on once the danger was gone.

We drove right on in and found a freshly killed reedbuck, about one third eaten. We made a circle around an area with high grass, where we felt the cat would retreat. Later (about five minutes) we returned to the kill, which by now, was completely devoured by the vultures.

Only then, did we check for tracks and found that it was a lion, and it had run straight away into a rather open, unlikely area. We tracked it for a while, but gave up as we figured it left the country.

About that time, we spotted a small herd of elephants—they saw us about the same time we saw them, at about 400 yards away. They were females and young and were moving around very restlessly, flopping their ears and raising their trunks to wind us.

We circled around to get the wind right and move in a little closer in the Land Rover. At about 100 yards, they decided we were too close and one old girl started a false charge, stopping after about 25 yards. We started driving away, she charged again, and this time did not stop!

**The old girl stopped her false charge at 25 yards, and then she charged again. The camera shook as we sped away.**

Duri sped away as fast as the terrain would allow, but she was closing the gap. James, the African game scout (Munduri descent), fired his military-type rifle at the feet of the elephant cow. She stopped, then madder than ever, started for us again—now with the whole herd right behind her.

Leaving at a speed more than Duri wanted to go on the rough plains, James fired again—this time turning the cow away from us. I think she was hit, at least with some bullet shrapnel.

Bob and I just enjoyed seeing the great quantities of game and didn't have any great desire to collect anything yet. Later on, Bob saw a good Mongalla gazelle and collected it with one shot with his .300 Weatherby. This gazelle is very similar to the Thompson's gazelle of Southern Kenya and Northern Tanzania—a thousand miles to the southeast.

By midday, we saw an unbelievable number of animals. Bob and I jotted down what we estimated seeing: 1 roan; 25 oribis; 3 duikers; 300 Mongallas; 100 tiangs; 12 elephants; 12 waterbucks; 15 zebras; 12 giraffes; and 50 reed-

bucks—over 500 animals of 10 different species in our first five hours of hunting.

Then a three-course lunch, a short nap and off again by 4 PM for the evening hunt. Bob and I, still just sizing up the area, saw a lot more game in a little different area. We must have seen 250 zebras total in six or eight different herds; a lot of giraffes, warthogs, bushbucks, besides most of the variety we saw this morning.

Jack did it again this afternoon. Three more trophies—bushbuck, waterbuck, and a white-eared kob (almost never seen in this area)—seven really fine trophies, several of which are in Rowland Ward's Records, all on his first day of hunting in Africa. Must be some kind of a record.

🐾 **Bob Chisholm with a fine tiang trophy.**

Arnie did it up right also. He got a bushbuck, grey duiker, and a Mongalla gazelle—four in all today for him.

**A white-eared kob taken by Jack Shelton in the Gemeiza area.**

03 February

Bob and I were up early. We wanted to hunt for another half day here, then head for the bongo area to the southwest of Sudan near the Zaire border. Everyone else up early also and out in different directions.

We saw four ostriches right off, then some giraffes, a couple of small herds of roans. Bob spotted a big tiang. He was a little uncertain as to try the 200-plus meter shot, as he hadn't had a chance to target in his rifle yet. Duri said to wait, and we would try to get closer.

Typical of an old animal, he didn't want anything to do with us and left the country. We spotted vulture activity and went over to check it out. About a third of a young tiang was there. We figured it to be a leopard kill because it was

a couple of days old. A leopard will nurse along a carcass like that for several days where a lion would eat it in one day. Even though leopards are very plentiful in most areas of Africa, they are on the protected list here and in most African countries because of pressure from the U.S. Fish & Wildlife, who don't know much about wildlife even in North America, let alone a remote African country.

We saw plenty of many different species of wildlife this morning. Bob did take a very good tiang with 19-inch horns. I collected a good Mongalla gazelle with 11½-inch horns. First time I used Duri's .264 Winchester Magnum and did a lousy job of shooting.

I found later that it was shooting three inches to the left, so made adjustments to get it on. Bob fired his and found it to be on.

Jack and Arnie did it again this morning. Jack got a good hartebeest—looks just like the Jackson's hartebeest found in Uganda to the south of here. He also got a good grey duiker. Arnie got a roan with 29½-inch horns, which is very good for this area. He also got a redbuck with a good, wide spread. That makes 16 animals in 1½ days of hunting. Not only that, but also 11 different species—12 if you count Bob's tiang.

With our gear piled in the Rover, Bob, Duri, Martin (African tracker) and I headed for Juba, arriving at 7 PM None of us realizing it, with the canopy flaps all rolled up, we were entirely covered with the red dust from the road,—we looked like a tribe of Dinkas.

The Dinkas sleep in, and otherwise cover themselves with ashes (which apparently acts as a bug repellant)—then for additional make-up they will rub dry cattle dung in their faces,

There are many native tribes in southern Sudan varying greatly in culture. Here
are photos of various women. The Mon-
golla live in savannah east of the Nile.

The Dinkas live right along the Nile.

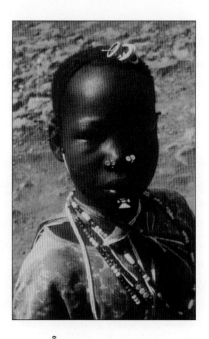

The Jur are in the
Bahr El Ghazal area west of the Nile.

giving a red appearance. They primarily live
from their cattle herds, bleeding the jugular
vein—mixing with cow's milk—and a little
of its urine to curdle it, to make their diet.
They all carry spears and will kill game at any
opportunity.

*The Forest Area in Southwest Sudan Near the
Zaire Border*

*04 February*
    Last night we stayed at the safari headquar-
ters. José had the shower ready and a comfortable
bedroom made up for us—and a dinner of Nile
perch. We were off by midmorning, heading for
Yambio in the southwest corner of Sudan near
the Zaire border.

*The first couple of hours were the worst part of the road as we headed southwest. We intersected the main highway from Uganda to Wau. It was also a dirt road. We hit it at the town of Jambo, proceeded on to Mundri (also crossed the Mundri River, in which we washed off a layer of dust), then to Maridi and to Yambio.*

*Maridi, as well as Mzara, were the two towns that had the fatal green monkey fever a couple of years ago. As we proceeded westward, the terrain became denser with trees. The Yambio area is actually in a rain forest.*

*The hunting concession that José has goes from the city of Yambio right to the Zaire border. His camp is only about 20 kilometers out of Yambio, and the concession is called Sukuré. A town of the same name is about two kilometers from the Zaire border on the main road, which is a very narrow track just wide enough for the hunting car.*

*We stopped in Yambio to check in with the head of the game department and to pick up our game scouts, which we are required to have while hunting. We also must pay nine dollars a day per scout. Only one was available and we*

**The Zandes are in the extreme southwest near the Zaire border.**

had to argue to get him. Their excuse was that we were too late in the evening.

The same game official lived in a grass shack right on the edge of town, and he rides a bicycle. His salary is 25 Sudanese pounds (about two dollars to the pound) per month. The money here, incidentally, is piastres (50 piastres equals $1 U.S.) and 100 piastres equals one pound. On the black market, we can get 70 piastres to the dollar. We arrived at the Sakuré camp at around 9 PM.

Dr. José Maria Talayero and his wife Elsa were here also to hunt. They are from Venezuela, and this is the second time they have hunted here in Sudan with this outfit. Antonio Ferreira and his wife Paki were staying in this camp. Antonio is a pro hunter, guiding the doctor and Elsa, while Paki is kind of a camp manager. Carlos Faria was also guiding the Talayeros.

The camp is a tent camp with all the luxuries including a grass dining room and a couple of portable buildings used for sleeping. This camp, like all the others has a generator for lights, refrigerator, etc. and a two-way radio. They (all camps) talk with Juba headquarters and each other, as well as Gassim (the safari companies agent) up in Khartoum at least three times a day. To bed after dinner and a shower (rigged up in a grass hut).

05 February

Up at 4 AM and out by 5 after a light breakfast. Bob and I hunted together this morning with Duri because of only having one game scout. We drove only about 20 minutes—left the car in care of Martin.

Duri's tracker is a Zande (the local tribe) named Saratiel. It wasn't five minutes before we ran across fresh bongo tracks. The area had been partially burned. That surprised me, as I didn't think they could effectively burn a rainforest area as they do the savannahs.

Burning is necessary in most all parts of Africa as the tall grass, when dry, crowds' sprouts resulting in no food for the game. Once the burning is done, new green sprouts immediately start growing. The burning does not harm the trees as they are mostly hardwood and will not catch fire. Thus, it was here, in some nice open meadows, where the bongo came in to feed.

After about 15 minutes of walking, we neared the end of a fresh burn. I stayed back a short distance, holding the game scout back as he was coughing and spitting. I was afraid he would spook everything out in front of us.

As I watched where the others were heading, I saw a flash of red darting off to the right in the bush in front of them. They stopped when they reached the bush and saw fresh bongo tracks. It was obviously a small herd of bongos—female and male—one of which I saw. To me, that is unbelievable, seeing a bongo within 15 minutes of hunting. We followed the tracks into some very dense bush, and then circled the area to be downwind from the path of the bongo. When in danger, they always go down wind, so they can smell their pursuers.

We lost that bunch, but as we circled into another area—more fresh tracks. We parallel their path by staying in the open. Moments later Saratiel froze and pointed, motioning Bob to come forward, handing him his rifle he had been bearing. *Bob just got a brief look at a male bongo darting off to the left, while the rest of the herd split to the right.*

*Since the area was very dense, there was no chance to go after them. We wove our way around to an area they were thought to have gone to hide. Duri, Bob, and I stayed in an opening, while the tracker and game scout went clear to the other side of the area and made noise, hoping to push the bongo, if any, our way. A male bongo track left the area, but unfortunately not in our direction.*

*It was around 10 AM and beginning to get hot. We headed back toward the car and saw some very fresh tracks heading into a thick area. Then we heard some shots from the .22 rifle that Duri kept in the car. Martin was probably shooting at some birds. Upon circling the area, we found a herd of bongo had just left the thicket—no doubt a result of Martin's shooting. A great and exciting first morning of hunting bongo.*

*We were probably never 10 minutes away from seeing fresh tracks. On the way back we saw two groups of baboons. They wanted us to shoot some of them for meat for the locals. This one hunting camp ordinarily does not supply much meat for the area.*

*The locals will not eat bongo, fortunately, as they are superstitious that the animals have leprosy, thus eliminating poaching almost entirely. That's why the hunting is good here. Upon returning to camp, we found that José had gotten an elephant. Took a shower, enjoyed a three course hot lunch, took a nap and out again at 4 PM There is no use hunting in the heat of the day. The game all bed down by then,*

*and the dew has dried off the leaves making them very crunchy and noisy. Now I have my own game scout, so I split off on my own with two natives, Martin and Titu, a Zande tracker. We checked out an area that hadn't been burned effectively. Terrific forested area with openings covered with a light bamboo. It was noisy and we couldn't see very far, but the area was loaded with bongo tracks. Coming back to the car through some dense forest was like being in the Tarzan movies. The sounds of birds and monkeys, along with the presence of Colobus monkeys leaping from tree to tree, made me forget I was bongo hunting for a while.*

*Back to camp shortly after dark. A quick shower and to the dining area for a much needed beer. The beer we have is smuggled in from Zaire and sold to us by Africans on bicycles coming up the main track, on which is this camp. The large bottles (about the size of a fifth) cost 80 piastres—about $1.60. The regular size beer cost about $2.50 in Juba.*

*Bob came dragging in telling about a herd of bongos he just missed seeing, but did see one respectable male—estimated to be about 25 inches in horn length. They were looking around at the end of an open meadow, when the tracker said that the bongo would "not be here, but there." As he turned around and pointed to where they just came from, the lone male bongo was just appearing out in the open. They looked it over carefully and determined it to be a little small—at least this early in the hunt.*

*It takes 27 inches for the Western bongo to go into the records, so that is the magic size to try for. Bob's group also saw a bushbuck, some bush pigs, and Colobus monkeys. For dinner,* we had bushbuck steaks cooked with onions and a sauce, along with Spanish rice. Lunches and dinners are always three-course—soup, main course, and fruit for dessert.

There are always cookies, fresh baked bread, tang, fresh lemonade, coffee, and tea available. The fruit is all fresh, bananas, papayas, pineapples, oranges, etc., served individually or in a fruit cocktail.

Last night Bob and I shared a tent, but since they have extras set up, I moved to another tent to give each of us more room to spread our gear. Laundry is done each day, so we got our last three days' laundry done and back.

## 06 February

Out before daylight with my African boys to an area to the north—on the road back toward Yambio, then to the west. We stopped at a

🦌 **The bushbuck is like a miniature bongo and offers equal sport.**

shamba, picked up a local guide, and proceeded on foot through a populated area. Saw plenty of tracks.

At another shamba, we got directions to go to an area that was supposed to be good for bongos. We couldn't find it, so returned to the shamba, and took a guide from there that knew the area. It was not productive there, but continued on to some other places. Saw a fair number of tracks everywhere, but the hunting was not professionally done. Martin had stayed behind, and he was the only one who could speak any English, thus my communication was not effective with my Zandes. Because of a lot of theft, Martin did not want to leave the car unattended in such a populated area.

The Zande people are farmers and hunters. They have little farms, called shambas, scratched out in some of the most unlikely places. The fields are small and rarely cleared off completely. A typical field will still have the stumps from the cut trees, some new forest growth coming up that is not being controlled, and a crop of some scattered coffee bushes. It will also have a few banana palms, a papaya tree or two; manioc plants, which produce a root that is eaten by the Africans; some corn or maize, etc.

Sometimes, it is hard to tell the farm growth from the natural forest. In the midst of all this will be the grass huts that may vary from a grass thatch roof only a foot or two off the ground with an entrance way cut on one side—to a room with grass or thatch-side or a mud-adobe type wall. Altogether, these are called shambas and are spotted throughout the area.

It seems that the bongo and the Zandes have learned to live in the same area with not much threat to one another. The Zandes do not have animals such as cattle, sheep, goats, etc. They are hunters, however, and, like the Dinkas, they all carry spears or bows. Many of them have nets. They get together with a group and stretch their nets over a game trail, or pass, and have a game drive. They have dogs that are quite small—look like a miniature dingo (Australian wild dog) crossed with a Mexican Chihuahua—and I have yet to hear one bark, even though I am told they will, if frightened. We have slipped in on many a shamba, so I guess it takes a lot to frighten them. Martin tells me the natives use the dogs for hunting and driving the game out of the bush.

## 07 February

I went, with my bongo battalion, (the name I assigned my African staff) way to the north, traveled north on the highway to Wau then branched off toward Lreungu. There they evidently have a leper colony. The area was more of a dense bush country; more like I hunted in Central African Republic in the Kota area, and it contains other varieties of game.

We picked up an African guide at a shamba. There were tracks, but nothing fresh this morning. Martin said last year they saw a great amount of bongo signs there, but the area was all dried out and so the bongos probably migrated to wetter ground.

I talked on the radio today to José in Juba and to Zeca and Arnie in Gemmeiza. Business talk to José, and he informed us the camp was being set up in the Nile lechwe area. It would be ready after we finished here, and we are to proceed there without delay.

When I went out in the afternoon, another tracker joined me—so I had Biadjo and Titu and, fortunately, the same guard, Antonio, did not show up. He is always coughing and I'm sure has hurt our chances of seeing game.

We only drove a few kilometers to the north and parked at the entrance to the Yubu coffee plantation. We walked through the usual forests and small openings eastward for an hour and a half. We went through a grove of huge wild lemon trees. On our return, we circled back through a big open meadow, with a lot of fresh green grass coming up.

We had seen a fair number of tracks going in, and they all seemed to be coming or going from this area. I sat on an anthill for a while waiting to see if any bongo came out to feed. Titu and Biadjo split out in different directions to see if they could see any activity in different areas.

They both returned and said we must return, as it is getting dark. We went down to intersect the trail in the direction that Biadjo just came from. Moments later, we were all stopped cold in our tracks. There was a bongo not more than 75 yards away feeding to his heart's content—a bull with about 25-inch horns.

I looked him over through the riflescope—and what a temptation, but at this stage of the hunt, I wanted to hold out for 27 inches, or better. I motioned to Martin to get the camera out, with which I shot a couple of pictures, knowing they might not come out good with the dim conditions.

The bongo continued feeding until he intersected our wind and took off. We moved slowly *to an anthill to look the area over, but saw no more signs of movement. Now we had to start back and 1½ hours of walking as fast as we could, mostly in moonlight (little better than a half-moon now) put us at the car at 7:20.*

*After our return to camp, Elsa came back with the story that she connected with a bongo about 28 inches, and darkness set in before they could find it. Everyone felt confident that they would find it at first light in the morning.*

*08 February*

*Generator on at 4:30 and in minutes I was eating and waiting for Martin. Our plan was to walk in by flashlight to the same place we had been the night before. At dawn, we were tiptoeing into the meadow. There were plenty of fresh tracks, some of which may have been made during the night—a big problem with the moonlight.*

*We did a thorough job of keeping the wind right, looking and glassing, as we worked our way through the mile or so of semi-open savannah. There had been a large herd of bongos at the far end of the opening since daylight, but we hadn't seen them. We were within 25 yards of a bushbuck and within 50 yards of another one—both of which finally darted into the bush. We followed the tracks of the big herd into the thick forest.*

*There would have been no way to approach them. The foliage was very dense, and the dry leaves were terribly noisy. We circled the forest to see if they exited and evidently, they had not. We took a different way back toward camp and came to some small openings.*

*Just about the time we let our guard down, Martin excitedly whispered, "There's a bongo." It was about 75 yards away, separated from us by some bush and tall grass. I could only see the body, showing its beautiful dark red coloration and vivid white stripes. Soon it turned to run off for the heavy jungle close by. At that point, I got a good look at the horns—they were almost identical to the one we saw last night, so again passed it up.*

*Upon inspecting the tracks, we found a set of larger tracks that went the opposite way. Perhaps a bigger bull had gotten our wind and split off from the younger one. We followed those tracks into a terribly thick forest that had us practically on our hands and knees to follow the elusive bull. Finally, we gave up and returned to camp.*

*Elsa did get a very good bushbuck—an old animal with worn down horns, 10 inches in length. The lorry (truck) had arrived in camp from Juba, bringing some fuel and supplies. The main cargo of the truck was heading north for the Nile lechwe camp that was to be ready (and built) prior to Bob's and my arrival.*

*About 4 PM when we were getting ready to go out, their Toyota comes roaring in and we hear them all chanting, "Bongo, Bongo, Bongo!" Bob was smiles from ear to ear, and once I looked in the back of the car, I could understand why—a 34-inch bongo! It is outstanding.*

*When you figure the largest one ever recorded, the world's record is 38 inches—Bob's is certainly one of the best ever taken. We snapped some quick pictures, making us a little late in getting out.*

*No one else got anything today. We had a little celebration tonight for dinner, giving credit to Bob and Elsa's trophies. They kindly assured us that the rest of us were bound to collect something tomorrow. Bob and I finished our vodka, and the wine was compliments of the Talayeros.*

*09 February*

*Changed to a new area to hunt today—drove a half hour toward Zaire and hunted the north side of the road. Within a half hour started seeing bongo tracks. Saw a couple of bushbucks, some baboons, and a yellow-back duiker. First time I had seen a yellow-back duiker and it was quite a thrill to see one finally on the hoof (seen plenty in the taxidermy studios).*

*It had the appearance of being jet black with the yellow coloration on the back vividly showing up. One of the bushbucks was undisturbed and I looked him over through the riflescope at 35 yards for a minute or so. Crossing through a forest, we found fresh bongo droppings. When we got to the opening, we found two sets of male tracks running away from us.*

*No doubt, they heard us coming through the noisy forest. Their tracks were heading against the wind then continued that way for a great distance. This surprised me as the natives say they always travel with the wind in order to smell anything following them.*

*They joined up with a herd of others—obviously some females and young in the bunch. We climbed an anthill to spot ahead, and to our surprise, there were two male bongos fighting about 110 yards away. They were obstructed by bushes. I looked at them with the binoculars and was satisfied one of them was a good*

*enough trophy, so I handed the binoculars to Martin and grabbed the rifle and told him to tell me which was the best, as they were going round and round while fighting.*

*By the time I got into position for shooting, they disappeared in the thicker bush. After talking over the strategy, we decided that Biadjo would try circling around them and try to scare them into the opening where we were. Shortly Biadjo returned and motioned for us to come. We followed and continued to stalk them through some tall grass. That was frustrating as it was noisy and the faster we went, the farther they seemed to be.*

*They were grazing their way into the forest. Our last chance to catch up with them, so we swiftly moved in on them. Before we realized it, we heard bongos in the tall grass on our left and on our right—we were among them! The wind was still favorable, but it had swirled around earlier, and regardless, they would get our scent soon.*

*The grass was about head high. We could see bushes moving and the occasional top of the back or set of horns of bongo. The females also have horns, so it got confusing. For the life of us, we couldn't find any of the males.*

*This is the first time I had seen females, but I hated to take one, especially when I knew there was at least one excellent bull within 50 yards of me. At a time like this, what do you do? You cannot talk it over with the others. You know that, whatever you do, it has to be done in seconds.*

*Shortly we would be seen or, worse yet, scented by at least one member of the herd—at which time they would vanish into the forests like ghosts. Each of us was frozen within a few yards* of one another, standing on our tiptoes, staring intently through the top of the tall grass.

I could see the head and neck of one bongo in the dark shadows of the forest. (We were out in the blazing sun, thus our eyes were not adjusted to the blackness of the forest that we were standing on the edge of). At that moment, Biadjo, about three paces to my left, pointed in that very direction—a signal, which we had worked out to indicate for me to shoot. I could not see the shoulder because of the tall grass, so mentally drew a line 45 degrees down from the head, where the center of the shoulder should be, and squeezed off. All hell broke loose as the herd crashed off in all directions.

I headed straight over to the spot where he last stood—no bongo. Biadjo angled off to the left, looking for blood trail. Soon we found blood and slowly followed the trail. Biadjo and Martin said it was a very big bull, maybe as big as Bob's. I told them I didn't think so from what I saw of the horns.

After we all mentally reenacted the scene, we determined that Biadjo had seen a big bull in the direction (but closer) of the one I saw, but it was cut off from my view. Twice we came close to it, but twice its keen senses warned it of our presence, and it bolted away.

A couple of hours later, we followed its tracks into a thick forest where I saw its silhouette and finished it off with two rapid shots. I had gotten my female for the museum—a perfect specimen and a big one at that, 27 inches of horn.

In the afternoon, we returned to the area we went the first evening here. Someone had done a lot of burning, which opened it up considerably. Plenty of bongo tracks.

Early we jumped a bushbuck and shortly after, a bunch of bush pigs. We jumped them within about 25 yards. The old sow seemed rather disturbed that we invaded her privacy, grunted, and growled at us as she reluctantly led her litter into the bush. Moments later, our path took us near her again and she got very vocal. I kept the gun ready in case she decided to try running us off.

Shortly after that, we were crossing a big opening that had a bit of thick bush sticking out in the middle of it. As we headed that direction, a whole flock of guinea fowl flushed and nosily flew into the trees. Just as we got to the point of bush, the crashing sound of bongos rushing into the bush was heard only about 20 yards away from us on the other side of the bush.

We checked the tracks and there were some nice bull tracks that had crossed the opening coming our way, just moments before. If we had been a couple minutes sooner, we may have seen them in the open. No doubt, the guinea fowl put them on the alert, keeping them next to the bush until they determined what had spooked them.

We proceeded and a few minutes later came into a herd of giant forest hogs —another first for me. There was a big old boar, a sow, and three others about half-grown. They were within 50 yards of us and undisturbed. We watched them for a couple of minutes before they scurried off.

Bob and Duri hunted situtunga today, but without success. The area where they wanted to hunt along the Yuba River, which is the small river that this camp is built on, was being fished by the natives—so no luck.

José and Elsa drew a blank today.

*Antonio fixed some sangria (a Spanish way of preparing wine with fruit) for dinner; after seeing it, Bob and I watered our Spanish burgundy with lemonade.*

*10 February*

*Headed right to the Zaire border this morning to the town of Sukuré, then turned left (south) for a couple of miles and took off on foot. Not long before we ran across fresh bongo tracks, which led to more tracks, a zigzag path for a couple of miles—quite a bit in the open, but through some thick stuff and eventually into the heavy timber. That is usually the pattern every day.*

*We now have a full moon, therefore, I feel that these elusive animals are doing a lot of their feeding at night—and for sure the water holes get their action at night, From reading the tracks, the herds scatter, often a couple of bulls will be off feeding by themselves, but they meet up with the herd by morning. I feel that, right now with the full moon, they are very close to the heavy timber by dawn. That is why we are only seeing them by tracking—and we are seeing them in the thick forest, or not seeing them at all because it is hopeless to get close to them for the noise we make.*

*We came across a pit trap (a deep pit dug and covered over with limbs and grass to capture game by having them fall through) with the skeleton of a bongo in it—what a waste. The natives obviously made the trap for bushbucks or wild pigs—so they get a bongo and then abandon it. We thought enough of this area to hit it earlier tomorrow morning and try to catch the bongos before they get into heavy forest.*

*On our return, we found that the whole population of the area were in Sukuré and also in a little village to the east called Bangui. This is Saturday and market day. They don't have an awful lot to offer, but whatever they have a surplus of that they can sell or trade, is brought out and laid on the ground, neatly displayed. Martin bought a T-shirt (his own) full of oranges and some honey in the comb, wrapped in leaves.*

*The area here on the Zaire border is mountainous and a little higher. I should say hills, as there are no tall mountains. Looking at the map, the watersheds on the Sudan side, all flow to the east and north into the Nile River and on the Zaire side to the west and south, flowing into the Congo River.*

*This area is really remote and primitive. These people are cut off from the rest of the world and lead a simple life in their little shambas, scratching a living from the land. I'm sure a traveler coming through here a thousand years ago would not have found it much different except for the roads, bicycles, etc.*

*In the afternoon, I went out only with Biadjo and Titu, to the area south where I have been three times already. I refer to it as the swamps, even though it isn't swampy at this dry time of the year. There is sort of a wide river bottom that winds its way through the Sukuré area, but has only an occasional water hole now.*

*During the wet season, starting in June, it is obviously a swamp, and judging by the elephant footprints, sometimes three feet deep, it is really swampy. Anyway, I saw a nice bull bongo as we crept into an opening, not 50 yards away. What* a beautiful sight. He had horns, I would guess, at about 26 inches. He was broadside, and I could have taken him easily, but I chose to pass him up.

Later we heard something approaching and as I sat ready, a yellow-back duiker came sneaking out. I got my camera out of the rucksack and shot him with that—at about 20 yards away. I wished Bob had been with me, as he wants to collect one. Later we snuck up on a noise in the tall grass and found warthogs at a water hole in the swamp.

Over one hour back in the full moon on foot—Martin was waiting with the car. Back at camp everyone feeling a little low from the lack of luck. Still no sign of situtunga by Bob and Duri. Poor Elsa, she missed another chance today, while tracking into a herd of bongo, at the last minute they had to run to get in the open for a shot.

With her having to carry her own rifle and try to keep up with Carlos and the Zandes, she missed her chance. To top it off, someone stole her camera out of her bag in the car. She had her bushbuck pictures as well as Bob's bongo still in the camera. I told her to go baboon hunting tomorrow and forget about bongo for a while. For sure, she'll be out though—has never missed a morning or evening hunt yet. Tomorrow, being Sunday, I think God will gift her with a bongo.

### TIME LAPSE

Elsa got her bongo. In at 3 PM with a real fine head—28½ inches. She was hunting elephant to the west of where we were when they jumped a lone bull bongo. They stalked into the bush where they heard it, and it was still there.

The first shot didn't quite do the job, so they had a chase that took them almost an hour, when she finished it off.

### 12 February

Up at 4 AM—got to our starting place before dawn. Started walking as soon as we could recognize tracks. Saw some fresh elephant sign right off—also some buffalo tracks. Duri says that these are typical of the Nile buffalo here, not the dwarf. Not a bongo track in the area. We walked for hours and never crossed one. Saw five waterbucks, female and young. Came across a nice bushbuck, so I went ahead and took it. With no sign of bongo, I didn't see how it could hurt by shooting. A lot of elephant sign in the area.

Back at camp Bob tells me about going to try and find the yellow-back duiker that I saw last night, and came across some bongo, just wandering around in the open. Two nice bulls—one well over 30 inches. He and Duri snapped a bunch of pictures, and they wished I were there. That's the way things always seem to go. Elsa came in with some more good luck—she got a giant forest hog. Her luck really changed for the better. José still hasn't been able to find that big one.

Out in the afternoon again with Saratiel, Titu, Martin, the game scout and an African boy that we have been taking along to watch the car. We went to the area that we hunted the first morning here. This area is near Saratiel's shamba, so he knows it very well.

The usual stalking from one burn to the next in among the small clusters of timber. There were some fresh tracks from the morning, which was very encouraging after not seeing a fresh track at all this morning in the other nearby area to the south of here. We finally had some action when we stalked into some heavy grass that had not burned well, and came across a group of bush pigs.

There must have been a dozen altogether—boars, sows and pigs—and did we ever have fun with them. We snapped a few pictures of them in the dimming light of evening. The pigs couldn't figure out what we were and didn't get our wind so they stomped their feet and snorted at us, trying to get us to leave their habitat. We finally walked out practically among them and Saratiel threw rocks at them to get them to scatter.

It's amazing how unafraid animals can be at times when they don't get the human scent. The bush pigs here are bigger and have a different coloration from those I've hunted in other areas. These are very orange in color and some white and dark on the face.

After causing our little disturbance in the area, we got down to some serious business (bongo hunting) as we marched our way back toward the car. We went through a bush thicket and just as we came into a freshly burned opening, Saratiel froze and pointed to the other side of the clearing. About 150 yards away stood a magnificent bull bongo facing us as if having seen us. I instinctively threw the rifle to my shoulder and aimed at the only target I had—right at the neck.

Even at that, I had to shoot through some grass that was obstructing everything but the head. Without hesitation, I squeezed off, and the bull whirled around out of view. I saw an anthill about 25 yards ahead that I ran to as fast as possible. The bull was standing broadside and, again, as fast as I could raise the rifle, I pulled one off, aiming just below the spine. He went down hard and out of sight. Had I seen him lying there, I would have shot again for insurance.

These older bulls will go 450 pounds—possibly 500. They are extremely heavily built and rarely do they go right down, even with the biggest rifle. The last thing I wanted was to have a wounded bongo disappear into the forest at dusk, where tracking would be near impossible. We ran to the spot and lying there was one of the most beautiful sights of my hunting career.

The horns were what I wanted with the top flaring out—typical of an older bull. After the backslapping and handshaking, expressing our happiness of success after so many hard days of tracking and fighting jungle, we posed the bongo for pictures, before all daylight was gone.

I asked if it would be possible to bring the car here. After some thought Saratiel motioned to Martin to come with him. About an hour later, in full darkness, the Toyota came banging through the brush. For the five of us to get the massive dead weight of the bull into the back of the bed was a real job, accomplished only after we rolled the animal next to a depression, that we back the hunting car into.

I taught the boys to sing "Bongo, Bongo, Bongo,—I don't want to leave the Congo." They chanted it, along with the tooting of the horn as we drove into camp—a proud bunch of hunters. I was certainly proud of them for all the work they put forth in search of this bongo. More pictures with the strobe in camp.

**" I am proud of my well-earned bongo, as are my boy's Saratiel, Titu, and Martin.**

*José got a nice bushbuck this evening. Carlos whipped up a good stout batch of sangria to celebrate the occasion. I came to find out they put vodka (or whatever else happens to be around) in it.*

*13 February*

*Out looking for yellow-back duiker today. They normally are found in the dense bush or forest areas near open areas, especially along river or swamp bottoms and always near water. Saratiel led us to such an area that we patrolled up one side and down the other. Saw two red duikers and numerous Colobus monkeys.*

*We came across a salt lick that had some huge elephant track in it. The lick was on a clay bank, where the elephants had been digging out a shallow cave in the wet clay bank. There were imprints of heavy tusks in the mud. The lick was at the edge of a dense forest in which we heard elephants breaking trees. I wasn't interested in elephant, but I knew Elsa was, so we went*

*back to camp early, hoping Elsa would be back also.*

*14 February*

*Valentine's Day and the last day of hunt here in Sukuré for all of us. Everyone out early to give it a last good try. Biadjo was back with Martin and me to an area where we saw a yellow-back duiker the other day. At one point, we saw a lot of tracks and Biadjo decided on a beat, as by then the animals would be bedded down in the thick stuff.*

*Biadjo and the game scout started their way to circle around the forest while I began over to the clearing where I was to stand. As I eased my way there, I saw the dark forms of what appeared to be either duikers or giant forest hogs (both black in color) slipping through the thick bush at the edge of my clearing. The wind had shifted about 90 degrees causing the scent of our beaters to go right into the forest, thus pushing out the wrong way.*

**Elsa and José Talayero with their huge elephants' ivory, each of hers weighing 151 pounds and his weighing 91 pounds. Squatted are their professional hunters, Carlos Faria and Antonio Ferreira.**

*We stayed put and let the beat happen before checking the tracks—yellow-back duikers. There were several of them in the bunch. We tracked them long enough to determine that they crossed over a swamp area to heavy forest. Upon returning to camp, we anticipated someone had success, as we had heard quite a number of shots earlier.*

*Elsa got her elephant. Carlos proudly displayed a piece of vine that they had cut off the length of protruding tusk, which was over six feet in length. It has to be a 100 pounder (100 pounds or more per tusk).*

*Carlos left three of the boys out to cut a trail for the vehicles to get to the location. After lunch Duri, Bob, Carlos and Elsa, along with the*

*skinners, headed back out to remove the tusks and other parts of the elephant.*

*As Paqi and I sat down to lunch, who drives in but José and Antonio with a bongo! José had smiles from ear to ear, as he showed off his 28-incher. Then when we told him of his wife's success, he really became excited, shouting "Dos elefantes, dos bongos—muy bien safari!" (He doesn't speak English).*

*It was late evening by the time they returned with the tusks—unbelievable! They must be 120 pounds each. Everybody in a happy mood and ready for a party. We have plenty of excuses— Valentine's Day, last day of safari here (and last day altogether for the Talayeros) and the taking*

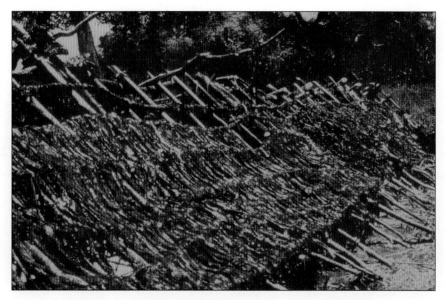

☂ **Making elephant biltong, the African method for jerky.**

of a record-class bongo and a huge elephant, not to mention Jack and Arnie are scheduled to stop here tonight. Therefore, the sangria is being made and it appears they are putting in all the left over booze.

*15 February*

Last night Jack and Arnie arrived in camp to hunt here. Bill Moss and his son Randy, along with their professional hunter Adrian Siabra. They were traveling with Dick Gilbert, whom I know, but Dick did not stop in. They all proceeded on to the Ezo camp, to the west of here. We stayed up very late catching up on all the hunt stories.

Jack had another story—he almost got thrown in jail for taking a picture of the jail-house in one of the towns before Yambio. Finally after he took the film out of the camera, exposing it to the light, and handed it over to the chief of police. They were left to proceed—but with an armed guard until they got to Yambio.

This morning we attempted to be ready to leave for Yambio at 7 AM, but as expected, it was not possible to get everyone organized, so it was about 8 AM. A charter aircraft was coming in to take the Talayeros back to Juba, where they had a connection to Khartoum and on to Europe.

*The Nile Lechwe Area in the West Nile Swamps*

It is interesting to note that their charter aircraft had to come all the way from Nairobi to Juba and on to Yambio, just to fly them 200 miles back to Juba. The approximate distance from Nairobi to Juba would be 800 miles. There are no charter aircraft in Sudan.

José Simoes was on the flight just to come over and meet with all of us, but we missed seeing him, as the aircraft had a tight schedule.

*The Game Department in Yambio asked us to take one of their officials with us to Wau, so that he could buy some fuel for them. We agreed, and it took us about another three hours for him to get the money to pay for the fuel. His name is Domonick, a black Sudanese. He rode with Martin and me in the short-wheel-base Toyota, while Bob, Duri, and Paloma, a shirttail relative of the Simoes's, rode in the other one. However, during our delay, we had time to witness the official weighing of the elephant tusks. José's 91 pounds and Elsa's an unbelievable 151 pounds each tusk!*

*We traveled westerly through the small towns of Nzara and Ringui—crossing the Ringui River at Mupoi, where there was a very large Catholic mission (the religion in Southwest Sudan is Christian—Catholic and Protestant), to the town of Tembura at which point we headed northerly.*

*At Tembura, Domonick wanted to stop and see the game officials, so we lost a little more time. The head of the game department was George Taban. All the officials spoke some English and most quite well, which was surprising to me in this extremely remote country. Taban asked me to ask Simoes, over the radio, to get him some kind of documentation as to who was authorized to hunt in the Bandalla Hunting Block to the northwest of Tembura.*

*His head office in Juba (for the whole Western Equatorial Province) did not inform him who had the right to hunt there. We drove on to the hunting camp at Bandalla, about 45 miles north of Tembura.*

*By now we were out of the rain forest and into a dense bush country, much like that which*

*I hunted in a hundred or so miles to the northwest of here a couple of years ago in Central African Empire. The Bandalla Block bordered CAE. At camp we ran into Bill and Randy Moss, who only stayed in Ezo for a few hours sleep. Mel Toponce was also there with Luis Mena and we met another Venezuela couple, Erasmo and Silvane Santiago.*

*16 February*

*6 AM—we start toward Wau, passing through Nagero, Bazia, and Bussere—then crossing the Bussere River. The people we have observed all through this remote and untraveled land was farming types, but they all hunt with their spears, bows, and nets.*

*Once we arrived at Wau, a noticeable difference in people was apparent. We now saw a mixture of different tribes. Wau, even though not strategically located (as a crossroads or trade center) is close to the same size as Juba—the two being the second and third largest cities in Sudan. (Sudan is the largest African country). We saw here a lot of the Jur tribe.*

*A statuesque, handsome people, tall and proud. They wore very little to cover their bodies, but did wear a lot of beads, coils and the like—much like I saw in the Karamoja of northwestern Uganda in 1962, when I hunted there. We also saw Dinkas, as well as Arabs and every other type of black. Colorfully dressed people crowded the streets along with practically nude natives. We had dozens of them ask us for a ride, but we did not even dare tell them where we were going or they surely would not have left us alone.*

The game department is called "Wildlife and Tourism." I asked Domonick if their offices took care of all tourism activities here.

"Yes, but no tourists other than hunters come here at all," he said. Here there is no transportation for surface travel such as bus and no railroad in all of Sudan except one small spur from Wau to Khartoum. The roads take the strongest four-wheel drive vehicles or lorries (trucks). There is no such thing as a good road in southern Sudan even though there is some improvement going on, but they are still dirt roads that get partially washed out each rainy season in the summer. The average road is so bad; to drive an average of 20 miles per hour would be over working the tough four-wheel-drive Toyotas and Land Rovers.

We had a short visit with the head of the game department, dropped off Domonick and proceeded east to the city of Tonj—a fairly large village of what appeared to be a mixture of Jur and Dinkas tribes—about 63 miles from Wau. We are now getting back into Dinka country as we get a little closer toward the Nile. From here, our route was along the Tonj River that flows northeasterly to our camp only about 15 miles from Tonj.

Rosha, the Portuguese maintenance man for Nimairico Safaris, along with his wife, Paloma, had built our camp on the bank of the Tonj in the last several days. We had brought the portable generator with us, which was promptly hooked up to the already installed lights and fridge. The refrigerator was found to have been broken en route—so no cold anything and no way to preserve fresh meat. Bob and I promptly skinny-dipped in the river while being observed by the curious Dinka natives that swarmed in by the numbers. I was not shy to expose myself in front of these people that wore no more than a draped cloth normally—but often completely nude. Since a Dinka woman was standing a few paces from us, Bob elected to leave his shorts on.

We found we had no cook in camp. Duri thought Rosha had brought one and vice versa, Paloma promptly volunteered to be our cook with the help of the camp boy. She was handicapped with the lack of refrigeration, local food produce, and skilled help, but did a fine job with what she had and satisfied our food requirements, which were not all that demanding.

In the next couple of days, Paloma got acquainted with several of the Dinka tribesmen that frequented the camp. One made an offer of 1,000 Sudanese pounds (about $2,000) for her. The following day she had a much better offer of 2,000 pounds. I told her to find out what that amount translated in head of cattle—a bartering media more commonly used by these natives—in order to determine what her real value was. While bathing in the river once, a Dinka woman stood around curiously watching me. I told Bob I felt she was about ready to make an offer for me, but never did—I guess I'm over the hill.

### 17 February

Out early altogether in one car to explore the area. Duri had only been here once for a day or two a couple years ago, so didn't know the area and to his knowledge, no one had ever hunted before. We had a local game scout and picked up a Dinka hunter who knew the area.

We spotted several hundred Nile lechwe across the open plains. They appeared to be a black line along the horizon. The Dinka indicated we must stop and said, "Maya" (water). Not really knowing what to expect, we grabbed our rifles and rucksack with cameras and started walking. Soon we were in water and later knee deep and sometimes waist deep, as we got close enough to start picking out an occasional good Nile lechwe head with the binoculars.

By now the sun was getting hotter and insects—mosquitoes, flies, and gnats began stirring and taking their share of us. Neither of us had carried our repellent. The entire area was an open swamp with an occasional higher piece of ground above water. The only concealment we had was some tall grass along the main waterways. The main swamp was an average of a foot deep (at this time of year) and had kind of a tangly floating grass. Each step had to be lifted out of water to prevent having to force our steps through the grass.

We made several attempts at a stalk on the lechwe herds, but each time the swirling wind or our exposure to their sight, sent the entire herd racing further off. The sun was getting hotter and the going much tougher. We did not carry drinking water with us. Bob had to come up with the crack, "Water, water everywhere and not a drop to drink."

After a while, we found ourselves split up—Martin and I approached the herd from one direction while Bob, Duri, and the two locals circled around in hopes of being in their path when we spooked them, which we surely would do sooner or later. When running away from us, the lechwe would angle off to the left or right, rather than running straightaway. Since their last retreat was to the right, Bob and the rest thought they would next go to our left.

I waited till I saw them stalking through some tall grass to our left some distance away, before I approached the herd. Once they were in position, I suggested to Martin that we crawl

**Duri and Bob wading in the home of the Nile lechwe.**

to some higher ground—the highest around— and try a distant shot, which would be our only chance as we had no cover to approach closer.

We were about 500 yards from the lechwe herd portion that contained a few nice bucks. A prone shot at that distance was the only chance— but what to rest the rifle on? When lying down, sight of the animals is lost because of the tips of the grass sticking above the line of vision. The lechwe were standing in water in most cases, resulting in less of their body being exposed.

I told Martin to lie on his side so that I could try resting the rifle on his rump—still not high enough. There was a good healthy clump of grass a short distance away that I snaked my way over to and set my flight bag on (which I used as a camera bag—waterproof, dustproof and all) and that was high enough. Even at that, the animals were constantly milling about and, more frequently than not, the male animals were amongst or behind the females.

Finally, one big male was exposed in the open, and I laid the cross hairs high on the back and squeezed off. The milling of the herd gave us no chance to tell whether I had hit or not. Martin wanted me to shoot again at the exiting herd (which incidentally did not choose to stick to their pattern to go Bob's way), but I told him I would not shoot again until inspecting the spot that I shot at.

Once the herd was out of view, we sloshed our way to the clump of high grass where I had shot—no signs of a hit. Perhaps the distance was greater than I thought and had undershot— or maybe the bullet had hit some grass and deflected, but I became certain I had missed.

Bob and Duri came over and we all proceeded again in the direction the herd had gone. Now there were much more tall grass areas and we could not see very far.

By now the insects half devoured us. At times, I would wipe them from my bare arms, leaving a dozen splotches of my own blood from crushed mosquitoes. It had been at least four hours since we had taken any liquid and we were as wet from perspiration above as we were from standing in the water below. The next half hour or so did not reveal any lechwe. We sent Martin and our Dinka guide back to the car to move it as close as possible to the direction we had gone so that we would not have to back-track all the way.

Moments later, we ran across a small herd of lechwe. We had previously agreed that I would take the first shot as my time was running out and Bob would be around for another ten days. I quickly paired up with the game scout and we worked our way to an opening that should put us within range. Part of the herd, a dozen or so females, saw us, and reversed their course, while the rest grazed off the other direction.

There was only one big male in the bunch. Just as I got to the opening in the grass and found the only high spot of ground around, the buck saw the females that had split off running, and he turned and ran their way. This offered a running broadside shot at least 200 yards away—my last chance, I was sure, to get my lechwe.

It took so long for us to get the kill; a vulture had already eaten one of the eyes out. Upon seeing the feet of the animal, it was apparent why he could run so fast through the swamp. These animals use about eight inches or so of their foot to support themselves. Their hoof is not only very long, much like that of the swamp-dwelling situtunga, because of the lack of their being worn down from hard ground, but the last joint or two of their leg flattens out giving a base that "floats" on top of the floating grass mat, when they are running. While walking or standing, they obviously sink, just as we do. However, when running, they are theoretically "walking on water."

I was very happy with my Mrs. Grey's lechwe, the official common name for the Nile lechwe. It is a trophy that is abundant in its limited habitat from the Ethiopian border on the east and where I am standing with my specimen on the west. The north-south range is not more than a few hundred miles at the extreme. Only the relatively few adventurous sportsmen that have ventured into this most remote area of Africa have had the rare opportunity to collect this unusual and fine specimen.

We skinned the trophy out for a life-size mount right on the spot. The vehicle came into view about a mile from us on the edge of the swamp. No need for Bob to stay so he headed that direction in the heat of the midday sun—an estimated 100°F in the shade and a mile and a half to the nearest shade. We were all extremely dehydrated and affected by the heat.

Every time I rose up from skinning, I had severe dizziness that forced me to immediately drop to my knees again. Bob had a pocket of gumdrops that he shared with me and were extremely helpful. It was 1 PM before we had the animal and all our gear packed to the car and a chance for water intake—some seven hours in the sweltering heat since our glass of tang at breakfast. The water made me temporarily sick. I felt that we were close to a heat stroke in our extreme exertion, fighting the swamps in the beating-down sun.

After finishing the skinning back in camp, we drove out in the afternoon in hopes of

The Jur guide with me and my well-earned Nile lechwe, more commonly known as Mrs. Grey's lechwe.

getting into the habitat of the white-eared kob. The local guide said that it would take us till about dark to get there—about two hours driving. In view of that, we hunted closer in and looked over some common kobs, oribis, duikers, waterbucks, and a lot of bird life—crested cranes, geese, ducks, and the like.

18 February

The sweet sorrows of parting from Bob, Duri and this wonderful safari faced me this morning. I had reservations on Sudan Airlines on a midday flight to Khartoum. After my good-byes to them and Paloma, Rosha and the camp staff, Martin drove me to Wau. Since we had 80 miles to travel, under uncertain conditions, I had him start very early. We also hauled the refrigerator in town to see if someone could repair it, but being Sunday, no one around to leave it with. The plan was then for Martin to stay until it was repaired before returning to camp.

We arrived in Wau about 10:30 and I had him proceed directly to the airport. To our dismay, the airport manager informed us that he received a radio message from Khartoum that the flight was cancelled (all flights to and from Wau) until further notice because of the lack of fuel for refueling the aircraft.

What to do? I had already extended the trip four days and I absolutely had to make my connection from Khartoum to London on the 20th and onward to Seattle, as I had a convention that I had to attend, along with Colleene, yet this week in Minneapolis. This triggered a series of events that I do not wish to repeat again soon. My only chance was to fly from Juba, some 562 miles away, tomorrow on a flight that I knew existed, and which the station manager confirmed would fly.

TIME LAPSE

(To avoid the gory details of a short cut over the worst road conditions, nonstop, flat tires et al.)

In Juba Carlos and José greeted us, told me to hurry to the airline terminal to check in. I said, "After a shower." We were brown with dirt and trail-dust and feeling miserable. I jumped in the cold shower and into city clothes. Fati, an Arabian co-worker of the company rushed me to Sudan Airways town terminal to check in.

The clerk sat there shaking his head indicating there was no space available. He said we had to check in by 8 AM (11:30 flight) in order to save the space.

At that point, I had few words. I said, "Where is the manager?" After 15 minutes with him, he said to meet him at the airport at 11. I got on the plane, but had to buy a new ticket, as my Wau-Khartoum ticket was not good on a Juba/Khartoum flight—about the same distance and on the same airline—typical of this primitive country.

The same primitiveness, however, has to be an asset, which makes it the unspoiled and great hunting country that it is. It is a great credit to a man like José Simoes, who recognizes the potential of this remote and forbidden country for the adventure that it offers the sportsmen who wish to be in nature with the unspoiled people and wildlife and to collect a few specimens as a remembrance.

# CHAPTER 4

# Africa— From Top to Bottom

My wife, Colleene, joined me on two exploratory trips in Africa in the fall of 1979. The first was to open an area to hunting in Sudan by the Red Sea, just across from Saudi Arabia, making it the northernmost hunting area in Africa. Two very good friends, Thornton Snider and Gene Rubeck, along with their ladies, joined us for this portion of our trip.

Our host for this arrangement was Nimerico Safaris, whom we had already been working with in Southern Sudan. José Simoes, a Portuguese professional hunter who previously operated in Mozambique and Angola before their downfall, managed this company. José's son, Duri, who grew up in the hunting circles, had now been assigned to manage this new program.

Our second maiden hunt took us to perhaps what will be the southernmost hunting arrangement in Africa. The area was a little known Autonomous Republic of South Africa, Transkei, located on the southeast tip of the continent. Our hosts there were two South Africans, Nic Ventor and Phillip Hommes, who were engaged by that independent country to start a hunting and tourist program in the Mkambati Game Reserve. The following is a copy of Chris's journal of the expedition, except for some parts left out, referred to as TIME LAPSE.

### Hunting the Red Sea Hills of Northern Sudan

*23 October, 1979 Seattle to London*

Colleene and I flew from Seattle on Western Airlines to San Francisco. The wrong direction to London, but we wanted to join Thornton and Helen Snider for our overseas flight. We spent a couple hours with them in the Clipper Club before boarding our 1:30 flight, which got us in London at 0730 in the morning –18 hours by the clock, which was 10 hours flying and eight hours time lost.

There we met Gene Rubeck and Terry Keichle for our British Airways flight to Khartoum, Sudan. Our trip was to go hunting and see new areas in Northern Sudan, the Red Sea Hills on the coast of the Red Sea and the sub-Sahara area north of Khartoum.

*25 October*

Finally in Sudan—43 hours after boarding our flight in Seattle by the clock. With 9 hours time change, that made it 34 hours en route—flying, in airports, to and from, with a short break and rest in London. As we disembarked, Gasmelseed Mohamed, better known as Gassim, greeted us even at this early hour. Gassim is a member of the staff of Sudanese International Tourist Company (SITCO). SITCO is involved in tourism and hotels and is a government company. Gassim is engaged by Nimerico Safaris to expedite hunting clientele through customs and assist them while in and out of Khartoum.

He was a welcome sight and with his assistance, we were whisked through customs without hang-up—in fact, we just bypassed customs. That was necessary as we were overloaded with excess booze, tobacco and ammunition. Our "yellow" cab just barely chugged into the Hilton Hotel where we were assigned our rooms.

We all mustered in Snider's suite to watch dawn break—from one side we looked down on the immense White Nile River while overlooking the Blue Nile River on the other side. The location of Khartoum is on the confluence of the two branches, which form the main Nile River that lazily winds its way north to Egypt and out to the Mediterranean Sea in the vicinity of Cairo.

### TIME LAPSE

*27 October*

Gassim picked Colleene and me up for a meeting with Abu Sinieva, Director of Wildlife for Northern Sudan—a friend of mine from the game conferences earlier in the year. José Simoes had arranged for Abu, along with other game officials and directors of SITCO, to come to the U.S.A. for the Safari Club International Conference in Las Vegas and Game Conservation International Convention in San Antonio. Colleene and I became good friends with them.

Had a very nice but hurried visit with Abu, who had a meeting arranged with his Minister, so we scheduled a dinner meeting with the whole group when we return to Khartoum after the hunt.

Our hunting licenses were issued in short order. We were each given two of the ibex special permits. The general license only cost 100 Sud pounds (about $125) and included a great number of animals. Royalties are paid for animals taken—those fees are also reasonable. From the

Game Department, we picked up Owen Rutherford, a Professional Hunter engaged by Simoes to scout out our next scheduled hunting area in an area north of Khartoum.

Back to the hotel for a quick lunch, checked out of the hotel and off to the airport. Our Boeing 737 Sudan Airways flight was on time at 3 PM Upon arrival at Port Sudan, on the coast of the Red Sea, we were met by Duri Simoes, José's son, and Zeca Carvalho—both of whom I hunted with in southern Sudan for bongo and Nile lechwe, among other game. It was great seeing them. Packed our gear in the two Toyota Land Cruisers and went to the Red Sea Hotel where we had to leave our passports for visas for the Red Sea Region farther north.

We had beer (Schlitz from U.S.A.!) while waiting for some sandwiches to take with us, as we planned to stop at Arous Village and stay overnight. Two and a half hours of rough, washed out detour road got us there about 10 PM This place is unbelievable!

A deluxe beach resort on the Red Sea literally in the middle of nowhere. It has 30 air conditioned cabana sleeping units to accommodate 60 people; very large open-air dining and bar area; all self-contained with generator, flush toilets, showers; a Marina with boats, motors, skin diving facilities, etc. One thing lacking—no guests and no apparent way to get them!

Arous Village was built by an Italian group with the best of everything going into it—but no workable plan as to how to use it. It is located in a nice protected cove about 45 km north of Port Sudan. It has been taken over by SITCO with some hopes of making it go. Nimerico Safaris,

being the general agents for hunting for SITCO, has access to the resort.

We broke out our booze supply and had cocktails with our sandwiches. They hadn't run the generator for a while so it wouldn't start. With flashlights, candles and lanterns we made out fine. There were only a couple of caretakers there, who made up beds for us, but Gene and Terri couldn't wait to get to camp. Zeca loaded all our bags and the two of them in one car and went on to camp arriving at 1 AM The rest of us made our way to the rooms and the next thing I knew it was dawn.

28 October

I wandered down to the beach and enjoyed the peacefulness of the quiet water of the Red Sea. Water was a clear pale green and calm, even though it is a tremendous, large body of water. A lot of unusual shaped coral lying around. After the rest got up, the caretaker served tea and Turkish coffee. Off by 7 AM northward and inland arriving at camp by 9 AM Saw several small herds of Dorcas gazelles as we neared camp.

Gene had good news for us—he went out early and shot two Dorcas gazelles, one of which was in the Rowland Ward Records—10½ inches horn length, a half inch over the minimum. So—fresh meat in camp and starting with success.

Beautiful camp nestled among some rocky outcrops near the base of the Red Sea Hills to the west of us, with private sleeping tents, dining area, showers, toilet, and other utility tents. Generator for power and quite a few added extras one doesn't normally expect in a hunting camp—refrigerator, freezer, and food of every description.

The driver, Setel, and Chris admire the record class Dorcas gazelle
taken by Gene Rubeck.

*We had kind of an easy day today. Sighted my rifle in—I'm using Duri's .264 Winchester and he just got a new scope mount, so I used a half box of the three that I brought to get it on. Thornton, I, and the gals drove out late afternoon to look for dorcas. This area on the plains around the mountains is just like the savannah areas in most parts of Africa right now.*

*This is a desert –could be considered sub-Sahara desert, but there has been plenty of rain recently, and it really bloomed out, and it's quite pleasant now. It has been raining off and on for a couple weeks. From what I can find out, they have two rainy seasons here—November and February. Therefore, we're getting early rains. While it's cloudy, which it was today, it was comfortable,—we are guessing in the upper 70s F.*

*We looked over 25 or so dorcas, but felt we shouldn't shoot unless we found one in the records. A couple could have gone over 10 inches, but we felt it was early enough to be selective. Gene climbed a nearby hill taking his spotting scope, seeing if he could spot any movement of ibex—he got some exercise, anyway. The main idea of the hunt in this area is for the Nubian ibex. The rugged mountains all up and down this area parallel the coast. The map indicates some of them over 7,000 ft.*

*Everyone in good spirits—another party before dinner while planning the hunt tomorrow for ibex.*

*29 October*

*Up at 4 AM Good hearty breakfast with canned sausages, fried potatoes, corn flakes with powdered milk and plenty of crackers, cookies and jams, honey, Tang—both orange and grapefruit—coffee and tea. I joined Thornton for the day's ibex hunt—our gals stayed behind to catch up on their rest. Gene and Terri went another way at the other end of the range from where we went. We stopped by the nearby native village to pick up the chief, who was to be our local guide. His name is Homar; the name of his village is Melangweib—which is also the name of the nearby mountain that we are to hunt. It was 5 AM and started to break dawn. Had a half-hour drive to the backside of the mountain where we started.*

*A couple hours hike from the car and part way up the mountain, I spotted five ibexes near the top of the rugged mountain—our first sighting and exciting for all of us. One big male at least in the bunch, but they were so far away, it was hard to determine horn size.*

*The mountain is 5,458 feet high and they had to be 3,500 feet above us. We planned a stalk, complete with signals from a man that we could place part way up the mountain, but aborted the plan when the ibex seemed to vanish out of sight. We climbed toward the top up a canyon out of sight of the top. Later we saw three ibexes top over the ridge. Two of them had big horns—Duri estimated to be over 40 inches!*

*We continued clear to the top to one side always trying to keep our wind away from the ibex. Hours later, we topped a lower saddle of the ridge. The only approach to the top was another*

*climb through rocky shale up the backside of the mountain. No signs of the animals having crossed over. Being in the locality that we were, we were actually closer to Homar's village than to the car. Homar suggested we go on down to the village, call it quits, and send one of the boys for the car to come pick us up.*

*To quit, after climbing over 5,000 feet, is something a mountain hunter does not look lightly on. I instinctively said, "bull shit" and pointed over the top of the hill where we last saw the ibex—you just never leave a mountain without looking over the whole area, providing there is enough daylight to safely get you off the hill.*

*I didn't realize it, but my insistence not to quit was not taken lightly by either the Chief or Duri. We did go over the mountain and looked briefly for the ibexes. We saw where they had been feeding but we did look into the various little valleys, where the ibexes could be bedded down, before making the long trek down. It was really too tough a day for the first day of hunting, but rewarding for Thornton and me.*

*October 30*

*Up at 5 AM Gene and Zeca headed out for ibex again. They only hunted a half-day yesterday—saw a few females. Today they were prepared to stay late—or stay on the mountain all night if necessary. We decided to take it a little easier today and hunt Dorcas gazelles. We had a lot of fun and saw probably 50 or more gazelles.*

*We got one, but several other good bucks gave us the slip. Thornton shot one with his .22 magnum—broke its back and put it right*

🐫 **The total livelihood for the Kurbab natives was from their domestic herds of goats and dromedary camels.**

in Northern Africa—unlike the black Africans found in areas farther south and throughout the rest of Africa. The color of these fair-complexioned northern Africans would be more like the typical American blacks that mostly are crossbred and not entirely black.

The hair texture of these Fuzzi Wuzzis is not the kinky hair of other Africans, but a finer naturally tightly curled hair. Their features are fine and they are quite a handsome race. They are nomadic, living with their animal herds, and their habitat is controlled considerably by the availability of water—which is anything but plentiful. Their main herds are camels, the one-humped dromedaries, but also they have a lot of goats.

In the late afternoon, we went out again in a different direction farther out on the plains. We didn't see as many dorcas as this morning—maybe 20 or so. I collected one a little smaller than Thornton's. After seeing the size of the ones we took, 9¼ & 9¾ inches in length, we knew that we had seen several of 12 inches or more.

It seems apparent that most of the dorcas are found out in the plains. Our camp is located right in the small rocky foothills of some pretty rocky and high mountains. The area reminds me very much of the southern Arizona country where I was born. The rocky volcanic mountains rise suddenly from the plains—and there are a lot of them.

I've looked at several maps, some of them show an indication of some hills, and you can hear references to the Red Sea Hills. However, I don't refer to range after range of moun-

down. These antelope are very small, probably under 75 pounds live weight.

The natives in this area are one of the Atam Kurbab tribes. They look just like the Fuzzi Wuzzi tribes that they claim are farther to the north. Their skin is light textured, the same as that of the Arabian African varieties

Colleene and a Fuzi Wuzi (Kurbab tribe) looking over a Dorcas gazelle that I collected on the arid plains off the Red Sea.

tains with peaks of 7,274 feet (Mount Jebel Erba) and 6,952 feet (Jebel Oda) with most of the range averaging around 5,000 feet and running from Ethiopia almost all the way to Egypt, as "hills." It is a mountain range even though an occasional plain or desert does break it up.

Gene and Zeca got in by late afternoon without success on ibex. They hunted the north end of the mountains where Thornton and I were yesterday, Melengweib. We're camped on the dry river Ankilbau, which changes name to Ballolab, as it gets closer to the Red Sea, which is about 20 miles, as the crow flies. Our water comes from a well made right in the riverbed.

*31 October—Halloween!*

Up at 3:30—Cornflakes for breakfast and off by 4:15. The gals didn't go, as we were

going ibex hunting—tough. Both cars went to Homar's village as the plan was—and it was the chief's idea—to have a drive for ibex today.

Thornton, Gene, and I, along with Setel (our African substitute driver, interpreter, handyman) and Juma (helper and interpreter), got in Duri's Toyota and about a dozen Kurbabs got in Zeca's car and we were off to their selected spot. By daybreak, we were on foot up another rugged mountain. We paired off with Kurbabs to go to our respective areas to stand. I got an older gentleman and a young boy. We communicated well and planned on going beyond if no ibex came our way.

No ibex came our way, so after the Kurbabs made their drive around the opposite ridge, hollering at the top of their voices to scare any ibex in the canyon our way, we headed over to the other side of the canyon, in the direction of *the high ridge where the beaters were to go. We saw a lot of hyraxes in the rocks at the creek bottom, a large rodent-like animal more closely related to hoofed species. They say they are the only other member of the elephant family, but they are small like a marmot.*

*We hiked up to intercept the beaters, who were hollering all the time at the top of their voice. I didn't know why I was doing this, as I felt there could be no living animal left in the valley. I wasn't really expecting any ibexes to be here, but suddenly, I looked up and there was a magnificent ibex 150 yards ahead of me, looking straight on. I was puffing and threw a shell in the barrel as I dropped to the ground for support of the rifle. During the seconds required doing this, the ibex bolted over the ridge, and out of sight—all this in two or three seconds. I stayed put, thinking that he could reappear— but he didn't.*

*We were in a draw that headed up to where all the beaters were. My Kurbab sprinted up the steep rocky slope to tell the others of the ibex we saw. They had seen it as well, and it went over the hill they were on. On the way back down the draw, for all of the Kurbabs shouting and running around, they jumped a female ibex! It must have been holed up in a cave.*

*It proves that the ibex have learned to live with people and will not necessarily leave the area, but hide to a certain extent. On the way back toward camp, we detoured off the "beaten path" and collected a couple of nice Dorcas gazelles. In doing so, we found Thornton's 7mm to be shooting way to the left. Back at camp, bore sighting showed it to be two feet off at 100 yards!*

*Our cook arrived today—happy occasion! They can't find help and were trying to even have a cook flown up from Khartoum, but this one became available in Port Sudan, so was driven up here by the manager of Arous Village. We had a nice dorcas steak dinner and lots of booze to celebrate Halloween. We even went around "trick or treating" the various tents— mainly Colleene and Terri did it. Colleene made a makeshift Halloween decoration—found a round rock, painted eyes and mouth on it, and put a candle on top.*

*01 November*

*Short night with last night's partying. Up at 3:15 AM and to the village of Homar before 5. We always stop by to pick up local guides from the Atam Kurbab village. The tribe has joined forces with Nimerico Safaris—they sort of adopted one another. It's probably the only income these people receive, except trading some livestock. They are hard working and nice to be around. Of course, none of them speak English and only a few speak Arabic (the common language in North Sudan). Our communications are through the two Africans, Setel, and Juma, who are assistant drivers that have been brought up from Juba and who speak Arabic and English. They are both full-time employees of the safari company.*

*We went to the same area we hunted the first day, but hunted the lower foothills of Melangweib. We had the chief and two other Kurbabs. As we proceeded up the valley, the chief sent one, and later the other, up side canyons, while the rest of us went to an opening in a basin. Thornton, Duri, and Homar went one way,*

 Homar, the Chief of the Atam Kurbab village, Melangweib, and Chris share Thornton Snider's excitement of the first Nubian ibex collected.

*while Juma and I went to the other side. The idea of the other Kurbabs splitting off was to move any game from the ridges up our way.*

*Juma and I located ourselves on a ridge where I had a good place to glass the mountains all around us. I could see Thornton's group on a ridge on the opposite side of the basin. Shortly after, I heard a shot! I couldn't see what Thornton was shooting at, but I could see his second shot was directed to the other side of that ridge. Duri stood up to get my attention and motioned for us to come over, so I knew Thornton had an ibex.*

*Juma and I went the long way around looking into all the little valleys and over the top of the ridge—no signs of anything freshly having been in the basin at all. By the time we arrived, the others were gone. I looked around,*

*spotted a few drops of blood, and tracked it over to the entrails, so Thornton had his ibex. By late morning, we were back at the vehicle enjoying Thornton's success.*

*Gene and Zeca went to another part of the range, hunted all day, but without success. The gals—Colleene, Helen, and Terri—have been patiently relaxing around camp while we've been doing the strenuous ibex hunting. They've been helping on some of the chores around camp, since a few things weren't getting done, like some of the laundry. Also, they would be sure that the ice and cold water and cocktails were ready for our return. We were always extremely dry and thirsty by the time we got to camp. Our daily consumption of liquid has got to be at least two gallons each.*

*02 November*

We hunted ibex fairly near Melangweib village. Today Gene hunted with Thornton and me, as the chief said the area was better with more people hunting. Good thing, as Zeca got sick and couldn't leave the car—just laid there—had a malaria attack, he thought.

After a couple hours walking into a confined canyon, Gene spotted an ibex skylighted high on the ridge of a steep side canyon. We all stayed in the bottom of the draw as we climbed closer. In the draw there were several crystal-clear pools of water in the distance of about 50 yards—the water above and below that was all subterranean. This is the first surface water I had seen here and did it ever look inviting.

Now it was 7 AM and temperature in the 70s F, but it felt hotter as we climbed steadily toward the ridge where the ibexes were. We saw more ibexes over to the right of the earlier sighting. The wind was now coming down the draw—as a rule, the wind blows downhill during the night, and as it heats up, it starts blowing up the canyons. Therefore, it was still favorable for us to climb up under the ibex, never moving while they are in view because of their keen eyesight.

Gene's guide, who was carrying his rucksack full of gear, was way out in front and heading as fast as he could for the saddle right at the top of the draw.

I told Gene to catch up with him and take that position. Since we had seen a nice head or two on the right side of the ridge, I suggested Thornton and Duri go that way. Juma, the African assistant, and I took sort of a side-hill position between the others. I saw no sense in scaling the cliffy area anymore, as I would only expose myself to possibly being seen by the ibexes. I wanted Thornton and Gene to get the first and best chance, so I stopped on a good vantage point below the other two.

After getting ready—i.e. cleaning riflescope and binoculars and getting a comfortable position out of sight—I started glassing. Immediately I saw a big male ibex not 75 yards to the left of Gene, who had now gotten in position in some rocks on top of the ridge. This ibex was looking right at them and, obviously, they didn't see it.

I whistled to Gene but apparently, they didn't hear me. The ibex started running up and across the cliffs on the opposite side of the canyon from my position. I shouted. "Gene, above you."

He didn't hear and obviously did not see the ibex. Through my binoculars, I could see three ibexes heading for the top, although I couldn't see well as I was looking into the sun that had just risen over the top of the cliff, making it near impossible to make out the forms of the animals in the shadows.

I rested my rifle in position in hopes of getting a shot off before they disappeared completely. The sun shining directly into my scope eliminated any possibility of getting a clear shot. Fortunately, a large male ibex skylighted itself and stopped momentarily. In a split second, I swung the scope to position and squeezed off. The magnificent animal dropped instantly and rolled some 30 yards down the cliff, coming to rest in the rocks. It was a very long and lucky shot—something between 300 and 400 yards, no way of pacing it across the rugged canyon.

Thornton Snider poses with Chris and his Nubian ibex.

Then I saw Gene and his guide rush around the rocks to finally see the other two ibexes. Another male skylighted himself to Gene at about 200 yards. The five seconds that it posed, there was not enough time for Gene to get in position for the shot. The ibex left the area. The chief, who was now with the others, worked his way over to inspect my ibex.

Everyone stayed put on the mountain for about an hour to see if there was any other movement of game. Finally Juma and I went on up to where Gene was and then over to the ibex. It was a magnificent animal and one that I was very happy to add to my collection of ibexes from other parts of the world—I already had the Persian ibex, Himalayan ibex, Spanish ibex, and the Siberian ibex.

After skinning the specimen out for a life-size mount and cutting the meat in smaller pieces, we worked our way out of the mountains and to the car. Thornton and Duri tried coming out a different way, ended up in a deep box canyon, and had to backtrack in order to get out of it.

03 November—My Birthday!

Up and breakfast at 2 AM To get everyone moving, Thornton shot a volley of .22 shots in the air. Since we were running a little low on provisions and the fact that the three of us planned on hunting together again today, Zeca, Terri, and Colleene planned on going to Port Sudan on a shopping spree.

By 4:30 the hunters—the three of us and five Kurbabs—arrived in one Toyota jeep to our starting point. Because of the heat of the *day, both animal and man must move around during the cooler time. The ibexes are rarely seen after midmorning when they bed down in the caves and shadows. The temperature ranged upwards to 100°F by midday.*

*Before dawn, which is around 5 AM, we were well on our way walking the river bottom that led us into the mountains. By 7 AM, Gene, and Thornton split off to a rocky pass area, while a Kurbab and I went around the other side of a rocky peak. A couple of the Kurbabs were sent a different route earlier to move any ibex in the lower foothills into the rockier peaks where we went.*

*I positioned myself on a rocky ridge with a good vantage point over the adjoining areas. Soon I spotted four male ibexes grazing up my direction some 500 yards away. They stopped on a ridge opposite me, giving plenty of time to look them over through the binoculars. Two of them were as big as or slightly bigger than the one I took yesterday and the other two, a little smaller. I could have easily taken one of them, but I would not unless I found a decidedly bigger head. These ibexes are so similar in color to the terrain, that each time I took my eyes off them, I had a hard time picking them up again.*

*Soon I heard the echoes of shots coming from the opposite side of the mountain. I was happy and really hoping both Thornton and Gene connected with some really good heads. Shortly one of our Kurbab "beaters" could be seen coming from below. He scared the four ibexes I was watching into a canyon beneath me. I watched carefully all around and never saw them again. We motioned to the beaters to go through the area below us to scare them*

*out—but nothing. That is a perfect example of the protection they have in the habitat. Whether they hid in the rocks or caves, or whether they slipped out of the area using hidden draws and their perfect camouflage to elude us is unknown, but is an example of the great sport that is offered in their pursuit.*

*We hiked around the mountains and were intercepted by one of the Kurbabs that happily told us the others got two really good ibexes. I met Thornton and we went up in the cliffs together and admired his fine head. Gene's was higher and around the cliff a ways. Shortly after we had Thornton's ibex skinned and ready, Gene, and crew appeared with his, likewise skinned and ready.*

*We all arrived late, as did the gals from Port Sudan, but it was birthday party time. They all got together and bought me a Galabia, typical man's gown. In addition, Colleene got me one of the knives that every man wears on his arm. I have collected knives from everywhere, so I was very happy with my present. Terri, Colleene, and Helen made me "King for a Day." The booze flowed freely and Furuk, the cook, prepared an elegant dinner. This is the second time I celebrated my birthday with Thornton, as he was on a hunt with me in the Soviet Union two years ago on my 50th birthday.*

*04 November*

*Everyone is satisfied with their ibex, even though we all had two permits each. We have four dorcas on our license, so today we all went out looking for them. They are never found in large groups—one day we saw about eight running together, but they soon split off into groups of two or three. Most of the time there would be two together—male and female or female with young.*

*This appeared to be their breeding season, yet on two occasions, we saw very young babies. Sometimes we drove 10 or 15 minutes without seeing any dorcas. They seem to instinctively scatter themselves, no doubt because of the normally arid conditions and sparse feed. They apparently do not depend on or normally get any surface water, but getting it all from dew and vegetation, as is the case with many desert animals.*

*05 November*

*Chief Homar of the Atam Kurbab tribe visited us on our last day in camp. The chief was a very pleasant companion on the entire hunt, as were all of the tribesmen that accompanied us. There were only about 175 members of the tribe scattered over an area of about 40 square miles, mostly in and around the Melangweib Mountain range. We presented the chief with a "Bakshi" a wristwatch brought along for that purpose. He learned quickly to read it and was very proud.*

*After some more gazelle hunting—both Gene and Thornton collected another one—We left in the afternoon for Arous Village to spend the night. An excellent dinner was prepared for us in the beautiful open-air lounge area. We were out of vodka and scotch, so Colleene purchased some at $37 per bottle! This, being a Moslem country, doesn't have liquor stores, so what little is available comes very dearly.*

*After dinner, we put up a Sudanese pound each (about U.S. $1.25) in a pool for a hermit crab race. The shells were numbered, all turned*

*loose in the center of a circle, and Thornton's speedy little crab won the pot by crossing the line first, after he put some Canadian whiskey on it.*

## TIME LAPSE

*07 November*

*After a morning of shopping, we caught a nonscheduled turboprop flight to Khartoum at 1 PM that had been put on to take the overload of passengers. Gassim and Owen Rutherford met us and settled us once again in the Khartoum Hilton Hotel. Owen presented us with the bad news that the Barbary sheep had been poached out in the area where we planned to hunt next. In the absence of a hunting program in the area, the locals considered the sheep useless and wiped them out. A leisurely evening, ending with a fine dinner of Nile perch in the hotel's Ivory Room, one of the city's finest restaurants.*

*08 November*

*Shopping and taking care of some business matters with Gassim took up most of the day. We were running a few days ahead of schedule, so Colleene and I decided to go on to Kenya to spend two days there before continuing on to Johannesburg in South Africa. The others changed their flights to return home right away via London.*

*09 November*

*Everyone up at 1 AM to be leaving the hotel by 2 AM Their flight got off on time at 4 AM, but ours was 3½ hours later at 8 AM—I would have liked to have spent the extra time in that comfortable bed in the Hilton rather than the* stuffy departure lounge of the not-so-modern airport!

The Sudan Airlines Boeing 707 was a smooth and comfortable three-hour flight. We crossed the equator just before arriving in Nairobi. I couldn't believe the airport. The last time I was in Nairobi was in 1966. At that time, a small stuffy airport, but friendly and very African. Now, a big metropolitan airport complete with boarding docks, to accommodate the big volume of flights as well as the jumbo aircraft.

The concourses were filled with every imaginable "duty free" shop. The taxi ride (less than 15 minutes) to the Nairobi Hilton, however, was just as beautiful as ever. Blooming flowers of every color lined the roadway—but it was rainy and cool—right here on the equator. The city was now a "City"—no grass-thatched huts on the outskirts (at least en route), many new high-rise buildings, and hotels. The shops were not the same either.

Kenya has vast quantities of wildlife, yet new government regulations forbid selling of any animal parts. Therefore, instead of the beautiful carved ivory, animal skin purses, and apparel, the shops are loaded with wood, stone and cloth items—not nearly as exciting and certainly not authentic.

A lot of the items we looked at were garments from Taiwan, stone carvings from South Africa, etc. However, there is still some good wood art and a few other souvenirs available. The animal parts are now going to waste, as far as the retail and export markets are concerned. The story is that the World Bank, that was loaning big sums to Kenya, is anti hunting and insisted that all hunting and animal products be eliminated.

## TIME LAPSE

### Fantasy Island and Much More

Transkei is not an island, but it is reminiscent of the TV series of the late 20th Century, Fantasy Island. Had the series been filmed here, they would have had a dozen more beautiful natural habitats to work with than Hawaii's Kauai Island. The beautiful terrain, numerous rivers and waterfalls right on Africa's Wild Coast, along with exotic wildlife, make this probably the single most enjoyable destination for a sportsman or nature loving person. The Klineburgers, having developed the reputation of advising, and developing new hunting programs in Africa, were contacted by the Transkei delegates to help them get started. Chris and Colleene answered the calls and here is how it all started from the continuation of Chris' journal.

### 11 November

Off to the airport by 7 AM for scheduled 9 AM flight. British Airways 747 was running one hour late but we relaxed in their first class lounge. The 3¾ hours flight to Johannesburg was mostly cloudy. We made an early connection to Durban on an A300 jumbo Airbus getting us in 1½ hours ahead of time.

Since we were uncertain of whether we would be met or not, I called Fred Holl, who is the radio contact for Mkambati Game Reserve. Fred informed me that Phillip Hommes was *on his way to meet our scheduled flight and described his appearance and vehicle so we would know what to look for.*

*Finally after a long wait—and no Phillip Hommes—a young girl asked if I was waiting to be met by someone. She introduced herself as Fredericka Bezuidenhout, Phillip's fiancé. Phillip was about ready to leave Mkamabati when it had been announced that our originally scheduled flight was two hours late. Phillip had car trouble and had asked Fredericka to meet our flight. She escorted us to the beautiful city of Durban and on to the new and luxurious Maharani Hotel in which Phillip had reserved us a gorgeous suite. It is huge, very deluxe and overlooking the entire waterfront of Durban, the ocean breakers and the ships anchored off shore.*

*Fredericka joined us for cocktails in the suite and later Phillip called and eventually made it to join in "to settle the trail dust." He then reserved dinner at the British Middle-East Indian Sporting and Dining Club. We had a wonderful evening getting filled in on much of the history of South Africa and especially the plans for their Game Reserve and Resort. Fredericka and Phillip treated us to some excellent domestic (Cape Province) white wine while ordering typical and well-prepared curry dishes—the specialty of the house.*

*12 November*

*In Durban today to see around the town and give Phillip a chance to get his Toyota Land Cruiser fixed. We checked out the beautiful sandy beaches, shops, and town in general. Had very American food today—breakfast, Eggs*

*Benedict and lunch, cheeseburger, but Colleene had more curry.*

*Fredericka works in a bank, so in the evening, joined with us once again for cocktails in the suite. Then off to the Bali Hai Restaurant, next door to the Maharani, for dinner. This restaurant was said to have been seen in Siam (Thailand) by the Director of Sun International Hotels, who, in turn, purchased it—had it dismantled and rebuilt in its present location. After a couple of "Cane and Cokes," we had a delicious dinner of barbequed ribs. To bed at a respectable time for early departure tomorrow to Transkei.*

*13 November*

*Met Phillip for breakfast—Eggs Benedict again, but split one order with Colleene, which was just right. Checked out of hotel, loaded gear in the Toyota Land Cruiser pickup and on the road. Stopped at a meat processing plant for the meat supply for the Lodge in an outlying area. Then proceeded to stop at wholesale vegetable market, discount liquor store, bait and hardware stores, etc., in every town south of Durban as we proceeded to Port Edward on good freeways/paved roads to the border of Natal and Transkei. Stopped there for a bite to eat and radio (C.B.) contact with Mkambati Game Reserve—and a visit with Marge Holl (who has been my phone/radio contact right along with the fellows at Mkambati)—nice girl.*

*That was the end of modern South Africa. We were now in a primitive Native State of Transkei, which is inhabited by the Pondo Tribe and was a Native Trust Area (like our North American Indian Reservations) that got its inde-*

*pendence October 26, 1976 and is now acting as an independent country—a Republic of South Africa. The distance (the way the crow flies) is only 25 miles to where we were going, but had to go 190 kilometers westward to Bizana and on to Magusheni, southward to Flagstaff and then easterly to the coast to Mkambati Game Reserve—all over rough dirt roads and arrived after dark.*

*We were greeted at the lodge by Nic Venter and Philip Elliott and the African staff and soon resting in the comfortable lounge area with a cane drink. Phil had radioed in on the C.B. about a half hour out. We had recognized Nic from 1973, when we had briefly met him in Luanda, Angola. He was there looking into a fishing operation at the time and we, along with our son Kent, were returning from a safari in Mozambique.*

*A cable had been awaiting us, asking us to hurry home as soon as possible. That kind of message is highly irritating, as it does not give any idea of trouble or not and can mentally ruin a trip. Therefore, I came up with the idea of radioing Marge Holl and having her telephone my office, since it was morning in Seattle (ten hours difference). Within an hour, she had the office on the phone and relayed information that appeared to need at least one of us for signing some papers before Thanksgiving—so we stayed on schedule.*

*We then sat down to a beautifully prepared lobster dinner, fresh from the Indian Ocean, on which we were now settled. The Elliott's are part of the staff here—an energetic couple. Another guest J.P. Klover, a friend of Nic's, who was here to help with fishing gear and fishing methods—both sport and netting. He is experimenting*

*with dragnets and gill nets to see how they can catch quantities of fish in order to feed volumes of guests, as the place develops.*

*We sat up visiting and learning about the plans for the development of the Game Reserve, while socializing over much cane liquor, which is made from sugar cane and thus is in the rum family of drinks. It has not got the sweet taste of rum—more closely resembles vodka and is likewise clear. Cane is inexpensive—about $5 a quart. To bed by 1:30 AM—time flies when with good company.*

*14 November*

*We were awakened at 7 AM with coffee in bed, served by one of the African servants, Doris. No one much interested in breakfast, so I had some bananas and grapefruit. The weather was sunny and beautiful for the day's inspection of the reserve. We took two Land Cruisers—Colleene riding with Nic and me with Phillip. They tuned on their C.B. radios so that we could talk as we traveled.*

*Hours of driving only revealed a portion of the most beautiful place. Picture a South Sea island and a beautiful African savanna and you would have an idea of what this area was like. It has several rivers that start in the higher elevations (highest probably 1,500 feet) of the rolling terrain and cascade their way down to the ocean. Each river has its own characteristics. The Mkambati River, about in the center of the property, is the most beautiful, coming through dense gorges—studded with palms, wild banana trees, and tropical vegetation of all types—and cascading over a series of falls that end in a beautiful cove in the Indian Ocean.*

**The Mkambati River makes its final debut as it cascades into the Indian Ocean.**

*The Mtentu River forms the northern boundary of the property, is more like a long narrow lake, and is tidewater for many miles of its length from the ocean. We cruised it in an outboard boat, which gave us the feeling of sailing up the Amazon River.*

*The Mgwegwe River is quite small and reminds one of a northwest mountain stream. It ends in a magnificent sandy ocean beach in a cove with breakers rolling continuously in.*

*The Msikaba River forms the southern border of the reserve and forms deep canyons that only differ from the Grand Canyon by its smallness and outstanding beauty. Both the Mtentu and Msikaba Rivers are the sanctuary for the Pondo cocoa palm trees, which grow no other place in the world than on their respective northern banks.*

*The easterly boundary is ten miles of what has to be the most beautiful shoreline of the Indian Ocean, having many coves, white sandy beaches, and many miles of jagged, rocky, and picturesque stretches with the surf continuously pounding away.*

*As one goes inland westerly from the ocean, the rolling grass-rich land rises lazily mile after mile. Each time one crests out, a new and different, magnificent view reveals itself—savannas, forests, hills, waterfalls, wildlife—each one a new experience, another chapter in a book.*

*The wildlife varied greatly—from a lone reedbuck bounding out of the bush, a small family of giraffes merging from an acacia forest, vast herds of blesboks, wildebeests, elands, gemsboks, hartebeests, greater kudus, impalas, spring-*

boks, baboons, duikers, and more. The day was mind-boggling! It was like a fairy tale. I can't believe the potential of a total adventure that this place can offer hunting and/or vacationing.

About midday, a Norman Brittan Islander airplane slipped into the airstrip dropping off a group of developers who are to establish a deluxe lodge to accommodate the influx of clientele that will soon start coming to enjoy and hunt this reserve. They were Cyril Manthe, architect; Charles Wilsenach, government architect; Alan Wilson, Umtata Barclay bank manager, Americo David and Charlie Mather, builders and hotel managers. A thunderstorm prevented them from leaving after they made their inspection of the site, causing them to be guests of the lodge for the night—enjoyable!

*15 November*

Coffee at 6 AM Cloudy and cool. Yesterday it was warm and sunny 'til about 4 PM when thundershowers started up, as it did the day before on the way here. It is now late spring, going into summertime, which is also the wet season. Being south of the equator, the seasons are the opposite from ours in North America. The more inland and the closer to the equator, the more predominant are the rains (monsoons). Transkei is a long way from the equator, which is 31 degrees north.

We went fishing in the surf at the mouth of the Mkambati River, which is one of the most scenic views I have ever seen—the Mkambati makes its "final debut," cascading over broad rocky falls into the ocean. A school of porpoises was at the mouth of the cove when we arrived. Phillip Elliott was our guide, who is very proficient at this type of fishing. A very skilled African assistant by the name of Vāsaline, helped. A misty rain, along with wind and an incoming tide, did not make for ideal fishing conditions. Even at that, we caught two blacktails, two shad, a small milk shark, and a barbel eel. The porpoises may have scared most of the fish out of the cove.

Later in the day, we hunted bushy areas near the coast and not far from the lodge. We got trophy class specimens of both reedbuck and grey duiker. These animals are very elusive and hard

« We could drive right to the specimen. From left, Phillip Hommes, Chris, and Nic Venter.

☞ **Colleene with a fine reedbuck taken right near the beach of the Indian Ocean.**

☞ **The author and Phillip Elliott with a fine blesbok.**

to see because of the high grass and little forest and bush areas that they live in. The rainy weather kept the plane grounded for most of the day until the weather started lifting in midafternoon. We ended the day with a late dinner of blacktail and shad fish caught this morning—another great adventurous day with wonderful people.

*16 November*

Because of the tremendous gorges cut out by the rivers, Elliott and I decided to go on foot to see more of the terrain and check out the wildlife off the beaten path. We left late morning after I ran a Klineburger Brothers, Inc. "school of taxidermy."

The staff knew the basic skinning methods, but new in the business, they needed help on the finer points, so I went through the complete procedure for the life-size skinning (duiker) and shoulder mount skinning (reedbuck). Also, showed them the proper use of the Wyoming knife—something they had never seen before. We had brought them a "skinning kit" which includes the Wyoming knife, two other knives, sharpening stone, skinning instructions, all contained in a case, and made up by our taxidermy division.

We drove to the Mkambati River and started hiking along the north bank. Two Africans accompanied us, bolo knives in hand. The river bottom is forested—"jungle" would be a more accurate description. We stayed as close to the river as possible, which wasn't very close most of the time, because of the rapidly rising terrain and portaging the waterfalls. The goal was to end up in the main north fork of the river where I had spotted the very top of a waterfall, through my binoculars the first day out. None of the staff had ever walked the river before.

We hacked our way through patches of jungle, climbed cliffs and, in general, went through some of the most varied, beautiful and interesting terrain imaginable. We saw thickets of yellow wood trees, an extremely valuable hardwood, as well as an occasional stink wood tree (even more valuable). There were many species of wild orchid, some of which were in bloom. The openings were studded with tree ferns, protected species. We also saw cydad palms—a prehistoric palm that is very rare. This area would be a botanist's paradise.

As we worked our way along, we mapped out a trail that could be used for horses and trekking alike, for hunting as well as sightseeing. We checked the animal signs and saw plenty of tracks and droppings of duikers, reedbucks, and bushbucks. We saw monkeys and baboons. I tried a very long shot at a baboon, which I missed. The Africans love the meat and I wanted a life-size skin. Because of the north wind, our smell was always going the wrong way, and that, along with the middle of the day timing, we didn't see any of the elusive, forest-dwelling big game.

By late afternoon, we reached the falls and what a beautiful sight it was! Even though this is the end of the dry season, there was a fair amount of water, which cascaded some 150 feet down into a big, deep pool. The opposite bank was studded with tree palms making a scene that didn't even seem real. Phillip said, with my persistence in discovering this spot, it had to be named "Klineburger Falls."

We had brought a walkie-talkie along and the last hour or so we had been talking to Nic and Colleene, who were to pick us up with their Land Cruiser. They were coming in from the top and with the use of the radio and firing a couple of shots we found one another. We figured out a way that we could drive within several hundred yards of the top of the falls, so there was enough daylight left to show Nic and Colleene our great discovery.

Back by dark to the lodge where Hommes and Leon Heunis showed us their afternoon fish catch—a jewfish (cod) two shad and a black tail. Leon is a photographer, writer and government worker and a good friend of Nic and Phillip.

*17 November*

Phillip Elliott and I started the day out early (5:30 AM) stalking through some of the upper forests looking for bushbucks but we saw no more than some tracks. This is the southernmost range for the bushbuck and they are very elusive and probably not too plentiful. The thick forests and abundance of feed, along with the fact they are nocturnal, made them a very difficult animal to hunt.

We then went on to photograph some plains-game and must have seen up to 500 at one time. Our take for the day was another grey duiker, a record-class reedbuck and a jackal.

In the afternoon, we all went fishing down at the beach, which we overlook from the lodge—about a half-mile away. They took down a barbeque and a complete bar set up. What luxury—having an African guide bait your hook and one of the girls bringing drinks while surfcasting in this beautiful place.

**The Mkambati River cascades 150 feet down cliffs to a serene pool. Because of my persistence to discover it, they named it "Klineburger Falls."**

They barbecued three kinds of fresh fish and lobster. What a day! We fished the outgoing tide and only in the late afternoon were we able to get far enough out in the rocks to have any luck. I caught a nice "salmon," about 15 pounds. It is not in the same family as our northern salmon. They also call it a cob, so I can't really find out what it really is—but among other things, it is a real scrapper.

🗣 **Chris with a 15-pound "salmon," locally called cob.**

*18 November*

*Up at regular time, 6 AM, with one of the Pondo girl servants awakening us with coffee, as usual. Of all the plainsgame that was here, the blesbok was the most desirable to both Colleene and I. Our hunting efforts till now have been primarily for "bush" game, which are a lot tougher to hunt because of the fact they stay in the small forest areas during the day and feed in the nearby grassy areas during the night. There-*

fore, they have to be kicked out of the bush in order to see them.

The "Plainsgame" generally feed during the day and use their senses, including very keen eyesight, for protection. They also usually run in herds, unlike the bush game, which are usually in singles or pairs. Most of the plainsgame was bunching up now and at times, we saw three or four different herds of various species all running together. The female were now dropping their young—what a great sight! While we were watching a herd of blesboks, we noticed one female that had lagged behind the moving herd in some thick grass. At closer inspection, we noticed a little wobbly baby trying to get to its feet. Seconds earlier, we would have seen it born. The mother ran off, trying to draw us away from the scene of the baby. She then trotted away and within three minutes of birth, the young one was trotting as well. On another occasion, a female hartebeest ran to get out of our path, while her baby, who was not more than five days old, came from behind and passed her speeding mother! It's amazing what nature does for the nonpredator animals, while predators, of which man is one, take a long time for their young to develop.

A few days ago, we saw the first young to appear. Within another month, these herds will increase by at least half again as many animals. The population of game will have to be kept in balance by cropping through the hunting program.

We worked with the skinners for a while, making the main cuts, and then letting them do the basic work. I inspected the skins from the other day and found they had not done a thorough job, so now we will constantly watch the progress.

In the afternoon, we saddled some horses to hunt the bush area close to the ocean. Colleene, along with Phillip and Nic went to the surf for fishing about five miles from camp. Elliott and I rode the horses and met the others at the beach by late evening. We only saw one animal in our little venture, which was an outstanding reedbuck. It would have been easy to take, but we didn't want any more of that particular specimen.

It seems that hunting by horseback will be a good approach, as, in this case, the game did not spook badly. The Africans here use horses extensively. This is the only place in Africa that I recall any blacks riding horses.

We arrived at the fishing site at twilight. They had a small variety of fish. The "bar" was set up so we had Cane & Coke to "settle the trail dust." Colleene and Nic got swamped by a wave, so took off for the lodge. The horses were turned loose to be picked up by the boys in the morning.

*19 November*

It started raining during the night and was a drizzling mist. After a leisurely breakfast and visiting, Phillip and I went out for a drive in some area where I had not been. We went inland and northward in the higher parts of the reserve, and ended up in a beautiful gorge called Vulture Gorge, whose name comes from the hundred or so Cape vultures that inhabit the cliffs of the upper Mtentu River. The Cape vulture is said to be almost extinct and therefore this reserve will be a good sanctuary for them.

We then followed an old track back toward the ocean. This road, as explained by Phillip, will be the main road into the site of a hotel that will be built on the bluffs at the mouth of the Mtentu. They will start the road construction after the rainy season, around March. The road led us near "Klineburger Falls," so we crossed over the hills in four-wheel drive to within walking distance and hiked on down through the forest, so that he could see it once again.

We then proceeded on down near the ocean and took the improved road back to the lodge, making about a four hour circuit—taking in about a third of the reserve. The late afternoon, after a delicious meal of lobster and all the trimmings, Phillip Elliott, "J.P." Kolver and I fished the outgoing tide in the bay below the lodge. J.P. is a fine old South African who was quite a legend in his day and one of the pioneers of the area. He lives near Cape Town and was an invited guest by Nic and Phillip. He was always happy and added life to the occasion when present. I caught three shad and one mullet—good evening's fishing. Business talks 'til the yawns got too frequent and one by one we faded off to the bedrooms—our last night in beautiful Transkei.

The Mkambati Game Reserve has an unusual background. The area was set aside some 20 years ago. On it was a leper colony and an agricultural test area for cattle. It is about 100 square miles of rolling terrain completely covered with lush grasslands, spotted with forests, especially in the river gorges where they get to jungle proportions. In the gorges themselves, there are vast areas that have been unexplored, as far as known, in the past 20 years.

The whole of the Transkei coastline is famously known in Africa, and by sailors throughout the world, as the "Wild Coast." This 150-mile stretch of predominantly rocky shoreline lies right in the path of ships, coming from the Indian Ocean and going around the Cape. Many a careless ship met its fate along the Wild Coast, the remains of which still lie there on the ocean floor. Just outside the bay below this lodge lies the wreckage of a Portuguese warship, the St. Joâ, in 30 feet of water off Msikaba Island. The wreck took place in 1562, ten solid bronze cannons have been recovered, and there still remain 19 more—a great chance for scuba diving expeditions.

A few miles up the coast is the steel hull of a Korean steamship that ended up on the rocks more than 20 years ago. Some of the old-timers (Pondos) around here remember the incident and tell about the funny little people with slanted eyes that abandoned the ship. They were all afraid of being massacred and ended up running off in all directions, never to be seen again by the locals.

The coastline has many beautiful coves and sandy beaches. The fishing in the deep sea off Natal, the republic to the north, and in Cape Province to the south, is very tightly restricted because of the heavy populations there—especially whites. In Transkei, however, there are no fishing regulations and no commercial fishing at present.

The Transkei got its name when this mysterious land was discovered and is named after the transverse of the Kei River, which is the southern boundary of the country. The northern boundary is the Mtamvuna River. The high

☉ **The remains of a Korean ship that wrecked on the rocks of South Africa's Wild Coast.**

*mountain escarpment running northeasterly forms the inland boundary. The whole of Transkei is a Native Trust area (like a huge Indian reservation) and always belonged to the native Africans. No whites ever owned land here. Three years ago, October 26, 1976, Transkei received its independence and is a separate country, unlike most of the republics and provinces of South Africa.*

*The development of this game reserve is one of the projects of the new government. The leper colony has been phased out and is only occupied by a few cured lepers and a basic staff. Within the next years, the facilities will be vacated completely and taken over by the reserve. There is no contamination of leprosy and has not been for many a year.*

*The agricultural experimental station will likewise be abandoned. Cattle, crowding out the game, ranged this area heavily. This was probably helped along by a lot of poaching of wildlife by the "cowboys."*

*Because of the leper colony and livestock operation, a considerable amount of money has been put into this one general area of the reserve—a lot of well-constructed buildings remain in good structural condition.*

*The lodge, in which we are staying, was beautifully built from sandstone blocks coming from the surrounding area. Nic and Phillip had it remodeled, as they did many of the other buildings in this particular complex, which is far removed from the hospital area. This complex was for administrative personnel and*

At the lodge, top from left, Nic Venter and Phillip Hommes along with Phillip Elliott and the Klineburgers look over their selection of specimens for their collections: reedbucks, blesboks, and duikers.

guests, so it turned out to be perfect facilities for this new operation.

Nic Venter and Phillip Hommes are working with the Transkei government to properly establish the entire reserve for wildlife, but to also turn it into a much-needed industry for the country. The government on a 35-year plan supplies the land and developments. Nic and Phillip are developing it to be used for hunting, photo safaris, fishing and vacationing in general for what it has to offer—and it offers plenty.

They moved here in January 1979 and have already done a tremendous amount. To begin with, they burned the entire reserve (grass that is). It was overgrown with matted old grass,

making for very poor feed for the wildlife. They remodeled the buildings in this complex. They built a network of excellent dirt roads. And, most important, have been bringing in much more wildlife to build the herds back up, as well as to add new species that were not found in this particular area.

Until now, they've put in approximately 1,500 animals and intend to keep bringing in more. They built a retaining fence across a section of the property to keep the animals (wild) from wandering into open native lands (where they would be instantly poached off) and to keep cattle from wandering into the wildlife habitat, as well as to keep poachers out.

*They are now in the final planning stages of their first exclusive hotel, the construction on which will start in about one month—the completion expected in about one year. This hotel will only have 20 units (10 single and 10 double), but will be exclusive—things like each unit having it's own swimming pool (fresh water), its own sauna, its own bar (free liquor) and the plan is to include everything with no way for a person to spend additional money while here, except gift purchases in a gift shop or trophy fees on some of the animals taken while hunting.*

*The hotel complex will be beautifully located on the bay at the mouth of the Mtentu River, right on the north boundary of the reserve.*

*A second hotel is already on the drawing board, which will be constructed at the mouth of the Mkambati River, overlooking the cascading waterfalls coming into the Indian Ocean.*

*A new airstrip will be built in a convenient location near the coast and strategically located for the hotels. Private aircraft will fly in all guests strictly on a "Fantasy Island" approach. They will have their own Immigration, which is a requirement in this independent country of Transkei. Much more can be said about the plans and the potential of this area, but there is not enough room in this book to describe it all—and there are no words that can effectively describe the beauty and mysteries of the area.*

*20 November*

*The day we have all not been looking forward to—the time of departure from the wonderful "Chapter in our Book." Oelleka had*

*the girls make fish cakes for breakfast from the shad I caught last night. Of course, we had the full line of food with them—scrambled eggs, bacon, fried tomatoes, and freshly baked bread.*

*The finalization of our business talks were sandwiched in, whenever possible. Our relationship and reason for being here was to exchange ideas as modeling the future of the game reserve, along with the resort and hunting program. We were brought here as experts in the hunting and travel field as fully the guests of Phillip and Nic. We finalized the details necessary for the 1980 hunting program and established the basis for the resort and future hunting program for 1981 onwards. It was agreed that we would be the general agents for the hunting in Transkei, but left open for the resort business in general.*

*We measured all the trophies for an on-going log of animals taken at the reserve. Colleene and I are the first hunters to ever hunt here from outside of Transkei—an honor that we are very proud of. Our chartered aircraft, a Cessna 310, piloted by Gary, a friend of Nic and Phillip arrived late morning. A last snack of lobster and fish cakes, along with the official Transkei drink, Cane and Coke, completed our stay at the lodge. Everyone accompanied us to the airport—even Doris, the #1 African servant.*

*The difficulty of goodbyes has never been harder for me. We know that we can't repay the kind of hospitality that Phillip and Nic have displayed, so we can only hope our departure has only partially made it a reciprocal acknowledgement and that we can be a good service to this great project that these chaps have undertaken.*

Departure at 12:30, Gary flew us past the lodge and along the waterfront for our last view of the Wild Coast and the great panorama of the rising landscape of the Mkambati Game Reserve.

32 hours later, we arrived in Seattle after an A300 Airbus (jumbo) flight from Durban to Johannesburg; South African Airlines Boeing 747 flight to New York, with a fueling stop at Ilha do Sal on an island off West Africa, then a Northwest Airlines 747 nonstop flight to Seattle.

It has been a great month from one extreme of Africa to the other—an unforgettable experience with great people in fabulous countries.

# CHAPTER 5

# Rwanda

*Known only for "Gorillas in the Mist" and tribal warfare*

I had fond memories of Uganda and being here in Rwanda reminded me very much of Uganda because of its beauty and abundance of game.

Rwanda is one of Africa's smallest countries, about the size of Maryland. It can hardly be found on the map. It—along with another tiny country, Burundi—are nestled between two of Africa's largest countries: Tanzania and Zaire (formerly Belgium Congo). Rwanda is heavily populated and one of the recognized critical problems of the country. There are 250 people per square mile of land and water combined. Except for the Reserves and National Parks, the country appears to be totally farmed or utilized for other industrial purposes. There is hardly a flat piece of ground in the entire country—it is either hills or mountains.

The farming is done all by hand and with difficulty, being on side hills and often very steep. Banana shambas stand out more than any other crop, because of the size of trees and the fact that everyone has them. Sorghum that appears like cornfields also stands out, but almost every other type of vegetable and fruit that grow in tropical or semi-tropical climate are grown here. Potatoes are plentiful and these make the best french fries, served with most of the meals we have had.

The earth is red in color and seems to have the food value needed to bless this country with a surplus of food. In fact, it is said that they support 450 people per square mile by its food production, resulting in a lot of export.

The country is blessed with a lot of water as well. Lake Kivu on the west boundary is 65 km long. In the east are many lakes, a good many of which are in the Akagera Reserve Park. There are many rivers, as every valley seems to have a stream or river.

Rainfall is abundant here. There has not been a day since we've been here that it hasn't rained. This is just south of the equator, where rains are not usually Monsoon type, but more frequent. Mornings have usually been dry and the rains come in the heat of the day and normally last less than an hour, then it clears up. The minimum elevation here is over 5,000 feet.

Fourteen years after the end of the tribal warfare between neighboring Burundi, under the able guidance of President Juvenal Habyarimana, the country was peaceful and prospering. In 1987, Bert and Brigitte Klineburger and Leonard and Hilda Milton, representing People To People Sports Committee, were the first to explore the hunting possibilities of Rwanda.

On that historic hunt, Bert collected "The Princess," Rwanda's record-size Cape buffalo, which Klineburger Taxidermy offered to make a full size mount for prominent public display. In 1988, the second safari was attended by Chris and Colleene Klineburger, accompanied by Robert and Beckie Chisholm, at which time Chris and Colleene mounted The Princess on location in Kigali, capital of Rwanda.

Just as Klineburger Worldwide Travel was ready to send hunters on a regular basis to Rwanda in 1990, civil war broke out between the Tutsi and Hutu tribes. President Habyarimana was killed and a carefully planned genocide by the extremist Hutu Power movement took place. Almost a million Tutsis and moderate Hutus were slaughtered, and 3 million more fled to Uganda and Zaire. Needless to say, this was another case of wildlife programs succumbing to political unrest. The following is Chris's journal of the last safari to take place in over 50 years in Rwanda, except for "TIME LAPSE" that advance to a later time.

*01 November (I arrived in Brussels after business meetings in Moscow, Russia)*

*Up early to transfer to Moscow's Shmeretyevo airport for my Aeroflot connection to Brussels. Our 727-like Tu-154 Russian built jet got us in Brussels on time. There I met my wife, Colleene, along with Bob and Beckie Chisholm who were checked in some four hours earlier at the Novotel Hotel at the airport.*

*After a little freshening up, our good friends Jacques and Micheline Henrijean fetched us at the hotel. They were very good clients of ours for many years and lived here.*

*So the red carpet was rolled out for us. Our first stop was for dinner at the Chez Leon, a great old (founded in 1912) typical Belgium restaurant in the old part of town—complete with cocktails, Belgium wine, and wild hare for the main course. Then a walk around Central Square, whose exquisite architecture dated back to the 1600s—probably something that would be extremely difficult to build in this era.*

Then they drove us around the various parts of this historic city, including the Brussels International Trade Mart near the former fairgrounds for the 1958 World's Fair. On it is the molecular-looking Atomium, which is a space age looking structure with globular shaped rooms suspended in space with connecting tubes containing elevators or escalators.

Within each globe (or molecule) is a two-story structure with exhibits, observatories, or restaurants. Micheline's father was a famous architect and the one that designed and built the Atomium. He died just a few months ago while Micheline was hunting bongo in the Central African Republic.

Jacques then took us to their beautiful home in an outlying area, where we had drinks and viewed their great trophy room. It was a separate building from their house. The complex was several rooms with an African motif—rustic hand-hewn wooden beams with bamboo thatching on the gabled ceiling that gave the effect of a grass-thatched roof.

They apologized continuously about the "run-down" condition, since only a few months before they donated a wildlife wing to the Royal Museum in Brussels and thus most of their full mounts, as well as many of their mounts of exotic trophies from around the world, left openings in their display.

Jacques then took us to the airport in time to catch our 10:50 PM Sabina flight to Rwanda—a great day.

## 02 November

We flew all night, lost another two hours on the clock and arrived at an intermediate stopover in Entebbe, Uganda, at 0830. We circled over huge Lake Victoria and had a good view of the beautiful savannas and bush of Uganda on our approach. What a great sight and it brought back wonderful memories to Colleene and me, where we had safaris and a business over 25 years before.

A 50-minute flight on the DC10 got us circling Kigali and once we penetrated the cloud layer that prevented our view between Entebbe and here, we saw the rolling hills covered with shambas (farm settlements) and the rich lushness of equatorial Africa. We had just crossed over the equator on this flight segment.

We quickly went through immunization check and by that time, the luggage was coming off the conveyor in this modern airport. The customs people were very politely looking through a few of our bags, which appeared to be more routine than worrying about what was in our luggage.

Just then, "Victor" Ngezayo Kambale introduced himself to us. He was one of our hosts for our stay in Rwanda—our main host to take us on our entire safari. "Safari" is the Swahili word for trip, usually connected with holiday and not necessarily to do with wildlife.

With Victor was Athanase Nyamacumu, a representative of Bureau of Tourism and National Parks, which encompasses their game department. At this point, our firearms were separated from us, as they had to be taken by Customs and later checked by the security people. Our gear was promptly loaded in a three-seater van. The gals rode to town in the van with Athanase and the driver, while Bob and I rode in Victor's Mercedes.

*The drive was a short 15 minutes, winding through the hills and valleys through shambas of bananas, beans, corn and every crop imaginable growing in the red earth, typical of East Africa. We pulled into our hotel, the Hotel des Diplomates, where our bags were promptly unloaded and sorted by rooms. While the bags were delivered to our rooms, Victor and Athanase escorted us to a veranda, where we ordered up an assortment of beverages, including locally made beer and Coke, along with mara goocha, a drink made from passion fruit.*

*Shortly after, Laurent Habiyaremye, the Director of Tourism and National Parks, met with us. Laurent was our other host for our stay here. Our visit was more than just hunting and gorilla viewing, as I was prepared to mount a full-sized Cape buffalo here.*

*The buffalo was a trophy collected by Victor and my brother Bert Klineburger. It was preplanned for the full specimen to be saved and eventually go into the airport terminal for display. The skin was shipped to the U.S.A., where it was tanned and prepared for the mount. At the same time, our taxidermy studio modeled and cast a form for the mount. Once the form was made, we cut it into four pieces that would nest together along with the tanned skin and other supplies and shipped to Kigali.*

### TIME LAPSE

(The next few days were utilized in lining up further supplies for the buffalo mount and securing a work area at the local tannery. Also, I gave instructions to some helpers to make a wooden base to be ready when we returned from our safari.)

*04 November*

*I gave final instructions for all that needed to be ready for me when we came off of safari, so that I could tie right into the mount. A little more shopping for some more booze and snacks, as well as fetching our guns from Customs security. We were off by late afternoon to the Akagera Game Reserve to the northeast for our hunt.*

*The countryside en route to Akagera was the same rolling hills covered with population—a few small towns and shambas as far as the eye could see. We arrived at the Gabiro Lodge about 9:00 PM.*

*05 November*

*Up at 5 AM to go hunting. It was a short night—only in bed at 11:30. Our cabana was comfortable, hot water and the likes, but they turn the power off at 11 or so at night and not on for us early risers in the morning. This lodge is in the Akagera National Park and the main guests are people coming here for game viewing.*

*So we were off in our Nissan three-seater van at twilight, eight of us including the driver, Victor, and two local guides. We drove out to the main north-south highway, which is the dividing line between the Park and the hunting reserve. From the highway east to the Tanzania border is the Park, about 40 by 125 kilometers. From the highway west, the hunting reserve averages between 8 and 15 km wide and is about 50 km from north to south.*

*So our main access to the hunting is traveling up the highway, which leads into Uganda, 65 km north of Gabiro. We began seeing game right away on the beautiful green savanna, spotted with acacia and other trees. Topi and* impala appear to be the most common species, as we seemed never to be out of sight of one or the other.

It hadn't been more than 30 minutes out when Victor spotted some Cape buffalo in a thicket of trees up a slope several hundred meters up a hill. In the shadows, we could not tell how many, but we did see some respectable horns on one, so decided to make a stalk. Bob seemed quite interested in collecting a good specimen of this variety to match it up with his buffalo trophy from Kenya, taken some 10 years ago.

The gals stayed in the van after we drove a half-mile or so up the highway out of sight of the buffs and downwind from them. They then drove back down the road to where we first spotted the buffalo, to park and keep the attention of the buffalo. Game here seemed unafraid of the traffic, as long as they felt to be a safe distance and with a good exit of forest behind them.

So we started our stalk by climbing up the hill to the same level as the buffs and slowly made our approach. As we got close, we slowed to a tiptoe, carefully keeping bushes or trees in front of us to keep out of sight. The guide caught sight of them and quickly went into a crouch. Bob jacked a shell into the chamber of his .375 Brown Precision rifle, made especially for him for this kind of hunt.

Just then, we felt the wind on the back of our necks. It had shifted, typical of what one can expect in hilly country. The buffalo got our wind and skirted around the hill away from us.

We quickly went straight up in an attempt to get over the hill, hoping to come down on top of them on the other side. A few minutes later we heard them crashing in the trees below

us, apparently having gotten our wind again, as the breeze kept swirling around with no definite pattern. We found their tracks, which headed for the Park, crossing the road not far from where the vehicle was parked. The gals got a good look at them as they crossed over.

We came down to the car, took a dirt track off the main road, and were never out of sight of game. Zebra was another thing that we saw a lot of. The impala were impressive. They are the East Africa variety, the biggest of all, so they all looked good, the mature ones, of course.

The local guide got real excited about one trophy in a herd and asked if we wanted to take it. Bob and Colleene both said no. So I decided to give it a try. When I got in position to shoot at around 100 meters, the grass was high enough to cover three-fourths of his body. Instead of aiming down into the grass a little, I held right on the grass line and over-shot.

My 7mm Remington Magnum Colt Sauer was sighted in 3 inches high at 100 yards, just enough to shoot right over the back. Fortunately, he didn't go too far, giving me another try. The grass was the same this time, but I lowered the cross hairs to what I estimated was low in the chest.

He was looking right at me, so the bullet entered right in the neck and right into the chest cavity—an instant kill. I was very impressed with the size. It was much bigger than I had gotten in Uganda back in 1961, just to the north of here.

## TIME LAPSE

So, back to the lodge just in time to have some lunch. In the afternoon, I went to the skinning area and supervised the caping out of the impala, while the others took a nap.

Bob and I went out at 4 PM for the evening hunt. We saw two female bushbucks, but no males. This was a thicker and swampier area, so we didn't see as many animals, but in one spot, we looked down in a valley and saw warthog, zebra, impala, and topi all at one time. It was a great day's hunting and we were all happy to be back in East Africa in such a pleasant and beautiful game-rich country.

This is Saturday and the lodge was packed and not our idea of being in the bush. We were the first ones in the restaurant, after having cocktails and snacks in our room from supplies we brought along. It took us about two hours to make it through our meal. Again, it was late getting to bed to prepare for another 5 AM arising. I laid in bed reminiscing over the great day. We must have seen over a thousand animals today.

06 November

Up at 5 AM again. Colleene stayed behind to rest her back that has been giving her trouble. Not 10 minutes out, we came across a pride of lions—two males and two females. They are protected and rightfully so. They need to build up their population from the recent times when they did not have the needed protection. They weren't far from the road, just lying down resting.

Our presence caused them to wander off toward a herd of topi. The lions obviously were not hungry and thus not hunting, but the topi herd started running off, except for three sentinels. Three of the males ran toward the lion to get their attention, and then would stop a safe distance away.

The pride paid no attention as they majestically walked their selected path. Once the sentinels saw the lions were not after their herd, they trotted toward their own. The lions were a beautiful sight and our day was made if we never saw another animal.

Shortly, we spotted a small herd of buffalo—six males with good horns. This excited Bob, so off we were for another stalk. We circled down wind and up the hill so that we could come to them at the same elevation they were. I carried the video recorder, while Victor took his .378 Weatherby to back Bob up, in case of a charge.

We made a great stalk, getting some 50 meters away. The herd was feeding away from us, not offering a good broadside shot. Bob picked out what he felt was the best one and put a solid into the chamber of his .375, since he needed the best penetration possible. He picked a target in the gut area, so the projectile would end up in the chest cavity. He squeezed off and the buffalo dropped, as I saw it through the video viewfinder.

Victor and the guide (François Nyanhve) started running up the hill in the direction of the fleeing herd. I couldn't understand it, as I hadn't seen the buffalo get up after it fell, although my vision through the viewfinder was not all that great. I went up to Bob and asked what was going on. He didn't know either, as all he saw was the trophy going down. We went over to where the buff last was. We saw blood but no downed animal.

Claude Shabantu, Victor's nephew, who came along and just got here last night, came to us and advised that we go down to the road. We talked it over and since the buffalo circled back paralleling the road, it seemed our best move to get back to the road to get the vehicle and go on to see if we could get ahead of the buffalo.

When we got to the road the van was already gone, so we hoofed it for a mile or so, when the van finally came back to fetch us. Beckie, who had a grandstand view of the whole affair, filled us in. The buff did, in fact, go down from Bob's bullet, but it got up again and ran off with the rest. There was a slight depression where the trophy rolled into and went out of our view. Then Beckie and staff headed north in the van in the direction the herd ran.

Victor and François stuck with them, and finally the blood trail led them to the wounded buffalo lying down as if dead. Beckie could see them approaching the trophy. Victor, being the experienced hunter he is, did not walk up to it, but fired a shot at it to make sure.

The buffalo had been playing dead, awaiting its pursuers. This is why many believe it is the most dangerous animal in the world. The buffalo sprang to its feet but was dazed. Victor put the finishing shot in the chest and this time he stayed down.

When Bob and I, along with the rest of the crew, arrived on the scene, we inspected the shots. Bob's .375 solid actually ricocheted off the tough, resilient skin. The bullet didn't actually bounce off the skin, but it changed direction enough that, instead of going into the chest cavity, it traveled just under the skin, rupturing it in several places and doing a lot of flesh damage all along the side.

The wound caused a lot of bleeding and weakened the buff to the point where he had to stop. Perhaps he would have died, but Victor did the right thing to finish him off and not wait for us. Buffalo are extremely tough and rarely does one go down with a single shot.

We were not far from a local village, so a number of the natives showed up to help in return for some of the meat. It was a nice old trophy and Bob was mighty proud of it.

The rest of the morning was spent looking over a tremendous amount of game. We probably saw well over a thousand animals, including a hundred or so elands. Bob had wanted an eland, but the quotas had been eliminated awaiting the results of a study currently being made.

Later this evening we met the girl from the World Wildlife Fund that was doing the eland study. We also met the Uganda Ambassador for Rwanda, H.E. John B. K. Katatumba. We had quite a chat with him and he remembered Jonas Brothers of Africa, the taxidermy firm that I started up in 1961.

Jonas was the name of our company, but since then we changed it to our own name because of much confusion due to two other Jonas studios in Colorado and New York. The Ambassador also remembered our participation in getting Uganda started in the safari business.

Henri and Emie Andrea, the managers of Gabiro Lodge, fed raw meat to the vultures every day right outside the dining room, so every meal time the vultures would hang around the complex and a couple of them would sit just outside the dining room door staring in.

We did not go out hunting in the evening, since it was Sunday and we had a pretty good workout already.

*07 November*

Started out at daybreak, shortly after 6 AM. Saw a small herd of buffalo right off in the dim light. We could see some really good horns in the bunch as they moved away from us. We decided against going after them, as they appeared pretty spooked and may travel for several miles before settling down.

We have seen hundreds of topis in the last couple of days, but one this morning really captured François' attention. Colleene elected to try for it. A short stalk got her within shooting range. She squeezed off on the 7mm and the topi buckled.

After the congratulations took place, the topi got up, shook itself, and took off to catch up with the herd. We were all dumbfounded and so the chase was on. After quite a while, we caught up with the herd and spotted the one wounded. The wound was high on the back. Colleene had forgotten the 7 mag was sighted in 3 inches high at 100 yards. The herd was restless and kept moving out. Colleene had to take a much longer shot this time, yet dropped the trophy in its tracks once again. This time it stayed down.

The size of the topi got Bob's interest up and he decided to look for a matching good head. As we went on, we came across a small group of zebras. Bob noticed an unusual marking on the stallion. Victor and François said it was a bad scar. Bob said he didn't care, as it would add to the trophy.

So we stalked closer. When Bob was ready to shoot, the zebra turned around and Bob saw the "scar" on the other side as well. He squeezed off and dropped the stallion with a single shot from Victor's .300 Weatherby, which he borrowed for these smaller animals, as his .375 was a bit much.

Upon approaching the zebra, we were delighted to see about a 20-inch patch of spotted markings on each side of the back just forward of the rump, instead of stripes. This was a most unusual specimen and one that none of us had ever seen the likes of before. Continuing on, we did find another large topi for Bob to try for. A short stalk got Bob into position and another one-shot kill.

After taking care of the trophies, we headed for the area where Bob had shot at the bushbuck the other day. En route a "big" oribi (they top out at about 25 pounds soaking wet) bounded through the tall grass. No one else wanted him, so I went after him with the 7 mag. It did not offer a decent target, as I could only see his head and neck sticking out above the tall grass. I tried getting closer, but each time it would move on, never less than about 80 yards, so I decided to hold down shooting into the grass, while allowing for the 3 inches high that it was sighted in for—now that is a lot of guesswork.

After two misses and a lot more walking and playing hide and seek, I found a tree to rest the rifle against. Still having to shoot into the grass and guessing a little, I did drill him through the shoulder. I saved the whole skin for a full mount, as I like these small antelopes that way to show off their tiny cloven hooves and delicate size.

I had collected an oribi in Uganda in the early 60s, but it only had one horn. The natives said it was bad luck—they proved right as problems arose—my Land Rover got stuck in a *warthog hole, we got lost in the dark, and we sat out all night in a thunderstorm. So, I am glad this one had both horns.*

## TIME LAPSE

*Our driving from Gabiro, which is within the Park, to hunting always starts out on the paved road. In fact, we see a lot of game from the highway and some of the stalks start out right from the paved road. So far, we have seen much more game from the highway on the hunting side than on the Park side. Of course, the hunting is only now being offered and the game does not know the difference.*

*The highway does not seem to bother the game at all. They cross over all the time. There is quite a bit of traffic, especially big trucks. There are some dirt roads crossing the hunting reserve, which I enjoy being on, although we did see a lot of the best trophies from the highway. In fact, we probably were never out of sight of wildlife while driving on the pavement and at times, we could scan the hilly terrain and see 100–200 or more animals at one time.*

*It was 65 km from Gabiro to the Uganda border. We did not go that far, as the road exited the hunting area and went through farmlands near Uganda. I would like to have gone to the border and just looked across and I know Colleene would have enjoyed it as well.*

## 08 November

*On the road again shortly after daybreak. Not a mile from the lodge we spotted a small herd of buffalo and stopped to glass. François got excited and was jabbering to Victor in Kenya Rwanda (the local language here, which is quite*

*similar to Swahili). There were ten or so males and several big heads stood out as being exceptional.*

*It had been decided that Colleene would go for buffalo if we came across a big one. She had taken Cape buffalo before in Uganda, back in 1965 on her first safari, but it was not real big, as the area she hunted, Semliki along Lake Albert, did not contain good trophies because the herd was isolated and was considered more of a forest buffalo, rather than Cape buffalo.*

*Bob handed his .375 to Colleene and said, "Go for it." Victor said there was a problem as this particular area was said to be reserved for the President to hunt. After a little more jabbering, they said, "Let's go." So I grabbed the video camera and followed them into the bush to get a closer look. There was no doubt that there were some good trophy heads in the bunch.*

*On certain animals, as an example the topi, it is hard to tell the difference between a good mature animal and a record class specimen. You might be only looking at a one-inch difference in length. Nevertheless, a Cape buffalo, with its large massive horns, is like many other big horned or antlered animals—when you see a good trophy, there is no question it is good. The medium sized animals present a lot of uncertainty and one needs to study them carefully to see if they are an acceptable trophy.*

*So in this case, there was no doubt that Colleene's trophy was there—it was only a case of deciding which one to take. Victor and François stopped on an anthill that had some bush cover and motioned for Colleene to get in position. I was watching all this from 25 yards back through the eyepiece of the video camera. Bob and Beckie had a good view of the stalk from up on the highway. Colleene got in a sitting position to rest one elbow on her knee and squeezed off.*

*I could hear the wop of the bullet on the buffalo. Victor and François started running toward the fleeing herd of about ten animals. Colleene just sat there with her hand on her head. I went up to see what happened. Her glasses were bent flat and she was shaking her head and asked me what happened.*

*The scope of Bob's rifle, as well as the stock, was not too good a fit for Colleene and she crept up a little too close to the scope. The recoil of Bob's short-barreled, custom-made Brown Precision rifle drove the scope back against her glasses that whacked her on the head and brought a little blood on her eyebrow. Aside from asking if the buffalo was down, she commented that Rwanda had the most beautiful stars. The buffalo, even though hit hard, split from the herd and headed for some thick bush. Colleene, still a little dazed, said, "Let's catch up with the others."*

*We followed the blood trail and soon saw Victor and François standing back from a clump of small trees. Before we could get there, the buffalo made a dash for it and Victor fired with his .378 and kept firing as it ran away. The trophy, obviously badly weakened, stopped down in a low grassy area awaiting our approach.*

*These old bulls (and buffalo in general) are tough and extremely hard to put down. Victor got there before Colleene, so he put the finishing shot in him from close range. Colleene's shot was well placed in the middle of the shoulders and, had we waited, the bull would have died, but*

*Victor did the right thing to put it out of its misery as soon as possible.*

*It is an extremely fine trophy and Colleene was one happy hunter. Bob and Beckie, along with the driver and skinners were right behind us in the Range Rover, which was able to drive right to where the buffalo fell. After taking photos and make the necessary cuts for skinning it out for a shoulder mount, we left the skinner to start carving it up and wait for the return of the truck to pick up the parts. We did take some of the meat to some natives that were somehow related to Francois.*

### TIME LAPSE

*Early in the hunt, we would come out just for an early morning hunt and return for a late breakfast at the lodge. That didn't work out at all, so we started bringing food out with the idea to eat by midmorning and continue hunting as long as we wanted.*

*We spotted a herd of 30 or 40 impala and saw there were several big males. Both Bob and Colleene were interested in taking an impala after they saw the great trophy I had gotten the other day. They weren't too far away, and it appeared we could go out a few hundred yards on the backside of the little ridge they were on and top over for a good shot for Bob. Therefore, we started out on that course with the gals lagging somewhat behind us.*

*Sure enough, we topped out above them, but the biggest bucks were milling around behind females and young and not offering a chance at a shot. At the same time, the herd was moving off around the point of the hill. So we backed off and took a course to intercept them once again.*

**Taking a break for lunch: Chris, Beckie, Colleene, and Bob.**

*By now, the sun was hot and the gals decided to head on back to the van.*

*We once again got into position, the same thing happened, and the herd kept moving on, perhaps looking for a cool place to bed down. We kept up this same maneuver a few times and the impala had crossed over a low plain and settled on the other side. Bob and Victor carefully approached them keeping out of view until they could go no further without exposing themselves out in the open. It was a long shot, but apparently the only chance. Bob squeezed one off and we could hear the wop of the bullet, so the chase was over.*

*By now Bob was really out of it, since he had not taken his insulin shot yet and was long overdue to take it and get some food in his system. This was the toughest hunt so far on this safari—one that we thought might be the easiest.*

*After the skinning and picture taking, we decided to take this trophy back to the lodge and check the buffalo as well. After a short rest, we went out for a late afternoon hunt looking for either zebra or impala for Colleene. We spotted a good-sized herd of about 25 zebras not far from the main road.*

*There were a couple of good stallions in the herd, so Colleene headed on with Victor* and François, with me following close behind with the video camera. Shortly we were within shooting range of one of the stallions. He knew we were there and he very cleverly milled in with the mares. Time after time Colleene tried to get a clear shot, but no such luck. The herd kept moving slowly away in the open and not much chance to approach closer without running the herd off.

François spotted another stallion on the other end of the herd, where there was a better chance of an approach, so off they went after that one. He didn't have many mares around him, which made it much better to get a clear shot. However, Colleene found herself out in the open and nothing to rest the rifle on for the rather long shot. François could see her frustration and offered his shoulder as a rest. This worked out great and gave her the steadiness needed.

She squeezed off and knocked the zebra down. It got up and required a second shot that Colleene promptly put in it, putting it down for good. It was a big, beautifully marked, pure black and white trophy and one that Colleene is mighty proud of. We waited for the truck to come to carry the trophy back to the lodge. That put us into twilight and no time for the impala.

We had one more day here and were given an option to hunt longer or take a tour through Akagera Park. If willing to start out early, we could take a boat trip into the swamps to view situtunga, a swamp dwelling, spiral-horned animal that is one of the most elusive of all African game. Bob got real excited about the latter so we cleaned the guns and put them away.

The restaurant at the lodge provided us with all our meals. They had a varied menu largely consisting of game meat. Buffalo, zebra, waterbuck, topi, warthog, impala and more were offered in different ways. Most of the meat was on the tough side mainly due to the lack of aging facilities.

Except for Colleene, who says she doesn't want her meat still kicking, we had what they called buffalo steak, American style. This was like the tartar steak, which is raw meat with spices and an egg yolk. That's one that was tender, as it was ground like hamburger.

Our favorite beverages were water and beer. The beer was mostly Zaire beer that cost 130 francs for a large bottle almost three times the size of American bottles. The water seemed to be a rarity here or in Kigali. It was never offered and when we asked for it, they would sell us a liter for 550 francs. For rough figuring, take 100 francs to the U.S. dollar. The exchange now is 73 francs to the dollar and the black market is 115 francs to the dollar. Anyway, it was a lot cheaper to drink anything but water. Coca Cola is made locally and it costs 60 francs in the restaurant.

09 November

We were up early and had breakfast in the lodge for the first time since we came here. Bob and Beckie had turned a lot of laundry in to be done and hadn't gotten it back and weren't about to leave without it. We checked and checked on it and they said, "It's coming, it's coming." Well, it was 9:30 before we got started.

We drove through some interesting terrain and good-looking game country, but for the first hour, the grass was high and appeared to me that it had not been burned. As a result, we saw very little game. In the hunting area outside the Park, the grass had been burned and that's what the game like.

It has always been customary to burn last year's grass once it is finished growing and has dried out. Once the burning is done, new shoots of grass immediately start growing and that's what the game like. Apparently, they are trying to keep the National Park completely natural, and it is driving the game out to areas with shorter grass. The burning, incidentally, does not harm the trees and bushes to any extent. The hardwood trees are just too hard to catch fire, even though the grass fires get extremely hot.

Finally, we got to a large swampy area where we started to see some waterbuck and buffalo. There was one herd of possibly 200 buffalo that filed past an opening just above the road. It must have taken 10 minutes for the herd to walk through, three or four abreast.

The roads in the Park are all dirt tracks, and apparently rarely maintained. As we went eastward, toward the Tanzania border, the hills became quite high, and the road took us right over the highest of them. As we got higher, the grass was shorter, and more and more game appeared. Once we topped out the last ridge, we had a beautiful view of a series of large lakes.

**Colleene's huge Cape buffalo.**

We delivered some buffalo meat to this typical shamba in the sparsely populated hunting area. The homes were wood thatch walls packed with mud and the roofs were the typical grass thatching.

*Rwanda is rich with water. These lakes are all in Rwanda, but a couple of them border Tanzania. There are nine altogether, the largest of which is Lake Ihema, about 25 kilometers long. Between these lakes are a lot of swamp areas, which contain possibly the largest concentration of situtungas in Africa. There are between 2,000 and 3,000 situtungas right here in the Park.*

*From our mountain observation point, while looking down on Lake Ihema, we were watching nearby small herds of buffalo, zebra*

*and topi, as well as a few oribis. We wound down the mountain road and soon arrived at the outpost residence of a Belgium biologist who had been here two years studying the life in the swamps, both flora and fauna.*

*He had been programmed to take us out to see situtunga in one of their habitats. However, he announced that we were far too late, as it was now noon. As with most game, by midday they are bedded down. In the case of situtunga, they live in the swamps and the reeds, most of which are high and give cover and protection.*

Their feet grow out very long and with these big feet, they can virtually walk on water. The hooves do not get worn down, because they rarely ever walk on rocks or even sand. We did board the boat that he was going to take us in the swamps with, cruised down the shoreline, and saw hippos racing into the lake from the bank. A lot of impalas were along the shoreline, as well as many water birds.

Back in the van we headed south along some of the lakes. There were a lot of monkeys in these low areas, along with a good variety of big game. Soon we started up to higher ground and arrived at our next scheduled stop, the Akagera Resort Hotel. Here we went in for lunch. There were very few people visiting here. It seems that only on weekends people flow here from Kigali on special tours. Not too many tourists, as such, come to this relatively unknown country.

After a delicious lunch, we exited Akagera National Park and wound our way through the shamba land, about a two-hour drive to Kigali. Victor left us this morning to attend a funeral, so we were not to see him for a couple of days. We settled back into the Hotel des Diplomates. It is located just a few blocks from the city center and on the same road with most of the embassies. The Belgium and U.S. Embassy were a couple blocks away. We did not have time to check in with the American Embassy.

## 10 and 11 November

I spent these days assembling the Cape buffalo form, as I finally got the fiberglass. The form was in five parts all nested together in a small crate. Therefore, my first order of work

was to put it back together and get it ready for the mount. I also soaked the tanned skin to try it on the form. The base was not ready yet—a simple job that I could put together back home in one hour or less. When first arriving in Kigali, I ordered the base, which is a simple wood frame with cross pieces to drill through for the leg-threaded rods to go through. I pushed them to get it done, but by the end of the day—still no base.

The gals and Bob went shopping and went to three different arts and crafts stores.

## 12 November

I got another five hours in on setting the buffalo up, 7–12 o'clock. The base got done, but only by my getting involved in putting it together. Therefore, I have the form all ready and the base covered with a wire mesh, so once we return for our next side trip, we will be ready to immediately start the mounting of the buffalo.

I put the wetted skin into the hotel cooler and got together with the others to prepare for a trip to the northwest of Rwanda where we are to attempt to view the mountain gorilla. At 3 PM, the driver and Authenus fetched us for a three-hour drive through the hilly farmlands and most interesting terrain and villages. In two hours, we passed through the town of Ruhengeri and got our first glimpse of the volcanic mountains in Volcanoes National Park, the home of the rare mountain gorillas.

Just weeks before we left on this trip, the movie Gorillas in the Mist was just released in the U.S.A. This was a story of Diane Fossey, the woman who dedicated her life to preserving the mountain gorillas. She lived with them for many years and established the protection and attention that they now have. The movie was filmed here in Rwanda, right where we are going.

We continued for the better part of an hour and arrived in Gisenyi, a nice town on the north end of Lake Kivu. We pulled into the Meridian Hotel and settled into our rooms at just about dark, but time enough to see the beautiful gardens of the hotel on the sandy lakeshore. The lake is part of the boundary between Rwanda and Zaire. In fact, the city of Gisenyi is right on the border, so the town is partly in Zaire. We drove to the gateway to Zaire, just a couple kilometers from our hotel.

13 November

Got up very early for a buffet breakfast, checked out of hotel, and we were on the road back to Ruhengeri and turned off on dirt track toward the forested mountains. We stopped at the Park headquarters where we picked up our local guide, also named François (same as our guide in Gabiro).

We met a team of American biologists who were studying one family of gorillas. They had a camp set up in the mountains where they stayed. There are about five different areas where they now allow people to go in to look at the gorillas. It is, however, on a special permit only and it is not for just everyone who wants to go.

We drove over much worse roads for another 15 minutes near the edge of the forest, where another post was set up for the game patrol for the area selected for us. Here we were given a couple of other guides/porters.

They gave me an instruction sheet that I read to the others. It contained the do's and don'ts of conducting ourselves in gorilla habitat and when with the gorillas, no physical contact, always stay behind the guide: do not run if attacked, no flash pictures, no eye contact, leave no human waste in area, etc., etc.

So we were off single file, eventually getting into thick forest. We walked about two miles when we neared a bamboo grove. François told us that the day before the gorillas were only 200 meters from this point. Just then, we heard the snap of bamboo very close by. François pointed and started making a deep-throated sound "M ā a a a m." He motioned to us to follow.

We had been instructed not to talk nor make any fast movements. We followed the snapping sounds of bamboo, and soon we saw the movement of a huge black form ahead of us. It was a silverback male. The old, large males take on a silver saddle of hair on their back.

He was in the process of pulling down a stalk of very large bamboo. As we inched forward, we watched him bite the stalk of bamboo in two and munch away on it as we would eat a stalk of celery. What a magnificent sight! He didn't seem to be much concerned with our presence, but he kept moving away.

Then we started seeing more of the family. The gorillas always live in family groups, headed by an older male. A little baby gorilla came following the silverback—then along came one about half the size of the silverback, apparently the mother of the baby.

The difference was obvious. The head of the old male was high and pointed toward the back. The female's head is very round and, actually, her whole anatomy is very round—sort of plump. The old male is taller and less fat. He weighs about 450 pounds as opposed to about 250 for a mature female.

As we followed them eating their way through the bamboo forest, we eventually saw the whole family of seven, which consisted of two females, each with a baby and two immature males. They are really a circus to watch, pulling down 15-foot high bamboo stalks, and then selecting the tender upper parts to eat. They broke the sections apart and chomped away on them, tossing out as much as they ate.

One of the babies climbed a stalk as if to try to pull it down like her mother was doing. It didn't budge, so it stepped over to a very small bamboo stalk. It was too weak to hold him up, and it went down with the little ape crashing to the ground. The baby was stunned and didn't move for a minute, and then it started moving around and got up.

On another occasion, one of the babies somehow got behind us, leaving us between the mother and baby. The mother called, and the baby came shooting past us to the mother. Just as the baby got even with the mother, she swatted it on the rear end and the baby went rolling end-for-end down the trail. The babies are just as round as a ball. I saw one roll down a slope—just being a kid.

The family, all except the old male, worked its way out to an open meadow where there was a variety of vegetation. Within the bamboo groves, there was very little undergrowth. Out here, there were a good variety of leafy plants that the gorillas appeared to enjoy. They pick a stem of leaves with their hands and feed themselves the same way we do. They occasionally would walk upright like a person, but most of the time their front feet would touch the ground when moving along. At times, however, they would use their foot like a hand, much the same as an ordinary monkey.

We went back into the bamboo grove looking for the old male. Once we went back in, the rest of the family showed up all around us as if to be following us. While we were among the gorillas, they didn't appear to pay any attention to us. We were instructed not to make eye contact with them. They would look at us occasionally, but were not concerned about our presence. One time, one young male came right up to François and touched his leg. Then it turned and went away. He carried a rifle in case of a serious problem.

There are estimated about 250 gorillas in Volcanoes National Park. There are also populations in Zaire, on the other side of these mountains, as well as in Uganda's Mountains of the Moon, which is part of these Ruwenzori Mountains.

That was a fabulous experience. We went out to a meadow and had our lunch before starting the long trek back to the car through the foothills.

Back in Kigali, we met up again with Victor. For the next several days, Colleene and I put in 12-hour days finishing up the Cape buffalo mount. Bob and Beckie had a relaxing time, including some sightseeing and shopping.

Once The Princess was completed (but not dry), Laurent Habiyaremye was anxious to show it off to all Rwanda. The life-size specimen was secured on the back of a flatbed truck and paraded all around downtown Kigali. The

The male mountain gorillas are greyer in color and bear a silvery patch on their back, dubbing them "silverback."

parade terminated at the City Hall for a reception and celebration, attended by most all the top officials, including the Honorable President Juvenal Habyarimana.

We had no idea of the tremendous importance they placed on the buffalo, making it a symbol for their tourism program. The only tourism Rwanda had to offer was their wildlife viewing, and hunting. Laurent's speech was highlighted by emphasizing our history-making safari and trusted it would lay the groundwork for a never-ending resource for Rwanda. Sadly, it was the last hunt to take place in the following 20 years to the time of this printing.

**The female and young gorillas stayed close together and seemed to constantly feed on bamboo and other forest plants.**

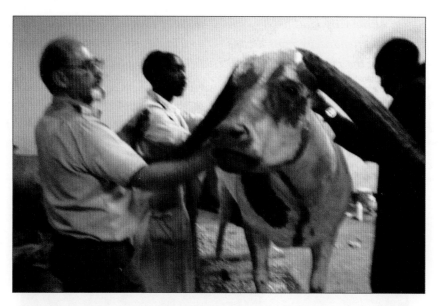

☉ **Chris doing the final sculpturing on the fiberglass form before applying the skin for the cape buffalo life-size mount.**

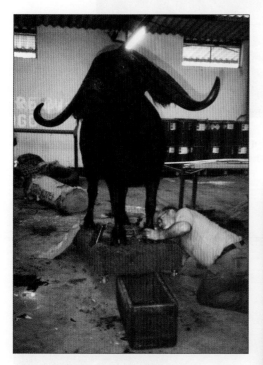

**The completed mount of Princess was placed on a flatbed truck and paraded all around Kigali for everyone to see.** ☉

☉ **Once the taxidermy work was completed, I bolted it to its permanent base.**

## REFLECTION
# People To People

**P**resident Dwight D. Eisenhower was one of the most visionary leaders of America. He believed strongly in the power of the citizen ambassador, people, and said, "People want peace; indeed, I believe they want peace so badly that the governments will just have to step aside and let them have it." He further emphasized, "If we can get people talking to each other, I am certain that most of the world's troubles would be over." In 1956, Eisenhower called a White House conference that included Bob Hope, Walt Disney, Joyce Hall (Hallmark Cards), and Jesse Owens (Olympic champion), among other American leaders and created People To People, with the purpose "—To create goodwill, friendship, and understanding between the people of the United States and those of other nations, using sports as the basic medium." The private entity was formed and Eisenhower became the

In 1970 an American People To People Sports mission met with Central African Republic President Jean Bedel Bokassa and his staff to further the country's only sport: hunting. Delegates from the left are astronaut James Lovell, Dr. Leonard Milton, Bert Klineburger, astronaut Stuart Roosa, Brigitte Klineburger, Joyce Wilson, and Irwin Wilson (not shown).

honorary chairman and encouraged each president thereafter to accept the chairmanship.

People To People was not limited to sports, but to any international exchange, including medical, educational, cultural, or any exchange that people can share. The program accelerated rapidly with widespread interest, so a separate entity was formed as People to People International, while People To People Sports Committee (PPS) would handle all sports-related activity.

When President Eisenhower made his official Alaska visit in Anchorage and visited our Alaska Museum, he felt strongly that we should get involved in the People To People Sports. As time went by, we got together with Dr. Leonard Milton, president of the Sports Committee, and became involved. Brother Bert went on to become a director and the treasurer. At the request of the PPS, sporting goods manufactures, along with businesses and individuals, donated generously. Under the banner of People To People Sports, teams of all ages were sent abroad and they hosted foreign teams in the U.S.A. Sports equipment of every sort was sent, or personally brought, to more than 25 developing nations, many times through American embassies in various countries, and often foreign officials became involved, often making front page news in local tabloids. In some cases, PPS was among the very first foreign exchanges. A case in point, Bert and Dr. Milton carried archery equipment to Bhutan, a tiny country sandwiched between India and Tibet, and whose national sport was archery. They went so far as to arrange for that country to enter the Olympics for the first time and even sent a coach to train them in Olympic-style archery. Well-known Texas hunter Stan Studer donated the costumes for the team for the Olympics.

One of our company's involvements was to encourage shooting sports and hunting wherever applicable. As it happened, in Central African Republic, hunting was the only sport, while in Zaire hunting was a leading sport. In the case of China, when we arranged the first ever hunt into the Manchuria region, we took mountains of sports equipment and presented it to the top officials in Harbin, Heilongjiang Province, at a special presentation (our soccer balls replaced goatskin balls filled with grass!). This led to a very close association with the Beijing sports officials and a partnership with them for the 1984 Summer Olympics in Los Angeles. We hosted some Chinese Olympic officials for a hunt in Texas on Studer's ranch, where Bert and Stan guided and prepared their specimens. The resulting taxidermy work was donated by Klineburger Taxidermy and the finished trophies were personally delivered by Colleene and myself at a special reception in Beijing.

PPS memories made great strides through the years and were great ambassadors of goodwill all over the world. This People to People concept was felt stronger than ever where we led hunting expeditions to remote areas where the people had never come in contact with foreigners, let alone Americans. Love and compassion were never felt more strongly than through the camaraderie we had with people from all walks of life, including herdsmen in the Afghan Pamirs, sherpas in the Himalayas, Tibetan monks, and Mongolian nomads. Wherever we went, the highest local officials welcomed us with banquets and open hearts— they truly wanted peace and openness for the world. People To People Sports, as a separate entity, came to a sad ending during the Clinton Administration in the 1990s when took away our tax status and we were no longer allowed to make tax-deductible donations to the cause. As a result, PPS was absorbed into People To People International.

# CHAPTER 6

# Other Fond Memories of Africa

At the time of this printing, memories seem to stand out as all there is left of Africa. Aside from a few exceptions, the people and wildlife of Africa have suffered greatly during my time of traveling that great continent, 1961 to 1988. During the colonial days, when Africa was nurtured and developed by European countries—Britain, France, Belgium, Portugal, Germany, etc—the people and wildlife prospered.

Slowly during the 20th Century, independence was given to the colonies. Volumes could be written about the fallacies of the ensuring aftermath, the deterioration of perhaps what was the greatest destination in the world for tourists and nimrods alike. Self-serving African leaders of every sort did away with the rights and freedoms of the people, as well as abolished good governmental policies. Sadly, many wildlife programs deteriorated resulting from the ensuring lack of game management.

Throughout most of Africa, a major source of income was a direct result of the abundance and variety of wildlife. Tourism, and especially hunting, was the backbone of wildlife conservation. Without either, the game became a victim to poachers, as well as hungry armies and natives. Here are a few countries that I had the privilege to hunt when they were stable, the people were happy, and the wildlife was abundant.

## Mozambique

Portuguese East Africa, Mozambique, was a rare treat for a hunter searching for an unusual variety of game. I had the opportunity to first hunt the southern part bordering South Africa along with Colleene in 1965, then again in 1973 for a safari in the northern part with Colleene and son, Kent, just before the overthrow of that country. I will write briefly about those expeditions in a following chapter.

## Ethiopia

In 1987, I was able to take time from my exploring of Asia to fulfill a dream of hunting in Ethiopia. John Cotten, longtime friend and hunting companion from the Seattle area, joined me on a trip to the Gambela area. This is one of the three savannah areas in Ethiopia located in the southeast bordering Sudan. The other two are the Omo River area in the south (bordering Kenya) and the Danakil

John Cotten and the PH check the size of an elephant track.

area to the east toward the Somalia border. In central and northern Ethiopia are high and rugged mountains that contain some unusual game including mountain nyala and walia ibex.

The natives preferred a primitive way of life. The author looks over dried vegetables that are ready to go into the cache.

Gourds filled with drinking water were essential, as our treks often lasted a full day.

**We conferred with local hunters and often used them as guides.**

We chose the Gambela area, as our outfitter, Colonel Negussie Eshete, reported a good elephant population, which was John's primary trophy to hunt. The area also had a good variety of plainsgame including roan, tiang, waterbuck, Mongalla gazelle, lion, leopard, and various small antelope, as well as zebra and giraffe. The area was very sparsely populated, even though the government attempted to displace refugees there from a troubled area in the north. They provided them good farmland and modern equipment, but it did not work, as the natives were not ready for modernization. They abandoned everything and went back to scratching out a living in small shambas, raising just enough for their own needs.

The hunt was successful and adventurous. John collected a variety of game, while I was very selective, as I had acquired most of the species previously, especially from Sudan, where I had hunted on the east bank of the Nile, and in the Acholi District of Uganda a little further to the south.

## Central African Empire

My brother Bert hunted Central African Republic (CAR), which was part of French Equatorial Africa in the early 1970s and represented the People To People Sports Committee on a program with President Bukasa of the CAR. It is a long story, but briefly, hunting was the primary sport of CAR. Their official meetings resulted in a partnership between president Bukasa and Bert, along with some foreign investors, to propagate the vast renewable resource of utilizing the wildlife.

A company was formed in 1975. For maximum success, all parties insisted that Bert manage the safari company. It was a major decision on Bert's part, but he left Klineburger Brothers Inc., which had been his lifelong work for some 30 years. He and his wife, Brigitte, moved to Bangui, CAR, where he painstakingly put together what was to be perhaps the most efficiently run safari operation in Africa. Not only providing deluxe camps, equipment, staff, and service, the field preparation and shipping of clients' trophies superseded anything existing in the past in Africa.

Bert had premade crates of every size awaiting the specimens from the field. No transport (plane or vehicle) would return to Bangui without being fully laden with clients' trophies. Once there, documentation was issued, crates closed, and air freighted on the next flight to their destination, sometimes arriving before the client returned home! The only other time in Africa that such effi-

In his early visits to CAR, Bert Klineburger was big on showing the natives write-ups' about themselves. He shows to the last remaining "Platter-lip" Ubangui woman a photo in Habari, the Shikar Safari Club magazine (left). He also shows the pigmies in the southwest rain forest of CAR a copy of the Klineburger publication To Those Who Hunt. (right)

ciency was displayed is when I set up Jonas Brothers of Africa in Uganda in 1962.

Bert managed the safari company (SACAF) for three years, during which time Central Africa enjoyed the apex of its safaris, never again to be repeated. In 1976, Bukasa's ego went to the extreme when he decided the country should be an empire—and he became the self-proclaimed Emperor. In late 1977, he put on a massive coronation for himself, inviting dignitaries from around the world. So now, the country became Central African Empire (CAE) and remained that way for a couple of years, before Bukasa was removed by a coup and returned to the old CAR.

The following is a transcript of my journal to CAE, with the exception of a few chapters (days) in order to shorten the story.

## Central African Empire

### 05 February 1977

*Arrived in Bangui, Central African Empire (CAE) at 4 AM. There was an accumulation of nine people—all going hunting in CAE. I started out with Jack Schwabland from Seattle at 2 PM on Thursday. We flew straight through, making connections from our Pan Am flight—Boeing 747—in London to an Air France flight—DC 10—to Paris. There Dick Dobbins, Wayne Ewing, and Dick Farr—all of L.A.—Jack Manning from Denver, Spence Felt, Joe and Raye Ringholz—all from Salt Lake City—met us. After buying out the duty-free shop at the Paris Airport (booze and tobacco), we boarded our Air Afrique flight to Bangui on a DC 8. We were met by brother Bert and Carlos Artejo, and helped through Customs—a tedious two-hour process.*

🐾 **From our hotel in Bangui we watched fishermen in their dug-out canoe on the Bangui River. Across the way is Zaire.**

Carlos had just joined SACAF to take over soon as manager. Bert started SACAF in 1975 and managed it himself, with the help of his wife, Brigitte, while building it up to the operation it now is.

It was after 6 AM when we were checked into our rooms at the Rock Hotel. The Rock is a fairly modern hotel right on the bank of the Bangui River, which separates C.A.E. from Zaire.

Everyone slept till about noon, when Bert and Brigitte met us for breakfast in the garden area. While having papaya and ham omelets, we watched the native fishermen fish with their nets in the river in front of the hotel. Brigitte exchanged money for us (240 CF francs to the dollar).

Later in the afternoon, they took us all sightseeing and shopping at the native bazaar. My duffel with hunting clothes was lost by the airlines, so Bert loaned me some clothes, which I had altered at the local native tailor.

We all bought a lot of souvenirs, mostly ivory carvings, which are a fabulous buy in C.A.E., probably the best buys in all of Africa. I bought mostly jewelry, necklaces, and bracelets. I bought over $700 worth for resale. The necklaces, made of various shapes and sizes of ivory beads, ran a little over $10 each.

From shopping, we all went to Bert's home for a cocktail party. It was a beautiful home about five minute's drive from the hotel. There we met Carlos' wife. In addition, we met the pilot, Louis Moureau, and his wife, Danielle. He's the pilot of SACAF. After cocktails, we all went to dinner at the hotel, where we had well-prepared food in the garden area and plenty of good French wine.

06 February 1977

Up at 4 AM, packed and checked out and met by all the transport and taken to the airport. The DC 3 chartered aircraft was being loaded

We were taken sightseeing and shopping for souvenirs, mostly ivory carvings, and jewelry.

At the Bangui airport, the chartered DC 3 was being loaded with a couple tons of
supplies along with our gear and us.

*with a couple of tons of supplies. In the air by 8 AM. There was a light fog in the area of Bangui. As we flew north, there was a dense haze from a dust storm and a 50-mile-per-hour wind from the Sahara desert causing the haze.*

*It was hard to see the ground, and the pilot wanted to turn back. Bert got his own map out and went up to the cabin to help the navigator, who was completely unfamiliar with the area, as was the pilot. They eventually found the strip at Golongossa. Schwabland and the Ringholzes disembarked.*

*They were to hunt in the two permanent camps along the Aouk River. This river forms part of the boundary between CAE. and Chad. Professional hunter René Ruchard is guiding Jack and PH Luis da Silva is guiding Joe and Raye. René drove me to the houseboat camp to show me around while the plane was being unloaded. The camp is just a couple of miles from the airstrip. There's nothing at Golongossa but a small native village. The strip is dirt and made to service this camp. The camp is a beautiful setting—very good accommodations in the boat, plus a cabana and some rondoval native-type sleeping quarters. Eighteen people can be accommodated there if necessary.*

*Rusty and Fran Gibbons along with Gene Worrell just completed hunting there and met us at the aircraft. In 14 days of hunting, they all got Lord Derby eland, roan, bushbuck, cob, and Gene got a lion. They also got a variety of other plainsgame. They then went for two weeks down in the Kota area. Also, completing a hunt in the Njojo camp (#2) were a couple of French clients with two beautiful girlfriends—*

*must have been French models by the way they dressed and acted.*

*I met most of the staff at the camp as well as René's American girlfriend, Ellen Wander. Also had a short visit with Luis da Silva, who was a professional hunter, on my last safari in Mozambique in 1973 with Safarique—the one my wife, Colleene, and son, Kent, were on. Everyone boarded the aircraft, but after taking off, the pilot refused to fly to the Kota camp because of the dusty haze, so we headed back to Bangui, a lot of disappointed hunters.*

*Bert invited the American ambassador to go along with us for the flight. His name is Anthony Quinton—42 years old—from Seattle. I had some very nice visits with him discussing hometown as well as African politics.*

*We were back at Bangui at 1 PM. Bert had left word to radio Brigitte at Bangui, so she was informed of our return. Within an hour, we were back checked into the hotel. Everyone took a much-needed siesta, then to Bert's at 6:30 for cocktails. The French clients were already there. One by the name of Emile Lagasse, an architect from Paris, and his girlfriend became quite friendly with me. The other one, Jacques Dessange, I was also able to communicate with, especially because he was taken by my gold watchband, a Klineburger product sporting gold heads of Cape buffalo and ram. Bert had a catalog of our jewelry, which prompted him to order a watchband from me. Jacques is the most famous hairdresser in France and does all the famous lady personalities.*

*The barbequed warthog was carried to the table in true safari style at our deluxe safari camp.*

*07 February 1977*

Everyone was up early after a much-needed night's sleep. The first full one I had in over a week. Bert was on the radio at 7:30 with our camp and got a good report of weather. To the airport by 9 and in the air at 9:45.

As I left the hotel, I was starting to climb in the Land Rover and Carlos pulled out, running over my foot. At first, it felt like my big toe was smashed. I didn't even look at it until after I was on the plane. I was afraid to, but it was OK. The already banged-up toenail was black, blue, and throbbing, but shouldn't keep me from hunting. In the aircraft with us were Rusty, Fran, and Gene Worrell, who were going to a different camp in the Kota area.

The three-hour flight put us on the Kaivadja strip at 1 PM. We were met by professional hunters Felip Parent and Franz Coupé, in addition to an old friend to most of us, Mario Lopes, who had guided for Safrique in Mozambique. Lunch was ready in the beautiful camp on the Kota River. A whole warthog, barbequed over the open fire, was carried to the table in true safari

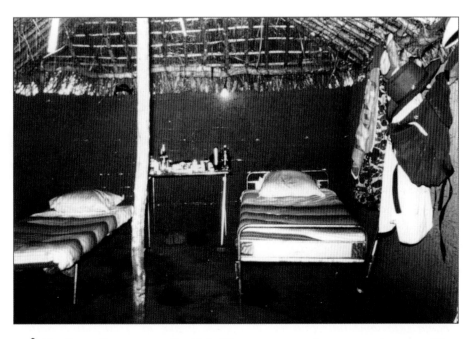

*Our kawadja camp on the Kota River was a semi-permanent camp with grass-thatched roofs and adobe-type walls and included spring beds.*

style, followed by all the trimmings, including a cold Nile perch fish salad and French wine.

Gibbons and Worrell parted after lunch to their camp, Bodi, about four hours away. Sighted rifles in and everyone went out to try the evening hunting. Farr and Ewing with Lopes, Manning and Dobbins with Bert, and Felt and I with Coupé. We went east to a small open plain. Saw a young bushbuck, two water-bucks, two hartebeests, and a lone bull buffalo. We checked out an old elephant kill to see if any lions had been around. Dick Farr took a cob du buffon in the record class. Wayne got a Francolin grouse with the .22. No one else did any shooting. Spence and I are looking primarily for Lord Derby eland and Spence wants a lion.

All were in by dark and after cleaning up, gathered around the campfire for cocktails and the usual hunting stories. The SACAF camp here at Kwaja is very deluxe, including a generator for electric lights, some permanent structures of the mud hut, native variety with grass-thatched roof, as well as some tents. All sleeping facilities with spring beds. Dining area was grass thatch roof with open sides—linen tablecloth, silver-ware and all the finest table settings. Dinner was four courses, with soup, main course—beautifully done, tender roan antelope filets with vegetables—cheese platter, and cake. After dinner—jokes by Dick Farr.

*08 February 1977*

Up at 4:30; breakfast at 5; hunting by 5:30. We drove the same way we went last evening, but well beyond into some hilly country. We saw a lot of game: 50 buffaloes, 15 hartebeests,

10 warthogs, 2 duikers, 7 oribis, and 1 reed-buck. I took a nice male oribi. I wanted a life-size specimen and took this chance to "break the ice."

Spence and I, being selective, looked for our main desires—eland, lion, elephant, and bush-buck. Anything else we saw, we enjoyed looking at and taking pictures, unless a real nice spec-imen turned up. The terrain is fairly dense with bush, so we didn't see but a small percentage of game.

Franz has our trackers looking as much for tracks as for game. He said the best way to get elephant or eland was to find a track that is fresh and follow it to the end. We didn't see any eland tracks this AM and only small elephant tracks. The elands eat gardenia leaves, as their favorite, so we stay with that kind of bush as much as possible.

**Lined up by the dining hut, from the left, Mario Lopes, Bert, Chris, Wayne Ew-ing, Dick Dobbins, Jack Manning, Dick Farr, and Spence Felt.**

TIME LAPSE

*09 February 1977*

Awake at 4:30; same routine. Delayed a little because Bert's car wouldn't start. After getting it repaired, we departed at 5:40, with the intention of hunting all the way to the Bodi camp where Rusty's group is. Franz drove slowly as the wind on our faces was quite cold. Just after crossing the Kota River, we saw a grey duiker. Ten minutes later, a huge bull eland was spotted at about 100 yards to our left. Spence was to take the first one we encountered, so he wasted no time in leaping out and got a shot off as the eland started disappearing into the forest.

The tracker said it was hit on the right rear leg. We left the car right on the spot, and ran to the point where we had last seen him. The tracker indicted he was running hard. Even though the ground was hard and covered with grass and leaves, the trackers were able to follow at a fast walk. No blood, but the tracker indicated that his right leg was broken. The eland had run hard enough to put almost a mile from the car, and then lay down. There was enough time for him to stiffen a little when approached.

One more shot with Spence's .338 Winchester Magnum finished him. What a magnificent animal! The Lord Derby eland has got to be one of Africa's most majestic animals—about a ton in body weight and beautiful coloration. Franz said this one would surely go in Rowland Ward's record book. A later measurement showed it to be in excess of 38 inches horn length, which is the minimum required. Being as close to camp as we were, Franz wanted to get their taxidermist from camp to see an eland in the whole. He had never seen one in the field. He fetched the taxidermist and some more help while we took pictures.

By 9 AM we had it all skinned, cut up and in the Toyota hunting car. Back to camp to take care of the skin and meat. Most of the meat went to the African staff. There are about 15 regular African staff and about 10 more that were brought in for construction of the camp—the native-type mud huts with grass-thatched roofs and the grass huts.

Each African will eat two or three pounds of meat per day. They smoke-dried most of the meat, called biltong in most of Africa. That's their way of keeping it from spoiling. We kept the loins for our own table.

Today another tracker joined us; now we had two trackers and two bearers. Their names are:

Pierre Masamba–tracker

Gabriel Nbesa–tracker

John Dieu-Donne Gnonia–bearer

Martin Yagao–bearer

They seem to all end up with given French names—probably a prestige thing with them.

## TIME LAPSE

*11 February 1977*

Franz explained to us the size of the Kota hunting concession, which is a huge area in the middle of CAE., available only to SACAF clients.

The roads are almost nonexistent. The road we were on is the main road to Bangui, about 1,000 km away. It is a single track. Deep ruts in about half of it—trees brushing both sides of the hunting car. It would be impossible for a passenger car to run on it. This road is typical of all the roads, which are very few, throughout CAE.

The country is very sparsely populated, with very little industry or agriculture, leaving little *need for transportation. The main highway, using the word loosely, running east to west from Cameroon to Sudan, is not much better than this one.*

*The whole of northern CAE. is dense bush country. There are some large trees, mainly Kava trees, in the lower areas and along the rivers. Other than that, it is all bush country of gardenia trees and many other varieties of smaller trees from 5 feet to 20 feet high.*

*On the average, we can only see about 100 yards into the bush. We are only seeing a small fraction (about 1 percent) of the country. Even at that, we are continually seeing some kind of game. Not a half hour goes by without our seeing at least a single animal—many times small herds.*

## TIME LAPSE

*Out at 3:30 again to the northwest on a track that we hadn't been on before. Thick bush, then a nice open area. Ended up at a small river. While I was standing up in the back of the Toyota spotting, I got hit in the face with a tree limb. These trees are all hardwood and don't have much give. The limb was about two inches in diameter and caught me across the nose and lower lip.*

*There was a little excitement while I dabbed off the blood, but soon we were on our way again, not much worse for the wear. We saw 103 animals today—35 hartebeests, 2 elands, 8 buffaloes, 6 warthogs, 2 Grey duikers, 1 red duiker, 2 bushbucks, 11 oribis, 21 water-bucks, 8 cobs, 5 roan antelope, 2 baboons and 1 hippo.*

*Spence and I were moved out of our tent today into our new hut.*

*12 February 1977*

*A great day of hunting—everyone out early. Dick F. and Spence went out with Mario, Jack and Wayne with Bert, Dick D. and I with Franz. We went down as planned on the east side of the Kota to a salt lick several miles below where we saw the eland yesterday. Masamba and Gnonia went with me. Dick and Franz hunted the river on the way back up to the lick where the eland were yesterday. My Africans and I headed northwest after crossing the river; we went directly away from the river. Right off, we saw a cob du buffon that would be way up in the records. I guessed 24 inches. Twenty inches makes the record book. We walked steady for about one hour to an area of bush perfect for eland.*

*Right away, we picked up a fresh track. The wind was wrong. It had just been feeding, not traveling. We followed it for a while. Shortly the strides stretched out indicating it was running, probably got our wind. We made a large arc, getting out of the wind pattern of the eland. We crossed the track again and the eland had settled back to feeding. The wind was better, but swirling around a little. It was feeding toward a dense bush area. It was interesting watching the Africans study the tracks. Where the eland would step on a plant, they would study the leaves that were bruised to see how old the bruise was.*

*We had already been on the track two hours; therefore, it made a difference whether we were five minutes away or a half-hour away*

**Crossing the Kota River in a shallow area**

from the eland. I spent a little time looking for tracks when we temporarily lost them but, otherwise, I would keep looking for the eland. The bush was so thick that it was a rare occasion I could see 50 yards between the trees. In another hour, the track stretched out once again to a running pace. It, no doubt, got our wind. They have an extremely good sense of smell and are very spooky. We followed the tracks for a while, but they indicated that the eland left the country.

We hunted a large arc back to the lick where Dick and Franz were. We came across another lick not far from where we lost the eland. Saw lion tracks, also tracks of elephants, waterbucks and many lesser antelope. We saw a lot of game as well—mostly cob, hartebeest, and warthog. A lot of buffalo sign.

We were back shortly after noon. From 10 AM on, it was very hot—probably the hottest day so far. I had a beer in my pack, but figured it would be too hot to drink, so didn't take in any liquid till I got back to the car after about seven hours of constant walking. Dick greeted me with a cold beer. I inhaled it!

## TIME LAPSE
*13 February 1977*

*Everyone out before daybreak. Bert took Jack and Wayne to look for the elephant that we saw last night. Mario took Dick F. to an area that had not been checked much to look for eland. Spence and Dick D. went with Franz, who took me, Masamba, and Gnonia and dropped us off to check out Saline Nord. Only a few hartebeests on the lick. The three of us took off on a foot safari to work our way back to camp. The driving distance to the lick was about 20 km. We started in a direction away from camp.*

*The Kota River, on which we have our Kawadja camp, runs southwest. The salt lick, as we are presently mapping out, is about four miles from the river. We hiked south-southeast (away from camp) for the first hour and three quarters, at which time we spotted the Kota River. We then turned northeast, paralleling the Kota River. This area had not been hunted, mainly because no road was within a few miles of the river. I wanted to check this area out, mainly because I seem to always have the desire "to see what's on the other side of the mountain."*

*We have only seen eland to date near the river, 'til now, so I had to see this section of the river that had not been looked at so far. Once we got there, we had our work cut out for us to work our way back to camp. All of us have a little of the Stanley or Livingston in us. This whole area had not been hunted in the past few years.*

*An interesting history of this area. Some 12 or so years ago, a French outfit started up. They set up a nice permanent camp and ran a lot of clients through here, but not so many as they needed to crop off enough animals. Sportsmen can't shoot enough to keep the herds in balance. A few years back a Frenchman bought the area and outfit from Cantar.*

**Chris' "Black Battalion" leaving Saline Nord and following the Kota River back to camp.**

*Cantar was a diamond explorer. (There are a lot of diamonds in CAE., one of the major export products.) Cantar took the world record Lord Derby eland out of this area, about 48 inches. Anyway, a Belgian, by the name of Van den Beilke bought into the latter outfit in 1973.*

That was the biggest year here in the safari business, but the outfit did not pay the government taxes, so the government took over all their equipment, permanent camp, and everything, thus, the area was closed down.

This was the first year, since then, that this area has been hunted. There is a problem now, and that is because hunting had not been done; the hunting is not as good as it was before. Why? Because the area had not been burned.

Burning the grass is very important in Africa. The grass grows tall during the rainy season. When it dries, the food value leaves it. An area that has not been burned has no food for the game. When it is burned, the new shoots come right up, along with small plants for brouse.

One would think that the trees would also burn up, but it's not true. The trees, as well as the grass, thrive on burning. They seem to be healthier after burning. Because of the lack of burning, the game has moved out of the area, somewhat. Still plenty of game, we're seeing, each of us, 75 to 100 head per day, and this is an area that is hard to see in. The burning will be done each November here, resulting in better and better hunting each year.

Getting back to my hunt, we had an adventurous journey back to camp. We saw a lot of game, a lot more than we would see if driving through a similar distance. Over every hill or into each new opening, the anticipation of seeing animals would be there. Rarely did we not see a herd of cob du buffon, hartebeest, or a family of warthogs.

We came in contact with the river a couple of times—beautiful river, the Kota. While filtering a glass of water, a hippo snorted, a beautiful African sound. A bushbuck male exposed himself. I was tempted to take him, but passed him up as being too small. Some old eland sign, but nothing fresh. Midday gets very hot, a hell of a time to be walking in the African veldt. We probably would have been wise to find a shady place to sit out the heat of the day, but we walked right on through it. We arrived in camp late in the afternoon after a tough, but adventurous journey.

## TIME LAPSE
### 15 February 1977

Yesterday the District Commissioners from Wadda City, a village 200 km from here, came to see what trophy fees have been paid. The various districts get 40 percent of the trophy fees, which clients pay for every animal taken. This money is possibly the largest income for the villagers. A lot of the meat and surplus skins from the safaris also go to the natives. Thus, the safaris firmly make the wildlife an important renewable resource for the country. The trophy fees vary from around $50 for a small animal like a duiker to well over $1,000 for an elephant.

Spence went out with Dick D. and Dick F. today with Mario. Their main purpose was to look for lion and/or lion sign. Yesterday we had put out an eland quarter for lion bait near a lick where I had seen a lion track on Sunday, a place that could be driven to on the east side of the Kota River. Bert took Jack and Wayne out looking for lion and eland.

Franz had to stay to take care of the trophy business with the (hung-over) Commissioner and his staff. He got a driver by the name of Dazagambia from Mario to go with me. We were out before daybreak to head northeast, same place we went yesterday, only not so far. We stopped in a big open plain, which was on the lower fringes of the area where Dick got his eland and where we saw all the tracks yesterday.

Not 10 minutes from the Toyota, we picked up the tracks of a small herd of elands. Two of them looked like bull tracks. It was difficult following them, as they had been feeding from side to side of a creek, partly on grass. We found very fresh droppings, an indication that we were close behind them. They kept moving and getting into thicker and thicker bush. Two and a half hours on the track (9 AM), we saw movement in thick bush.

I saw a hartebeest, I thought, but Masamba and Dazagambia motioned me to crouch and move forward. Masamba handed me the rifle. We moved into position and sure enough I saw two hartebeests looking at us, but Masamba took my binoculars, looked, and pointed to a dark mass about 50 yards away. I threw my scope up. It looked a little like the shape of the neck and shoulders of an eland. I couldn't see horns. Maybe Masamba saw a good set of horns, but with the language barrier, there was no way to ask. I speak no French, let alone Sango, the local language. (All four boys spoke no English.)

All kinds of thoughts ran through my mind, including the fact that it could be a female, which is against the law to shoot. I waited to see if it would turn its head in order to get a look at the horns. I definitely did not want anything but a trophy-class animal. Suddenly the hartebeests that were staring at us spooked and took off running, taking the eland with them. It was a big bull. I got a glimpse of it just as it charged out of sight.

Masamba motioned for me to follow, and we broke out in a dead run. We ran in a direction paralleling the eland for about a quarter mile. We never saw the eland during our chase. We intersected their track again and followed at a fast pace for a couple of miles as long as the tracks indicated. The herd was running. There was no need in us being too quiet, as far as our footing was concerned. It is extremely dry and there are very crunchy dry leaves all over the ground, so we just let her crunch! That was a mistake, however, as the herd had come to a screeching halt in a thicket to wait and see what the danger was. They took off running into thick bush, with no chance for a shot. Now we all sensed that we really had our work cut out for us.

An eland during its daily routine might cover 10 or 15 miles, as they are constantly on the move. Being scared, they could easily go 25 miles. I felt that 'til now, they had not gotten our wind; therefore, it was my feeling that they might settle down sooner or later, especially since it was getting into the heat of the day, at which time the game all like to find a nice cool place and settle down.

One of the bearers, Yagao, indicated by a hand motion that the elands were long gone. There was a discussion in Sango among the four Africans. They sort of looked at me with a "What do you want to do?" look. No doubt, they took into consideration that this heat could be a problem for me if we struck out on a several hour chase. I don't know what the temperance gets to midday, but I would guess at least 90°F in the shade, and this bush offers no shade.

I felt fine and knew that I could always call it quits later (not that my pride would let me), so I merely pointed to the tracks and said, "Track." They smiled and gave it thumbs up. We walked a steady pace for a couple of hours, during which time the eland tracks indicated they were traveling.

They headed due south and crossed the road that we drove in on. Along about noon, the tracks indicated that they started feeding a little. We had now been on the tracks a little over five and a hours. We were on the biggest male track, which was bigger than my hand laid out flat.

I noticed that the rest of the herd—we figured there were eight altogether—had not followed the herd bull. It is a typical reaction for certain species for the herd male to do that. I was glad in this case, because it is a lot easier to follow one animal, and stalk it, than a whole herd.

The sign was very fresh so we knew we were close. Every footstep was carefully placed, even to the extent that Masamba would often move the leaves to one side with his hand to keep from making any noise. Suddenly he froze. Dazagambia grabbed me by the arm just as I saw the bull. He had not sensed us. I handed my binocular to Masamba as he handed me the rifle.

I looked through the riflescope as he looked through the binocular. I glanced over to him and he nodded. I centered the crosshairs on the massive shoulder and squeezed off. He went a very short distance and was dead by the time we were able to run to him. The shot was about 100 yards and not too badly obstructed by bush. What a happy feeling to have collected this magnificent specimen.

I didn't have a tape measure, but I guessed the length of horn to be close to 40 inches, which would put it well within the record class. After getting pictures of all the Africans with the trophy, and an attempt to have one of them take a picture with the trophy and me, I sent Dazagambia and Yagao back for the Toyota.

We caped the bull out, cut the meat up, and had plenty of time to rest before the car arrived. We were all very happy for our success. Every time I caught the eye of one of the Africans, they would smile and jabber on in Sango, as I would jabber on in English. We all knew what each other was saying, as we had worked very hard and covered a lot of ground to obtain this trophy.

TIME LAPSE

*17 February 1977*

*Mario took me to the east looking for elephant. We went on an old road that hadn't been used in years. The boys had to do a lot of cutting, mainly on trees that had been knocked down by elephants. It's amazing how much damage the elephant can do to a forest. They'll take down good-sized trees 8 to 10 inches in diameter, eat a few leaves, and then pull down another. Sometimes they will butt the tree with their head, breaking it off, and often grabbing it with their trunks and pulling it down. I remember back in 1963 in Uganda, seeing an entire forest that had been wiped out by elephant. The trees that were too big to knock down, they would strip the bark, causing them to die.*

*By afternoon, we got into some dense forest—perfect elephant habitat. We encountered some nice tracks. If the front foot tracks measure 18 inches or more, it is usually a big bull. Working our way into the forest, we soon heard disturbances. A little crashing of the bush and we heard the sucking sounds of their feet being pulled out of the mud.*

*We headed into the bush—the three Africans, Mario, and me. Right on the edge of the dense forest, after a bushbuck jumped out right in front of me, we saw the huge tracks of the elephant. Mario's head tracker, then I, then Mario, followed by the other two Africans all filed into the bush. The area was so thick; to see 20 yards would be impossible.*

*The elephant tracks sunk at least a foot into the muddy bottom of this dense forest floor. Quietly as possible, we followed the tracks—over fallen logs, through streams, always in the deep mud. Before long, we came to a sudden stop behind the tracker. We came face to face, about 15 yards away, to a cow elephant. Everyone took a complete about-face and got out of there. She may not have made out what we were through the thick foliage as the wind was right. She had very long ivory, but thin, as is typical of a female.*

*We worked our way around to another set of tracks. Followed them to where we could hear the elephant feeding, even saw brush moving. We moved around to within 10 paces of the elephant, but could not see it. We were dangerously close; it was getting very late, around sundown. We decided to evacuate the forest, as it would be dark before we could get back to the car as it was.*

*As we got out into the opening, Mario stated that we would return in the morning. He said, "We know there are big elephants in*

**Wayne on the harmonica and Bert on the guitar gave good entertainment around the campfire.**

*there." Tonight we had a celebration: It is Jack Manning's anniversary. Bert and Wayne played music and everyone sang. Bert on the guitar and Wayne on the harmonica. To top the evening off, we had crêpe 'suzette brandy. What a day!*

*18 February 1977*

*Up at 4 AM—Mario and I were out before 5. Bert and Jack were out looking for a fresh eland track. Franz took everyone else with him. By daybreak, we were looking for fresh elephant crossings, as we drove on the road to Oudda— same as last night. Stopped at the same small river that we hunted downstream from yesterday. We headed the opposite direction: west. Soon we were on elephant tracks, a good day old. We followed them for several hours. The tracks went back and forth across the north branch of the creek. In places, the forest was very dense, not nearly as thick as the place we went last night. There were a lot of buffalo tracks, but we did not see any buffalo.*

*Three different times we saw Colobus monkeys jumping from tree to tree. In crossing an unburned area, we spotted elephants. In making a half circle around them, to keep the wind right, we got a closer look. There were two cows and two calves. We kept going into a dense area along the creek. There was plenty of fresh sign.*

*We got the wind right and headed into the dense area. In addition, it was very thick. We heard elephants! Their stomachs rumbling, brush snapping, and an occasional vocal sound. Mario and Dazagambia listened and pointed at areas ahead of us in a semi-circle. We had elephants directly ahead, to the left and to the right of us. All less than 50 yards*

*away. We approached the sound to the left. Spotted a bushbuck. We got within 10 yards of it; there were a pair of them, barking as they ran away.*

*We got a glimpse of a couple of the elephants—cows. We circled on out of the forest. Mario says that some of these dense areas are just like the rain forests in the south CAE., where they hunt in the summer for elephant and bongo. Just as we came out into a clearing, a red duiker appeared right in front of us. It was only about 20 paces away. It was feeding and didn't give us as much as a glance as we approached it. I got my camera out and walked up to within five paces.*

*He was irritated by my approach and the click of the camera, so he started wandering away, not missing a bite as he grazed, an indication the game here had not had contact with mankind. We headed out at a 90-degree angle from the creek looking for bull tracks. Sure enough, we found the track of a lone bull— about one day old. Fortunately, they were heading somewhat in the same direction where we left Mario's Land Rover.*

*He was traveling, and only occasionally did he stop to feed. Two different times along his trail, he picked out a good size tree, close to 12 inches in diameter, and busted it down. Mario said that they do it by banging against it with their heads. These trees are all hardwood and are tremendously tough. Mario said he couldn't buck one of these trees with his Land Rover!*

*Dazagambia was doing the tracking, although Mario and two other of the African boys were helping. All of them are extremely skilled in following an elephant track, and it amazes me how they can do it.*

*I am reasonably able to follow a hoofed animal track, but I would never attempt to say I could follow an elephant track any distance at all. Their wrinkly track on the hard ground takes a good deal of study by me. However, Mario and the boys can walk at a fast pace and follow the track, and a fast pace we went. It was midday, and one of the hottest days we've had. We followed the track up a valley, over a ridge and down the other side. This ridge was the highest ground around here. This is considered savanna country but it is more small rolling hills, fairly dense bush, forests, and an occasional dense forest.*

*The track continued at a fast clip, and it never changed from being a day old. Mario said that at a normal walk, they travel at about 7 miles per hour. Elephants are a restless animal, especially the bulls, and change country quite often. Franz said that one time down in Zambia, on the open plains, they drove alongside an elephant that was running, and they clocked him at 35 miles per hour for 5 minutes before giving up.*

*They are a tough and rangy animal and are not to be compared in any way to the zoo animals, which are Indian elephants. African elephants normally cannot be captured or trained. They are all wild. Speaking of tearing down trees, it is easy to identify the areas where the elephant frequent, as every fourth tree is torn down. It is a good thing there are plenty of trees in this country, or there wouldn't be any forests left.*

*We gave up hope of catching up to this bull. In returning to camp, we saw a small leopard along the road. They are very abundant here, as in other parts of Africa, but the U.S. Fish & Wildlife Service has listed them as endangered, so it is illegal to take then into the U.S.A.*

## TIME LAPSE
*20 February 1977*

*The plane is due in to pick us up today. Up early at 4 AM—everyone went out for one last chance. Spence and Franz went out to check two of their baits on the east side of the Kota. Bert took Jack back to the bait that had the leopard on yesterday in hopes that a lion may have run the leopard off.*

*I had considered not going for elephant, but only hunting for bushbuck nearby. Bert suggested I go look for elephant—in Bert's own words, "Don't give up till the left engine starts on the DC 3." Therefore, Mario and I were out at 5 AM before daylight. We went on the northeast road, same way we hunted yesterday. One of the Africans said that the fresh sign that we were on last night was heading northwest toward the Kota. So we drove along, even by headlights from the car, we were looking for tracks.*

*At dawn, Mario saw tracks out of the corner of his eye as he drove by. We got out and looked them over. Just then, Franz drove up behind us, and we discussed the tracks as looking a little old. Franz drove on. Then, no sooner did his Toyota get out of earshot than we heard the trumpet of an elephant. They must have crossed the road just about the time we were talking to Franz and Spence.*

*Without speaking a word, we gathered all the guns—my .458 Kleinguenther, Mario's .460 Weatherby, and his .458 Brno. The trumpeting was only a couple hundred yards away. It kept moving to our left and farther away at times. We were soon on their tracks. They were feeding, yet they were moving faster than we were, walking at a good pace. Soon we closed the gap to within a couple hundred yards. Our visibility was limited to a maximum of 100 yards.*

*The excitement of such a chase with the almost continuous trumpeting is hard to put in words. Tension was mounting as we closed the gap. We could hear trumpeting and trees breaking to our left and to our right. We spotted one of the herd, then another. They were bulls. Their huge bodies never stopped as they fed along. They moved out of sight again. We knew there were several bulls, but couldn't tell how big the herd.*

*In a situation like this, it is impossible to look the herd over to select the biggest. We put on a little speed and caught up with them again. We saw them pass through an opening. Then one with a good set of ivory passed. Mario pointed and Dazagambia said, "Oui!" The herd slowed down and grouped up. We had a brief look at the whole herd. Several good elephants. First Mario pointed to one near the back of the string. Then he pointed to the first one, and whispered, "Brain shot." There was a small tree obstructing his head. The distance was somewhat less than 100 yards. I moved a little to the right and centered the iron sights on the ear hole. I fired and the bull lunged. The whole herd of ten bulls made an about-face and ran back the way they came, including our bull.*

*We temporarily lost sight of them. We ran as fast as we could follow them. We spotted a lone bull—it was the wounded one. He was broadside at about 60 yards. Mario whispered, "Brain shot." I moved toward a nearby tree to steady the rifle, as I was breathing hard. Just then, the bull saw us and before I could raise the rifle, the mad bull was coming toward us at full charge! Mario and Dazagambia both stepped up alongside me and we all raised our rifles and fired at the same time into the head of the massive beast that seemed to already be towering over us, but fell to the ground about 15 yards in front of us, shaking the ground with great force. He tried to get up and Dazagambia and I both fired again into his head.*

*The boys and Mario, speaking in French, were wild with excitement as they shouted to one another as they obviously were relating to the thrill of the charge. As we stepped up to the great beast, Mario wrapped his hands around the girth of the tusks and exclaimed, "35 kilos!"*

*With the DC 3 coming in today, we were not able to wait until the tusks were cut out. I gave Mario the instructions to save the feet, trunk, and ears, to remove before the natives moved in to save all the meat. It was a happy occasion and a tremendous finale for me as the Africans waved the elephant tail in the air as we drove into camp. The others were all back in camp upon our return. Unfortunately, they were unsuccessful in getting a lion. Jack's leopard was back again on his bait. They watched it for a long time before it got their wind.*

*Wayne was making a big hit with all the African staff in camp. He has a color Polaroid camera and was giving the boys pictures of*

**Mario Lopes is mighty proud of our success of stopping the charging bull at 15 yards.**

*themselves for souvenirs. Parting was tough for all of us. We all became much closer as only a safari can do. We made some great new friends in the professional hunters and the African staff. We are all enriched by memories and trophies that will help us relive this great occasion for the rest of our days.*

*Another special thing for me today—my son's sixteenth birthday.*

*Happy Birthday, Kent!*

*Recap of animals I saw during the 14 days in this area of CAE.: 4 lions; 1 leopard; 302 kongonis; 265 buffaloes; 75 warthogs; 8 red duikers; 30 grey duikers; 13 bushbucks; 40 oribis; 142 waterbucks; 3 reed bucks; 213 cob du buffons; 13 roans; 12 elands; 34 elephants;*

*9 hippos; 3 Colobus monkeys; and countless baboons.*

*These figures are a summary of a daily log that I kept of all major animals seen. Not counting baboons and minor game species, the total was 1,167 animals, an average of more than 83 animals per day. There was more variety of game birds than I had seen in other parts of Africa including guinea fowl, dove, quail, various types of grouse and sand grouse, rock chickens, snipe, etc. Considering the relatively dense bush in this particular area, that is a lot of game. We could rarely see clearly farther than 50 yards. The game was relatively undisturbed and would last forever with proper cropping practices.*

Bert Klineburger began hunting CAR in the early 1970s when he collected this fine bongo.

After successfully managing the safari company for three years, Bert and Brigitte returned to the U.S.A. at the end of 1978 to pursue a safari consulting business in San Antonio, Texas. One of the foreign partners of SACAF brought in a Frenchman to manage the safari operation after Bert's departure. It seemed that he was more of a puppet to the partner than a manager, as he catered to him, allowing him unlimited shooting, including taking 36 elephants. Furthermore, that partner managed to finagle all the other investors out of their stock.

Chris' son Kent and his PH Jean Luis Masson pose with Kent's Lord Derby eland taken on a safari to Central African Empire shortly after the author's hunt.

*Following that, the government closed elephant hunting to outsiders while poachers moved in and destroyed one of the greatest herds of trophy elephants remaining in Africa. Another sad story of an African country going bad, resulting from a government allowing game management to deteriorate with poachers running rampant. Not only has wildlife suffered, but also the country lost income from that resource.*

*Although there was organized hunting, while safari operators were constantly patrolling the area there was no poaching to speak of. Marc Techenart, a Frenchman that had a concession next to Bert's in the rain forest area, told Bert a few years later he went back to visit his area and broke down crying when he saw skeletons of whole family units and no sign of living elephants.*

## Zimbabwe, the former Southern Rhodesia

I had hunted all around Zimbabwe but had never been there, even though we sent numerous clients there for hunting in various times since the mid 60s. The country had been on again, off again, but now in 1980 it seemed safe to resume hunting.

We had started working with a South African operator, Ben De Wit of Southern Africa Safaris, who worked with landowners in both Zimbabwe and South Africa to utilize their areas for hunting. I arranged for a few clients of ours to hunt with Ben's outfit, including Bob, Jack and Andy Phillips, Klaus Mein and Frank Hibben, coinciding with a hunt of my own at the same time.

My main desire was to collect a greater kudu, which I was not able to connect with in two different hunts in Mozambique. Ben suggested I come at the same time as Frank Hibben. I agreed and requested that I go out on my own with a native tracker only, the type of hunting I had done mostly all over Africa. The time was set for early September 1980. The following are excerpts from my journal as certain events happened.

*I had landed in Johannesburg after long flights from Seattle, Chicago, and New York before catching the lengthy flight to South Africa. Ben De Wit met me then delivered me to the Carlton Hotel where he said Frank Hibben and Marilyn Rapier were waiting to visit with me—so more cane (the local rum-like drink) and a little dinner while having a very enjoyable chat with them—but I had been up the last two nights and was mighty tired.*

*Frank is a longtime friend, customer, and hunting companion. We hunted Marco Polo sheep together back in 1968. At 11 PM, we finally split and went to our rooms—did that bed ever feel good!*

*Wouldn't you know it, I woke up at 1:45 AM and couldn't go back to sleep. Therefore, I rearranged my packing, showered and changed into safari clothes and finally at 6:30 went down to check out. Shortly after, Frank and Marilyn followed and we hailed a cab to take us to Lansaria airport, which is on the opposite part of town from Jan Smuts airport where we had arrived last night.*

*The cab driver got lost and we ended up going through some back dirt roads and finally* *found it—cost 30 Rand ($40). We met the pilot, Phillip Koornhof of Western Air Charters. We loaded our gear in his Beech Baron and were off by 9:30 for our 1½-hour flight to the town of Messina right on the Zimbabwe border.*

*Ben had driven a Toyota Land Cruiser up during the night from Johannesburg—an eight-hour drive. He had just arrived a half-hour before we did. Our instructions were to buzz the Impala Lily Hotel, which we did and were met shortly after landing by Ben's son, Anton.*

*Back at Impala Lily, we met up with Klaus Meyn, and Nancy, whom we had arranged a short hunt for. Klaus is our Seattle district sales manager for TWA airlines and quite a hunter. He was trying for leopard, but was unsuccessful—did get two fantastic warthogs, two impalas, and a zebra stallion. Klaus and Nancy had to leave today.*

*The Impala Lily is the name of a small stock plant that has a massive trunk with high water content. It provides impalas, among other animals with water during droughts. It has a beautiful pink flower in the spring. In fact, now the blossoms are ending with winter (south of the equator).*

*We were served sandwiches and Coke, while visiting with Klaus, Nancy, and Anton before they left. Then we serviced the cars, the bar—picked up cane, scotch, and Coke—then headed for the nearby border of Zimbabwe for the exiting formalities from South Africa and entrance into Zimbabwe—a half-hour long process with guns, vehicles, et. al.*

*The town on the Zimbabwe side is Beit Bridge, named after the only bridge between South Africa and Zimbabwe. The Limpopo River forms the border between these two countries and flows on down to Mozambique and into the Indian Ocean. I had hunted the Limpopo along with Colleene back in 1965 in Mozambique. The hunting area was just a short distance to the west of Beit Bridge.*

*Our hosts were Peter and Betty Carimus at their estate, River Ranch. It lies right on the Umzimgwane River and the land they own is 57,000 acres between the Umzimgwane and Limpopo Rivers. We were impressed by the fact that they had to put an eight-foot high game fence around the building complex to keep the game out. Peter and Betty showed us around the accommodations—private rondoval cabanas for the guests, skinning and meat processing room with large walk-in cooler, large home with screened-in veranda on two sides and beautiful garden area. Peter showed us a small herd of elands not 200 yards from the facilities.*

*They had an excellent buffet cold lunch presented in the garden area—very pleasant. Temperature about 75°F and crystal-clear, dry air. Elevation here is about 1,500 feet. After lunch and getting our gear unpacked, we all headed out for a look-see. I rode with Peter, and the others with Ben.*

*We checked the area out toward the Limpopo—plenty of game. Just driving around, we saw plenty of impalas, a couple of small bunches of greater kudu cows, a bushbuck, some warthogs, and several steenboks and duikers.*

*The area is dense bush, and this is the height of the dry season. It is dry, almost no leaves on the trees and bush and the grass seemed to be entirely gone—yet the animals were fat and healthy looking. What little feed there is has a lot of strength. The rainy season is just barely starting, so before long the area will start greening up once again.*

*Betty had prepared a special treat for us—stuffed impala leg. Cocktails were set up in the garden area where we exchanged hunting stories and really began to enjoy the companionship of these wonderful people.*

*I was awakened by coffee service in bed at daybreak. The plan is to go right out and not fuss with breakfast and be in for a late morning brunch. I felt good as I surprisingly had a good nights sleep—except for being awakened at around 3 AM by jackals wailing.*

*We all went out in Ben's Toyota Land Cruiser. There were two trackers—Finias for Frank, and Elias for me. These blacks are the Venda race and are very nice people. All the black staff was very happy and nothing has changed since the independence earlier this year. More about that later.*

**Some female and young impala take a drink in a drying water hole on the River Ranch.**

*We headed for an area with some rocky hills, which the kudu like. Saw game continuously on the way out. Elias and I were off-loaded at the downwind end of a small range of hills, while Ben took Frank and Marylin cruising. The wind was rather strong, making for good stalking into it but caused the game to be restless. We found some good kudu bull tracks—they had been through here this morning.*

*Elias was a good, skilled tracker and moved cautiously at what I considered just the right pace. Saw a few small bunches of impalas early but no kudus near the hills. After leaving the hill area and getting a ways out onto the densely covered plains, we came to some nice blue wilde-beest (gnu). Looked them over through the dense thorn bush before they got our wind and took off. I was really only looking for greater kudu, so just enjoyed looking over the other game.*

*So far, today we passed several bunches of impalas, a few duikers, a klipspringer, a bunch of baboons, and these gnus. They pretty much disturbed the area ahead of us, so we started an arc back toward our rendezvous point, keeping the wind as much as possible to the side. Most animals, when spooked, go into the wind so they can scent anything they approach.*

*We had to be careful not to go downwind. Otherwise, we could be certain not to see any game, as their scent abilities are very keen. Their sight is also extremely good, along with their hearing. With all that in the favor of the wildlife, hunting in this dense bush can be very tough.*

*I have great admiration for a good tracker, as they have senses often approaching those of the game. As an example, Elias often knew game was in a certain nearby thicket that I had neither seen nor heard, and certainly did not smell. He would stop, move side-to-side, staring into thick thorn bush—move ahead, and soon point into the thicket. Only after careful study of the bush and usually after there was some movement did I detect what Elias seemed to sense being there.*

*Our scheduled meeting with our car was at 11 AM, so we started moving a little more rapidly. I detected the "grey ghost" appearance of a kudu that apparently had sensed us moving though the thicket, so I signaled to Elias to stop. Then we heard the pounding of the hooves of a large herd leaving the area. We chose not to follow them, as it would not have been right to hold Frank up.*

*Our rendezvous point was an intersection of several roads and cattle fences. While waiting for Frank and Ben, I saw as much game cross through this area as we had seen all day—a jackal, a hundred or so impalas, one of which was outstanding, and I almost shot a kudu cow. Frank told us they'd seen about four magnificent kudu bulls, one of which was very heavy and long, moments after they drove away from Elias and me early in the morning. Frank had not planned on shooting a kudu, but now changed his mind.*

TIME LAPSE

*I shot a big male baboon, as Ben and Frank wanted one for leopard bait. Baboons can be a very obnoxious pest, and they must be constantly cropped off. The landowners limit the number of leopards that can be taken, as they are the best predator against baboons. Frank collected a* nice impala with the idea that additional meat might be needed for baiting.

There are a lot of leopards here, which are allowed to be shot without restriction. However they are at present wrongly on the U.S. endangered list. In the midafternoon, we all drove westward to the Sentinel Ranch, which is near the Botswana border. John R. Bristow owns this ranch, and it is another hunting concession used by Ben De Wet.

This is the area where the Phillips party had just hunted and did very well. Bristow was expecting us, as he was anxious to show us around and especially get acquainted with me (as an agent for him) and give me a tour of the area.

He started out by showing us the remains of his mansion that had been burned out by the terrorists during the war. He explained that he was gone, and one day his son, who was also

🐾 **Baboons were very abundant and not much afraid of human activity as they are rarely hunted.**

living there, left to go to South Africa when the terrorists made a raid. They tied up all the African help and took two drums of aviation fuel into the house, punched holes in them and ignited the fuel. What a horrible, needless waste. I am ashamed to say that the U.S.A. sided with the terrorist movement.

John showed Frank a room full of artifacts that were collected by one of John's sons who is now away at school. Frank was a professor of anthropology at the University of New Mexico. Frank had already found some stone utensils that he figures could be over 10,000 years old. He says he is still looking for the "real old stuff."

John and one son, Linley, took us on a tour of the property showing us wildlife of many sorts—kudu, eland, ostrich, impala, bushbuck, zebra, and more, but it was very windy by now, and the game was not out in its usual quantities. They showed us new hunting camps that they are building out of bamboo and grass on the Limpopo. John explained that he has now sold all his cattle and is in the process of taking down all the fences. He said they used to have great herds of sable antelope but killed them off, along with a good amount of other game so that they would not compete with the cattle that they were required to put on the land when they started some 25 years ago. John is in the process of bringing sables back to the property.

We were back at River Ranch after dark following the 45-minute drive between ranches. As usual, Simon the cook had our open-aired cocktail lounge all set up and he had the barbeque going. The wind was still blowing

☆ **A crocodile resting along the Limpopo River on the Sentinel Ranch.**

and it was quite chilly. I broke out my insulated vest and put the safari jacket over that, which was just right. While Ben put some eland steaks on to barbeque, the stories went on.

Peter had a funny thing happen today. They have these big concrete water tanks used as holding reservoirs to feed the smaller troughs found throughout the property for the game. Some baboons were trying to drink, but the water was about four feet down from the top. From the hill above, he was watching the baboons trying to get to the water. One baboon held onto the tail of the other and lowered it down to the water. Several of them did it that way.

After breakfast, we went early to the same general area that we had been hunting. The weather (wind) calmed down so we felt the kudus should also settle down to a more normal pattern. We all agreed that the wind spooked the animals and that the wind caused too much

☆ **A young, lone cape buffalo along the Limpopo River.**

noise around the hills causing the kudus to stay away from them.

We drove Frank and Finias along with Marylin to a hill that would be the focal point of my stalking around the hill area. Bonasio and I were dropped off at our starting point. As the usual pattern went, we jumped a bunch of kudus in the thick stuff, cows, and young bulls. Saw an assortment of other game—impalas, duikers, and warthogs.

We crossed through the hills a few hundred yards below where Frank was and worked the area in sort of a cloverleaf pattern always coming back near where Frank was. After no success near the hills, Bonasio and I struck out to the flatter area. We had gotten into a torn-up area with a lot of fallen trees, which looked like old elephant damage and where there were a lot of fresh kudu tracks.

After following the tracks a short distance, we came right onto the herd. First, we saw one cow right out in the open feeding, and, surprisingly enough, she did not see us out in the open. Then we saw a few more cows, but we were able to hide behind some thorn bushes. Bonasio worked through the bush to see whether he could spot some more kudus.

About that time, the cows sensed us and started trotting off. Bonasio motioned me to come quick. Just as I got there, I could see a real nice bull vanishing into the thick stuff before I could get my rifle up. We cautiously, but speedily followed them. Not 10 minutes later we caught up and saw the bull vanishing from the scene once again, bringing up the rear of the pack.

We continued and, again, in another 10 minutes saw the bull in really thick bush looking right at us. The only part of him exposed was his head and neck. I swiftly raised the crosshairs as low as I could place them on his neck and squeezed off. The bull turned and vanished instantly. Bonasio had seen that the bullet hit a branch of a thorn tree and was afraid it deflected the bullet.

We quickly went over to inspect the area where the bull was and sure enough, there was blood. A very short distance away, we found the magnificent kudu. While I dressed it out, Bonasio went to get the car and the rest of the group. After pictures, we loaded the whole kudu into the Toyota and went back to the ranch.

They have good processing facilities with a hoist high enough to hang the kudu for skinning. I worked with the African skinners on the proper method for trophy skinning. Also demonstrated the use of the Wyoming knife, which was in a skinning kit I gave them.

## TIME LAPSE

For the past decade or so, communists in nearby African countries such as Tanzania, Zambia, and Mozambique have trained terrorists. The idea was to send bands of these trained (brainwashed) terrorists to mix with the local blacks, terrorizing them and forcing them to put them up and take care of them while carrying on their activities.

These activities varied from demonstrating against the (excellent) Rhodesian government to killing and destroying everyone and everything they could. This was a hard type of battle to fight for all the citizens, black and white of Rhodesia because of the inability to determine who the terrorists were. They were not a uniformed army in any way. One of the worst things they did to us was to kill thousands of innocent people by planting land mines almost everywhere. As indicated earlier in the case of Peter Bristow, homes were burned and mortared. The black citizens of Rhodesia were very happy with their progress under the whites.

Now, earlier this year, after many years of trying to fight off the terrorism, the government gave in and gave the power to the blacks. During all this time, the United States and most European countries sided with the communist terrorists, putting a ban on trade with Rhodesia and put every conceivable pressure on the government to give in to the terrorists and give them independence. Western countries did the same in most other parts of Africa and now Africa overall has gone back many decades in time, with famine widespread in most of the now "independent" black African countries. The black citizens such as our trackers, skinners, cooks, etc. are happy once again to work for the whites exactly as before, depending on them for guidance, education, and food in their stomachs. However, how long will it last?

Peaceful conditions existed at the time of my hunt in 1980, when Robert Mugabe became president and was hailed as a symbol of the new Africa. Under the independent government, President Mugabe slowly destroyed the entire infrastructure of Zimbabwe, terrorizing the

Ben De Wit, Chris, and the kudu that took the author three safaris to collect.

*businesses run by whites, confiscating the land owned by foreigners, and murdering many.*

*In the years following, I heard the terrible news that Peter Carimus and his family had been murdered and their farm confiscated. What black populations have not escaped to neighboring countries are unable to make a living under the lowest poverty conditions. At this time Zimbabwe has the world's shortest life expectancy—37 years for men and 34 for women. The widespread famine has caused wildlife and other natural resources to dwindle to the lowest ever. Another sad story of unwanted independence by the population.*

*We go on hunts and come home bragging, to anyone who will lend an ear, about what a great hunter we are—fearless in the face of the lion of Africa, the tiger of India, or the bear of North America. We enter our trophies in B&C or Rowland Ward record books and,*

# REFLECTION
# Professional Hunters

Even though a great deal of my hunting has been self-guided, I want to make it clear that I have the greatest respect and admiration for guides and outfitters, without whom hunting the world over would be chaotic, dangerous, and, to say the least, unsuccessful. One might ask what the difference is between a guide and an outfitter. At times, they might be one and the same, and occasionally an outfitter might be a one-man show.

A case in point was a dear friend and outfitter, Ed Cretney of Brule Creek, British Columbia. I first booked a hunt with him for bighorn sheep in southeast B.C. He had horses, tents, and know-how of the country. I had a great, yet unsuccessful hunt and wanted to return. The horses were a real pain and kept us camped too far down from those high, lofty-loving critters we were after. So next time I told Ed, "Next year I'm bringing the outfit and you'll be the guide." Our outfit, bedroom, kitchen, and food (freeze-dried) all came neatly packed in two backpacks. Ed and I backpacked from one end of the mountain range to the other, staying high in sheep country all the way. His vehicle was left at the starting point and mine at our scheduled hunt's end.

On our first hunt, Ed was the guide and the outfitter. On the second hunt, he was the guide, but I was the outfitter. Guides are a key ingredient to the success of a hunt. First off, they know the country like the back of their hand. In addition, just as important, they usually understand the habits of the game, which is critical. A "guide" might be a professional hunter (PH) of sorts, or a native "tracker." A PH will very often depend greatly on the skills of a tracker. From many of my own experiences, I have been amazed at the determination and ability of native trackers. Once a track is identified as one worth pursuing, their mental attitude is "at the end of the track, there will be that animal." PHs also develop the skills of the trackers, but use common sense like, "We'll die of thirst if we continue," or "We'll never get back to camp by dark."

Normally a licensed guide will be the hunter's companion and protector for the duration of the hunt, whether assigned by the tracker or the outfitter himself. Whether called a professional hunter or guide, they are indispensable for the hunter's success and safety. Many guides have lost their lives or been badly maimed by following dangerous game that had been wounded by their client.

They also have the ability to determine at a glance the size of animal, whether it is trophy class or not. Last but not least, they have the hunter's comfort, safety, and ability always in mind.

An "outfitter," whether a one-man show like Ed Cretney or a massive operation like Uganda Wildlife Development, is amazing, to say the least. They literally provide a self-sustaining community in the middle of nowhere. Whether the camps are taken in by pack train, lorry (large truck), or bush plane, the comforts of home are present, the magnitude of which varies greatly.

Outfitters' and guides' licenses are commonly issued by government agencies only to qualified and proven people. It is also common to award exclusive concessions or hunt areas to qualified outfitters in many parts of the world. These operators usually are the greatest conservationists, knowing that their resources must continue to be sustainable.

I like what Colleene wrote about professional hunters in her Uganda journal:

*. . . The professional hunter is expected to be a man of many capabilities, managing staff, shoeing horses in Canada, flying airplanes in Alaska and above all know what the game will do before they do it. One of the most vivid incidences of this was done by Ajay Kumar, my gentleman Shikar in India when he said the tiger would not come out in certain places but would come out here, pointing to a space between two trees–and that is exactly where he appeared as if he knew all the cues. The PH has to be a doctor, psychiatrist, and above*

*all share the enthusiasm of the sportsman who feels this is the only hunt in the world and that the PH has been looking forward to it as long as he has. They have to find the game, pamper the hunter when he can't, and keep everyone smiling.*

*But, among all of the professional hunters, there is one group that stands apart–a special breed of cat, known as the "Great White Hunter." Here is a man who eats, sleeps, and breathes his profession. He looks, dresses, and acts the part. He is admired by all he meets and is the hero of books written by Hemingway, Ruark, and others. He is a legend in his lifetime and have people all over the world convinced that he is some sort of a god. I am one of those people who believes in them . . .*

if they are large enough, receive awards from these two organizations or Weatherby or Shikar Safari Club or any other of the numerous clubs designed by and belonged to by hunters. But, no matter how we brag and carry on or how many times our name appears in record books, the real hero of the situation is the professional hunter. Without him our hunts would be cold, colorless, and miserable and, nine times out of ten, game-less. The professional hunter is the means to the end—the person depended on to deliver the goods in the most comfortable method possible and then expected to be able to take professional-type hero pictures with us posed dramatically beside the animal he has led us to and pointed out for our inexperienced eyes to see.

So, to make up for the injustices I have caused, I will try and explain the professional hunter and give credit where credit is due.

The professional hunter is expected to be a man of many capabilities, managing staff, shoeing horses in Canada, flying airplanes in Alaska, and above all knowing what the game will do before they do it. One of the most vivid incidences of this was done by Ajay Kumar,

my gentleman Shikar in India when he said the tiger would not come out in certain places but would come out here, pointing to a space between two trees—and that is exactly where he appeared as if he knew all the cues. The PH has to be a doctor, psychiatrist, and above all share the enthusiasm of the sportsman who feels this is the only hunt in the world and that the PH has been looking forward to it as long as he has. They have to find the game, pamper the hunter when he can't, and keep everyone smiling.

But, among all of the professional hunters, there is one group that stands apart—a special breed of cat, known as the "Great White Hunter." Here is a man who eats, sleeps, and breathes his profession. He looks, dresses, and acts the part. He is admired by all he meets and is the hero of books written by Hemingway, Ruark, and others. He is a legend in his lifetime and has people all over the world convinced that he is some sort of a God. I am one of those people who believe in them. I have had the privilege of hunting with them, of eating with them, and of listening to their vast experiences in the special world they live in.

# CHAPTER 7

# The Good, Bad, & Ugly

As we enter the end of the first decade of the 21st century, here is an overview of the wildlife conservation and hunting status of various African countries that had good wildlife resources in modern times. However, while some utilized this valuable renewable resource, others failed for whatever reason.

**The Good.** These countries have stable governments with sustainable wildlife resources and have well run hunting programs. It is also well to note that, in most cases, the revenues from hunters and hunting is of the greatest economic value and creates jobs and food for these rather poor countries. Wildlife populations are stable or growing, because the very small percentage of specimens taken by foreign hunters makes no difference in the numbers of game, but provides most of the money for conservation.

*Tanzania* contains the largest herds of game in the world and without changes will remain that way indefinitely. Hunting and other tourism is its largest industry. *Ethiopia* has a stable government and unusual game in this mountainous country. It also has excellent savanna areas in the Omo River valley bordering Kenya, the Danakil area in the east, and the Gambela area bordering Sudan, and they have handled the wildlife wisely.

*Zambia*, the former Northern Rhodesia, has good government-controlled hunting areas that are leased out to private operators. Their hunting revenue brings more income than all other forms of tourism.

*Botswana* is a very sparsely populated country with vast wildlife resources with a well-run hunting and wildlife program, which is being reassessed in 2009.

*Namibia*, formerly Southwest Africa, continues to propagate game to all time highs, mainly through hunting/conservation programs award by private landowners, but also through government areas that are leased to private operators.

*South Africa* is a shining star in sustainable use of natural resources. It has risen from a minimal hunting area in the mid-20th century to possibly the largest hunter's destination by the turn of the century, largely through the efforts of private landowners recognizing wildlife as the prime use of land, as well as the stable government.

*Cameroon* is a stable former French colony that has surfaced more recently for good savanna hunting in the north and rain forest game in the south and has continuously improved with the presence of hunting.

*Gabon, Benin* and *Burkina Faso* have stable governments and offer good hunting for a limited number of animals.

**The Bad.** These areas of Africa were once excellent hunting destinations for some of the most abundant and unusual game with happy and peaceful people under colonization. After getting independence, self-serving and brutal dictators destroyed the country's infrastructure, including the wildlife programs. Their unscrupulous armies killed off great quantities of animals, sometimes for their own food, but often just to kill. These countries are slowly getting their act together, realizing that to go on, they must make use of their sustainable resources. They are slowly developing the hunting/wildlife conservation programs.

*Uganda* is slowly solving its government mishaps and striving for peace among its people, while beginning to allow hunting on a limited basis.

*Mozambique* is improving tourism and hunting little by little in this war-torn country, which once was dependent on both as a major income.

*Zimbabwe*, under terrible conditions caused by President Mugabe, still allows hunting to go on in government areas that are leased to operators. One daring to hunt there is encouraged not to spend any time in cities, but to be taken directly to hunt areas.

*Central African Republic* continues to allow hunting during these unstable times and there is possible danger for hunters and operators with the presence of well-armed poachers.

*Congo* is included here because the government is stable, although in the absence of hunting, wildlife had been considered valueless. The Congo is now considering allowing hunting to utilize this renewable resource.

**The Ugly.** Include countries whose governments have gone bad and, in most cases, have allowed decimation of their wildlife programs. In some cases, it appears that perhaps the governments themselves closed hunting, so that they could go in and kill off the elephants for the lucrative ivory trade at the time.

*Kenya* was once the ultimate destination for an African safari, and actually the first in the heyday before the openness of sport hunting after WWII. However, for some reason, they closed hunting in 1979 without warning. The rumor I heard was that Kenya needed big funding from the World Bank. The story went on that the Bank was anti-hunting and so to get the funding they would have to disallow hunting. Well, whatever the story, wildlife populations have dwindled enormously—positive proof that hunting is conservation, as wildlife becomes valueless in its absence.

*Zaire,* now the Democratic Republic of Congo, is in a state of chaos since 1973 when President Mobutu closed hunting, and without the presence of game management, the wildlife has been destroyed including elephant populations that at one time had large numbers of big tuskers.

*Chad* was once a destination with exotic desert animals in the northern sub-Sahara Desert and excellent forest and plains game in the south. With the closure of hunting, in the early 70s, and poor game management, it is questionable how much game is left.

*Sudan* was once one of the greatest destinations for hunting in the suppressed south, witnessed earlier in this book. However, political turmoil has shut down all hunting in the south, and in most areas wildlife has declined, including the elephants that apparently have been poached by the same ring that took Central African Republic and Zaire. However, reports are that a large population of plains game is doing well east of the Nile in the swamp-protected areas near the Ethiopian border, as it is almost impenetrable for people to live or travel there. In the Muslim north, hunting still goes on for the Nubian ibex and gazelles.

*Angola,* which was Portuguese West Africa, was a fantastic destination for hunters of diverse and abundant wildlife. However, since their independence in the 70s, hunting was closed and wildlife decimated for lack of value and management.

*Rwanda,* after almost two decades of strife, unrest, and lack of government control, is home wildlife to that have likely suffered greatly as in the other war-torn countries.

This is certainly not the last word on African wildlife, but an idea of circumstances at the end of the first decade of Century 21. It does show that countries with stable governments that have intelligent wildlife programs and that encourage hunting have better game populations and benefit financially from the renewable resource.

# REFLECTIONS
# Too Many Elephants?

**R**ecently at a gathering, I was told by an uninformed antihunter that elephants were endangered. I responded to her deaf ears with my knowledge, but to no avail. Let me explain the difference between Indian and African elephants. They appear the same, except at first glance one can see the ears of the Indian variety are about half the size of those from Africa. What one mostly sees in the zoo and circuses, and being used as beasts of burden, are normally Indian elephants, which are tamable, and may be endangered in the wild.

The African elephant is another story. At the time of this writing, in several areas of Africa, they are multiplying at an alarming rate. I conferred with brother Bert on the situation. He is still active in Africa (still guiding at times in Tanzania)

**An entire forest in Uganda was wiped out by elephants. The trees that they could not knock over by butting, they would girdle the bark off, killing the trees.**

and a director of Conservation Force. Here are some of the statistics that he provided. The African Elephant Specialist group of the World Conservationist Union indicates that elephants are increasing at an alarming rate in many areas. Botswana has an estimated 140,000 and Tanzania about 130,000.

In Africa's protected areas, where they can make proper surveys, they estimate about 600,000. Therefore, the count could total a million or so. No doubt, they are endangered in some areas, like where CAR, Sudan, and Zaire come together, where poachers pretty well cleaned them out (all unstable governments with lack of game control). In some places like Botswana's Chobe area, culling will no doubt have to be done to preserve the habitat. Elephants are very destructive of their habitats, often wiping out entire sections of forests, as well as low-growing shrubs, plants, and grass that sometimes takes years to recover. They can also destroy water resources that they and other game depend on. This affects the habitat of all wildlife, including birds, primates, and mammals.

Hunting does nothing to reduce the herds, as the trophy hunter is looking for a good set of tusks. Maybe one out of every thousand elephants is collected as a trophy. Here are some facts that affect elephant populations. To begin with, the world market on ivory is down, as poaching is controlled pretty well in protected areas. In addition, it takes a long time for an elephant to grow sizeable tusks. The males are the ones that grow big tusks. (Females have small tusks.) Elephants live very long lives, maybe up to 100 years. The old adage was that it took a year for every pound of ivory on each tusk, i.e., a "hundred-pounder" (weight of each tusk) was a hundred-year-old elephant. But modern data has proven that often a hundred-pounder was no more than 50 years old, which is still a long time to wait for these expanding herds to produce the ivory to view or collect. Therefore, what do you do, let them overpopulate and destroy their own habitat, as well as that of the millions of other wildlife, and quite likely die of starvation? Or do you keep them in balance? Perhaps my antihunting acquaintance should solve this difficult problem.

# CHAPTER 8

# My Year in Transkei

*by my son Chris Kent Klineburger*

Icouldn't believe it when Dad said, "Get your desk in order and turn your files over to Skip (Jennings), you're heading for Transkei in a couple of weeks."(For the big picture of Transkei, see Chapter 4 "Africa—From Top to Bottom" in this section of this book, starting on the date of 11 November). His idea was for me to oversee the trophy handling of clients specimens, which included training skinners and educating the staff on shipping and documentation, all very critical under new rules for trophies coming into the U.S.A. and other Western countries.

What kind of a background would a 19-year-old kid have to take on the responsibility such as that? Well, looking back, I guess Dad trained me well. I started hunting Africa in Mozambique at the ripe old age of 12 and even got my first dall sheep and caribou in Alaska before that. I grew up in the hunting business and learned through practical experience. As my high school days were nearing end, the subject of ongoing education surfaced—college or on-the-job training. My goal was to be part of the company, so the decision was easy—school could not teach me the complexities of our business.

One month out of high school, Dad took me on the exploratory hunt in Kashmir for that type of experience. (See Chapter 8, Part IV.) He then turned over the African Division of our travel agency to me for sales and outfitter coordination. After my folks did the maiden hunt in Transkei, they handed me that new and exciting program and the bookings came easy. I had the 1980 season fairly well booked by February of 1980 and the season was to start in March. It was like Dad saying "Get over there and make sure your clients' trophies are well taken care of."

So off I went with a one-way ticket to the independent Republic of South Africa, Transkei. It is a Native State of the Pondo Tribe, sandwiched on the Wild Coast between Natal to the north and Cape Province to the south. No Europeans ever owned land here. However, two South Africans of European descent formed a partnership with the newly formed Pondo government to develop the Mkambati Game Reserve as a much needed tourist industry. The two, Nic Venter and Phillip Hommes, took me in like family. I arrived just before the first safaris were to start and was assigned a building for the trophy care, part of which was open air. Two Pondo men were put under my care. They already had a big walk-in cooler ready to age the carcasses, along with an adjoining butcher shop. The plan was to only eviscerate the animals in the field, and then bring the entire animal into our compound for skinning and washing the carcasses and then hang them in the cooler.

The first several weeks seemed to be non-stop animals coming in each day, about noon from the morning hunts and then by cocktail time in the evening after the afternoon hunts. With my evenings pretty well occupied with skinning, I was quite anxious to get my boys well trained so I didn't have to be watching over them, so I could spend my time socializing with my hunting clients. My mornings were free, so I spent considerable time out in the field studying game movements and looking for exceptional specimens. When space was available in a hunting car, I would go along and help spotting game and do the field care of animals taken.

Once I was freed of training the skinners, Nic and Phillip asked if I would help supervise some other projects including removal of some old cattle fences, building bridges, making racks for drying meat, and more. The main staff of Pondos was furnished housing right in the compound, but many native laborers lived in a village that was an abandoned leper colony. A number of them worked with me on various projects. They would invite me up for any local celebration.

🦶 **Don Sutherland dances with the Pondo women at the abandoned leper colony village.**

🐾 **Kent Klineburger and Roy Hinds with the hartebeest that Kent guided him to**

We would supply them with meat for such an occasion and they would do a non-touristy song and dance for us. They also supplied us with fresh bananas and other produce. They were wonderful people and fully trustworthy.

A long-time friend and client of ours Louis Stumberg brought his 14-year-old son Eric to hunt. I was out with them along with professional hunter Phillip Elliott when I told them about an extraordinary reedbuck that I had studied on various occasions. I guided them to the spot and made them wait till I knew he would appear. He did and Eric collected him with one shot. (In my many visits to their home in San Antonio, we always reminisce that occasion).

As client numbers began to increase, my services for guiding increased and soon I acted as a full professional hunter right to the end of the season in the spring (fall in the Northern Hemisphere). I believe my first client to fully guide was Roy Hinds from Texas, whose notoriety was setting the standards for white tail deer conservation for game farming. He collected an outstanding hartebeest along with a full bag of South African specimens. Among others that I guided or helped guide include Harry Tennison, president of Game Conservation International; Frank Hibben, the Dean of Anthropology at the University of New Mexico; and the families of Stan Studer and Bob Phillips, both of which were well known Texas sportsmen. It was a special treat when uncle Bert Klineburger and Brigitte came and hunted with us.

During any slow times, we kept the clients busy fishing off the rocks on the coast. We never knew what we might catch—actually couldn't identify a lot of them. Some people came just for fishing. One of them was a fine girl that claimed to be Frank Sinatra's secretary. The following January I attended the Safari Club International convention in Las Vegas, where she tracked me down and comped me with front row seats to see the Man himself.

The staff at Mkambati was overwhelmingly good and I was proud to be a part of it. We gave service that was unbelievable to our clients. Nic told me, "Your folks told us, 'Give

🐾 **Kent was the PH for Mauricio Escamez for this wildebeest taken at Mkambati.**

the clients outstanding service and respond to their every need, set your prices accordingly, but do not nickel and dime them to death with extras,' so that's exactly what we did, including free booze of their choice. They also said that this place was like the TV series *Fantasy Island* and how they greeted their visitors with champagne, so we decided to do that, as well." Sure enough, when the clients landed, we were there with champagne and snacks overlooking the falls and the beach, all of which set the stage for what they could expect for the rest of their stay. So everything, including the charter flight from Durban, was included, except the trophy fees for animals collected. Besides excellent results from a wide variety of wildlife representative of South Africa, we kept the clients busy fishing, horseback riding, beach combing, and socializing around the campfire. They were among the happiest hunters Africa has ever seen.

Before the end of the season, however, there was some uneasiness with Nic and Phillip. The lodges that were to be built on the Mtenta and Mkambati Rivers were put on hold. Some new people were showing up and we saw less of Nic & Phillip. A sporting goods dealer from Durban and a Botswana hunting operator showed up with some Transkei officials, rather secretly getting into everything. To make a very long story short, by season's end, Nic Venter and Phillip Hommes were out of the picture and new management was in place.

Apparently, a promoter got to Transkei officials and convinced them that everything was being done wrong at Mkambati. My company was told that hunts would no longer be one to two weeks in length, but be no more than 5 days long *and* be tied into a Botswana safari, which would be a requirement! That combination virtually shut down the wonderful hunting operation being enjoyed in Transkei. The new managers did accept the hunts that we had booked for the 1981 season on the old basis, but it was impossible for us to convince clients to book with the new requirements. We resigned as the exclusive agents for Mkambati. To our knowledge, the new program completely failed and from all we can find out 30 years after the wonderful beginning in 1979, the Mkambati Game Reserve and the potential income to the poor Republic has gone to waste.

# CHAPTER 9

# Around the World in 80 Days

## UGANDA

In mid-October, 1965, my wife, Colleene, and I commenced on a historic trip that would take us from Seattle across the Atlantic on hunting expeditions in Uganda, Mozambique, Iran, and India crossing the Pacific and returning to Seattle on New Years Day, 1966. This chapter will serve as our transition into Asian explorations, which unknowingly were to be the greatest accomplishments of my life. The remainder of this book will dwell deeply into the little known last frontiers of the world, but for now, here are brief stories of this 2½-month trip around the globe. Not only did we go around the world, but also we traveled high in the Northern Hemisphere and way down in the Southern Hemisphere.

Our trip first took us to Rome, Athens, and Cairo for looks back into the history of civilization. After enjoying the ancient ruins and interesting culture of those people that were by far the most advanced of the known world thousands of years ago, we headed to British East Africa. Our first stop was Nairobi, Kenya, where we enjoyed a stay at the New Stanley Hotel, the historic icon of early explorers, especially hunters.

I had business that needed my attention in Arusha, Tanganyika, so I went there while sending Colleene ahead to Kampala, Uganda, to commence her safari with Uganda Wildlife Development (UWD). Before Colleene arrived, the professional hunters were debating on who was going to be stuck with ole' Chris's wife, who would no doubt be a stuffy and boring, yet demanding, undesirable member of the opposite sex. They put her off on Nicky Blunt, the youngest and newest member of the staff.

Well, when the manager, Ken Jesperson, brought this beautiful, lively lady into the office all jaws dropped! The PHs (Professional Hunters) stumbled all over themselves while making her comfortable and supplying drinks and snacks, while Nicky shyly sat in the corner with a big smile on his face. Nicky was a very shy gentleman, but as professional as any PH ever was.

Nicky drove Colleene to the Semliki Hunting Reserve, the better part of a day's journey over lush savannah and bush country to the very west of Uganda. Semliki is a depression surrounded by mountains on three sides and Lake Albert on the west, which is the boundary with the Belgium Congo. To the south are the Ruwenzori Mountains or Mountains of the Moon, snow-capped, and right on the Equator, also home of the mountain gorilla, extending south to Rwanda. A beautiful lodge had been built there for UWD guests, with private rooms and a dining/bar area.

Here is the beginning of Colleene's journal describing the Semliki area and the start of her hunt:

*The grass is very high and has not been burned yet. Flowers grow profusely, decorating the countryside with deep exotic colors and blooms. Even the greens and browns are more intense and alive in Uganda. Everything and everyone—even the air—is more alive—tingly with the extreme zest to be alive. I guess I must believe in the "Mystery" of Africa. It is not something you see like the snake charmers of India, but a feeling that fills you with intense desire to be part of the mystery, to take part of a wondrous world where living and being happy are the two important things, not wealth, or personal esteem.*

*The White Hunters are marvelous. I could listen for hours to their stories of hunts, hunters, and animals. All told with sound effects with the White Hunters acting out all the parts. Of course, they are the heroes in each episode. Nicky is not the same extrovert as the others. He feels deeper, I am sure, and is more in unison with the country. He is supposed to be very shy but*

**PH Nick Swan jokingly volunteered his help to guide Colleene's safari.**

A lodge was built by Uganda Wildlife in the Semliki Hunting Reserve to accommodate hunters or tourists.

Nicky Blunt was a shy gentleman, but as professional as any PH ever was.

*I found him to be quite talkative and most delightful company.*

*The four of us, the African boys, Kenga, and Charles are always with us and are a happy and relaxed lot. This is the first time in ages I've been relaxed around strangers. It all changes when we return to camp and see all the others, though.*

*We sighted in the rifles, and Nicky had me "dry" fire the 30-06 a few times before he let me shoot. I know they were all concerned about my shooting but I managed to bring a smile to their faces when my bullet bored a nice clean hole next to Nicky's in the bull's-eye. All Nicky said was "Let's go hunting" but I could tell he was very pleased and for the first time could relax knowing I could shoot a gun. He didn't have me shoot the .375, as he is afraid I'll get gun-shy from the recoil—he is quite thoughtful.*

*We looked over the game today and decided on a beautiful Uganda kob. The kob is very graceful and is so abundant that I am sure you see at least 2,000 head each day from the roads. Since Kenga had on a light shirt, I told Nicky that I could carry my own gun—after all! So, the two of us took off through the elephant grass at a very fast pace in such heat.*

*Nicky had drawn me a picture of each of the animals I can shoot and pinpointed the place I am to shoot them. After our stalk, I was delighted at the perfect and still broadside shot the kob gave me and managed to bring its life to an end with a one-shot kill. Both Nicky and I were delighted and Nicky surprised too I'm sure.*

Several days after Colleene's visit began, I arrived in Kampala where I had a series of meetings, including an inspection of Jonas Brothers of Africa facilities that I had established three years before. Then I was furnished a car to meet up with Colleene.

I stopped for a visit in the high plateau at the base of the Ruwenzori Mountains with an old acquaintance, Bill Pridham. He owned a tea plantation near the town of Fort Portal. Bill is a legendary wildlife control hunter that worked with the Uganda Game Department to help keep herd populations under control, including taking rogue elephants that continually wipe out the natives' shambas. I then continued down the steep escarpment to the Semliki valley and to the Semliki lodge that had been built since my 1962-63 visits here.

It was exciting to hear the hunting stories about Colleene's hunt so far and other tales of safaris past and present. She had already collected several species of plainsgame, as well as got a nice forest elephant, sub-species of the larger pachyderms that roam around the rest of Uganda.

She went on to collect other plainsgame, including cape buffalo. While hot on the trail of a lion, we got distressing news that we had to leave early because of flight changes. We were scheduled to fly direct from Entebbe to Johannesburg, but the flights were canceled. The only connection available for several days was a flight from Nairobi the day after tomorrow and no connecting flight was scheduled from Entebbe to Nairobi.

The only way to get to our scheduled hunt in Mozambique was to charter a flight. The only aircraft available was a Cessna 170, so we said, "Bring it on." The next morning

« Nicky gets up high to spot for game in the beautiful, unburned savannah of the Semliki Valley. Colleene is dwarfed by the anthills. Kenga and Charles join Nicky in admiring Colleene's trophies. Even though their buffaloes are isolated in the Semliki Valley and more of a "dwarf" variety, they are considered Cape buffalo.

the small bird arrived for our lengthy flight, well over 500 miles, crossing the entire width of Uganda and halfway across Kenya to Nairobi. When crossing into Kenya, the pilot commented, "Hope we don't have a forced landing here, this is Kikuyu land, where the Mau Mau uprisings recently took place."

The Mau Mau was an insurgent organization bound to force the expulsion of white settlers from Kenya. The Mau Mau was put down, but one of its leaders, Jomo Kenyatta, became president last year when Kenya got its independence. So it was uncertain just how receptive these Kikuyu would be if three foreigners showed up in this hostile land. However, the flight went well without a sputter.

In Nairobi, we couldn't get into the New Stanley, as some sort of celebration was going on—maybe the Indian New Year. We settled for the only room we could find in the East Indian part of town. Couldn't sleep much because of continuous fireworks all night.

## MOZAMBIQUE

Our reservations had been made by UWD for our flight to Johannesburg. While sitting in the bar at our Jo'burg Hotel Europa having a Lion Beer, Colleene jokingly said, "I guess the only way I'll down a lion is to down a Lion (beer)."

Our connection to Lourenço Marques, Mozambique, was in order. We were met by our host José Ruiz of Nyalaland Safaris, who graciously showed us around the major town in the south of the country. Over dinner in the courtyard of our hotel, José explained the

magnitude of his hunting areas. Mozambique was just coming into its own as a major destination for safaris and certainly, José's operation was one of the top players.

Nyalaland Safaris was named after one of the concessions, Nyalaland, which itself was named after a spiral horned antelope, nyala, common only to this region of southwestern Africa. The safari company has three concessions, some bordering Kruger National Park along the South African border and along the Limpopo River, a major watershed from South Africa and Rhodesia.

The Nyalaland Concession is 8,000 square miles and was never hunted until now. The Mavue Concession is 5,000 square miles and the Chicualacuala Concession covered 12,000 square miles, 25,000 altogether for the exclusive use of the safari company.

The next evening we were put on a night train heading north to near our first camp. We were awakened at 3 AM in our berths and told to be ready to disembark. We were greeted by PH Manuol "Mac" Figueira and taken by hunting car to the Assane camp. Another PH, Harry Manners greeted us, escorting us to the dining hut for breakfast.

The camps throughout the concessions were permanent, African-styled quarters, all a different style, some rondoval/adobe type, others squared/thatched walls and all with grass-thatch roofs. This is Portuguese East Africa, and when this country was colonized, they introduced the best of Portuguese hospitality and cuisine.

During our three-week stay, we hunted four different camps; besides the Assane were

The Assane Camp had an elephant skull on top of an anthill at the entranceway.

The Chicualacuala Camp was by far the best safari accommodations we ever experienced.

Everyday our clothes were washed and pressed by the staff using a charcoal iron.

The hunting car was dwarfed by a huge baobab tree that is common to southern Mozambique.

the Mpuzi, Lilau, and Chicualacuala camps. When moving to other camps, we were escorted by Vasco Cardiga, brother-in-law of José, in hunting cars.

Other professional hunters at our disposal were Antonio SaMello, his son Luiz Pedro SaMello, and Harry Lee-Wingfield. Colleene and I were the only guests at the time, so one can imagine how spoiled we were. We collected game of all types from Cape buffalo and eland to small ones like suni and duikers and, of course, the nyala. The lion once again evaded Colleene, as our hosts wouldn't let us stay in any one camp long enough to concentrate on lion.

A considerable amount of our time was spent filming our safari to make a 16mm movie for promotional purposes. They offered for us to stay as long as we wanted,

Chris was intrigued to collect a nyala, the namesake of Nyalaland Safaris.

but our planned schedule to hunt in Asia could not be changed.

## A RETURN TO MOZAMBIQUE

In order to keep yarns about Africa all together in this book, an interruption of the 'round-the-world trip is being placed here to tell of a rather historic event in Mozambique. By 1973, guerrilla warfare, spurred by communist trained terrorists, seemed to be resulting in an end to the freedom of this peaceful land that was colonized by Portugal in 1505 after being first explored by Vasco da Gama seven years earlier.

This year 40,000 Portuguese troops had arrived in Mozambique to fight the rebels. I had been putting off hunting the northern

**Colleene stands fascinated by her huge cape buffalo.**

**The common eland were abundant from all four of the hunting camps.**

area of the country since my last visit eight years ago. I contacted my good friend Adelino Pires who headed Safrique, a well-established safari company, and the date was set for July of 1973.

Colleene and son Kent, now age 12, were to join me. In addition, to join us on the hunt was good friend Charlie Duke and his wife Dottie. Charlie is the astronaut that walked on the moon during their three days in the Apollo 16 program, exactly one year ago.

Curtiss, Donna Scarritt, and Sam and Rose Pancotto, all old acquaintances of mine, also were to hunt with Safrique. Charlie offered to do a film presentation and talk on the Apollo Space program in Beira, the main city in northern Mozambique, after our safari. So our safari was promoted there, telling about the showing and our safari.

Now here is an occurrence that there seems to be no human explanation for. The Dukes, traveling via Rome and Athens, and Klineburgers, routing through Madrid, were all to arrive at a scheduled time in Beira. The following morning our charter aircraft had been scheduled to take us to Nhamacala, Safrique's northern concession #6. While we travelers were taking in Europe's historical past, a weird thing happened. While we all had accurate itineraries in hand, both parties missed their days of departures and called Safrique's headquarters in Beira that we would arrive a day late.

Not being easy to book the only charter aircraft in Beira (or possibly in all of Mozam-

bique), the staff had to make a decision to utilize the charter and the camp awaiting us by sending a group of Spaniards, also there for hunting, in our place. When the charter arrived at camp and the hunters disembarked, terrorists awaiting them in nearby bush opened fire with machine guns, killing one and wounding several!

After our arrival and hearing the terrible news, it was my feeling that the terrorists' plan was try to kill Charlie, an American space hero, in order to get international publicity for their cause. Later as I reminisced about the tragedy, I truly felt that it was Divine guidance that kept us safe, throwing us off schedule. Fortunately, the wounded Spaniards rapidly recovered. The deceased hunter was the personal doctor of the late Generalissimo Franco of Spain.

The Portugucse military warned against continuing any safaris, but after all our insistence, they supplied each professional hunter with a machine gun and hand grenades. They also assigned a well-trained mercenary to accompany Charlie for the duration of his hunt. The mercenary explained his function had been to resemble terrorists while going into a village that had been taken over by the guerrillas and saying "Where are my buddies?" then going in and wiping out an entire unit of terrorists.

All our camps were now changed to concession #10 near the village of Gano, bordering the Indian Ocean where there were no signs of guerrilla activity. It was a beautiful camp, well laid out with permanent cabanas

Our camp at Concession #10 was a deluxe permanent camp with all the comforts of home.

with walls made of bamboo. It could accommodate up to a dozen guests at a time with hunting available in all directions.

The terrain was vast plains, with those near the coast interspersed with swamps that the waterbuck, reedbuck, and buffalo favored. Inland was drier with large quantities of Sable antelope, zebras, impalas, hartebeests, bush pigs warthogs, bushbucks, and various duikers and other smaller antelope.

We collected all the game we wanted. We took time to do the skinning of trophies out in the field so that we could take our surplus meat and drop it off in various small villages spotted around the concession.

Charlie and Adelino struck out in a fly camp for a few days to look for kudu and other game not available in #10. It was a little

Because of intermittent swamps on the plains near the ocean, amphibian vehicles were necessary. These monsters were driven across water the same as on land.

Colleene Klineburger and Charlie Duke swap the day's experience while awaiting a deluxe lunch.

José Pires and the boys gather around Colleene's biggest
sable antelope.

chancy with the terrorists' activity, but all came out OK. They spent one night in concession #6 where the Spaniards were raided, however, all was quiet. The mercenary said the terrorists were cowards and only struck innocent and unarmed people.

**Here are a couple of journal entries from our trip:**

**Colleene:** *Day 4—July 13, 1973*

*I guess the 13th is an unlucky day for me, and it started out so beautifully. Chris got a bushbuck about 45 minutes from camp. Then Kent got a big red duiker with one shot. All was beautiful with the world until we saw sable. I offer no excuses for myself other than shear stupidity and that's not good enough for me. Since everyone said I had to shoot, I did, and before it was over, I had killed two sables. José had to finish off one for me. The other one, the wrong one, went down with one shot. What can I do now?*

**Kent:** *Day 11—July 21 1973*

*Dear Diary,*

*Today we were chasing a reedbuck around and jumped another one. José said shoot thinking it was the same one. Killed it with one shot in the neck. It was 11½ inches. We met Curtis and Donna under the big tree on the edge of the planes and had lunch. On the way back we saw a bunch of wart hogs. I shot three times at a big female—missed the first time, hit him the second time in the rump then went after him and shot him just before he went down the howl (hole). Donna got drunk tonight.*

Our hunt went very well and safaris continued for the remainder of 1973. However, hunting closed in 1974 after the Portuguese were forced to give the country independence. Here is the way the terrorists worked. They were trained (in other African countries) to mix with the villagers. They went into villages and took control of the people by telling them "Do what we say, or die." They forced the villagers to say "We want our independence," even though the villagers were happy and didn't even understand what "independence" meant.

Western countries kept listening to the plea for independence and pressured Portugal to make them independent. So after 470 years of help and colonization by Portugal, in 1974, they signed a cease-fire and gave independence, effective June 25, 1975. The head terrorist Samara Moises Machel became president.

The people stood up and, under the Mozambique National Resistance (MNR),

**Kent Klineburger, age 12, collected a well-rounded bag of trophies, including the warthog and Cape buffalo.**

started a guerrilla war against the socialist government, which finally weakened. By 1992, Mozambique finally returned to a liberal government and the situation began improving. In the meantime, there were 16 years of warfare, poverty, and a deletion of the majority of wildlife. With the reintroduction of wildlife conservation, most species began coming back and doing well.

## INTO ASIA–IRAN

The third week in November we exited Africa and entered Asia as we continued our Around The World trip. Our destination, Iran, was an unlikely place to go hunting at the time, as it had never been open for foreign sportsmen. Here is the story leading up to this historic hunt.

Among our worldwide taxidermy clientele were people like Prince Abdorreza Pahlavi, a renowned international hunter and the brother of the Shah of Iran. In a visit to our studios in Seattle, he requested that we train a couple of Persian taxidermists in order to do their museum work. We agreed and along came the Tajbakhsh brothers, Nourala and Hedayat, for their apprenticeship. They became like family to us.

Right away, we talked about hunting in Iran and soon evolved a plan for an exploratory hunt for Colleene and myself. We had the blessings of Prince Abdorreza to hunt for mountain game, which by now we had become quite passionate about. The Tajbakhsh family was in the lineage of the Persian royalty of old.

Our selected guides were cousins of Nouri and Heda, as we called them. Upon arrival in Tehran, Hossein Tajbakhsh, who spoke excellent English, greeted us. He settled us in the Commodore Hotel and treated us to a fine lamb kabob dinner and a short tour around the neighborhood on foot. The most prominent custom observed involved the women, almost all of which were covered with their black chadors, covering everything except their eyes. Fortunately, Colleene had slacks on. Even so, the eyes were upon her.

The next day we were picked up and headed east to a village belonging to Amir Tajbakhsh, called Shazand, Arak. The farther from Tehran, the more it seemed we were stepping back in time. Off the main road, there were more donkey carts than cars.

Passing through villages, beautiful rugs were laid on the roadway for cars and donkey carts to run over. It was explained that once the rug was completed, the wear and tear of the traffic on them served to tighten up the weave. As tough and well made as they are, apparently they are no worse for the wear, and once cleaned they are like new and ready for the market. In one village we passed through, they had Colleene wear a shawl over her head, explaining it was a very holy town and a woman is forbidden to go uncovered.

We arrived at Amir's village late in the day and settled into relatively nice quarters. Our bed was a pad on the floor with soft wool blankets. The toilet was ground level with a place marked on each side where your feet go

From our second story room, we had a view of Amir Tajbakhsh's walled village and his adjoining farm. Note cow dung being dried for use as fuel for their fires.

when you squat. We had been advised to bring toilet paper, which we were thankful for.

A well-prepared meal was awaiting us in Amir's dining area. It was a tasty rice dish called pelow, with lamb and vegetables all cooked together. Much fine talk around the table of many things, but mostly about hunting and what we were to expect. The sheep in this area are the Armenian sheep, a subspecies in the urial sheep family. We were given the option to set a camp up in the mountains or stay in the village.

The Armenian sheep were found in a relatively low mountain range right near Amir's village. Therefore, we decided to stay in the village and hunt out from there each day. We could drive his jeep to the base of the moun-

tains and hunt on foot. Colleene put her vote in for a mule to ride.

Hossein also owned a village just a few hours drive from Amir's village and we were to hunt ibex and sheep later on from his place. The quarters that we stayed in were the same used by Prince Abdorreza Pahlavi, who uses Amir on many occasions as his personal guide in a nearby controlled game area.

The mountains that we hunted were fairly small and virtually surrounded with small villages every five or ten miles. While hunting, it was common to see villagers with their burros in the mountains digging bushes for fuel. Not many of the local residents hunted, but still the wild animals were quite alert and spooked easily.

In the first day of hunting, we topped out a ridge that gave us a beautiful view of the valley lying below us. Quite a number of draws converged within a quarter of a mile of the crest that we were on. Therefore we spent

On the mountain ridge, Colleene and Hossein Tajbakhsh (to her right) relax while some spot for sheep and others prepare lunch.

a couple of hours glassing in these draws and on opposite faces. Several experienced hunters from the local villages were with us and they turned out to be some of the best spotters and trackers, and what terrific mountain men they were. The Persians are known climbers and climb they did as a necessity and a pastime.

Two rams were spotted shortly after we had a full course meal on the ridge—chicken, lamb kabob, and rice. The rams were down at least half way to the valley below. The wind, approach, and everything seemed to be in our favor so the stalk began. Everything seemed to go great except when we got to where they should be—no rams. We had spotted a villager digging bushes off in the direction that the rams were heading, and it is possible that they had spotted him and turned back, but where they went we never knew.

The next several days in different areas on the mountain went in a similar manner. One day we were able to watch a large band of sheep for several hours while trying to work out plans for a stalk. It was interesting from the standpoint of seeing just how they can share these mountains with people and domestic herds.

The sheep were spotted a half-mile below us in a very large canyon. We thought that perhaps they would start moving up toward us so we just sat and watched. After a while some villagers came down the bottom of the canyon with a large herd of sheep and goats while the wild sheep just

sat and watched. No sooner did the domestic herd pass through the valley below than the wild band ran at full speed all the way down to the bottom of the canyon right behind the domestic sheep, and up the other side.

After the domestic herd went down about another quarter-mile, the wild sheep came back across the canyon at full speed again as if they were making fun of their civilized counterparts. They continued to run up our side of the canyon, but about a mile downrange. They settled down to feeding and resting, but our stalk, again, was to no avail. Colleene was in position and got a couple shots off, but missed the running targets.

During our pleasant stay at Amir's village, we always had great fun with these fine people, with evening and morning meals well prepared and time to visit. Every morning it was up early so we could be ready to start up the mountains by dawn.

Small villages were established most every place suitable for farming. The farm owner builds a village for his workers and their families, thus owning a village in addition to the farm.

One morning breakfast was a roasted sheep head. It was placed on the table right in front of Colleene's place. (We always were positioned in the same places at the table). When I spotted the morsel, I tugged at Colleene with a "Why don't you sit over here?" as I pulled a chair out for her. With her sleepy eyes not yet quite in focus, she replied, "I always sit here." As she plunked down, she was staring eye-ball to eye-ball at the delicacy. Even though it was not a good substitute for ham and eggs, we found that a baked sheep head was a delicacy and a tradition for many Asians.

The people here typically live in walled-in villages outside the main towns. The visitor never sees individually scattered farmhouses. Their buildings are always grouped together in a tightly compact stockade with high adobe walls where at night even the goat and sheep herds are brought.

The landowner, like Amir, actually owns the village and the livestock. The other people in the village work for the landowner, who provides for them. For a bathhouse, we were escorted to a large, earthen steam room, a sauna of sorts, with a separate room for splashing water on yourself to rinse off. Colleene was the only female, so we took turns. I assume they had another communal bathhouse for the villagers.

On another stalk on a different day, I missed one single ram that was lying down—shot right over the top of him. We would have set a camp in the hills, but all of us thought that we would have our sheep within the first

⚲ **Rather than make the steep climb from the valley floor, Colleene put in for a mule.**

day or so and we could move on to other game, but every day it was up and down the big mountains.

Colleene rode a mule, and there were times I wish I had taken one to keep up with those untiring Persians. One day about mid-afternoon, we spotted a small band of sheep down near the base of the mountain below us. Being late November, with the days short, we knew we didn't have much time so we started the stalk without even seeing what the sheep were going to do.

Just after starting down, we saw a couple of medium sized ibexes, which are not too plentiful in this particular area. We skirted around them and continued down. Because of our experiences in spooking these animals, we decided that the old man, Mohammed— about 75 years old and very spunky—and I would go down for the stalk, while another would stay within sight above and signal us as to where the sheep were. This turned out to be one of the most interesting experiences of the trip.

Neither of these fellows could speak English so it was sign language between Mohammed and me. It was obvious that they had done this many times before as they had their signals really down to a tee. We made our approach downward on the opposite side of a hogback from where we had last seen the sheep.

Every couple of minutes Mohammed would stop and look at our spotter above. He had no interest at all in looking over the ridge to see if the sheep were there, but just went by the signals from above. If our spotter took

his hat off with very deliberate arm sweeping motions and set his hat down on the ground either below him or to the right of him, or to his left, then that was the direction that the sheep were from us.

The interesting part was that once we got into position and the spotter felt that we were ready to top out on the ridge, he never made another motion. By this time, we were so far below the spotter that we could just barely make his motions out with the binoculars, and I wondered how he could possibly tell how close we were to the sheep.

Mohammed was so confident that we were in exactly the right place and so cautious at this point of the hunt that he just nudged me to top out and shoot. I eased up over the rocks and leveled off on a beautiful ram that had just gotten up just 15 yards away. I dropped him in his tracks with the first shot, and a second beautiful ram ran up and stood right along side of him. I wished Colleene were along as it would have been duck soup for her to get the other one.

She had gone down another canyon in hope that they might be able to find signs of a ram she had hit the day before—no doubt, fatally. Yesterday, we had run out of time due to darkness and couldn't follow the blood trail any longer. They did find her ram, but scavengers had gotten to it, ruining the skin.

After looking over this fine ram, it was obvious why we had done a poor job of shooting. They were less than half the body size of a North American sheep, about three feet high at the shoulder. This would cause a person to misjudge the distance and size of

75-year-old Mohammed holds my rifle while the spotter raises the head of my Armenian sheep.

the target. The Armenian sheep has horns like the Mouflon sheep, but instead of the curl coming forward toward the neck, they go back above the neck or shoulders. Seeing these sheep from a profile view, the horns almost look like a halo sitting just on top of the head.

Our original plan was to quickly collect our sheep here and then continue on to Hossein's village, where he had red sheep, another of the urial family, as well as the Persian ibex. We were running too short of time to accomplish that, as our shikar in India was critically scheduled and not changeable. Therefore, we elected to spend our remaining time here and do some sightseeing in Tehran with the promise to return.

We spent our time establishing procedures and tariffs for an ongoing hunting program for foreigners to enjoy. We visited with Prince Abdorreza and saw his rather

The Tajbakhsh family formed the first hunting operation, Iran Professional Hunters, Ltd., for which our company was their agent. Our brochure shows the unbelievable low price of $2,836 including airfare for a 25-day arrangement. Note that the Persians referred to the Armenian and red sheep as mouflons, since they were in the family of moufloniforms. »

I soon returned to Iran to collect other sheep specimens. Nouri Tajbakhsh, who had been training in our taxidermy studios, came to guide me on a red sheep hunt in the Royal reserve east of Tehran.

Chris and his Persian guides with a specimen of Esphahan sheep taken in west central Iran.

This urial sheep was taken in the east end of the Elburz Mountains.

↑ **Persian ibex (bezoar goat) in the esphahan area.**

crowded trophy room, which he explained was to be expanded. However, many of his specimens would end up in the planned Royal Museum.

His Highness was in charge of the Forestry and Game Department and gave his approval of an ongoing program allowing foreign sportsmen to hunt the abundant wildlife, which include various subspecies of urial, ibex, red deer, wild boar, wolf, gazelle, and the possibility of permits for panther, cheetah, and brown bear. Our visit was the historical opening of an Asian country in modern times for wild sheep and goat hunting. At the time, India was the only country in all of Asia open to hunting.

## TIGER SHIKAR IN INDIA

It was certainly with "sweet sorrow" that we left our fine hosts in Iran, but we promised to return often for our ongoing relationship. We changed our flight to arrive a day early in Bombay in order to be rested for our month-long schedule in India.

Our plan was to hunt in Madhya Pradesh (Central State) for two weeks, and then fly to New Delhi where the headquarters was located for Allwyn Cooper Ltd., our shikar operator. Then we would visit with its owner, Vidya Shukla, who was also Minister of Home Affairs for India. From Delhi, we were to go to the foothills of the Himalayas for another two weeks to hunt by elephant-back.

On our way to town from the Bombay airport, we witnessed considerable poverty as we viewed residential areas of crowded tin shacks along a small waterway, obliviously polluted with floating algae. As I pointed out domestic ducks in the dirty water, I told Colleene, "Remind me not to eat duck in the restaurants." We settled into the Ritz Hotel, which was very clean and well laid out.

After contacting our shikar operator in Delhi by phone and receiving our transfer information to the hunt area, we walked out to see the town and find a bank for some rupees. There were a lot of beggars, several on every block. We gave money to one twisted and crippled guy that almost appeared to be tied in a knot. On our return later on, we noticed the same guy sitting up taking a break, having a cigarette—our first, and good, lesson in this form of entrepreneurship!

Two days later, our driver picked us up and took us along farms and forests deep into south central India. Once out of the city, we saw no more of the slums that we observed in the outskirts of Bombay, nor did we see any begging.

Oxen carts on the single-lane highway slowed our travel from Bombay to our roadhouse.

Farther along, we saw workers along the road and they seemed to include as many women as men. Surprisingly, the women were always clothed in very colorful and long saris, yet barefooted. Very often, we observed that some people's mouths were red, as if bleeding. Our curiosity was satisfied by the explanation that they were chewing betel nut. Apparently some sort of "upper."

All along the rather narrow two-lane road, we were rarely out of sight of people walking to or from the frequent small villages that also seemed bustling with activity in markets of every description. Over-laden donkeys and buffalo-drawn carts were always an obstacle that slowed our travel more than anticipated, causing a late evening arrival well after dark.

Ajai Kumar, our gentleman shikari (an honorable name given to their Asian profes-

sional hunters), greeted us at our forest house. He excitedly reported that he and his staff members had just returned from building a

Ajai Kumar. Our "gentleman shikari" chats with Colleene around the fireplace in our roadhouse accommodation.

machan in a nearby area where a cattle-killing tiger had been located.

Over a well-prepared meal that included curried beef, rice, and all the trimmings, the talk was serious hunting instead of the usual welcoming camaraderie—leisurely chatting about the trip, family, etc. Ajai explained that this marauding tiger had been raising havoc with the villager's sacred cattle and had just killed one in a small valley. The site offered perfect conditions for a daytime beat, which had been arranged for daybreak the next morning. The exciting anticipation of such a great start on our shikar overshadowed our former thoughts of a long and relaxing night in our soft bed, draped with mosquito netting.

We were greeted at wee hours with hot tea in our bedroom and after quickly adorning ourselves in camouflage. We gulped down a continental array of pastry and fruit, then crowded into our American-made jeep. All of Ajai's talk was centered on what to expect and how the beat was planned.

The day before, they had already engaged the beaters from the village and had a couple of his staff orchestrating the functions of the villagers. He explained that it was a perfect location for the beat, as the tiger had killed the cow in the bottom of a small valley.

He said the tiger was a very large male and would no doubt make its lair close to the kill to protect it from other scavengers, including panthers and other tigers. At the head of the draw was a nice "saddle," an opening between two ridges, one on each side of the valley. Very likely, the saddle would be the exit route the tiger would take in leaving the area. On the far side from the draw is where a tree machan was built, overlooking about 50 yards of cleared area in the saddle.

The beat itself would be a triangular-shaped pattern where the various villagers would be located, with the base of the triangle being the wide part of the valley near its bottom, while the other two sides would be along the ridges that converge at the saddle.

Partway down from the top of the ridges, about every 20 yards or so, a "stopper" would climb and sit up in a tree. The function of a stopper is to turn the tiger back into the intended direction of the beat if he tried to exit the area by topping over the ridge. Usually a clap of the stoppers hand would do the trick.

The beaters would line up across the bottom of the canyon to form the base of the triangle. At the magic predetermined time, the beaters would start up the valley talking to one another and hacking on trees as if cutting trees for wood. This is something tigers are familiar with, as villagers are constantly in the forests for wood.

We walked about a half-mile from a dirt road to the machan at dawn. It was a nicely built platform built about 12 feet high in a multi-trunk tree. They had tied crossbeams to various branches, and smaller split logs served for the decking, all hardwood from nearby. A bench was made to accommodate Colleene, Jay (as Ajai was nicknamed), and me.

A ladder was also built of natural tree limbs. At this point, we quietly climbed into the machan. In a low voice, he told that there were no sides to the platform as the tiger would not look up for danger. He also indicated the approximate area where the tiger should appear from the dense cover about 40 yards in front of us. He said the tiger should look ahead and around cautiously, then rather quickly, cross the open area below to seek the dense cover behind us.

He said we would not hear the tiger, but it would just appear. He cautioned against shooting the tiger in the head, as one that becomes wounded from a jaw shot will certainly become a man-eater.

"Go for a heart shot," he said, after he is out in the open.

I was to be ready, the .375 magnum magazine fully loaded and a cartridge in the chamber, and none of us were to make any noise or fast movements. We had already agreed that I would be the first to shoot.

As I was psyching myself for instant action, many thoughts went through my mind—won't hear from him; he will just appear; don't shoot in the head; wait till he's out in the open and shoot for the shoulder.

I was ready with my gun and my body at about the correct angle to slowly rise and shoot. Jay touched my arm as we could hear the beaters in the distance with an occasional shout and smacking of trees. In a very short time, I heard the snap of a limb. I slightly rotated my body to better positioning to the sound and raised the rifle.

At the edge of the forest the head and neck of the magnificent beast appeared, coming right out from behind a tree. However, he stopped and cautiously looked all around, and then it looked up right at us. Jay whispered, "Shoot." Its shoulder was not exposed, but to avoid a head shot, I moved the iron sights as far back on the neck as possible and squeezed off.

The tiger turned and retreated into the beat area. Once the beaters heard the shot, they had stopped and were silent. They saw the tiger returning so they started shouting to turn it back our way. It did, but not through our saddle, but coming along the ridge to my left at top speed.

As I swung the rifle to take a running shot, Jay was in my way sitting next to me, so I stood up and shot just as the tiger was disappearing into thick brush. We heard the whop of the bullet hitting him, but we also heard sounds of him crashing through the brush farther down.

We quickly descended from the machan and all decided there was no hurry in following the wounded cat. If he were well-hit, he would soon lie down and die. If we rushed in too quickly, he might be sitting waiting for us and return the favor in one giant lunge.

We inspected the tree where I first shot and, sure enough, I had hit it when I was swinging toward the shoulder. The tree was perhaps 7 or 8 inches in diameter and the bullet did pass all the way through it, but may not have had much energy left when entering the tiger.

Jay commented that this tiger had no doubt been shot at before from a tree machan the way it had looked up at us. He had never seen one look up in the trees before as a source of danger.

By now, all the beaters and stoppers had caught up to us. He had them sit and wait quietly for further instructions, while we set out following the tracks of the wounded cat. It was apparent that it was running on three legs, so probably with the cat running at top speed, my swing forward on the animal was not far enough and the bullet entered the hindquarter as it was angling away from me. As we followed the tracks and blood trail, we could see it was not slowing down.

In conferring with local guides and villagers, they had a hunch it was heading into a thick area with a lot of brush and tall grass. However, as we could literally step on the tiger before seeing him, the area would be unsafe for either tracking the animal or allowing beaters to go through. If he were healthy enough to charge, he would no doubt kill someone before he could be dispatched.

After a great deal of discussion by everyone, including the village chief, a plan had been made. The villagers had a small herd of water buffalo that they would fetch and herd near the area where the tiger was thought to be. The idea was for Jay and me to get in the middle of the herd with a couple of herdsmen, and we would go right through the patch.

Three things could happen if the tiger was alive and in there: We would run the tiger out to hopefully a better place to hunt him; the buffalo would spook if they got wind of the tiger and we would perhaps know its whereabouts and go for it; or the waiting tiger would charge a buffalo and we could dispatch it. The fourth thing that might happen is we would find it there, dead.

We moved the jeep to the designated rendezvous point. By now, our breakfast had worn off, so we had a prepared lunch that awaited us in the cooler. The buffalo herd arrived and we planned how we would zigzag through the area. We left Colleene in the jeep with her 30-06—not a tiger gun, but a well-placed shot could stop almost anything. Several of the boys stayed there with her.

I felt a little strange being herded like a buffalo. The area was a little swampy. There were about 20 buffaloes. Jay and I each would stay about one buffalo in from opposite sides and as close as we could to the front of the herd, just behind the leaders of the herd.

It seemed hours were spent on this sojourn until we felt we had covered as much as we could and to no avail. We had kept our eyes open for tracks and blood, neither of which appeared. Back at the jeep, Colleene told of a muntjac coming out into the open. She could not determine whether the horns were of trophy size, so she passed. The muntjac is also called a barking deer because of its sharp barking sound when it warns that danger is near.

Shikaris utilize that warning as a sign that a tiger or panther might be near. A large male may not be more than 35 pounds body weight. It is a deer with antlers just a few inches long and, oddly, a pair of long canine-like teeth. On the way back to camp, Jay stated we must go all out to get this wounded

**The right front footpad had a scar on it that helped keep track of "Scarfoot."**

tiger, because if a man-killer showed up in the area, the villagers would determine it was my tiger that turned on them. Jay had sent a couple of his trackers to follow the tiger's trail as far as they could.

Back at the roadhouse, our cook had prepared a chicken tandoori dinner for us, a delicious treat, the Indian version of chicken cacciatore—sort of. The British built these roadhouses back in India's colonial days, so that officials would have nice accommodations while traveling about the country. I believe the purpose is the same now for officials and their guests, but they are also available to our host, Allwyn Cooper Ltd.

They are strongly built of concrete, round in shape, with bedrooms, bath, and kitchen around the perimeter, open in the center for dining and relaxing around a fire-place. In addition, there was a concrete deck all around. Although there was a permanent caretaker, our host furnished our staff and provisions.

Jay explained how well the game management was handled. All of India was divided into areas called hunting blocks. They maintained a wildlife census for each block. Hunting quotas for all game were determined annually for each block. In the case of tiger and panther (Asian leopard), they might allow one, two, or sometimes no cats to be taken in a certain year, with high priority on troublesome cats, like the cattle-killer we were after.

Aside from the cats, India has a lot of forest and terai game including sambar deer, muntjac, wild boar, wild buffalo, gaur (a bovine), chital deer, blackbuck, and more.

All along the Himalayas, mountain game includes argali sheep, serow, ghoral, tahr, bahral, and markhor, as well as gazelles.

Our block is quite large and right in the center of India. The area is semi-tropical, covered with vegetation, including teak and kowa trees. Bamboo forests support a lot of big game as well as primates and game birds such as peacocks and the chicken-like kala teeters and colorful gamecocks.

Our trackers returned and reported that the tiger traveled a long way before the track was lost. The blood trail diminished, but he was traveling on three legs, indicating the wound was in the left hind leg.

Our hunting block was spotted with small settlements, with people scratching a living with little farms, domestic stock, and logging. Their transport consisted of animal drawn carts.

A trailer loaded with machan building supplies.

We purchased live goats for tiger bait.

The building of a tree machan.

Positioning ourselves in the machan for construction of seating.

Ajai Kumar and Colleene have a snack on the hood of the Jeep before heading into the woods for a beat.

They said the right front footpad had a deep scar across it, making the identification of this tiger's tracking easier in the future. We nicknamed him Scarfoot. The next day's plan was to search the areas in the direction he went but also spread the word among all villages and with all who worked in the woods (such as loggers and bamboo cutters) to keep alert and report any findings.

Therefore, that was what happened and in the days that followed, we did get reports in several cases of the spotting of pugmarks of Scarfoot. Each time we reacted with a plan to best capture our prey. Many a night I spent in a tree machan. A number of drives by beaters were performed, and several times we tried to actually track him down to his lair.

One night while I was in a machan, our staked live goat made a big fuss, but Scarfoot did not come to make the kill. Inspection of the tracks showed where he had come close enough to look over the area, and left after not liking what he saw. He was one very smart cat.

As our scheduled time of departure was growing near, we all decided it best to scratch the plans of going on the elephant-back hunt in the terai and devote our time right here, where we must get Scarfoot. Being constantly after my prey, it was hampering Colleene's chance at success on tiger even though she did spend some nights in machans and participated in game drives, being spotted in possible zones for the cats' escape route.

Here is one episode that turned out successful for Colleene. One morning when we were getting a little rest after being up all night in a machan, a phone message was received that a cat, apparently a small tiger, had just killed a buffalo.

It was actually the responsibility of the shikar operator to investigate such matters. We concluded that if it was determined that the cat must be taken because of it being a threat, Colleene would go for it, even if it were a small tiger.

Jay said the location was quite a distance away and that we should be prepared to stay all night, if necessary. Therefore, off we went through mostly back roads for what seemed about three hours where we visited with the village chief. He said that this was the first recent problem that they have had, but they know of a village some distance away that had considerable problems from a big panther and he was concerned that maybe that cat had moved into this area. We were supplied a local guide to direct us to where the buffalo had been killed. We were able to drive close, but had to walk maybe a half-mile on a well-worn cattle trail.

We quietly approached what was a yearling buffalo that maybe weighed 300 pounds. Only a small amount of it had been eaten. After inspection, Jay said they felt sure it was a panther, but certainly a large one leaving such large tracks.

The area was quite flat with no trees large enough near it to make a tree machan. We dragged the carcass out into a more open area and built a ground machan within a stand of bushes, by adding more tree limbs. This made a nice round blind with room enough

After arriving in the remote village where a cat had killed a buffalo, the village chief provided a man to guide us to the location.

for two people in plain view about 40 yards from the buffalo.

By the time the blind was made, it was twilight. Monkeys started chattering nearby. Jay said to me, "The panther may be coming—you go with the boys back to the jeep, talking and whistling as you go, imitating wood cutters leaving the woods." He snapped out the instructions to the three natives with me and tugged at Colleene to enter the blind.

Following instructions, we got to the car shortly before dark. The one Indian started the car and went maybe 100 yards, turning off the engine and coasting to a stop. We gathered some wood and just as we started a fire, we heard two shots from the distant machan. We put the fire out and headed up

the trail by flashlight. To our amazement, there were Jay and Colleene standing over a huge panther.

Excitedly, Colleene told the story. After sitting on the ground in the blind about 10 minutes, something came from behind right up to the blind. Jay flipped his rifle over to the direction of kind of a whimpering sound. Looking at Colleene, he shook his head "no," but put off the safety ready to shoot. They could hear its heavy breathing, then the animal left.

Jay turned his attention back to the bait. At almost dark, the panther ran out of the bush, stood right over the buffalo, looked all around, and settled its stare right at the machan. Colleene had already had her rifle in readiness, so she leveled onto the cat's shoulder and squeezed the trigger—all this in seconds.

After the cat was down, Jay fired his rifle, just to make sure, although Colleene's shot was fatal. The animal that had approached from their rear was a hyena that Jay could see through the bush and had gotten ready to shoot if the hyena decided to join them.

Jay dispatched helpers to fetch the jeep that they were able to bring all the way with the help of a little clearing with their machete. We eviscerated the cat to rid it of all the body heat possible, loaded it whole into the jeep, and started the long trip back to the roadhouse.

Upon skinning the panther out the next day, we found lead buckshot embedded in the skull on the side of the nose and in the roof of the mouth, and the right canine tooth was broken completely off. The bones had all mended, so the damage was done at least six months. Jay said this panther could certainly become a man-killer if not already one. He said he would try and find out more from the general perimeter, but we heard no more.

I had also taken a panther, but I cannot come up with an exciting or dangerous tale of my heroism. One night in a tree machan hoping for Scarfoot to show up, I heard the crunching of bones at our bait. My companion touched my arm, a signal we had worked out when he was ready to turn on the spotlight. Rifle raised, I nodded. As the light illuminated the

panther, it was an easy shot at about 30 yards distance.

After almost four weeks of patrolling a great perimeter, following occasional leads, driving at night with spotlights near where there were signs of Scarfoot, organizing beats, many nights in tree machans, decisions had to be made. We canceled our onward flight to Bangkok where we were to spend a couple days over Christmas in the New Nana Hotel.

Even though our time had been tense and tiring, not to mention disappointing, it was an enjoyable time viewing a great variety of wildlife and learning the culture of such interesting and determined people. They were a happy, proud, and hard working people, scratching a living from the environment. We did collect muntjac, chital, and sambar specimens. The sambar is a wiry haired deer similar in ways to an American

**Having taken her panther at the last minute of dusk, Colleene waited till dawn to get this photo along with Ajai Kumar.**

Colleene holds her hand alongside the huge paw and shows the broken canine tooth of the panther.

elk, with heavy horns of only a few prongs on each antler. The chital is a whitetail-sized deer, reddish with white spots and similar horns to the sambar, but thinner.

I spent all night Christmas Eve in a machan, where Scarfoot was thought to be, with no luck. Some wild pigs had come and shared the meal intended for our cat. After we napped at the roadhouse, a runner came reporting that at dawn a bamboo truck driver saw a large tiger that was limping as it crossed the road. We rushed to the reported location and sure enough, Scarfoot's tracks were found. He was walking on all four legs.

Knowing that the cats were nocturnal, we knew that he would find his nest for the day, so everyone's knowledge was pooled to determine where. The thought was that he would go straight in from where his tracks led to a rather shallow valley with thick cover in its center. Stalking was out of the question as there were exit routes for the tiger in every direction. The only answer was a beat. The exit area for the cat and the only place open enough for a clear shot would be right on the road that the cat had crossed early this morning. The plan was to collect a hundred beaters who would quietly go in and form

**Author and Jay looking over Chris' panther as it is brought out of the woods in the morning.**

a giant U-shaped circle around the valley. Colleene, Jay, and I would position ourselves along the road about 75 yards apart, standing in the brush along the far side of the road.

It took the rest of the day for the monumental chore of organizing such a complex drive. What made it so complicated was that, to begin with, the beaters must enter the area undetected and find their location in the perimeter, but then their movement and sounds, or lack thereof, would begin slowly from the base of the circle toward the road.

We three sentries positioned ourselves along the road and awaited the sound of a single shout from the head beater on the farthest side from us. The beat was on, and it was now dangerously close to getting dark. I was centered on the road, with Colleene to my right and Jay to my left. I stood there tensely, praying, "God, if I am ever deserving

The local villagers carried the whole sambar out of the forest.

» Chris and Ajai with a muntjac or "barking deer." Their "bark" often warned us that a cat was nearby.

⚜ **A segment of the beaters was given final instructions by
the head huntsman to form one side of the semi-circle.**

of a Christmas present, please finalize this episode as you are willing."

The beat was much quieter than previous drives, with no chopping on the trees nor the widespread vocal orchestra. As my eyes constantly scanned from side to side, safety off and rifle in readiness, suddenly the tiger was exactly in front of me, crouched in the

⚜ **I got my Christmas present a day late. Back at the roadhouse, our
only chance for a photo was using the headlights of the car.**

bushes and looking straight at me with only his head and neck exposed.

Having myself psyched up to react to any sight of the cat, I raised the rifle and fired, jacked another shell in the chamber, and shot again as a safety measure. Jay and Colleene came running, and soon stoppers appeared on the roadway. On inspection of the front paws, it was Scarfoot! When I explained the crouched position of the tiger, Jay said, "He was ready to spring on you." I felt that the other possibility was the tiger was lying flat to prevent my spotting him. Nevertheless he moved no more.

The driver, having heard the shooting, brought the jeep to us. We quickly got the camera out, but darkness was already on us. Without flash, we couldn't get photos. Colleene and I made some quick decisions on the remainder of the rest of our itinerary. We asked the driver if he would mind driving all night to get us to Bombay. He agreed, so it was back to camp, where we did our packing and made our salutations to Ajai and the staff.

We did take time to make photos of the tiger using the headlights of the jeep. We went right to the airport in Bombay and our luck continued—a flight was available, connecting in Bangkok, to Hong Kong where I had business appointments with a company called Foo Kee that was manufacturing various taxidermy supplies and gifts for us. In addition, we were to rendezvous with my brother Gene, along with Alaska outfitter Ron Hayes and big game hunter Pat Salvino from Seattle. All three were on their way to India for a shikar with Allwyn Cooper. All was accomplished in our Hong Kong stay, including Colleene and I getting custom-made pure silk suits for $45 each.

On 30 December, we were off to Tokyo where we were staying at the New Japan Hotel to celebrate New Year's Eve. To our amazement, in checking in, there was our good friend Pat Brady, sidekick of Roy Rogers, and a member of the Sons of the Pioneers. He informed us that all of the famous musical group was there for an engagement in Tokyo.

Before even going to the room, we went to the bar, when Bob Nolen showed up and joined in. Over the next 24 hours, we had more visits and talks about our mutual friends, Roy and Dale. After celebrating New Year's Eve there, we had an early morning flight on January 1, 1966, Tokyo time. After crossing the International Dateline, we arrived in Seattle to celebrate New Year's Eve December 31, 1965, concluding our trip around the world in 80 days.

# PART IV

# THE DAWN of ASIA

Perhaps Inner Asia was the least known part of earth by outsiders in the nineteenth and early twentieth centuries before communism pretty much closed the doors for many decades. However, thanks to early adventurous hunters in the late 1800s and up to the mid 1920s, much was chronicled in those important first years of discovery. I started a library of those old books, including Roosevelt, Andrews, Lydekker, Morden, Littledale, Carruthers, and many more. With topographic maps, I traced their footsteps and recorded wildlife distribution across Asia. Yet with all that data, there were many blanks and unknowns.

What happened in history and in the lives of the Klineburgers could only happen once in the twilight of Asia hunting. As one reads through this priceless record of an extraordinary time, he will travel the unknown. As Ralph Waldo Emerson once wrote, ''Do not go where the path may lead——Go instead where there is no path and leave a trail.'' That pretty much describes the Klineburgers as they virtually opened Asia to hunting. The late Elgin Gates, one of the leading sportsmen of modern times, in a keynote speech, dubbed the Klineburgers as ''Gamemasters of the World,'' a name that followed them around the globe.

Asia was about the challenge of the unknown, the lure and mystery of faraway places, and sharing the experience.

To me, Asia was mind-boggling. The Soviet Union alone covered 11 time zones—-almost halfway around the world. Inner Asia contained the Argalis, Urials, and Mouflons, while the Far East was the habitat of the Asiatic bighorns. Wild goats were spread from Europe to the eastern extremities of Asia—over 40 different subspecies of mountain game, while North America contained only five. There also seemed to be countless forest and plainsgame, including cats, bears, gazelles, canines, bison, and numerous members of the deer family from moose to tiny musk deer.

The pioneering spirit, that all of us hunters have, gave me the drive and ambition to focus on the hunting opportunities Asia had to offer.

My brothers and I did not have a big picture in mind or a game plan, but took one opportunity after another—-one country after another. As learned in Iran, it was political connections that would open the doors. Hosting the King and Queen of Nepal on their Alaska hunt certainly opened that door. We also utilized the People to People Sports Program established by President Eisenhower to connect with officials in countries like China, Mongolia, and Afghanistan.

It was not just a case of "who you knew" but "what you knew" on the subject of hunting. I came to find out that I knew more about wildlife and their distribution than most government officials knew. Most importantly, I knew that wildlife is a renewable resource and a profitable resource. The Sportsman Financed Wildlife Program that I presented included financial and material benefits, but most importunately education to the local people. This resulted in the best poacher becoming a guide and the best game protector. The local people gained respect for the animals, proving our point that the presence of a hunting program puts a value on wildlife and worth protecting.

# CHAPTER 1

# Afghanistan

Except for India, Asia has virtually been unhunted and certainly the least traveled by outsiders. The most distinctive breakthrough materialized when back in 1967, we were able to negotiate a hunting program in Afghanistan for the Marco Polo sheep and other game.

Of innermost Asia, the Pamirs have always been the most romantic locality. It is the home of the *Ovis ammon poli,* named after the great Venetian traveler Marco Polo, who first reported on these magnificent wild sheep. Aside from Polo (who was thought to be a liar), no outsider had ever seen, much less hunted, this magnificent beast until Captain Wood, in 1837, penetrated the source of the Oxus River and brought back a head of this wild sheep, enabling the naturalist Blythe to name it.

It was late in the 19th century before other expedition's penetrated Inner Asia that hunted the Pamirs in China and Pakistan and the Asian countries that became part of the Soviet Union. By the early 20th century, the areas were once again closed to outside travel. Great heads of Marco Polo sheep had been picked up measuring 75 inches and 70 inches with tremendous curls dipping down on the ends. The largest horns recorded were brought out from the Afghanistan Pamirs, but travelers were not allowed to go there. The early expeditions usually took several months, starting from India, western Russia, or the eastern China coast.

Then in 1926, Inner Asia was briefly opened with great American expeditions—the Morden & Clark expedition and the Kermit & Teddy Roosevelt expedition. Since then, the great mountain ranges of Asia have been virtually closed to travel of any type.

However, in 1959, Elgin Gates and Herb Klein received permission to hunt the southernmost fringes of the Marco Polo sheep range in Pakistan's Hunza region right on the China border. A highway from China to Pakistan now runs through Chapichingal Pass where Elgin hunted, driving the sheep northward near and into Afghanistan and China.

Through negotiations with the Afghanistan government, we introduced a sportsman-financed hunting and wildlife conservation program that had never existed before in that country. The program included allowing foreign sportsmen to hunt the Marco Polo sheep and all other non-endangered game. The other game included markhor, ibex, snow leopard, a grizzly-type bear, wolf, urial sheep, and gazelles.

The resulting profits would provide game management for all wildlife, not just for the animals hunted. We entered into an exclusive contract, which included conducting surveys of proposed hunt areas, supplying equipment not available in Afghanistan and education for all aspects of outfitting. By 1967, we did exploratory trips all along the Hindu Kush mountain range and into the Pamirs, collecting specimens, surveying wildlife, and educating locals as to sustainability and value of this renewable resource. The Hindu Kush is the "backbone" of Afghanistan traversing

the country west to east from Iran to China. It divides the land from the fertile north that borders the Soviet Union, to the arid south that borders Pakistan. The Range's eastern extremities are the southern edge of that finger of land that protrudes to the right as one looks at the map. That "finger" was one of the silk trade routes that connected Europe to China in those early days of exploration and trade. The northeastern end of that finger is the southern edge of the Pamirs, which is an extension of the great Himalayan Range. The east end of that finger is known as the Wakhan Corridor and part of Badakhshan. Several exploratory trips were taken by

**The Klineburgers visited many ancient sites, including the Salsal Bamyan Buddha that was carved in the 2nd and 3rd centuries in the heart of Afghanistan and at 53 meters high became the largest statue in the world. This photo taken by Chris Klineburger is among the last taken, as the Taliban demolished this and other statues in the year 2001.**

the Klineburgers throughout the game-rich Hindu Kush and Pamirs.

Sport hunting was entirely new to these people—they could not understand why anyone would want a set of horns and endure such hardships. Till now, these mountain herdsmen shot every animal they could for meat and skins with their primitive muzzle-loaders.

We would find the best local hunter to be a guide. Back home we would call him the best "poacher," but since there were no game laws yet, he really did no wrong. After receiving many benefits, this hunter would no longer shoot the game, but would encourage all others to protect the wildlife. These guides soon learned hunting and stalking techniques as we instructed them and supplied them with binoculars, spotting scopes, and footwear.

All the game was very spooky, as they shared the same habitat with the locals. Aside from making cloth and fine wool rugs, it seemed the main occupation of the Afghans was supplying food—farming and livestock. Any place that could be terraced or irrigated was farmed; otherwise domestic herds of goats, sheep, cattle, camels, and yaks made use of the vegetation in the plains and mountains. The ever-present muzzleloaders were readied to take pot shots at game everywhere. The alert and wise game kept their distance, so the most skilled hunting techniques were essential.

One of my early experiences—and a memory that will live with me forever—was my first sighting of Marco Polo sheep. It was at 17,000 feet at the head of Tulaboi Valley when our staff foolishly went over a hill riding their yaks in plain view. Across a beautiful horseshoe-shaped lake, a herd of "poli" came to alert in glacial moraine just below an ice field. Much too far to shoot and impossible to stalk, we watched through the spotting scope. There were 25 or so in the herd and all rams. They proceeded away from us single filing on the smooth ice, which gave us a perfect silhouette of the long spiraling horns against the white. Many of the rams were trophy class but the one bringing up the rear had such massive and long horns, it seemed double the size of the rest. We watched til they became tiny specks as they disappeared over the horizon of ice, yet the horns of that big ram could still be seen! In discussing where the herd had gone, the locals did not know, as they said they never went there, as even the surefooted yaks probably could not make it.

Field care of specimens was high on the list of teachings for the staff. We singled out skinners, and spent tedious hours instructing them, as well as supplying them with proper knives and ensuring there was plenty of salt to cure the skins. Another important subject to be addressed was learned by us early in our travels—sanitation and health. It seemed diarrhea was ever-present, even though we thought we took every precaution. In one incident, after they followed my instructions to scald the dishes after washing, I saw a helper drying the dishes with a filthy rag and even spit on the plate to get a nice shine! From then on, our dishes were scalded in our tent and left to dry in a dish rack, never leaving our sight.

â **The Klineburger caravan leaving civilization as they head for the Wakhan Corridor.**

For the high Pamirs, because of where our base camp was at 14,500 feet and often-crossing passes at 19,000 feet, we supplied oxygen equipment and instructions on its use. We supplied medical kits and frequently conducted clinics for the staff, curing infections, stomachaches, and headaches. We took extra clothing and footwear and when leaving an area, we would leave everything behind for the staff other than the clothes on our backs. I took western saddles, which worked very well on the yaks. I took packsaddles, and taught them the use of the diamond hitch.

The Marco Polo sheep hunt in Afghanistan was truly a modern day expedition, even more so than hunting by dog team or skin boat with the Eskimos, or trekking into the Himalayas with Sherpas. In our exploratory days, we blazed trails and took much time surveying, yet those to follow still had the better part of a month to make the trip. Half

**Thrashing grain by animal hooves was among many primitive lifestyles seen for the first time by outsiders.** »

of the time was traveling to and from the Pamirs, through the most primitive conditions where people lived much the same as those in the time of Christ.

We eliminated several days of travel by using a Twin Otter aircraft owned by Royal Afghan Airlines to go from Kabul to Faizabad, the last point that any outsider was allowed to travel, aside from we hunters that had the blessings from the King. From here, it was traveling along that narrow finger of land protruding north easterly between Tajikistan on the north and Pakistan's Hunza on the south and extending all the way to China.

The first several days were by four-wheel drive vehicle. The only vehicles available with four-wheel drive were an American International panel truck, British Landrover, and a Russian Jeep. Much of this was without

Our International truck fared well crossing rivers early in the day before melt-off floods each afternoon.

A large boulder in the raging river prevented the truck from completely washing away after the narrow track collapsed. Afghan manpower rebuilt the road and righted the International truck that went no farther.

Our remaining vehicles, the Landrover and Russian jeep, got us to Qala Panja, where we negotiated for horses and donkeys to continue along the Wakhan Corridor. Chris checked out Bactrian camels, but the rugged trail ahead was too difficult for them. The author taught the use of the Diamond Hitch on equipment we furnished.

The easy going soon transformed to extreme danger as the Wakhan closed to a narrow gorge where the trail was carved on the rocky cliffs above the raging Wakhan River.

👁 The last civilization in the Wakhan was Baba Tangi where we outfitted with local guides and yaks. We hired this Badakhshan hunter who claimed to have killed 150 Marco Polo sheep with this matchlock muzzleloader.

👁 A last look at the Wakhan Corridor as we begin an ascent over 10,000 feet into the high Pamirs.

👁 At an altitude of 17,000 we stayed at a herdsmen's yurt camp when first entering the Pamirs.

👁 We cross the 17,800 feet high Sargus Pass and have our first look at the Pamirs. The yaks are the only suitable beasts to sustain themselves in the thin air.

« Badakhshan guides pack a yak at our Sargus camp. Pamir translated: "pa" means foot, which is the high plateau, and "mir" is king, which is the mountain masses that rise from the plateau.

Our final camp for hunting was in Tulaboi Valley at the 14,500 level.

Hunting usually starts in pitch black by 4 AM, riding the smooth, surefooted yaks up the valley until daybreak where one hopes to find the sheep feeding in the valley floor before climbing to the peaks to bed down for the day. The Marco Polo sheep is in the family of argalis (Ovis ammon), all of which seem to constantly be on the move. The poli is the highest living wild sheep and no doubt chose this remote part of the earth because of its shyness.

A single ram or small band can find a small, isolated meadow and live happily, its only worries being snow leopards or the occasional pack of wolves. Their keen senses and swiftness resulting from their long legs keeps them safe. A big ram can approach 300 pounds in weight, so predators are more likely to take ewes and lambs. The Himalayan ibex also lives in the rockier areas of

roads altogether, having to cross rivers early in the day before afternoon floods, caused by snow and ice melt. Once we reached Qala Panja (Five Rivers), the borders were less than 15 miles apart with the towering Hindu Kush rising sharply to the south. A gunshot distance to the north was Tajikistan, a republic of the Soviet Union.

It was travel by animal back from here on. At first horses were used along the Wakhan Corridor, a relatively low valley between the Pamirs and Hindu Kush, to the last settlement, Baba Tangi (Narrow Gorge). Here the expedition was resupplied with local guides and yaks for the higher altitudes.

The first day from there was a torturous climb over 17,800-foot Sargus Pass into Sargus Valley, where camp was set near a 17,000-foot herdsmen's yurt camp. Then there was another day's travel to the confluence of Sargus River and Tulaboi River. After that we trekked up the Tulaboi Valley where a tented camp would be used to hunt from the 14,500-foot elevation.

**At the head of Tulaboi Valley at about 17,000 feet elevation was a beautiful horseshoe-shaped lake that I named Lake Colleene (my wife's name), and on the far right, a high snow-capped mountain I named Mount Picher after Bill Picher who died here when accompanying me on a return trip. Since little had been named here, the names were said to have been officially accepted.**

The western saddles that we provided were much appreciated and worked well on yaks.

Chris spots for Marco Polo sheep across Lake Colleene.

A skull of a young ram that no doubt fell prey to predators—snow leopards or wolves, whose tracks were frequently observed.

I preferred what I called a "sport model yak," which was completely adequate for riding and easier to handle than the old bulls.

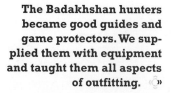

The Badakhshan hunters became good guides and game protectors. We supplied them with equipment and taught them all aspects of outfitting.

the Pamirs. Their heavy scimitar-shaped horns can easily measure well over 40 inches in length.

The ideas of our program of wildlife development were carried out in many areas of Asia. We learned much in every bend in the trail, expanding our knowledge and passing it on to the officials and locals alike. Afghanistan, unknowingly to the Klineburgers, became training grounds for us. At the same time we were teaching them, we learned what we had to teach. After several years working with the Afghans, we were ready for about anything else Asia had to offer.

The author with two of his Marco Polo sheep. The largest was 59 inches around the curl of each horn.

The Himalayan ibex were found in the rocky outcrops of the Pamirs, as well as throughout the Hindu Kush mountain range. Chris' specimen was an easy load for a bull yak.

**The author did the first exploratory trip in Afghanistan for markhor in the Nuristan area of the Hindu Kush Range, collecting these specimens.**

# REFLECTION
# High Altitude Sicknesses

**M**ost hunting for caprinae is done at high altitudes, where there can be a danger of mountain sickness (mild) or pulmonary edema (acute). The reason is simply that there is less oxygen in the air the higher one goes. Most everyone has minor problems when getting into the thin air. These can range from lack of energy, breathlessness, dizziness, and headaches to nausea, which fall into the category of altitude or mountain sickness. Normally, getting more oxygen into one's lungs will take care of the problem or at least help. The best first aid is forced breathing, taking deep breaths. If available, small doses of oxygen will normally do the trick. We often see athletes take oxygen on the sidelines. The Denver Broncos have a special home team advantage at Mile High Stadium over those sea-level teams.

To me, mountain sickness was just something to patiently get over with, till I had a rude awakening when a hunting partner of mine died of pulmonary edema in the Pamirs of Afghanistan. I immediately began reading and found that little had been known until research had begun in India in the early 1960s. They had been airlifting troops to the troubled India/China border, an instant 10,000-foot ascent or more. They lost hundreds of troops and thought the cause to be pneumonia because of lung congestion. In a follow-up study, they found the problem to be pulmonary edema, the lungs filling with fluid, and found that fatalities can be reduced to a minimum if the body is dehydrated.

My research continued, and I found that my theory of patience is the best adaptation to the altitude. A person's red blood corpuscles carry the oxygen from the lungs to all body parts. As a person goes to thinner air, the body automatically begins increasing the number of the little red carriers. So gradual ascent became part of our hunting programs in any areas in excess of 10,000 feet. Also important was a portable oxygen supply.

In another study by climbers on Mt. Rainier in Washington, it appeared that altitude sicknesses were somehow acid-related, and Rolaids (not any antacid) were the chosen medicine. I personally found immediate relief with Rolaids when climbing thousands of feet by helicopter over mountain passes.

Early symptoms of pulmonary edema are much the same as mountain sickness and if not remedied may become worse. Watch for these signs of hypoxia (a deficiency of oxygen reaching the body tissues): coughing up sputum, low temperature, mental confusion; inability to urinate, swelling, face turning flush, gurgling in breathing.

Remedies include taking a diuretic (Lasix recommended) at the earliest sign of water retention, taking Rolaids on a regular basis on first sign of any related discomforts, and taking short doses of oxygen (a few minutes) during early signs of hypoxia. Start planning evacuation to low altitudes if symptoms do not improve. If symptoms worsen take continuous oxygen and begin the descent or call for evacuation.

# CHAPTER 2

# Outer Mongolia

When Mongolia surprisingly opened its doors to travel and hunting in the mid-1960s, the Klineburgers were right there to offer their expertise. The first hunts during the first several years were conducted in the Gobi steppes, an area easily accessible by Russian-built jeeps. This arid area from the Altai Mountains south into Inner Mongolia can be described as giant stair steps of deserts descending lower and lower, each separated by a ridge of mountains. These mountains, actually low hills, are the habitat of the Mongolian argali sheep, Ovis ammon darwini, and Siberian ibex, Capra siberica hagenbecki. Also throughout the area are many snow leopards and gazelles on the plains. These rather small argalis are somewhat larger than the North American bighorn sheep, both in body size and in horn size.

Those first hunts were about as crude as one could ever expect for accommodations and food. We had to take our own sleeping bags and depended mainly on freeze-dried foods that we took along.

On the other hand, the Mongolians were good and willing hunters. We camped in rather poor tents near nomad herdsmen's camps where we could get local guides and the use of their sturdy ponies. The saddles weren't bad as they were padded, but the stirrups were of marginal use, usually suspended by an un-adjustable rope or rawhide, always the wrong length.

The herdsmen's camp accommodations were roomy yurts that we hunters were usually able to finagle our way into by offering our

^ **The first hunts in Mongolia were conducted in the Gobi Steppes in the south part of the country for the Mongolian argali sheep, Ovis ammon darwini, and ibex, Capra siberica hagenbecki. We obtained guides and horses from the nomadic herdsmen.**

able from the U.S.S.R. via Irkutsk, a major Soviet city on the southern shores of Lake Baikal, not far north of the Mongolia border. Also, train transportation was available from Beijing, China. There were a few roads, mostly dirt, from Ulaanbataar to nearby towns, but farther from the city roads ceased to exist. The firm, gravelly gobi (meaning desert) was fine for driving on. If the ruts got too deep, no problem—just move over.

The capital was the residence of more than one-third of the country's population. Aside from this, a handful of other "cities"

camaraderie along with our well-stocked supply of arhi (Mongolian vodka) and Marlboro cigarettes. This was always a welcome chance to warm up and stretch out.

We became like a family to these people who were as curious about us as we were to them. After an arhi or two, we could usually get them to sing in their chant-like way, then we would try singing to them—they had no way to know how bad we were!

These people, except for our interpreter and drivers from the capitol Ulaanbataar, lived their entire lives in remoteness away from all the spoils of civilization. They were fun loving people and loved to hunt. They welcomed the hunting program that provided diversity to their mundane life style.

Ulaanbataar was the only major city in Mongolia and the only link with transportation from outside. Frequent flights were avail-

**The Bactrian camels were for carrying heavy loads and sometimes for riding.**

On the early hunts, simple tents were used and we supplied our own bedding and much of the food.

Chris and his guides with a typical Mongolian argali sheep from the South Gobi.

The small blacktail gazelles were found in abundance on the steppes between the low mountain ridges.

Bert Klineburger with his outstanding Ovis ammon darwini.

were spotted around this land mass, which is double the size of Texas.

In the '60s, the total population hovered around 2 million in a country that ruled most of the known world for almost 200 years back in the 13th century. In 1206, Genghis Khan struck out to conquer all of Asia from Vietnam in the south to Poland in the west, beginning the Mongol Empire. This was 22 percent of the entire world's land mass.

The Qing Dynasty built the Great Wall to stop the "Tartars," however it didn't work. Genghis Khan was one of the first, if not the first, to establish game conservation. The story goes that hunting was forbidden until a certain time of the year. The "season" started when it was time for war games.

The mounted and skilled warriors with their bows and spears would surround a huge area, closing in on the game. The highest-ranking officers stayed within the circle using their ability to ride at top speed and use their weapons to kill the game. Then the lower ranks would move in. Once the game began to escape the perimeter, the least-ranking soldiers pursued the wildlife. Of course, most of the game escaped, but the hunt was a way to train the troops and made them the world's dominant military force.

In the entire south Gobi, where all our hunts took place for the first few years, there was one major town: Dalandzadgad. The communist government's Mongol Airlines had some turbo-prop, high-wing, Russian-built planes, which served outlying towns that were hundreds of miles from the capitol.

Hunters were soon allowed to travel on the airlines, getting them within a few hours drive to their proposed hunt site, which would be already set up and staffed. The designated interpreters/guides for the hunters would usually meet the clients upon their first arrival in Ulaanbataar and be their companion throughout their stay.

A couple of days were always spent in Ulaanbataar for shopping, picking up arhi, cigarettes, and souvenirs from the Dollar Store, a place where only foreign currency was used—nothing cost only a dollar. We exchanged some money for Tugriks, the local currency, because if we gave tips to the local guides in the hunt area, our money would be useless to them.

Our guide would also take us sightseeing, which consisted of the monastery, where the monks constantly seemed to do their audible, chanting prayers with spinning prayer wheels. We were also shown the residential parts of town, which consisted of thousands of yurts.

Some apartment buildings existed, but the people preferred yurts as being more desirable and efficient. There was usually evening entertainment, which we were always eager to see. This varied from Mongolian-style wrestling to concerts to circuses to operas to ballet. The guide would then fly with us to our arrival town and guide us

« **At the Juulchin head office in Ulaanbataar, Chris signs the partnership agreement with the directors, Tsend Ochir and Luvsandash.**

The colorful herdsmen welcomed us in their community.

The author's first camp in the High Altai was set by a herdsmen's camp to utilize their horses and guide service.

We were welcomed like family inside the warmth of the herdsman's yurt.

on the hunt. Any guide who stayed on the hunting program became a highly skilled big game guide.

Our host was the government agency, Juulchin Foreign Tourism Corporation, which handled all tourism in Mongolia. However, in all those early years, the only "tourist" that I encountered was a photographer who ended up getting into trouble for taking pictures of the people. Apparently, the communist government did not want the "wrong" idea of their country being spread. I did see a lot of foreigners arriving with me on incoming flights, but they were construction workers, Russian officials, and geologists.

Speaking of photography, the hunters seemed to have no trouble with still pictures, as we schooled them early on to do it discreetly and not to go around poking their cameras to someone's face because they may not even know what a camera is.

I always took a Polaroid camera along with a lot of film. Out in the bush, I would take a photo of someone without him knowing it,

☂ **Our spare binoculars were utilized by the interpretor and local guide in the lofty heights of the Altai**

☂ **A fine Altai ibex, Capra siberica siberica.**

☂ **My two guides were as proud as I was for collecting the first Altai argali taken in modern times.**

then hand him the picture. They would look at it curiously and someone would point out "that's you." Then they all wanted pictures, and it became easy to use our other cameras freely—but they couldn't understand why our 35mm cameras didn't produce an instant photo.

I explained to the vice-director of Juulchin, Luvsandash, that it would be a great promotional thing for the hunting program if I could bring a 16mm movie camera and do the filming. (We had been doing extensive filming of our world travels and were quite good at it). Movie taking was illegal in the late '60s, but Luvsandash actually helped me smuggle the camera and film into the country, so I actually took the first movies of this remote country.

By the end of the '60s, I finally got permission to hunt in the Altai Mountains in the far west of Mongolia. This was the home

« **Dr. Arthur Twomey and Chris pose along with the guides with the collection of horns taken on this historic trip in the Tonhil area of the High Altai.**

My recommendation to accommodate the hunting clients in yurts resulted in the best camps in all of Asia.

Inside the roomy yurts, hunters enjoyed spring beds, wood stoves, and carpeted rugs on wooden floors.

of the Altai argali, Ovis ammon ammon. My hunting partner for this history-making trip was Dr. Arthur Twomey, representing the Carnegie Museum.

We were flown to a town in the mid-Altai where our Juulchin staff had already gone ahead with two Russian jeeps. Incidentally, the airports in all the outlying towns were unpaved causing the aircraft to land on a gobi strip. This hard packed, gravelly ground presented no problems for those high-winged, turbo-prop aircraft.

We drove two days west to the Tonkil area of the Altais where we negotiated

Hunters were allowed to fly to the nearest settlement of their camps on the Russian built turbo-prop aircraft. Note the hard packed gravelly "gobi" surface utilized in lieu of pavement.

**The wapiti found in the forested areas throughout northern Mongolia are almost identical to the North American elk.**

with a local herdsman for his services and horses. The hunt was on and over a two-week period, Arthur and I each collected two Altai argali sheep and two ibexes, Capra siberica.

Even with one of the jeeps carrying two drums of extra fuel, we barely made it back, driving all the way to Ulaanbataar, passing through the ancient remains of Karakorum where the Venetian, Marco Polo, spent 17 years during Genghis Khan's time.

Our ensuing early trips in Mongolia paved the way to a program that injected millions of dollars annually into this country, which needed hard currency badly. At the time, agriculture and livestock were the main exports, along with leather products made from the hides of livestock.

Luvsandash agreed to improve camp conditions. I told him about our desire always to spend our camp time in the local herdsmen's yurts. He said, "Do you really think the clients would want to stay in our yurts?"

"Absolutely," was my answer, and he not only agreed, but also promised to have a trained cook in camp.

In our annual returns to Mongolia, Bert and I were delighted to find camps of yurts with wood floors that were carpeted with woven Mongolian rugs, spring beds, dining table, and chairs: the best hunting camps in all of Asia right into the 21st century.

Klineburger Worldwide Travel entered into a partnership with Juulchin helping them to set standards and develop new programs for all the wildlife under the able guidance of

On their first visit to America, our Mongolian guests, Bataar and Luvsandash enjoy some Klineburger hospitality. Bert Klineburger entertains them and shows off his all time World record moose.

Bayartogtokh Ayush, who had taken over as vice president of Juulchin. By 1980, surveys showed Mongolia to have 40,000 argali sheep, of which 40 percent were in the Altai; 80,000 ibexes, with 60 percent in the Altai ranges and the rest in the south Gobi; and 100,000 blacktail gazelles and at least that many whitetail gazelles. Wapiti, which are almost identical to the North American elk, were estimated at 130,000.

We started an air-rail wapiti package that included air transportation on China Airlines from San Francisco to Beijing; a couple days in China, including tours to the Great Wall; an overnight train ride to Ulaanbataar; and a 10-day itinerary in Mongolia, including one elk trophy with a price tag starting at $3,500.

A hunter could easily get a chance at a trophy-size elk, usually six-point (each antler), or better. (It bears noting that a similar hunt for elk in North America at the time started at about $5,000, plus licenses.) This program alone eventually brought up to $200,000 a year to Mongolia on the hunts alone.

However, free trade showed its ugly face in the late '80s, when poachers started killing the bulls while they were still in velvet. The horns were exported to other Asian countries where the ground horns were used for medicinal purposes, including as an aphrodisiac. The population of elk dropped to about 50,000 before the government took charge of protection in the late '90s.

Free enterprise also disrupted the rest of the hunting program. When Juulchin handled hunting exclusively, hunts and wildlife conservation were well-managed, but the collapse of the Eastern Bloc countries affected cost of operations. Mongolia was completely dependent on the Soviet Union for fuel, vehicles, and most supplies, so costs increased dramatically.

Permits for the wildlife and hunt areas were issued to independent Mongolian outfitters, so Juulchin became only one of many to offer hunts. In addition, the interference of the U.S. Fish and Wildlife Service by restricting the number of wildlife they would allow into the U.S. from Mongolia had a negative effect on the hunting programs.

## REFLECTION
# Our Attempt in the Movie Business

The artist's sketch was the Klineburgers' idea of what Genghis Khan may have looked like, along with his warriors who ruled most of the known world from the beginning of the 13th century. The sketch was done by artist Robert Allen from Yakima, Washington. We engaged Robert to do a series of paintings, including those early-man drawings used in the foreword of this book.

In those early days of sport hunting when many destinations were little-traveled by outsiders, we had the mind to document many of our early expeditions on 16mm movie film. We apparently did quite well at filming. Back in the early 1960s we put together three short films: *Equator to the Arctic, Shikar,* and *Safari to Nyasaland.*

These 40-minute films were shown in small-town auditoriums, sometimes in schools. This was before the Discovery Channel, History Channel, National Geographic, and countless others that got on the bandwagon.

So people were hungry to see what the rest of the world was all about. It was also before all the antihunters got on their high horses and disrupted the balance of nature. Those early audiences had good intelligence and came out in great numbers to see good hunting films that also included documentaries of life in remote areas.

☝ **Chris and Colleene Klineburger in authentic Afghan clothing promoting the motion picture *The Great Shikar.***

A group of interested people got together and partnered with us to form a film company called World Adventure Enterprises to utilize our footage for movies and documentaries. The first production was a motion picture called *The Great Shikar,* which was all about Afghanistan and the Klineburger expedition for Marco Polo sheep. The late, great newscaster and adventurer Lowell Thomas narrated it. You old-timers will remember Lowell on Movietone News, covering WWII.

The film did not do all that well in theaters as it was too much of a documentary. The Khan montage above was used to help tell part of the history of Afghanistan when it was conquered by the Mongol Empire.

The drawings of the evolution of man as a hunter in the opening of this book were made for another film that we started, which was called *Man the Hunter,* but with the antihunting movement gaining ground in the early 1970s the film company decided to close down. However, the film on Afghanistan was so historic that a video company in Dallas, Texas, by the name of Outdoor Visions shortened it and made it available as a DVD and VHS, still under the title *The Great Shikar.*

CHAPTER 3

# The South Pacific

Most islands in the Pacific had very little in the way of mammals living on them. Early settlers and sometimes governments introduced wildlife to make use of the excellent habitat. In the case of Australia and New Zealand, which had mostly marsupials, many varieties of wildlife were introduced to make better use of the varied plains, forests, and mountains. Predators being nonexistent, game flourished in the lush conditions. The Klineburgers, always wanting to help develop new hunting destinations, took keen interest in these large landmasses. Chris took exploratory trips to both countries and here is his report as it was written at the time.

**"DOWN UNDER" HUNTING REPORT (circa 1966)**

Australia and New Zealand have been somewhat controversial hunting areas with the widespread commercial hunting of the introduced and native game in those countries. At one time, the game was shot or poisoned. Now commercial hunting is still going on and the meat and hides are being sold and exported in most cases.

By the early 60s there seemed to be a slight hint of wildlife conservation in government levels. This is especially true in Australia where crocodiles are on a tightly controlled permit basis and kangaroos are being protected in some areas.

However, individuals, who have blocked off land and have more or less told the government and individuals alike to stay out and leave the game alone, are carrying out the most vivid examples of conservation. These areas, in most cases, are set aside for nonresident guided hunting. The principle that they were going on is that the animals are worth a lot more as a trophy than the meat that they have been selling. My trip to these two countries was very enlightening, and I found the hunting and outfitting second to none. In the following paragraphs, I will cover the areas and outfitters separately.

In New Zealand, a couple of devoted outdoorsmen by the names of Gary Joll and Ron Spanton formed a company called New Zealand Trophy Guide Service. They got a few investors together and bought 58,000 acres of land in prime hunting country. The area contained Himalayan tahr, chamois, and red stag. Although the area had been commercially hunted heavily through the early 60s, it now abounds with trophy-class animals of all three species.

This area, 20 air miles from Mt. Cook, is in the South Island's Southern Alps. It had been a sheep and cattle ranch. The game animals were being killed off because of their competing with the domestic stock. Gary and Ron sold off around 7,000 head of sheep and most of the cattle, maintaining only a few thousand sheep, which are restricted to areas away from most of the game animals. Now, here is a good lesson in land use: The domestic sheep bring around $6 per head as compared to over $300 per head for a trophy-class wild animal.

In the hunting area, they built a lodge with all the comforts of home. In addition,

**Early New Zealand pioneer Gary Joll poses with Chris and his chamois.**

they have conveniently located cabins in the main valleys. They use four-wheel-drive hunting vehicles or horses, whichever seems to be more convenient for the occasion. Ron and Gary try to personally guide all clients, and their ability as guides cannot be beat anywhere. I found the hunting there to be equally as good and challenging as any place I have ever hunted. Furthermore, I got animals that are extremely difficult to obtain in their natural habitat, as in the case of the tahr.

**Dr. Robert Speegle shares Chris' excitement over collecting a Himalayan Tahr from New Zealand's South Island.**

🪃 **Australia's pioneer operator, Don McGregor, by an anthill near a billibong. The barefooted Aussie never wore shoes until his wedding and then as our guest at the first Game Coin Convention in San Antonio.**

There is a lot of other game available in different areas on both the North and South Islands, and Trophy Guide Service has arranged with other landowners to hunt for the respective species, providing game is abundant enough and trophy heads available. We went to a black fallow deer area near Lake Wakapitu on the South Island and found conditions excellent. We drove to the west end of the lake and were met by the landowner in his Super Cub for a 10-minute flight. The accommodations were very good in an older home from where we saw some large trophy heads. Up in the mountains is a hunting cabin where I counted 26 fallow deer within 500 yards of the cabin, including a few nice heads.

Other game available on the South Island are moose, elk, and wallaby. The elk obtain some nice racks, but the moose just go about medium size on North American standards. I did not go into the moose and elk areas, which are in the extreme southwest areas of the island. Wallaby is available in several areas.

The North Island contains some good areas for sika deer, sambar, and rusa deer, where Gary and Ron have arrangements to hunt on private land that is not commercially hunted. Ron is from the North Island and was a commercial hunter for the government before he became sports-minded. I did not hunt there, but he told me the hunts could be rewarding for those who like forest hunting.

The seasons for the best hunting are in their fall and winter (our spring and summer). The deer are in hard antler by mid-February and hold their antlers into September. Chamois, tahr, and wallaby can be hunted any time of the year. The rates are very reasonable for this high class of outfitting—around $100 per day. Ten days is enough for the hunt at the

**The Asiatic buffalo was introduced in Australia's Northern Territory to make use of the vast grasslands.** 🪃

☉ **Chris with a specimen of dingo, one of the original wild dogs.**

South Island lodge, but 30 days is necessary for a combined hunt on both islands for most of the game. A nearby helicopter service is available for lifting people who cannot climb to the mountaintops, and one can hunt their way back down to the lodge.

In Australia, a similar situation exists. Don McGregor, up in Arnhemland in the Northern Territory, has a 40-mile square area

**Chris's Aborigine guide was his partner as they trekked Arnhemland.** ☉

☉ **The author poses by an awesome anthill, possibly the World's largest.**

in which he does not allow any commercial hunting. His area abounds with Asiatic buffalo, wild boar, wallaby, and dingo. If an experienced African hunter were dropped off in Don's area with no hint of where he was, he would swear he was in the lush bush country of Africa. Climatic conditions and method of hunting are also similar. You would expect an impala to go bounding off or a waterbuck to pop up out of a swamp at any time. The buffaloes are not unlike the Cape buffalo and do appear frequently, whether you expect them or not. Crocodiles, both seagoing and fresh water, can be taken by special permit.

My buffalo went down in a likely spot. After all, they are water buffalo!

Bob Penfold, an early developer of Australia's wide variety of wildlife, started out with his homemade hunting car. Colleene Klineburger, seated, ready for the hunt.

Don built the beautiful Patonga Lodge on a billabong ("lake" or "still water" in Aborigine) as the clients' base. The area is reached by bush plane, less than an hour east of Darwin on the continent's north shore. Hunting is done by four-wheel drive vehicles and on foot during the dry season—May 1 to December 1. The rest of the year it's by riverboat and on foot. During the wet season, it is hot and can get really wet, making it an undesirable time to hunt, but no problem for getting a good buffalo and other game.

Fishing and bird shooting is also very good. The main species of fish in the nearby waters are barramundi, saratoga, and brim. The best time for fishing is May 1 to September 1. There is tremendous waterfowl shooting from August 1 to November 1, mainly for Magpie geese.

A hunter can expect a buffalo well into 70 inches around the front curve. Mine was 77¼ inches, taken while stalking for wallaby. The dingo seems to be abundant and can be seen while driving the hunt area. I got one while sneaking up on the remains of my buffalo. Wallabies (Agilus variety) are plentiful, and a good male will run more than two feet in height. I also got a wild boar weighing around 250 pounds, but they will go well over 300 pounds.

Like New Zealand, prices in Australia with McGregor are very reasonable, with an all-inclusive eight-day hunt for $1,000. Combination hunts to the two countries work out well together, with the best times from May 1 to October 1. In three weeks total elapsed time, including air travel, you can hunt both New Zealand and Australia. A sportsman can be reasonably assured of collecting tahr, chamois, red stag, buffalo, boar, wallaby, and dingo, besides having an unforgettable experience in both countries.

These pioneers, Don, Gary, and Ron, are making history in their respective countries. They are demonstrating conservation to their governments. Conservation usually starts because of, and is financed by the sportsmen.

**Colleene with her boar collected with a handgun.**

They are making game sanctuaries, while their governments have little regard for the wildlife. In addition, finally, they are bringing a lot of hard currency into their countries with a better land use.

With the changing hunting scene throughout the world, the little known "Down Under" countries will certainly come into their own in the international hunting picture—especially if these "pioneers" are successful in their crusade to protect and properly cultivate their wildlife.

Some 40 years later as we enter the 21st century, Australia and New Zealand, along with other island sanctuaries such as New Caledonia and Papua New Guinea, have prospered, just as I predicted. There are now dozens of hunting operators offering nimrods a chance at 15 species of antlered and horned game.

One visionary sportsman, Joseph J. Malek of Sidney, Australia, was so enlightened by the potential of the "Down Under" wildlife, that he and his family created an award honoring a collector of all the species taken by fair chase and contributing to conservation practices. The "J. J. Malek South Pacific Grand Slam Award" was first presented in 1984 shortly after Joe's unexpected death. His wife, Diane Malek, carried on the tradition presenting the award every year thereafter at a major hunting and conservation convention in the U.S.A.

The South Pacific Grand Slam includes sambar deer, chital deer, red deer, wapiti, tahr, hog deer, whitetail deer, fallow deer, rusa deer, chamois, Asiatic buffalo, banteng, wild boar, and feral goat.

Wildlife continues on the increase with a likewise accelerating interest in hunting, making the South Pacific a major destination for sport hunting—another example of a sportsman-financed wildlife program. Sadly, New Guinea is out of the picture as of this writing because of terrorist activity, which prevents hunting and most travel around the island.

**Diane Malek presents the Malek Award trophy to the 1991 recipient, Mahlon "Butch" White. The Award is presented annually at a major hunter/conservation convention.**

On the subject of introduced Asiatic buffalo, Bert Klineburger pioneered the hunting on Brazil's Amazon delta.

## REFLECTION
# Tamales in Afghanistan

**A**s a desert rat being raised on the Mexican border of Arizona, my ultimate cuisine was not McDonalds, but zesty Mexican food. The closest thing to "fast food" in those days was the tamale cart that infrequently came past 711 Cole Ave. in Warren, Arizona. Mom's tacos were a hit, as she fried the ground round right in the corn tortilla, which soaked up the meat juices. When leaving Arizona to live in the great Northwest, I suddenly had to adapt if I wanted life's essential—Mexican food. So cook it I did—usually from scratch.

Finding the best ingredients, I did it all, from nachos and tortilla soup to handmade tamales. My reputation preceded me to the point of being talked into donating Mexican dinners to charitable auctions, including wine tasting from my homemade wines. The latest that Grace and I hosted went for $1,400 (for a party of four) bid up by Captain Ron and Terry Rismon of Black Diamond, Washington.

It seems I've constantly collaborated with the camp cooks in strange places around the world to come up with a Mexican combination plate they didn't know they had. One such case was in the Nuristan area of Afghanistan near Jalalabad on the Pakistan border.

This was the first exploratory trip into that portion of the Hindu Kush mountain range. At the end of a rugged four-wheel-drive track, we came to a remote village clinging to the edge of the high rocky mountains. We were welcomed to pitch our camp on a recently cultivated field, next to a standing crop of dried corn.

We were searching for markhor, a rather rare member of the *Capra* genus. We found guides who were willing to assist us, so they invited us into their home for nan and tea. I was delighted to sink my teeth into their nan (bread) and found it to be of corn, exactly the taste of Mexican masa!

With the dried cornhusks available in their field and time for us to stay put while the guides scouted the mountains for markhor before we moved in with fly camps, I was determined to make tamales. After mustering a meat supply (chicken) and available spices, I soaked cornhusks and made a huge pot of meat sauce. Before cooking, however, I invited the villagers' wives to witness the routine in case they wanted to get away from their rather bland diet. The women were too shy, although they were not the chador-laden women of the cities, so the men said they would sit in and pass the info to their wives.

We had a huge pot, the bottom of which I lined with rocks and water. This way I could steam the tamales, the required cooking procedure. I smeared a layer of the uncooked masa on the soaked husks and applied a spoonful of meat sauce, before rolling each one to its final form. Then I layered the six or eight dozen tamales in the steaming chamber, cooking them for a couple hours. The "banquet" was a huge success, with the (all male) guests delighted over their newfound cuisine. Through the interpreter, I quizzed many to see whether the procedure would be passed on. The response varied from "By all means, they will have their wives make them" to "No way would my wife go to that much trouble to cook for me." My curiosity has always had me wondering whether I created a new Afghan dish in that remote corner of the world.

# CHAPTER 4

# Opening of the U.S.S.R.

**H**ungarian born Guy Jonas, founder of the taxidermy studio that we took over, Jonas Brothers of Seattle, once stated, "If ever the Soviet Union opens its doors to hunting, it will be the world's greatest hunting grounds." Amazingly, less than 20 years later in 1970, I personally was the prime factor in opening the doors for foreign sportsmen to begin collecting specimens from behind the "Iron Curtain."

Brother Bert's and my activities in Outer Mongolia in the late '60s had us traveling through Moscow, which was the only entryway into that country. I spent considerable time in Moscow with the heads of Intourist, the Soviet agency for all travelers, whether for business or pleasure. I even spent time in Alma Ata, Kazakhstan, and the largest of the Asian republics, discussing their wildlife potential. Not only did I meet with Intourist personnel, but also with wildlife officials such as Vladimir Fertikov, head of Glavakhota, the board of wildlife reserves for the Russian federation, and also in Kazakhstan, the Minister of Forestry, Alexander Amanbaev, and the president of the Wildlife Department, Valery Savinov.

The wildlife officials were eager to allow hunting, but they said they could do nothing without a directive from Intourist. My main contact in Moscow was Valery Uvarov, Intourist's director for all of North America and Latin America. We became very good friends and he was able to negotiate an expedition in and around the Caucasus Mountains in the southwest of the U.S.S.R. (Union of Soviet Socialist

Republics). It was for two people: Dr. Arthur Twomey, representing the Carnegie Museum, and myself.

Since all travel in the Soviet Union had to be pre-planned and prepaid, it was not possible to book our trip in the normal fashion, as there were no established tariffs. After several tries, Valery was able to get this information: It would be 5 rubles per day for a huntsman, 5 rubles for a horse, 25 rubles for hut accommodations, 25 rubles for a jeep, etc.

"OK," I said, "How long, how many huntsmen, horses, jeeps?"

They could not answer, so Valery said I would have to go find out myself. He booked us for six weeks of deluxe hotel accommodations in the nearest cities to the reserves that we were to visit. He told me to take a lot of our travel vouchers (similar to blank checks) along and pay on the spot for services received, then report our accounting back to him when we returned to Moscow.

This process probably never happened before in the U.S.S.R., and I was honored by his trust and cooperation to fulfill my dream hunt. (Because of this maiden trip, I established the first written tariffs for hunting in the U.S.S.R., and our agency became the first to book organized hunts as a general agent.)

Russians do like to hunt, and a number of reserves had been established in recent times, mainly for the use of the Republics' hierarchy and certainly not for the common folks. It was in these reserves that Valery was able to get permission for our hunt and for other foreigners to follow. Here is a brief story of this history-making trip.

*It was mid-August of 1970 when, after a few days business in Moscow, we arrived in Baku on the shores of the Caspian Sea. This is in the Republic of Azerbaijan, which translates into "Land of Fire," because of the eternal gas flames early travelers saw coming from the ground. We were met by Rafik Kapharov who was assigned to be our personal guide and interpretor for ventures into the Kubinsk Wildlife Reserve in the eastern end of the Caucasus mountain range.*

The Caucasus is a high, rugged mountain range, much like the Cascades of Washington and British Columbia. The snow-clad mountains run northwesterly from Baku for a few hundred miles. The mountains and the surrounding foothills have been known for a wide variety of unusual game.

I do not know what Valery Uvarov had said to the local authorities, but we soon found out that our trip was regarded as very important for the future of a Soviet hunting program. The "Red Carpet" (not a pun) was out for us from the beginning and they responded to our every wish, as if we were the Soviet hierarchy they were accustomed to serve.

It took us two days to reach and establish our base camp. Several jeeps were provided to take us to a village called Derk, where we were provided with horses to ride and pack our outfit into our campsite in a rugged draw as high as possible in the Caucasus, where there was still a flat enough place to pitch our tents.

**The Caucasus Mountain range in the southwest of the Soviet Union is among the World's most rugged and makes an excellent sanctuary for the elusive tur.** »

This rugged area had recently been set aside as the Kubinsk Wildlife Reserve, the habitat of a pseudo sheep called the Dagestan tur. Every day we went out to a different area and each time we saw tur. The mountains were literally covered with these magnificent animals and an obvious need existed for an aggressive hunting program.

Man was their only natural enemy. There were no wolves and the bears here were satisfied with the great amount of vegetation. We did see the Asian mountain grizzly, which is called "brown bear," but the fur was quite shaggy and unprime, so we elected not to collect any here, as we were to be in at least two more bear-hunting areas later.

We stalked the tur extensively and worked with the local guides in developing techniques for them to spook the game out of their rugged habitat into areas that are more accessible. By the time we could get up these vertical mountains where the tur had been grazing, they had often settled down into treacherous rocky gorges, where it would be extremely dangerous for us to venture. Therefore, we constructed some rock stands in natural crossing places, such as saddles and trails from these gorges.

The Soviet guides would then surround the opposite sides of the gorges, exposing themselves, making noises and often firing their shotguns in hope of moving the game

in our direction. This method worked quite well and has been developed into a science through the years that followed. Twomey and I collected excellent trophies for the Carnegie Museum and for personal use. The tur is about the size of the Rocky Mountain bighorn sheep and has horns with about the same mass. Even though it is considered a goat with the scientific name *Capra cylindricornus*, it is much more like a mountain sheep.

We were the only foreigners on a flight from Baku to Mineralney Vody (Mineral Water). From the airport, we were driven about 25 miles to the resort town of

Chris Klineburger and the first tur collected on the history-making trip that opened the U.S.S.R. for hunting.

Pyatigorsk, where we spent a delightful night. The next day, we were driven several more hours to Ordzhonikidze, a city overlooking the north central Caucasus.

Following a couple of days of discussion, we headed to a newly built deluxe lodge at Saniba inside a game reserve in the Autonomous Republic of North Ossetia. This is a progressive part of the Soviet Union, and they had a newly established game department, members of which were to be our guides and hosts for our stay in the area. (In our previous visit in Azerbaijan, there was no game department. Our guides and hosts while in the mountains were from the local hunting society, which at the time was a hunting club assigned to oversee the Kubinsk Reserve.) We were escorted to the game department headquarters, which consisted of modern premises with large statues of wildlife in the garden area.

The Saniba Lodge overlooked the meadows and lush foothills, as well as the towering snowy peaks of the central Caucasus. Within the view, we could see the habitats of tur, chamois, maral deer, roe deer, Russian boar, European bison, and brown bear. In the mountains, we had to use our own ingenuity in making a spike camp, since they did not have any tents available. We built a sort of overhang over a cave where seven of us slept in an area not quite big enough for two.

After looking over the tur, we found them to be the same variety that we had seen in Kubinsk. We had hoped to find the

The Saniba Lodge in North Ossetia was built as a retreat for Soviet hierarchy but made available for our use and other foreign hunters to follow.

west Caucasian or Kuban tur but, since we did not, we elected not to take any more tur specimens.

The areas available for tur hunting are quite expansive compared to Kubinsk in that the starting points were accessible by two good roads that can take hunters relatively

near to the tur hunting areas. We had horses available to take us from road's end to our spike camp. We saw signs of maral stag in the high valley floors, but we did not take time to hunt stag, as we were scheduled to do that from the Saniba Lodge.

From the lodge we collected brown bear, boar, roe deer, and maral stag. They used every method of hunting conceivable, which included stalking in early morning and late evening and driven hunts during the day. One day they took us to a distant area and had us go out by horseback, a treat that they used for visiting dignitaries. A side trip with a fly camp got us into the chamois area down range.

**Dr. Arthur Twomey, center, and the Soviet guides with a Russian boar taken in the Krasnaya Polyana Reserve.**

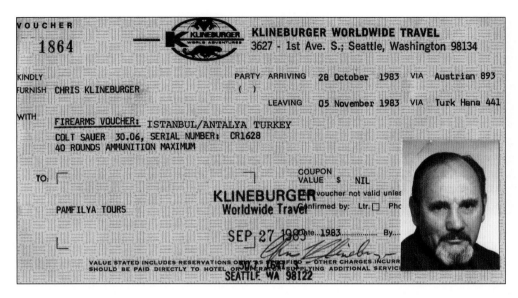

The firearms voucher that I created similar to this one, using our agency voucher, became the official firearms permit in the U.S.S.R. for the hunters and even for those transiting to Mongolia.

During our hunt, we had received several messages from the next area to be visited, encouraging us to go there as quickly as possible. Therefore, we rushed things somewhat and left before our hosts were really quite ready for us to leave.

We were driven southward over the Caucasus, through many hairpin turns to the city of Tblisi, the capital of Georgia. Then we were flown to Adler near the resort town of Sochi on the Black Sea, before being driven to the headquarters of the Krasnaya Polyana Reserve in the forested foothills on the west side of the northwest end of Caucasus.

This reserve is part of a large area, the Krasnodar State Forest Hunting Reserve. The director of the reserve explained that their main trophies were the brown bear and Russian boar. Now in late September,

the animals fed mostly on the wild fruits, berries, and nuts that were ripe at this time and hunting was at its best, the reason for the urgency to start the hunt.

As in the other reserves, we were treated royally at their headquarters for a day or two before being taken to our first camp, which was a newly built cabin in the forest in an area surrounded by wild pear trees and chestnut trees. We practiced the usual stalking and driving of game as well as sitting at night in nut tree groves while waiting to hear the munching of nuts by bears and/or boars. Another "camp" was out of a beekeeper's farmhouse—our lunch consisted of honeycomb and all the fruit, nuts, and berries we could pick as we ate our way through the day.

Game was abundant, but we did not take a bear since we had already shot bear in the last area. We felt we had taken our share, much to their disappointment. We did take boars, which are extremely impressive trophies as they are large and well furred unlike the so-called "Russian boars" that have been transplanted to many parts of the world and are usually as scraggly looking as a barnyard pig.

The demand for time in these three areas consumed most of our allotted time on our visas, as well as our budget, so we canceled

**I visited those same reserves often in the ensuing years, then in 1977 took a group to hunt in the Saniba area in North Ossetia. Included were notable hunters such as Thornton Snider, Art Carlsberg, John Cotten, Mel Topance, Don Williams, and Pete Papac. Here I checked out a newly built stand used for hunting.**

**Pete Papac with a mountain grizzly taken in the Caucasus' foothills.**

our other planned stop in Krasny Les to the north and part of the Krasnodar State Reserve, which specializes in maral stag and roe deer. Since we had collected those animals in North Ossetia and now had a good feel for the overall situation in the U.S.S.R., we returned to Moscow with our report. As a result of these exploratory trips, I structured the first official "Tariffs and Conditions for Hunting in the U.S.S.R."

In the years following the grand opening, sportsmen flocked past the Iron Curtain from all western countries. As part of our general agency agreement, we wholesaled the hunts to other agents. However, as time passed, the officials at Intourist gave in to demands of appointed travel agencies to deal direct. European agents asked, "Why should we deal with an American company and have to deal through the American department of Intourist?" So I agreed, but my agency

This huge Russian boar collected by the author was mounted life-size and donated to the international Wildlife Museum in Tucson.

Don Williams with his maral stag.

still offered the product to any agency that desired our services.

However, in the first years of hunting, Intourist did not have a department to handle hunting arrangements, so I kept involved in maintaining the schedules. Rafik Kapharov, my first tour guide in Baku when the hunts first opened, moved to Moscow and kept in touch with me. I talked Intourist into making a separate department for hunting arrange-

Chris with a Caucasian chamois.

ments and I got Rafael, as we called him, the job as manager.

Firearms permits were an early-on problem, as our hunting clients were the only foreigners bringing in guns. To keep in tune with what Soviet Customs were familiar with, I created a "Firearms Voucher." It was done on our agency's voucher, listing the serial numbers, make, and caliber, along with the number of rounds of ammunition. It also displayed a passport-sized photo of the hunter and our official agency seal—a Firearms Permit was born!

**Art Carlsberg helped carry his roebuck from the forest.**

**The 1977 hunt ended the day of the author's big 50th birthday. Alexander Kupaev, the head of the game department, presented Chris with some of their finest locally distilled brandy.**

This worked perfectly and hunters were allowed to take their firearms along with their other luggage everywhere they went, including their hotel rooms. Vouchers were necessary for all visitors and each one listed the type of service, date, and location of service. Without the prepaid vouchers, one could not enter the U.S.S.R. or travel within the U.S.S.R. Therefore, our Firearms Vouchers became very recognizable by Soviet Customs and eliminated problems. Even our Mongolia clients had vouchers for their guns while traveling through the U.S.S.R.

A year never passed in the 1970s that I didn't travel to Moscow and parts beyond. I would make it a point to travel to most hunting destinations occasionally to visit with department heads and sometimes the hunt areas themselves. I would also travel to most of the Asian countries that were known to have wildlife of great interest to foreign sportsmen, even though hunting was not yet permitted.

The Asian countries were all the "'stans" in the south central U.S.S.R., including Kazakhstan, Tajikistan, Uzbekistan, etc. I escorted an occasional hunting group to areas in and around the Caucasus, as well as to forest areas. The clients included some high profile hunters such as Thornton Snider, Pete Papac, John Cotten, Art Carlsberg, and Clayton and Modesta Williams.

**A surprise birthday party had been pre-planned by the Game Department and Intourist officials, along with his hunting pals.**

Art Carlsberg failed to get a tur on the North Ossetia hunt due to heavy snows, so Chris escorted him to the Kubinsk Reserve in 1978, where he collected this fine silver medal tur. Shortly thereafter, Art died from a fall in the rugged Caucasus. Art's last ride was on a makeshift stretcher on the back of his horse.

I kept encouraging Intourist to develop further hunting programs, but progress was slow because of the socialistic mindset of the people—why do more and work harder when my pay will remain the same?

Finally in 1979, the big breakthrough I had been working on was agreed to. In a high-level meeting in Moscow, Valery Uvarov, who now had been elevated to the vice-director of Intourist, agreed to start

Chris again returned along with Colleene to the Kubinsk Reserve with Clayton and Modesta Williams, notable Texan's and International hunters. Here, Claytie, with his signature cowboy hat, makes the long ride from Derk to the hunting camp.

Rafik Kapharov, the young Azerbaijanian interpretor on our historic 1970 hunt in Kubinsk (on horseback), returned with us in 1983 when he was the manager of Intourist's hunting section (holding a Game Conservation International banner). From the left, Chris, Modesta, Rafik, Clayton, and Colleene at the newly built, permanent stone accommodation for the hunters. Clayton and Modesta both collected gold medal turs.

a new program of my choosing each year thereafter.

In addition, he appointed Alexey Mesyatsev to be head of all hunting tourism, and he would work directly with me. I knew Alexey for several years as he accompanied me on some hunts and was my guest on a trip to Seattle. Valery requested me to do a "Hunting and Wildlife Manual" that would show the wildlife distribution throughout the Soviet Union with detailed information about each sub-species. I agreed and said it would be in his hands by year-end. He also stated that the expansion of the program could start only in the year 1981, as every possible resource of Intourist would be fully occupied until after the 1980 Moscow Summer Olympics.

No sooner did I return home from the would-be results of the historic meeting, that the U.S.S.R. launched a massive occupation of Afghanistan. The whole world came down on them with the ban on the Olympics along with trade and travel embargoes. At the same time, Intourist did a complete reorganization to handle the Olympics, putting Alexey into a high position handling tourism and never let him back into the hunting section. As a result of the immense pressure on Valery during the pre-Olympic time, he suffered a couple of heart attacks, placing him into semi-retirement.

Many hunters submitted to the travel ban in the years following the Olympics, so hunting in the U.S.S.R. experienced a downturn and the promise of new openings was on the back burner. Even during this slowdown, I kept in touch with annual trips to Moscow and various other destinations within the U.S.S.R. We also made many proposals on expansion and improvement of existing programs. With the dwindling hunting program in the hands of Kapharov and his assistant Vladimir Snegorinko, both of whom were under the socialist syndromes of "Why work harder and still get paid the same?" I wrote the following official overview to the Intourist authorities in early 1987:

## OVERVIEW OF U.S.S.R. HUNTING PROGRAM

It is worthwhile to go back through the history of the hunting program, as mistakes in the past are responsible to a certain extent for the current picture. We have been privileged to work with Intourist from the inception of the hunting program. I personally have had more continuous contact with the program than any individual within the Soviet Union has. In addition, my company and I have been involved in the inception of all the hunting programs that have existed in the last 28 years in Asia and many in other parts of the world. We have seen many hunting programs come and go, and we have seen many travel agents and travel promoters come and go. As a result, I feel that we have a good hold on the hunting situation around the world.

We sincerely want to continue to assist the Soviet Union in every way to fulfill their goals in hunting and other sports travel. The following is only an overview, but it contains serious facts that must be carefully studied.

## PROBLEMS

Hunting had a good start around 1970 in a half-dozen different locations. I established the first tariffs for Intourist and put tremendous amount of effort and expense into promoting the program worldwide. The program was clumsily handled by Intourist in the years to follow as there was no person or department within Intourist actually in charge of the hunting nor enthusiastic about success, profitability, or expansion. By the late '70s, the combined effort of Valery Uvarov, Alexey Mesyatsev and I developed a better rapport with the existing reserves and laid the groundwork for an expansion into much more profitable areas of hunting.

In the late '70s, the hunting section of Intourist was organized to at least have personnel to coordinate booking of the small programs that existed. In 1979, it was agreed to start one major program each year. However, with the Moscow Olympics only one year away, it was determined that nothing more could be handled until after the Olympics. At that time I was requested by Mr. Uvarov to make a hunting manual for the Soviet Union to show the distribution of game and a little about each animal. During the next year, political problems caused a drastic decline in the hunting. From 1980 onward, completely new personnel involved in the hunting and related programs, as well as more political problems that compounded the situation, were contributing factors to a declining and very sluggish program.

Lack of variety in the hunting that was available, as well as the lack of the most valuable game, was a large contributor to the decline. During the latter years of the program, the success for some of the more difficult animals like tur and bear started dropping off. Reports from unsuccessful hunters indicated more time needed in the hunting areas, but nothing was done to increase the time and resulting hunter's success. Without success, the word spreads around rapidly in the hunting circles and more and more people lose interest in coming to the U.S.S.R.

The U.S.S.R. has not had the best atmosphere of friendliness around the world. Events that have taken place in the past 8 years have hurt the image of the U.S.S.R., and hunters travelling through the Soviet Union on their way to Mongolia have constantly commented on the unfriendliness. I personally know that the Soviet people are not unfriendly, but it is the impression that people get, mainly because of the lack of any real personal service in the major cities. This may not seem important, but it does contribute to the lack of enthusiasm of people wanting to come hunt there.

With the decline in success and less interest in hunting, overall prices were increased substantially earlier this year, after most of the clients had been booked from a year ago and some since 1985 for the forthcoming season. As a result, some of those people canceled, and it turned away many that might have booked yet for this season. A review of the Kubinsk booking schedule for this year is an indication of people resisting the sudden increase in price while success and the reputation of Kubinsk was on the decline. A review of the bear hunting schedules for this year, even after closing down your biggest bear hunting program in Baikal, is an indication that the drastic increase in trophy fees, after a poor show of success in 1986, is not to the liking of the hunters. The amount of hunting that Intourist has to offer today is less than it was 10 years ago, which does not say much for progress.

Many proposals have been made since 1970 regarding the great potential of hunting in the Soviet Union. If there is an interest in making the hunting section a highly profitable business, a review of the presentations that have been made in the past 10 years is essential.

Refer to "1978 U.S.S.R. Hunting Program, Proposed Expansion," and Five-Year Plan. Also refer to the large bound book showing "The Purpose and Need for Hunting in the U.S.S.R."

Refer to the 1980 Hunting Manual. (This was made up at the request of Mr. Uvarov.)

Refer to the 1986 Proposed U.S.S.R. Marco Polo Sheep Hunting Program, dated 23 September.

Refer to the file on Trout Unlimited. We have been encouraging Intourist to take on good fresh-water fishing throughout the years and it seems an organization like Trout Unlimited can move in right past Intourist and work its own deal with other Soviet departments.

Refer to Mountain Travel Expeditions into the Caucasus and Pamirs (where the Marco Polo sheep habitat), who evidentially are bypassing Intourist and working directly with other departments.

Refer to our Kelly Sampson's recent letter regarding the Waterfowl Shooting Program in Manych. The main problem is new unprecedented high trophy fees.

Refer to price and information sheets on neighboring countries Mongolia, China, Nepal, and Turkey. They are all successful. Mongolia started a couple of years before the U.S.S.R. in its hunting program, and has constantly improved. They know where the best profits are and that is in the sheep. They have two different species of Argali sheep that they manage very well, and are now doing around $1 million per year just on the two sheep species alone.

Their forest hunting programs, right along the Siberian border, are constantly expanding and producing extremely well and have very reasonably priced hunts. Please take note of the relatively low trophy fees, paid only after the animals are taken on forest hunts. Their six-day stag hunt, which *includes* one stag, is very well priced and is the same as the Iziubre offered in Baikal. From the forest and South Gobi sheep and ibex hunts, they even offer a 20

percent discount from the first of November onward to encourage late-season hunters. Their current hunting program is grossing around $1,500,000 and is expected to be around $2,000,000 this year. What Mongolia has to offer is very small indeed, compared to what the Soviet Union has to offer.

## SOLUTION

Without any question, the most important thing that you must do is add some excitement to your hunting program. This can be done by adding new and different animals, many of which are found only in the Soviet Union. You could start even with the lowly saiga antelope. If priced right, you could probably get a constant flow of hunters combining it with other hunting.

You should start one sheep species, which is your top dollar item in the Soviet Union. I would highly recommend the Asiatic bighorn, which are found in numerous quantities in many areas in Eastern Siberia and the Kamchatka Peninsula. Another good and easy possibility would be the urial family, of which you have at least three species. The Afghan urial found in Turkistan, the Transcaspian urial in Kazakhstan, and the Armenian sheep in Armenia and possibly Azerbaijan. The top choice however, would be the Marco Polo Sheep in Tajikistan.

As for your old programs, they have to be reviewed to give maximum success for the clients. Keep in mind that success is the greatest advertising you can do.

The second thing that needs to be done is better handling of the hunting clients in places like Moscow and the city of arrival for the hunts. Hunting is a very personal thing and you need personnel who are willing to give personalized service at all reasonable hours. Everywhere in the world, except the Soviet Union, hunters are taken in hand and shown the best time possible during their stay in the respective countries. Perhaps if Intourist cannot do it (and they have not been able to do this at all in the past except on remote cases in the smaller cities of arrival) you should look at an independent agent in Moscow, now that there is more free enterprise taking place.

You need to have more variety of game in any specific hunting area. At one time, North Ossetia was quite exciting with four different animals that could be hunted at one time. As time went by, fewer and fewer of these animals would be available on any given hunt. Several of the forest areas have two, three, and four animals, but it is not likely that a person can hunt more than one or two during any given time. In Mongolia, a hunter can go for 14 days, hunt 6 different forest animals, and have an excellent chance of getting 4 or 5 of them or even all 6—that is excitement!

And lastly, your promotions need to be looked at very seriously. We have put more into promoting the Soviet Union internationally than all the rest of the world put together. Yet we have been on the same basis as everyone else, even new agents that come and go. In the past, we have advised you that if you had an agent like ourselves that could be made an international coordinator for your hunts that we would spend whatever money necessary internationally to give you the kind of publicity that you need. The way it stands now, no agency is going to spend much money for promoting the U.S.S.R., especially with the declining success and the limited hunting program currently available.

In summary, you need more and better programs. They must be priced right. You must be better hosts and obtain more and better publicity worldwide. If you do not make efforts *now*, I am afraid it will be too late.

It always has been and always will be a pleasure to work with Intourist and its various departments. We stand ready to go into more detail on any subject matter or program you wish to discuss.

Sincerely Yours,

Chris Klineburger

President

During two decades of constantly negotiating with the Soviet officials to make it truly "the world's greatest hunting grounds" as predicted by Guy Jonas, the lack of progress gave me plenty of time to explore other areas in Asia. Later in the book, you will read about the exciting "new era" of U.S.S.R. hunting. In the meantime, enjoy many other exciting Asian and European adventures.

# REFLECTION
# The Birth of a Book

After many groundbreaking expeditions into underdeveloped areas around the world, we realized that the events were not being properly chronicled, as many of them were a definite mark in history. Each adventure had the makings for a book. That was what we needed—a book. Therefore, we engaged a bindery to make customized, hardcover blank books for us, and our clients, to use as a diary of the trips. These journals, as we called them, were custom made for each hunt with the country and the year on the spine, and then on the front face was inscribed "HUNTING JOURNAL," then the person's name and our logo with "A Klineburger World Adventure."

The 100 blank pages were for whatever use a person desired, from a day-by-day account of everything done, names of mountains, rivers, towns,

and the people involved— or use it as a picture album. I personally have a few dozen of these journals that I methodically kept current on a daily basis, usually under difficult conditions after the long and tiring day's activities, often at midnight, knowing I had to be up at dawn.

In doing this book, I had considered including all the journals as written, which were done on the major expeditions that I did in my late years of travel.

**These blank books, "hunting journals," were supplied to all of our hunting clients to record the day-to-day activities of their expeditions.**

However, the book would need to be multiple volumes and, I do admit, would be boring at times. However, I felt some of these journals are worth printing, so the reader will follow my footsteps on a few trips, with the exception of some "Time Lapse" where some days or time of the trip was omitted. The first journals were issued in 1974 and the first one written was my Nepal expedition in March of that year and is included in this book.

# CHAPTER 5

# Nepal

This expedition was in search of the bharal, better known as the blue sheep. Other specimens sought were the serow and ghoral. The habitat of these animals is the Himalayas and the Tibetan Plateau to the north.

There has never before been any organized hunting in these areas. Only a few people in the past, with special diplomatic permits, have been able to penetrate this high, remote country for the bharal. Only now has hunting been allowed for foreigners for the bharal and other game in the rugged Himalayas. Our expedition was the exploratory trip, setting the stage for Nepal's hunting program.

Our outfitter, Tej Jung Thapa, had considerable background with wildlife in Nepal, as he had worked for the Forestry Department and has outfitted for treks into both the Terai region and mountains. My contacts with Tej were only by correspondence, starting around the spring of 1973. The introduction was through my good friend, John Blower, who had been working for several years for the United Nations, studying Nepal's wildlife.

I met John in 1962 in Uganda when I set up Jonas Brothers of Africa in Kampala and went on my first safari. Blower was the head of Uganda's game department and worked with the newly formed Uganda Wildlife Development, Ltd. John, knowing the value of sportsmen-financed Game Programs was influential in opening the mountains of Nepal. When John informed King Birendra of my desire to hunt, permission was immediately granted, not only for my hunt, but also for others to follow.

Thapa picked the spot to start our hunt directly south of Dhaulagiri Himal, in the Gurja Himal. He hired 30 sherpas from Kathmandu to carry the supplies into the base camp. It was a 14-day trek, which he headed up, to a Tibetan immigrant village called Dhorpatan. Having already collected all of the available wild sheep of the world, I was overly excited about this rare opportunity to get one of the most coveted game animals, which had rarely been hunted before.

I arrived in Kathmandu on 18 March, 1974, two days ahead of my good friends and hunting partners, Dr. Robert "Doc" Speegle and Mahlon "Butch" White. The time was spent making final preparations and obtaining my hunting license, which bore the magic number of 1, the first hunting license ever issued in Nepal.

Since Thapa was already at the base camp, our host while in Kathmandu was Mahesh Busnyat, a very capable assistant to Thapa. Mahesh was invaluable there to help with all my needs. Here is my Nepal journal:

*20 March, 1974—Kathmandu, Nepal*

*Doc and Butch arrived. Busnyat and I met them at the airport. None of Butch's gear arrived. Jimmy Stewart, of motion picture fame and a good acquaintance of mine, and wife Gloria and daughters were supposed to be on the same flight, but were not there. After Doc and Butch settled in the Shanker Hotel we had lunch, and then went sightseeing. We saw*

*what seemed a thousand temples and observed a cremation by the river. They just swept the ashes into the water when done. Good idea.*

*We met General Sushil Shumshere in the evening for dinner. I'd previously met Shumshere when he was a colonel accompanying King Mahendra and Queen Ratna of Nepal on their Alaska hunt my company hosted. The general took us to the Yak and Yeti Restaurant, which was converted from an old palace and operated by Boris of Kathmandu. Boris spent the evening with us talking over his hunting experiences.*

*21 March*

*We met the flight from Delhi and still no baggage for Butch. Jimmy, Gloria, and daughters were on the flight, also Avi Kohli, a friend of mine from New Delhi, India, for many years. We had a brief visit at the airport and saw them to their connecting flight to Tiger Tops. Butch spent part of the day trying to find some gear to rent—found an inadequate sleeping bag, a pair of canvas boots, and a bright orange rain shirt. Doc and I had enough extra gear to supply Butch—but the gun was a big problem.*

*General Shumshere had us out again for dinner. First, we went to the palace of Khagda Shah. His wife is the sister of King Birendra. Luck would have it that he had a 7mm Remington Magnum rifle and offered it to us for Butch's use. I was carrying a 7 mag, so had plenty of ammo. We then went to the home of Shumshere who had a lot of trophies, mainly from India. After a few drinks, we all went out to dinner to an Oriental restaurant with Tibetan type of food.*

Our Nepal hunt started at Dhorpaton after flying from Kathmandu by Swiss made Palatis Porter turbo prop aircraft.

## 22 March

About a two-hour flight to Dhorpatan in a Pilatus Porter aircraft with turbo-prop engine. Dirt strip in a wide valley. Camp was set up two miles from the strip. Camp was very well equipped and staffed—all three of us had our own sleeping tent. Tents were from a Dhaulagiri mountain climbing expedition and were of the best quality. Elevation at Camp #1 was 9,400 feet—the airstrip was at 9,200 feet. The weather is warm and dry, but getting cloudy.

For a conditioning hunt, we went out for a wild boar hunt in the rather steep foothills above camp. I saw the ears of two boars passing through some thick stuff. No shot. News that local guides spotted some bharal about one day away. Sighted-in rifles late in the evening. Food was well prepared with folding chairs and TV tables around the campfire!

## 23 March

Started early moving camp. Hunted along the way to and above timberline. Saw some ghoral tracks at timberline around 11,000 feet. My local guide, Bala, showed up bare footed and bare legged. Yesterday he had to finish plowing his field and couldn't join the hunt.

The Tibetan immigrant village of Dhorpatan was located in the first fertile valley at the base of the Gurja Himal. The foothills of Dhaulagiri Range.

After a couple of days acclimatizing ourselves at the 9,400-foot level, we began the long trek deep into the Gurja Himal.

*He is Tibetan. Bala is a rugged type, 46 years old—same as me.*

*The three guides and we three hunters went on ahead of the sherpas that had the camp and supplies. As we approached the pass of 13,000 feet, where Camp #2 was to be, the fog set in and we couldn't hunt anymore. We overshot the campsite by about 1½ miles. We found enough wood from an old settlement to build a fire. It started to snow lightly. No sherpas showed up, so we sent Temba, Doc's guide, back to find them. By the time he returned to fetch us it was snowing and blowing hard.*

*When we got to the campsite, they already had a couple of tents up. Some of the sherpas*

**My Tibetan guide, Bala, showed up barefooted and in shorts.**

Bob Speegle and Butch White prepare to hunt for blue sheep after a night of full scale Himalayan blizzard. 25,000-foot high Dhaulagiri is in the background.

were still arriving—very fatigued. The cook was in no condition to cook, so we broke out Doc's butane stove and had freeze-dried stew. Blizzard all night.

A word about the sherpas—a sherpa is a packer, an occupation that is highly respected in Nepal, where mountains cover most of the country and roads are extremely sparse. Therefore, sherpas are essential. In carrying loads, they do not have pack boards, but carry a large basket on their back, suspended only by a leather strap around their forehead. There are no sherpas among the Tibetan immigration village, so they are all brought from Kathmandu.

*24 March*

Sunny and bright out—took several hours to dig out and put up the rest of the tents and find shoes for my guide. 10:00 AM we started hunting. Doc, Butch, and I split three ways to try and locate bharal. Clouds started forming by early PM, then fog and blizzard. Climbed to over 14,000 feet. Weather forced us back to camp.

This camp is right on a high ridge. Looking north we see mountains of the Gurja Himal, ridge after ridge. Then maybe 50 miles away is the Dhaulagiri Himal rising sharply with five major peaks over 25,000 feet in elevation. When flying to Dhorpatan, we passed Annapurna, another major himal. While in Kathmandu, Butch and I took a charter helicopter to a "hotel" which is a major take-off point for Mount Everest expeditions. We were not allowed to stay there because of the extreme danger of going that high without acclimation.

*25 March*

We went the same way as yesterday in hopes of getting farther. Started at 8:30. All three covered more ground before once again being forced back. Butch saw a good lone bharal, but it got their wind at 100 yards. Doc saw a lone serow near timberline. Timberline was about 11,000 feet. I gave Bala a pair of wool socks today. He got blisters yesterday wearing shoes without socks. He had a different pair of shoes today.

*26 March*

We got out at 7:30 today—getting system worked out. Fresh eggs every morning. We brought 200 in, so it doesn't look like we will have a chance to try out Doc's freeze dried Spanish omelet.

We discovered our waiter has gonorrhea! Doc is treating him and insisted he have nothing to do with the kitchen. Slaughtered a buffalo calf that was brought in for meat. They lead the meat supply in—don't have to carry it that way or worry about it spoiling. Had fresh hamburger for dinner—no grinder, cook chops it up with his khukri, the national knife of Nepal and carried by all.

Chris and Bala, now with shoes and red socks, get ready to split off from the others. Far right is "Doc" and Butch is fourth from right.

*27 March*

Wild dogs had driven a domestic cow all the way from Dhorpatan to our camp. Wild dog tracks found all over the hills yesterday and today. Tej says they will kill bharal and probably stir them up for us. I see bharal tracks that were made yesterday. Fog moved in with blizzard earlier than before. This was the fifth day of blizzard—mornings always clear and cold, afternoon's blizzards set in and drive us back. Can't get enough distance from camp before clouds close in on us and then, blizzards. The head sherpa says when a storm sets in it lasts five days in the mountains—if not five, then seven—if not seven, then fifteen days. He said that there was one day of fog after a storm.

*28 March*

Fog in early morning. First time it was no use in going out at all. Tej did send some local guides out for spotting farther out than we have been. If they don't find anything to change our mind, we move camp to Camp #3. Camp #3 is actually lower than Camp #2, even though it's farther into the Gurja Himal. We named Camp #2 "Camp Blizzard." Temperature pattern has been below freezing at night—usually around 25°F in the morning. Sun is usually out in morning and it warms up enough to almost melt the snow from the open hillsides by early afternoon. Then fog, wind, and snow whip up in afternoon again and cover everything. We fight our way back to camp in the blizzard.

*29 March*

Dense fog at 6 AM. Tej wanted to try a "spooking" operation for sheep in a cliff area that cannot be hunted successfully by spotting. Butch and I were spotted at two different points at the head of the canyon while sherpas and guides were sent around and exposed themselves to spook the game. All went well until our guides got cold and told us the hunt was over and time to go back to camp. Much later, the sherpas returned to camp and informed us that three bharals came past our post!

Doc went up with his guide to check out five sets of tracks that crossed over the hill above camp. Fog kept him from following the tracks. Snow started about midday and continued off and on.

Butch and I did see 28 ewes and lambs and one small ram about three years old. My first sighting of bharal—quite a thrill. My guide tried to get me to shoot one. I had a serious talk with him through Tej.

Our local guides were Tibetan mountain men. They herded sheep in these mountains in the summer, so had a complete understanding of the terrain, but were not familiar with trophy hunting. They couldn't speak one word of English. Normally, when going out each day we would go in pairs—guide and hunter. Tej stayed behind and kept things well organized. We only traveled by foot, which was good—no animals to worry about—just hiked and hunted. We didn't understand each other's language, so we didn't talk—just hunted.

*30 March*

Beautiful day at 6 AM. It had stormed until 4:30 AM. All three parties climbed to the west of camp. Doc and Butch dropped off the other side to look at cliffs where eight rams were thought to have gone. I split out to the north, deeper into the Gurja Himal. Looked over a lot of new country in the area where we're supposed to move to Camp #3 tomorrow. Some got snow blind.

Bire, Butch's guide, was also with me. I was impressed. He was more like a guide—22 years old. Bala knows the area but is very primitive—can't use binoculars, can't speak a word of English. All he does is pack my camera bag—no doubt has good eyes. Covered a lot of country—20 miles plus or minus—but saw no signs of life.

Butch threw snowballs at me in the "john" tent. We ordered some booze up from Dhorpatan again. The "diluted" cost three rupees a quart. We ordered "undiluted" but got six quarts of diluted. Taken straight, it tastes like the stuff they had in canteens in North Ossetia, U.S.S.R.—Bad! We made martinis with olives (whole bunch)—didn't help much. Best way we found was with fruit juice or squash.

We had sherpas going to town every day or so bringing us more of the liquor made there. We found out later that the small (?) quantities that we were obtaining were the total surplus of the distillery. Evidently, the capacity was not all that great. We did share our supply somewhat with the staff. We had an occasional call from the cook or camp boys requesting a little nip.

*31 March*

Moved camp today to Camp #3. We all went out ahead and hunted three different areas. Butch's guide, Man—Tibetan guide—had eye trouble. Probably snow blind, and wasn't much use other than carrying his lunch. Doc had diarrhea and left a trail all the way from one camp to the other. We went through the cliffs and sure enough, we saw where the bharal were staying during the bad weather.

Bire went with me and we went clear out one side and back the other of the northwest range from Camp #3. Very long day—walked steady all day—maybe 20 miles.

Camp #3 is much better than Camp Blizzard. Several sheepherder houses at this camp. These are shelters used in the summer by herdsmen to stay in—built of rock with wood shingle-type roof. They are called goaths. One was used for our cook shack. Tried mango squash with local booze—tasted good.

*01 April*

Tej said there had been a leopard all around camp during the night. He probably didn't know what an April Fool's joke is, so it probably was the truth. We still had our live lamb, goat,

and chickens in camp. They would be enough to draw a leopard in.

We started early—all three parties in different directions. I headed due north along the western face of the main Gurja Himal. Walked in and out of rocky gorges for over four miles. Bire was guiding now and Bala was packing. Hadn't seen any fresh sign. Finally spotted a herd of eight bharal! Two were very good heads. They were in the second draw away from me. I had plenty of time—they had not seen us.

Even though I had never seen a bharal ram before, there was no question in my mind that the two large ones were excellent trophies. The horns curled wide and far back. They turned upward at the tips, which I knew was an indication of a very good specimen. Bire and Bala stayed back out of sight very obediently.

The sheep were quietly grazing and the wind was favorable. I looked with the binoculars, then with my riflescope. It was difficult determining which was the biggest. One of them had indications of battered up horns, and that one looked the longest. He seemed to be the leader of the band, so I made my decision to take him. This was the first test for my new 7mm Colt Sauer rifle. I was confident in its accuracy, but a little unsure of the distance, not knowing the exact size of one of these rams. I knew it was well in excess of 200 yards, but sure it wasn't 300 yards. Therefore, I held right in the middle of the shoulder when he turned broadside. A brisk wind was blowing right into my face as I gently closed my hand. The ram lunged downhill and went out of sight behind the ridge separating us.

**Chris with the first bharal on the first hunting license issued in Nepal.**

*The rest of the sheep scattered very slightly, then stopped and stared in the direction of their leader. They stayed for the better part of an hour, not appearing to be very nervous. Most of them at one time or another disappeared behind the ridge separating us to go down and inspect the old ram. I purposely stayed out of sight until the sheep left on their own accord, so as not to allow them to associate the loss of their leader with man's presence. The sheep probably only very faintly heard the shot because of them being upwind and the distance involved. Finally, they left, first walking in single file, then trotting by the time they topped over the ridge.*

*The anticipation was about to get the best of me waiting so long to get my ram if he was there at all. He was—and what a beautiful specimen. He hadn't gone 20 yards from where*

*he stood when I shot. Ironically, bharal number one on license number one in the first organized hunting program for this coveted animal.*

*We skinned the sheep for a life-size mount and had it back in camp by midafternoon. Everyone was happy in camp—it called for a celebration. I supervised cooking a Mexican dinner, which all three of us savor. I had been able to locate in the supplies everything except corn flour, but used their unleavened whole-wheat flour for the tortillas. Had chili soup, enchiladas, and chili con carne con frijoles. Had this all arranged for Doc and Butch when they got in about dark. Doc broke out a bottle of Wild Turkey bourbon! What a great day with such fine people.*

*Tej did know about April Fool's jokes and he did a good job of fooling us in the morning!*

*02 April*

Butch headed out for a three-day spike camp to hunt the main face of Gurja Himal. Doc went out to follow the second ram in the herd that I took mine from. I skinned the head out after taking more pictures. Saved full skin, but left the head unskinned yesterday so Doc and Butch could see it. Had lunch with Tej, and then Bala and I headed down to timberline looking for other game, especially serow and ghoral. No signs of life. Doc returned without luck—followed the tracks for a mile to a cliff area. They ran out of time and couldn't continue.

Very cold and windy today. We have experienced almost every day sudden changes in temperature. When the sun is out and not windy, it is very comfortable. When topping a windy ridge, it is extremely cold.

*03 April*

26°F. Beautiful clear morning, but windy. Temperature has always gone below freezing every night. There seems to always be wind here. At night, our tents rattle with the wind. During the day, the chill factor adds to the low temperatures. We have had to have layers of lightweight clothing to take off or add on when required. Wool pants, wool socks, and two-piece duo-fold underwear are uniforms of the day.

Tej decided to send Doc out for a three-day spike camp to work the adjoining ridges with Butch. His outfit consisted of two sherpas, one interpreter/guide, and one local guide. The reason for the extra sherpa was they had to take tents—one big one for the four Nepalese and my small two-man for Doc. Butch's camp were using goaths—the sheepherder's huts. He took one sherpa, interpreter, and a local guide.

I headed down to timberline again looking for ghoral with Bala. He tells me there is no serow in the areas we are hunting. I was back by 3 PM. No ghoral or signs. Tej and Bire went glassing for bharal at the "bank." The bank is a cliff area where the bharals hole up when they can't be found anyplace else. They saw nothing.

Tej had the cook fix some snacks from the bharal stomach. The stomach is first boiled to get rid of the fuzzy stuff from the inside. Then they cut it in strips, hang it a ways above the fire in the cook shack, which sort of smoke-dries it. Then he cuts it in little chunks, fried it with seasoning and served. It was good-tasting, but a little chewy. Bharal stew for dinner. Very Good!

*04 April*

28°F at sun up. Getting a little warmer each day. A few clouds though. Started out at 7 AM to glass some cliffs below where Butch was hunting. By 8 AM it started snowing. Bala dug his boots out of the pocket in his robe. He had been barefooted. We found a goath and holed up. Built a fire. It kept snowing and found its way through all the cracks. Storm hung on and it then got foggy, so we returned to camp.

It seems that goaths are spotted at regular intervals around these mountains. We were always within a couple of miles of a goath. They are built from poles and sided with bark. The roofs are very similar to our cedar shakes. They are all very airy on all four sides—not built for wintertime. The snow and wind come right through. Most of the roofs leak.

*In Camp #3 there are three of these huts being utilized. The cook operates out of one of them. That's the most popular spot in camp. We have a dining tent set up right outside the cook shack. I'm now sitting in the cook shack keeping out of the snow and so are the chickens. Every day or so another chicken hits the pot. The snow is drifting in, and we are all moving closer to the fire. No doubt Butch and Doc are holed up as well. About three inches of fresh snow outside now—late morning. There is occasional thunder and lightening, which is often the case.*

*Butch returned about 4 PM—guide Man was sick most of the time. Snow loused things up today—first day he saw 12 sheep. Everything went wrong. After a shot of Doc's Wild Turkey and a bath, the world seemed to still be OK to Butch.*

*Tomorrow the plan is for Butch and crew to head out earlier and plan on spending whatever time necessary in the spike camp.*

*05 April*

*26°F and clear. Butch was off at 6 AM I started down to timberline at 7 AM. Butch took Bala with him, as Man was still sick. I had loaned my binoculars to Bire, Butch's shikari. The main reason I was staying close to Camp #3 was because of not having my binoculars. Butch had been quite handicapped, having never received his gear from Air France. Jeta, my personal boy, accompanied me. I was a little sick today—didn't see anything again, so returned by 2 PM.*

*Yesterday, Bala said he would never wear shoes again and showed me his blister sores on his heels. He came to the mountains without shoes, but after the first storm, Tej supplied him with*

*leather boots and no socks. His feet sloshed up and down and caused bad blisters on his heels. Next day I furnished him with socks and Tej found some canvas boots that most of the others use. These worked fine for him. Therefore, the last couple of days while we were hunting low, Bala went barefooted. Yesterday, after telling me he wouldn't wear shoes anymore, (and probably thinking that our storm was now over) as soon as it started snowing, Bala had his boots on again. The bulge in the back of his robe had me wondering.*

*Doc returned about 4 PM. They had seen six sheep—one big ram. Temba and he thought they had it in the bag. Just then, the interpreter came running up the mountain shouting that he saw the sheep, and spooked all six. Doc could have killed him, but realized the kid had never been hunting before. That was Doc's first sighting of sheep.*

*06 April (07 April)*

*This is being written on 07 April because I didn't have the strength last night to do it. Cold and clear. Doc was preparing for his new fly camp to the northwest and off the area we've all been hunting. It seems that as we've spooked the sheep, they've all headed that general direction. I started out by 7 AM with Jeta, with the idea of putting some distance between here and ourselves. We certainly did that. Walked steady down stream to the southeast fighting our way up over passes and then down through tangled creek bottoms. By noon we ended up on an open face, which was on the opposite of a big ridge from Dhorpaton. Had lunch and glassed the wooded cliffs on opposite mountains.*

By 1:00 PM we spotted a lone ghoral on the mountain to our left. Had to go down through a canyon and back up to the top of that mountain. He spotted us at about 200 yards and ran for the cliffs. If I had my binoculars, I probably would have spotted him in the clump of bush. I had borrowed Tej's binoculars, but they had been water damaged and were blurry.

I momentarily had my crosshairs on him as he hesitated for a split second, but I didn't have time to squeeze off. I did not want to chance a running shot, so as not to disturb the area. To date, there has only been one shot fired in the mountains and that was my firing at the ram I got. We looked around the cliffs where the ghoral headed, but could not find him.

It was 3:30 and we could not take a chance on spending any more time, as camp was a very long way. We pushed very hard to make camp by dark. At 7 PM I had over done it and was completely wet with perspiration, legs all knotted up and just plain fatigued. I couldn't even talk as I had been breathing so hard my vocal cords were even fatigued. Had a cup of local booze. Two cups of tea and went to bed without dinner.

The ghoral that we saw was at an estimated 12,000 feet, which was about as high as ghorals range. Generally, they range from 10 to 12,000 feet, which is from timberline to 2,000 feet below. They will not likely be found above timberline. They hang out in or close to the cliffs and rock outcrops.

Yesterday I had gone from Camp #3, which is 12,400 feet down to an estimated 10,000 feet, back up to about 11,500 feet to spot, down 1,000 feet and back up to 12,000 feet where the ghoral was. Then dropped back down at least 1,000 feet and back up to 12,400 feet at Camp #3. According to my pedometer, I went 16.1 miles. Our vertical was about 5,000 feet as well as our fall—through some very tough country. All this at high elevation for someone from sea level. That was too much!

In talking over the location of the animal that we saw, as well as the coloration, Man and Tej felt that it was not a ghoral but either a tahr, serow, or the remote chance of it being a musk deer. Musk deer have no horns, and I was sure that I did see horns on this one. The horns on both the ghoral and serow are much like our North American mountain goat—and strangely enough, both in the same family of Rupicaprinae.

The ghoral is small, about the size of a Thompson or goitered gazelle. The serow is at least double the size, about like a big North American mountain goat. If this was a serow, I feel it was a young billy or a nanny. The local people call the serow a tahr. The Himalayan tahr is called jharal.

## 07 April

Cold and clear. I stayed in camp today to rest up after yesterday. Six days left before our charter aircraft is scheduled to pick us up.

The plan is now for me to head out on a spike camp for the rest of the time, traveling through serow and ghoral habitat on my way back to Dhorpaton in a round about way. Butch is due back tonight if he runs out of hunting country or gets his ram. If he gets his ram, he might join me. I had loaned him my trail mat, binoculars, Herman Survivor boots for this last *fly camp. He already had my chukka boots. This all worked out fine as long as only two of us were going out on spike camps, but not enough gear for three of us to split entirely.*

*At 5 PM, we saw a smoke signal from Butch's camp. We had worked out a plan that if Doc returned with a sheep while Butch was out, we would send up a smoke signal from Camp #3 at 5 PM. Therefore, the fact that Butch sent up a smoke signal indicated that he no doubt got one.*

*We could see Butch's camp even though it was the distance of about eight miles walking. Tej was out spotting this morning and thought he heard a shot in that direction about 11 AM. Tej and I are sitting in the cook shack having a drink of local booze to celebrate Butch's success. We ran out of mango juice for chaser, so we drained the juice from a can of pineapple slices. Anything is better than drinking it straight.*

*Tej was just telling me about the potatoes that we have been eating in camp, that he got from Dhorpatan. They raise mainly potatoes there. To store them, they dig a deep hole in the middle of the cowsheds and bury them. The cows come in all winter and do their thing. When Tej's outfit wanted to buy some potatoes, the locals led them to the shed and said, "Start digging." Our potatoes look good after all the camp staff had to go through to get them.*

*Honey works pretty well with the local booze. The head sherpa was right; the storm did last off and on for 15 days. The last two days were beautiful. Butch's camp is two ridges away, and we can see each other with spotting scopes.*

**The author, Bob, and Tej Thapa pose with Butch and his ram.**

*08 April*

26°F. and clear. Finally, about 10 AM spotted Butch and one sherpa returning. I could not leave on my side trip till I, at least, got my binoculars and trail mat. Went out to meet Butch part way. He got a good ram of 23½ inches, each horn length. He got into a herd of them and made his shot straight up. Got a scope cut and bled badly. He didn't think he had hit the ram, because he couldn't see after he shot. He got another shot off as another good ram came through. He hit it and it went down.

Upon inspecting the area, they found a blood trail indicating he had also hit the other ram. They had a tough time getting to it but found it ok. It wasn't as big as the second one. We had a spare permit just in case of a problem such as this. We sent four more sherpas from Camp #3 to help bring the camp and meat in. Butch was happy, but bushed, so he decided not to go on the fly camp with me. He had to make sure that the skins were skinned, salted, and dried. I helped, as Bire had not returned yet with my binoculars.

By midafternoon, my binoculars finally returned, but not the trail mat. I didn't want to wait any longer, so left for lower country. With me were two sherpas, guide Man, and Kesha. Kesha was the waiter (who had gonorrhea) and was going to be our cook. We stopped to camp before dark where Jeta and I went the other day.

They kept a big fire going all night to keep warm. The locals rotated between sleeping and caring for the fire. I took two sleeping pills hoping to soften the disturbances I was sure the smoke and fire would scare any game out of the country. We had seen some serow tracks in the creek bed nearby. They have the shape of a yak or cow track but much smaller—bigger than a mountain goat, though.

*09 April*

Up at daybreak. Kesha brought along corn flakes! I had some with freeze-dried peaches. Man and I hiked straight up from camp and in five minutes spooked a serow. With all the commotion in camp, none of us expected to see anything until we topped out. We had been walking very hard and I was lagging several paces behind Man. By the time I ran to where he was, I was puffing too hard for an offhand shot. The serow went over the ridge. We looked all around the cliffs and found where he had been bedding down. After seeing this serow, I knew the one I saw the other day was definitely a serow.

The staff was anxious to move to goaths downstream, where they say is better ghoral and serow hunting. We spent six torturous hours crossing the river dozens of times and climbing out of gorges through the densest bamboo groves. The entire length of our trek was through rugged gorges that made for the worst traveling. We saw fresh tracks of a Himalayan black bear. We arrived at 5:30 at our designated camp. A well-made and well-used goath. We were not far from civilization—no doubt there's a village a little farther downstream. The goath had a layer of cow dung in it that we had to remove.

No one would believe the amount of food these people can eat. Each one would eat a large plate of rice heaped about 4 inches deep, and a side dish of meat and potatoes—sort of like stew.

☉ **My guide, Man, and I pose with my hard-earned ghoral specimen. I donated the full mounted specimen to the International Wildlife Museum in Tucson.**

On top the main ridge we spotted another serow about 1½ miles away—he didn't see us. Man said we could stalk him from the opposite ridge tomorrow. We hunted the other direction. Jumped two ghorals. They make the funniest grumbling sound when scared. Couldn't get a shot off, as it was very thick. Fought cliffs, bamboo thickets, and bushes for hours.

Just as we decided to head back to camp, we jumped another ghoral. He made the mistake of skirting around the open hillside. I had a good running broadside shot at about 75 yards and stopped him in his tracks with the trusty Colt Sauer. The weight of the ghoral was less than 100 pounds. Man wanted to carry the animal whole back to camp. My small group was quite tickled over my success.

"Mukluk telegraph" informed us that Doc, three sherpas, and Bire went on a fly camp to a different area looking for bharal. The main camp moved back to Dhorpatan. My crew said they had to go back to Dhorpatan on the 12th. They said they were out of rice. I told them we were going back on the 13th and if they needed more supplies they could send a sherpa after it. I cut off one of the back straps from the ghoral and fried it for dinner. Excellent.

*10 April*

Clear and cold—still frost every night. Elevation must be around 10,000 feet. Man and I went out early. Spooked two serows. Man was visible at about 600 yards and they left the country. He is just too careless—after careful spotting, he stands on ridges, which will clear the valley of game. These animals—all of them—are extremely spooky. They will all leave the entire area at the slightest view of man.

*11 April*

Went after the serow that we saw yesterday. Made a perfect stalk with wind and everything right. Man saw it go into a depression about 150 yards away. It didn't come out, so Man got impatient and went down the ridge we were on to look up the draw and try to spot it. He came back. I made a stalk around and above where it was. I had perfect control of the whole area. No serow. I motioned for Man to circle underneath. Still, no serow. Either he was spooked out earlier when Man went below him or he just wandered off somehow on his own.

We spent the rest of the day going through forest areas. Found serow tracks and fresh droppings. Bamboo groves everywhere and a constant battle going through them—smaller in diameter than my little finger but thick as hair on a dog's back. In addition, sticker bushes! There must be a dozen different kinds. Everything from Devils Club like to a thorn bush type. Then there are groves of very large rhododendron trees—I didn't know they grew so big—in bloom now, too.

Back at camp—ghoral chops for dinner. Rice holding out well!

## 12 April

Climbed to an area adjoining our first day's hunt in the area. Got very high—glassed hard all day and didn't see a thing. This is the last day of hunting and am depressed that I could never get my sights on a serow. I feel in every case it was human error that prevented me from getting one. The first one that I jumped, when I was with Jeta, the camp boy, I didn't have my binoculars and just couldn't see. All the rest was a case of foolish exposure. It seems to be customary for the local guides to very carefully approach a place, look it over good, then stand up and totally expose himself.

Had ghoral hamburger for dinner. The cook very painstakingly chops the meat with a khukri (native knife). Ghoral meat is very tasty. Rice holding up exceptionally well!

## 13 April

Up early. Packed and hit the trail to base camp via the village of Damdu, which was upstream (east) of Dhorpatan. Easy going by trail all the way. Good thing, as I had a damaged knee. Hurt it coming down the rugged canyon to the last camp from Camp #3. It got progressively worse as Man and I really hiked hard for the last several days.

Butch was boar hunting. He was the town hero. He shot a fox that was eating the chickens and a boar that was destroying crops. The local farmers are plowing now and planting potatoes. Wild pigs come in right behind them and eat the potato eyes. Butch was back by early afternoon and we had some well-prepared boar meat.

I took a bath in a basin and shaved—first time since I left Kathmandu.

Doc's sherpas returned with great news that Doc got his ram. Cape was in two parts and we didn't get the straight story until he got in. He and Bire came out on a ridge on return to Camp #1, looking for serow or ghoral. Luck really turned for the better for Doc, as he got a ghoral on the way down today. Doc looked lean today. Looked like he lost about 15 pounds. He had been in fly camps continuously for 11 days, Butch for eight days, and I had been for five days.

I hadn't seen Doc for a week. He was lean, bushy, and proud. He worked harder than the rest of us. He got his sheep on a ridge above a cliff and when it fell, it went down a rock chute and busted it all to heck. Doc didn't want to chance going down to the sheep, so they fetched the sherpas to retrieve it. They skinned it out and brought it back. The head *was torn loose from the rest of the body. It looks like pieces of head skin will go back together ok for a mount. Skinned out his ghoral and took pictures.*

*A young girl—in her early 20s—from Oregon wandered into camp. She had been trekking around Nepal for a year. She did not have the required trekking permits to be in the area. She joined us for dinner and a drink before returning to her quarters down by the airstrip.*

*Bad rainstorm hit—snow in mountains. I made enchiladas for dinner—hot batch. Brought in all the local booze we could get for a party for everyone. We drank the town dry. Booze came directly from the still. Last gallon came about midnight. Whole camp—about 30 people—joined in the party. Dancing, singing, and drinking. They got the three of us out to do their dances. Only thing missing were the girls! They used plastic water containers for drums—very effective. Butch sacked out about 11 PM—smart! It was after 1 AM when the party broke up.*

*We were given some prayer rocks to take home. Carved in the rocks in Tibetan was "Oh Lord, save me please."*

*Maybe they figured we needed to be saved after drinking all that local booze!*

Following our history making expedition, Ozzie Davis and Joe Quarto arrived and were the fourth and fifth hunters to collect the bharal and other game. I came up with guidelines and suggestions for Thapa and his assistant Busnyat to improve hunting techniques, especially for the local guides, and emphasized conservation of wildlife. Busnyat split off and started his own hunting operation, Himalayan Safaris. Both Thapa and Busnyat's operations went well and they spent much time educating the locals on the sustainability of wildlife. We first hunters had it tough, as the game was scarce and spooky from constant poaching. Five years later, the bharal and other game populations had increased noticeably and hunting became much easier, another example of conservation prevailing in the presence of a hunting program. The "game wardens" were the locals who prospered and saw value in the wildlife.

Another country and wildlife program has disappeared by the time of this writing. There had been a constant rise in communism (Maoism) in the late 20th century in Nepal. By the year 2000, Maoist training camps for terrorists found the remote hunting area as ideal for this operation, closing down hunting and without doubt taking a heavy toll on wildlife. Now the King and royal family have been driven from power and the Maoist military leader has assumed the position of Prime Minister. As seen in Iran, Afghanistan, and now Nepal, Asian countries can tumble, as have many in Africa.

ᐱ While on the subject of the Himalayas, brother Bert collected this takin in Bhutan by special permission from HIH King Wangchuck. Dr. Leonard Milton also took one. They were the only two taken in over 60 years in Bhutan and to the time of this printing.

ᐱ Nepal also opened its terai areas to hunting. Here, two of my long time friends and hunting companions, John Cotten with a blue bull (Nilgai) and Thornton Snider with a forest serow, shared their photos.

# CHAPTER 6

# Spain

As far back as written history goes, the most populous places encompassed Europe and the subcontinent of Asia. Little was written about wildlife and hunting, but without management, one could be certain that residents and armies killed everything they could for survival. Yet the cunning abilities of mammals contributed to their survival until man finally recognized the value of wildlife.

Some governments set aside refuges, but just as important, many landowners recognized a superior land use by making private game reserves. Also in Europe, hunting was a highly respected tradition throughout history and remains that way to this day. More and more land is being set aside for wildlife by private landowners and governments alike for all to enjoy for hunters and nonhunters alike.

Spain is a model example of flourishing wildlife due largely to those that love wildlife most, the hunters. Back in the late 1960s when the country was unknown as a hunting destination, Spanish ibex (Capra pyrenaica victoriae) became overpopulated in the Gredos Reserve. The far-sighted game officials came up with the only sensible solution, to issue permits for hunters to crop off the surplus in this fine national park. Before that, however, brother Bert was one of the early recipients of a permit and collected his ibex in 1963, through contacts with the family of the late Generalissimo Franco.

In the late '60s, two of our renowned Spanish clientele invited Colleene and me to be their guests in Madrid and to participate in

᠀ **Ricardo Medem and Chris Klineburger with the first Spanish Ibex to be taken on private land adjoining the Gredos Reserve.**

traditional cazarias and monterias. Our hosts, Ricardo Medem and Valentin de Madariaga were internationally known hunters, and later, both became recipients of the coveted Weatherby Hunting and Conservation Award. Cazarias are driven bird shoots by farm fields where native red-legged partridges and introduced pheasants abound. Monterias are driven big game hunts in forest areas designed to cull surplus red deer, roe deer, and wild boars. At these gala social events, I discussed the possibility of sending foreign sportsmen.

Not long after, I received a phone call from Ricardo saying that he had a permit for me to hunt Spanish ibex adjoining the Gredos Reserve, where the animals had drifted and begun overpopulating the area. I jumped at the chance as my great love was hunting mountain game. Ricardo personally guided me on the successful hunt, when I once again brought up the subject of offering Spanish hunts to outsiders.

Although Ricardo had a successful John Deere equipment business, in 1977 he decided to start a needed hunting operation called Cazatur (hunt tourism). We began sending him clients. His operation got the attention of other landowners, and set the model for the hunting business, which grew enormously in Spain. Paralleling this, of course, was more and more game conservation.

In January 2009, I visited with Eduardo de Araoz, who guided for Ricardo, and purchased Cazatur from him in 1988. I asked a couple of questions and this was Eduardo's response:

Dear Chris:

It is and has always been nice to visit with you, learn from you, and because of it, respect you as the pioneer of what we call today "The Hunting Industry." I wanted to get you correct numbers so I wanted to check them out first, which I did. I am answering your questions:

1) How many outfitters operate in Spain as partially a spin-off from Ricardo's early efforts?

Today, eleven different outfitters are coming to the conventions in America. Many more act as "agents" in Spain arranging hunts to the Spanish hunters. There are more than thirty today. Directly coming from Ricardo's efforts I can say Cazatur is still there as you know operated by me, Alfonso Fabres, and Alfonso Fabres Jr., Felix Lalanne, and Javier Angus who slid out of it two years ago. Indi-

In 2008, Eduardo Araoz, second from left, joined 300,000 Spaniards from all social levels to demonstrate against the new game department in hopes of restoring proven game management.

rectly, there are three others who worked at Cazatur under my direction, two of them decided to operate by themselves and another joined an existing outfitter in Spain, Javier Lopez de Ceballos, who also worked under Ricardo's direction. The rest got the wind of the business from seeing us operate in Spain.

2) What is the gross income to Spain as a result of the hunting industry?

The Spanish hunting industry employs today an estimate of 100,000 people. It generates 5% of Spain's Gross Income and the industry is moving "5 billion Euros"!!!!

3) If you have any comment on the quality of the Spain Wildlife Department, I would like to hear it.

4) It has evolved a lot throughout this time. At first (Cazatur was founded in 1977) there was one single Wildlife Department for the entire country of Spain.

This department was based in Madrid, the capital, and those who run it were Hunters first, Landowners second and Wildlife engineers who had a degree in Agricultural and Forestry Engineering. This meant they knew what they were talking about and regulated the wildlife species and their habitats with knowledge and hands on the job. The National Hunting Reserves were established from 1965 to 1975. The man responsible of doing this was Dr. Ing. Jorge de la Pena Paya, who was able to create them by fulfilling the promises of generating jobs amongst the locals in those areas, some becoming game wardens, others helping in the building of the road systems needed to access those remote places and indirect jobs created with the hunting activity itself.

Today, they (game officials) have a degree, but have not left the city life, do not understand the correct management of the renewable natural resources, and start regulating it all in such a way that if you want to follow their regulations, it is IMPOSSIBLE to do so.

As a result, last year, in hopes of restoring proper game management, 300,000 hunters from all social levels in Spain marched together in a demonstration against the new hunting law, in which restrictions had been imposed against the traditional ways of hunting in Spain.

Humbly,

Eduardo de Araoz

# CHAPTER 7

# Yugoslavia and Turkey
## (Circa October 1983)

O f my hunts in Europe, one notable trip was with a fine group of high profile hunters of the time, all members of the International Sheep Hunters Association (ISHA). We were to first hunt in Yugoslavia then on to Turkey for another hunt. My group consisted of Thornton and Helen Snider, John and June Cotten, Jim and Clarice Wilkenson, Dr. Jim Conklin, Ray Bond, Joe Shaw, Bob Chisholm, and my wife Colleene. The following is a report of the ISHA group hunt.

Our group completely filled the Crossair/Fairchild turboprop aircraft. As we winged our way eastward from Zurich, we had a beautiful panoramic view of the snow-laden Alps off our right wingtip—first Switzerland, then Italy, and finally the Yugoslavian Alps.

After landing in Klagenfurt, Austria, we cleared Immigration and Customs with ease (even with rifles) and were met by our host, Werner Fleck, who had our bus waiting for a short transfer to a prearranged hotel. The Austrian hospitality was topped off by a welcoming banquet in the Hunt Room of the Hotel Musil. The cocktail party and Austrian-style banquet was also attended by three of the officials from the Yugoslavia Hunt Reserve where we were heading, as well as Hans Fanzoj of the famous Johann Fanzoj Firearms Manufacturers of

Ferlach. A two-piece typical band and a birthday cake for Helen Snider highlighted the banquet.

The next morning, we said goodbye to Helen, June and Colleene who were to tour Austria during our hunt in Yugoslavia. Then we boarded our bus and in 45 minutes stopped in Ferlach at the Fanzoj firearms factory. We Americans have almost forgotten what real handwork is like. Words cannot describe the tremendous amount of skilled labor put forth to make each piece a custom-made master-piece. A stop at the rifle range to assure us all of "one shot kills," and we were off to nearby Yugoslavia border. A winding mountain road took us to Loinle pass, 1,368 meters, and to the Yugoslavia Immigrations and Customs, neither of which any of us saw—we drank schnapps at a bar and exchanged money while Werner easily got our gun permits and cleared us through.

Another hour's drive brought us into the small Alpine town of Bled, beautifully situated on a lake and overlooking the Alps. We went directly to the game department office for briefing and coordination of the hunt. The game department staff are the actual guides who take the hunters out. At this point, the three hunters who elected to take Alpine ibex (*Capra ibex*) split off indi-vidually to go to three different areas adjacent to Mt. Triglov, 2,863 meters, and the highest point in Yugoslavia.

The other five hunters continued into the foothills passing through one ski resort and ending up staying in the Sport Hotel at another ski resort. The 1984 Winter Olym-pics was scheduled in Yugoslavia; so much expansion was taking place. Because it was the off-season both for skiers and summer vaca-tioners, we had the entire hotel to ourselves. After we dropped off our gear in our private rooms, our guides met us for the afternoon hunt. Everyone went out individually. The hunting was done by driving around, stalking and sitting in open meadows awaiting move-ment of game. In many places throughout the game reserve, well-made strategically located stands were constructed, some quite high in the trees. Game found in this forest area is the mouflon sheep (*Ovis gmelini musimon*) roe deer, red stag, and chamois in areas near the rocky outcrops. Joe Shaw was the lucky hunter to get a really fine mouflon ram the first evening.

Because of the change in weather, fogging in and snowing the first full day of hunting, ibex hunters Thornton Snider and Ray Bond had problems getting close enough to big ibex, which had changed areas on them. After a few days of really working the area hard they decided to come to the forest area to hunt. On the other hand, Jim Conklin had great luck, having collected a nice chamois on the way into his mountain hunting chalet the first evening, as well as getting a really nice ibex before the fog closed in the next morning.

In the week of hunting everyone got the game that they put in for, mainly sheep, except Thornton and Ray on the ibex, but most people got more game than they had expected. In the week of hunting there was plenty of action with 17 animals in all being taken. Joe Shaw, Jim Wilkinson, and I only hunted for

**Bob Chisholm congratulates Chris for collecting a medal-class mouflon ram in Yugoslavia.**

mouflon, Joe getting the first, and I was lucky to get the biggest, a 190 CIC points medal-class ram. Bob Chisholm got his mouflon, a roebuck and was the only one to collect a red stag. Ray Bond got his second desired trophy, the roebuck. The next-highest scoring animals, except mouflon, were Jim Conklin's chamois and ibex, both of which were just a couple of points under medal-class.

The accommodations and services were just great. The game department has various small lodges spotted around the entire country available for their use. Even the "Ibex Camp" had small lodges with private bedrooms, with bedding, good food and a cook. The guides were extremely knowledgeable of the area and knew where to look for the game. The people are extremely friendly and helpful in every way. We were the first Americans to hunt here, so I spent considerable time teaching the guides proper skinning for shoulder mounts and life-size mounts. Taxidermy, as we know it, is new to Europeans. Traditionally, they just saved the horns and skulls that were cleaned and bleached and put on a panel. These are referred to as European mounts.

The Director of Game, Ivan Fabgam, invited us all to a luncheon at a restaurant one day, and then he escorted us to his big, beautiful home where he had a trophy room displaying animals he has collected on several African safaris and an Alaskan hunt, as well as many outstanding European trophies. Ivan presented me with a beautiful bronze of a chamois.

Yugoslavia was a socialist country, but without the hard-core regimentation seen in

**The Director of Game for the Bled, Yugoslavia Area, Ivan Fabgam, gave me these photos that he took just a few days prior to our arrival: Alpine ibex, red stags and a family of chamois.**

the Soviet Union. (After the collapse of the Eastern Bloc countries, Yugoslavia became free and eventually split, and this area became Croatia.)

After returning to Klagenfurt, Shaw, Conklin, Bond, and the Wilkinsons returned home, while Thornton, John, Bob, and I flew to Vienna where we rendezvoused with the gals and flew on to Istanbul. At that point, Guy Rodrick from the Bay area joined us. Organized hunting in Turkey had only started the year before, and we were eager to be among the first to hunt there for the bezoar ibex (Capra aegagrus aegagrus).

Upon arrival in Istanbul, a representative of Pamfilya Travel, our Turkish host, expe-

dited us through Customs. We had several hours before our connecting flight to Antalya, so Yasar Sobutay, the Director of Pamfilya, drove us around showing us part of the old city of Constantinople and the famous Bosporus Channel, connecting the Mediterranean to the Black Sea. Before taking us to a very typical Turkish dinner. At Antalya, we were once again met and escorted to the beautiful resort hotel, Talya, right on the bluffs above the Mediterranean. After a few welcoming drinks of raki, the licorice-tasting national drink, we were glad that we had chosen to take the first day off and relax.

We spent time in the Bazaar, which is a number of small shops trading in the typical Turkish wares—carpets, copperware, gold, and silver jewelry, handicrafts and souvenirs of every sort and well-priced. The Turkish carpets of many different varieties are among the best in the world. The ancient city of Antalya is referred to as the Turkish Riviera

Thornton Snider poses with the author and his outstanding ibex specimen.

breakfast, as the restaurant did not open early enough. We were picked up between 4:30 and 5:00 AM every morning and within a half-hour we were at the game department headquarters, adjacent to the hunt area. There we met Suleyman Karakaya, the Director of Wildlife for the Thermesos area. (Special note: Suleyman is the father of the then young Kaan Karakaya, who eventually became the leading hunting operator in Turkey. He also outfitted hunts in many parts of Asia under the name Shikar Safaris.)

At this point, we were each joined by a personal guide and two packers and were distributed by car to our take-off places for the day's hunt. The hunt plan changes from day to day, depending on the pattern of hunting in prior days. The staff all works for the game department, and they know the

and the area is called Pamfilya, where our hunting area, the Taurus Mountains, rises abruptly nearby.

Our deluxe hotel was our hunting camp, so we had prearranged room service for

In the Taurus Mountains near Antalya, Turkey are the ruins of the ancient city of Thermesos. This amphitheater, carved from solid rock, is now the habitat of the bezoar ibex, Capra aegagrus.

**Bert Klineburger went two years later to help explore a new area in the northeast of Turkey in the high mountains that rise above the Black Sea. He collected this grizzly type bear.**

area and the game very well. They have excellent eyes for spotting, and they could often see game that we had a hard time spotting, especially when the animals were bedded down in the woods.

The ibexes are plentiful in the area and all of us saw them every time we went out. I believe we all saw really big billies, a few of us missing some outstanding trophies. They claim to have horns measuring in the 150-cm class, and I have no doubt that that is true. The ibex that I got was 111 cm, almost 44 inches, and it was very young. Everyone in the group got an ibex, with Guy Rodrick taking three. Hunters are welcome to take

more than one trophy. The game department depends on the large part of their income taking more than one.

The terrain is generally not very difficult, although some areas could be very tough. The average hiking time is generally less than a couple of hours, normally starting out before daylight, with the idea of being where the ibexes are once the light is good.

The guides like to stay out all day long, quite a bit of the time sitting and glassing or waiting in places where ibexes might move through. The packers carried all the lunch and drinks, along with rifles and anything else to make it easier on us. They don't speak English, but a small vocabulary was worked out both for guides and hunters.

The Director of Game, Karakaya, informed me that by 1984, they planned on having two other entirely different areas at their disposal to hunt. This way they can let areas rest from time to time. They also plan to have the guides start learning English in their idle time, during the off-season.

One part of the hunting area is the Thermesos National Park, which is the site of one of history's most impressive ancient cities, dating back a few hundred years before Christ—and it is taken over by ibex. We were told that Alexander The Great was unable to conquer this city because of its fortress-like location in the cliffs high in the rugged mountains. Alexander finally won by girdling, thus killing, their native olive trees, destroying their olive and olive oil business (and livelihood).

To the time of this writing, hunting and wildlife populations have increased due to proper game management, which is financed with hunting revenues.

# CHAPTER 8

# The Demise of Afghanistan and Kashmir

**F**arther east in the subcontinent of Asia things were changing in Iran, Afghanistan, and India in 1979. The fine and progressive kingdom in Iran had just been dethroned and the country was taken over by a hard-line Muslim dictatorship. Businesses were nationalized and the hunting industry and all its benefits to wildlife were gone. Afghanistan was on shaky footing with an unknown future as a result of a Russian invasion.

On the positive side, I was encouraged by a new relationship with willingness of the J&K States (Jammu, Kashmir, & Ladakh) of India to open their doors to hunting for exotic species of sheep and goats as well as forest and plains game. I was requested to produce a detailed wildlife manual for a sportsman-financed wildlife program, which would include a five-year hunting and conservation plan.

Our maiden hunt in Kashmir had already been agreed-upon, and our longtime friend and outfitter Avinash Kholi from New Delhi was to handle the arrangements. On the hunt would be a previous hunting companion Mahlon "Butch" White, his wife Patty, and my son Kent who had finished his education and was now working full time in our travel agency. Business talks were scheduled in Afghanistan before our arrival in India. The following is parts from my hunting journal, as written as Kent and I left London: (Circa 05 July 1979.)

*Airiana's Boeing 727 was close to on time. Many passengers, mostly Afghans or hippy-looking Westerners. Routine stops in Paris and Tehran. It was interesting to see the airport at Tehran. This is just after the nationalizing of all businesses in Iran, following the revolution that has been taking place over the past year.*

*Very few foreign aircraft at the airport—one KLM (Dutch) that was sealed up and one Air France that was being serviced. Iran Airline planes parked all over the place as well as military aircraft and transports. I talked to the Airiana Station Manager for Tehran, who boarded the aircraft and who I knew for a good many years. He felt that the situation would be fine in Afghanistan, but didn't know what to expect in Iran, as there were two parties fighting for power.*

*We finally touched down at Kabul Airport at 9 AM Saturday. As every time I've arrived in Kabul in the past several years, I was met again by the same representative of Airiana Airlines as I walked into the terminal. He informed us that Hassan Kaseem, President of Afghan Tourist organization, had come to the airport to greet us and was waiting in the lobby, We quickly obtained our visas at the airport at $7 each and continued into baggage claim where we found three of our bags were missing, including our rifle—7 mm Kleingunther.*

*We were expedited through customs, not checking our bags because of who we were and met Hassan. After going through the formalities of filling out the lost baggage forms and having a coke with Hassan in the restaurant, our driver took us all to the Intercontinental Hotel, where I received my usual welcome and handshakes from the many familiar people whom I had known in the past.*

*Hassan joined Kent and me to the room, where we found flowers, fruit basket, wine, chips, and nuts already set up in our room to welcome us. We talked business for a couple of hours, and then continued in the restaurant for lunch, where Kent and I had a chicken burger.*

*Khorami called and I asked him to stop by for a drink. Khorami is the manager of the hunting program so we had a good visit regarding hunting matters. We had dinner by the hotel pool, where they had an "Old West O.K. Corral Barbecue." They really did it up right—dressed the Afghan waiters in Western clothes, had a makeshift covered wagon along with other decor plus a barbecue of beef and other meats with all the trimmings. Had a sort of Afghan version of a disco band and were quite good. We were beat, so headed to bed early and had an enjoyable nights sleep.*

*08 July*

*To Hassan's office at the newly acquired premises for Afghan Tourist Organization. They converted one of the old hotels into the tourist offices, and it is a decided improvement over the old crowded ones from before. Hassan's office was decorated with trophy mounts from Africa and India. They probably were confiscated from* the home of (Prince) Sultan Mahmud Ghazi, who was fortunately out of the country during the Coup of April 1978. Most all the members of the royal family were done away with after the revolution.

I understand, although no one would admit it, that (Prince) Salahidan Ghazi was executed. Salahidan and Sultan (brothers) were both very good friends of ours. In expressing my sorrow for the killings that took place, I was informed that the new government must kill their enemies in order to carry on without interference.

After a short meeting with all the higher staff of Afghan-tour, Hassan, Kent and I were escorted to the offices of the Ministry of Transport (soon to become Ministry of Transport and Tourism) where we visited with Mr. Khoson, the Deputy Minister. We had very positive talks about Tourism in general and the current problems with the hunting program.

The big problem is that there are rebel forces that don't agree with this new government and they are trying to overthrow it. Because of that, there are some problems in the outlying hunting areas around Jalalabad and the Hindu Kush mountain range in general. We came up with the idea of trying to hire a military helicopter that could take the Marco Polo sheep hunters all the way to Qala Panja in the Wakhan Corridor, eliminating four days travel each way.

In the afternoon we had meetings with the President of Wildlife, Mr. Khoson, and Jeffrey Sayer, FAO Wildlife Officer. Present at all meetings except the Minister's meeting were Ali Hijab, Director of Touristic Services; G.R. Amiri, Vice-president of Afghan Tourist Organization; and usually S. Arif, presently General Director of

Accounting and Administration. The meetings went very positively and our General Agency relationship was solidified and it was clearly put across that hunting was vital to their game conservation as well as the financial benefits.

In the evening a special banquet was set up in our honor at the Bagh-e-Bala Palace. This palace, of the 19th Century vintage was that of King Abdur Rahman who died in 1901. The palace was preserved in its mountain setting, overlooking Kabul, and later (very recently) made into a restaurant for special occasions, operated by the Hotel Ministry. Most all from today's meeting were present, including the deputy minister. Upon return to our hotel room, a note informed us that our Airiana flight the next day was delayed from 9:00 to 12:30.

*09 July*

Another meeting with President Kassem to finalize a few matters, then he joined us to the airport. Our rifle case showed up, but not the two main suitcases. I had predicted a 1:30 departure (their always late, even on their late schedule) but I was wrong, it was 2 PM when we finally took off. At New Delhi customs and baggage claim, another hour was consumed. A young pretty sari-clad Indian girl that had been waiting 3½ hours for us in the hot humid arrival area met us. Her name is Meenkashi Kaushal of Amber Tours Pvt. Ltd., which is an agency that has widespread tours in India, besides being general agents for Pan Am Airlines, whose premises are shared with Avinash Kohli's Wildlife Adventure Tours, the company that we deal with and our hosts for our stay in India. We were taken to the beau-

*tiful home of Avi where we were to stay. Later Butch and Patty White of Pueblo, Colorado and long time friends and hunting partner (Butch) arrived from their hotel.*

*We had a lovely, well-prepared Indian dinner of about a half-dozen courses, after a couple rounds of cocktails and followed by tea in a restful sitting room. To bed for a good nights sleep even though we perspired in this tropical heat to the extent our beds were wet by morning. A cool shower didn't help much.*

*10 July*

*Up early, repacked to leave a few things behind. The coffee was served in the room. During the night Avi went to the airport to fetch Debbie and Jennifer Colussy, daughters of the Director of Pan American Airlines from New York. Butch and Patty joined us all for breakfast, after which we headed for the airport where Meenkashi expedited us and our 60 kilos excess baggage through the Indian Airlines check-in and sent us all on our way to Srinagar, Kashmir, our stepping-off place for our expedition into the Himalayas.*

*This is to be the second "first" for Butch and me. We, along with Bob Speegle of Garland, Texas, were the first hunters to go into the mountain regions of Nepal, back in 1974, for a blue sheep hunt, initiating the program there in the Himalayas. Now we are heading in another section of the Himalayas in the mythic Kashmir, Jammu and Ladakh provinces of northern India and border exotic areas like Hunza, Tibet, and Nepal, The areas straddle the Himalayas and contain high plateau country to the north and south of this greatest range of mountains.*

*We were met at the Srinagar Airport by Ghulam Rusool (Russell), who had a bouquet of flowers for all of us. He claimed our baggage while we waited in the small airport lobby sipping non, a cool soft drink. The climate here at 5,000 ft. elevation was much more comfortable than Delhi—I would guess 75-80°F and dry.*

*Three taxis took our gear and us to a roadside dock where we were transferred to comfortable gondola boats that took us through the exotic channels of Dal Lake to our houseboat that was to be our home for the next few days. In no way can words convey the beauty and uniqueness of the houseboats that are owned and operated by Russell and Haji Ramgon Guru.*

*They were large, roomy and exquisitely furnished with hand made and hand carved furnishings. Kent and I had our own totally self-contained boat, as did Butch & Patty. Debbie and Jennifer shared another houseboat with Avi.*

*A phone call instructed us to go to the office of Mir Inyatullah, the Director of Game Preservation. We had a wonderful discussion with him, and I presented him with a portfolio that I had worked up for him with regard to a proposed Game Management Program for his area of jurisdiction, which is all of Kashmir, Jammu and Ladakh, which I will refer to only as Kashmir in this journal.*

*It was soon apparent that we were on the same wavelength as we talked along. It was basically said that he would go along with my proposal of working only with the unit of Avi's Wildlife Adventure Tours and my Company for their hunting program, which, in simpler terms, is an exclusive for all hunting in Kashmir.*

*He said, however, that two things should be done: 1) have a shoot with him in a special preserve the day after tomorrow (tomorrow is a Moslem religious holiday-there are about 70 percent Moslems here, the rest being mostly Hindus), at which time we will get final authority as to what we can do (his reasoning was that, by having the meeting in the office there would be too many disturbances); and 2) that we communicate with his boss, Dr. Kamal Mustafa, Chairman of the Board for Wildlife and Recreation.*

*So, after a really fine Indian-style lunch (more like a heavy dinner), Butch, Avi, and I headed to Mustafa's mountain home toward Pakistan in a town called Tangmarg. His home was on the point of a hill that had a breathtaking view overlooking a valley with terraced farms, opposite of which were some higher peaks of the Himalayas.*

*He wasn't home, but we were told he was up at the resort of Gulmarg, where we went and found him busily giving instructions to workers at this beautiful alpine resort that had golf and trekking in the summer and skiing in the winter. He greeted us and invited us for coffee at the lodge of the resort. He also, like Inyatullah, welcomed our thinking and help on their wildlife program and granted us "carte blanche" on our desire to hunt. Butch requested the opportunity to hunt markhor (which is on the protected list) and he said O.K. He also agreed to come to our meeting on the 12th.*

*11 July*

*After a well-prepared breakfast on the boat, we all went shopping for footwear. Our two bags are still lost. Butch came to the rescue with*

*pants and shirt for me and Avi lent me a jacket, underwear, etc. From shopping, we went trout fishing to an area to the east of here in a valley nestled right in the Himalayas.*

*Srinagar is in a large open valley with high mountains all around. To the east and north is the Greater Himalayas Range. To the west and southwest is Pir Panjal Range right on the Pakistan border. Peaks of approximately 20,000 feet can be seen in both ranges from Srinagar.*

*We drove about 100 km, first southeast on the main road to Delhi, then cut into the mountains in an easterly direction through the town of Anantnag and a little northeasterly through Kukarnag and on to Kungun, then fished in a most beautiful small mountain river at about the 7,500 foot level.*

*Russell had caught a half-dozen fish right away, which were promptly fried and added to our picnic lunch. Then we all split in different directions and caught enough for dinner and then some. Back to the houseboat by 9 PM for a Kashmir dinner of Kabob, chicken curry and all the trimmings—after the trout course.*

*12 July*

*We went visiting Mr. S.S, Gergan the third person here who is on the game board and is influential in our efforts to begin a game program here. He is a delightful old Ladakh gentleman that probably knows more about game in Kashmir than anyone else. At one time he was the Chief Game Warden and wrote the only report on wildlife here back in 1962. He has been writing books and indicated he would like to do one with me on Hunting and Conservation. As with the others, our association turned into a "love affair" and he was invited to go hunting with Avi's outfit at any time.*

*Part of the afternoon was spent looking at carpets, made in Kashmir. Butch and Patty bought one 12x15, all wool, 400 knots to the square inch—fabulous these rugs—as good or better than the Persian, Afghan, Nepalese, etc.*

*Bashir, an individual who had been part of the scene around our houseboats, has 250 families manufacturing carpets, and he ships to some of the top department stores around the world including the U.S.A.*

*At 3 PM we were all packed for the hunt, but first our plan was to have business talks with the game directors at the Dachign Game Reserve in the foothills near Srinagar. Gergan, Nyatullak and Dr. Mustafa—the three "big guns" in the Wildlife Department were present. Our meeting was on the lawn of a rest house in a secluded canyon, which looked up into the lofty foothills of the Himalayas.*

*It was apparent that all three had gone over my presentation and had made their decision. It seemed that exactly what I suggested in my report paralleled their thinking entirely. They announced that they would adopt my plans to use Avi's Organization as the official appointed outfitter for the government, provide we were his sole representatives worldwide.*

*In other words, they placed their entire hunting program (nonresident) into our hands. We proceeded to go down the list of animal quotas to be allowed for next year—1980 season from March to November.*

*It was pointed out that I should have included some animals that they wish to be* hunted, *but that were not on my list. After all the formalities, they drove us around and showed us some game that were contained in enclosures—brown bear, Kashmir stag, musk deer, nilgai, and black bear. They then asked if we could join them for a drink.*

*I suggested that we return to the houseboat, where we enjoyed conversations about everything from Spacelab (it was scheduled to fall to earth about now) to religion to hunting. It was well after midnight before we broke up and drove 2½ hours to Lihinwan, a small village at the end of the same road we took fishing the day before.*

*The exploratory hunt was as much fact-finding trip as well as the possibility of collecting a few specimens of the area. The timing was proof, which we had already determined that mid-July was the wrong time to be hunting, but the period was set to coincide with the scheduled business talks with the wildlife officials. I had to leave the hunt partway through, as I had important business meetings scheduled with officials in Moscow, Russia.*

Kent, Butch, and Patty continued exploring the area after my departure.

The following is the report of the trip to the wildlife officials, made in parts by both Kent, and myself.

## HUNT REPORT WARWAN AREA-KASHMIR

This exploratory trip took place 12 to 29 July 1979. The general conditions during this period of time were not too conducive to hunting. The weather was very good except for a few rainstorms. The area was very

⌃ **The herdsmen were active in the mountains carrying supplies by their trusty yaks that were adaptable to the high elevations.**

populated with people, both with caravans taking supplies into the area, and herdsmen with their flocks of domestic animals. In other words, at this time of the year, the wildlife is pushed back to the highest elevations and the most remote areas that they inhabit.

We drove into Lihinwan where we rented horses and hired grooms, who also acted as local guides. Here we also met two Game Scouts that had been assigned to us by the game department–Abdul Ahad Wani and Mohammed Hashim Wani. We went eastward over Muragan Pass, approximately 12,500 feet elevation. The range of mountains that we passed over is locally called Muragan. This trail continued down to Inshan on the Warwan River (called locally Chinab River).

Part way down we encountered a local man with a shotgun. Upon questioning him, we found that he did not personally have a permit to carry it. In the same area, we met Dr. A.R. Sheikh, Veterinary Surgeon–Sheep Husbandry of Warwan. He was working with the local herdsmen as well as experimenting with some imported sheep herds from North America. Dr. Sheikh advised us that his herds had been bothered by both black and brown bear and that they had lost numerous sheep to the bear. He offered his assistance in helping us to locate the bear, which would in turn help the herdsmen if we could thin them down somewhat.

We used the Inshan Rest House as our base camp. From there we split into different parties to explore the area. Two Game Scouts, along with some locals, went to Marwah (Madwa) and either up the Rin Nai Valley or the small river valley to the north to the Apan area. Kent Klineburger went with a team of local scouts to the north about 7 km to Mingun Mulla (Mungil Nai). Chris Klineburger, along with Mr. and Mrs. Mahlon White, went another 7 km up the Warwan River and turned off at Manbalwas River (Kozuz Nai).

## *REPORT BY KENT KLINEBURGER*

**At the beautiful Murugan mountain pass in the Kashmir's Warwan area of the Himalayas, Butch and Patty White lie down to rest, while Kent Klineburger helps to redistribute the loads.** ⌄

Butch and Patty White with a mountain grizzly that Butch collected.

The Whites and I made the main hunting party and went back up to the Mingun Mulla Valley from where my scouting group had just returned. We continued to the high reaches of the valley where we spotted five ibex. The locals said they had seen two male ibex in the vicinity the day before and nine the week before. Scouts then saw nine more ibex and indicated some with good horns. When making a stalk on the herd we saw some local herdsmen making a game drive toward the ibex. Mr. White fired a warning shot, far above the heads of the local hunting party, and they turned and ran off. It was said by the locals that these local hunters were driving for musk deer, which they could sell for a sizable amount of money. This activity scared the ibex out of the area and therefore, we abandoned this valley and returned to the base camp at Inshan. By now, reports were back from the Game Scouts that were down in the Marwah area with reports of "plenty of game."

Our hunting party then went south 24 km, near the confluence of the Warwan River and the Rin Nai and stayed at a rest house at Madwa before going easterly up the Rin Nai Valley or Apan Valley, where we went southeasterly into the higher reaches of those valleys. The locals referred to the area as Apan, but it may have been up the Dund Nai or the Agannet Nai Valley.

We spotted ibex again in the high areas up near the glaciers. It appeared that the Whites would be able to collect specimens from this group, but the weather set in for two days. When the weather finally cleared

Avinash Kholi and Chris with a bearskin. The bear was quite well furred for July due to the cold conditions in the Himalayas.

and we approached the area where the ibex were, we found local herdsmen in the same spot and never saw the ibex again.

Time had run out for us by then, so we returned to Inshan and then on to Lihinwan.

Following the exploratory expedition, all data recorded by myself, Avinash Kohli, Mahlon White, and Kent Klineburger was received for the following report made to J & K officials.

## CONCLUSION

The Exploratory Expedition was a success in as much as the presence of wildlife has definitely been confirmed.

It is apparent, however, that:

1. Local herdsmen and hunters are putting maximum pressure on the animals and forcing them into the most inaccessible places.
2. Local hunters are killing whatever animals they possibly can, without proper authorization.
3. Protected areas must be set aside for the wildlife.

## THOUGHTS FOR IMPROVEMENT

The area is huge, and further scouting should be done at different times of the year. We feel that July is a poor time because of the heavy occupancy by people during that time. It would be desirable if a team of Game Scouts could be sent out in October of this year, equipped to travel fast and light, and be able to continue on in a circuit through the general area with constant spotting for all types of wildlife, reporting game counts and all conditions.

We suggest that at least two hunting parties go into the general area in 1980, one in May, and one in October. We also suggest that the clients be allowed to shoot any "reasonable" wildlife (one specimen of each animal per client) that might be encountered. It is apparent that there is no possibility of this type of approach hurting the game population in any way. The resulting presence of hunting parties and the benefits derived from such scouting parties would be of great benefit to the furtherance of the propagation of wildlife in the area.

We feel that definite rules should be set up to prevent the herdsmen from taking over the entire wildlife habitat. Perhaps one or a combination of the following suggestions might be adopted:

1. Domestic stock not be allowed above the 13,000-foot level in specified areas.
2. Domestic stock not be allowed beyond a certain point in the higher valleys such as 5 km from the ridge at the end of the valley.
3. Two or three valleys to be set aside in each small range of mountains exclusively for wildlife preserve.
4. Game Scouts be assigned to patrol the areas during the grazing season.
5. Deputize veterinary personnel and other government officials and/or employees in the area to help protect the wildlife.

Because of the almost total lack of wildlife protection policies in the past, we feel that with the execution of even minor protection practices the wildlife will come back in good numbers. The country, in general, is a beautiful wildlife habitat and should flourish with proper protection and proper utilization.

Respectfully submitted,
Chris Klineburger

*My Five-year Hunting and Conservation Plan, the Hunt Report Warwan Area-Kashmir, and my Conclusion and Thoughts for Improvement, along with a detailed report and request from the J & K Wildlife officials was submitted by the Kashmir officials to the India central government for final approval.*

*Who knows what went on in the minds of many uninformed and backward-thinking officials behind desks in New Delhi, but laws were immediately passed to outlaw any big game hunting in India, possibly as a result of pressures from Western countries. This is a perfect example of shortsighted leaders preventing sustainable use of wildlife and the resulting conservation of it. The J & K State officials were dismayed at their leaders' self-centered and bad decisions, which resulted in the suffering of wildlife throughout a great section of the Himalayan Range.*

*Now 30 years have passed with no concern for sustainable use of this valuable, renewable resource by the central government of India.*

# CHAPTER 9

# China—
# The Beginning Hunt

**P**aralleling my encouragement to the Soviets to expand the great potential for hunting in the U.S.S.R. (with little success), my attention turned to China. It would be far too detailed and even boring to tell of all contacts I made to open doors to serious negotiations for a wildlife program in China.

Since it was a socialist country like the Soviet Union, I felt the ones to deal with would be the national tourist agency China International Travel Service (CITS), which served the same purpose as Intourist in the U.S.S.R. and Juulchin in Mongolia. By the late '70s it became apparent that Chinese officials in general were quite "standoffish." They were polite and seemed to be good listeners, but did not put forth any real encouragement.

During these frustrating times, I learned that a good friend, H.I.H. Prince Abdorreza Pahlavi of Iran, hunted Littledale's argali sheep in China's Tien Shan Mountains in 1979. I learned this through Nouri Tajbakhsh, the taxidermist who accompanied the prince and whom we had trained in our Seattle studios. Another acquaintance, Robert Lee, who owned Hunting World, an outdoor equipment business, hunted Marco Polo sheep in the China Pamirs in 1980. Lee had been dealing in China for products for his own business. I learned that in both cases, the hunters made their own direct arrangements with the local authorities in Xinjiang Province, bypassing the central government altogether. Even though it was tempting to go to Urumchi, the capitol of China's northwest province, I felt it better to keep working with the central government in Beijing, knowing that they would eventually take charge.

I eventually learned that China's government was more complex than the communist countries to the north. I was directed to China Sports Service (CSS), which was the commercial wing of China Sports Federation (CSF). The International Olympic Committee was also under CSF. The authorities felt that perhaps the new subject of hunting would be handled by CSS.

Then we were referred to the next piece of the puzzle—the Ministry of Forestry, who had the overall authority over wildlife in China. I had made contact with Dr. Qing Jianhua, the General Director of the Forestry Department. Within Forestry there were two other departments that I made contact with. One was the Wildlife Administration Division (WAD) where I was referred to a director, Wang Wei. The other department was the Wildlife Conservation Association, who had a director also with the name Wang Wei. (Later I referred to the two as Big Wang Wei and Little Wang Wei. The WAD Wang Wei was a little bigger and older).

My financial capabilities at this point were becoming rather thin and I contemplated giving up on China. After all, I had just lost my two biggest Asian programs,

Iran in 1979 and Afghanistan in 1980, both falling to political takeovers. Two of my dear friends who were devoted to new frontiers encouraged me onward. They came to the rescue and donated funds to help finance the ongoing complex negotiations. These two were Thornton Snider and Robert Chisholm, both of hunting notoriety.

Once we got closer to cooperation by the various departments, but not knowing which would actually take charge, we sent a cover letter to CITS, CSS, and WAD with a copy of our proposal. (I was told early on to make short presentations to the Chinese, that long ones would be considered too complex and pigeonholed).

Since sheep and other mountain animals were of prime interest and since most officials didn't seem to know what species existed in China, I included a list of sheep, which would be the central focus on a wildlife program, since they were the most abundant in the many mountain ranges. (The below list was in accordance to the studies I had made.)

April 1983

### SHEEP SPECIES OF CHINA

*ARGALI SHEEP*

*Ovis ammon hodgsoni*–Tibetan argali
    Location: Southern Tibetan Plateau
*Ovis ammon littledalei*–Littledale's argali
    Location: East Tien Shan
*Ovis ammon ammon*–Altai argali
    Location: Northwest China in Altai
    Mountains along Mongolia border
*Ovis ammon jubata*—Gansu argali

Location: Gansu Province, Tibetan Plateau

*Ovis ammon camosa*—Mongolia argali
Location: Inner Mongolia in desert mountain ranges

*Ovis ammon poli*—Marco Polo sheep
Location: Pamir Mountains, West Xinjiang

*Ovis ammon karelini*—Karelin's argali
Location: Western Tien Shan, Kok Shaal Tau and Teke Tau

*Ovis ammon sariensis*—Sar Mountain argali
Location—Sar Mountains, N.E. Xinjiang

### URIAL SHEEP

*Ovis vignei vignei*—Shapoo urial
Location: South and western Tibetan Plateau

### PSEUDO SHEEP

*Pseudos nayar*—Blue sheep or bharal
Location: Tibetan Plateau from the Himalayas to the Qillian Shan

The above is a general guideline of sheep species that should be readily available for sport hunting programs. Areas listed are general. Other subspecies may be available or other scientific names may be used.

The great nation of the Peoples Republic of China stands almost entirely alone of not having a hunting conservation program. The importance of such a program is emphasized in the pages to follow. It is our desire to be able to assist in the establishment of such a program.

Sportsman-financed wildlife programs have set entire wildlife programs and conservation standards. Enough income can be derived from foreign hunters to eventually pay the cost of conservation for all wildlife in the areas hunted. It should further be pointed out that the presence of a hunting program results in an increase of the wildlife. This is a result of the education passed on to the local people, making them aware of the great value of the animals as trophies instead of meat.

China contains various wildlife species that are attractive to foreign travelers. Among them, as well as the most important, are the various wild sheep species. Among these great hunting areas are the Tien Shan, Pamirs, Kunlun Shan, Himalayas, and some of the nearby sub-ranges of Min Sha, Tsinling Shan and the Heng Shan only to mention a few.

In the Tien Shan Mountains, in the Xinjiang Province, near Urmuchi, there are the Littledale's argali sheep, Karelini's argali sheep and Siberian ibex, as well as many other species of game. Incidentally, Prince Abdor-reza Pahlavi of Iran hunted there in the fall of 1979.

In southern Gansu and Shensi Provinces, in the Min Shan and Tsinling Shan, there are bharal sheep, Takin (Budorcas Bedfordi), Serow (Nemorhaedus Argyrochoetes) as well as roe deer, wapiti, bear, and gazelle. In the Great Tibetan Plateau are argali sheep species, shapoo urial and bharal, as well as gazelles, antelope, ibex, snow leopard, and other wildlife. In the high Pamirs are the coveted Marco Polo Sheep, ibex, and bear.

In the forested areas of Jilin and Heilongjiang Provinces, the Tien Shan, Pamirs, and Tibetan Plateau are found various species of deer, as well as bear and boar.

It has been said by the Chinese, "We shall tolerate not a single inch of unused land." Hunting is a valuable land usage. As an example, each wild sheep hunt, along with other available game in the same area, would bring thousands of dollars as income to China. I recommend trying two exploratory hunting expeditions, one in the Tien Shan Range and one in the Tibetan Plateau:

## TIEN SHAN AREA. EXPLORATORY HUNTING EXPEDITION

### Animals Available:

Littledale's argali sheep * *(Ovis ammon littledalei)*

Karelin's argali sheep * *(Ovis ammon karelini)*

Ibex *(Capra siberica merzbacheri or almasyi)*

Tien Shan stag *(Cervus canadensis songaricus)*

Roe deer *(Capreolus pygargus tienshanicus)*

Gazelle *(Gazella subgutturosa yarklandensis)*

*Itinerary:* Flight arrival should be in either Urumoi or Aksu, depending on the known concentrations of argali sheep by the authorities. From either place it appears that there is an adequate road system to penetrate reasonably near the concentrations of sheep, so that horseback travel can be kept to a minimum.

The only recent known hunting expedition into the Tien Shan was in 1979 by H.I.H. Abdorreza Pahlavi of Iran. His expedition followed the same paths that a couple of expeditions followed back in the mid-1920s. Their goal was Kargai Tash Mountain (Oaragai Tash; Trees of Stone). Their routing was from Aksu northward across the Muzart Glacier into the Tekes Valley, eastward, and then southward to Kargai Tash. This was all done by horseback. Now it is felt that there is a road into Xinyuan (Kunes) just north of Kargai Tash.

These sheep are thought to be the Karelin's Argali, which are generally felt to be in the Borohoro Shan and possibly in the Bogda Shan and westward along the Kok Shal Tau and along the eastern borders of Kirgizistan and Kazakhstan.

Many Ibex are found nearby all of the sheep areas and made available. Stag, roe deer, and gazelle in the adjacent forests and plains would be of interest, if time allows.

The length of this portion of the expedition would be three weeks and possibly less, depending on the accessibility and concentration of argali sheep.

## TIBETAN PLATEAU AREA. EXPLORATORY HUNTING EXPEDITION.

### Animals Available:

Gansu argali sheep *(Ovis ammon jubata)*
Bharal sheep (Psuedos nayar)

Tibetan gazelle

*Itinerary:* It was mentioned that Golmud would be the starting point for this portion of the expedition; however, it would be more desirable to enter the plateau from the north at Dunhuang. It is felt that the Gansu argali might range from the Kunlun Shan all the way north to the Qillian Shan. If bharal were found in the same vicinity of the argali, then that species would be of interest. Tibetan antelope, wild yak and gazelle would also be desirable while on this portion of the trip.

The length of this portion of the expedition would be three weeks and possibly less, depending on the accessibility and concentration of argali sheep.

Respectfully,
Chris Klineburger

## THE BEGINNING HUNT

Outside help also came from other sources besides Snider and Chisholm. A good Chinese-American friend, Lit Ng from central California, had also been traveling to China and even encouraging the opening of this great resource. Then finally the People To People Sports Committee came into the picture. Dr. Leonard Milton, president of People To People and also a hunter himself, along with my brother Bert who was a Director of People To People, both had been working with the China Sports Federation through the International Olympic Committee on various exchange programs. Without going into the lengthy details, finally, the first ever-organized big game hunting in China's long

A photo taken in Harbin, Heilongjiang Province at the People-To-People presentation of sports equipment. From left, Ernestine Studer, Bob Leonard, Modesta Williams, Stan Studer, Bert Klineburger, Lit Ng, Thornton Snider, Leonard Milton, Guy Rodrick, CSS official, Bob Chisholm, and kneeling with a China Sports Service official is Clayton Williams.

‹» **This beautiful log lodge was finished just in time for our arrival. It had all the comforts of a fine hotel, yet they apologized for not having the landscaping done.**

history was established in the fall of 1984 in Heilongjiang Province (Manchuria).

The historic hunt was dovetailed with a People To People exchange in the capital city of Harbin attended by officials from the Sports Federation and Forestry Department, along with the American hunting party that represented People To People. The hunting party brought mountains of field and track sports equipment to donate to the poverty-stricken athletes in the area. Our group consisted of myself, Bert and Brigitte Klineburger, Dr. Leonard, and Hilda Milton, Thornton and Helen Snider, Clayton and Modesta Williams, Stan and Ernestine Studer, Bob Chisholm, Guy Rodrick, Bob Leonard, Lit Ng, and his daughter and son-in-law.

We had been informed earlier in the year that the hunting programs would be handled by the Wildlife Administration Division (WAD) and that a hunting lodge would be built in the forest area in Manchuria where

we were to hunt. After the People-To-People ceremonies, banquets, and sight-seeing in Harbin, our hosts boarded us on a rather antique steam engine-driven train that took us well north of Harbin into rolling, forested hills, called the Taoshan area, where we were greeted by our hosts and taken by van to a newly built log lodge, apparently just finished. However, the outside landscaping was yet to be done. It was very well laid out with large sitting area with fireplace, a dining area, numerous private sleeping rooms, and sufficient bathrooms. It was obvious that WAD was very serious about the program and desired to do their best.

The animals available in the area were elk-like wapiti *(Cervus elaphus xanthopygus),* Siberian roe deer *(Capriolus pygargus bedfordi),* wild boar *(Sus scrofa),* and brown bear (Ursus arctos), along with native Chinese ring-necked pheasants. Local guides would

**One of the vans used to take us to the hunt areas.** ‹»

⌃ **Dr. Leonard Milton and his guide pose with Len's elk.**

⌃ **Lit Ng and his guide pose with a big wild boar.**

escort each hunter or pair of hunters out by Chinese-built jeeps and vans along logging roads to a point where they continued on foot. It was apparent right away that the guides were not experienced in any aspect of trophy hunting, so it was a case of us trying to teach the hosts proper stalking techniques. Field care of specimens was another obstacle, as guides would be quick to slash throats and often chop the heads off before the client could get his camera into motion.

The Chinese are the best hosts one can find anywhere around the world. As a matter of fact, their whole routine was built around entertaining us, with fabulous cuisine three times a day and nightly cocktail hours. Unknowing that we were there to hunt as hard and long as possible and to

**Chris's guide took him to his home in a nearby village to meet his family and his hunting dog.** ⌄

**Brothers Bert and Chris walk the Great Wall once back in Beijing.** ⌄

⚲ **Clayton and Modesta Williams along with their guide, give thumbs up to Claytie's fine stag.**

collect trophy-size animals, they were little prepared for the chase. At any rate, the time was enjoyed by all and wouldn't have traded the experience for anything. Some good specimens were collected by everyone of most game, except bear.

Bert and I had private meetings with the management on hunting methods, and with each trophy taken, we would give skinning lessons. We left them with skinning kits and diagrams for processing shoulder mounts and life-size mounts. I promised to follow-up in writing about our discussion and recommendations for the future. I told them I would return next year and meet with all concerned and go over expansion of outdoor sports programs for Heilongjiang. Then we had a meeting with all the staff and the guests, letting all speak up.

**The following is the written report of my recommendations, which is not unlike many guidelines I used in my Sportsmen Financed Wildlife Program used throughout Asia.**

*To: Officials of Wildlife Management and Tourism, Heilongjian Province*

*This is a summary of the seminar held after the first experimental hunt in Taoshan area, chaired by Mr. Lu Shou An on 16 October, 1984.*

*It was emphasized at the beginning of the meeting, which was attended by all of the staff and guests, that the suggestions by the guests would be focused on ideas for improvement for the future. Therefore, the lack of praise was intentional. In general, the service and accommodations were excellent. It was felt that the staff did their very best under the conditions.*

## GUIDES AND GUIDING

*The hunting guide is the key to success. Success is the single most important factor for a client to travel halfway around the world to hunt in China. There is little hope for the future of the program unless each client has a good chance of getting a trophy-size animal of each species available or that he desires.*

*The guide must always be with the client, not 10 or 20 meters out in front of him. The client's rifle must also be close by, in the event that it is being carried by one of the staff. The hunting pace must be that of the client, not of the guide. Moving too fast usually results in the game seeing the hunters before the hunters see the game. If the client is breathing hard, his shooting* ability is restricted in case he has to take a quick shot. The pace should be slow enough so that the guide uses all of his ability to determine if there is any game ahead. Hunting is done with the eyes, not with the feet. The hunting party must not top out over a ridge until carefully scanning the other side.

The guide should always remain calm and not get over-excited when seeing game, and should pass his calmness on to the client.

A guide should know a few basic words of English, as well as some hand signals, to be able to communicate with the client to show him which animal to shoot or what the next move is.

The guide must know the proper field care of trophies. He must know how to properly skin an animal for a head mount or a full-size mount. He must communicate in advance with the client before making any cuts or dragging an animal down the hill. He must know the proper method of salting to completely salt-cure the skins and method of drying the skins in the field. (In the case of Bob Chisholm's red stag, which was supposed to be saved for a full-shoulder head mount, the skin was completely destroyed by improper skinning and was useless for mounting purposes).

The guide must know the hunting area, as well as the habits of the game. He must also learn as much about the client as possible in order to choose the area to hunt, that best suits the capabilities and desires of the client. Each night the guides should all get together and work out the game plan for the next day's hunt. The guide should always keep the client briefed on what is going to happen. Most importantly,

since the client is seeking the largest specimen possible, the guide must be able to judge trophy quality.

## HUNT AREAS AND CONDITIONS

In the 1984 hunt, it appears that only the fringe of the wildlife area has been hunted, those areas easy to drive into. It appears that the hunting will mainly be done from mid-September through November, in order to utilize the hunting season at its best. Since this is during the change of weather conditions, it is probably also during the change of habitat of at least some of the wildlife. A continuous study should be made to know where to find the best concentrations of game. New areas should be constantly looked into.

It has been decided to try to limit the hunting parties to six clients at one time, in order to have the best possibility of results. It is recommended that an advance party of wild-life personnel go ahead of the hunting parties, during the 1985 season, to investigate the game situation in other areas and report back to the hunting parties. Until full knowledge is known of the game habits and the available hunting area, extra efforts will be needed, especially in the 1985 season.

In the areas that are known to be hunted, it is important to spend some time in advance of the season to cut trails. In most cases, it is merely a case of walking through the popular hunting paths with a machete, cutting down the bushes that cause noise against the clothing and slow the hunters down.

It was recommended to utilize horses wher-ever possible, allowing the hunters to be able to cover four to five tines as much area as by foot. In general, wildlife has much less fear of horses than they do people.

It was suggested to use fly camps if necessary (fly camps could either be a cabin or a shelter in remote areas, or tent camps that could be taken along to set up where desired). These would increase the range for hunting tremendously to penetrate deeply into undisturbed new areas.

If hunting is being done where forest work is being done, the hunting must be done prior to the arrival of the workers in the morning, while no hunting will be done in the evening in these same areas.

From observations on the experimental hunt, the wildlife appeared to have considerable fear of man, possibly indicating that there has been hunting of these animals by local people. If this is so, that is more reason why deeper penetration into the wildlife areas will be important. (While firearms were being carried by the guides, they were very quick to want to shoot at any game that moved, male or female, which may have been an indication that they had been shooting at the animals right along. That, of course, was completely unacceptable conduct of a hunting guide).

## HUNTING METHODS

Stalking is the most practical and acceptable method of hunting. Success is directly related to seeing the game before it sees the stalker. Moving slowly, constantly glassing and looking is important for success.

Waiting on a stand in a pass or by a game trail can be very effective. This can be effective by having one or more "beaters" surrounding an area, causing the game to pass near the hunter.

Tracking can be most effective and should be utilized whenever possible, especially after any snowfall.

During the experimental hunt, the pattern of hunting generally was to go out and back the first hours of the morning, and then again in the late afternoon. The negative effects of that type of hunting can be considerable. It can be more tiring to have to climb twice in one day. The wind generally goes up the valleys and hills in the afternoon, the same direction as the hunters must go, which puts the wind behind the hunters and to the animals. By being up in the mountains already in the afternoon, the hunting party can be above the animals already awaiting them to come out in the open. Enough supplies can be taken into the mountains for the party to eat and take a nap at midday, being fresh for the afternoon hunting. By using this method of hunting during the day, more penetration can be made into the mountains in a single day.

## SAFETY

Hunting can be considered a dangerous sport for two reasons. The environment itself could be the cause of an accident by a person having a fall, getting drug by a runaway horse or attacked by a dangerous animal. The other danger is the misuse of firearms. Safety rules must be established wherever they might apply.

This hunting outfit is a professional organization and should apply safety measures to prevent as many accidents as possible. We have seen a case in the 1984 season, where one of the staff was hit by a shotgun shot. Had the *guide applied a simple safety rule, that accident would have been prevented. The guide should have known that one of the staff was in the bush and prevented the client from taking a shot.*

*The guides and other staff members, on a hunt, should take every measure to prevent the possibility of an accident.*

*In summary the guides and staff must do everything necessary to become fully educated in order to have maximum hunting success for the client on a safe and happy adventure.*

*Respectfully submitted,*
*Chris Klineburger*

## REFLECTION
# Klineburger's School of Taxidermy

Our mission to establish hunting and wildlife conservation in undeveloped areas around the world required much in the way of education. The operators didn't really know what they were getting into, as they knew little about trophy hunting, guiding techniques, and field care of specimens. We supplied equipment and training for most aspects of outfitting.

**Bert Klineburger showing the Manchurian staff the proper method for caping a Siberian roe deer, taken by Bob Leonard.**

The author giving skinning instructions for a life-size mount from a bharal specimen collected in Quinghai Province on the Tibetan Plateau.

Bert and Chris showing the Tadjik guides the final steps in the field preparation of a Marco Polo sheep full skin for a life-size mount.

**The Russian guides took great interest in learning trophy care, as instructed by Chris on the historic first hunt on the Kamchatka Peninsula.**

Proper handling of skins and horns was of paramount importance once the animal was taken—after all, that's what the hunter went for. Even though the local guides usually had some hunting skills as extraordinary poachers, being herdsmen in the wildlife habitat, they knew nothing about skinning for trophies. Here are a few pictures of skinning seminars in various parts of Asia.

I had quite a compliment from Dr. Jim Conklin, a world-renowned sportsman and head of the selection committee for the Safari Club International Hunting Hall of Fame. While hunting in remote areas of Asia he was amazed to find skilled skinners. In asking, "Where did you learn skinning?" they responded, "Chris Klineburger taught me." "Where did you get such fine skinning knives?" "Chris Klineburger gave them to me." We packaged in suitable field containers, knives of different descriptions from Schrade "Sharp Finger" to Wyoming knives, as well a skinning charts and salting procedures.

# CHAPTER 10

# Over the Hump

After our groundbreaking hunt in the fall of 1984 in Manchuria, my years of negotiations with the various bureaucracies seemed to be falling into place, resulting in an important business trip in May 1985. Colleene joined me for business talks and new explorations in Beijing as well as in the provinces of Shandong and Heilongjiang. Here are a few excerpts from our travel journal (our meetings in Beijing were badly messed up by a flight misconnect en route):

## CHINA 1985

*08 May, Beijing (after arriving two days late due to airline problems).*

*After a long process of trying to locate the hotel restaurant, that was in an unmarked other wing of the hotel on a second floor, we missed their 8:30 closure. Almost all locals staying at the hotel and very little English spoken. We bought some packaged orange juice and some little packages of snacks. Colleene's first bite caused her to inspect the little wafers more, only to find they contained shrimp—she is violently allergic to shellfish! She was able to spit out most of it, so no problem. I called every connection I had to try and establish lost meetings and make connections with our guide that no doubt gave up on us upon our no-show.*

*I made contact with a Miss Deng Ton (I probably have the spelling wrong as the phones are very static, Chinese speak too fast, pronounce words funny and pronounce letters differently from us) at ph.754250, China*

Sports Services, my main connection here and business associate for hunting, who informed me that Mr. Qin, of Wildlife Administration Department was out of town, as well as her boss Madam Zhong Tao, and Kong Quigwen another good friend in CSS, But she did say our meetings were set for our return next time to Beijing a week later.

I then got hold of Mr. Tu Mingde and Mr. He Zhenliang, members of International Olympic Committee, for whom we brought a black buck head mount and a Barbary sheep panel mount. They had already made a dinner appointment for us for tonight but had canceled because of our no-show. However, it was rescheduled for tomorrow in the Ye Chen Sportsmen's Restaurant near the Eastern Gate of Tien Dan Park. When I told them that we a) had to check out of the hotel by 5 PM (and had no place to go after that as no hotel space available), b) we had a ton of baggage including their two heads and c) a train to catch at 1:10 AM after midnight. They said they would bring a minibus at 5 PM to pick us up and see to it we got on our train. That was half the battle, now if we could only find our guide who has our tickets!

I made contact with Mr. Zhang Yaomin, Deputy Director of the North American Division of China International Travel Service, whom I had broken an engagement with yesterday because of our no-show. He set an appointment for 1:30 with taxi instructions. By now it was 11:30 and lunch opened in the restaurant. We ordered four main meat dishes, figuring them to be the normal small portions, plus soup and rice, Huge plates came and we chopsticked our way through about half of it and ordered our

check before the soup came—oh yes, we had two very large beers.

We had an English-speaking person give instructions to our taxi driver to get us to the CITS main office. He missed it by almost a mile, causing us to walk through the 80°+ weather to meet Mr. Zhang at the door a half-hour late, in this land of usual punctual meetings.

We presented our Klineburger "Image Book" and some other brochures that we had on China programs already in process. Our purpose here was to get a direct relationship with the Head office of CITS. We already have a working arrangement with the CITS Branches in both Shandong and Heilongjiang Provinces. But if we have tourists going on any other arrangements in China, that are not largely in one of the other provinces, we have to work through another travel operator. As a result of our meeting, it is now established that our agency can now handle any individual arrangements in China—a great accomplishment.

Upon return to the hotel we received a call from our guide's aunt, Miss Kong Lingyu. Shortly afterwards, Miss Kog Wei, our guide called and informed she had our tickets and would be accompanying us to Shandong and will be our guide there. We arranged for her to come to the restaurant about 8:30, where she would join us.

Mr. Tu picked us up at 5 PM sharp. We had uncrated and assembled the Barbary horn panel mount, which was big and complicated. Mr. Tu petted the trophies all the way to the restaurant, telling us of his and Mr. He's hunt in Texas on the Valdina ranch guided by my

Mr. Tu Mingde of the International Olympic Committee, under the China Sports Federation, picked us up at the Da Du Hotel in Beijing along with our luggage and the blackbuck and barbary sheep heads.

brother Bert last summer. At the restaurant, he took the trophies in to show everyone and keep in the private dining room we had for our small group.

*Awaiting us (being late because of peak hour traffic—thousands of bicycles, trucks, animal carts—what a mess) were Mr. He and Mr. Yuan, two of the very top people in China Sports Services. CSS is the commercial wing of China Sports Federation. CSS is supposed to handle all hunting and fishing arrangements in China. CSF does all the competitive sports— track and field, Olympics, etc. Mr. Tu and Mr. He are two of the very top people in the China Sports organization.*

*We had a fabulous meal of well over a dozen different courses. One never knows when the end is nearing, so we over-ate as we proceeded, only* to find more and more coming. Beverages—you bet, started with beer, which was cool and refreshing, the two kinds of wine, red and white, both sweet. That not being enough, a rice wine (also sweeter than sake of Japan) came on, it being served warm. The toasts were numerous and frequent, switching from one drink to the other. We all finally reached our capacity of food and drink.

*In the meantime Miss Kong showed up and Mr. Tu worked out a deal to turn over his minibus and driver to Wei, with promises of more getting together later on in our trip, especially an early visit with Mr. Yuan to get our main business talks rolling, Wei, our pretty little 23-year-old guide had us driven around. We visited the Tiananmen Square, Beijing Hotel (the biggest here) and the Great Wall Hotel (the most modern and expensive), as well as the Jinlin (Beijing Toronto) and the Jian Gau next door with the Mod restaurants. By then it was time to check into the train station, fighting our way to our sleeper car—had to carry our own gear including our 100-pound giant suitcase. WOW! It was good to get on four bunks— Colleene and I took the two bottom and Wei a top one. Pretty soon a knock on the door ended up putting a military officer in the other top bunk!*

*Colleene and I had decided to have our official Silver Wedding Anniversary today, as it was really still 07 May back in Seattle on the other side of the dateline. Everyone wished us well and many toasts at our welcoming banquet. It sort of turned that into an anniversary celebration. Since we were married in a strange place like Nome, Alaska, it was really*

**Chris and Colleene Klineburger dining at the Sportsman's Restaurant with He Zhenliang (with glasses), Mr. Yuan and Tu Mingde (who is taking photo). Mssrs He and Tu are Directors of the International Olympic Committee, while Yuan is head of China Sports Services. Note blackbuck head behind Chris and barbary sheep in back.**

*great to share #25 with such wonderful people here in China.*

Our trip to the coastal city of Qingdao (formerly Tsingtao) was for the purpose of establishing a fishing program in the Yellow Sea. I was anxious to see this area after having been here on my navy ship in 1946 overseeing the evacuation of the Chinese Nationalists from their last stronghold following the communist takeover. Our trip here was to coincide with an international fishing tournament hosted by the local Fishing Association and handled by CSS. Colleene and I, along with a couple of Japanese, were the only "internationals" attending. The deep-sea tournament came to an abrupt end because of an unseasonable gale. The fish available in the Yellow Sea are flounder, perch, mackerel, brim and yellow croaker. Our trip here included a banquet attended by all the top brass from the local CSS and CITS and

the General Director of Foreign affairs for Qingdao. We did do some surfcasting from the rocky outcrops north of town. I bought a few of the local made fishing reels, said to be unchanged from what they claim to be the first ever fishing reel invented in China centuries earlier.

Once back in Beijing we connected directly to a flight to Xian, which has a history dating back 8,000 years and the capital of China through 11 dynasties. More importantly, only 10 years ago some peasants were digging a well and discovered an underground vault containing life-size figures of terracotta warriors. Excavation to date has uncovered thousands of soldiers with different faces. It is believed that China's first emperor, Qin Shi Huangdi had the army placed in battle formation all around his tomb to protect him. Qin's Dynasty was 221 B.C. to 206 B.C. and the first to unify China under one leader. We felt

**Pagoda Pier in Qingdao brought back great memories of when Chris's Navy ship anchored there 30 years earlier during the Nationalists' exodus.**

it a must to witness this historical site in destinations for our clients. The other local attractions included the Hua Qing Hot springs, Wild Goose Pagoda, an evening performance, Tang Dynasty music and Dances, and the 600-year-old City Wall.

Upon returning to Beijing, a meeting had been arranged for us to meet with the manager in charge of hunting for China Sports Service, Madam Zhong Tao. Kong "Kevin" Quigwen and Chu Siming, both of whom I had met before and who were our guests in Seattle last year, also attended the meeting. The meeting went well and our relationship was firmly established with CSS for whatever role they may have with regard to hunting and fishing. Madam Tao informed us of a banquet schedule for us upon our return from our onward trip to Heilongjiang.

The next day we flew to Harbin where we expected to spend several days reviewing the hunting program for the forthcoming season. We were met by Zhao Xinlue, a friend from the hunt last fall, who informed us we were scheduled to catch a train at 12:30 to Inner Mongolia. They wanted to show us a duck hunting area they felt would be of interest to foreign hunters. We were delighted about the plan, but had to quickly shop for some jackets, as we had not planned to be sitting in duck blinds with the wardrobe we brought. We found two down jackets with detachable hoods, $23.00 each. Zhao took us to the CITS office to join the manager, Mr. Lou Binsheng, with whom I was acquainted with from the fall hunt. They took us to a luncheon, where we met Mr. Pan Weili, the Deputy Director of the Wildlife Conservation Department of the Provincial Forestry Bureau. Both Misters Pan & Zhao were to accompany us on the trip. They had special visas issued us, as we were told we are going to an area that had not been visited by foreigners in modern times.

While on the clean and comfortable, day-car train, Mr. Pan explained the situation

**Chris and Colleene were honored with a banquet attended by all the top officials of China Sport Services, China International Travel Service, and the General Director of Foreign Affairs for Qingdao, China.**

&#9775; **Miss Kong Wei, our guide/interpretor who accompanied us to Qingdao from Beijing, shows off what is said to be the oldest known fishing reel, unchanged from centuries ago in China. Note her Klineburger Worldwide Travel jacket and hat, the type of gifts we spread around the world.**

that was interpreted by Zhao. We were going to an autonomous (self governed) Mongolia County of Derbete. The area was known as Lianhuan Hy, which translates to "Chain Lakes." There is a lot of marshland, but mainly 17 lakes all linked together covering 830,000 hectars. The industry in the lakes is fish farming and the waters contain 40

different fish. Various carps are the main fish that grow up to 20 kilograms. He mentioned crucian carp, common carp, silver carp & grass carp, plus blackfish and a sort of catfish. Because of all the waters the area is blessed with, it is a major flyway and nesting grounds for both ducks and geese from both the Siberian Arctic and Alaska.

The train ride was a nonstop four hours through fairly flat farming and grazing land before we disembarked in Tai Kang. We were met by a mini bus and taken to an inn, where they had a nice suite arranged for us. Everything fine except the plumbing, none of which worked and certainly not an uncommon occurrence in Asia. However, they did bring in vessels of hot water for our bath and had the ever-present thermoses of hot water and an assortment of tea.

Mr. Bai, the director of Foreign Affairs for Durbete, met us at dinner. He brought two Chinese made over and under 12-gauge shotguns for us to use along with a supply of shells. The loads happened to be for clay pigeons and we were told no magnum shells were available here, as no hunting for waterfowl has been allowed. He assured us that he would have proper loads for any hunters that we may send. We quizzed Mr. Bai as to why they had a Foreign Affairs Agency since no foreigners had been there. He explained that they were a self-governed region, and that certain protocol was necessary even for dealing with the Chinese nationals, as well as planning to have foreign countries send visitors there. After many "gombays" and a dinner of "thousand year-old eggs," sea

The author was provided a Chinese-made over-and-under 12-gauge with trap loads to hunt waterfowl in the Chain Lakes area of Inner Mongolia.

world, we should offer a combined shooting and fishing program.

The weather became overcast just this morning and now the wind was starting up. We were late for the best shooting time and the ducks we saw were heading for the protection of the reed areas pretty much out of reach. We stalked some black or white ducks (that's what they called them and didn't seem to be up on scientific names). These were very large, about the size of the smaller geese, like snows and emperors in North America.

We shot a bunch of times at ranges where I normally prefer my three-inch Magnum, and I just "dusted" them to the point that they didn't even seem shook up, and only flew a short ways, landing again for another stock & the same performance all over again. Later I patterned my gun on an old adobe wall to see what it was doing. At 25 yards, the pattern was over

Chris and Colleene holding fish caught in Inner Mongolia in an area known as Lianhuan Hy, 17 lakes covering 830,000 hectares.

cucumbers, and beef tendons, the plan was made for the early morning hunt.

Here are notes from Chris's journal—

*18 May, Durbete, Inner Mongolia*

*After a typical Chinese breakfast, including the "thousand year old eggs" we were off in Chinese-made jeeps for a 21-kilometer drive to the wetlands. As we approached the lakes we saw many net-traps spotted around. These are usually a length of net posted in the ground to guide fish toward an enclosure that somehow they get into and stay till collected. We had indicated to Mr. Bai our desire to catch some of these fish, which he agreed to. Our thoughts were, that if people were to travel halfway around the*

Chris signing the official contract for hunting and fishing in Heilongjiang Province and Inner Mongolia with the Directors of China Sports Services and the Wildlife Administration Division.

two-feet in diameter and high and to the left. There were thousands of a few different types of "snipes" that we shot several of that this light shot could handle. Anyway, during the beginning of nesting, we really didn't want to upset the situation here.

In the meantime, the wind got very strong and there were some vicious whitecaps on the lakes. The plan was to use boats, which was promptly abandoned. We fished in some smaller ponds from the shore with very good luck. Midday we had to find shelter in an old adobe

At a celebration banquet in Harbin, Mssrs Lou, Zhao, Pan and Jin, along with others, gave me a photo taken when they presented me with a banner months earlier when they were our guests in Seattle. The banner effectively stated their appreciation for all I had done for them.

« While in Beijing Chris and Colleene took in many activities, including visiting the Forbidden City and fishing on the lake at the Summer Palace.

building that was being set up for an office for the fish farming, for our "picnics" that everyone was prepared for. Wang Qian was our guide—he was the ex-director of the fish farming operation and a lover of duck hunting.

Rain started, which was good, as a sand storm was underway and made any further looking around impossible. We returned to Tai Kang in heavy rain and settled in after a hot bath and a couple shots of Mao Tai, followed by an excellent dinner. After dinner they asked us how we liked certain well-prepared meat. After our positive answer, they said it was dog. In China, dogs were not pets. There were a few hunting dogs, but most dogs were raised for meat.

Then we discussed the recommendations on the proposed hunting and fishing program, which we told of the requirements to satisfy sportsmen to come this far to enjoy. They asked if we could return in the fall and spend a lot more time to really get into the actual situation, as it would be. We said that we would try, but, at any rate, work with them on developing a successful program.

This area is much more primitive than other parts of China that we visited. They did not use the brick structure found elsewhere, but their homes and villages were much more like we had experienced in Iran and Afghanistan. Mud/adobe structure, a lot of walls used around homes and villages. People lived off the land. Very little modernization that is flourishing in many parts of China.

Back in Harbin we had a delightful couple of days sightseeing along with our business talks about the future of tourism and hunting. Banquets are the traditional

 **Another Chinese invention—not the ordinary popcorn machine. The kernels from the hopper, when ground, generate the heat that "pops" it, then comes out in a stream that the operator artistically rolls in a sort of hive as seen in the basket.**

one always wonders if the seriousness of the program is getting across to our new partners. Anyway, our final banquet with Misters Lou, Zhao, Pan and Jin was delightful with a multitude of courses, including Peking duck.

After our return to Beijing, we had plenty of time for the fabulous sightseeing and shopping, punctuated by meetings with the various departments of government that we were now dealing with, including CITS, CSS, WAD and CSF, as well as other tour operators like China Women's Travel Service, which we ended up using for most all our sightseeing tours and transit clients en route to Mongolia. All departments took a liking to us and promised to fill our desires to expand the hunting program.

The negotiations in China were long and hard, but wc finally felt we were "over the hump" and now awaited results in our request for sheep hunting. Our final banquet was back at the Sportsman's Hotel and in the same room where the Olympic chairmen entertained us weeks earlier. Mr. He hosted the banquet and we were surprised to see the room had been made into a trophy room featuring the mounted specimens from his Texas hunt that we carried here. Other guests for final talks included Mr. Kong and Madam Tao, all sharing respect and devotion on both sides of the table.

Chinese way of business gatherings, that include many toasts to "camaraderie," "the future of hunting," "to Chinese/American relations," "new friendships," etc. etc, but

# CHAPTER 11

# China's First Sheep Hunt

The following is Chris' journal as written (except for some time lapse) for the first organized sheep hunt allowed in modern times. The long awaited permission was given less than two months prior to the scheduled hunt, which was to begin in early November. Chris hurriedly lined up two companions to join in this historical expedition, Bill Taylor and Bob Chisholm.

*29 October 1985*

*I had to get up at 4 AM to make my PSA connection to San Francisco. Colleene drove me to the airport with my seven bags, five large duffle bags of expedition gear, besides my own suitcase and gun case. Bob Chisholm, a longtime friend and hunting partner from Wichita, Kansas, and Bill Taylor from San Francisco are meeting me there to catch our Pan American Airlines flight to Tokyo, with connecting flight to Beijing. I purchased all the gear for the hunt for all three of us. We are taking all the necessary camping gear as well as food, since the Chinese hosts are not expected to have most of what we will need for comfort and nourishment. I talked my way out of paying excess baggage charges in both Seattle and San Francisco.*

## TIME LAPSE

*Our Pan Am 747 connection was on time and we had a smooth 4¼-hour flight to Beijing. As I walked off the plane, there was an old acquaintance Robert Aman waiting for us. Robert is from Seattle and is here for a year, working in cooperation with CAAC Airlines. He is a Boeing aircraft engineer and is assisting them with their new 767 aircraft that are just now going into service. I had sent Robert a telex a few days ago telling of my visit. He was anxious to visit with some Americans, especially hunters.*

*Just as we finished the formalities, I recognized Mrs. Chen Huijuan of the Foreign Affairs Department of the Ministry of Forestry, who I met in May when I was here on a business trip, working on getting some of these trips started. Mrs. Chen was accompanied by Mrs. Chang Jun and Wang Wei, all of which came out to greet us. They verified with the officials that our firearms were authorized. They had a small 12-seater bus reserved for us, half of which was filled by all our gear. We said our temporary goodbyes to Robert and all worked our way to the Huilong Guan Hotel, while discussing the plan for the next couple of days.*

*Chang, who is to be our interpreter and guide during our time in Beijing, is the official in charge of Foreign Affairs for the Beijing Forestry College. Wang Wei is in charge of our hunt and assistant director in the W.A.D. (Wildlife Administration Division). He will travel with us to Qinghai Province and coordinate the hunt.*

*31 October*

*Even though we were chasing the sun and gained nine hours on the clock, we lost a day by traveling across the International Dateline. Temperature at night was near freezing. The weather is clear. We had an "American Breakfast," eggs, toast, a dab of ham and french fries, with coffee. Chang was promptly there to pick us up at 8:15 and we head for the Ministry of Forestry office for a meeting with Dr. Qin Jian Hua, the General Director of W.A.D. along with Mr. Xu Xuechi, who I had known from a visit to the Game Conservation International Convention in San Antonio last March.*

*He and two others from China came over to see what this big game hunting was all about. I also had meetings with him in May when I was here. We discussed the entire hunting arrangement and emphasized in front of Wang, who was present in the meetings, the importance of all the aspects of hunting and that we would be working with Wang and the local staff to teach them hunting techniques as well as skinning, etc. We were disappointed that Dr. Qin himself would not be on the hunt, as it would have been a great opportunity to really emphasize the importance of expanding into the argali sheep hunting, where he could see first hand what he is getting into in running a hunting operation.*

*I presented Dr. Qin with a "China Hunting Manual" that I have started and only completed the sheep and ibex section so far. I made Mrs. Chen promise that she would read it and translate it for Dr. Qin while we were in the mountains. Along with the manual was*

⌗ From Xining, the road rose sharply onto the Tibetan Plateau. Bob Chisholm, Miss Liu Xiao-Li, our interpretor, and Wang Wei stretch their legs alongside our van.

a presentation showing the difficulty in selling blue sheep *hunts as opposed to the great success that they could enjoy by starting hunting for some of the eight different sub-species of argali that they have within the China borders. We then settled the finances, for which I had to carry cash over.*

*01 November*

*Last evening we had tentatively planned on having Peking duck dinner with Robert Aman and his wife; however, we finally gave up on it after missing one another on the phone all day*

*and the fact that our hotel was so far out and the risk of no taxis being available. Therefore, we had dinner at the hotel, a couple of shots of Wild Turkey bourbon that we brought and an early night to bed.*

*Cold and clear again this morning. We had our entire luggage packed and awaiting our bus at 8 AM. After dropping by Pan Am and Lufthansa to reconfirm onward flights, we took in the Temple of Heaven complex. This was the place where the Emperors came and cleaned their minds and bodies for a spell, then prayed for a good harvest. From there we picked up*

« The massive high plateau, over half the size of the 48 U.S. states, average 10 to 11,000 feet high, with mountain ranges rising above that. Hay is stacked in preparation for winter.

**We observed thousands of livestock in their winter range on the Plateau. Some Bactrian camels, sheep and herds of yak, which are their form of cattle for meat and milk.**

Wang Wei at the Forestry office and went to the airport for our flight to Xining. Robert met us there for lunch and made sure we got on our flight OK.

Our flight was a small Russian built propjet. Got off at 2:30, one hour late. The flight stopped at a town out in the flatlands, Tai Yang. Disembarked long enough for a cup of tea and back in the air once more for Lanzhou. Many of the names of cities, provinces etc. have been changed in the past decade. Peking is now Beijing. Tai Yuen is now Tai Yang. Lanchow is now Lanzhou and Hsining is now Xining. Qinghai province was Tsinghai. It is said that the current spelling is correct, but in the old days, foreigners could not pronounce the words correctly, so they used their own English spelling.

As we boarded the aircraft we were told that our final destination today was Lanzhou and tomorrow we would go to Xining.

## TIME LAPSE

*(Our flight to Lanzhou went well, but our connection to Xining failed to materialize, so* we finally drove, thus losing two days from our itinerary).

*03 November*

We met in the evening with Wang Wei and Mr. Wang Ya Xue, the Assistant Director of Forestry. We talked over final plans for our 7 AM departure in the morning. We bought a half case of canned beer and a bottle of brandy. Earlier I tried to find some vodka. Nobody seemed to know what that was. Therefore, I bought three bottles of what looked like it at 4 Yuan ($1.30) each. Laying sideways in my

**Our camp had six Mongolian style yurts and three larger frame tents. The staff consisted of camp help, guides, a doctor, and an experienced cook. Wang Wei is in white.**

🔊 **The sturdy ponies were a terrific help getting us around the Burhan Budai Shan range,**

carry-on bag they all leaked a little, enough to smell the stuff. It smelled like some very horrible liquor I have had before here in China that was called Mao Tai. Anyway, we'll take it to camp and see if anyone wants to drink it. We also bought a couple of cartons of cigarettes, local ones to hand out.

*04 November*

Gear all loaded, carry-on in our Toyota van and the big stuff in the Toyota pickup; we were on the road at 8 AM. It was an interesting 11-hour drive. We were soon out of the bustle of Xining and putting on elevation, passing through frequent small villages at first, then sparse settlements toward afternoon. What we were never out of sight of were herdsmen and their flocks. We saw yaks by the thousands. Because of the high elevation, the yaks do better than cattle, so the milk and "beef" are from yaks. We saw a lot of domestic sheep and a fair number of the Bactrian camels—two hump variety.

The people were colorful. Some wore skin clothing and many wore what seemed to be the more typical outer garment, a fleece-lined long coat, some with a colorful trim. We went through several mountain ranges. The plateau appears to average around 10,000 feet in elevation, with the mountains protruding high above that. In the area we went through they are probably 13,000 to 14,000 feet, with an occasional peak going above that. The highest peak in the range that we are hunting in is 5,730 meters—18,900 feet.

Our route took us westerly to Qinghai Lake, a huge lake that appears on every map. We traveled around the south side of the lake (there is a road around the north side also, but evidently very mountainous) and westerly to Tianjin, where we turned south to Dulan. From Dulan we went about 100 km south and then west on the main road to Golmud. We left the paved two-lane road and went about 20 km south into the Burhan Budai Shan Mountains.

The rough road led us to our camp that a large staff had been working three days to set up. There are six Mongolian yurts and three larger frame tents. The latter were used for dining, cooking, and guides quarters. Bob and I shared a yurt, while Bill had one all to himself. These yurts are the same design as the ones used by Mongolians, except they only had a double thickness canvas wall and top. The ones used by the natives have a thick wool mat between two layers of canvas. The yurts all had a stove, spring beds, washstands, tables, and all the comforts of home.

When the expedition was first arranged only two months ago, we were told to bring tents, sleeping bags, and whatever else we needed. No doubt, the officials had second thoughts and decided to go all out. Besides the guides and camp staff, they sent in a well-experienced cook and even a doctor. Even though the beds were equipped with a comforter and extra wool blankets, we rolled out our sleeping bags on top of everything, making a super comfortable bed. They had a well-prepared dinner awaiting us. After dinner, they explained tomorrow's hunt plan.

*05 November*

We split in three different directions, three in each group. With me were Jia Bo and Zheng Jie. We hunted west from camp, working our way up the bottom of a valley with a lot of side valleys and hills rising 1,000 to 3,000 feet. The base camp is 3,218 meters, or 10,620 feet, and everything is up from there.

We barely got into the valley when we saw four blue sheep near the top of a hill to our left. I didn't see horns through my binoculars, but the guide said they were male and had good horns—all through sign language, of course. He also indicated there was no horse trail up to where they were.

Since I was in relatively poor shape and just coming to high elevation, I was not eager to strike out on foot all the way up that mountain and I think Bo knew it. Although it went through my mind—how could we possibly pass up a good blue sheep trophy? I held hunting license #1 in Nepal on the maiden trip for blue sheep back in 1974, while here in the high plateau, we have license #'s 1, 2, & 3.

So here we are on a trip that only five days are left of actual hunting time because of the travel delays we've had, to collect three blue sheep trophies. My only satisfaction of not going after them was that by not disturbing them, maybe they would hang in the same area and be available in the next day or so.

We proceeded up-canyon and soon topped over a little ridge, spotting a herd of around 40 ewes, lambs, and small rams on the mountain 600/800 yards above. I could not understand why so many sheep would be around here, as these mountains were grossly over-grazed by the local herdsmen, with hardly a blade of grass an inch long. Zheng Jie was also with us and it was evident that he knew nothing about hunting. He stood right on the ridge and scared the herd away. Then through sign language, I showed him how we must always stay out of sight of the sheep. Bo, who was obviously a good hunter, had a talk with him, so we had no further problem of that sort. As the morning progressed, we saw several more herds of sheep—to my amazement!

About midday, we were at the end of the canyon where it took a turn to the right and rose to a high ridge above. We left the horses tied up to take a careful look up the draws—more sheep, but all ewes and lambs. Edging on up a little farther, more sheep came into view in a little side draw. Moving on up a ways to get a better look, I saw an instant glance at ram's horns before he disappeared out of sight.

Up a little farther to see if we could get a better vantage point. By now, we were quite a ways away from the horses—about halfway to where the sheep had disappeared. The other herd of ewes already vacated the mountain upon sight of us, but we didn't feel the rams were even in sight of them and certainly had not seen us. So we were at the "point of no return," we had to go on up and look into the draw where the rams disappeared, assuming they were bedded down for the afternoon.

Believe me, the going was rough for me—lungs and legs both. I had no way of telling the altitude, but I would guess around 13,000 feet. The air is thin, less oxygen, so the lungs have to work a lot harder to get enough for the body to function. The legs aren't getting much oxygen, besides being weak from nonuse—so moving was slow.

Bo was very patient, understanding the problem as if he had years of experience, yet this was hunt number one for sheep in China!

**Bo and I were mighty proud of the well-earned specimen of North Tibetan Blue Sheep, Pseudois nayaur szechuanensis, the first taken in modern times.**

**My guide, Bo, had good eyes for spotting sheep.**

He knew the exact spot to approach the draw. The terrain takes on a totally different look, to where it looks almost flat through the binoculars or the naked eye, but when you get there, you find a very different situation with a lot of deep draws.

Bo merely indicated to put a bullet in the chamber and pointed to the edge of the draw, as if to say, "I got you here. It's your baby now."

Making sure I had my breath and was relaxed for whatever occurred, knowing that I may have to pick a target and make a split-second decision. Nothing there! They had obviously moved out when we were on the backside of the ridge going up. It was about 3 PM. We were tired, disappointed, and hungry. Zheng had been carrying one of the rucksacks I brought, with our lunch—canned meat and cheese, so we relaxed and had a little bite.

Bo pointed "up" or "down" and I pointed up. As long as we came this close to the top of the mountain, I saw no sense in not utilizing

The horses were summoned to get us and the sheep back to camp.

every moment of daylight—you just don't find blue sheep in camp! As long as you're in sheep country, there's always a chance.

After another hour of climbing we topped the high ridge. It is always misleading, but it looked like we were on top of the world. A beautiful view to the south into the main part of the Yi Ke Gao Mountains. That is the name the locals give the range, but it appears to be just a part of the Burhan Budai Shan. A big mountain lies to the south of us. I wondered if it was the 5,730 meters one indicted on the map. I could see no other high mountain in the clear air.

We edged our way over the ridge and Bo's keen eyesight immediately picked up some sheep. He motioned for me to move alongside him. A brief look through the binoculars indicted some respectable horns. My immediate survey of our position indicated, if I were to take a shot at the distant target, I would not be able to drop to a prone position, because of the rounded profile of the hill in front of me. Looking down about 20 meters, there was more of a sharp point of the ridge that I could rest the rifle on. Backing off and bellying my way down, I found a spot much more to my satisfaction.

Even though the sheep had only seen a couple of heads from the eyes up at a distance of well in excess of 300 meters, they sensed the danger. In the many sightings of animals all day long, it was obvious the game was very spooky and extremely alert. Nothing happens on these mountains that the sheep don't know about—a typical situation where local herdsmen share the same habitat and a simultaneous poaching situation.

The rams, about 10 in number, split off from the rest of the herd of ewes and lambs and angled off down the hill, actually coming a little closer. Not too spooked, they stopped and looked at the would-be danger of the small profile on the ridge that we formed. I grabbed my fur-trimmed down hat to make a rest for the fore end of my 7mm Remington Magnum.

**The guides frequently had me to their quarters for a drink, but especially to celebrate the success of collecting a sheep.**

*With scope set on 7 power, I quickly scanned from front to back at the procession of rams to pick out the biggest ram. I could see no difference, so I turned the crosshairs to the lead ram. Even though the ram looked tiny in the scope, I was aware of the flat trajectory of bullets at high altitude and was careful not to overshoot, so held right in the middle of the shoulder and squeezed off before the obviously restless ram bolted off.*

*With the kick of the rifle and my quick reaction to get another bullet in the chamber, I saw only snow flying up beyond the target and the ram charging into forward motion. Getting my attention back on the action, I saw one ram charging down the mountain, while the rest went splitting off up hill. At an excited few words from Bo, I looked around and saw him holding up his thumb and a big smile on his face. What I had seen was the bullet, after having gone clear through the ram, knocked snow up and above the ram's back, making me think that I had missed.*

*The ram did bolt down the hill, but only for about 25 meters, where he lay dead with a direct heart shot. I was one excited sportsman with the thought popping in my mind that I was the first to ever get a sheep on an organized hunting expedition in modern times in China. That, along with the fact that I was the first to take the first blue sheep, a different sub-species, in the opening of Nepal 11 years ago, made this moment very special to me, even though I am definitely not competitive with my fellow sportsman. I would have even been happier, as I thought on my way back to camp, if Bob*

*or Bill would have gotten one sooner than me today.*

*More sign language indicated Bo would go back and get the horses, while Zheng and I would go take care of the sheep. Even though it was estimated only around 300 meters away, it took us a long time to work our way through a draw and to the spot where the ram lay. I had my little pocket camera that I recorded the trophy with and then I field dressed him out.*

*A long, but satisfying, trip to camp after dark found Bob and Bill happy with my success, but unfortunately unsuccessful themselves. Bob had seen several sheep, but none that he could take a chance with. Bill had seen an estimated 250 sheep during the day, but mostly on the "other side." I had seen approximately 100 sheep this day.*

*06 November*

*I reluctantly stayed in camp today, because of the necessity of skinning the ram. Bob and Bill were out bright and early heading to a different area than yesterday. It seems no matter which way you go from camp you'll find sheep. The herdsmen had already left the high country and were either going to market or to their winter pasture—wherever that would be, I don't know as it appears everything high and low has already been grazed off.*

*Jia Bo stayed in camp to learn how to skin trophies for taxidermy purposes. Some of the other helpers in camp got involved and seemed to take a real interest. We used the mess tent for skinning. I spread out one of the tarps we brought to keep things clean. For flooring in all* the tents was woven grass matting, except by our beds there was heavy wool felt matting.

I skinned the ram for a full-size mount, so they got the full instructions. I would also make all the major cuts, and then do one part of skinning and let Bo take charge of the rest. I would bone out a hoof, and then he would do one. The same with around the horns, eyes, and lips, then turning the ears, lips, and nose. Ultimately the salting, rolling up the skin, and the draining and re-salting to follow. Bo never lost interest, and I feel he could now do a complete skinning job by himself.

I set up one of the sleeping tents and the bigger dining tent that we brought. Even though we now had no use for them or most of the equipment that we brought, I wanted to spread it out so as to show Wang and Gong, hopefully to be used for Argali sheep expeditions in the future where packing in would be essential. The big polyester sleeping bags that I brought were used by all three of us and were all that we needed, even though the temperatures dipped well below freezing in the yurts during the night. All the water was frozen solid in the tents during the night. The only source of liquid was our thermos.

The Chinese have the world's best thermoses available everywhere along with their delicious green tea. We would always start our day out with the packaged hot chocolate mix that we brought. In camp, they even brought in a generator and wired all the yurts with electric lights, as well as a few lights outside.

Both Bill and Bob were unsuccessful today. Bob stalked two small rams and could have shot at the undisturbed targets, but they were not as big as he would like early in the hunt and the distance was a lot farther than he cared to shoot. Bill again saw well over 200 sheep in the area he went today, but no chance for a shot.

We spotted about 25 sheep, ewes, lambs, and small rams on one of the hills above camp. I set up Bob's spotting scope and looked them over. This was quite exciting for the camp staff, especially Xiao-Li, as they otherwise may never have seen a blue sheep on the hoof.

## TIME LAPSE

*08 November*

Up very early, this time we split to go three ways again. With Bob's ankle bothering him, he couldn't go to the Big Mountain, but I wanted to go back there. Fortunately, the weather cleared up beautifully—but the coldest morning to date. We didn't stop to glass til we got within view of the Big Mountain and surrounding area. We saw several herds of sheep in different areas, one of which had a few respectable rams, but we elected to go up our route of yesterday to get a good look at the Big Mountain. Once up on the face of our spotting mountain, an increasingly strong wind caused it to be extremely cold. The chill factor of the wind at 1°F per mile an hour, I am sure put the effective temperature below 0°F.

## TIME LAPSE

(After many failed stalks, around 4 PM we located some rams that offered a good opportunity, so on with my journal).

We were now on foot for the rest of the stalk. Daylight was diminishing, so I knew there would be only a chance of getting to where the sheep were and hope that conditions would be favorable and light enough to see. We crossed over the ridge at the point where we had last seen the rams disappear. No sight of them, but the tracks in the snow indicated they were farther down.

Around another little ridge, Bo pulled back, indicating the sheep were in sight. As before, he merely motioned me around him, as if to say his job was done, it was all mine from here on out. Peeking over I could see sheep within shooting range about 200 meters away, but I could also see the hill was too flat for me to rest the rifle on. Looking down, I could see a sharper point that should be ideal.

Working down, I wasted no time in cranking the Redfield scope to 7 power, then gun barrel first, I moved into position. I scanned the herd quickly through the scope and there was only one ram in plain view, but the light was so dim I could not get a clear view at all. I had to put on my amber-colored shooting glasses and could now make the target out clearly enough.

Hat under fore end, I had a perfect rest, but the ram was facing me head on giving too small a target. I waited for him to feed around to give me a side view. He was on a steep slope and I was looking down at an angle, so when he quartered down the hill, I figured it would be the biggest target I could expect. In effect, I was looking down on the ram's left shoulder, so leveled the crosshairs on where I though the heart would be from this angle and squeezed.

With the kick of the rifle and darkness, I saw nothing but sheep scurrying all over that hill and rapidly vanishing from the scene. I looked up at Bo and saw his big smile and his thumb up in the air! The ram died instantly and rolled about 25 meters down the hill where he lay in a heap. We heard the rattling of rocks over the ridge so went over it to see the herd of about 25 sheep, maybe a good ram, turning back under us. We went along the ridge and straight down to the ram. Luckily, I had my little Olympus pocket camera, with flash, as I would not have enough daylight without it.

While cleaning out the ram, Bo smiled when he pulled out the fragments of the heart—a perfect hit! The assistant guide was there with the horses in time to load the ram on Bo's horse as the last bit of daylight diminished.

So here we go off the mountain in the dark. No moon, but the stars at this elevation cast off enough light so that we could barely see the contrast between light and dark. There were patches of snow around, especially on game trails, so that helped. We all slipped and fell a little as we patiently walked off the mountain, the worst and most dangerous part.

Once at the bottom and relieved, Bo pulled a half-frozen bottle of beer from his bag that we all enjoyed while we tightened the cinches on the horses. We were now on familiar ground for the horses, so we rode on out.

My rear-end didn't take it so well because on one of my falls, my feet went straight up in the air and I landed on the ice right where "the hip bone is connected to the leg bone." For a while I thought I had broken something, but I just ended up with the sorest rear-end I've ever had.

About a half-hour from camp, a "rescue party" intercepted us. Several of the Mongolian staff were concerned about us and came to see if they could help. They were delighted with our

The camp doctor (in back) accompanied
Bob Chisholm to monitor Bob's diabetes. Doc
and Wang Wei celebrate his success.

results and jogged our horses into the view of
a lighted and welcome campsite. Several of the
staff was on points above the camp with lights to
direct us in like beacons. Everyone was still up
and waiting for our return.

The greatest news was that both Bill and
Bob also shot rams today, making it a perfect
day. Everyone sat up telling yarns of the day's
hunts, while the guides and I had some good,
hot supper.

Animals saw, taken or seen signs of on this
trip:

blue sheep—Pseudois nayaur szechuaninsis
white-lipped deer—Cervus linnaeus
wolf—Canis lupus linnaeus
giant chukar/Snow chicken—Tetraogallus
himalayensis G.R.gray
red fox—Vulpes vulpes linnaeus

09 November
I had already promised to make breakfast
one morning and show the cook how to make a

good western omelet. I chose to make a Mexican
type, so in digging around the kitchen I found
some spicy little hot pepper, onions, tomatoes,
garlic and cheese and proceeded to make a big
omelet of sorts that back home I call huevos chin-
gados! Everyone enjoyed it. Over breakfast, Mr.
Gong suggested that we finish things up in camp
and leave late in the afternoon for Dulan, so it
wouldn't be such a long trip back tomorrow.

We skinned the last trophy and re-salted
Bob's and Bill's that were caped out yesterday. I
spent time with Gong and Wang demonstrating
the tents and other pack-in equipment that we
brought. I explained that we were leaving the
equipment with them in Qinghai Province to be
used for pack-in hunts for argali when opened—
hopefully next year.

The staff had a big banquet for us in
midafternoon. They pulled all stops and had a
magnificent feed, with blue sheep ribs being the
tastiest part of the 12-course meal. It was hard
to say goodbye to these wonderful people. We
handed out a bunch of gifts we brought for the
occasion. Our trip to Dulan took about three

The staff join Bob, Bill, and Chris for one last
photo with the horns of the North Tibetan
Bharal.

🔊 **This lady made fresh noodles in one minute from a ball of dough, the same process that Marco Polo introduced to the Venetians that became the spaghetti of this day.**

hours, half on the dirt road, crossing the half-frozen creek 10 or so times. Once on the narrow paved highway, the 100 km to the east, then north to Dulan went smoothly.

10 November

Left Dulan at 7:30. It was a nice day and interesting to watch the local people doing their chores. Every village was threshing wheat in their primitive ways. Drove 100 km along the south shore of Qinghai Lake, crossed the 3,300 meter (11,000 feet) pass through the Sun and Moon Mountains (Ri Yu Shan), and then wound our way down through more and more civilization to Xining, arriving at 2:30.

A real bath felt great and to remove our whisker stubble. We were advised that a banquet was arranged for the evening. The table was set in true Chinese banquet style with an elaborate food centerpiece, centered on a "lazy susan," and surrounded with many cold dishes to start with. At our table was Mr.

Jie Zheng Jiang and Mr. Wang Yu Xue, both section leaders in the Forestry Department, as well as Zheng Jie, assistant director, and Wang Wei and Xiao-Li.

The meal went along as most Chinese banquets with a steady flow of tasty hot dishes—a dozen or more—interrupted only by a series of toasts with Mao Tai, the local hard liquor. Toasts are usually standing up and traditionally its "bottoms up" with the word Gambey, which translates exactly as "bottoms up."

Then came the highlight of the meal. A sort of elaborate version of a fondue pot was placed on the table with a ring of boiling water. The "hot pot" was surrounded with various raw meats. We were led over to an adjoining table that had a dozen or more different sauces or spices, all in bowls and marked in Chinese.

They explained what each was. We were to select what we wanted in our own bowl to build a sauce of our liking. A lot of this was guesswork, but we took what seemed to blend. The thinly sliced meat was put into the boiling water a few pieces at a time and everyone was on their own to grab pieces with chopsticks, dip in their own concoction, and eat to their hearts content. A great evening with some wonderful people.

11 November

Up early, as I had meetings with Mr. Jie and Mr. Wang first thing. Bob and Bill were taken by Xiao-Li to the carpet factory, one of the more famous in China. The carpets here are some of the better oriental rugs found *anywhere. My meeting covered suggestions on better structuring of the blue sheep hunts and scheduling for 1986. In addition, of course, encouraging them to pursue the argali sheep hunting.*

*At 10:00 two directors of the Northwest Plateau Institute of Biology showed up, and Mrs. Wang San, Secretary of Foreign Affairs and Dr. Cai Gui Guom, director of the Institute. We had known about them and the institute through Dr. Richard Mitchell, the Scientific Authority of the U.S. Fish and Wildlife Service, who has had many dealings and exchanges with the institute and many of the staff members.*

*When we first arrived in Xining, I had calls into them, but being a Sunday, we did not make contact. While we were in the mountains, however, a meeting had been set up for our return. Bob Chisholm has offered a sponsorship through Dick to have one of the Institute members come to the U.S.A. for exchange education. The meetings became more interesting as both of them spoke good English, so we now had some real experts in wildlife to help get some of my points across.*

*After lunch to the train station to catch our 42-hour ride back to Beijing, which we felt to be the only safe way to, finally, get there and not depend on CAAC Airlines anymore!*

*Our compartment was small, but adequate. There were four bunks for the three of us—Wang Wei stayed in a separate compartment. We needed all the storage space and the extra bunk to store all our gear. The trip was*

One last banquet in Xining with the traditional hot pot. First you cook your selected meat in the charcoal heated water, which makes the broth, and then cook the freshly made noodles.

*interesting, taking us easterly and a little south to the lowlands of eastern China.*

*This is the area where most of the billion population of China live and it is the agricultural area. Therefore, it was farmlands and villages and farmlands and villages. There didn't seem to be much difference in the way people lived throughout the areas of China—mostly small towns and villages, the houses mud/adobe type of construction along with a lot of brick structures. The history of bricks goes back thousands of years in China, so they probably invented bricks like they did everything else! Some of the people in these hilly areas carved their homes into the hills, so all that was showing was the front, usually nicely decorated.*

*The train made hundreds of stops, while we used up our Wild Turkey whiskey supply that we brought from the states as well as a bottle of brandy bought here earlier. Eventually at 5:30 AM on the morning of 13 November, we pulled into "Grand Central" where Mrs. Chen*

*Huijian and a driver met us. They hauled us to the Friendship Hotel, which was a big improvement over our first hotel here.*

*We spent the day sightseeing and shopping. We were back in time for a banquet set up by the Ministry of Forestry at a fine Chinese restaurant. Present were Dr. Qin Jianhua—Director of Wildlife Administration, Mr. Guo Fushan—Director of Foreign Affairs—Forestry, Mrs. Chen Huiyuan—official, Foreign Affairs—Forestry, Mr. Wang Wei—wildlife guide and escort, and Mr. Xai—Assistant Director of Wildlife Administration.*

*This was the official and final "success party" for the first officially organized sheep hunt in China of all time. We had plenty of well-prepared food and liquor. The standard beverage placing, for a banquet, from right to left: a small stem glass for the "hard stuff" Mao Tai, a little larger stem glass for wine usually red and sweet, a regular glass for orange soda, and a tall glass for beer. We had plenty of "Gambeys" and a little time to report on the blue sheep hunt and business talks.*

## REFLECTION
# Chris's Library

**O**ne would think I was a librarian with case after case of books lining the walls of my Treasure House. Of the old world books, my favorites used for my research on Asian wildlife include:

*East of the Sun and West of the Moon* by Kermit and Teddy Roosevelt
*Ends of the Earth* by Roy Chapman Andrews
*Tibet and the North West* by Alexander Kinloch
*Across Asia's Snows and Deserts* by William Morden
*Unknown Mongolia* by Douglas Carruthers
*Innermost Asia—Travel and Sport in the Pamirs* by Ralph Cobbold
*Big Game Hunting in the Himalayas and Tibet* by Gerald Burrard
*The Great Arc of the Wild Sheep* by James Clark

As for my own writings, I have written many articles for magazines and scientific publications. I have never before published a book, but have contributed chapters to many books, including the following:

*Grand Slam of North American Wild Sheep* by Bob Householder
*Great Rams & Great Ram Hunters* by Robert Anderson
*Wild Sheep of the World* by Raul Valdez
*Horned Giants* by John H. Brandt
*In the Hearts of Famous Hunters* by Dickson Griffith
*Big Game Hunting Around the World* by Bert Klineburger
*This is the Greatest Hunting Era* by Bert Klineburger
*International Hunter* by Bert Klineburger

# China Argali Sheep Exploratory Hunt

The established hunting in China went well in 1986 and 1987, especially in Qinghai province for blue sheep, Tibetan antelope, and white-lipped deer. However, I was frustrated for lack of progress for more variety of sheep hunting, but now I understood that the Chinese did not just jump into a new program.

Finally, however, in January of 1988, I received word from Dr. Qing Jianhua, the head of wildlife for all of China, that a long-awaited hunt for argali sheep was now approved. This was one of the two proposed exploratory hunts that I recommended exactly five years before. It was to take place at the end of March, only two months away, and would be in Gansu Province on the north edge of the High Plateau.

Only four licenses were available for the little known argali found there, the Ovis ammon jubata. From the long list I had of the "first to hunt China argalis," I chose four of my past hunting companions, Robert Chisholm, Clayton and Modesta Williams, and Mahlon White. I might add that Thornton Snider was to have one of the first permits, but a recent operation on a bone in his ankle prevented him from accepting. With the high demand, I felt it better that I not use one of the four permits for myself. Bharal and gazelle would also be available in the areas.

The following is taken directly from my journal of this historic expedition:

*28 March 1988*

*We met at the San Francisco Airport, within a half hour of each flight arrival. I flew in from Seattle on Alaska Airlines, Clayton & Modesta Williams from Midland, Texas via Dallas, Bob Chisholm from Wichita, Kansas via Denver, on which flight Mahlon "Butch" White from Pueblo, Colorado boarded. Lit Ng had come up from Monterrey, California, where he lives, to San Francisco a couple days before and stayed in his apartment that he maintains there.*

*We all met at CAAC Airlines counter and piled up a great heap of luggage! 23 pieces in all—or was it 24? Somehow we could only count 23 in our minds, but had 24 tags. Clayton said Modesta was the 24th bag! They charged us for three pieces of luggage—$276 to Beijing, which wasn't bad since we must have had over a thousand pounds of weight. We all brought a lot of extra gear. I had six bags myself, only one of which was my personal gear, the rest being equipment for the expedition.*

*30 March*

*Arrived Beijing late, about 0100 this morning. The flight made two stops, one at Tokyo Airport and the other at Shanghai, where we cleared Immigration. At baggage claim we could see two of our old friends from the W.A.D.—both named Wang Wei, one is the top man in WAD and the other with the Wild-*

*life Conservation Association, also in Wildlife Administration of the Ministry of Forestry. The top man went with Bob and me on the blue sheep hunt back in '85, at which time he was an assistant.*

*A big mini-bus got our gear and us to the Sheraton Great Wall Hotel. Even though we had reservation slips for $100 per night rooms, they claimed they had no record on their computer, but put us up at the $130 rate, which we all figured was a gimmick to get more out of us. Since we had turned down the last meal on the flight, most of us went to the all-night coffee shop and had a delicious hamburger, along with some of the Crown Royal whiskey that we brought from the San Francisco duty-free shop.*

*To bed at 4 AM. Up by late morning and we all hung around the hotel until our departure to the airport for our 6:55 departure to Lanzhou. During the day we reorganized our gear to see what we could leave behind that was not needed for hunting. The accountant from WAD came and relieved me of the big bucks that I brought to pay for the hunts.*

*Later Richard Mitchell, the seventh member of our party, joined us. Dick had come ahead of us and has done wildlife studies with the Academy of Sciences, with whom he has done several study trips since 1980 in Qinghai Province. He had heard about our expedition and asked if he could come along, so we greeted him as a member of our party.*

*Dick has quite a diversified wildlife background, and has been with the Scientific Authority of the U.S. Fish and Wildlife Service. This past year he has been put out* on loan to the Smithsonian Institute, but still active in USF&WS. He is as curious as the rest of us to learn about this unknown argali sheep species. It has been known to exist, but no known studies have ever taken place nor have there been any known expeditions to collect specimens.

We arrived at the airport, now with 26 bags, including those of the WAD staff—200 Yuan overweight cost, about $60—not bad!

A comfortable 2½-hour flight to Lanzhou on a British 146, high-wing, and four-jet aircraft—great for short runs. Ling Tien Wen, a pretty young lady with the Foreign Affairs Division, who was to accompany us and assist in interpreting, met us at the Lanzhou airport. We had a mini bus, 18-seater, and driver to escort us to the Shugli Hotel in Lanzhou, about a full hour's drive.

It was not a very good hotel, especially because the plumbing was mostly shot—a typical thing throughout Asia that has never been mastered. A pleasant late dinner—Chinese style of course, was waiting us. We had been tapping the Crown Royal since we had gotten on the flight, so we didn't stop now. To bed by midnight.

*31 March*

Our bus and second car, a Chinese-made Jeep Cherokee, met us at 9 AM and we proceeded to a welding supply company, apparently the only place we could get our oxygen bottles filled. Clayton and Modesta brought some sophisticated oxygen equipment along, and I brought some along as well. It was not known what elevation we would be

We traveled by road two days along the ancient Silk Route from Lanzhou to Dunhuang. At a stop in Wu Wei, Bob Chisholm, Ling Tien Wen (interpretor), and Butch White stop for a snack at a sidewalk café.

hunting, but we knew we would be based at a minimum of 12,000 feet. Such equipment is not normally needed, but when it is, it can be life saving.

We were not allowed to go into the plant for the oxygen, so we had Ling guide us around the streets of Lanzhou on foot. We had asked earlier about Qinghai noodles, so she found a small café that made their own. We went in and ordered some and asked if we could observe the lady chef making them. This is a unique process of making noodles by hand. It is a process of taking the dough in a roll about 18 inches long, about one inch in diameter—like one giant noodle. She would then stretch it out with her two hands, quickly double it and stretch again, having two noodles half the size. She would then double that, having four noodles, then eight, and then 16 and at around 32 noodles she would have the most perfect spaghetti shaped noodles. She cut off the ends that she had in her hands and put the noodles into the boiling water. I don't think the whole process took more than about 10 seconds. They were delicious!

It was noon before we hit the road toward our destination—three days driving—two days on paved road and one strictly four-wheel drive on makeshift dirt roads. We went north and westerly from Lanzhou to Wu Wei, a good-sized town along the old Silk Route. In fact our whole journey for the two days was on this historic route that dated back as far as history has been recorded.

The route was one of the two ways that early travelers could travel through central Asia to connect the Far East with Europe and Asia Minor. This is the southern of the two routes. With the gigantic land mass referred to as the Tibetan Plateau, over half the size of the U.S.A. and with a minimum elevation of 10,000 feet, the route was just off the north slopes of the plateau, which parallels the Kun Lun Shan, the Altun Shan and the Qillian Shan ranges.

Just to the north of the Silk Route is the huge Xinjiang Desert, a forbidden area, to say the least. The other route was to the north of the Xinjiang Desert, along the southern plains of the Tien Shan range, perhaps a thousand miles to the north.

Traveled to Wu Wei before stopping for dinner. We were in sight of the snow covered Qillian Shan range on our left all the way. It is the northern rim of the Tibetan Plateau. The average peaks in the Qillian Shan are around 16,000 feet, with some getting to over 18,000 feet.

We drove on till 11 PM and stopped at the Zhang Ye hotel in Chiu Chuan. This city is also known as Jiayuquan and is one of the major cities in the area. We went right to bed. This was a very nice hotel—the plumbing worked well, and I took a shower.

## 01 April

We got off at a decent time and traveled westerly, again in view of the Qillian Shan all day. We were also in view of a lot of ruins of sorts that were a reminder of the old days of the Silk Route when travel was on foot or on an animal back. There were beacons (towers used for direction as well as warning of enemy coming), temples and even stretches of the Great Wall. The wall in this area was made of "hammered earth," more of an adobe/clay.

We traveled through Dunhuang and then west and south to Supei, which is a small town at the very west end of the Qillian Shan. The mountain range, which is an extension of the Qillian Shan, is the Yeh Ma Shan. A river valley from the Great Altun Shan to the southwest only separates this western tip of the Qillian Shan.

The two great ranges overlap one another by about 150 miles, with the Qillian on the north and the Altun to the south. The extension on the east end of the Altun is called the Tang Ho Nan Shan. Supei is the last main settlement before rising up into the northern part of the great Tibetan Plateau. The town lies in the flats at 7,200 feet elevation.

We arrived at an inn and greeted royally, given separate rooms and advised dinner was *waiting. The rooms were very plain, concrete block floors, hard bed, and washbasin with thermoses of hot water, cigarettes and candy on the table. No bathroom, but an outhouse 100 meters away—his and hers. Another 50-yard walk to the kitchen/dining complex where we had a good Chinese dinner, with the usual tasty Chinese beer and soft drinks, often their Chinese-made Coke or Pepsi.*

*02 April*

*Below freezing this morning. After a nice breakfast we proceeded to change our gear from the Mitsubishi bus to four-wheel drive Chinese Jeeps—one pickup-type with canopy that took most of the gear. The smaller versions that we were to ride in had very little luggage space behind the back seat.*

*At 10:00 we had a scheduled meeting with the mayor of Supei County. Our talks took place in a meeting room in the inn around a long table with the usual tea in cups with lids. The television crew that was summoned all the way from Lanzhou was on hand and cameras humming to record this historic event.*

*We talked about the importance of success on this first trip, so that specimens could be studied to establish the origin and rightful family of the sheep that is known to be here, but with no history of specimens ever collected. We expressed our gratitude to be the ones to accomplish this. The T.V.—or should I say video—film crew was scheduled to record the entire event. They had their own Jeep Cherokee—China-made.*

*We were off and soon winding our way up from the 7,200 foot elevation of Supei,*

**Two young lady servants placed us in our respective yurts. Modesta Williams stands with them in front of her and Claytie's yurt. The people on the north part of the Tibetan Plateau are Mongolian type.**

*following the main river system until we hit 10,000 feet elevation where the valleys widened. We were now heading east-southeast paralleling to our southwest the snow-covered Tang Ho Nan Shan, the easterly extension of the Altun Shan.*

*To the northeast was the Yeh Ma Shan, the westerly extension of the Qillian Shan. We were now in the Tibetan Plateau and would remain between these two great mountain ranges. Smaller ranges, hills if you wish, cropped up out of the Plateau all the way, especially to the north obstructing our view of the Qillian Shan.*

*These hills, we were told, were the habitat of the sheep, both argali and bharal (blue sheep) families. As we progressed upstream until late afternoon, we saw less and less human population, not that there was much to start with.*

An occasional herdsman with sheep, horses and Bactrian camels (the two-humped variety found in all of eastern Asia) were seen in search of the limited late winter food supply in this quite arid terrain.

The streambeds were dry, with just a small stream in the main river where it wasn't frozen over. We occasionally were in view of a frozen spring, which produced water until it froze, either like a giant white mound or flat like a glacier. The temperatures on the plateau had obviously been below freezing night and day. Late afternoon we arrived in a small village, a commune that controlled some fenced-in white-lip deer herds for antlers (used for medicinal purposes) and some domestic sheep. We stopped briefly to rendezvous with our caravan of Chinese and American jeeps, before heading north across the frozen river.

Just before dark, which comes about 8 PM because in China they all go by Beijing time a couple thousand miles to the east of here, we arrived to our very elaborate camp, consisting of three large Mongolian yurts for guest quarters, and eight other large, insulated military-type tents to house the staff, cook tent and dining tent. This is the second time the Chinese officials told me to supply all the camping gear and, at the last moment, felt they must make an elaborate camp. Previously, I had shown them photos of what their northern neighbors, Mongolia, supplied for the hunters, so perhaps they did not want to be outdone.

Nice looking young Chinese girls escorted us into our tents, which were heated with coal stoves and furnished with spring beds, wash basins and lockers that locked. The wind was fierce, blowing dust across the plains. It was explained that it is usually windy here. The camp nestled against one of the small ranges and faced a plain that varied from one to three miles, depending on the direction you looked across to the next small range. The range across from us blocked the view of the Qillian Shan, but we could frequently see the peaks of the Altun Shan depending on where we were,

Bob and I shared a tent (yurt), as did Clayton and Modesta, while Butch, Lit and Dick took the third one. Dinner was announced in the dining tent, which was welcome after the long day, with only granola bars and candy to carry us through. The same young girls waited the tables and brought course after course of Chinese food.

**Our camp set up only for our hunt consisted of three yurts for the guests and eight large frame tents for staff quarters, cooking and dining. Chris' horse was typical of the sturdy, Mongolian ponies found here.**

*After dinner I had called a meeting of all the guides and hunting staff. Having done these new hunts many times before, I knew the importance of having proper communications well established in the beginning, as well as informally getting acquainted with one another.*

*Subjects covered were trophy hunting, skinning, hunting methods, and the all-important patience the guides must have with us "dudes" from sea level that suddenly were at a 12,200 feet camp and going higher yet into the thin air. We all elected to have a rather easy first day of hunting, getting a good night's sleep and not kill ourselves off before having a chance to get acclimated. We stocked our stove full of coal one more time before crawling under the comforter, topped with a wool blanket.*

*03 April*

*27°F with 10-mile per hour wind in morning. The guides had the horses in and grained by the time we were ready. The horses were small, but sturdy. The saddles were the typical Mongolian type that required a pad in the small seat. The tack, in general, was good and sturdy.*

*Bob, Butch, Claytie, and Modesta, the four hunters (the maximum they would allow to hunt), all headed out in different directions in the range behind camp. I went out with Bob along with the two guides. Each hunter was assigned a guide and assistant guide.*

*Not three quarters of an hour out of camp over rather easy terrain, we came in view of Butch and his two guides, who had*

*been paralleling us less than a mile away. As I watched his lead guide round a knoll, I saw him suddenly turn back and motion the other two back with him. I knew he had seen something so I grunted to our guides to stop and look.*

*We then spotted two argali rams at the head of the valley to our left about a mile away. Butch was probably about 500 yards away from them. In putting the binoculars on the sheep, I could see they were looking right at us. We goofed and allowed ourselves to be out in the open and no way to hide from the rams.*

*They had been feeding; now they lay down to keep an eye on us. I motioned to the head guide, Haroqing, to fetch the spotting scope. Cubudai, the assistant guide, had it in his saddlebag so rapidly got it and put it on the tripod.*

*What a beautiful sight! The thing that greatly pleased me was the totally white neck on the larger of the two rams. I could also tell that the white fur was long and formed a sort of mane all around the neck, being the longest on the front. This one feature meant that it was not related to the Ovis ammon that are found north of here in Outer Mongolia, which all of us had hunted and collected in the past.*

*I had always hoped the great deserts to the north would have been a barrier that would have prevented the migration of both the Altai argali (Ovis ammon ammon) and Gobi argali (Ovis ammon darwini) into the Tibetan Plateau.*

*It was very pleasing to me to see that this species had the white frontal neck mane that* was noticeable in specimens of the Tibetan argali, found a couple thousand miles away in the southern part of the plateau and even on the Marco Polo sheep found a thousand miles to the west of here in the connecting mountain range known as the Pamirs.

By coincidence, Bob and I had just hunted Marco Polo sheep less than six weeks before in the Soviet Pamirs. We had collected specimens with full winter coats, on which this same white mane was predominant.

We could see that Butch's party had backed off of the sheep after looking them over through their spotting scope. Bob indicated he would like to take a closer look and perhaps try to take the bigger of the two rams. Haroqing indicated through sign language (we had no interpreter while hunting) that two of us must stay here in view of the sheep. As long as they had us in view at long range, they felt safe.

Bob and Haroqing rode away at an angle until out of view of the rams, and then started their circle up and behind the next mountain over, to get above them. I could tell through the scope that the largest was a full curl, but no flare and did not seem to be too heavy. The other was 3/4 curl, and definitely not one to consider the first day of the hunt.

Bob and Haroqing came into view above the rams on horseback, and then dismounted. Haroqing crept over to an outcrop of rocks to check position, while Bob held the horses. Suddenly he motioned for Bob to come quickly. Bob, not knowing what was up or what to do with the horses, came over leading them. The

Bob Chisholm and our guides, Haroqing and Cubudai, ride past a young ram head that was felt to be a wolf kill.

wind started swirling by the time Bob took his rifle and had a look. The rams picked up their wind. They leaped to their feet and were in an all-out, dead run down the mountain, actually toward us. They crossed a gully onto an outcrop and looked us over, then turned and ran out of sight. I doubt if they ever saw Bob, only got their wind.

Bob and guide kept on going higher to do more glassing so Cubudai and I caught up with them. We spotted Clayton and Modesta, who apparently ran into one another on a far ridge.

We crossed back through the mountains to the side of the plains. We spotted two rams way out crossing the plains to the next range. I felt they might have been the ones we spooked. We also saw on the plains a herd of wild ass, about 20 or so. Also a herd of camels, maybe wild—I could never find out. There were about 25 and way out on the plains.

As we circled back toward camp, a group of three argali rams appeared coming from the plains to the same ridge we were heading for. We struck out over the top of the ridge hoping to head them off. When we got to the other side, there was no sight of them. They no doubt saw some of the horses or our campsite and turned back. One of them had a nice dark body and a full, white frontal mane.

Back in camp just before dark. Claytie was back, but Modesta and Butch not in. Darkness came and still out—a good sign that they may have gotten something. An hour or so after dark there were shouts that the hunters were coming in.

The two of them and their guides rode in together. Modesta had gotten a blue sheep. Butch was mumbling that his rifle was playing tricks on him. He had gotten a shot at a blue sheep and missed. When we got to camp yesterday, we all fired the rifles—Butch's gun was off at first, then crept back to zero, so we assumed it was OK. I had carried Claytie's spare 7mm Rem. Magnum today, so Butch asked if he could use it tomorrow. Modesta's bharal was nice and heavy, an old one with 22-inch main beam. Wang explained that the farther north, the smaller the blue sheep. This area is as far north as blue sheep get. This is close to maximum size here.

04 April

19°F, 10 mph+ wind—Early start today, except Modesta, who decided to stay in camp

and watch over the skinning of her sheep, which Dick volunteered to do. Incidentally there were 15 rams in the band that Modesta and Butch hunted, but mostly medium to small. We all three struck out across the plains today. Butch to the left, Bob and I in the center and Claytie to the right.

In a straight line, it took almost an hour to get to the mountains on the other side. We headed for the "big mountain," which was about 1,000 feet tall, rising from the plains, but certainly not as high as this range gets, once you get back into it. We started glassing halfway across the plains and continuously as we got to the mountain and on up it.

**Clayton Williams with the first Gansu argali, Ovis ammon jubata, taken in modern times by a foreigner. Later Claytie got a bharal ram and a red fox.**

⌃ **I had staff members go out and pick up horns of larger rams to help judge sizes of trophy sheep. Some went over 50 inches around the curl, even though dried and rotted for several years.**

We went right over the top. On the other side, Haroqing spotted a bunch of sheep on a mountain into the range about a half-mile away. He insisted there were four good rams, but did not want to take the time to use the scope on them till we got closer, so we proceeded to lead our horses down off the mountain. Once we got to the bottom and ready to look them over more carefully, we spotted Butch and his guide way ahead of us.

At closer examination, it appeared the sheep were gone and no use for us to go forward. So we made a left turn, crossing Butch's tracks and went in and out of seven high ridges and valleys during the rest of the day, crossing from one to the other, paralleling a high ridge to our right. Late afternoon we headed out of the mountains toward camp.

The angle that we had been traveling took us to a point three hours ride from camp— saddle sores, you bet! Butch was in camp telling of being on that herd two different times, but no luck. He saw about 25, including females and young. Claytie got an argali. Beautiful white mane. Only 4-1/2 years old, triangular horn—different from the argalis to the north in Mongolia. He saw 50-60 rams!

*05 April*
10°F, 20 mph wind+, Very cold, low clouds and socked in on the higher peaks. Decided it would be foolish to go out today. During the night when one of us would wake up, we would put coal on the fire. Even at that, this morning the water in canteens and basins were all frozen. It started snowing a little, but the wind kept it moving.

We skinned Claytie's sheep out in the dining tent. I spent time with the guides showing them the proper method of skinning. Modesta's bharal wasn't completely skinned, so we completed that. When we had gotten here, none of us had ever seen a set of ram horns, so as to know what to look for. We had made it very clear that we depended on the guides to advise us on what to shoot, but for sure older rams.

Claytie's guide had encouraged him to shoot the one he did, even after our explicit talks the first night. Claytie was disappointed that he collected a relatively small ram on the second day of the hunt, when we had at least 10 days to collect quality specimens.

In the meantime we started seeing horns lying around the hills from winterkills, wolf kills etc. We asked the locals to bring horns of larger specimens to camp. Today they drove around and picked up several in a jeep. So now we had a lot to compare to, as well as study the horn configuration. I was very happy to see several sets that averaged over 50 inches around the curl of each horn, even though they had dried and rotted for several years. From all indications it would be possible to find these sheep with horns in excess of 50 inches!

So now we all had something to go by in horn size. Also in what we saw in sheep and further discussions with the guides, it was established that the older rams had the whitest neck manes and darkest reddish brown bodies. Claytie and I negotiated for him to have an opportunity at a larger ram. They finally agreed but wanted $15,000 if he took one! He declined and said he would only hunt blue sheep and gazelle from here on out.

Modesta and her guides decided to walk out of camp for a short hunt—stayed out for a few

**Modesta collected the biggest ram taken, 52 inches around the curl and heavily broomed on the tips; She also got the first bharal taken in the area.**

hours, with no luck, although they did see some rams, one of which they estimated could have gone 45 inches. Dick had followed along—his first time out. Dick had brought test tubes and alcohol to take skin samples from the sheep, which will be diagnosed to help identify this family of sheep.

The weather did not improve much, so it was a lost day. The guides, in general are quite good and reasonably skilled in stalking the game. Their eyes are quite keen and they have proved good at spotting the game at long distance. Except for their poor judgment on Claytie's ram, we have been quite satisfied with the overall arrangement.

06 April

-5°, 10 mph wind—Out early after a day of rest. Claytie went for blue sheep, east in the same range we are camped. The rest of us crossed the plains again—Butch left, Modesta right and Bob and I again in the center. When the guides' drove across yesterday picking up sheep horns, they spotted four rams on the "big mountain," so Bob and I went in hopes they didn't move too far.

These sheep, like all argalis are constantly on the move—no grass grows under their feet. We went over the mountain again, this time heading a little more to the right, which put us in a big valley, heading deep into the range. We then circled left up a high snowy valley—windy and cold! Topped out on the main ridge of the mountain and almost got blown off by the high winds.

Saw Butch's tracks on the ridge, where he was earlier and said he saw us. Our circle now had us heading back towards camp, but we were a long ways away. We saw 14 medium to small rams today. They got our wind and spooked. It took us three hours riding to get back to camp— late. Butch and Claytie were back with no luck. Darkness came and no Modesta. We were all in hopes it was because of luck. Later the shouts came from the returning hunters. Modesta got her ram—a 52 incher, and heavily broomed! Boy, were we excited.

They took it late and in a different place, so they covered it with a blanket to keep the wolves away, till they can go back tomorrow and get it. Now things were getting interesting. Claytie watched five wolves today surround a herd of camels. One big old camel kept coming out chasing the wolves! Finally the wolves gave up in disgust and went off looking for something more their size.

*07 April*

2°F, 10 mph wind, sunny—Bob and I went out farther to the left across the plains, pretty much due west directly across, just about the same area that he had hunted yesterday. We headed for a big red mountain and went around it and followed the range on the back side it's entire length, putting us a terrific long ways from camp.

We were quite close to the river that was frozen over that we drove over coming in. We saw a lot of tracks, but no sheep in the mountain. Then as soon as we got out of the hills at the end of the range, there were 10 females and young rams. Haroqing instantly got a glimpse of them as he topped over a rise and made a quick 180° turn on his horse and

**Mahlon (Butch) White collected a younger ram with a beautiful white frontal neck mane.**

got back down out of sight. We glassed them from about 400 yards. Nothing looked good, but we felt it worthwhile to circle them by walking down a ravine and coming up on them downwind.

In doing so, we stalked about 3/4 of a mile. Just as we came up on them they spooked, I think because they got wind of Cubudia and the horses and not from us. There were no rams big enough for Bob, so we started back toward camp a long ways away.

Soon we saw another six females and young. There was one ram, about a four- year-old that was not of interest. We did stalk a lot closer by putting a small hill between us and them— again not good enough. We let them see us, and they then traveled about three miles across the plains before really getting down to feeding again.

Butch took the first Tibetan gazelle ever recorded from here, besides taking a blue sheep.

We rode hard and long—four hours back to camp, arriving an hour or so after dark. They all thought we had luck for sure, arriving so late. But Butch took a ram today—a very heavy and broomed 42-incher, with an outstanding long white neck mane—beautiful.

Dick had gone out today with Modesta's outfit to help skin. Claytie didn't do any good on blue sheep—saw some, but too small.

*08 April*

15°F, no wind, cloudy—Really feels warm today after sub-zero weather and getting used to the cold and altitude. All of us by now are feeling better, as our red blood corpuscles increase in number, carrying more oxygen.

It always takes about five days in high elevation to begin to accomplish this. But I had diarrhea now for three days and it does not seem to be going away naturally. So I talked to the doctor and he gave me a few different types of pills, one of which was yeast to help me get a little of the food into my system. I have been weak, as I believe most everything I ate was going right through me.

Claytie, Modesta, and Butch, having each gotten their argali, decided on a change of pace and went out on some big flats today in search of Tibetan gazelle. They went by

Bob Chisholm and I hunted long and hard for argali in these high rolling mountains. Finally he got his ram the last night, too late for photos.

**At a movie set near Dunhuang, Claytie pulls a cart while Butch gets the battering ram ready.**

vehicle. This left the mountains all to Bob and me.

Dick Mitchell got enough sheep samples and got itchy feet to go on to his next destination which was Urmuchi in Xinjiang Province far to the north of here. Which meant they had to drive him back to Dunhuang to catch a train. Lit had the notion that a trip to Dunhuang to thaw out and get a nice bath and have a night in a hotel room would be an exciting change, so he joined Dick.

## TIME LAPSE

On 08 April Butch got a gazelle with 14-inch horn length, which should be high in the records. On 09 April Claytie and Butch got blue sheep with 22-inch horns that seem to be about the maximum size for these North Tibetan bharal.

*(10 April continued)*

Bob not back yet and darkness fell. Lit and the others only got back to camp at 4:30 this AM—they had gotten stuck in the river and Lit for sure was not rested and sorry he took the trip. We all were sure that Bob had got his sheep so

broke out the Crown Royal and started celebrating in his behalf.

We went to dinner and as we about finished, the lights of his jeep could be seen across the plains. He got his ram, not big but it was his and the hardest earned of the whole trip. So now all had the main trophies that we set out to get. Everyone had itchy feet to head for Dunhuang tomorrow. So I elected to stay up and work with the locals to get the sheep skinned and salted. To bed after midnight and super tired.

Some of the guides took a real interest in the skinning and once shown how to do a certain phase, i.e. take knuckles out of feet, turn ears & lips, they would do quite a good job. On the other hand, we could not just leave a skin and expect someone to skin it out and see that it was all taken care of or even salted. They needed supervision.

## TIME LAPSE

*12 April*

Today is Bob's birthday, so we made plans for a Peking Tien duck dinner along with the Chinese Hot Pot, which is a special way of

Wang Wei, along with the rest of us, board Bactrian camels to explore the sand dunes near Dunhuang.

cooking at the table. We went shopping and went out in the afternoon to a place that looked like a big, old fort, but found it to be a recently built walled city that was used for a film set. The film had been made in partnership with Japan and will come out soon. No matter how many times I asked, no one seemed to know the name of the film.

The city was well-done in mostly adobe-type construction, but with Chinese style temples and a lot of warfare equipment. Several of the buildings and structures were purposely burned in the film. The set is now being rebuilt for a tourist attraction.

*13 April*

We are stuck here till Thursday when the weekly flight goes to Beijing. Only last week did the flights start for the year. When we arrived for our hunt, there was no flight. Right after breakfast, we boarded our bus for the Magao ruins. The cliff area was honeycombed with Buddhist temples that dated back to the Fourth Century A.D. At one time this was a garden spot with springs and a lot of natural vegetation. With the overgrazing through the years, it was turned into a desert wasteland. The sand blew over the hills and cliff areas burying the ruins, which were only recently discovered and excavated.

*We returned for lunch and went to the sand dunes and crescent springs. Once there, we boarded camels to look over this interesting area. The entire area around Dunhuang is like the early days of the Silk Route. It was a green, lush paradise—what man can do to destroy what God has given us!*

*Back in Beijing, I had China Women's Travel arrange a side trip for Butch, Clayton and Modesta to go to Xian to see the amazing museum Qin Terra Cotta Warriors and Horses.*

*I had many meetings with various departments. Finally the last evening, Dr. Qing Jianhua of the Forestry Department hosted a most wonderful celebration banquet for the successful beginning of the new hunting programs. The gala affair was attended by a number of the wildlife officials, including the two Wang Weis. They provided us with the first CITES export permits issued by China for the trophies. China is a signatory to the Convention on International Trade in Endangered Species (CITES), whose members include most all nations that have wildlife populations.*

*CITES intended purpose is to watch over their wildlife and determine threatened or endangered statuses of it. The members are supposed to work together and respect each other's activities with their wildlife. They agree to issue export and/or import permits for non-endangered specimens taken by hunters. So Dr. Qing proudly presented us with this documentation to accompany the trophies that Chisholm and I agreed to take back as luggage to the U.S.A.*

## USFWS RAISES ITS UGLY HEAD

*As Bob Chisholm and I arrived at U.S. Customs in San Francisco, we had a well-attended reception committee from the U.S. Fish and Wildlife Service that promptly confiscated all of the hunting specimens from this historic trip. Hitting only the high spots, here is the story. Only a couple of months prior to the hunt, permission was granted by the Chinese and the plan for the hunt was made. It was just prior to an international wildlife convention in Nevada, where the announcement was made and publicized widely.*

*The Service secretly made their plan to grab the specimens and try to prove them not to be the Gansu argali (Ovis ammon jubata) but one 1,200 miles away, the Tibetan argali sheep (Ovis ammon hodgsoni) that was not endangered in China, however, the Service listed it as such. To make a long and costly story short, the hunters took the U.S. government to court and won the case. The federal judge severely scolded the Service for the terrible, underhanded, and wasteful tactics.*

*The majority of all the argali sheep subspecies and populations are found within the borders of China and nearby mountain ranges. The remaining argali habitat radiates out from China in bordering countries such as Mongolia, Afghanistan and the Asian Republics of the U.S.S.R. There are about 14 sub-species of argali thought to exist, with 12 of them in China.*

*One might think that the problems caused by the Service was a direct result of Richard*

Mitchell accompanying this expedition while still employed by USFWS and on loan to the Smithsonian Institute. However, it was quite the contrary. Dick, as we called him, was a biologist with the Service and he became the senior biologist in the Scientific Authority. If I, or any of my staff in our Taxidermy or Travel Section of my company, wanted clarification on the status of any wildlife, we would always try to speak to Dick, knowing we would get the true and an unbiased opinion.

Others in the Service would often talk in circles and in some cases give misleading information that we felt was done purposely in an attempt to get us to violate the law. Dick always fought for what was right and the ever expanding and seemingly anti-hunting Service staff never overturned his decisions. As a result, he became increasingly unpopular with the insiders in the Service.

The Smithsonian Institution in cooperation with Academia Sinica (the Chinese Academy of Sciences) set out to study the wildlife in Qinghai, Xizong, and Xinjiang Provinces, which encompass the majority of the wild sheep habitat of China. The Smithsonian requested the cooperation of the Service, so Dick became on loan to the Smithsonian from 1986 to 1988, while still employed by the Service. He made a number of field trips to China and was well respected by the Chinese partners.

On hearing of our expedition, the Smithsonian requested me to include Dick as a member of our party. The data that he collected, including tissue samples, photos and populations of wildlife were invaluable to the ongoing surveys. The resulting studies contributed to the proof that the Gansu argali and Tibetan argali were indeed two different subspecies. Dr. Jiu Feng further proved it in her Ph.D. dissertation at the University of New York at Buffalo, using DNA analysis.

After the service lost the Gansu argali case against the hunters, they went after Dick, claiming he prejudiced their case and furthermore brought tissue samples illegally into the U.S.A. For eight years Dick was the target of investigation by six agencies, mostly within the Department of Interior, and costing taxpayers over 18 million dollars trying to persecute him.

They lost that case and forced Dick into retirement. In paralleling that, however, convinced not to use the field work of Dr. Mitchell and the Chinese Ministries, the Service set out to list all argalis in China as endangered in Rule: 55 FR 40890; October 5, 1990. It bears noting the Service apparently was the only government agency that had no overview committee to answer to, so they went on unchecked.

The Chinese wildlife program suffered by losing American clients, who are a major source of revenue to support the program. My interest in continuing in developing more argali programs in China now began to falter, knowing my fellow countrymen would be prohibited from importing them. At the same time, however, perestroika was now in full swing in the Soviet Union, where I had what seemed to be unlimited opportunities in developing new areas, so I focused my attention there.

## REFLECTION
# Endangerment of Wildlife

**T**hroughout this chronicle are messages concerning conservation and sustainability of wildlife, but most important, sportsmen financing of wildlife programs. As far back as research goes, man has always been a hunter. In pre-management times, humans have killed all the wildlife they could, yet almost all the species survived. As populations explode, by the late twentieth century, governments around the world recognized the need for broad controls over wildlife.

In the case of the U.S.A., which was not unlike most countries of the world, the U.S. Fish & Wildlife Service (USFWS), under the Department of the Interior, regulated migratory fish and wildlife that was in its own lands and waters. Each state had its own fish and game department that ably regulated its own indigenous species.

In 1973 USFWS passed the Endangered Species Act (ESA), which seemed to be a well-intended measure to determine species that were truly endangered or threatened around the world. At the same time, the Convention on International Trade in Endangered Species (CITES) was established to encourage countries around the world to establish their own ESAs as such, and all join together to prevent illegal trafficking of species that are truly endangered.

That was all well and good until the ever-expanding bureaucracy of USFWS decided that the other countries of the world didn't know anything about their own wildlife populations and began dictating to them their endangered statuses. So instead of honoring a fellow nation's CITES export permit and allowing the specimen to enter the U.S.A., they reverted to their own determinations that were dead wrong in numerous cases.

Back in the 1980s I was in Washington DC conferring with the under secretary to the Department of Interior, whose platform was to "Clean up USFWS," when he said, "Chris, there are 20,000 people working here and I don't know what they do." In other words, they used him as a figurehead, and distanced him from their self-centered activities.

Instead of encouraging proper sustainability of wildlife programs of developing nations by honoring them, the USFWS has actually destroyed programs, resulting in endangerment of various species. This is a direct result of the absence of value of the wildlife, because the local people will not protect it as they do when prospering with the presence of a hunt program.

# CHAPTER 13

# Big Change in the U.S.S.R.

As changes were promised for self-government by Mikhail Gorbachev, my activities in the various Soviet republics increased with frequent trips to the "Asian countries," those "stans" in the south bordering China, Afghanistan, and Iran. My contacts were with the officials most directly involved with wildlife, including forestry, sciences and game departments. It appeared all my contacts were anxious to get out from under the strict socialist government that lorded over them since the 1920s when they first joined the Soviet Union. Aside from the wildlife and other resources, the Asian countries were the "breadbasket" of the U.S.S.R. and the major source of crude oil.

I made it known to Intourist that I was prepared to deal directly with the various republics, but still preferred having one partner (Intourist) to work through. Rafik Kapharov, being fully in charge of hunting activities, finally realized his Hunt Section of Intourist was in danger of competition. So late in 1987, after many years of a do-nothing attitude, he agreed to the Marco Polo sheep program in Tajikistan that I had been pushing for. The following are transcripts from my journal of that historical event.

*October 1987*

*This is the first expedition for Marco Polo sheep (Ovis ammon poli) since the mid-20s in the Russian Pamirs. Our group was carefully selected to take this exploratory trip.*

*There were only three permits issued for each Poli and ibex. ("Poli" is often used as a common name for Marco Polo sheep), I had already collected three Marco Polo sheep myself in Afghanistan, so I had three permits to carefully allocate. Sheep hunters are a breed of their own. Because of the importance of having the right people on this all-important expedition, my list of possibles resulted in the group that made up the party: Robert "Bob" Chisholm, a long time friend, client and hunting partner and Darwin "Curley" Miller, like Bob, Curley dates back a long time.*

*Both Bob and Curley lost out on the Afghanistan hunts, both scheduled to go in the year of the '79 Revolution. (Like this current Poli program, my company opened the hunting program in Afghanistan in the late 60s). Frederick Fortier, a very active sheep hunter now, and good client through the years, was my final choice.*

*Albert "Bert" Klineburger, my older brother by a year and a half, volunteered his expertise to help make the hunt successful. So it is the five of us that made sudden plans to make this greatest of all modern-day expeditions in the U.S.S.R.*

*My part of planning was far beyond getting in shape and lining up the right boots and parka for the trip. After discussing it in great detail over the phone with Rafael (Rafik Kapharov) several times at 3 AM Seattle time, it was determined that we had to furnish the entire accom-modations, complete mountain expedition types of gear and food. So I had tremendous detailed planning to make everything come together. The entire outfit from soup to nuts, from tents to toilet paper, was assembled in a dozen extra-large duffle bags. I had to provide such critical items as oxygen equipment, multi-fuel stove and lanterns and special gear to provide comfort and safety in the 13,000-foot base camp and who knows what higher fly camps.*

*23 October*

*(Our group had been traveling since 19 October trying to land in Moscow, which had been fogged in, while we were stranded in Frankfurt.)*

*Weather OK and we landed in Moscow—four days late. The baggage claim and customs area loaded with people. No baggage carts for our 24 pieces of check-in plus 8 or 10 pieces of carry-on.*

*No signs of anyone from Intourist to meet us. After we waited for close to an hour in customs line, they decided to run a big soccer group in ahead of us. We got indignant and started shoving our guns through the x-ray along with their cases. We got their attention, so when they did let us through they cleared our 1,000 pounds of gear without a question. I had been concerned, since we had tents, equipment of every sort that was supposed to be prearranged for Intourist to receive it—but no Intourist!*

*Once through customs, an associate of mine, Alexander Lubvny "Sasha," met us. He is just a private citizen that Colleene and I met several years ago. Since then he has been assisting our* travel clients. He was a tremendous help to us, as we had no more reservations, since we did not arrive on time, so their crude system of handling people does not allow for changes. Anyway, we got three limousines to carry all our gear and ourselves.

We had small rooms at the Intourist Hotel. Still no signs of a representative of the Hunt Section of Intourist, nor were there any messages. We got to work with the airline desk and found that the flights to Dushanbe (Tajikistan) were planned to be operated on a nonscheduled basis until they had all the people moved about that were backed up. It was decided that we would go to Domodedovo domestic airport tomorrow morning and Sasha would accompany us and make sure we got on a flight to Dushanbe, the capitol of Tajikistan.

*24 October*

Still no word from Intourist. Sasha met us at 9 AM. This time it took five normal size cars to get us and gear to the airport. Sasha asked Bob for $200 to bribe the attendants to get us on the first flight. It was scheduled at 4:15 and we got seats. Curley bought a half-dozen cartons of American cigarettes, most of which Sasha took or distributed to porters and attendants at hotel and airport. Then Curley gave Sasha $50 to get a ride back to the city—approximately 30 miles away. Boarded flight on time for 3-1/2-hour flight, plus losing three hours on the clock, arrived after midnight.

Sasha or someone from the Intourist desk at the airport called Intourist in Dushanbe

and told them we had better be met. Sure enough, Rafik Kapharov was waiting for us, along with a driver and mini bus. They took our carry-on luggage and us to the Tajikistan Hotel. Rafael, as he likes to be called, and I returned to the airport and brought the luggage back to the hotel—finally 2:30 AM in bed!!

*25 October*

Up for 9 AM breakfast. Met Safar Tabarow, Intourist guide that will accompany us to the Pamirs. He took us around the city on a tour ($40 for a three-hour tour in mini bus). Explained that Dushanbe as it is now is a modern city, only started building it up in 1926 after their revolution. The name translates to "Market Day" as this was a meeting place for trading by the mountain people (herdsmen) and the farmers that tilled the fertile valley soil here. It is also located near the north-south

**1987 It was a real treat to have brother Bert accompany me on an exploratory trip, the first Marco Polo sheep hunt in modern times to the U.S.S.R. Here we visit Red Square in Moscow.**

*trade routes that followed the foothills of this great mountain range.*

*The Hissar Mountains surround the city. Snow-capped peaks stood out around 25 miles away—looks cold up there! What little remained of the old town was leveled to make way for apartments, office buildings, schools, theatres and sports arenas. This is one of the more well-planned cities in the U.S.S.R. that I've seen, and it is a pretty city with a lot of parks and trees everywhere—population 650,000.*

## TIME LAPSE

*(The same storm that hit Moscow settled in this area with snow and fog in the mountains, so four more days of delay had us sightseeing and taking in museums).*

*27 October*

*The area we are to hunt is the Balyandkiik Reserve on the north edge of the Pamirs about 500 kilometers from here. It is between the*

**While weathered in at Dushanbe, Tajikistan, we visited the Hissar Museum Preserve. A 1500 A.D. fortress built for all the Mirs of Bukhara, used up to 1922 by the last Mir Alim Khan.** ☙

*two highest peaks in the U.S.S.R., Mt. Lenin 23,772 feet and Mt. Kommunizma 24,590 feet. (In 1998 this name was changed to Pik Lmeni Ismail Samani). These are second only to many of the peaks of the great Himalayan Range, southeasterly from here. This area, I am estimating at 300 km north of where we hunted in Afghanistan, which was at the southern edge of the Pamirs.*

*To the south and west of Balyandkiik Valley, including on and around Mt. Kommunizma is the largest glacier in the world, the Fedchenko Glacier. It is an ice field, like frosting on a cake. It is 70 km wide and up to 500 meters thick. Balyandkiik Valley is, in my estimation, about 100 km long, starting at a ridge at around 18,000 feet elevation and flowing northwesterly to the Muksu River. The two valleys to the north are the Kaindy and the Sauksay, both containing Marco Polo sheep and ibex. All three of the rivers flow into the Muksu River, the waters of which eventually come through Dushanbe.*

*30 October*

*I could still see the mountains from my hotel room, so eagerly got up before daybreak. Took a walk while day broke and saw blue sky for the first time since I left Seattle. Got all repacked and called the others. We finally got word from the airport to come on out.*

*We got out to the Aeroflot helicopter and stood around for at least another hour and a half before everything and everybody arrived. It was after noon before we took off. Just about normal for the Soviet Union. The MI-8 copters* are really big. Over 20 feet of cargo/passenger space long and about eight feet wide. There were 15 people, including the three-man flight crew. We had about 1,000 kilos of gear. They tell me the load capacity is 2,500 kilos, over 6,000 pounds.

They informed us that we were not allowed to take any photos in the airport or in the air. I didn't care about the airport, but sure wanted to take photos of the mountains, especially Mount Kommunizma. It was a beautiful flight. At first we could see all of Dushanbe, which I was surprised to see how big and spread out it was. Then a lot of farmland before we got into the valley of the Muksu River, which is actually way upstream.

The big river that flows through Dushanbe is the Surkhandar River. Before that it is the Surkok River, but it changes name after picking up many other side rivers and streams. The Muksu and Kyzylsu join together to form the Surkok River. The valley most of the way was populated with big, then smaller, villages. Farming in every flat spot and some of the hills were terraced off for more farming.

We flew at 10,000 to 13,000 feet. Mt. Kommunizma was an awesome sight, over 10,000 feet above us with its northern, rugged face plastered with gigantic rock outcrops and busted-up glaciers. It is so steep on the north side that the glaciers were not the long, flowing type that normally fill valleys, but chunks of ice 500 feet thick that shear off when they over-hang. The last half-hour of flight was past some of the ruggedness and steepest mountains I have ever seen. No doubt this is good ibex habitat. Game trails could be seen on the open faces.

The flight took just short of two hours to get to Camp 1, where we were scheduled to spend three nights to adapt ourselves to higher altitude at this 10,000-foot level. The Muksu River basin is very wide here—a good mile across. The river itself in this low water period is an average of 50 yards across and not too deep. In the spring runoff, I would imagine this would be some sight.

The camp consisted of a very large yurt, 18 or 20 feet in diameter; equipped with kerosene stove, spring cots with mattresses. The five of us, as well as the doctor, Jarkov Renaut, and Safar, both of which flew up with us, slept in the yurt. They had a separate cook/dining tent and a couple sleeping tents for the staff. They also brought a cook in, but ordinary things like making pancakes (to go with the canned bacon we brought in) was over his head.

We spotted some ibex, mainly female and young, but enough to excite us into planning a hunt for tomorrow. Bob and Curley were not so much interested in ibex, but Fred would take one if he had a chance at a big one. Fred hunted Mongolia just one month ago and, even though he was lucky in getting a massive Altai argali ram, he did not find a really big ibex. These ibexes are in the same family group as those in Mongolia, Capra siberica, but they are a different sub-species, probably the C.s. formosani.

Since the food supply was rather skimpy of fresh foods from Dushanbe, we broke out freeze-dried packets that we brought—Bert's supervision of reconstituting it and the lack

At the 10,000-foot elevation acclimation camp, I had my spotting scope trained on ibex that Fred Fortier was hunting. From left, myself, Darwin Miller, brother Bert, Bob Chisholm, and the interpretor.

of a proper measuring cup, we ended up with Turkey Tetrazini soup. It was good, anyway.

*31 October*

Fred and I donned our hunting clothes and headed out with Michael Frolov, head guide and number two man in the local game department. A second guide, Tagag, joined us as we headed east toward the head of the Muksu River. That is the confluence of the Sauksay, Kaindy, Balandkiik, and the Fedchenko Rivers. It is also where the mountains take command and no more wide river bottoms.

We walked for close to two hours in the river bottom, which is not the best footing— either rocks or soft sand. Not much snow on the ground to hamper walking, but enough to require us wearing our outer shells of pure white clothing.

We started seeing ibex as we approached the escarpment separating the Sauksay and the Kaindy Rivers. Nothing but nannies and

kids, so we kept on until we got to the Sauksay River.

Michel had a pair of very cleverly designed rubber boots in his pack for our use in river crossings. They are lightweight and large enough to go over the outside of our boots and pull up over the top of our knees. (How I wish I had something like this in some of my Alaska hunting days). The Tajiks wore rubber boots that came up to their knees—loose fitting and something we dudes could never climb in.

Anyway, to cross, we had to find a wide place in the river, usually rapids, where the water was shallow enough. Even then, we would have to throw big boulders into holes, then hop across from rock to rock and wade the shallower places, using a walking pole for a third leg. With only one pair of pullover boots, one of us would go, and then the boots were brought back by one of the guides for the other. There were four branches of rivers to cross altogether to get onto the mountain.

Once we got up into the hills we spotted more ibexes, but no mature billies. We had traveled from 10 till 1:45 and could see the camp as a dot through binoculars way down the valley. It did not seem advisable to continue on. We had now seen 35 ibex. Michael indicated through our usual sign language (Safar did not accompany us on the hunt) that we should take a young billy for camp meat. Since Fred had one ibex included in the hunt, he wanted to make it very clear that this would not be his trophy ibex—Michel (Michael, as we called him) said, "No tariff."

We got into position on an ibex lying down, but it was too far for such a target, well over

↑ **At camp one, I demonstrated the setting up of tents I supplied, large dome tents and 3-man tents, all double walled, expedition type.**

300 meters. We went back down and circled around to a point less than 200 meters. Fred leveled off with a lying down shot and got the ibex. It never got up after being hit with a perfect heart shot.

We had a little lunch while skinning out the ibex. All the meat was saved, only a few bones left lying on the mountain. Three-fourths of the way back we were met by the film crew. These were five Russians that came down from their home city in the Ural Mountains in north central Russia.

Their mission was to make a wildlife/hunting film in the U.S.S.R. Probably more than one film will be produced, but one will be for the promotion of hunting at the World Hunting Congress to be held in Las Vegas in January of 1988. It will be a 15 or 20-minute film to be shown in the Film Festival as well as in the U.S.S.R. booth. My company will be setting up the Soviet booth with full-mounted specimens of U.S.S.R. trophy animals. Raphik will personally be coming over to represent the country and provide first-hand hunting information.

Getting back to the film crew. There were five photographers altogether, three of which were in Camp 1 before us and two accompanied us in the helicopter. They seemed to be quite professional taking 35mm negative movie film, as well as still pictures. They had taken shots of us arriving and around Camp 1. Now they wanted to get some shots of us traveling and spotting for game.

Sure enough, while spotting, we located seven big ibex trophies on the mountain across the basin from camp. Too late to hunt now, but if they stay till dark, they will make for a good hunt tomorrow. We watched them through dinner (again freeze dried—but not "soup" this time) and right up till dark. There was a half moon, very bright and clear out, so we expected the ibex to feed for part of the night.

## TIME LAPSE

01 November

Fred and Michael returned late afternoon very tired having been on a wild goose chase all over the mountains, thanks partly to my signal being displayed on a wrong assumption—and no ibex trophy.

Something was stirring late in the evening, that I couldn't figure out until they escorted me to the dining tent. They had a big birthday celebration for me—a well-kept secret indeed! My 60th birthday was actually 3 November, but since our scheduled departure to the high camp was tomorrow (back to their home bases to start editing film), they wanted to honor this event tonight. Vodka, caviar and a great dish

A surprise "60th" birthday party was thrown for me at Camp 1. Myself, interpretor and Michael Frolov, the number 2 man in the Tadjikistan Game Department.

of Tajik pelow (pilaf) made from ibex meat, was there in generous proportions. Typical of Russian hospitality, there were many toasts wishing me and all of us well, followed by some gifts, to all of us, of lacquer-ware spoons—a very typical Russian gift. They also gave me a set of shot glasses in a container in the shape of a large (oversized) shotgun shell.

We compared ages, Bert being the oldest at 61, then me, Curley at 59, Bob at 56, Fred at 39 and the Soviet staff, photographers etc. ranging from 26 to 35—a great and thoughtful occasion. Bob had brought birthday cards from wife Colleene and son Kent. He also brought one from himself, his wife, and his office staff—Curley brought one also. Someone must have been talking! Colleene obviously "spilled the beans"! Anyway, I was honored that everyone took the time in these adverse conditions to have such a memorable party.

The pelow was loaded with whole cloves of garlic, typical of Asian food. Bob is very

allergic to garlic and it makes him ill, from even small quantities. He got very ill during the night, throwing up periodically all night long.

02 November

The helicopter is due in today to move us to Camp 2 and on to the fly camp high in the Pamirs. We started right off to get the gear sorted out for three separate fly camps—Bob and me together, Fred alone and Bert and Curley together. Tents, food, sleeping bags, and all the essential clothing and gear to go, all unnecessary items to be left behind.

Bob was feeling better first thing this morning, but as the hours went on, he started feeling worse again and having dry heaves, which is an indication of altitude sickness. A quick decision had to be made—should he go up another 3 to 4,000 feet and take a chance on real problems, stay in Camp 1 (practically by himself) or return to Dushanbe's low altitude.

This was a horribly difficult decision for Bob, as he has been trying to get on the trail of a Marco Polo sheep for over 10 years. He was scheduled in 1978 to go to Afghanistan for the Poli, when he broke his arm playing polo. Since no one ever thought that the Afghan program would ever come to an end, Bob postponed for a year.

In 1979 the Soviets invaded Afghanistan and ended all tourism, including hunting. Bob figured he has put it off this long, he better take care of his health right now so that he will be able to do it another year. So he made the decision to return to Dushanbe and wait for us—a very tough decision for an active hunter like him.

The helicopter arrived at 11 AM, the time that it was scheduled. Since the lift capability of the copter is greatly reduced at the thinner air, it had to make one trip with some of the staff and equipment before taking the rest of us. By early afternoon the four of us, our gear and the remainder of the staff were off to Camp 2. We did not fly up Balandkiik, but up Kaindy valley, which parallels it to the north. Michel claimed that the Poli did not go into the more rugged Kaindy. It was indeed a rugged canyon, but good-looking game habitat. We flew right over the spot where Fred and I hunted ibex a couple days before. We saw ibex and a really good billy just a little ways above where he dropped the "meat" ibex!

At the head of the Kaindy, we turned south through a pass, which was directly in line with Camp 2. We landed at the camp, which was equipped with a yurt, about half the size of the one we had in Camp 1. We off-loaded the gear in piles of which went to the separate fly camps. By now we decided that we would only have two fly camps, where Fred and I would camp in a place where we could strike out in four different directions. Bert and Curley were to camp several miles downstream from us.

While flying in, we saw several groups of sheep from 5 to 10 animals in a group. Mostly all rams—what an exciting scene! The entire Pamirs were blanketed with snow. The valleys were gently rolling and comparatively flat.

Camp 2 is located roughly halfway from the mouth to the summit.

At this point it actually splits into two separate valleys easterly, one being Zulum Archa, the northern valley, and Balyandkiik, the main southerly valley. It is at the confluence of a lot of other side valleys. It is a good spot to hunt from, providing they get some animals to ride, preferably yaks, the very best animal for high and rough country. We had no riding stock, so it was all by foot for us.

Camp 2 had three tents as well, one of which had been torn down by a mountain grizzly. The staff was hard at work to get the radio to work. It was supposedly strong enough to contact Dushanbe, several hundred miles away. Less powerful radios were to be in the fly camps, to give total communication with each other, Camp 1 and Dushanbe.

By late afternoon Fred, myself, Michel, another two guides, Vladimir Brizgalow and Rahman Beroi, and an assistant/radioman, as well as our gear, were boarded onto the copter and on our way to spike it out. As we approached our campsite, a dozen or more Poli rams broke out of a draw and ran away right under the chopper. What a sight!

Needless to say, they were out of sight in a moment. We quickly unloaded our gear and sent the copter on its way. In looking up on the hill opposite our campsite, another herd of sheep, another dozen or so rams, was topping out into a canyon to the south of us—exciting to say the least.

Everyone pitched in to set camp up before it got dark on us. Since we had all the gear for

The big MI-8 helicopter dropped us off at the site of our spike camp.

two fly camps, we had two dome tents. After popping up one for Fred and me, we offered the other to the staff. The staff supposedly had all their own gear, which did not turn out to be true. They had one small canvas tent, which would have been almost impossible for them to even be able to crowd themselves in side by side to sleep, let alone have their gear inside and cook. They happily put up the other dome tent and ended up with a fairly comfortable camp.

We got our Coleman single burner kerosene stove lit up, closed ourselves in out of the bitter cold, possibly 20° F below zero, and cooked up a batch of beef stew from our supply of freeze-dried food. Since we wanted to conserve on dirty dishes, we marked a line halfway across the cooked dinner and each ate his half out of the pot. That, along with a cup of hot chocolate, was dinner.

We each put a quart bottle of water in bed with us to keep it from freezing. Additionally, we filled a thermos with hot tea and filled a pan with water (which would be solid ice within

an hour) to set on the stove in the morning. A bottle or canteen with water, sitting out, would be a most worthless thing at these cold temperatures. The stove actually warmed the tent up enough to take our outer coats off.

Going outside to go potty was a real experience! Fred had the problem of having to go frequently. In the process, one of the zippers, the main one on the tent flap, broke. To keep the wind from entirely blowing through, we zipped the mosquito net fly, which kind of held the other fly close together.

The wind stirred up all night long, causing a flapping tent and a howl that made our cuddly Quallofill sleeping bags feel very good.

Bert and Curley were flown to their camp four or five miles down the valley from us. They took the oxygen equipment with them. We had brought only one regulator, along with four bottles, which when properly filled would be about 13 hours of straight oxygen. In Dushanbe, we had a terrible time getting the bottles filled. It appeared to be entirely over the head of Raphik to get it done.

**The Marco polo sheep hunting camp.**

*We explained that airlines, hospitals, welders and many others used oxygen. As it was, they did not fill the bottles to 2,400 pounds per square inch as instructed, but only about 1,800, reducing our supply down to two-thirds capacity. We had a worse problem with white gas. Even though Rafael said "Do not worry, have confidence, you will have white gas." As it was we had none and suffered in camp from the lack of it.*

*03 November*

*We were up at daybreak and ready to hunt. Fred found ice in his rifle bolt mechanism, and it wouldn't fire. Michel got some kerosene and bathed the whole mechanism, making everything ok. We then spotted five rams bedded down on a hill less than 1,000 yards away from camp. They were too small for this early in the hunt. The tips just past a full curl and barely flattened out on the tip.*

*Vladimir Brizgalow was my guide. I was now able to hunt, using Bob's permit. Vladimir was a big man, over six feet tall, lean and a rugged-looking person. He was not a Tajik, as he had reddish hair and beard—probably a Russian or Scandinavian type from northwestern U.S.S.R. The other assistant in camp, whose name I failed to note came along. We started out in the direction taken by the herd of sheep that were feeding at our campsite when we landed yesterday. The tracks led us northeasterly into the valley that is the pass between Balandkiik Valley and Kaindy Valley—the same pass that we flew yesterday in the copter coming into Camp 2.*

*We spotted a herd of ibexes in the rocky side hill of the pass. There were about 20 altogether. I saw horns, but did not give them a second*

Because of the presence of snow everywhere, we wore white coveralls in order to blend in.

*look, as I was only looking for Poli. Soon we spotted a single ram across the canyon about a mile away—not too big a trophy, but worth keeping an eye on. The tracks of yesterday's rams led us quite a way into the valley.*

*Vladimir spotted a band of rams coming from the direction of Kaindy Valley coming toward Balyandkiik on the opposite side of the canyon. There were nine rams, but nothing really big, all less than 50 inches in horn length. We decided to stop on a knoll and just watch for a while. We had been hiking for about three hours now and I really welcomed a rest. It was slow moving for me. My legs were OK, but shortage of breath in the thin air was my limiting factor, as we were pushing snow all the time.*

*Soon eight more rams were coming across the same route as the previous nine, which was from our left to right. These were big! No question about size of most of them. When you see a big trophy, there is no doubt. They all had a flare to the horns and a few of them pointed down nicely on the tips.*

*The Marco Polo sheep has the most spectacular horns of all the wild sheep. When the horns spiral out and turn down at the tip, it is a breath-taking sight for any mountain hunter.*

*They angled up higher on the other side of the valley than the younger herd earlier. The distance straight across was at least a half-mile. We elected to stay put as sheep have the best eyesight of all the big game. Even though we had the white clothing, they could easily catch our movement. We were in the open and except for a gorge in the bottom of the valley, there was no cover at all between us and the sheep, so we were pinned down until they were out of the valley.*

*More sheep appeared in the distance coming from the same direction. They were female and young coming in single file over a rise. I counted, as they appeared—10, 20, 30, 40—55 altogether marching in single file much lower than the rams.*

*Then 11 more ewes and young boiled out of the gorge below us—83 Marco Polo sheep in view at one time! I was so excited and intent at looking at the big rams that I forgot to take my camera out until most of the sheep had passed. A dozen or so of the female and young bedded down about 300 yards across from us, so I took pictures of them.*

*Once the "wave" went around the edge of the mountain onto the other side, we made our move. Unfortunately we had to give up some of that hard-earned elevation we gained by dropping down into the gorge below and start climbing up the other side.*

*The sheep were all out of the valley now and heading toward a northern branch of Balandkiik, Zulum Archa. Vladimir indicated that Fred went straight toward that valley. I gave little chance of catching up with the big rams, unless they bedded down, so I hoped that Fred would be in position to intercept them.*

*The sheep that we saw here were definitely in a migration pattern coming from the rugged mountain in the head of Kaindy Valley (where Michel told me earlier that there were no Poli) It could be that the three round trips yesterday by the chopper through Kaindy was the cause of the movement.*

*Climbing up the other face of the valley was tough on me. I was following Vladimir, taking two steps to his one, so I was bucking snow, which was between one foot and two feet deep. I could feel the pressure on my lungs and, especially, my diaphragm. Finally we rounded the ridge onto the south slope—less snow, but lousy footing on the steep rocky hillside. There was just enough snow that we didn't know what was under it—a great way to turn an ankle, or much worse slip and fall.*

*As we entered Zulum Archa, we spotted Fred on top of a knoll. I assumed he had not made connection with the rams, as nothing was in sight. When we approached nearer, I called "Didn't you see those rams?" His answer was "Yes, I got a hellava trophy!" How happy I was for him. He is the first foreigner to take Marco Polo sheep in the Soviet Pamirs since the Roosevelt expedition some 60 years ago!*

He truly did have a great trophy. It was a tight curl with the tips pointing almost straight down. He had fired twice, but we did not hear the shots, probably because we were in the other valley at the time. Fred supervised the skinning job and had the full skin off the carcass—Michel and Rahman cut the meat up. They were glad to see my guides show up to help pack everything out. It was two hours steady walking over fairly easy terrain back to camp. My day's walking was in the shape of a big triangle, with a lot of ups and downs.

It was getting dark when we arrived in camp. While shedding our ice-covered outer clothing outside, we spotted 15 rams on the mountain south of our camp. They appeared to be emerging from a side valley that we had not looked into. In the dim light it was hard to judge horn size, but some looked good. The guides were shouting among themselves about

**Michael Frolov joins Fred Fortier in the first photo of the first Marco Polo sheep taken in the Soviet Union in modern times.**

something. I indicated by putting my hand on my mouth to be silent. Michel brought a two-page note written in Russian over to me and explained in a few English words along with sign language that Curley was sick down in Camp 4. One guide came through our camp during the day to get two more bottles of oxygen from the main camp (Camp 2) and dropped off the note. It indicated that the copter would come in tomorrow and pick Curley up to take him out. They got on our radio and talked to someone. When radioing, they would shout loud enough that if the radio didn't work, their voices would carry to the other end! We didn't give much hope for the sheep still being around after all the commotion.

Fred and I talked over what to do and decided there was nothing we could do tonight. If we did try to go down, we would have to take bedding, tents and other provisions. We were not equipped to pack our outfit around. Also there was the chance that one of us could get hurt on the trip down in the dark on the trail.

About midnight we heard Safar's voice calling my name. He and the doctor were on their way from Camp 2 with two bottles of oxygen that had been taken from the helicopter when we first arrived. Safar thought that Curley had heart trouble, which really concerned us. We gave Safar a thermos of tea and some candy bars. He also told us that the radio had not worked in their camp because they had forgotten one of the parts. So they took our radio along. We finally were able to sleep some after being assured that the copter was coming in the morning with another doctor from Dushanbe.

Happy Birthday Chris! It was a great day except for the bad news about Curley. Seeing 104 Marco Polo sheep in one day was a sight I never expected to see.

04 November

I got out of bed at the first light and went out glassing for sheep. I was thrilled to see nine rams on the hillside up the valley. They were moving in the direction of Camp 2. There were definitely some good trophies in the band. Fred did not want to hunt today, but rather take care of his skin, which still needed some attention around the head and feet. Vladimir asked if he could take his rifle along and Fred agreed. He showed Vladimir that there were three shells down in the magazine and none in the chamber. He pulled the trigger to make sure the mechanism was not frozen up again. He then gave Vladimir his belt holder with spare bullets. I then took the gun and showed him the safety—forward to fire and back for safety. He seemed to be a very experienced guide in every way. In fact, Fred and I continuously praised the ability and helpfulness of the guides, unlike the almost total incapability of Intourist.

So with me today was Vladimir, Rahman (Fred's assigned guide) and Michel—all the top guides. I felt they wanted to put everything possible into obtaining success for me, because of the many delays and hardships that we have

had up till now. Vladimir asked if the sling could be extended as he carried the rifle all the way over his head instead of just over one shoulder. I showed him he had to loosen the screw in the sling and it could be made longer. He indicted that was too much bother, so he led off with Rahman behind him, then Michel and me in a line. In the two times we've been out, Michel always stuck close to me, making sure that I was always OK, and to see if he could help me.

I had kept watch on the rams as they rounded the mountain toward Camp 2. If they stayed on course would pass just a few hundred yards above the camp. We walked for about one hour at a steady pace in the river bottom, sometimes crossing the ice on the edge. I was the slowest of the four of us. My sea-level lungs were still lagging in this thin air, so I tried to pace myself so that I didn't get super tired. Even at that, there would be times that I would literally be gasping to get enough oxygen.

Vladimir and Rahman, about 35 yards ahead of Michel and me, started to climb up the slope out of the river bottom. While I was looking down to assure good footing, the sharp crack of a rifle echoed from the two ahead of us. In looking up I saw one of the white-cloaked figures sliding down the steep, snow-covered bank. In a split second the second figure slid down.

All within a second or two, many thoughts passed through my mind. Why did one of them shoot? Did he fire at one of two young rams that we had jumped in the river bottom just a short while before? Did the kick of the rifle *throw him slightly off balance, just enough to cause him to slip on the slick side hill? Did the one falling cause the other to fall down and slide down as well? Did the gun go off accidentally, causing them to slip? Then the thought of disgust passed through my mind, with the sound of the gunshot causing the rams we were pursuing to spook.*

*A shout from them and a distressful moan from Michel changed my mood from disgust to distress. Then shouting rang out between Michel and one of them, while Michel darted forward and I instinctively followed, knowing the situation was serious—one of them must be wounded!*

*Rahman was kneeling over the limp body of Vladimir! Then Michel, both testing for signs of life. I knew when they stood up, fell back and raised their hands upward to heaven, that Vladimir was no longer with us. Shock possessed us all, followed by silence, as we all three wandered off a ways, each having words with God.*

*Michel and Rahman went over to the river, where there was a hole in the ice and reached down, throwing handfuls of icy cold water into their faces. Reality came to me. We had to take Vladimir's body out. He was a huge man and we could not carry him out. There are no trees to make poles, no bushes to make a biviak. We were miles from camp. The only hope would be the helicopter, hopefully, that was summoned to pick up Curley.*

*I called the two guides and, mostly through sign language, pointed toward Camp 2 and Camp 3—"radio"—"helicopter." They nodded, motioned for me to stay here and both trotted off in opposite directions. I took my outer parka off and spread it over the head of Vladimir. Where was the rifle? I took Vladimir's walking stick and started digging through the snow. No rifle. Finally I spotted the sling showing out of the snow about 30 feet above, on a small ledge. I couldn't take being in view of the body anymore, so gathered my pack and rifle and switch backed up the hill. I pulled Fred's rifle out from under*

**Rahman has words with God over the body of Vladimir Brizgalow, while shocked Michael Frolov sits above in the rocks. The tragic ending of this historical hunt. (Note: Because the hunt had to be called off, Bob Chisholm and Chris returned the following spring for a successful hunt.)**

the snow, but left it lying basically where it was, as I wanted others to see where it had fallen at the time of the accident.

I went to the flat area above the riverbank. A brief scan assured me that it would be perfect for the helicopter to land. I took my ski pole, which was furnished me in Dushanbe for a walking stick, and blew up a gigantic orange balloon (that wife Colleene had given me before my departure from Seattle, after printing "HERE I AM" on it) and attached it to the pole, placing it in the middle of the helipad.

I worked my way over to an outcrop of rocks, still in a daze, and spread out my gear. I put a bullet in the chamber of my rifle, thinking if I was intended to get a Poli ram on this trip, he would come strolling across the slope above me—my only hope on this trip.

In the next couple of hours, a thousand thoughts passed through my mind. What kind of fate is this for me? Death is not new to me on hunting trips, I wondered how many people who hunted all over the world, even knew a person who died in a hunting accident. The chance of a hunter being on the scene of such a death is probably 1 in 10 million. I shook my head—this was the third time a similar thing happened to me!

The first time, some 20 years ago, when I first made my way into the Afghanistan Pamirs, a couple hundred miles south of here, with hunting companion Bill Picher from Orange Cove, California, was a horrible experience. We were hunting Marco Polo sheep under very difficult conditions. We were five days by yak down to the nearest civilization. Bill developed (with little known at that time) pulmo-nary edema. Shortly after I recognized Bill had a serious problem, while I was organizing his evacuation, he died in my arms.

The second time, about seven years ago, my good friend and hunting companion, Arthur Carlsberg of Los Angeles, California, and I were hunting for the second time together for tur in the Caucasus Mountains of the Soviet Union. Art had taken a really nice Silver Medal tur. On the way down on the very steep slopes, Art fell right in front of me and couldn't stop himself and went to his death a thousand feet below!

In both cases, long, drawn-out evacuations, hardships, depositions on top of depositions and trying to avoid the press, were the things that made a very bad thing worse, not to mention the dread of and eventually facing the widows and families of the deceased.

Even though I only knew Vladimir a short while, the camaraderie of huntsmen brings people rapidly together. Together, you rough the elements, outsmart the game, share your binocu-lars, split your candy bars, drink out of the same canteen, share the excitement of spotting that trophy ram, etc. etc. You become the closest of companions, sharing the same wonderful inter-ests! I felt deeply for Vladimir and his family—I had learned he had a wife, five-month-old child and six-year-old child.

Why did Vladimir have a bullet in the chamber? Why was it off safety? When I checked the rifle below, it was off safety. In reconstructing what probably happened, Vladimir and Rahman had just reached the small ledge, climbing the bank. He obviously had the rifle in one hand and his walking stick in the other. He probably slipped and jammed both the stick and the butt of the rifle into the ground to catch himself. The rifle discharged and sent the bullet right up through the bottom of his chest and out the top of his shoulder. There is a possibility some ice formed in the mechanism causing it to go off easily—who knows?

About 2½ hours had passed and Rahman called to me from the bank above the river. He motioned for me to come down. I went over and saw that Fred was coming up the bank. He was beside himself. He didn't know whether it was I or one of the guides who was involved. Nor did he know the extent of the accident. The language barrier was a real problem. He had brought a sleeping bag thinking one of us would need the warmth and comfort.

We made a feeble attempt to try to drag the big corpse up the slope, but no possibility. I don't know how much time passed, but later in the afternoon we heard the helicopter. From the sound, we knew it had landed in Curley and Bert's camp. It then took off and came up the valley, following the river. We all got out waving in our little snowfield. It homed right in on us and landed.

Neither Curley nor Bert was in the copter. Through sign language and a few known Tajik and Russian words, we got the message that they were going to report in to the base camp, and then evacuate both Curley and Bert. They also indicated that Curley had pulmonary edema, the oxygen saved him and he was OK. I motioned to them to bring a rope or hoist to bring the corpse up to the flat.

Another hour passed and the chopper returned with a sling and rope. It took all of us including the three-man crew of the copter to pull the big huntsman up to the flat. All boarded and we went to Camp 2 to visit with Michel, who had gotten the message through for us on the radio. The weather was beginning to deteriorate once again. Fred and I had a serious talk about whether we should abandon the hunt at this time.

Not to mention the helicopter flying up and down the valley several times and scaring the game out of walking reach, we analyzed the continuous problems that we had right from the start:

- A four-day delay in getting to Moscow
- Another four-day delay getting to camp
- The mini bus having the collision on the way to the airport
- Bob getting sick and having to turn back
- Curley getting pulmonary edema
- Now this tragic accident
- The weather turning bad—we might be here till Thanksgiving!

We decided to go back and leave some of the bad luck for someone else. We talked to Michel and the pilot about stopping at our camp, so that we could pick up our personal effects. They agreed.

Curley's guide was in the chopper and advised us that we should stop at Camp 4 and pick up some more of Curley's items that were left behind in his hasty departure. So we stopped at Camp 3, while the chopper's blades were still turning, Fred and I did the world's record packing job of as many personal effects as we could lay our hands on. We left all the camp gear, including sleeping bags, stoves etc—a couple of the staff stayed in the camp.

Into the air again and landed five minutes later down the valley in Camp 4. The blast of the copter practically blew the camp down! Curley's guide disembarked and got his personal effects (Curley's, that is) and brought them to us and bid farewell. The flight down Balyandkiik was interesting, since we had not arrived this route. The valley soon became narrower and less and less sheep country.

The sheep like the wide rolling valleys, as opposed to the narrower and rugged gorges. The valley became very steep and the mountains rose sharply above us. The river bottom is a rough and rugged gorge. Earlier we had talked about the possibility of riding yaks up in the future from Camp 1 to Camp 2. Now I had doubts about that possibility—just too rough.

As we neared the end of Balyandkiik Canyon (not "valley" anymore), we got a great view of Fedchenko Glacier, or at least the last few miles of its foot. Then a right turn brought us out into the familiar wide river bottom of the head of the Muksu, and then we got sight of Camp 1.

Bert and Curley met us, and we all embraced and expressed thanks that we were all healthy. Curley was feeling quite good, but very weak. No doubt his lungs were still partially filled with fluid—the deadly symptom of pulmonary edema. The oxygen supply had been removed from the helicopter earlier for his use. A doctor was sent here from Dushanbe.

The pilot announced another delay—Dushanbe was weathered in again! This time heavy thunder showers, presenting a dangerous situation and no possibility of returning tonight. In taking count of sleeping bags et al, there was just barely enough for the guests and none for the chopper crew. They decided it best for them to fly the corpse to the nearest town, Dzhirgatal, about a half-hour flight down river, and stay there.

Vladimir Snegerenko, the assistant to Raphik Kapharov in Moscow, had come down to get a look at the sheep program, so he had made it this far. I was glad to see him, as he was a good friend for many years. He was very ill-equipped clothing-wise, so I gave him a bunch of gear from boots to caps.

Food was very skimpy here, except for freeze-dried and other food we had brought. I got the dinner-making process underway, while Bert and Fred did the final skinning on the feet, ears, lips etc. on the sheep and salted it down. By bedtime I was really rummy, and the terrible accident today still had me in semi-shock. I could hardly sleep, reliving the accident.

In the morning there was a slight skiff of snow. I made instant oatmeal with dried banana chips, along with some canned bacon. It was midmorning before the chopper arrived, so I had a lot of time to visit with Vladimir. I gave him a list of all the gear that we brought, along with instructions for storing it for next year's hunts. I also gave him my ideas for properly structuring the program, alternating valleys and not putting too much pressure on any one area. I asked him to talk it over in detail with Michel and finalize the hunt plan now.

*There were two coroners who arrived with the helicopter. They asked Fred and me to go to the dining tent to start the inevitable depositions. I knew this was coming. The pilot stopped our deposition and said we had to leave.*

*Thank God we headed in the direction of Dushanbe, but did stop at Dzhirgatal and finished the depositions. The pilot was chomping at the bit and very upset with the delay, which did hurry along the depositions. I was glad that the body was not put on the helicopter. There is a road to here from Dushanbe, so no doubt they sent to corpse down by road.*

*Upon arrival in Dushanbe, a whole host of people, doctors, ambulances and a bus were there to meet us, including Rafael. The Soviet version of "Medic 1" checked Curley over and found his lungs to be clear. Everyone wanted to hear the first-hand story of what happened in the accident. Upon arrival at the hotel, Fred and I were asked not to drink, as the coroner and prosecuting attorney were to take depositions. Damn!*

*Bob was there with open arms—very happy to see us in good health. He presented me with a birthday present he carried all the way from the States, a bottle of Crown Royal Canadian whiskey, and a favorite of mine. We did not dare drink in the hunting camps, especially at high altitude—a dangerous thing indeed—and I was ready to unwind after all the frustrations! Fred and I spent until around 10 PM in the depositions. We missed dinner, but headed for the "Dollar Bar."*

*The head of the game department (Michel's boss) met us and visited, in addition to supplying us with an export permit for the trophy. Rafael joined in and we enjoyed many rounds of good ole "Stoli" (Stolichnaya) vodka and camaraderie till about midnight. They agreed that Bob and I could return for a spring hunt around late March, along with Curley, if he wanted to try again.*

*We sent a letter to Vladimir's wife expressing our condolences.*

I returned to the Balandkiik Reserve in the spring of '88, along with Bob Chisholm, where we successfully collected Marco Polo sheep specimens. That trip was important for two reasons, not only to test conditions for spring hunting, but also to meet with the Tajik officials privately.

This time there were no Intourist representatives present, so I had the opportunity to review their future desires. It became apparent, with Perestroika clearly in view that they did not desire to work with Moscow. However, they were uncertain just how to proceed, as they were in the process of restructuring their own government. I discussed a broader hunting program, which not only would expand the Poli hunts deeper into the Pamirs, but also to hunt the lowlands to include markhor, urial sheep, ibex and bear. Plans were made for an exploratory trip in early fall.

Pete Papac and Ray Follosco were scheduled to hunt in September for Marco Polo sheep (still through Intourist), so I planned to accompany them to Dushanbe. The two brought their wives, Virginia Papac and Dolly Follosco, but observers were not allowed on the Poli hunts, so Intourist arranged sight-seeing for the two gals and me.

This so-called sightseeing was for me to look over urial sheep and bear areas all through the foothills of this most mountainous republic. The gals and I checked out areas all along the Uzbekistan and Afghanistan borders, as well as right up to Tajikistan's steep escarpment that eventually rises to the impenetrable Mount Kommunizma.

Further talks with the Tajiks revealed their definite plan to break away from Intourist and Moscow in general. Yet it appeared they were not quite ready to handle the wildlife program and would continue to work with Intourist for the time being.

Back in Moscow I met a Russian couple that had contacted me and requested employment with my company. They were Peter and Irina Afonin, a young couple who were positioning themselves for entrepreneurship. Peter was a biologist working for the game department concerning future business, while Irina was a nurse, and most importantly, they both spoke English quite well.

I ended up hiring Peter to come to Seattle where he would be my liaison for the ever-increasing Soviet contacts who mostly did not communicate in English. I took Peter on a trip, visiting officials in Kazakhstan, Kirgizstan, Uzbekistan and Azerbaijan with the idea of him being my spokesman concerning future business.

I should have known better, but to my surprise, the high officials did not want to deal with a Russian from Moscow. Even though Peter was allowed in the meetings, he was often stuck in a corner and my communications were through a local ethnic interpreter. They had enough of Russian dominance and wanted to deal with the American, Chris Klineburger. Peter was important to me back in Seattle, as the Russian language was universal even with the Asians, but communications were always signed by me, not Peter the Russian.

## REFLECTION
# Shooting at High Altitudes

**I** supplied a great amount of information for people traveling to under-developed countries. Many things are different at high altitudes, including rifle performance. The hunting in much of Asia was often 10,000 or more feet higher than experienced in North America and Europe. Here is one information sheet relating to shooting:

Rifles will have a much different performance at high altitudes than they will at sea level. To give an idea of the difference in drop of a 150-grain bullet from a 7mm Remington Magnum at 16,000 feet as compared to sea level, the following is an indication of how much higher a bullet will shoot at the higher elevation:

400 yards—plus 4 inches

600 yards—plus 16 inches

800 yards—plus 44 inches

1,000 yards—plus 114 inches

(In other words, if you were sighted in for 400 yards at sea level, you would be shooting 4 inches high at 16,000 feet at that distance.)

As one can well see, at the greater distances a rifle shoots much flatter in the thinner air. This is because of less air resistance. Most of the misses at these elevations have been because of overshooting.

Because of the complete lack of trees or even bushes, much of the shooting is at fairly long range. A person should be well equipped to shoot at longer distances and, if at all possible, try to have it figured out beforehand, in view of the fact that you might not have the time to make calculations at the time you stalk.

Sight in your rifle again as soon as you get into high altitude at accurately paced-off distances to see what the comparative trajectories are for your rifle and loads. In case you have a rangefinder in your scope, this distance between brisket and top of shoulder on a mature Marco Polo ram is 24 inches, and on an Ibex 18 inches. (Most rangefinders are calibrated to 18 inches.)

# CHAPTER 14

# A Historic Change; The CIS

After more than 70 years of strict communist rule the Union of Soviet Socialist Republics (U.S.S.R.) became the Commonwealth of Independent States (CIS). Perestroika, Mikhail Gorbachev's program of economic, political, and social restructuring became the unintended catalyst for dismantling the former totalitarian state. Gorbachev introduced policies designed to begin establishing a market economy by encouraging limited private ownership and profitability in Soviet industry.

This change was a major opportunity for me and a definite blow for the Hunt Section of Intourist, whose progress was too little, too late. Having done my homework and especially keeping in touch with many of the republics, I had almost a free hand to establish programs for the most desirable wildlife. In 1988 and early 1989 my time was occupied with many organizational trips to the CIS. My first trip with a joint venture went smoothly to the far east of Siberia in the Autonomous republic of Yakut. The following are some journal entries of that hunt, as well as of business meetings in my temporary Moscow office in the apartment of Irina Afonin:

*20 August 1989*

*After 20 years of negotiating with the Soviets, I am now en route to Siberia for the first expedition for Asiatic Bighorn sheep. In the late sixties, I first started my talks with Intourist, the official Soviet travel agency. Valery Uvarov, the head of the New York Intourist office at the time, made arrangements for me and a client, Dr. Arthur Twomey representing the Carnegie Museum of Pittsburg, to explore the three hunting reserves that were established in the U.S.S.R. for use by their hierarchy. Valery said, "If you want to know about the hunting, you will have to go find out for yourself."*

*He then arranged for a six-week visa, and we were off to the Kubinsk Reserve in Azerbaijan, the North Ossetia Reserve in the Autonomous republic of N. Ossetia and the Krasnaya Polyana Reserve in Russia all in the Caucasus Mountains. The result of that trip was the opening of hunting and I established the first tariffs of the U.S.S.R. hunting program. (See Chapter 4 in this part of the book). Since then, I worked with various republics and Intourist, tutoring them on the importance of sustaining their wildlife.*

*Last March I was in Moscow on a travel agency conference and visited with my good friend Valery Uvarov. We reminisced over the years of frustrations working with Intourist and their sluggishness in making progress. I asked Valery what he would do if he were I to expedite hunting in the U.S.S.R.*

*He said flatly, "Do joint ventures," meaning I would get nowhere continuing with Intourist.*

*This gave me the green light to aggressively pursue many leads that I had developed over the years.*

*Earlier this year we hired a young Russian man from Moscow, Peter Afonin, to help beef up our U.S.S.R. Section of Klineburger Worldwide Travel. On that same trip in March, I visited Peter Afonin's wife who made appointments with some of Peter's associates in the Wildlife Department, where Peter used to work. That and a well-known reputation of our own, started contacts flowing in from various geographic areas, including an area in northeast Siberia, where a joint venture formed a division, Concord Hunting Services. To make a long story short, we arranged an exploratory expedition into a remote area beyond Yakutsk in the Autonomous Region of Yakutia.*

*Even though it was a last-minute plan, I was able to get a few hunters to join, including dear friends and hunting companions, Bob Chisholm of Wichita, Pete Papac of Montesano, Washington, and Warren Parker of Kansas City who has been very active in the formation of the Foundation for North American Wild Sheep and now one of the officers of Safari Club International.*

*The plan was for Peter Afonin to accompany me on this trip to pick up first-hand hunting experience. His visa was not approved when I left. I have the whole week ahead for appointments in Moscow and I wanted Peter in on them, as well.*

*I purchased all of the expedition equipment to outfit us on this journey including most of the food. I have seven large checked-in bags,* weighing in excess of 300 pounds. I checked them in at the sidewalk at United Airlines for my connection to Vancouver, B.C. to connect with Lufthansa to Frankfurt and on to Moscow. The $25 accompanying my ticket did wonders with the skycap—no excess baggage charge!

## TIME LAPSE

At Moscow—first, through Immigration and then claim my "cargo" at baggage claim. I was able to find two pushcarts, and then had a time holding on to them, as people tried taking them. Once loaded, I headed for the uncertainty of clearing Customs with all the hunting gear. Having a firearm always helps to divert their attention, so that's all they looked at and seemed uninterested in all my huge bags.

I found Irina Alfonin waiting with several men. The one, Yuri Puchkov spoke perfect English, as did Irina. Yuri is the doctor scheduled to go with us to Siberia, so he was used as a translator. Vladimir Treschov, the head of the Concord Travel & Hunting Services was there to greet me. There was also a representative of Nash Dom, another joint venture company that had previously contacted me to develop a hunting program.

We were able to cram all my gear and the passengers into two compact Russian cars, with no room to spare. A half-hour drive got us to Irina's apartment, which was to be my headquarters for the week to follow. It is in the back streets of a large apartment complex, not unlike hundreds of others all over the Moscow area. The flat is a modest 6th floor apartment, two bedrooms, kitchen, living/dining room, toilet and bath. My bedroom is their late son's

room—a hit-and-run motorcyclist killed him earlier this year.

Irina's friend, Eldenora (Elja) had been busily fixing dinner and awaiting our arrival. We all crowded around the small table filled with nicely decorated typical Russian food. After a couple of toasts, in true Russian down-the-hatch style, we devoured the cuisine and carried on hunting talk till midnight—by now well over 30 hours since I had left my bed in Seattle.

*22 August*

I was wide awake at 4 AM. According to my body, it was still daytime and no time to be sleeping! Oh well, a good time to get my files in good order for the many talks scheduled for all week long.

At 10 AM our driver delivered us to the Concord office complex a two-story office building on the Moscow River, a 10-minute walk to Red Square, as central as one could be. A plush meeting room was set up and in attendance were Vladimir, Alexander Koklov, and Yuri, as well as Andrei Babenko, with whom we had all our first communications and established our working relationship.

Also in attendance was Victor Naishuller, vice-chairman of Concord. Concord Cooperative is a joint venture with a foreign company that specializes in trade and service of small appliances. They have offices in several locations throughout the U.S.S.R. Our talks now centered on final plans for the expedition, as well as other programs that would give Concord Hunting Services year-round activities.

*Apparently these foreign cooperatives are approached by local game departments asking for foreign hunters, which leads to them inquiring with the Moscow departments that handle wildlife matters, resulting in our name coming up. These joint ventures have only really gotten into operation this past year, so recently we have had many contacts directly and indirectly from co-ops like Concord asking if we would become involved with them on hunting programs in various geographic locations of the U.S.S.R.*

*Once Concord indicated they had connections in Siberia, I jumped on the chance that we might get permission to hunt for the Asiatic bighorn sheep, a trophy I have attempted to get open for the past 20 years with Intourist, with complete failure. To make a long story short, we got permission to do an exploratory trip to an area a few hundred kilometers beyond Yakutsk in northeastern Siberia.*

*Alexander then drove me back to the apartment where another joint venture group was awaiting my 3:30 appointment. This was with ASK Cooperative attended by Sergey & Alexei Nazarevsky and Michael Savostyanov. Among the areas that they do business, Kyrgyzstan SSR caught my attention, as it is an area that has both argali sheep and urial sheep, along with some other game—they promised by next Monday (five days from now) that they would have more info on hunting possibilities and scheduled another meeting.*

*While finishing up over dinner with the ASK group, Ali Jeidar from Azerbaijan SSR arrived for an evening meeting. Ali is from a newly formed company called Association Azerbaijan and they are developing additional tourism and wish to expand into hunting and fishing. His director had met me years before in Azerbaijan where I first went in 1970 in the inception of the U.S.S.R. hunting program. He offered new areas for tur, bear, stag, roe, boar, and waterfowl—he wanted me to go into a joint venture with them. Today was just a preview of what I was to do for the remaining of the week—up till midnight every day with meetings with several groups per day.*

*23-26 August*

*All week long, meetings from morning to late night. One evening, the Nash Dom joint venture group—Nicoli Guriev, Sergei & Irina Gasevich and Sergei Ganusevich—drove me on a city tour and then took me through Arbat walking street, the Soviet version of Greenwich Village of New York. Then to Sergei and Irina's apartment near the Kremlin, where we had dinner and drinks along with business talks. This group are real hunters and will probably be some that we can work with in the future.*

*Michael Frolov, the head of Hunting & Wildlife Department of Tajikistan SSR, came to Moscow to see me. I have been negotiating with him to arrange a direct relationship with his republic to be their general agent for all the hunting there. This is the place where we did the first exploratory trip for Marco Polo sheep in 1987 and where I returned to hunt in March of 1988. It appears my negotiations are progressing well.*

*Another republic to contact me was Georgia SSR. Alexander Abuladze came to tell about the current possibilities there, which are limited to falconeering, fishing and game viewing, as a result of the recent ban on guns because of the revolutionary activities in the area of Georgia, Armenia, and parts of Azerbaijan.*

*Besides several meetings with not-too-likely candidates, we had very positive meetings with people and organizations that could influence the future of our Soviet relationship. Glavakhota, the main Board of Hunting and Reserves for the Russian Federation (about 3/4 of all the Soviet Union), came in strong with the proposals of Vladimir Fertikov, the organization's Deputy Chief.*

*Vladimir wants to work directly with us and said, "The Government will always be here, while the joint ventures will come and go." He wants a representative from our organization to go to the Baikal region and see their first*

**Of the countless business meetings I had in Moscow, one of notoriety stood out. Vladimir Fertikov, the Director of Glavakhota, wanted to work directly with me. From left, myself, four chiefs of Glavakhota with Vladimir on the end, and Irina Afonin, my coordinator/translator.**

*proposed area for brown bear, Asian wapiti, moose, Siberian roe deer, etc.*

*Another very interesting meeting was with the head of the Military Reserves for all of the U.S.S.R. There are scores of reserves set aside for wildlife that are available for military personnel. Apparently it is a rare military person who hunted these reserves, some of which are quite remote. So now they want foreign hunters to utilize these reserves.*

*It would be impossible (and somewhat boring) to go into much detail about the many meetings that I had, so I will mention only a couple more. Alexander Lisitsin, the Head of the North European Section of Intourist, a friend (and hunter) whom I previously had visits with, would like to quit his job with Intourist and go to work for us in whatever capacity we could use him—and he would be good.*

*Valery Uvarov, whom I made mention of previously, would like to quit his Intourist job and form a joint venture with us for developing a good, solid wildlife program throughout the U.S.S.R.*

*Living in a Russian home has been very interesting. Irina has been telling me about the shopping and lack of availability of goods. Our menu has been heavy on chicken, which is about double the cost of beef here—so she thought by getting the most expensive meat, it would be the right thing to do. The beef is lean and tough, so it is understandable that it is low cost. I guess that's why beef stroganoff is popular here, as it is nothing but a stew—a way to use tough meat.*

Bananas become available in the local store occasionally. Last time she waited three hours in line and they ran out just before she got to them. A long wait in line is an every day occurrence. When something good is available, she will buy a year's supply. Irina said sugar is rationed now. She feels the reason is to prevent the people from having enough to make their own wine, vodka and brandy. Her parents live in an apartment a 15-minute walk away. She told of them making wine so we went over to check it out. They had about 20 liters of choke cherry wine working in a couple of big jugs under their kitchen table. We sampled some left over from last year, and it was delicious.

Living in the small flat was also Irina's sister Kate and her husband. Also here right now was their cousin Corska, just now out of serving his mandatory two years in the army. This was a stop en route to his home in the Stravapol Region of the North Caucasus. He took a liking to me and gave me his military hat. He also likes to cook and kept asking us to come over to eat. One time we had ¾ of an hour to spare, so we dashed over to try a drink he made in a hollowed-out watermelon. It was a mixture of champagne, wine and some spices, a tasty drink as was the watermelon afterwards. Corska came over to our apartment and cooked a delicious lamb steak and hash.

Whatever is left over from the night before ends up on the breakfast table. That's the way it is here—nothing is wasted. There was a rather dry white cheese appearing on the table at most meals. She explained that was the only one available in the market now. Everything seemed to be that way, probably the way it was 50 or 100 years ago in the U.S.A.

One of the joint ventures, Nova Forya, a perfume manufacturer among other things, invited me to a sauna on Sunday. They said it was a traditional way to have business talks. They picked me up early and took me to the private club reserved for them for the day. We started out in the steam room followed by a dip in the pool. Then I was ushered into a room and placed against a wall. A pretty blond lady proceeded to massage me with a high-pressure hose. Following that it was in a tub, where she used a pressure nozzle all over my body. Back to the steam room and then back in the pool again. Then we settled in a tearoom and commenced business talks. One of them was a Georgian and he broke out a bottle of Georgian wine, the best known in the U.S.S.R. They had a video set up and showed some film of traditional and modern ballet and a troupe of Georgian dancers. The Georgian fellow was one of the stars in the Georgian troupe. They were looking for connections to get their shows in the U.S.A. and wanted me to try to help make contacts. Their other business is travel, so most of our talks were centered on what I could do for them.

About midday, I was surprised to see Elja (the lady who cooked dinner the night of my arrival) and another girl come with a group of men—I had been told this was for men only! They went through the whole sauna bit like we did and then Elja joined us. I guess I should mention the dress here is swim trunks—Elja looked great in a scant bikini.

Cocktails before dinner at the home of Yuri and Irina Puchkov, when Pete, Bob, and Warren arrived in Moscow. Yuri was to be our camp doctor, while Vladimir Treschov would be the head guide. From left, Yuri, Vladimir and Elena Treschov, and Irina.

*27 August*

*In the evening the three hunters were scheduled in. Vladimir and his wife Elena picked Irina and I up and we proceeded to the airport. 1½ hours after the Lufthansa flight arrived, Pete, Bob, and Warren went right through customs, guns and all, without the officer looking at anything. After driving them to the Central House of Tourists Hotel and checked them in, we all went to the home of Yuri Puchkov and his wife Irina.*

*It was Yuri's birthday, so they had a great party that we all enjoyed, with all the fancy Russian cuisine, vodka, brandy, champagne—the works! They had a few of their very close friends present, so everyone enjoyed being in the home of a Soviet.*

## TIME LAPSE

*29 August–Afternoon*

*At the hotel we had a farewell banquet set up for all the staff and the wives, then depar-*

*ture for the Domodedovo airport for our "scheduled" 7:55 PM flight to Yakutsk. We were running a little late and the staff was getting concerned. I said, "Don't worry, the flight will be late." (From a lot of experience with domestic flights here in around 20 years of continuous traveling to and in the U.S.S.R. Late? Yes, would you believe 5½ hours?*

*Alexander must have known about a delay, he had a big carry-on bag full of booze, sausages, and bread. We found a room upstairs in the airport terminal that wasn't being used, so set up our private party room and whittled away at the time waiting for our now 1:45 AM departure. Our baggage was 310 kilograms overweight, which cost two rubles per kg, 620 rubles!—About $1,000 on the 1.65 exchange rate, but we used black market rubles.*

*Once on the aircraft, we were crowded in the world's most uncomfortable airline seats. Poor Bob and Pete, both big and over six feet, had their knees crammed into the seats in front. Even though it was a scheduled dinner flight, they still had to force onto us a now well-aged chicken and rice dinner at 3 AM, just when we were starting to doze off. With the six-hour flight and six-hour time change, it was 2 PM when we arrived in Yakutsk.*

*30 August*

*We were met at the aircraft, which incidentally is an IL62, a conventional-sized plane* with two twin-pod engines on each side of the tail section, Soviet built, of course, sometime after World War II. Yuri Korkin, head of Wildlife for Yakut Region and his assistant Alexey Spiridonov, met us.

Yuri explained the area: Yakutsk has 200,000 population. There are 70 different dialects, and 40 percent are Yakute, a Mongolia/Eskimo type. There apparently is no major industry here, but being the capital of the Yakut Region, it is the center of trade.

Yakutsk lies on the Lena River, the largest in Siberia, which is a navigable river so barges bring supplies from the southwest, all the way to the Arctic. Yuri told us that they have no roads coming here, but when the river freezes in the winter, trucks use the river as a highway, or at least the riverbanks. He said that where the trucks cross the river, they even have an artificial freeze-up established to accelerate the freezing of the "bridge."

**Our camp was exactly on the Divide of the Suntar Khayata Range that separates the Pacific and Arctic watersheds. The camp was between two lakes, one draining to the Pacific that we named Lake America and the one draining to the Arctic, Lake Russia. Pete Papac, Bob Chisholm, Warren Parker and I stand under the flags.**

They then put us on a mini bus and transferred us to a different airport where our helicopter was waiting. They presented us with an ivory carving of mastodon ivory, which is a Baljanai, sacred hunting god. When getting an animal, the owner is to put blood on the nose and thanks for success and request continued success.

The helicopter is an MI-8, which is 7½ tons in weight and has a carrying capacity of four tons. There were about 10 of us and all our gear, so we had a pretty good load. Yuri explained that the first part of the flight was 350 km, a two-hour flight to the town of Teply Kluch, which translates to Hot Springs.

At that point, we changed the flight crew and took on a pilot who is a well-known hunter in the area, Peter Stetsuk. He explained that he was the one that took H.I.H. Prince Abdorreza Pahlavi on his hunt, which I was aware of at the time, about 13 years ago.

The Prince took two sheep and a caribou, which I saw in Tehran at the time and talked to him about his hunt, Peter was famous for his wolf hunting—he takes 40 or 50 a year. Our ongoing flight is another 120 km. This was a scenic ride into the foothills, then into the higher mountains in the southeastern end of the Verkhoyanski Mountains.

We arrived in the camp, which was a beautiful setting on the side of a lake. They had tents for every function, even an outhouse. The staff was very helpful in everyway and constantly tried to help.

They had a tent set up for us to sleep in, but it would have been awfully crowded with all our gear. So we broke out the three dome tents that

I brought, as well as one of the three-man tents. Pete and Warren took a tent each for themselves and Bob and I shared one. The three-man tent is being used for storage of our food and other supplies.

Once set up they had a champagne welcoming party for us. After a round of toasts, they had me raise the flags—U.S.S.R. and U.S.A. flags side-by-side. This was followed by a nice dinner, the meat being from a caribou that they took for camp meat.

We then talked about the hunt plan, the physical capabilities of each hunter, the size of sheep that we might expect, safety, proper skinning of trophies and guiding techniques, including how they are to assist the clients.

This being an entirely new experience for all the staff, it is a learning process for them, as well as the entire Concord Hunting Services. We overdid the welcoming a little too much, as Vladimir kept breaking out more brandy and vodka, as well as the champagne. Mostly we did it Russian style—a toast with each drink and the "Down the hatch!"

### 31 August

Up at 7AM, mild temperature, but we were fogged in. The helicopter had stayed overnight because of our late arrival, so Peter suggested to make our hunt easier for the day, that he fly us out a distance and we would walk back to camp. So while waiting for the fog to lift they gave us a geography lesson. I broke out what maps I had and they explained that we were exactly on the divide that separates the watersheds.

From our south the streams flow to major rivers that empty into the Pacific Ocean via the Okhota River. This river flows to the city of Okhotsk on the Okhotsk Sea, which is the huge inlet between the Kamchatka Peninsula and the Mainland.

Our camp is between two lakes, which are the headwaters of streams that go in opposite directions, going both north and south. These mountains where we are the Khrebet Sunstar Khayata, which is the southeastern range of the Verkhoyanski Mountains.

From the mountaintops here we can see Gora Muskaya to the northwest and it stands 2,959 meters. Glaciers can be seen coming from its peaks. In the distance to the northeast is Gora Druza, which is 2,745 meters high.

The streams to our north flow into the Indigirka River that, in turn, flows to the Arctic Ocean. The streams just to our west flow southwesterly into the Argun River, which we flew over between Yakutsk and Teply Kluch. That river flows into the Lena River, which flows to the Arctic Ocean.

Before the helicopter left us, Peter dropped us off at points where we could hunt our way back to camp. They dropped Bob and me off on the backside of the big mountain a couple of miles to the east of camp. They had seen a couple of big rams when they first came to set up camp. The noise of the helicopter stirred up a small herd of female and young caribou. We proceeded to work our way back through a saddle at the timberline level.

The biggest trees here are tamarack, which may get 50 feet tall and are seen in all the valleys and some of the side hills, probably all

*There are apparently no wolves in the area, which was music to my ears, as they can be deadly on the game population.*

*Nicolai, a young Russian guide and I split off a little from Bob and Valery, his guide. Neither of our guides could speak English, but Nicolai made motions that maybe he and I should go up and over a big mountain to our right. I said OK, and we started climbing and eventually worked our way to a high saddle the other side of the mountain.*

*Our original idea was to skirt around the mountain and come back towards Bob and Valery to see if we could locate the two rams seen here before. But we were very high on a ridge that continued a long way to the north, so we kept indicating to one another that we should*

**Andrei Treschov, Vladimir's brother, was the camp chef, who cooked everything over an open fire, like the kabob he is working on.**

**Elaborate desserts were daily fare, like these cakes with a sheep head artistically displayed in the icing.**

*under 5,000 feet elevation. Our camp is about 4,000 feet. Starting at about the 4,500-foot level is a scrub pine that grows like bushes close to the ground and might be present up to about the 5,500-foot level.*

*Almost everywhere from the valley floors to the mountaintops is lichen, the thickest I have ever seen. It is usually four to six inches high and retains a lot of water in its underside that makes it extremely slippery. It is just like a sponge and works great to wash the blood off the hands.*

*It is the greatest feed for caribou and one would think they would be in here by the thousands. The sheep also eat the lichen, but there is plenty of low brush, berry bushes, and grass.*

*just keep looking over the rise. We continued this all day, carefully glassing as we went. Eventually we were all the way out on the end of the ridge and did not see any game except those caribou earlier.*

*We back-tracked up the ridge part way and then dropped down into the valley to our right, following game trails all we could but when we ran out of trails it was steep and slippery on the moss. Then we walked up the rather steep creek bottom back to camp by late evening.*

*Pete and Warren were flown out to a more distant sheep mountain, and I was tickled to hear that they both got a ram. Pete's is long and heavy, about 39 inches by 38 on the shorter side. Warren's was a lot smaller than he thought it was when glassing it, but his guide said it was big. So he took it, only to find out that it was less than desirable for the first day of the hunt. Everyone planned on taking second rams, so obviously the mistake will not be made again. On a new trip like this, one expects misjudging problems, as trophy hunting is new to most of the staff.*

*Bob and Valery did not see the sheep, but they did see a moose that was working his way out of the area too late for them to follow it. The days are long here in the Arctic so I had up till 10 PM to give them their first instructions on trophy skinning, in this case for life-size mounts.*

*Alexander and Sergei went out spotting on the ridge to the west of the ridge that Nicolai and I were on. They spotted some ewes and lambs and a couple of caribou.*

TIME LAPSE

*(The next couple of days were spent hunting all the nearby ridges and valleys for sheep, caribou, bear and moose with no luck)*

03 September

*Weather very good—almost no clouds in the sky. Just below freezing at night and pleasant during the day. While walking and climbing we removed our outer jackets, but sitting on a windy ridge we piled the layers back on. We had a little rain in the beginning, but it dried out and we have been having perfectly clear days.*

*Surprisingly, we have been seeing a lot of bear and caribou sign in the areas from timberline on down. Since we covered the ridges nearby in the last couple of days and are not seeing the rams, we struck out in the lower areas to the east and southeast of camp. Bob and I went out together and Pete and Warren paired up.*

*Bob and I went around the upper lake in the direction we were the first day, but kept low and went to the semi-forested hills to the south from there. There were a lot of game trails as this is sort of a pass, with the lakes on one side and the mountains on the other side. Game moving from one watershed to the other is likely to come this way as any other way. This was the line of least resistance.*

*We saw a couple of older piles of bear droppings and then a tree along a game trail where a bear had been rubbing. We felt we would most likely come across caribou in this area, but our excitement for bear rose to a high tempo. The rub marks on the tree was up to about my shoulder height, where there were* bits of brown hair from the bear—that was a big bear!

These are the Asian brown bear and classified as Ursus arctos, same as our North American grizzly, but there is a difference and the sub-species needs to be determined. So far none of the staff has knowledge of sub-species.

We got into some fairly thick tamarack groves that had a lot of caribou trails and was a perfect crossroads for game, but our visibility was too limited. Vladimir suggested we get out on the edge of a big opening in hopes of seeing movement of game on the forest edges in late afternoon.

After sitting there for awhile, Vladimir suggest that Bob and I stay put, and they would make a big circle in the forested areas, hoping to kick caribou out to us. We must have waited an hour when we heard some shouting and commotion over a hill on the opposite side of a meadow that we were watching.

Shortly we saw a bear running over the rise and coming at a slight angle to our left. I grabbed the camera and Bob his gun. Not having fired his rifle yet, I think Bob was a little over-anxious and shot at the running bear at about 300 yards away. He failed to lead it enough and hit it on the back foot.

This turned the bear a little more toward our direction. Bob kept firing at fairly long range until his rifle was emptied. By then the maddened bear obviously saw where we were and turned right toward us. Bob was frantically trying to get more shells in his gun as the bear was rapidly closing the gap.

To this point Alexey was holding my gun. As I finally set the camera down, Alexey indicated that I should take the rifle. I rapidly put a shell in the chamber and plopped down on my rear end to get a steady shot if necessary. I followed the bear in the scope from about 50 yards away. I did not want to look over at Bob to see how he was coming along with his reloading.

As the bear made his last turn from a slight depression, he came charging right at us. At about 20 yards from us, and seconds away, I squeezed off my 7 mag and simultaneously I heard Bob's .300 mag report. Both shots into his chest stopped his forward motion and even raised him up a little. He was instantly dead at about 10 yards from us, as we all gave a sigh of relief. That moment of silence with the bear coming our way is a memory I think Bob and I will always visualize.

The trophy is very dark in color, almost black with silver tipped fur mainly in the center of the back. It is a young male, probably 10 years or so old. Bears are like men; they don't obtain their full size till about 20 years old. Actual carcass measurement 56 inches nose to tail (base of tail). Back home a "squared" measurement after skin removed, greatest length plus greatest width, divided by two, would be about a seven-foot square or seven foot bear. It was very well furred for the beginning of September, typical of a far north bear.

By now we had almost forgotten about caribou. Our guides did a great job in locating the bear and getting on the far side of it, giving their wind to the bear and making commotion enough to send the bear running our way. We all pitched in on the skinning and Valery had his work cut out packing it back in his big back pack. He is a real character, and we nicknamed him "Big John."

Bears likewise were found to be different in coloration. The bear Warren Parker collected on the Arctic side of the Divide was very light colored, (posing with guide Alexander Khoklov, holding rifle). The one Bob Chisholm got was exactly like the dark colored, silver tip grizzlies found in the interior of southern British Columbia and Alberta.

We were glad to hear, upon our late return to camp, that Warren had also taken a bear on his way back from taking a sheep—all after going out with caribou in mind! His bear we figured was fully matured, 68 inches in length nose to base of tail and very broad. Surprisingly it was quite light brown in color, so now we are confused as to characteristics that can help us in distinguishing the sub-species.

Warren's sheep is 15 years old, same age as the one Pete got earlier, an indication that conditions are good here allowing them to get to the maximum age of sheep as we know it in North America and other parts of Asia.

It was celebration time in camp and we consumed an abnormal amount of vodka, with toast after toast celebrating a great day's hunt. As customary after a successful hunt, a shot of liquor, vodka in this case, is thrown into the fire while giving thanks to the Yakutia hunting god and asking for continued hunting success.

Bob and Warren did it well along with all of us doing our share of toasting the same.

04 September

Pete continued hunting caribou today to the south of camp, while the rest of us went north toward the Halija River area, where all the sheep have been taken so far. Prior to the start of the hunt, the staff had scouted the area and had seen a band of eight rams. They felt that these sheep might have broken up in smaller bands and come a little closer our way.

We followed a side ridge out that headed northerly from the big ridge that we had thoroughly hunted in the early part of the hunt. At the end of the ridge were a small valley and a lone hill just beyond. We stayed on the end of our ridge using up whatever time we had to spare to sit and glass for any activity of any kind of game.

**The author getting ready to give trophy skinning instructions to the guides on Bob's bear.**

About midafternoon, near the top of the lone hill, appeared a couple of young rams. We put the spotting scope on them and determined them to be too small for taking this early in the hunt, maybe 30 inches in horn length. We kept watching them and to our surprise a third and a fourth ram appeared. The two young rams were sentries for two big mature rams. They were definitely of trophy size, one bigger than the other.

Bob had "won the toss" so the big problem came up as to how to get to them. In studying the terrain, we figured we could easily get off the hill we were on, going down a side gulley and working our way out to a little high point in the valley below. Vladimir suggested that only he, along with Bob and me, make the stalk. So we stripped down to a minimum and soon were down to our vantage point.

The rams were feeding across from the same level where they first appeared. It would be a dangerously long shot at a steep angle uphill and looking a little into the sun. So we figured we were pinned down and were really at a loss what to do. Then much to our surprise, the rams started down the hill in our direction. They were moving as if being disturbed. There is a possibility that the wind swirling around the hills, took our scent around behind the sheep, causing them to come our way. Whatever the reason, we were tickled to see them coming our way.

Once to the bottom of the hill, which would have been a quite acceptable shot, they made a turn and started angling even more in our direction across the flats. Because of the angle that I was in relation to Bob, I could see that I would be in Bob's way for his shot. So I had to roll back out of his line of fire. The big ram was leading the way, so I waited till Bob got his first shot off before even getting into position to shoot.

**Vladimir Treschov began his guiding and outfitting business on this trip. He became our partner and went on to be one of the leading operators for hunts in all the CIS (former U.S.S.R.).**

It was not entirely surprising that we collected two different subspecies of snow sheep near the Suntar Khayata Divide. I took this Yakut snow sheep, with triangular shaped horns and dark pelage, while Bob Chisholm got an Okhotsk bighorn with rounded horns and much lighter pelage.

*At just over 100 yards distance, Bob squeezed off on his ram, after which I sat up and immediately shot right at the confused second ram. It went down immediately, so I put my attention to Bob's ram, which was obviously hit, but starting to run away. I was still somewhat in Bob's line of fire as the three rams were going off to our left. So he had to wait till they passed my position before he could shoot again.*

*During all this time I had not paid any further attention to my ram until I saw a glimpse of movement out of the corner of my right eye. In looking up, I saw my ram running back up the mountain he came from! I quickly rotated around and got another shot into him just before he went over a ledge. I kept my attention on both rams at this point. So both rams were down. By then Warren and the other guides came running down off the hill to greet us.*

*After taking pictures of Bob's on one side of the valley and mine on the other side, we took blood and tissue samples for a study that is being organized by Cornell University back in Ithaca, New York. The samples will be the first of a series that I am coordinating for all the foreign sheep to help determine the various sub-species. In this case, a probable tie-in with the North American sheep. The study is a project of the International Sheep Hunters Association (ISHA).*

*Once we got our two heads and skins together, it was very obvious that these two specimens are entirely different in horn shape and skin coloration. Also, Bob's was larger in body size and horn size. It is apparent to all of us that we are in an area bordering different sub-species of sheep. We feel that one of them could be from the O.n. alleni sub-species to the east of us, while the other is either the O.n. lydekkeri or the O.n. borealis which have unknown distribution points to the west and north of us. It is our intention to study all specimens possible and learn what we can from available data while we are here.*

## TIME LAPSE

*06 September*

*Nicolai and the two Sergeis struck out early in the morning to search the area to the southwest from camp, looking for caribou. They have some walkie-talkie radios to communicate with each other and hopefully from camp if they don't get too far away.*

*The helicopter came in. So we flew out with some of the three-man tents and sleeping bags that I had brought looking for places to hunt farther out. We dropped Pete off in a place about one day's walk from camp to the northeast of here. We then flew around scouting the areas southeast of here and in the direction our guides went this morning.*

*We flew to a low area that was pretty well covered with tamarack trees. I spotted about 10 caribou females and young with three pure white ones in the herd. I assumed they were reindeer that had gone wild. Soon I saw a few log cabins and a wooden corral. It was obviously a camp of reindeer herdsmen. No signs of life, as they probably moved out for the season.*

*Alexey said that the herdsmen wanted hunters to shoot any reindeer that have gone wild, because they will come into the domestic herds. They will take as many as they can, which eventually will go wild as well. He said the government herds were all branded and the private herds would notch out the ears with different markings.*

*The reindeer herdsmen are Evenks, a nomadic-type people. There are about 150,000 Evenks in Yakutia, which is about 12 percent of the total population. There are 1,200,000 people in Yakutia. Of which there are 400,000*

*Yakuts. The Yakuts are an Eskimo/Mongolia-type people.*

*Alexey Spiridonov is a Yakut, the only one in our staff. The rest of the staff are Russian types, four from Yakutia and the rest from Moscow. The Yakut republic, Yakutia, is an autonomous republic of the Soviet Union and part of the Russian Federation, as is all of Siberia. It is a very large republic and rich in certain products. Most of the diamonds from the U.S.S.R. are from Yakutia, but unfortunately not where we are hunting*

*I saw a cow moose in among the tamarack trees. This looked like perfect moose country. They call them elk here, actually Elch, which is typical of all over Asia. We landed on the bar of a river and picked up Nicolai and the two Sergeis.*

*They had walked an awfully long way, looking over a lot of country, but did not have good reports of caribou. They saw an occasional small herd of cows and calves and a few small bulls, but no trophies.*

*These caribou definitely remind me of the mountain caribou in northern Canada, not only living in sheep country but not found in large herds. The Yakutians tell us of huge herds of sometimes a thousand or more caribou up on the Arctic coast region, which are apparently more like our barren ground caribou of northern Alaska and the Yukon.*

*So we were not encouraged to be dropped off on a spike camp and flew back to base camp.*

*Pete surprisingly came in very late today with a really fine caribou. They caped it out and brought the head back. I was impressed with the size of the horns and cape. It appears that body size, are bigger than the North American caribou.*

*The plan was for a couple of the guides to return tomorrow to fetch the meat. They have not wasted any meat from any of the sheep, but bear meat was of no interest to them. These bear probably eat a lot of meat, including caribou when they get a chance.*

*Right now, however, there are a lot of berries ripe. The berry bushes are quite small, averaging four or five inches off the ground and not really loaded with berries. There are blueberries, and then a shiny blackberry, as well as a red colored berry- all quite small.*

## TIME LAPSE

*08 September*

*I tried talking Alexey out of his Yakutia knife, but it was too sacred to him. Their traditional knife has a long, pointed blade, with a handle made from wood from the root of the birch tree. The sheath is wood, but lined with leather. I collect knives, so I started bargaining with Sergei, who had one that he personally made and the leather cover on the sheath was a cow's tail, rawhide. I finally made a deal by giving him my "Game Skinner" knife, sort of a modern version of the Eskimo ooluruk, and a sharp folding knife.*

*We got to talking guns and Vladimir broke out the rifle that he used the day before, which he said was a special rifle. With Yuri interpreting the inscription on the inset brass plaque, it read," To esteemed Nikita Sergeivitch Khrushchev at his 68th birthday from KGB of the Soviet Ministers (SM) of U.S.S.R., April*

*1962." It is a 7x57 BRNO, which is made in Czechoslovakia.*

*It was by a stroke of luck that Vladimir obtained the rifle through a higher up connection that he had. Vladimir explained the rifle had been presented to Khrushchev by Semichastny, the Chief of the KGB at the time. In October 1964, Semichastny was the instigator to have Khrushchev removed from power! He was the only high official to be present when Khrushchev arrived at the airport in Moscow, escorted him to the Kremlin when he was removed from power.*

*Unbeknown to us, a big celebration party was planned for tonight, as tomorrow is departure day. When evening came, a better-than-ever table was set up. Normally Andrei who was usually assisted by Valery presented the food in an artistic fashion. The cold cuts, tomatoes or whatever was artistically placed on the plates. Tonight was no exception, but the quantities were increased and the table lined with bottles of brandy and vodka.*

*Everyone was in good cheer. But first the trophies were all lined up outside and hung or set up for photos and recognition of the success. Then they moved the Soviet and American flags around so they would fly above the trophies. Another table was set with champagne and cups (sorry no champagne glasses). Yuri popped the cork, and the celebration started.*

*When in at the dinner table Andrei came out of his shell. Whether planned or not, he became the keynote speaker for the occasion. He started a toast that took all of 15 minutes giving*

*credit where due and honoring guests and staff alike.*

*The one memorable thing that he said was something like this—"Like the two lakes that we are camped between that are joined by a stream, the American visitors and the Soviet hosts are joined by a common bond of understanding and camaraderie." They talked earlier about naming the lake we were on "Lake Klineburger," but my thoughts were naming the twin lakes "Lake America" and "Lake Russia."*

*Dinner was great, but what really topped it off, Andrei created a cake for each of us with a sheep head on the icing, and our initials on our respective cake. What a party and what a thoughtful staff. The whole trip has been going this way. They just can't do too much for us—by far the best I've seen in the U.S.S.R. and most*

*other places in the world. Intourist, the government agency, could never have done this.*

*09 September*

*Helicopter scheduled in by late morning, so breaking down camp and packing up was in order. I first got onto the job of packing trophies, which went smoothly with the help of the trophy bags, tags, etc. that I had brought along. The remainder of the packing went smoothly with the exception of a rainstorm that came up when we had everything laid out and our personal tents down.*

*Fortunately, they left up the big dining tent, with fire going. 11 AM came, then 12 and on to the afternoon and no helicopter. We had high clouds, but nothing that would bother helicopter flying. There were two helicopters scheduled. We were all somewhat depressed*

**The lowering of the flags signified the end of the hunt.**

*thinking that we would not get to Yakutsk tonight.*

*The talk was how many tents would we need to put back up when around 4 PM the drone of the helicopter was heard in the distance. I quickly started rolling up a couple of sleeping bags, that had already been unpacked, and getting a few other things ready.*

*Only one helicopter came. It was explained that the weather was socked in entirely from Yakutsk to Tepley Kluch until a short while ago. One of the helicopters was to come from Yakutsk, which didn't happen. Peter, of course, came from Tepley Kluch.*

*We loaded the gear into the back end of the helicopter and then 17 people, including the flight crew, boarded. We left behind a few of the guides and some of the gear and warmed up for takeoff. Remember the carrying capacity is*

*only four tons and the somewhat thin air in the mountains reduces the capacity.*

*Peter got those blades going fast as possible before changing the pitch, and if a helicopter could moan, this one did! We broke loose from the ground and backed up over the water but apparently we could not get high enough to tip forward and get some forward motion, so Peter touched down again and made a second try and was able to find a path between the tamaracks to get moving forward, which, in turn, gave us what we needed to get some lift.*

*He headed as directly as possible to the Halija River, following it down to the Tiri River, which flows in the direction of Tepley Kluch. Once there, we could see the problem they had with fog earlier. There was a low fog bank, probably averaging 200 or 300 feet above ground that we had to fly under all the way to Tepley Kluch. Once there, it was obvious we were enjoying some reasonably dry weather in the mountains, while the lowlands were drenched with rain.*

*We refueled and got off as quickly as possible for the two-hour flight to Yakutsk. We dropped off a few of the passengers, so we were a little lighter. There was rain and low clouds between the two towns.*

*Upon arriving in Yakutsk, we were met by Yuri Korkin who gladly heard our success story. He said we had to go direct to the other airport to check on new schedules that had changed on September 5 and our flight tomorrow at midnight was no longer in existence.*

*Fortunately, they had openings on three flights 10 PM tonight, 8 AM in the morning and 12 noon. I chose the 12-noon flight, and everyone agreed it was the best choice.*

*So off we were to our rooms at the Yakutsk Hotel. Yuri advised us that we had to take a bath now as the hot water was turned off at 10 PM, and we were to meet at 9:15 for dinner.*

*All the way to the hotel in our mini bus everyone was looking over the good-looking ladies—Yakut or Russian, they did look good after a couple weeks out of touch. The rooms were modest and clean. When I started the water, there was no hot water at all. Oh well, I've gone this long using the cold mountain stream water, so a cold shower it was. A shave and a change of clothes.*

*Yuri and Alexey met us by our rooms and presented me with a beautiful carved wooden vase. Then all of us were presented a new, traditional Yakutia knife. Then we were escorted to the lobby, through a doorway, down a dark hall, up a flight of stairs to a night club blaring*

*with the sound of Russian rock music—and pretty girls all over the place!*

*Our table was beautifully set right on the edge of the dance floor. It was apparent that they knew we were foreigners, as several of the single girls would dance together right by our table.*

*We had the usual toasts from the various brandy, champagne and vodka bottles that adorned the table. It was too noisy to talk much business, and the band never did take a break. After dinner some American songs were played in our honor and some of the girls dragged us on the floor for a dance. The chubby, blonde Russian girl that got me wouldn't let me sit down, so finally Alexey interrupted and said we had to talk business. Yuri then suggested we leave. He said that he "saved" us by having us leave.*

## TIME LAPSE

### 10 September

*In Moscow a large bus picked us up and took us to the Central House of Tourists Hotel, where we rested till picked up at 5:30 to go to Vladimir and Elena Treschov's home for a party. All the gals had been working hard to prepare a welcoming banquet for us. They really went all out for us and had an array of food, that if merely sampled, would be too much. There were ample quantities of champagne, brandy and vodka that found their way into our glasses for many toasts for the friendships formed, the success of the hunt and to further maiden hunts throughout the U.S.S.R. that we all hoped to participate in.*

*11 September*

*My day was filled with meetings, including one with a delegation that flew up from Alma Ata, Kazakhstan to meet me and offer an exclusive for the hunting in that Soviet Socialist Republic. Irina arranged for Elja to come and help prepare a final dinner for me with caviar, smoked salmon and sturgeon for openers, chicken (remember the expensive meat) and rice and a beautiful cake. Valery Uvarov came for one last meeting—he will depart for Greece in two weeks to be the Intourist representative there for a couple of years.*

*The hunters did some last minute shopping. They got dollars exchanged for six rubles to the dollar—probably on the black market, but they didn't know for sure. The bank rate is $1.60 to one ruble. They managed to spend it all on gifts and souvenirs.*

*We all met at the airport at 5:30 for our 7:20 departure on Lufthansa. All the staff and their wives came to the airport to see us off— just one example of the entire opposite from the handling that our clients and I have received from Intourist in 20 years of dealing with them.*

*It is a whole new world with Perestroika taking hold after more than 60 years of stern communist rule. We have all traveled many times in the U.S.S.R. and all agree that this arrangement and all the people involved was among the very best experiences that we have had worldwide. Never have the people involved—as well as their families—taken us in their homes and humbled themselves in such a way.*

# CHAPTER 15

# Kazakhstan—Two Exploratory Expeditions in Inner Asia

A ll of Inner Asia was of extreme interest to me, but Kazakhstan led the list. Earlier in this chronicle I mentioned visiting this republic in 1970. There was willingness to begin a hunt program at that time—all they needed was the go-ahead from Intourist in Moscow.

Periodically I visited the officials in the Kazakh capitol of Alma Ata in a never-ending renewal of my interest and information exchange. Kazakhstan is the largest Soviet Republic, aside from Russia. It lies in the south center of this vast nation and borders Turkmenistan, Uzbekistan, Kirgizistan, and China on its east boundary.

The western border wraps around the Caspian Sea while it extends eastward almost to Outer Mongolia. Northerly, it penetrates well into Siberia. Its terrain consists of everything from forests to savannah. Most important, it has numerous mountain ranges, especially along the thousands of miles along the southern and eastern borders. Likewise, a great variety of wildlife exists, including urial sheep, several varieties of

On an early visit in the 1970s to Kazakhstan, the museum officials in Alma Ata were very helpful in my study of the distribution of Asia's wildlife. Here we are holding a specimen of Semipalatinsk argali found in the far north of Kazakhstan.

argali sheep, ibex, wapiti, Siberian roe deer, jaran gazelle, saiga antelope, and more.

The Kazakhs fairly well confirmed their eagerness to work with me on their wildlife program when they sent a delegation to visit with me in Moscow on September 11, 1989 and then later during my visit to Alma Ata in November, I established a general agency agreement. At that time, the exploratory trips for urial and argali sheep hunts were established to take place at the earliest possible time, which were set for March 1990.

Our two planned hunts were for Trans-Caspian urial sheep in the far west of Kazakhstan and then another area in the far north for an argali sheep that apparently had no recorded history of ever being hunted by a foreign expedition.

Since the whole exploratory expedition would take a better part of a month, I had difficulty in recruiting enough hunters to stay for both hunts. So those that would accompany me for the entire time would be old-time hunting buddies Bob Chisholm and Pete Papac along with Allen Means from Reno, Nevada. Then for the urial portion would be Andy Samuels from Youngstown, Ohio and Craig Leerberg from Colorado Springs. Then joining us for the argali hunt would be Russ Underdahl and Milan Sablich, both from the Midwest.

After the usual flights from the States and my essential business meetings in Moscow, on 09 March we started on the history making expeditions, we boarded our flight in the new Soviet jumbo jet. I'll start now on my journal entries:

*The one strange and different aspect of the configuration of this jumbo jet is the boarding up a short stairway into the belly of the aircraft, where there are baggage racks and where you are expected to leave off your carry-on luggage, then you go up a stairway into the main cabin for seating. The four-hour flight was smooth and we arrived in Alma Ata about 9:30, having lost another three-hour time change.*

*Igor Zelenko and Sergei, an interpreter, met us. Igor is the head of a joint venture, Dalso Pacific that is in charge of Intourist, by providing accommodations, transfers, interpreters etc. We were taken to the hotel, where Igor and I got into planning strategy for business talks the next day. He had some food and vodka brought to our room where we planned our talks, while the others went to the hotel bar.*

*10 March*

*The weather is mild here and the sun was out part of the time. Alma Ata is a beautiful*

I made frequent visits in Kazakhstan with Wildlife and Forestry officials in developing their hunting program. Here with Chris are the top people including Valery Savinov (next to Chris), the Game Department Director, Yuri Stepanov, Valery's Vice-Director, and Tulegan Kupaev, the head of the Wildlife Protection Department of the Council of Ministries. This meeting established my general agency agreement.

city, right on the north edge of the Tien Shan Mountain range. The snow-covered mountains tower over the town. Igor and Valery Savinov, the head of the Kazakh Game Department, met me in the lobby of the hotel. We proceeded to the Forestry Department office building where meetings were set up with Tulegen Kupaev, the head of the Wildlife Protection Department of the Council of Ministers and several of his aids, as well as Yuri Stepanov, assistant to Valery.

It was very important to convince Kupaev that hunting as a sustainable renewable resource was imperative to their Wildlife Program—i.e. foreign hunters would bring in enough hard currency to finance their entire conservation program. The sheep are quite abundant now, but to get permission to hunt them and get proper export licenses, special permits had to be obtained from Moscow. There is a lot of sentiment against hunting by Moscovites, so this meeting was essential, and it was successful.

Mr. Kupaev asked me how wildlife is managed in our country. It was apparent that his newly formed department was starting from scratch. I suggested we work out a program for a delegation of their people to come to the U.S.A. on a fact-finding mission and spend some time with one or more of our game departments. I agreed to get it established and funded. They then suggested that I try to get funding for establishing an experimental game farm. They agreed to fly me around by helicopter to choose a site for such a game farm for sheep in a mountainous region.

After our successful talks we had lunch at a Chinese restaurant, specializing in Xinjiang

The mayor of Shevchenko (left) welcomes Chris and Valery Savinov to the remote city.

type food. Xinjiang is the Chinese province bordering Kazakhstan to the east.

Back at the hotel, we took a sauna, and then went to the hotel restaurant, which had a band and dance floor. Plenty of single girls, but the fellows didn't dance much, although we did a lot of heavy drinking and had some girls visit with us at the table.

## TRANSCASPIAN URIAL SHEEP

*11 March*

After breakfast Valery and Sergei met us with a microbus, in which we loaded our gear and headed for the airport. Valery and Sergei went with us on our three-hour flight to the west, which was probably halfway back to Moscow. We paralleled the Tien Shan for a while, then across plains, south of the Aral Sea, which we could see to the right of the aircraft, then onward to Shevchenko on the eastern shore of the Caspian Sea.

Shevchenko is out of bounds for foreigners, so we had to get special permission to go there, which was the reason we could not fly direct from Moscow there. We expected warm weather, but were surprised to see people bundled in warm clothing as we taxied in.

We were greeted by a large group of people outside the baggage claim shed. The Mayor of Shevchenko, Alexander Gordiev, was introduced to me. He proceeded to tell me that we were the first Americans known to visit the area, and they were very excited about it. He said a few other foreigners had been there, mainly some Europeans who were directing the building of a chemical plant.

Also there, was Alexander Korsakov (Sasha) a taxidermist from Moscow, who was sent to further develop his skills in field care of trophies and to assist me. Sasha works for Vladimir Treschov of NTL Hunting Services with whom I recently formed a partnership. Other delegates of the area that met us were Victor Raketin, Inspector of Hunting; Alexander Ivasenko, Director of Hunting Economy; Arganbay Kadanov, the Main Hunting Director; Daugaliev Kuanysh, General Director of United Forestry Economy. These staff members were all working in the Forestry/Game Department for the Gurevsk Hunting Area.

Our mountain of gear was loaded in a mini bus and we were driven some 25 km to the city of Shevchenko and directly to a very nice small hotel right on the Caspian Sea. The Mayor had a splendid banquet set up for us in a special dining area, with all the trimmings, including cognac, vodka, champagne and wine. There were many rounds of

**The gang's all here. From left, Victor Raketin (Inspector of Hunting), Craig Leerberg, Al Means, Pete Papac, Bob Chisholm, Andy Samuels, Arganbay Kadanov (Hunting Director), and his children, Berig Kadanov and Chris Klineburger.**

*toasts welcoming us and wishing us happiness, health, success, health to our families, peace in the world, etc. This was just a preview of what we were to expect for the entire stay in Gurevsk and Shevchenko.*

*After the banquet (this was really lunch, as we had gained back three hours of the four we lost traveling from Moscow to Alma Ata), Gordiev insisted we see a little of his beautiful city. It is nicely laid out along the Caspian shore about 50 km south of the Mangyshlak Peninsula, that finger of land protruding westerly into the Caspian.*

*He showed us a few of the landmarks and buildings of significance, then walked us in the cold offshore winds to the pounding surf of this huge inland salt sea, which is actually below sea level. On another spot along the shore, he took us to a place frequented by the swans native to the area, which were once endangered and now doing well.*

*We then proceeded out of Shevchenko 25 km up the coast and stopped at a resort hotel*

*that was to be our accommodations for the night. This hotel was only used normally in the summer season for the truck drivers and their families, sort of the Soviet version of the team-sters union. The Forestry Department had best of connections with them and had permission for our full use of it.*

*We had doubled up in rooms that had four beds giving us room to spread our gear and get ready for the hunt. They had put in some small space heaters that were hardly adequate to raise the chilly temperature more than 5°C.*

*After settling in, we were ushered to a base-ment level where another banquet had been prepared. This one was attended less by city officials, but more by Forestry/Game Depart-ment people. They were now getting the point across to us that it was an exciting occasion for not only having American visitors, but the first hunt ever to be organized here. In the many toasts throughout the multi-coursed dinner, we were welcomed in many ways as the forerunners of the future in their wildlife program.*

*After dinner and many rounds of toasts in the true Soviet traditional way, i.e. with lengthy recognitions and good wishes, it was bottoms up! Most of the guests left for bed, but Pete and I hung on for a while longer and one of the most important figures in the Department showed up, Arganbay Kadanov, with his son, Berig.*

*He is the Main Inspector for Forestry and Wildlife. He had heard that I collected knives and had inquired about locating a hunting knife with saiga antelope horn handle. (I had been looking for one ever since seeing one owned by a guide while opening the Marco Polo Sheep hunting in Tajik SSR in 1987). I was pleasantly surprised to be presented one of these rare knives.*

*The toasts went on for a considerable length of time and I was pleased to see how much importance was put on Berig, only 15 years old to be involved in our program. Berig spoke fairly good broken English. I invited him to join us in the hunt and his father was agreeable and asked if I would write a note to his teacher—jokingly, of course.*

*Pete and I, along with Sasha, then took advantage of the sauna that they had heated up and prepared for us. It was now getting well past midnight, but they insisted on more drinks before retiring.*

*12 March*

*Last night I was presented the head of a sturgeon fish (that the Caspian is well noted for) so it was made into a fish soup for breakfast, along with oatmeal and various cold cuts and smoked fish.*

*Finally we were off to the hunt area, the Gurevsk region on the northern base of the Mangyshlak Peninsula about a three-hour drive. The mini bus and two Russian jeeps were our caravan. About midway we left the paved two-lane road that went north of Shevchenko and turned northwesterly, leaving behind all forms of civilization—which there was very little of anyway.*

*We had occasionally seen some stray camel herds out on the forbidden plains as well as a few horses. Much of the area was once under the Caspian, which has continually lowered throughout the centuries. Its salt content has been left in the ground making it poor soil for most growth, but yet there were some hardy plants and grass that feed some domestic animals and wildlife.*

*Fuel tanks and reserve cans full; we went over some very poorly maintained dirt tracks that eventually took us into a steppe that was no more than a thousand feet high. It was a high plateau that had many breaks or small canyons that were the habitat of the Trans Caspian urial sheep, the Ovis vignei arkal.*

*We drove into a canyon that had a river, only trickling at this time of year. We were told it completely dried up in the summertime, when temperatures in the general area got to 120°F.*

*I rode in the lead jeep, and no longer than 10 minutes into the canyon, I spotted some sheep. I motioned to the driver to stop. Valery shouted "Bharan," meaning sheep.*

*We piled out only to see the sheep band up and head up the rugged mountainside. In glassing them, some big heads could be seen as well as their flowing frontal neck mane.*

*Al had thought to have his binoculars in hand for the trip in, and he shared them with* the rest of us. There were about 50 sheep in the herd, with the males mixed with females. I commented that I probably had never seen that many sheep in a herd before.

As we proceeded, we kept an intent watch and frequently saw small groups of a few up to 10 sheep at a time. It seemed we were never out of sight of urials, which the locals referred to as "mouflon."

At one juncture we saw two large bunches of sheep, which banded together to make an estimated 100 sheep all in one herd. In less than an hour's drive through the range, we estimated seeing around 250 head of sheep.

We also observed several small herds of horses and camels in the same habitat. My thought at the time after seeing the rather skimpy feed supply that they should not allow domestic stock in this Urial Reserve.

**Our accommodations at the Gurevsk Reserve on the Mangyshlak Peninsula were one large, well-decorated yurt, lined with Kazakh carpets on the walls and dirt floor. We would roll up our sleeping bags and breakfast was served on the floor.**

We arrived at our campsite at the head of a small box canyon in the early afternoon. I was surprised to see a large yurt set up to accommodate us. The camp staff was awaiting us with lunch prepared. It reminded me very much of Mongolia, which is a neighboring country to the east. The Kazakh people look basically the same as the Mongolians, and the dress of the women in camp was very similar to the Mongolians.

After unloading our mountain of gear from the bus, we were ushered into the yurt, where a beautiful display of food was set on the table (a table cloth on the floor) around which were pads for sitting. It is customary for people to take their boots off when entering the yurt, but with our heavy boots and all the bother in unlacing and lacing again, we did not honor their custom.

The food was fine with clean and sanitary plates and utensils. There was the ever-present brandy and vodka, and we accepted a small welcoming toast.

It was now midday after our three-hour drive from the hotel, so we split up and went out hunting. Bob and I went together. No sooner out of camp by jeep, we saw some sheep about 1,000 meters away.

I took out the spotting scope and saw a couple of fair rams in the herd of about 15. I was surprised to see the rams running with the ewes and lambs at this time of the year, as the ewes were getting ready to drop their lambs. The plan was for us to hunt the valley floor of the canyon adjacent to camp, while the others went in subgroups of two to the surrounding hillsides.

This area is a high plateau with many breaks or canyons that have been washed out through the ages. As a matter of fact, part of the washing out has been by the Caspian Sea itself, as its level has continuously gone down, even though constantly fed by some major rivers and with no outlet.

So some of these canyons were under water at one time. The rock structures are unique with many caves and unusual formations. The steep canyon walls are the escape for the sheep and are difficult for man to traverse.

We drove up the canyon to the end of a very rough road and took to walking. Just a few hundred meters from the jeep, we spotted a large herd of sheep a long way away near the top of the rim. They were on the move, possibly from seeing one of the other hunting parties.

We were at a good vantage point, so we decided to stay put and look for movement of sheep that might settle down in a place where we could make a stalk. In looking back on the canyon wall beyond the jeep, we were very surprised to spot some sheep. They had just moved our way from around a point about 500 meters from the jeep and were in perfect view of it. They did not seem to be uneasy, so perhaps they thought it to be a big rock, since there was no movement.

I trained the spotting scope on them after crawling on my belly to the top of this rise we were behind. I was impressed with a dozen or more big rams in the herd of about 50 animals, ewes and lambs included. It appeared much too far to shoot and we were pinned down and not able to move any closer.

I crawled back to discuss in sign language and by writing distance numbers in the dirt to try to find out their opinion of how far they were away. They indicated 500 meters, but I could

not believe they were that close. I went back to my viewing point and studied them through the spotting scope, which was 20 power, and my eight power binoculars and through my variable Redfield scope screwed up to 7 power.

Fortunately, the best rams had bedded down giving me time to study the situation over. I determined the two biggest rams from studying both the mass of the horns and how far the curl went out away from the head.

What I felt was the second largest was a very light-colored animal. It was almost off-white as compared to the more reddish tone of the average body color of most mature males. The one I picked out as being the largest had heavier horns and seemed to have an equally larger curl.

Since they were undisturbed, I asked Bob if he wanted to try a shot. He declined, so I took my down jacket and down-filled cap off to make a cradle for my rifle on top of the rise, as I didn't want to have any human error in my try. I put the cross hairs about one foot above the shoulder of the ram I selected and shoved the rifle butt firmly against my shoulder as I lay prone on the crown of the hill.

I carefully squeezed off, and the thunder of the shot caused the entire herd to break out in a dead run across the face of the canyon wall, It was impossible for me to see where the bullet hit, but in studying the area through the binoculars and later the spotting scope, I determined I made a clean miss.

After watching the movement of many sheep all afternoon, we returned to camp the way we came. I thought back through the excitement of the day and the great number of sheep that we had seen. I estimated seeing well over 300 sheep today, without doubt more wild sheep than I had ever seen on a single hunt in my life! The rest of the group had varied experiences, and no one took a ram today. The staff all joined us for a very good dinner of traditional Kazakh food and the ever-present vodka and cognac.

*13 March*

Now that all of us had a chance to look over some big rams, we had considerable discussion as to what to look for in a big ram. The general belief of the guides is that if the frontal mane—that is, the lower hair on the front of the neck—was long and black that it was an old male, while those with that same hair being white, it would be a young ram. So we all went off with the idea that the blacker the frontal mane, the older the ram and supposedly the bigger.

In looking over horns at long distance yesterday, I definitely had difficulty in distinguishing a good mature ram from a really big outstanding ram. In looking straight on, the mature rams all had the same look, with the horns forming an outward circle on each side of the head.

The end of the horns, being quite thin were not visible even through the spotting scope at 800 or 1,000 yards away, thus it was hard to determine whether the horns flared out on the tips. A ram with a full curl, plus the tips flaring out, would certainly be a big old ram. So for one, I had preprogrammed my mind that if I had a good shot at a full curl ram that had a black frontal mane, I would go for it.

Today, Bob stayed in camp. He had been constipated and felt it best he not go out. They

had me go out in a smaller four-wheel-drive car. We headed out toward the flats of the Caspian coast. Went westerly for a ways, then drove back onto the high plains, with no mountains in view in the direction we were going. A Russian jeep was following, and I figured one of the other hunters was in it.

Soon we came to the edge of one of the huge breaks and for the first time I got a real view of what the Ustiyrt Reserve area was really like. On top and away from the breaks it appears to be a vast grassy plain, spotted with an occasional herd of camels or horses, many of which are wild mustangs. The plain, however, is cut out by many long canyons that were carved out by the violent shores of the Caspian Sea when ages ago it was much higher.

My driver, and Daugaliev Kuansh, who was head of the wildlife section of the Forestry Department, kept waving the other jeep back as we would go to the edge of the breaks looking for sheep. Finally it became apparent that the other jeep did not have one of the other hunters, but other officials of the Forestry and Game Department, including Savanov and Berig.

I felt a little uncomfortable having all the top people in Kazakhstan watching my hunt. Daugaliev spotted a herd of sheep in the bottom of a canyon and motioned for my careful approach. I crawled on my belly, exposed my eyes over the rise, expecting to see some rams at close range, after I had put a cartridge into the chamber of my 7 mag.

It took me a while, after seeing nothing on the near slopes, to realize that the herd was over a kilometer away at the base of a mountain in the center of the break. He indicated I should shoot, apparently thinking our modern, scope-sighted rifles could do wonders. I refused, but spent time looking over the animals.

I walked to the edge of the head of one break and saw two animals at quite close range that at first appeared to be two ewe sheep. They saw me, and upon them starting to run, I recognized them as being Jaran, a gazelle that is of the gazelle subguttorosa family found in this area. These were male and good looking trophies that I would be allowed to hunt, but I elected not to try for them, so as not to disturb the area for sheep hunting.

Around 2 PM we walked to a point that protruded well into one of the breaks. A herd of sheep was spotted on an opposite face, over a kilometer away. Soon more sheep appeared from our side of the canyon, from a place that we could not see because of the way the mountain on our side dropped off. Rams started to appear, as they grazed from our side of the valley to the flats at the bottom, and some up a ways on the opposite face.

Daugaliev indicated we should move back out of sight. We were now in the shadows, so we crawled back and soon were out of view of the sheep. We circled around the backside of the point and went around to a place that was about straight across from where a few rams bedded down. I indicted to Daugaliev to stay back and I crawled out on my belly to a rock outcrop that I visualized as a good place to rest the rifle.

I carefully looked the resting rams over with my nine-power Leupold binoculars and selected the one with the blackest frontal mane.

He was lying broadside at a sharp angle down the opposite face near the bottom of the canyon. Carefully studying the situation, I determined that the distance was in excess of 600 meters. It was a sharp downhill shot, and my bullet would have little drop so a shot at that distance would not be unrealistic.

I took plenty of time to get a good rest for my Kleinguenther 7mm Remington Magnum, which has been a faithful, accurate rifle. I put my down filled cap under the fore end to cushion it from the sharp rocks. I carefully placed the crosshairs right on the upper part of the shoulder of the ram and gently squeezed the hair trigger. The scope slammed against my shooting glasses and forehead so I momentarily lost vision of the ram, but soon saw him rolling over and indicated thumbs up to my guide that the ram was down. I figured I had a scope cut and the telltale blood rather disturbed Daugaliev, but I indicated no problem.

In looking over the situation, we determined we could not get to the ram from where we were, but would have to drive all the way around and drive up the bottom of the canyon. That ended up being a one-hour drive back to camp, where we found Bob feeling much better after the doctor and lady hosts nursing him along all day. Bob joined us in continuing on to the flats leading to the canyon where my ram was. We spotted 10 Jaran gazelles on the plains and tried to head them off.

No luck there, so we started into the mouth of the canyon and spotted a large herd of sheep feeding on the floor of the wide canyon. We stopped the vehicles and walked back to *a vantage point. When we got to our viewing point, the sheep had already left the valley floor and were part way up the hillside. The other jeep that followed us did not take any precautions to stay out of sight, so that was probably the cause of them to move farther away.*

*We continued up the canyon and worked our way over some very difficult conditions to get close as possible to the dead ram. We located it without any problem, as earlier we had studied the various landmarks to identify the actual spot.*

*Once up the side of the hill, we located the ram and, although it was a fully matured ram, I was disappointed in its size, as it was barely a full curl and just five years old. At that long distance where I shot from, as I looked up the steep cliffs to the other side. I felt it was unbelievable that I hit the ram, let alone be able to see the horns as well as I did.*

*I took blood and tissue samples of the specimen for DNA tests that I had prearranged for studies through the International Sheep Hunters Association (ISHA). It was getting very late, so aside from field dressing, I took the whole carcass back to camp in the jeep for life-size skinning and field care. Furthermore I wanted to spend time with Alexander (Sasha) Korsakov on skinning methods for taxidermy purposes.*

*I was very pleased to find that Pete and Andy also met with success today. Pete had a really nice ram, with nicely flared out horns, but his animal had a bad fall down the rasp-like rocks and his skin was badly damaged for a life-size mount. Andy's trophy was almost as*

*big, and it was a specimen that he was mighty proud of.*

*The Chief of Enforcement, Alexander Ivanenko, was waiting in camp and had a party waiting for us in the yurt. We put the trophies near the yurt in the cold night air where they would be safe from wolves and then sat down to another beautiful array of food.*

*This time however was the cooked head of a sheep (domestic) sitting in front of my place. It was explained that I was given the honor to follow the tradition of the Kazakhs to cut off the various parts from the head and present them to the other guests of the table. If I gave an ear to a guest, this would improve his sense of hearing, an eye for better seeing, a nose for better smelling, etc. Each guest Kazakh accepted it with much gratitude by taking it in their hands and going back to their seat with much pleasure.*

*Alexander presented me with a hatchet-like apparatus, a traditional weapon of the Kazakhs. At the same time he gave Bob a large pipe that could be used for smoking a cigarette or tobacco (or possibly used for some kind of dope). These people were so pleased to see us here that they felt every meal had to be a party and there was always plenty of brandy and vodka.*

*Today I estimated seeing about 250 sheep. In talking to others, it was near the same. The other hunters did not hunt the breaks in the plateaus, but more on individual mountains that were formed the same way as the breaks, but the Caspian had washed and eroded all around, making rather small individual mountains up to a few miles across.*

*14 March*

Bob and I headed west today along the north shore of the peninsula. I questioned Daugaliev again about the number of urial sheep in the area. Earlier they said there were some 10,000 sheep here, a rather unbelievable number. They confirmed that their estimates were fairly accurate, but maybe they could be off a little, perhaps only 9,000 or maybe 12,000, but felt they were not far off. This area is approximately 400 square kilometers and they explicitly said that the 10,000 sheep are only here, not other areas with other populations.

As we drove across the plains we saw an abundance of camel herds and horses. They indicted the horses were mustangs and as wild as they were, I believe that to be true. At the sight of our vehicle, they would start running.

We soon came close to two rather large table mountains and stopped for glassing the nearer of the two. We skirted around the first one and drove to a low pass between the two mountains. I immediately saw some rams sky-lighted on top of the second mountain. I had just enough time to train the spotting scope on them before they disappeared over the top. They definitely looked promising, as good trophies. Then we saw more sheep down in the valley that separated the two mountains.

There were a few nice rams, and they had not seen us. Bob loaded his rifle, and we stalked as far as we could go to the end of the pass. They were definitely too far for a shot and we had not much chance of getting closer without being detected.

Even though the wind seemed favorable, and we didn't expose more than our heads over the crest of the ridge, the herd spooked and ran up and out of sight on top of the second mountain. After a lot of sign language and a few known Russian terms, it was decided that Bob would go down to the area near where the last herd was feeding and wait in a likely place where the sheep would probably pass if spooked from one mountain to the other.

Then I was driven around to the far side of the mountain where I could approach it, climb on top, look into various draws and, in general, hunt for myself, but hopefully drive the sheep Bob's way. I was dropped off with an assistant guide on the high side of the mountain that made climbing it quite easy. Once on top, it was flat as a pancake with low ground cover and apparently good feed for sheep.

There was no game in sight, so we crossed the top diagonally to a place that would be exactly opposite the side where Bob was. We cautiously looked over the side, which gave us a panoramic view of the plains beyond. I spotted sheep right out on the plains several hundred meters from the base of the mountain. There were about 75 animals, including a mixture of rams, ewes and lambs. We kept moving that direction getting a different view of the surrounding area and seeing many more sheep on the flats.

The mountain I was on was actually two "table-top" mountains, each fairly round, joined by a high pass connecting the two. At this point we were looking across to the steep sides of the second part of this mountain. I spotted rams on a bench a few hundred yards down from the top, but probably 600–700 yards from me. I studied them through the spotting scope. There were some big rams, without doubt. At this point,

🐑 **My largest Transcaspian urial sheep (Ovis vignei arkal)
had a wide curl and long, white frontal neck mane.**

*I had about 100 sheep in sight with possibly a
third of them were rams.*

*I bellied up to the edge at the closest point
across from where the rams were lying, and I
determined which I felt was the biggest ram. I
was uneasy about the distance I had to shoot,
which I estimated to be between 500 and 600
yards. The angle was down at about 35 degrees,
which would lessen my bullet drop by about
40 percent. So, even though the distance was
almost twice that far, I figured I could aim the
same as if the animal were about 300 yards. I
turned the scope to 7 power and rested the fore
end of the rifle on my down-filled hat. Lying
down, the ram gave me an awfully small target.
I carefully closed my hand on the hair trigger
and instantly felt the bite of the scope on the
bridge of my nose—— another scope cut!!*

*The herd exploded into a maze of move-
ment all over the hillside. I didn't see a ram
down and damned myself for possibly missing.
I did notice, however, a few rams standing on
a point looking back down the hill. My hopes
rose, as often in such a case of a lead ram being
down, the rest of the herd will wait for him to
come and lead them out of the danger.*

*I swiftly raised the binoculars to study the
hillside below. Sure enough, there was a ram
lying there. He was apparently crippled, but
more likely hiding and hoping the danger would
pass. Neither the guide nor myself had exposed
ourselves, so the sheep did not know the source
of the danger. I took very special care in placing
the crosshairs again on the ram and squeezed
another round off and this time the ram rolled
gently over, and I knew I had my ram.*

*By now both herds of sheep had topped
out and vanished some place over the plateau
beyond. Shortly a shot rang out in the valley to
my right from where Bob was. I was thrilled*

Everyone collected fine specimens of the Transcaspian urial in Kazakhstan, the first taken in modern times by foreigners. In front of yurt are Pete Papac, Al Means, and Chris Klineburger, while a late evening photo shows the trophies of Andy Samuels, Bob Chisholm, and Craig Leerberg.

*and hoped he had connected with a ram. There were no further shots, which often is a good indication of getting something with the first shot. I indicated to the guide who was with me to go to Bob and help him and also try to locate the driver of the car and get him to drive around the mountain as close as possible below my sheep.*

*I worked my way down the steep and rocky slope to my ram. He was a beauty! I field dressed him and waited, thinking that the jeep would arrive. Soon it did appear in the distance, but went out of sight again, as there was no direct way to get to the mountain because of many deep ravines. I contemplated skinning the trophy out, but decided to wait and enjoy the luxury of having a skinner in camp.*

*Later the vehicle came from another direction and made it close to the base of the mountain. We carried the sheep down and met Bob*

*and the driver. Bob's sheep was great and he was one happy person. He had in his hand the heart of his sheep, showing me how his bullet went right through the center of it. Bob is a terrific shot and given a chance, he always gets his game.*

*Back at camp, we were thrilled to see that Al and Craig had gotten their rams today as well. Craig's was a very nice ram, but Al was disappointed in the size of his. I asked permission for Al to shoot another sheep and Valery Savinov agreed. As usual, it was party time again, with everyone having gotten their urial.*

*15 March*

*Cold and snowy this morning. We expected rather warm conditions here, but it has been quite cold and with the seemingly ever-present wind, the chill factor puts it down below freezing most of the time. Bob and I started out back* toward our table mountains of yesterday. Al went the other direction toward the lone mountains a little inland. Pete joined Al just to keep busy and maybe see a chance to take a Jaran.

## TIME LAPSE

*Back at camp a sudden decision was made to break up camp and go back to the hotel. Within minutes the yurt was coming down. They told Al it was OK, that there was a place he could still hunt tomorrow by driving out from the hotel. Somehow they must have called ahead, as our rooms had been made ready.*

*We took a sauna, which felt very good. Then we were taken into Shevchenko to a home. Again a cooked sheep head was placed in*

front of me for carving and handing out to the various table guests, and it was received with great thanks.

*16 March*

*Al was not awakened early as promised, which disappointed him. At breakfast we were told we had an early afternoon flight arranged to Alma Ata, which would get us on our way a few days early. On the way to the airport, another custom was observed. The bus was stopped along side the road and a final toast of vodka and the goodbyes were made. Then we proceeded to the airport where the Aeroflot plane was waiting for the three-hour flight.*

*We arrived early evening and Igor was awaiting with the announcement that Andy and Craig had a flight arranged back to Moscow within an hour and that our flight to our next destination, Karaganda, was scheduled for around 6 AM. Most of our gear was left in a heap at the airport, and we went into town to the hotel for dinner.*

## KARAGANDA ARGALI

On 17 March Al, Bob, Pete, and I were on our flight from Alma Ata to the far north of Kazakhstan to the city of Karaganda. Igor Zilenko, who was not allowed to attend our previous hunt at the Caspian because of

《 **On the plains of Kazakhstan are large herds of saiga antelope, tough, short-legged animals that can outrun a vehicle. They have wax-like horns and a Roman nose snout that gives a breathing capacity like no other mammal. Here the renowned sportsman Jim Conklin shows off a fine specimen.**

travel restrictions, was well established here and took over as host.

Also joining us in Karaganda were Russ Underdahl from Minneapolis and Milan Sablich from Bloomfield Hills, Michigan. Igor settled us in our hotel and announced that a banquet was arranged with the mayor in our hotel. It was a gala affair emphasizing the first foreign visitors to come to the region, assuring us that Karaganda was at our disposal.

Igor then took me to his home and showed us several picked up horns of the argali in this area, the Semipalatinsk argali (Ovis ammon collium), the northernmost of the argali family of sheep. He said they estimated there were more than 7,000 sheep in the general area and that the locals did not hunt, so they were on the increase.

I told him we had to do something about the common name of the argali, Semipalatinsk, which I did not like, let alone could

Zakan, the Chief of Agriculture for the Zakan area in the far Northeast of Kazakhstan, opened his home to accommodate the first foreigners to visit the area. From left, Al Means, Pete Papac, Chris Klineburger, and Zakan (with suspenders).

not pronounce, so I told him I was now officially changing the name to Karaganda argali. He laughed and said his joint venture company, Dalso Pacific, would honor my request.

The next day we were promptly moved by a caravan of Russian jeeps and a van to the next major town to the east, Karakarelin, whose prior name was Sukur-Kuduk. Again we were placed in a hotel and told this would be our base camp.

On the one side the idea seemed good to me, as it was full winter here with snow everywhere. I did not relish the idea of staying in the tents that I had brought with temperatures well below freezing and the ever-present icy cold wind. On the other hand I was concerned about low, rolling hills as far as I could see. I expected high, lofty mountains, typical argali sheep habitat that I experienced in Tajikistan, Mongolia, Afghanistan, and China.

As always, a banquet had been arranged, this time with the wildlife officials as such: Alexander Voriz, Chief of Forestry; Alexander Berbir, Chief of Hunt Section; and Arkin Basheav, game master and head guide. Both Alexander and Arkin were newly appointed into departments resulting from the planning of this exploratory hunt. In their many toasts,

I raised my glass and thanked them for "officially changing the name of this argali sheep from Semipalatinsk argali to Karaganda argali." There was a lot of chatting taking place between Igor and the officials and

**Zakan had hundreds of well-trained Arabian horses under his care as Chief of Agriculture. Note their version of the lariat.**

finally laughter, nodding and raising their glasses, "To the Karaganda argali." It was now official.

From Karakarelin we drove different directions by jeep to nearby hills, none of which had high mountains. One range was Gura Kuzil Taz (translated Red Stone) near the village of Miriburak. Another was Kara Gash/Harnishti Mountain Reserve. Still another was hills near the village of Karkaralinsk. Single-track snow machines were made available to go up the valleys. From there we could climb to the ridge tops where the wind had blown much of the snow away making hiking much easier.

On one occasion, I was taken by snow machine up a long valley deep in snow. From what appeared to be a big snow bank, I saw smoke rising. We pulled up to it and walked through a snow tunnel and knocked on the door. An elderly woman greeted us and jabbered with my guide. After seating us

at a table, she immediately scurried around her cooking stove, which also provided heat for the house. In what seemed less than five minutes, she had a noodle entrée and hot tea in front of us. Not speaking Russian, I determined through motions that her husband was out with their domestic stock in search of wind-blown faces exposing vegetation.

On another occasion, Pete, Bob, Al, and I were taken far to the east to a settlement called Zakan, named after the chief who apparently governed over the area. Zakan took us into his home, where his living room became our bedroom. On one wall there were stacks of mattress pads and blankets, which was our bedding. Food was also at his large dining table for the several days we spent there.

Our interpretor explained that all travelers through this remote part of Asia carried only their day provisions and other necessities or cargo, as the rule of the land was for residents to supply food and accommodations.

**In the far north of Kazakhstan, in the Karaganda area, heavy snows presented feed problems for domestic herds. Huge tractor drawn trailers of hay were brought to the Karagach area where we were hunting argali sheep.**

🐾 **Lunch break was simple. Hang pot from bumper, start up blowtorches, and have hot water in minutes!**

There were no inns or hotels for hundreds, and perhaps thousands of miles through this remote wilderness. Zakan was the Chief of Agriculture, and hundreds of well-trained Arabian horses were under his care, which supported most of the livelihood of the people here.

He provided mounts for us to use while hunting, which was a perfect way to get around the rolling grasslands punctuated with hilly outcrops. The area was more arid with less snow, providing good year round pasture for the domestic stock and wildlife.

Another time Russ, Al, and I were driven to the remote village of Karagach where we were put up in a home after the day's hunt, again lining up their mattress pads on the floor. However, Russ didn't care for this kind of living and had his driver take him back to Karakarelin, several hours of nighttime driving.

This area had heavy snows, so huge hay trailers were pulled in by tractor to save the domestic herds. Our hunt area was across what appeared to be a huge frozen-over swampland, so Al and I were ferried across by snow machine.

We saw argali sheep in every place we hunted, but they were scattered. We only hunted from places where a road could take us, and there were very few roads. The habitat of these sheep is probably 10,000 square miles, with hundreds of hilly outcrops.

Typical of all argalis, they have long legs and can cover a lot of ground, which they regularly do. We all collected good rams,

**Chris with a Semipatalinsk argali, (Ovis ammon collium) that he was successful to rename as the Karaganda argali.** 🐾

**Milan Sablick took the largest specimen of Karaganda argali. Note the white frontal neck mane, typical of most argalis.**

which, to my knowledge, were the first ever to be preserved. We also saved tissue samples for the ongoing study by the International Sheep Hunters Association of the world's wild sheep.

The rounded horn cross-section, curl of horn and flaring at the tips is typical of all argalis. The presence of a white frontal neck mane was also similar to most all argalis from the Tibetan Plateau, the Himalayas, the Pamirs, the Tien Shan, and up to here. The pelage color, however, was distinct for this far north sub-species. They are basically a solid grey, with a very light frosty grey on the upper body, then darker toward the underside. There is white on the back of the legs and solid white on the lower legs, as well as on the belly and front of the neck and snout.

Bob and Milan collected two big Russian boars. No other game was seen, although

grizzly-type brown bears are present, but currently sleeping in hibernation.

## OTHER KAZAKHSTAN EXPERIENCES

Kazakhstan rapidly became a popular destination in Asia for the next few years for hunters through my efforts. However, the bureaucrats eventually found ways to mess it up. The last time I went to Kazakhstan was in the fall of 1993 when the new independent governments were clumsily taking charge.

I escorted (ex) Governor Tom Bolack of New Mexico on a hunt, first at the forested Badger Reserve near Moscow and then on to hunt different areas in Kazakhstan. The two areas we were to hunt were the Shevchenko area near the Caspian and a new area in the southeast that had just become available.

The latter area took in the Baguti Mountains that lie on the north edge of the Tien Shan Range and south of the famed Ili River and Borohoro Range on the China border. I had read much about this general area that

**Both Bob Chisholm and Milan Sablich took big Russian boars. We were able to fetch this one with the use of a horse drawn sledge.**

had been hunted last in the mid-1920s before socialism shut it down till now.

To give an example of how the new independent governments were making life more complicated, read an excerpt from my journal of that trip. Keep in mind that the native Kazakhs now were positioning themselves in a newly structured government and at the same time the various departments were fighting over who would be in charge of wildlife and hunting. They also detested the Russians that were previously in charge and certainly those Moscow Russians that were running my hunt.

One night on the way back from hunting ibex, my jeep was stopped at a roadblock and my rifle was confiscated. Here are some journal notes:

*On the gun situation of the 22-250 that had been confiscated, they would not release it to Vsevolod, who tried to repossess it the next day. They said I had to be present to get it. So a day later when we went to fetch it, we were informed it was taken to police headquarters in Alma Ata—the capitol of Kazakhstan.*

*So another trip was necessary. We were well over an hours drive from Alma Ata. We went to the central police station where we were to meet with the proper authority to get the rifle. We were escorted to the high authority's office where a lot of jabbering took place, and it was apparent to me that they were making an international incident out of this simple situation.*

*It bears noting that all the officials now are Kazakhs, instead of the predominant rulers I have known from just a few years back,*

*Russians. You can see the "hand writing on the wall," since these Asian countries only broke away from the U.S.S.R. in the past year or so, they want to do their own thing, right, wrong, or otherwise.*

*The top bureaucrats said we must have a firearms permit issued by Kazakhstan, not Russia. (It bears noting that the Magical Tour staff, when getting our visas from the Kazakh Consulate in Moscow asked if there was any further firearms license necessary for Kazakhstan, and they were told it only required the Russia permit, which we already had).*

*So Vsevolad brought this up and the bureaucrat blew his top and read the riot act to Vsevolad and made him shut up and sit down. Vsevolad is Ukraine and it was apparent these people wanted to be the rulers, and that the Russians and other Soviets that had ruled them since the 1920s now had to take orders from them.*

*The top guy now calmed down and explained to me, through interpretation from Sergey, that I had not violated any rules and the firearm would be returned to me but "I will deal with this terrible violation of the law (Vsevolad) separately."*

*He basically said, and did read from their written law, that rifled firearms were illegal in the country, only smooth bores were permitted. I told the official that this was unfortunate. We must now cancel and stop any other foreigners from coming into Kazakhstan for hunting, as it would be impossible for the sportsmen to hunt with smooth bore firearms and not spend great amounts of hard currency here.*

*He assured, however, they can issue a special permit for hunters. I said, "Fine, please issue us the proper permit and inform your hunting operators and your Kazakh consulates of your procedure." He then backed down and said they were just in the process of establishing this procedure (obviously something only being formed in his mind at the time!).*

*In the two days to follow, even though the official told his people to give me the gun, we went through hours of sitting around while many different Kazakh officials put their two cents worth into the matter.*

*I told the coordinator we were dealing with that they obviously had no procedures, no permit system, no one that could make decisions and asked what we can expect in the future. He assured me that in two weeks time they can issue firearms permits for our clients from the time of application. I said, "That sounds pretty efficient for a five minute job!" Finally we got the rifle, and it is the good thing we had the four-day delay here. We truly set history and developed a procedure that they never thought of before.*

The money used here in Kazakhstan is a ruble printed in 1992, apparently by the Bank of Russia, which differs only slightly from the Russian ruble. The exchange rate currently is 3,000 rubles to one U.S. dollar, as opposed to 1,250 Russian rubles to one U.S. dollar.

The staff told me I could not use the Russian rubles here when I had them stop to buy vodka. After exchanging some dollars and buying vodka, the clerk gave me Russian rubles in change! When exiting Kazakhstan on Aeroflot Airlines, while buying some peanuts and beer from the stewardess going through the aisle with her cart, she looked at my Kazakh rubles and explained she could not take them, as, "They were old rubles."

However, after the 1990 opening of Kazakhstan, many other opportunities awaited me in these Asian countries, while we expanded programs in those already started. With similar frustrations in Asia as witnessed above, along with the U.S. Fish and Wildlife Service's interference in foreign wildlife programs, my enthusiasm to forge ahead was dwindling.

# CHAPTER 16

# The Opening of Kamchatka

For the better part of a century, the Kamchatka Peninsula, on the far east of the Soviet Union, had been closed to all outsiders. The north-south land barrier had been a crucial military zone protecting the country's eastern boundary. The wildlife, including moose, caribou, brown bear, and the coveted Kamchatka bighorn sheep, had been undisturbed, except for limited local hunters. There are virtually no roads on this landmass, which is perhaps 10 times the size of the Alaska Peninsula, with a very small population. I was finally successful in arranging the first ever hunt in modern times to take place on this forbidden, yet desirable, destination. Here is my journal as written on this trip in 1990, except for some time lapses:

*July 31, 1990*

*The long awaited Kamchatka bighorn sheep hunt has finally become reality. 20 years of working with Soviet Intourist ended up being a fruitless effort to get the renowned Kamchatka Peninsula in Far East Siberia open for sheep hunting. The Kamchatka bighorn has been the focal point for hunters the world over since I opened the Soviet Union for hunting in 1970.*

Following Perestroika (allowing private business) and our partnership with Vladimir Treschov in National Hunting Service, the Kamchatka hunt was approved. I contacted the people that were high on my "Kamchatka list" and selected these participants; Bob Chisholm of Wichita, Kansas; Pete Papac of Montesano, Washington; Phyllis Tucker of Muncie, Indiana; and Dixon Granstra of Sheldon, Iowa. As observers, Dixon brought his wife Esther and Pete brought his fiancé, Virginia Schneider. Additionally a film crew from Great Northern Productions, Mike Degutis and John Helegren joined in to document this history-making event.

## TIME LAPSE

My group met in Moscow, where special visas were obtained for the out-of-bounds destinations, along with sightseeing and shopping. The evening of 2 August we went to Domodedovo Airport and boarded our plane.

We talked nice to the flight attendant and she blocked off some of the good front rows for us. The flight was seven hours and over the Arctic. We had midnight sun all the way, as we were looking over the top of the earth, seeing the sun all the time on the North Pole horizon. This was the second polar flight we were on since leaving the U.S.A.

We arrived in Magadan at 11 AM having lost eight more hours in time change. No one from NTL accompanied us on the flight, but Vladimir was there waiting along with some of his Moscow staff. We claimed our bags and had to go back through security to get back out to the charter aircraft, which Vladimir had arranged for us to continue up to the head of the Kamchatka Peninsula.

When going through security I kept the passports out of sight and ushered my group out the door as fast as they came through. Vladimir had them busy checking his rifle and gun permit, as it is not usual for a Soviet citizen to be carrying a gun around. So we got through Magadan without a hitch, a place where we did not have permits to be.

We boarded our AN 28 twin prop charter with all 16 passengers (plus two pilots) and our mountain of gear. The capacity is supposed to be 2,100 kilos, but we had about 2,700 kilos, so they only filled the fuel tanks half-full. This aircraft cruises at 300 km/hr., has 14 passenger seats, but there were 16 of us plus gear that filled every available space, including the aisle!

Our route was northeast to Takhtogamsk on the coast to Chaykukha on the northwest base of the Taygonos Peninsula. This small village had a fair-sized airstrip. Vladimir explained that it was used during World War II by the U.S. Air force as a base against Japan.

This was a fueling stop for us, so in a half-hour we were airborne again, crossing the Taygonos Peninsula, and crossing the northern tip of the Sea of Okhotsk to Kamenskoye, which was another very small village. This one just had a dirt strip and was not capable of taking very large aircraft. It is on the Penzhena River, a major drainage from the Arctic. The actual town that we landed in was Manily, slightly west of Kamenskoye. Our helicopter was out on a run before our arrival, but soon showed up.

*Esther Granstra and Phyllis Tucker disembark the huge MI-8 helicopter that brought us from Manily at the head of the Sea of Okhotsk to our camp on the Kamchatka Peninsula.*

*Soon we loaded all our gear plus a few timbers to be cut up for firewood, and lifted off. The MI-8 helicopter is bigger than the AN-28 fixed wing aircraft with a larger carrying capacity of three tons, of which one ton is fuel if tanks are filled.*

*We were off and now traveling 1½ hours southeast to the Enychavayam River, where camp under Vladimir's supervision, had been set up by the local staff. It is a beautiful layout* and a well-constructed camp. The sleeping tents for the guests are American-made, expedition type that my company sent over, while the rest of the equipment is Soviet made. There is one large tent for dining with tables and benches, plus a cook tent with three wood cook stoves side-by-side, as well as five sleeping tents for the staff. An outhouse was made out of sight, covered and waterproof. An excellent camp in the usual NTL professional fashion.*

*The sun was out and temperatures were in the 50s F—and the mosquitoes were out in numbers. They explained this was the first day with no rain in three weeks and we were credited with bringing the sunshine. A nice dinner, featuring fish and soup was enjoyed by all before retiring for a good night in camp.*

*This long-awaited destination was now another time zone away, now 20 time zones from my Seattle departure point, only four time zones short of going around the world! As of now, no flights arrive from overseas on the east coast of U.S.S.R., except one from Niota, Japan into Khabarovsk, in the southeast of Siberia. It is impossible to take rifles through Japan, so the*

*Our sheep camp was well laid out on the Enychavayam River. The five tents on the right are mountain expedition type tents that the author supplied.*

Atlantic routing was our only possible way to travel.

Camp elevation is about 1,500 feet while the mountains average 3,000 feet that go up on both sides from camp that was at 62° Latitude, 169° Longitude.

*04 August*

After the first good night's sleep in the better part of a week, I welcomed sleeping in 'til about 8 AM. After a breakfast of porridge and abundant trimmings, we gathered around the flagpole, where American and U.S.S.R. flags waved, for a welcoming ceremony. This included introduction of all the guests, guides, and staff, along with discussions on the requirements of the hunters for a safe and successful hunt. We were paired off in groups, each hunter with two guides, and then individual discussions in these sub-groups as to the hunt plan. Yuri Puchkov, our doctor from Moscow, also speaks good English, so he was the main interpreter for our discussions. Vladimir speaks broken English and a few of the Moscow staff, a few words.

Dixon's group decided to cross the river and hunt an area where sheep were spotted a few days earlier. They had some tall rubber boots for the crossing. The other three sub-groups hunted the mountains behind camp, where sheep also were spotted. I joined Bob and the film crew and we headed straight into the central part of the rather small grouping of mountains. Phyllis and Pete's groups formed pincers in each direction north and south to come into the mountains from those directions.

Vladimir Treschov and Chris glassing for sheep that were found in all directions from camp.

With the heavy filming gear, Airoflex camera with all the attachments and Nagra recording equipment, moving was a little slow for our group, but we inched our way through the low growth of brush and scrub pine in the lower areas. There were a lot of ripe berries and cranberries. There were many wild mushrooms, which the guides happily picked and put in their packs.

Once out of the creek bottoms, we took to a rather steep ridge up that was easy footing. Vladimir struck out ahead of us in hopes of spotting sheep to help set our direction, while Oleg Boychev (local doctor as well as guide) and Pyotr Vyatkin stayed with us.

We took a slow pace, resting occasionally while looking for signals from Vladimir in case he saw something to change our direction. He topped out, glassing carefully, took the main ridge to the right. About ¾ the way up our ridge, we stopped to observe all of the many ridges and valleys in our view. We saw Vladimir circling back to our right, eventually taking him back toward camp.

While we sat there a very large wolverine crossed one of the peaks to our right, running as if something scared it. It was large and very old, as the patch on its back was a creamy white, typical of a very old male.

A little later Phyllis's group appeared on a far ridge to our left. They glassed intently and had some lunch. Then they disappeared, apparently going deeper into the mountains. So now, it was our time to move up to that saddle on the high ridge above us.

Pyotr went on ahead with the film crew, while Bob, Oleg, and I stayed a little behind. Pyotr soon came running back telling us of "baran" (sheep) being there. He indicated that one was bolshoi (big). We hurried to the saddle and saw that they were all the way across on a high ridge about 1,500 meters (one mile) away.

Through my nine power Leupold binoculars, I could clearly see a heavy set of horns on one of the rams in a group of four. Over to the left of them, about 500 meters, was a ewe and lamb. The rams topped out on a high peak, then worked their way down and out of sight. We waited and observed to see what movement of sheep or people might occur. We knew that Pete's group was someplace on the other side of that ridge. It wasn't long 'til I spotted Phyllis and Vladmir "Walter" Koscheev on the far left of the same ridge going in the direction of the sheep, but about a mile behind them.

Pyotr and I discussed the best we could in our respective language (neither knew the other's language) what to do. We agreed that we should continue climbing our ridge, which joined the side ridge that both the sheep and Phyllis were on. We felt that if the sheep were disturbed by either Phyllis or Pete, the sheep might come our way.

Therefore, once we were at a good vantage point, I snuggled in out of the cool wind behind a rock where I had a good view of Phyllis's ridge and the various ridges coming off the main ridge. Now I could see Phyllis's group, which eventually came to the exact spot where the rams had disappeared earlier from our view. Bob and the guides along with the film crew were well situated waiting for action, whatever it might be.

I watched intently to see if Phyllis would get in shooting position, but soon they started to traverse the near side of the peak where the rams were last seen. They came to the next saddle and carefully glassed once again. Soon Phyllis got into shooting position and fired once, then twice. They did not move, so my hopes diminished in her getting the ram, but soon they went over and out of sight.

Upon our return to camp, about 8 PM, Pete's group was still out, but Dixon was back—and what a wild story he had. He got a bear, and Vladimir had just finished the final skinning process—a seven-foot bear, which is not big for this area. It is a beautiful blonde color, even though unprimed for this time of the year.

Here is the story that Dixon and his guides told: They went up the canyon across from camp looking for sheep. Dixon spotted a nice ram in the distance at the head of the canyon. They started that way when they spotted a bear. At further inspection, it turned out to be a female with three, second-year cubs. So Dixon said no as a trophy. The bears were quite a way above them, but they did decide to try to get a little closer and take some pictures. They barely got started and really weren't paying much attention to the bear that was about 150 yards above them at a steep angle.

They were lying down behind a ledge and talking to one another, when Dixon saw his guides' eyes get a big surprised look, and he looked around and saw the bear running down the mountain at top speed right at them. They got up and Anatoly grabbed the gun. Dixon reached over and flipped the safety off, and then Anatoly forced the rifle into Dixon's hands.

He raised the rifle and fired quickly at the bear 30 or so yards away. The bear never seemed to be phased and kept coming at full speed. Dixon immediately jacked another shell into the chamber and fired again at point blank right into the chest at a couple of yards away as the bear made its final leap. While the charge was taking place, Anatoly was off to one side waving his arms and hollering at the bear trying to distract it and even threw Dixon's binoculars at the bear.

While the bear was coming down the hill and all during the commotion, the bear was roaring, growling and grunting. After firing the final shot while the bear was lunging toward him, Dixon poked the gun barrel toward the bear, and it went right into its throat. He fell on his back and put his legs against the bear pivoting it past him.

In looking back at the bear, Dixon remembered seeing the bear throw the rifle into the air, which apparently went all the way down

its throat, stopped only by the riflescope. At that point, the bear turned back on Dixon, landing right on Dixon when it died.

Alexander Vyslanko, the other guide, had gone way ahead and was way up the mountain, but had been watching the bear sequence in his binoculars. He was horrified and came running at top speed down the mountain. Both Anatoly and Alexander were more excited than Dixon and were both sure that Dixon had received critical wounds as he was covered with blood.

Feeling his limbs, pulling his clothes back and checking him over, they found the blood was all from the bear, as it had gushed out from the very large bullet hole in the chest right from the ruptured heart.

After settling down from the excitement, they watched the three cubs wander off, apparently unconcerned. This is usually the time the mother bears run the cubs off, so they may have been through that process already. They skinned the bear out and ended their hunting for the day. Dixon was apparently in good condition, except for a sore knee and a few muscles. He showed us his gun, which was saturated with blood inside and out.

The camp staff reported hearing four more shots from up on the mountain beyond where we had come from in the direction where Phyllis and Pete were. Finally, around 10 PM we spotted Phyllis's party coming across a mountain in the basin in our view from camp.

The guides appeared to have heavier packs than before, so we assumed she had her ram. The fact that Pete was out so late, we had hopes he had success as well. About 11 in the last

☾ **Vladmir Koscheev and Phyllis Tucker with the first Kamchatka sheep (Ovis nivicola koryakorum) taken in modern times.**

twilight, Phyllis came into camp with the first ram. They had skinned it out and brought the full skin and just part of the meat, figuring to send someone up tomorrow for the rest of the meat.

It was too dark for pictures, so we listened to Phyllis' story of what happened. She had not hit the first ram she shot at. There were four rams in that bunch and she selected the biggest, which was about 300 yards at a steep angle down hill. After shooting, the ram ran off, and her second shot was about 500 yards away.

After failing to find any trace of blood, they continued on the same ridge, which brought them closer to camp. They kept checking carefully for sheep and found a lone ram feeding on the opposite side of the ridge. It may have gotten wind of them and saw them, so it took off running. She hit it three of the four shots, one of them grazing its horn.

She had a heavy-horned 14-year-old ram, the first taken in modern times of a Kamchatka

bighorn. Pete came in shortly after, telling he had seen the same sheep that Phyllis collected.

## TIME LAPSE

*06 August*

At 6 AM, Peter and Dixon were off with their guides in their respective areas in different directions across the river. Weather was good, partly cloudy but no rain. The rest of us waited around, as the helicopter was scheduled to come in. Phyllis wanted to try for bear, so her guides took her downriver, and it was planned that if the helicopter did come, they would look for them, pick them up, and take them farther down.

We kept spotting, and we did spot one lone ram late in the evening on a high ridge behind camp. The helicopter did not arrive. We spotted Pete's group coming across the river flats with sheep horns showing on top of one of the packs. Shortly we saw Dixon coming from the other direction and it looked like their loads were heavier. Both parties arrived within a few minutes and both got nice rams! So what a hunt!—Three rams in three days. Phyllis returned later without luck.

We finally had time to study the sheepskins as both parties saved full skins. There are variations in coloration between the two, but the most vivid thing that caught my attention is that these sheep are a definite gray in color. The main coloration on the legs, head, and body is a solid medium gray. The rear half of the back turns slightly tannish, mainly on the tips of the hair. Both had white on the muzzle and a little on the ear tips, as well as a very small white rump patch that goes in a stripe a short way down the inner back leg.

*Pete's ram had a pure white patch between the horns. He said that all the rams in the herd had that same white patch. On the other hand, Dixon's sheep did not have the white between the horns, but his did have an indication of a thin white stripe down the back of both the front and back legs. The gray color is very interesting in comparison to the chocolate brown color of the sheep we collected in Yakutia two years ago, a thousand miles to the west of here. I spent several hours skinning and instructing the guides on proper field care of specimens.*

*07 August*

*Weather remaining good. It has been cloudy the majority of the time, but the rain has been limited to some small sprinkles. Most of the guests mustered in the cook tent, which is warmer but much smaller, waiting for the helicopter to come in. The helicopter arrived with a large load of wood. It only had about 50 minutes of spare gas. We had hoped to use the helicopter to take Bob and me a distance from camp and either*

Pete Papac and his guide return from a hard, but successful, days hunt in the mountains on the other side of the Enychavayam River.

*make a spike camp or take us to a place where we could hunt our way back to camp. All three of the successful sheep hunters are interested in bear, so they all boarded the helicopter and flew down river with the idea to drop one or more groups off if good bear sign is found. However, there were no signs of bear, so they came back, except Pete's two guides that were dropped off to bring the meat out from Pete's ram taken yesterday.*

*It was about noon before Bob and I started out with Vladimir and Alexander Ovcherov and Alexander's son, Andrei. In addition, the film crew, Mike and John, joined us, as it may be a good opportunity to film some sheep. We went up the same canyon we hunted the first*

Dixon and Pete with a pair of fine Kamchatka sheep. Note pure white patch on the head of Pete's ram.

day, but instead of taking the side ridge to the top, we continued up the main draw. It opened into a nice basin with grass and steep side hills, a paradise for sheep.

Soon we spotted a ram partway up the mountain, traversing from his bed on a shale slide. The sun had been out for a while, so apparently it was getting a little warm for him. He fed a little as he moved around to the shady side and soon settled in a green area that had a lot of grass and low brush. Through the binoculars, I saw the ram pick a mushroom and eat it.

We moved a little ways up a side draw, out of sight of the ram. We had the wind in our favor as it was going straight up the draw we were in, which is typical for this time of day. Generally, the wind goes down in the morning and up the canyons in the afternoon.

Bob and Vladimir eased over the top in great position, about 250 yards from where the sheep was settling down. I came up behind them just in time to see the big ram lying down. Bob squeezed off and the ram never moved, except for a few rolls down the hill.

The ram is 11 years old and apparently, he would not have lasted another winter. His chewing teeth were about gone, which would have made it hard for him to get the vitality needed to survive the severe winters they have here. After skinning out the ram, we got back in camp just in time for the scheduled dinner at 7 PM.

## 08 August

Pete and Dixon went out after bigger sheep and Phyllis struck out for bear again. A second

Oleg Boychev took time to catch some greyling that gave us some delicious variety in our menu.

ram is allowed, and if one is taken, a trophy fee of $5,800 is to be paid. Pete's group headed into the hills behind camp, while Dixon wanted to go back to the same area he got his ram, as they had seen a big, lone ram after he had taken his first one.

Phyllis went the direction where Pete took his ram across the river, as there is a large basin that they felt would be good for bear. Since the three main directions from camp are being covered, Bob and I stayed back to spot and finish taking care of the skins and horns.

In early evening, we saw a group coming out of Mad Bear Canyon and assumed it was Dixon.

*As they got within a mile or so, I could see it was Phyllis, which was a surprise. She headed way to the right into the mountains and came out way to the left. They got into camp just as we were starting dinner and heard her story. They did not see any bear after going well into the basin, so decided to cover some high country making a circle to the left.*

*They came to a tall wood structure on a far ridge, which I assume is a beacon. From studying the contour maps, she was, no doubt, on the divide that separates the watersheds. On this side, the water flows to the head of the Sea of Okhotsk, while the other side flows into the Pacific. That was a tremendous long distance, but Phyllis held up with no problems and didn't appear to be tired at all. She's small and I doubt if she would go 110 pounds soaking wet, but she's tough and keeps up with the best of them.*

*Pete came into camp alone, reported he had taken a second ram just around the corner from camp, and just over the ridge from where Phyllis got her ram and Bob took his. Mike and John had gone along with the Bolex movie camera and got some shots of live rams. He came back shortly after Pete while the guides stayed back to do the preliminary skinning. We sent two more helpers out to pack the meat.*

*Pete had made a spectacular shot at the lead ram running at about 300 yards. They had seen the rams earlier and two of them were butting heads. When they made their stalk, they lost sight of the rams, but were looking over some ewes and lambs. Unknown to them, the rams were just barely under the ridge below them, about 15 yards away!*

*Mike had come over to one side and saw them—and the rams saw him. While he got his movie camera ready, the rams made a break for it. By the time Pete got a good view of them, they were on the other side of the draw running at top speed. He heard them say "Number one" so he led the lead ram a little and rolled it over. It almost went end-over-end and never moved once it hit the ground. This ram was very heavy, but did not measure as big as his first ram.*

*Finally, we saw Dixon coming in the distance and he made it into camp about 10:30. He reported finding the big ram, but upon close inspection, they found that one horn had been broomed off about halfway back, while the one horn had a spectacular flare. Dixon figured it would go over 40 inches, but would not make a good trophy because of the one horn, so he passed it up.*

## TIME LAPSE

*10 August*

*Vladimir awakened John and me at 5 AM to go sheep hunting in the range behind camp. After a snack for breakfast, Konstantin Treschov, nephew of Vladimir, joined us, and we headed straight up the canyon behind camp. Three of the five sheep taken, including the biggest one taken so far by Phyllis, were taken in the range behind camp, and a lot more rams were spotted there than anywhere else.*

*In a little over one hour, we topped the first ridge, constantly glassing for sheep, or any other game, for that matter. We saw nothing, so we turned northeast and followed the ridge to the top, putting us near the summit of the range,*

**Mike Degutis and John Helegren, the film crew, handle the Airoflex camera during the filming of the expedition.**

which is about a 1,500-foot rise from camp. Still nothing, so we continued on the main extension down the other side of the main ridge. We could see a lot of country, and it was beautiful sheep habitat, but no signs of sheep at all. With all the hunting and shooting, the sheep no doubt got smart and left.

We heard two shots earlier down in the main valley up-river from camp. Once we topped out on the north side of the ridge, we saw some people that had just unpacked some horses and were setting up camp. Vladimir thought they could be geologists. Then in the distance, far up the valley above their camp, we could see a massive herd of reindeer. There were many hundreds in the herd and they seemed to flow along the bottom of the valley. The campers were obviously the reindeer herdsmen.

We were back at camp shortly before noon, when we heard a helicopter coming in. They had some passengers, one of which got out and came and spoke with us while the turbines of the helicopter kept running. He reported that a bear in a village killed four people across the

divide to the east in the past week, two of them just two days ago.

They were limited on space, but wanted bear hunters from our group to go to the village to try to eliminate the man-killing bear. Bob, Pete, and Dixon quickly volunteered and were joined by Vladimir and John with his Airoflex camera. They quickly grabbed their guns and a little gear and boarded the helicopter. Apparently, some of the passengers were survivors of one or more of the bear victims.

In the late afternoon, several of the staff were busy making pelmeni, a meat pastry that is a typical main dish in Siberia. The guides were the ones making them, so Esther and Virginia joined in to help. They started with ground sheep meat (a meat grinder is part of the camp gear) that has some spices mixed in.

A special dough is made and rolled out in two-inch rounds. A teaspoon of meat is placed in the center, and the dough folded over and sealed. They made hundreds of these. They were then put in a boiling pot of water for a few minutes and taken out. Butter was put over a bowl of these, and then served with some broth that they were cooked in. Delicious!

The helicopter returned late in the afternoon and still had the Koryak passengers aboard, so they all got off to have tea and snacks. The village that had the bear problem was weathered in. So they went to another town to refuel, then flew around looking for bear in the general area, but the fog never did lift, so they had to abort. One of the Koryak people had a younger brother that was killed by the bear, so he was trying to get there to visit the victim's family.

👁 **Four Koryak Eskimos came to visit us from their reindeer camp several miles to the north.**

👁 **Phyllis, Virginia, and Esther picnicking with two Koryak ladies.**

*On the way back to our camp, they spotted Phyllis and her guides standing over a bear that she had just taken. They landed and loaded the whole bear into the helicopter and brought it to camp. It was seven feet in length and a trophy that Phyllis was happy with. When the helicopter took off, it headed toward the Pacific again, so maybe it cleared enough to get into the village. The pilots had said they might come back tomorrow and give the bear hunt another try.*

*Four native people walked into camp, two adult men, a young boy, and a 19-year-old girl. They are from the reindeer camp, so we fed them and had quite a visit. They reported having about 3,000 reindeer in the herd and were having problems with hoof disease. They had radioed out to get some veterinary help and had killed several deer to send in on a helicopter that was ordered. The helicopter did come in the early evening, flew right over our camp, and we could see where it landed above the herdsmen camp.*

*Most everyone wanted to go to visit the Koryak peoples' camp to take pictures of them and the reindeer herd, so it was planned to do it in the morning first thing, so they could be back in case the helicopter returned for the bear hunt.*

*There was a Siberian husky dog in camp that appeared to be quite tame. Part of the time, it was left running loose, and part of the time it was tied near one of the guides' tent. I had walked past it many times when it was tied up, but today I went by it and it attacked me. It got me right in the thigh. It made a bad wound, so Oleg and Yuri worked it over and even had to put in some stitches.*

## TIME LAPSE

*12 August*

*Bob and I got up early to go out again for sheep. Bob was looking for a bigger ram, while I was still working on my first one. Just getting ready to leave camp, we saw some of the Koryak people coming on horseback. We had thought* they left with their herd, as we had seen them break up their camp yesterday morning.

They had come to get us and take us to their camp, which was situated about five miles up the main river bottom. We woke the others up while the Koryaks enjoyed some breakfast. Bob and I stuck with our plans, but all the rest went to film and visit the Koryaks and the reindeer herd.

Bob and Vladimir headed straight back into the mountains from camp, while Oleg and Alexander Vyslanko joined me to hunt a tall mountain upriver where a scouting party saw some sheep. We crossed the river and stashed the rubber boots, except for Oleg, who always wore them, even while hiking in the mountains. We climbed to the top of the highest peak. Alexander had kept out in front of us a ways, scouting what was ahead.

This mountain system is a lone ridge not connected to any of the other mountains around.

It consisted of twin peaks with a deep saddle in between. Oleg and I sat on the first peak glassing, while Alexander went to the second peak. Suddenly we saw three sheep quite far down the second hill and they were obviously disturbed.

I looked over carefully through my nine power Leupold binoculars and reported to Oleg, "Bolshoi nyet" (not big). They were 700 or 800 yards away and there was only one good ram with two younger rams. They soon took off down the mountain, crossed the river, and went upon the mountain system behind camp. I watched them 'til they topped a ridge and were out of sight.

From where we sat, we were looking down on the reindeer camp and herd. In fact, we watched the others as they went all the way from camp to the Koryak camp and watched them filming.

We saw another wolverine, an unheard of thing to see two wolverines in a single hunt,

**The Koryak natives herded some 3,000 reindeer that must be kept on the move constantly searching new pasture.**

let alone a hunter ever seeing one. Alexander motioned from the other peak for us to come over. Perhaps he had spotted another ram, so down we went from our peak, through the saddle and up his peak only to find that he had seen some very fresh tracks and beds and thought the sheep were still on the mountain. The sheep probably had gotten his wind early, spooking them off the mountain.

We dropped once again into the saddle, where we had lunch. I got to thinking that maybe I made a mistake in judging the horn size of the ram, as the horns did appear quite big from the rear. Therefore, I suggested we go after him—a big undertaking, but I was getting desperate and didn't want to lose any hunting time. So off we went, down to the river, this time without rubber boots. No problem—Oleg carried us across the river over his shoulders!

We headed for the end of the mountain, beyond where the three rams had crossed over. This area is a couple of side ridges beyond where I had hunted three days before. Once we got on top, we looked over several ridges of beautiful sheep country. We glassed for a half-hour or so and saw no signs of the rams. Therefore, reluctantly, we followed the ridge in the direction of camp.

Once at a place where we would angle down to the river bottom, I stopped to glass one more time. Oleg had already started down and motioned for me to come. Alexander had gone farther up the ridge and was just getting back to where I was.

Just by chance, I looked at the first ridge across from us, which I had already looked

No problem of crossing the river without rubber boots. Oleg carried Alexander and I across on his back!

over before. A spot that looked a little out of place caught my eye. The lighter grey of the youngest ram made a contrast that stood out, and then nearby, the darker coloration of the other two rams gave their presence away. It is amazing how they blend in and how without movement, they fit right into the surrounding terrain.

They were bedded down, which I did not expect at around 6 PM. In general, we had found the rams especially would feed first thing in the morning and be bedded down midday, only to start feeding around 4 or 5 o'clock in the afternoon. By far, the majority of sheep have been seen during feeding times.

Rarely did we ever see sheep during the middle of the day even though most of our hunting was at that time. It is no wonder that we wouldn't see the game much when bedded down, the way they seem to dissolve into their surroundings.

Apparently, the ram's pattern was upset when we spooked them at midday, running all

**Chris and Oleg Boychev with well earned Kamchatka ram.**

that distance and probably feeding once they got into this area. How they did not see us could only be due to the fact that all three rams were asleep. The distance was about 800 meters, so I could not distinguish the horns. We motioned to Oleg to come up.

The wind was strong, and it was apparent that we had to get on the other side of the ridge from them. I saw a point on the ridge that would make an ideal shot. The rams were about 100 meters down from the ridge in a very open area.

Just pointing at the route of the stalk was understandable to all of us as it is a common communication among hunters. Unfortunately, we had to expose ourselves until we dropped down off our ridge, but apparently the sheep did not observe us.

Once out of view of them, we hurried down the ridge they were on, crossing over to the backside. A few hundred meters along the ridge and we came to the point I had selected to top out. I eased my head up slightly over a low bush, just enough to see the big ram. He was sound asleep lying with his head toward me, with his horns covering his shoulder area. It was an odd position with his chin buried in the shale so that his horns rested on the ground.

Much to my surprise, the two younger rams jumped to their feet, ran a short distance and stopped to look right at us. I was well hidden and I am certain the wind was right, so I assumed one of the guides behind me must have exposed himself too much. I quickly shifted from binoculars to riflescope. When I first topped out, I had slid the .300 Weatherby Magnum right up along side me ready to grasp it.

Amazingly, the big ram did not move when the other two ran off. As I studied him through the riflescope, he sure looked good and was a trophy worth taking. Moments later he raised his head, looked around a bit and laid his head down once again, this time a little to one side, exposing the point of his shoulder.

I had a perfect rest and assumed the distance to be about 200 meters or so. The scope should be right on at that distance, so I placed the cross hairs right on the point of the shoulder and squeezed off. The ram rolled a few times and never moved. There was no need to hurry, although I kept my eyes on the ram. I looked at the two guides and they were all smiles, showing thumbs-up for a great stalk and a beautiful trophy.

**Celebrating the Opening of Kamchatka the final day of the historical hunt.**

We took pictures and relaxed for a few minutes before the tedious job of skinning the ram out for a full mount. In removing the skin, we found the expanded bullet just under the skin of the rump area. We found that the bullet hit the top of the heart and traveled all the way from the point of the shoulder to its rear end—great bullet performance and an accurate rifle. Since my gun and gear never did show up before we left Moscow, I had borrowed Phyllis's rifle, since she was done hunting.

We cut the meat up in sections and left most of it under some rocks, so we just took the hide, head and hindquarters. Alexander said he would return tomorrow for the rest of the meat. On the way back by a stream, Oleg found a patch of Zelatoi Koren plants, so we started digging roots and ended up with about a kilo of them.

The roots are used for medicine and are said to give stamina when one is tired. It can be taken raw or dried and made into a tea or put into vodka, then take a teaspoon of the vodka when needed. It was about 10 PM when we finally got back into camp—a very long day of almost continuous walking and climbing. I thank God for such good health at 63 and still being able to climb around the mountains I love so much.

I ate outside with the guides, as the rest had already eaten. They immediately cut the liver into bite-sized pieces, fried it in butter and put mayonnaise over the top during the final simmering. We ate it right out of the pan and

« The first five people to collect specimens from Russian's Kamchatka Peninsula. From left, Chris Klineburger, Phyllis Tucker, Dixon Granstra, Bob Chisholm, and Pete Papac.

how delicious it was. Phyllis broke out a liter of vodka and a bottle of champagne and joined the guides and me for a little celebration and fellowship.

Finally, Bob and Vladimir showed up with another ram. Bob got a real beauty, the second largest one taken on the hunt. The reindeer viewers were very happy with their visit—a perfect day for everyone.

*13 August*

A day of rest for most. I skinned trophies along with my students of the School of Taxidermy. In the afternoon, some of the staff brought their table from outside, joined it onto the table in the dining tent, and put a tarp over the top of it—they were getting ready for the celebration banquet. Victor was busy with cooking all kinds of goodies.

At 5 PM the fun started. The guides brought a 10-gallon milk container up to the table, in which they had made a wine from tomatoes.

Recipe:

First day of hunt:

*Mash 1 kilogram of tomatoes,*
*Add: 6 kg. of sugar,*
*6 liters of water,*
*2 sections of yeast*
*Let it sit for at least seven days.*

They call it Braga—I named it Tomato Jack. It is very smooth, pleasant and it really has a kick to it!

Pete saved a bottle of Crown Royal and Vladimir broke out a couple of bottles of champagne. We managed to polish off all of it during the course of the evening with one toast after another. The meal was great with red caviar in hard-boiled eggs, meatballs, sheep cutlets and grayling fish—a great evening with a wonderful group of people.

*14 August*

The helicopter is scheduled at 11, so we were up early. We had a closing ceremony with all the trophies lined up between the American and Soviet flags, flying side-by-side. We took pictures, and then Vladimir and I gave farewell talks. Yuri presented a clay model of a sheep to Phyllis for getting the first ram. It also turned out to be the biggest ram with the highest CIC score.

The helicopter was on time for the 1½-hour flight to Manily, where our AN-28 was waiting for 3 more hours of flying, plus another stop at Chaybukha again for refueling.

We were met at Magadan with a bus and a very nice hostess from Aeroflot who escorted us to their VIP lounge for a four-hour wait 'til the Moscow flight took off.

She arranged for a dinner to be prepared for us in a bar, while we were entertained by an X-rated Italian film on TV—another surprise of new things happening in the Soviet Union. Our IL-62, with two twin-pod jets on the sides of the tail, took off right on time at 9 PM, scheduled to arrive in Moscow at 8 PM, gaining one hour after all the time change.

In the springtime, I returned to explore Southern Kamchatka and took four hunters for hunting the huge brown bear. My companions were Marvin Ripkin and three Mexicans, Carlo Alvarez, Victor Lopez, and Julian Pasquel. We arrived in Petropavlovsk and flown to the West side of the Peninsula and set up camp at a trappers cabin and it was on foot from there. Fishing provided good cuisine and red caviar.

 **Marvin Ripkin with his bear. They compare in size to the Alaska brown bear.**

 **Chris with one of the Mexicans.**

 **Russian guide and Mexican hunter.**

# CHAPTER 17

# Kyrgyzstan

My cup runneth over in 1990. I had more opportunities in the Soviet Union than I could possibly handle. That is when I formed a partnership with Vladimir Treschov, who had split off from the Joint Venture Concord after handling the Asiatic bighorn hunt in Siberia's far east in 1989. He formed a hunting operation of his own, National Hunting Service (NTL).

Joint ventures were too restrictive, as they normally dealt only in specific geographic areas. NTL could still work with joint ventures, but also explore other areas and work directly with local governments. Already in 1990 I had more time scheduled in the U.S.S.R. than at my home office in Seattle, including two major exploratory trips to Kazakhstan and the Kamchatka Peninsula.

Vladimir took full charge to get the Kyrgyzstan (Kirgizia) program started. The borders of this mountainous country lies completely within the enormous Tien Shan Mountains and is sandwiched between Kazakhstan, China, Tajikistan, and Uzbekistan. The Tien Shan Range is among the world's largest, being about 1,500 miles long and a few hundred miles wide in places. About half of the mountain range extends into China.

Only five percent of Kirgizia is cultivated for farming while the rest is mountainous, some of which is so high and rugged that it is impenetrable on foot. Parts, however, are good grazing land for domestic stock, including horses, cattle, domestic sheep, and yaks. With the mountains

In Bishkek, Kirghizstan, Dr. Gennedy Vorobiejov, chief biologist for Kirghizstan and a hunter himself, shows Chris his huge Mid-Asian ibex, which could be the all-time world record. It measured 62½ inches long and 11 inches around the base of the horn.

He had maps and various studies, of which he had copies made for me.

Gennedy was a hunter himself and showed me a prize specimen of his, an ibex with a main beam length of 159 cm (62½ inches) and base circumference of 28 cm (11 inches). The age rings indicated it to be 14 years old. In my estimation it could be the all-time world record ibex. Gennedy assured me all the wildlife in Kirgizia was abundant and he applauded our plan for a foreign sportsman-financed wildlife program.

Our reconnaissance through the mountainous terrain was in the huge MI-8 freight

Gennedy gave me this photo of a 59½-inch ibex taken in 1926.

comes wildlife, providing a natural renewable resource for this poor country, now in need of trade following their independence.

In early summer of 1990, we did a reconnaissance trip through much of the main range of the Tien Shan. Arrival was in the capitol, Frunze, which lies just off the north slope of the mountains near the Kazakh border. Frunze was the name of a Russian military officer, so the plan now is to change the name back to its prior name, Bishkek, a Kyrgyz word for a stirring stick used in cooking.

I had a meeting set up with a prominent biologist, Dr. Gennedy G. Vorobiejov, who is an expert on wild sheep of the Soviet Union. I was eager to visit with him and discuss the dividing lines of the various sheep and ibex.

helicopter, the only machine capable of flying at the required high elevation of 15,000 feet or more. Gennedy sent his son, Alexander (Sasha), along to guide us and later to be a guide for the hunting program. We immediately rose to 10,000 feet to clear the first pass into the magnificent Tien Shan.

As far as the eye could see were snow-covered mountains, many of which rose thousands of feet above us. We headed south crossing several Khrebets, which are mountain ranges within the Tien Shan, some of which are as big as the Cascade Range of northwest U.S. and southern British Columbia. Those we crossed en route to the Naryn region were the Kirgizskiy, Terskey, and Moldo-Too Khrebets.

We encountered ibex in most every rocky area. These are the dark brown-colored ones known locally as the "black ibex," the Capra siberica formosani. I was excited seeing numerous heavy-horned males, some of which were near a full curl. We went fairly direct to the Naryn area where the first Marco Polo sheep hunts were to be conducted. This area is near the China border and not far from the northeast border of Tajikistan.

After a fueling stop in the town of Naryn, we kept going south right to the China border. The terrain was much more sheep-like— that's high rolling mountains favored by wild sheep everywhere. We were rarely out of sight of what I consider the most magnificent and coveted big game trophy animal, the Marco Polo sheep. These are the Ovis ammon poli humes.

As we crossed three Khrebets of the Tien Shan, there were snow-covered mountains as far as the eye could see.

Not much more than a couple hundred miles to the southwest of here, in the Pamirs of Tajikistan, we did the exploratory trip there for the O.a. poli blythe. It seems the major difference in these sub-species is in horn configuration, The blythe has more of a triangular horn cross-section and is thinner, while the humes is more rounded and heavier.

We saw many herds of sheep of a couple of dozen or more, including ewes, lambs and young rams, as well as smaller herds of only rams. The animals looked very healthy, and there were plenty of huge rams.

After landing at potential base campsites, we turned eastward and headed up-range to the Uzengyu-kuush Khrebet. We now had crossed over into the Issyk-kul Region of Kirgizia, which is a self-governed area that encompasses the whole eastern third of the country.

At this point we did not have hunting rights for this year, but negotiations revealed a promising future. This area of the Tien Shan is important to us, as the area to our east, where the range spills over into China, is the dividing line between the Marco Polo sheep and the Tien Shan argali, better known as Karelin's argali (Ovis ammon karelini).

We were now in the Kakshaal-Too Khrebet of the Tien Shan, the summit of which to our right is the border with China. Farther south inside China is the Aksay River Plateau, the famed trade route reported by Marco Polo and more recently by the Roosevelt's and other early expeditions in the mid 1920s.

None of those explorers entered the areas we are in, as they were restricted to the Chinese parts of the Tien Shan. The Tien Shan Range is about half in China, extending almost to the border of Outer Mongolia. Close to 800 miles of the range is largely within Kirgizia, while spilling over into Kazakhstan to the north and Tajikistan on the southwest. It ends in Uzbekistan in its western extremity.

As we traveled east-northeast, everywhere along the Kakshaal-Too we observed herds of Marco Polo sheep and in the rocky outcrops were ibexes. We were now getting into the habitat of the white-backed ibex (Capra siberica alaiana). This was apparent by the yellowish-white saddle, predominately on the backs of the billies. Other game included a grizzly-type bear, wolves and wild yaks.

After what seemed to be an hour of flying, we approached a tremendous mountain barrier that was certainly the end of the sheep habitat. The mountains, which were largely cliffs, stood on end as far as the eye could see and were capped with snow and glaciers. This is the Khrebet Sary Dzhaz that extends a hundred or so miles and on into China, where the Chinese border makes a sharp turn to the north.

As we turned north paralleling the massif on our right, by contrast there was a vast valley and plains on our left. It was easy to see why this great expanse was the natural barrier and dividing line separating the Marco Polo sheep and the Tien Shan argali, whose habitat begins in the Khrebet Ala-Too, and wraps around the north edge of the Sary Dzhaz in an easterly direction and on into China.

We did not see any sheep in our route through the Ala-Too and from further research, I concluded that the Karelin's argali is only found near where the Kazakhstan, Kirghizstan, and Chinese borders come together and range easterly from China's Sary Dzhaz.

As we turned to the northwest we came to forested canyons, a sight that we did not see in the southern part of the Tien Shan. It was explained this area had Russian boar, roe deer and Asian wapiti.

We soon saw in the distance some cultivated areas, the first we had seen in the many hundreds of miles we had now traveled in our huge semi-circle around the country. I was told only three percent of the Issyk-Kul Region was in agriculture, while five percent of all Kirgizia was farmed. The leading produce here is apples; while potatoes and wheat are also grown.

As we approached Karakul near the eastern shores of Lake Issyk-Kul, we were nearing the end of our fuel supply, which

Upon arrival in Karakol, the capitol of the Issyk-kul Region, the Chief of Tourist Management, Bolotbek Moldokeev, had me quickly get ready for a banquet that included the Governor and the Minister of Tourism. Bolotbek presented me with the best gift they could come up with, a wild boar lower jaw, while the Governor looks on.

included an additional, huge tank inside the helicopter. In Karakol we were met by the Chief of Tourist Management of the Council of Peoples, Bolotbek Moldokeev, and two biologists, Nikanor and Victor Titov. An interpretor Yuri Morgachev explained a banquet was arranged immediately after settling-in at the hotel.

In addition to the officials of the Tourist and Wildlife Department, Issyk-Kul's Governor and Minister of Tourism attended the meeting. The banquet was a gala affair.

After many toasts and assuring me that our company would have exclusive hunting rights, they presented me with the best gift the region could provide: a tusked lower jaw of a wild boar. Then I presented the governor a bottle of Jim Beam whiskey, a carton of Marlboro cigarettes, and a Klineburger Worldwide Travel hat.

Not to be outdone, the next day the locals presented me with a mink hat of typical Russian style, made locally from ranch minks that were raised here.

Vladimir Treschov took charge of the Marco Polo sheep and ibex program. He held nothing back in establishing excellent camps in the Naryn area for the 1990 season while my company went to work booking the hunts. For the first time, hunters had the luxury of riding horses from excellent base camps while hunting Marco Polo sheep.

On the poli hunts in Tadjikistan, to the south, we were told that horses or yaks would have to be brought in from Kirgizia, but they never went to the trouble. Vladimir arranged separate ibex hunts in areas closer to Frunze, but they were more of a fly camp and without horses.

The 1990 hunts in the Naryn area went off without a hitch, and the hunters enjoyed 100 percent success. By the fall of 1991,

Bolotbek escorted me around all the attractions near Karakol, including this zoo. The zoo director, to my right, had a grandson born during the night, so he told me he was going to have it named "Chris!"

In the fall of 1991, Vladimir Treschov established this deluxe Marco Polo sheep camp that included horses, in the Uzengyu-kuush in the Kokshaal-Too Khrebet of the Tien Shan.

Vladimir and his capable staff had similar deluxe camps established with horses in the Uzengyu-kuush of the Issyk-Kul Region for Marco Polo sheep and ibex.

However, the Moscow bureaucrats made a blunder that confused and mislead biologists worldwide. In early September 1991, there was a Caprinae Study Group conference in Beijing, China that was attended by Moscow biologists. They presented a paper that drew an arbitrary north-south line right through the Uzengyu-kuush, saying that on

the left is the Marco Polo sheep and on the right is the Tien Shan argali!

As stupid as the thought was, it appeared the other scientists took it as gospel. Now the wild sheep will magically change from the O.a.poli to an O.a. karelini as they step over the line, not to mention our 10 clients starting to arrive in October are now hunting a different species than they originally contracted for.

This kind of mentality is known worldwide by bureaucrats thousands of miles, if

Heading into the mountains in search of sheep and ibex.

Sheep country. Those specks in the snow at the right are Marco Polo sheep.

not halfway around the world, from situations they know nothing about. In this case, instead of conferring with knowledgeable people like Gennady Vorobiejov, a well-respected biologist and perhaps the leading authority on the argali sheep in the U.S.S.R., Moscow biologists moved the line hundreds of miles away from the original preestablished natural boundary, which was far to the northeast.

Regardless of the confusion of the identification of the species, the hunting went well in both the Naryn and Issyk-Kul regions. I visited the camps in the fall of 1991 and was extremely well pleased with the accommodations and staff members at the time. I went on to explore a remote and isolated area in the Sary Dzhaz Khrebet and collected outstanding ibex specimens. (For more information see "The End of the Chisholm Trail," which follows).

Hunting in Kirgizia continues to this day and has become a major source of much needed income. However, in 1999, the U.S. Fish & Wildlife Service discontinued issuing CITES import permits for sheep from the Issyk-Kul Region, making it impractical for Americans to hunt there.

## REFLECTIONS
# The Mysteries Behind the Iron Curtain

Early travel in the U.S.S.R. back in the '60s was awkward and sometimes scary. However, once I became familiar with the system (or lack of system), I used every opportunity to the advantage of my clientele, as well as my own. As an example, they did not have a firearms permit because no one brought guns until we started traveling to Mongolia through the Soviet Union.

I used our travel agency voucher to list guns, ammo, passport number, destinations, etc. before applying a passport-size photo and embossing it with our agency seal. The never-before-seen document expedited our clients' firearms through customs, allowing them to accompany the hunter wherever he went, including hotel rooms. We had created the official firearms permit.

At the airport arrival (as well as departure) areas before entering customs, were Berioska stores, referred to as dollar stores, i.e., only foreign currency could be used. An assortment of gift items, imported spirits, and tobacco were available. Therefore, that was the place to stock up on gifts to take to friends or friends-to-be. The only American whiskey available was Jim Beam and the only cigarettes were Marlboros, so we spread these delectables to remote extremities of the vast country.

In those days the Soviet currency, the ruble, was not exchanged in the world market. Therefore, the socialized government set the exchange rate, at the highest they felt they could get away with—around U.S. $1.60 to one ruble. As foreign currencies became more and more in demand, a lucrative black market emerged.

At first, the exchange was about equal but as time went on, many rubles were purchased for a dollar. We took advantage of those realistic exchanges and then when entrepreneurship surfaced in the late 1980s, the private operators who received payment in foreign currency paid their expenses with black market rubles, making many times their normal profit.

The government travel agency, Intourist, handled all travel arrangements in the U.S.S.R. and it had offices in all destinations where they had established tours. An interpreter was always furnished when taking a tour, including a hunt. They were schooled that the perfect place on earth was the U.S.S.R. and about how polluted and bad the rest of the world was.

After finishing a hunting trip with a group of successful American businessmen, their worldly knowledge was greatly improved. We hunters went where no other tourists ever went or were even allowed to go. Once out of the system (the canned tours), we found the mentality of Soviets to be much more like us westerners, eager to share their homes and enjoy camaraderie.

I developed great friendship and respect with the Intourist officials in Moscow. Our clients had special handling wherever Intourist had influence. Many times when a group of our clients flew domestic with Aeroflot, the Soviet airlines, they were given special seating (no first class). Upon arrival at the destination, none of the passengers made a move to disembark. After a short period with sounds of luggage being moved from the holds, an Intourist agent would board to fetch the clients and lead them off the aircraft to a vehicle, which already contained their luggage.

One time a group of us were running very late to catch a flight to the point the agent said the flight was already closed. I told one of my companions, Pete Papac, a burly logger from Washington, to go out to the plane and stand in the doorway and make them wait 'til I was able to make the agent check our luggage and get it on the aircraft.

I did a little name-dropping and the interpreter caught on. He went along with my story. Upon boarding we found that they even moved passengers around to give us special seating.

American diplomats visiting the U.S.S.R. were very restricted on where they could go. Therefore, the U.S. established a similar protocol, which included only certain cities (sinful Las Vegas wasn't one of them), and they were restricted from traveling more than 25 miles from the city center.

Our agency often got calls from the FBI saying, "I understand you are going to have a Russian official visit you." We had not yet known, but being familiar with the system we knew that the traveler would have to make a specific itinerary, apply with the Soviet immigration who in turn would request a visa for the U.S., and the FBI would be notified to check things out.

This process took a long time, so our friends at Intourist would wait to see if they could even get the visa, before bothering us. We always had an open invitation for them to be our guests.

We had fun with one official who was to be a guest in my home on the High Lonesome Ranch, which happened to be a little more than the 25-mile restriction. We had a good friend in the sheriff's department whom we set up to knock on the door with patrol car lights flashing. He asked whether a certain Russian visitor was present. We let it go on long enough for the handcuffs. The deputy escorted our comrade to the car before he turned and said, "Let's go have a party!"

# The End of the Chisholm Trail: A Hunt for Wild Yak in Inner Asia

**T**his article was written for the Weatherby Foundation for a publication they produced on their 50th anniversary of awards given for hunting achievements and wildlife conservation. The book was to have stories of each recipient. Since Robert Chisholm had received the prestigious award and was no longer with us, I was asked to write the chapter for him. The story below took place at the opening of the Issyk Kul region of Kyrgyzstan (Kirgizia), one of the most remote areas of Inner Asia and perhaps never hunted by foreigners. This region is the eastern half of Kirgizia and contains one of the world's largest fresh water lakes, Lake Issyk Kul. The lake is so big and deep, that the Soviet navy used it for submarine testing and training, yet it is thousands of miles from an ocean.

Hunters are forever looking for something different to hunt. Last October (1991), when I was in the Issyk-Kul region of Kirgizia in the Tien Shan Mountains, I saw herds of wild yaks, when I was flying in to a newly established Marco Polo sheep camp.

The author had a long history of camaraderie with Robert Chisholm on social occasions and hunting trips around the world. On the left, Ed Weatherby presents Bob with the most prestigious award a hunter could ever receive, the Weatherby Hunting and Conservation Award.

Bolotbek Moldokeev, the head of tourism, which now includes the hunting program, had flown into our camp in the Kakshaal Too mountain range to visit with me. He told me about a remote location in the Sary Dzhaz Mountains where he wanted to take me. The mountains bordered China, he explained, and formed an area more than 100 miles square that was so rugged it was virtually impenetrable by humans. However, there was a pocket of land, isolated within the escarpment that had abundant ibex, snow leopard, and wild yak.

No humans had touched it in more than 40 years. Prior to that, a man named Han Jantai and his family had lived and died there, around 1950. At the end of WWII there was a border dispute between China and the U.S.S.R., and the Soviet border patrol had started to build a frontier post in that isolated pocket. They soon abandoned the idea as being foolish, since nobody could get to the area except by helicopter, and if they did, they couldn't really do anything.

When Vladimir and I returned to Karakul, the capitol of the Issyk Kul region of Kirgizia, Bolotbek had already made arrangements to fly us into the Sary Dzhaz Mountains. We took provisions for a simple fly camp and flew into the area in a big MI-8 freight helicopter, camping at the base of 15,181-foot Maibash (translated as Flat Top) Mountain. The campsite was directly below the Chinese border, which was the summit of Maibash.

On the exploratory trip into the heart of the Sary Dzhaz escarpment in Kirghizstan, Chris collected this Mid-Asian ibex, Capra siberica alaiana, which measured 51½ inches and ranked #2 in the records at the time.

We were all very enthused about the area. I named it the Koyu Kup Reserve, after the Koyu Kup River where our camp was located. Bolotbek said he would set up a full camp in the reserve.

I asked about the possibilities of taking a wild yak and received a favorable response from Bolotbek. He agreed to issue permits for an exploratory hunt. I checked with two of my longtime hunting partners, Robert (Bob) Chisholm of Wichita, Kansas, and Peter Papac of Washington State, and both responded favorably for the yak as well as the opportunity to collect that sub-species of ibex. This would be the first-ever wild yak hunt to our knowledge in modern times. It bears noting that both men were among the 50 people to receive the coveted Weatherby Award.

**A welcome banquet in Karakul, Kirghizstan, for celebrating the first ever-official hunt in the Sary Dzhaz Mountains, was attended by the Governor and other officials. Pete Papac, left, and Bob Chisholm were my companions on this historic hunt.**

From the chopper we saw hundreds of ibexes and a few small herds of yaks.

During our short stay, I collected a 51½-inch ibex, the Capra siberica alaiana subspecies, which ranks as the largest of all the ibex. The local people call them "white-backed ibex" (because of the light-colored saddle) to distinguish them from the "black ibex," C. s. formosani that are found toward the west end of the Tien Shan Mountains. My ibex specimen ranked Number 2 in the records at the time. I am certain much larger ones are there,

**These are the foothills, but beyond is the impenetrable escarpment of the Sary Dzhaz Mountains.**

The Koyukup Camp was established in a wide opening in the middle of the Sary Dzhaz Mountains and was surrounded by rugged, impenetrable cliffs.

The only other sighting of wild yak I have had was in Afghanistan's Hindu Kush Mountains in the late 1960s while searching for ibex and urial sheep. At that time, my fellow hunters and I did not have permission to collect yak, so we watched two old males for a short time on the heavily wooded hillside below our trail.

Our hunt was set for us to arrive in Kirgizia in early March of 1992. We flew into the capitol of Kirgizia, Frunze. We were to be met there by a helicopter, but weather conditions forced us to drive through a mountain pass to meet our helicopter, which was "parked" on the side of the road. From there we flew to Karakul where we socialized with and received the good graces of the governor of the Issyk Kul region for this special official opening of the new reserve.

Our helicopter flight into the reserve took us through some of the most forbidding

country one could ever imagine. There were rugged snow- and glacier-covered mountains as far as the eye could see. As we came near the camp area in a vast opening, we spotted four wild yaks on a rugged mountaintop, but they appeared to be in a place that was impossible to hunt. These were obviously all bulls, as the horns stood well above their heads.

On landing, I was surprised to see that a beautiful camp had been set up for us in one of the most remote parts of the world. There were about ten "buildings" including Mongolian-style yurts and other shelters similar to yurts but shaped like cabins. Both yurts and cabins had canvas outer shells and were lined with felt pads almost an inch thick. Inside, a wooden framework held the shape. The cabins had wooden floors, wood- and coal-burning stoves, spring beds with mattresses, a table, chairs, and all the amenities. Pete took a cabin for himself. Bob and I shared one, which we normally do on these hunts, so I could monitor Bob's diabetic condition.

The camp consisted of about 10 structures, including Mongolia style yurts. They all had wooden floors, stoves, spring beds, and chairs.

☼ **Horses were flown in one at a time in the huge MI-8 freight helicopters. They were shod with spiked shoes that gave good footing on the frozen rivers and streams. Chris and Bob ready for the hunt.**

One large, heated yurt, equipped with a long table and benches, was used for dining. A separate tent was used for cooking. There was a large camp staff, several of whom I knew from my preceding visits, including Nikonor Gidnev, the head guide for the hunting program. All the staff members were eager to get us settled. Pete commented that it was the best hunting camp he had ever seen—and he had seen many. Everything had been brought in by helicopter.

The next morning after a fine breakfast, the wranglers wasted no time in rounding up the horses, which also had been airlifted in one at a time by helicopter. They had already decided that Bob would be the first to take a yak and Pete would be the first to take an ibex.

Pete and his guides headed up a canyon looking for ibex while Bob and I headed down the canyon in search of yak. It was winter, and there were lots of ice floes in the creeks and river bottoms. The way the ice piled up was picturesque, but it made for difficult going.

After a couple of hours of riding down the canyon, we spotted a herd of yaks in a side canyon. They were far away, and it was decided I would take Bob's spotting scope and head to a ridge opposite their position for a better opportunity to judge their size. The guide, Bolotbek's brother, Marat, accompanied me.

After a rather slow climb, due to the thin air around 10,000-foot altitude, we finally came out on a ridge at the same level as the yaks. They were only 400 yards away. After studying them with the spotting scope and binocular, we decided that one or two were satisfactory specimens, and though we had nothing to compare them with, we were certain that at least two were bulls.

We signaled down to Bob and the other guide to come up by horseback. After they joined us, Bob and I studied the animals one more time and then decided that he should take one that was off by itself. Bob moved to a place he could get a good rest for his rifle, but because of the conformation of the mountain, he had to shoot left-handed. He carefully squeezed off, and on hearing the plop of the bullet, we knew he had hit the bull. It lunged forward and started to move up the hill, so I suggested that Bob take a second shot.

There were 10 yaks in the herd, but only the wounded bull moved. Bob's second shot dropped the animal, which rolled a considerable distance down the hill. Only then did the rest of the herd show any concern about the unusual happenings. We stayed hidden so as not to cause any unnecessary disturbance.

Soon the rest of the herd walked down the mountain to Bob's bull. It was obviously dead. However, three of the others nudged it with their horns and foreheads urging it to get up. Only after their attempts failed repeatedly did the rest of the herd finally become concerned and move off.

These animals had never seen a human before nor heard a gunshot. Therefore, they associated neither with danger.

We went over the crest of the hill and commenced the tedious effort of working our way down to the ice-covered bottom. The bull was only about 30 feet up the opposite side but was in a very precarious place, so we rolled it down to the bottom of the draw. This ended up being a mistake, for the slipping on the ice-covered creek bottom made the skinning extremely difficult. The ice was not only slick but was sloped, and our cleated

boots did not give us much purchase. It was a young bull, not nearly the size of the ones we had seen from the helicopter the day before.

Bob was a very happy hunter nonetheless. He was the first to collect a wild yak in modern times. After the congratulations were made and the pictures taken, the tedious job of skinning it out life-size and saving all the meat began. I supervised the skinning, though the guides were quite capable because of my training them previously in Marco Polo sheep hunting camp. The people were eager to learn and conscientious in their work.

As Chisholm often did at the strangest times, during the skinning he broke out with the old trail song, "Oh, come along boys, and listen to my tale, I'll tell you all my troubles on the Ol' Chisholm Trail. Come a ti-yi-yippy-yippy-ye—"

As we started down the icy draw, I found it extremely difficult to stay on my feet. Finally, I slipped, did a split, and injured my left groin muscle. Walking became painful and very hard. One of the staff finally brought my

**Bob Chisholm with the first wild yak ever collected in modern times. From left, head guide Nikonor Gidnev, Bolotbek's brother Marat, Bob, and Yuri, the interpretor.** »

Pete Papac with his wild yak specimen.

horse, and I hesitantly climbed on and rode down the icy gorge. The horses were shod with special shoes designed for the terrain, with inch-long spikes that cut deeply into the ice. Without them, the horses would have experienced the same difficulties that I did.

The gorge had steep, rocky sides, so we were forced to follow the ice floe all the way to the bottom of the canyon. At all times we kept our toes barely in the stirrups so we could jump free if a horse slipped. There were no accidents, thankfully, and we enjoyed a safe ride back, even though my leg was killing me whether I walked or rode. Back at camp, we were cheered and congratulated by the staff.

Bob and I lay down for a rest but soon heard Pete and his guides return to camp. Pete had also had a great day and had seen a couple of outstanding ibexes. However, they were at a long distance, and apparently the wind had

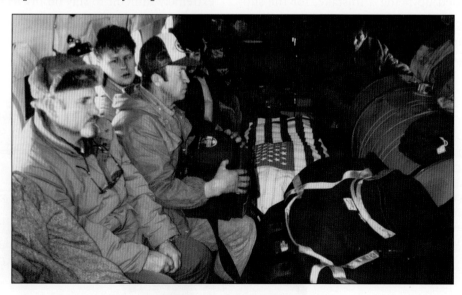

The end of the Chisholm Trail and the last ride for Robert Chisholm, who died of heart failure doing what he loved most—hunting.

changed, causing them to move even farther away. Peter had been suffering from a cold, and deep breathing in the thin air didn't help.

Dinner consisted of some of the fresh yak meat with all the trimmings. There was plenty of Pepsi Cola, as the staff knew Bob was involved with the Pepsi Cola Company (that took over Pizza Hut, of which Bob was a co-founder). Since it is now produced in the U.S.S.R., they gave him a pitch that a Pepsi plant should be established in Kirgizia.

We discussed plans for the next day and decided Bob and I would stay in camp to finish skinning his yak and to allow me a chance to rest my injured groin. Pete would go back to the same area to search for an ibex. In good spirits, we retired early.

Our cabins were nice and warm, and the camp staff kept the stoves well filled with coal. Bob and I snuggled into our comfortable beds and chatted for a while, reminiscing about the day's hunt. After saying goodnight, we dozed off.

Just after midnight, I awakened as one of the staff came into our cabin to add more coal to the fire. I heard Bob take a half-dozen deep raspy breaths. I asked, "Bob, are you OK?" I received no response. Sometimes when traveling, Bob's insulin shot would exceed his food intake, resulting in a coma. After a brief attempt to force some applesauce into his mouth, I found that his breathing had stopped. I could feel no pulse.

The camp doctor was quickly fetched, and we administered CPR, but to no avail.

Bob's heart had failed. God had called him back home—to the end of the Chisholm Trail. His own trail had taken him practically everywhere on the world's seven continents, hunting for virtually every known type of game animal. We all felt he went the way he would have wanted—hunting.

Since we could make radio contact with Karakul only at scheduled times in the evenings, we knew we would not be able to evacuate for another full day. I encouraged Pete and his guides to go look for that same herd of yaks, which we knew held another acceptable bull. Bob, I was sure, would have wanted it that way.

Pete made the hunt and was successful in taking a yak trophy.

We made contact with Bolotbek, and I requested he contact the newly formed U.S. Embassy in Frunze. I specifically asked them to get in touch with Bob's business partner, who was to pass the sad news on to his family and that I planned to be on the phone with them as soon as possible after my return. After reaching Karakul, I was able to talk to Bob's wife Becky and son Rob. They agreed to have the body cremated and Bob's ashes spread in the Koyu Kup River.

Perhaps some future hunter in Kyrgyzstan will hear an echo of that sad refrain. "Oh, come along boys, and listen to my tale, I'll tell you all my troubles on the Ol' Chisholm Trail. Come a ti-yi-yippi-yippy-ye."

(Note: the name of the city Karakul was later changed to Przhevalsk).

# CHAPTER 19

# Uzbekistan

**B**y 1992 most of my objectives in hunting programs in the Soviet bloc areas had been fulfilled except for two of the Asian countries. Uzbekistan was a high priority for me, as little was known about the wildlife from the western descending arid foothills of the Tien Shan Range to the Caspian Sea.

Turkmenistan was also interesting, but in my studies the most desirable wildlife would be two subspecies of urial sheep, one of which was the same as we established in Kazakhstan and quite likely also available in Uzbekistan. There should also be some Afghan urials, the Ovis vignei cycloceros, the same as we found exploring Afghanistan in the late 60s. Our partner, Vladimir Treschov, had good connections in Turkmenistan, so he took on that program on his own.

Aside from those two "Stans," a term used when grouping all the Asian countries of the CIS, our focus was in enhancing the programs that we now had established, such as adding the huge brown bears to our Kamchatka program and add more of the Asiatic bighorn subspecies to our offerings.

On a circuit of the Asian countries in 1989, I took Vladimir with me to acquaint him with my many contacts. Resulting from our stop in Tashkent, Uzbekistan, I came away with a contract to begin hunting there. I turned the follow-up over to Vladimir to establish an exploratory hunt. In the years to follow I kept getting reports from Vladimir that the Uzbeks were not yet ready and other stories.

Finally, in the summer of '92, Harv Hollek and Irina Afonin of my travel company were in Kirghizstan on business, so I had them stop in Tashkent to learn what went wrong. Having received their independence following our '89 visit, the Uzbeks no longer wanted to deal with a Russian from Moscow.

This was not the first time I ran into similar situations in the Stans. It was nothing against our partner who happened to be a Muscovite, but some Asians had been lorded over by Moscow so much they figured they had had enough. The Uzbeks happily signed an updated contract providing they would deal directly with us and not with our Russian partners. That set the stage for the first hunt to take place here since 1908 when Douglas Carruthers traveled through and wrote his book "Beyond the Caspian."

On short notice, I invited Rudolf Sand from Copenhagen to join me on the exploratory hunt. Rudolf, a past Weatherby Award recipient, had collected most all the world's big game and made me promise to include him on one of these new programs. Furthermore, Americans were not allowed to bring these sheep into the U.S.A., after the U.S. Fish and Wildlife Service passed the Argali Sheep Act.

The date was set earlier in the season than I wanted, but the Uzbeks were anxious to get started early to allow time for further hunts this season. So our arrival in Tashkent was 17 August 1992.

Boris Ovchinnakov and Elena Ilukhina met us from Soyokh Extrem, translated

I chose not to explore Turkmenistan, a Soviet Republic bordering Afghanistan and Iran, where both the Transcaspian urial and Afghan urial (Ovis vignei cycloceros) exist. Here Peter Bollinger shows off a fine specimen of the Afghan urial.

extreme travel, an Uzbek company established for doing the unusual. They had already engaged in some trekking and mountain climbing trips, so they became the designated hunting operator.

We were accommodated in a nice walled-in compound that resembled a small inn with a house, garden area and some additional outbuildings, including more bedrooms and staff quarters. We were the only residents and were treated royally, including meals and all desired services.

All meetings with me were held there, relating to all hunting and wildlife matters, including with Atajon Atajonov, the Director of the Game Department, Gosbiokontrol. Atajon made it a point that final talks would be made upon my return from the exploratory hunt to discuss wildlife distribution and quotas for future arrangements. He specifically wanted me to take time to visit with one of their leading experts on wildlife, Kuchkur Kurganov, the Director of Senchof/Farish Reserve, which takes in about half of the Nuratau Mountain Range. Our hunt will take place in the areas outside the Reserve in the same range.

To review the history of the wildlife in this area remains relatively easy—there is none! Aside from a few people like Douglas Carruthers who pretty much sailed through the area to get to more exciting places, very little attention was given to these desert ranges that exist in a rather large area between the Caspian Sea and the great escarpments of the Tien Shan and the Pamirs.

Of the sheep in the Nuratau Range that I was to explore, there were contradictory reports, some saying the sheep were argali-forms while others claim them to be urial-forms. However, they were referred to as Severtzov sheep or Bucharan sheep.

My goal was to clarify the situation once and for all to the outside world. I was happy to hear Atajanov's opinion that they were an argali. The argali sheep family has by far the largest wild sheep on the globe with Mongolia's Altai argali getting to several hundred pounds, with horns alone weighing 60 to 70 pounds on an older ram. The animal we are now studying probably would top out at 100 pounds, and about 32 inches at shoulder height. Quite likely, this would be the smallest of the argali family.

Our flight to the Nuratau Range on the big MI-8 helicopter took us over a vast culti-vated valley that was known as the bread-

Flying from Tashkent to the Nuratau Mountains, we crossed the "bread basket of the CIS." In the distance is Lake Aydarkul.

basket for the defunct Soviet Union. The area is blessed with unlimited water and fertile plains, along with a temperate climate. We passed on the north side of the huge Chardarinskoye Reservoir, crossing its outlet, the Syrdarya River, the second largest river in central Asia. It flows north to the Aral Sea, which is the second largest body of water in central Asia. The Caspian Sea, some 1,200 kilometers to the west, is the largest. Neither the Caspian nor the Aral Sea has an outlet and both have huge rivers flowing into them. They are both salt water and have been continuously lowering through the centuries. Some scientists think they are connected underground.

Two guides, Alexey Sveshnikov and Anatoly Grinsberg, had joined us on the flight and both spoke a little English. Elena Ilukhina, who spoke perfect English, also accompanied us for the entire trip. Combined, the three were good tour guides, and they kept me abreast of the byways. Our route now was southwest, taking us across another huge body of water, Lake Aydarkul. Anatoly said it was a great waterfowl area with all its marshes and backwaters. He encouraged us to send hunters in the fall when the birds migrate south.

Once we crossed the lake, we got our first glimpse of the Nuratau Range. I had my topographic maps, on which the range looked quite small, but it was quite impressive as we flew up side canyons to its summit. In the low valleys there were some small villages with little farms and orchards. As we approached the high meadows, present were herdsmen with domestic herds of sheep, goats, cattle, and horses.

After some time we began flying around in circles, obviously lost. Our base camp had been set up prior to our arrival, but where? Finally we landed at a herdsman's settlement, causing all his domestic stock to stampede away in every direction.

Near Kichiksai, the villagers turned out to witness the strange arrival of foreigners. Elena, our interpretor, poses with them by the huge MI-8 helicopter.

The wind and noise from the huge helicopter was a new experience here for man and beast alike. The herdsman felt he knew where the camp might be, so he boarded the chopper and in about five minutes we found the camp in a canyon, where the staff waved us on to a village at the mouth of the canyon. We landed near a small village, Kichiksai, translated as Little River.

During a 45-minute wait to be fetched, the whole village turned out to observe the strange goings on. We were quite a curiosity, as they had never seen a foreigner before. I always carry balloons, chewing gum and the like to hand out, so I made quite a hit.

Alexey Nazarov, the field director for Soyokh Extrem, met us with two, four-wheel drive vans. After bidding farewell to the helicopter crew, who had another two hours of flying back to Tashkent, we drove about 10 kilometers on a very rough creek bottom before arriving at a nicely laid-out camp, with three tents, outhouse, shower and dining table under a shade tree.

We were introduced to the staff, including our local guide, Kakhramon Nabiyev. Plans were made for the hunt and considering the physical condition of us two, Rudolf was to hunt from the base camp while I was to go out on a fly camp. Another local guide, Radjhabay went with me, along with Anatoly and Anvar Zhilkibaev, a driver who stood in as an assistant guide. We eventually obtained the use of a couple of riding horses and a donkey from a herdsman, so I was able to see a considerable amount of Nuratau Range.

**Two horses and a donkey were supplied by a herdsman for Chris' ten-day fly camping that allowed him to cover half of the Nuratau Mountain range.**

We kept on the move during a week or so of scouting the area, staying a few times as a guest in herdsmen's settlements. They welcomed us by offering us their ayvan for sleeping quarters. An ayvan is the traditional eating-place, always open on one end, offering shade and ventilation. Their "table" is a cloth or rug on the ground with cushions for seating. The natives also offered us food, a custom that I found in many parts of the Asian countries.

A traveler doesn't really need to bring supplies, as they will be fed and housed wherever they may go. We did have our own sleeping bags. I had brought four from America, as the local bedding is often of questionable sanitation.

Food was often a dish called Beshbarmak; "besh" is "five" as in "five fingers," "barmak" meaning, "take." In other words, take it with your hands (no eating utensils here!). Beshbarmak is lamb. All parts are cooked separately—head, liver, kidneys, tripe, etc., and are served on a noodle of the flat variety. This is put on one common plate in bite-size pieces. Prior to eating, a pitcher of water is passed around to wash one's eating hand.

When we were not a herdsman's guest, we would drop into a draw with a running creek and sleep under the stars. I was surprised to see this arid area had running streams in August, the hottest and driest time of year. Although there were a lot of barren, rolling hills and high meadows in this area we are allowed to hunt, there are mostly rocky outcrops.

Because of the ruggedness of this end of the range, there are very few herdsmen that utilize it for grazing their flock. This also brings up an interesting point, in that we were not seeing wild sheep on the open slopes. Normally sheep like to be out in the open, using their keen eyesight as their defense against danger. We saw sheep every day, but usually finding them in rugged areas, hiding in the rocks. We did not see large bands of animals, possibly no more than a dozen at one time.

The officials estimate the population to be around 2,000 heads. We did not get into the Senchof/Farish Reserve, which is about half of the Nuratau Mountain Range. I am guessing this range is about 100 miles long and maybe half as wide. Its elevation is 6,990 feet and does not vary much from one end to the other. I did not find out the elevation of the base of the mountain, but my guess would be around 4,000 feet.

During the summer, the herdsmen and their families lived in the mountains. This family produced cheese and other dairy products from their goats and cattle and had to deliver their products to a village ten miles away. Part of Chris' fly camp facility was in an ayvan, an open ended shelter.

I spent considerable time studying these sheep with binoculars and spotting scope. Only on one occasion did I get photos, lucky shots of a young ram that fed close to me. I ended up taking a ram, a five-year youngster after the "big ones got away." These sheep were among the spookiest I have ever hunted. Having lived among herdsmen and wolves throughout time, they learned how to survive and did outsmart me on several occasions.

The coloration of the sheep is almost solid reddish brown. The rams have a slight indication of a frontal neck mane, which is an off-black color. Their muzzle is cream colored, as is a small patch around their short, black tail. The horn cross-section is slightly triangular, which might have led some early explorers to believe they were in the urial family. However, one must realize that the Marco Polo argali found 1,000 or so miles to the southeast of here have triangular horns.

I did see one wolf briefly after driving it from its bed in the dim light of morning. They are not big, maybe half the body weight of a timber wolf. Wild boars were found in the creek bottoms, but were not numerous. Chukar partridges were also found in good numbers and are native to this part of the world.

After finishing exploring a good portion of the Nuratau, we returned to the luxuries

Chris got a lucky shot at live Bucharan sheep when they grazed close enough. The ram was perhaps 3 to 4 years old.

Local guide Radjhabay and Anatoly Grinsberg receive skinning instructions from Chris,
while Alexy Nazarov, in back, looks on. The
body weight of the ram was a little over 100
pounds.

of the base camp and I was delighted to see
that Rudolf had collected a nice specimen.
I was informed that Kuchkur Kurganov, the
director of the reserve was anxiously awaiting
my presence. So, after I took a shower in the
makeshift facility and the best meal I've had in
10 days, Alexey took me by van to the reserve
headquarters, which was Kuchkur's home.

Our meeting took place on an unusual
ayvan, which was a deck built of native wood
right over a roaring mountain stream. Our
meeting was accompanied by a variety of
fresh and dried fruits, vodka, and nan (the
local bread called Lekeshka).

Aside from sharing scientific wildlife
data of Uzbekistan with one another, the
talks turned to the subject of the reserve, and
he then solicited my help. The reserve now
included little more than lines on a map and
a set of rules for those who share the area. He
wanted to build a large holding pen to keep a
number of sheep for scientific study. He also
wanted obtain equipment such as binoculars,
radios, guns, posting signs, and even vehicles.
He would build small cabins in a few places
around the perimeter of the reserve for their
game guards.

I explained how my Sportsman Financed
Wildlife Program was intended for the
purpose of protecting all wildlife, not just
those that were hunted. I promised I would
help wherever I could, as well as insist that
part of the funds from the Severtsov argali
hunt program be channeled into his reserve.
He had some very urgent needs, so I gave
him $300 from my diminishing cash supply.
I would have given more but just couldn't
spare it. However, $300 equates to 62,000
rubles at the current exchange of 207 rubles
to one dollar, so it will go a long way.

Just as important as it was to get the first
hunting program underway here was to find
answers to the unsolved mysteries about the
vast, 1,500-mile-square area between the
Tien Shan Mountains and the Caspian Sea.

Resulting from discussions with every
knowledgeable Uzbek, along with my own
studies from old world writings, here are a
few comments:

North of the ancient city of Buchara
to the west are small mountain ranges, the
Tamdy Tau and Uuminga Tau, both of
which have sheep called the Tajik argali
(Ovis ammon kuzukum) and the Buchara
argali (Ovis ammon buchariensis). Some say
that these sheep are the same as the Severtsov

⌃ **Chris with the first two specimens of the Severtzovi argali, Ovis ammon severtzovi, taken in modern times.**

argali while others say they are different. For simplicity, let's call them Bucharan sheep because of their proximity to Buchara.

Quite a distance to the northwest on the cliffs of the west bank of the Aral Sea are sheep known as the Ust Urt sheep. There is controversy about whether they are an argali or urial as no one has been able to come up with a scientific name for them. If they are urials, they would, no doubt, be the Ovis orientalis arkal, the trans-Caspian urial, for which I began a hunting program in the spring of 1990 in Kazakhstan.

To the north and slightly east of the Nuratau is a desert mountain range called the Karatau, and sometimes called the Black Mountains, because of the dark grey rocky terrain. Sheep in this area have been called the Buchara argali, which I feel is wrong. I

prefer another name that it has been known for, the Black Mountain argali (Ovis ammon nigrimontana).

The size of that argali is basically the same as the Severtsov argali. The Karatau Range is under the jurisdiction of the city of Chimkent, which is in Uzbekistan, while the actual range is across the border in Kazakhstan. It seems that country boundaries did not consider ethnic groups and judicial boundaries.

Another example of that is right here in the Nuratau. The people here are actually Tajiks, not Uzbeks. Back in November of '89 I was exploring an urial area in Tajikistan and we came into Uzbekistan to get into the mountain range. In questioning whether we should be there without proper visas, the answer was it did not matter, as the people are Tajiks, not Uzbeks.

There is another range south of, and paralleling, Nuratau that has sheep but no one that I talked to knew the identity of the species or the population. There are other smaller desert ranges near the Caspian, but, again, no data.

Back in Tashkent, Atajonov, the Director of the Game Department, suggested I return, and they would conduct a survey of all the mountain ranges as well as for forest and plains game along the Syrdarya River basin, which flows northward to the Aral Sea.

Tissue samples I collected from the Severtsov sheep did reveal that the sheep was indeed an argali.

# CHAPTER 20

# The World's Caprinae

Caprinae are the various sub-species of the wild sheep and goat families. In the old days, the North American species were well-documented by the *Boone and Crockett Records of North American Big Game.* The Asian Caprinae were somewhat documented by *Rowland Ward's Records of Big Game* compiled from the sketchy reports of those early expeditions that took place from the late 1800s to the mid-1920s.

As for the wild sheep of Asia, James L. Clark, a renowned taxidermist who accompanied an expedition in the mid-1920s, published the most comprehensive account of Asia sheep. His book, The Great Arc of the Wild Sheep, came out in the mid 1960s, a time when I started hunting Asia and when I had already done research similar to what Clark had done.

At the time I became involved in Asia in the early 1960s, the data available was all there was, although confusing and contradictory, a start. As Asia unfolded before us, as documented in this chronicle, my interest in defining the Asian Caprinae intensified. As mentioned earlier, I joined with some colleagues to form the International Sheep Hunters Association (ISHA), now combined with the Wild Sheep Foundation, whose purpose was not only to join those with a common interest, but also to study the Asian Caprinae. We made up specimen kits to take samples for DNA studies, along with logs for recording horn configuration and pelage, as well as population and distribution data.

From information that I collected, along with other members' data, and the resulting scientific studies, I compiled the attached lists of Caprinae. It must be noted that these lists are not complete, but are limited to wildlife that has been available to sportsmen in recent times. Missing are subspecies that may still exist in remote areas, which include some serows, gorals, ibexes, and argalis in the transcaspian. and tahrs.

Currently, several hunting and conservation clubs have compiled Caprinae lists, including Safari Club International, the Wild Sheep Foundation, Ovis, and CIC.

# THE SHEEP OF THE WORLD

The wild sheep have made their home in the most remote places in the world - in the high and lofty mountain ranges of the Northern hemisphere. Their keen eyesight and alertness contribute to their choice of high open country. As James Clark pointed out in his book, "The Great Arc of the Wild Sheep", the mountain ranges that form their habitat, as displayed on the map, form the shape of a great arc very much like the flare of a sheep's horn.

Many regard wild sheep as the greatest animal in the world. Conservation, their shyness, alertness and intelligence have contributed to their increase in numbers. Controlled hunting and photography of these elusive sheep have now been made possible in these modern times. And these surplus animals finance a portion of many wildlife programs.

The spectacular beauty of the majestic wild sheep, their wariness, and the harshness of their habitat contribute to their mystique. That, coupled with the difficulty of their quest only adds to their desirability. To approach an elusive, old ram of maximum age is a challenge unequaled by most any other sport. Klineburger Worldwide Travel continues to be the leader in helping sportsmen the world over rise to this challenge.

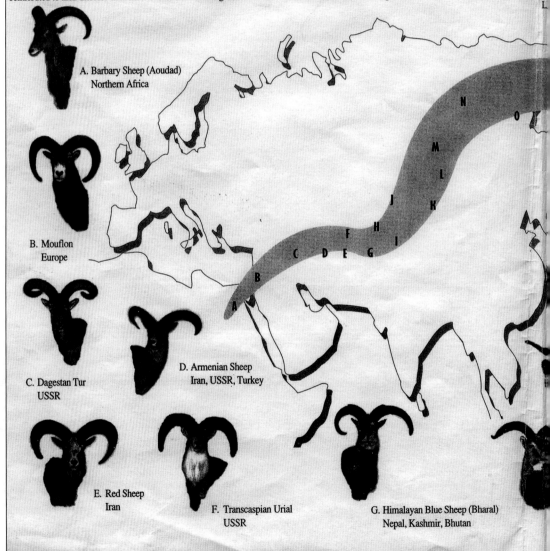

A. Barbary Sheep (Aoudad)
Northern Africa

B. Mouflon
Europe

C. Dagestan Tur
USSR

D. Armenian Sheep
Iran, USSR, Turkey

E. Red Sheep
Iran

F. Transcaspian Urial
USSR

G. Himalayan Blue Sheep (Bharal)
Nepal, Kashmir, Bhutan

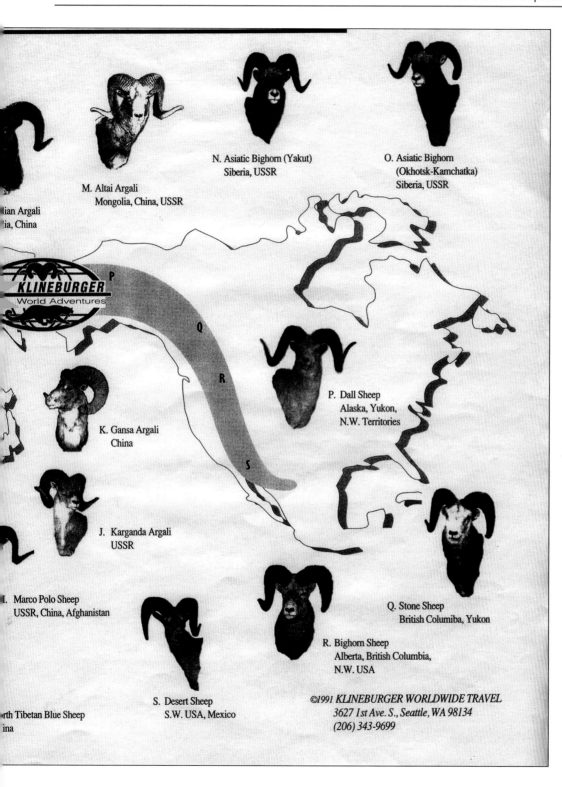

N. Asiatic Bighorn (Yakut)
Siberia, USSR

O. Asiatic Bighorn
(Okhotsk-Kamchatka)
Siberia, USSR

M. Altai Argali
Mongolia, China, USSR

lian Argali
ia, China

P. Dall Sheep
Alaska, Yukon,
N.W. Territories

K. Gansa Argali
China

J. Karganda Argali
USSR

I. Marco Polo Sheep
USSR, China, Afghanistan

Q. Stone Sheep
British Columiba, Yukon

R. Bighorn Sheep
Alberta, British Columbia,
N.W. USA

S. Desert Sheep
S.W. USA, Mexico

rth Tibetan Blue Sheep
ina

©1991 *KLINEBURGER WORLDWIDE TRAVEL*
*3627 1st Ave. S., Seattle, WA 98134*
*(206) 343-9699*

| Sheep of the World–Ovis | |
|---|---|
| **ARGALI FORMS–*Ovis ammon*** | |
| **Altai Argali** | *O.a.ammon* |
| **Gobi Argali** | *O.a. darwini* |
| **Marco Polo Argali** | *O.a.poli blythe* |
| **Humes Marco Polo Sheep** | *O.a.poli humei* |
| **Gansu Argali** | *O.a. jubata* |
| **Sair Argali** | *O.a. sairiensis* |
| **Tian Shan or Karelini Argali** | *O.a. karelini* |
| **Littledale's Argali** | *O.a littledalai* |
| **Tibetan Argali** | *O.a. hodgsoni* |
| **Kuruktag Argali** | *O.a. adametzi* |
| **Karaganda Argali** | *O.a. collium* |
| **Karatau Argali** | *O.a. nigrimontana* |
| **Severtzov Argali** | *O.a. severtzovi* |
| **Kunlun Shan Argali** | *O.a. dalailamae* |
| **PACHYCERIFORMS—nivicola** | |
| **Kamchatka Bighorn** | *O.n. nivicola* |
| **Yakut Snow Sheep** | *O.n. lydekkeri* |
| **Okhotsk Bighorn** | *O.n. alleni* |
| **Putorana Snow Sheep** | *O.n. borealis* |
| **Koryak Bighorn** | *O.n. koryakorum* |
| **NORTH AMERICA PACHYCERIFORMS—dalli and canadensis** | |
| **Dall** | *O. dalli dalli* |
| **Stone Sheep** | *O. dalli stonei* |
| **Fannin Sheep** | *O. dalli fannini* |
| **Rocky Mountain Bighorn** | *O. canadensis canadensis* |
| **Desert Bighorn** | *O. canadensis nelsoni* |
| **California Bighorn** | *O. canadensis californiana* |
| **MOUFLONIFORMS—*Ovis gmelini and vignei*** | |
| **European Mouflon** | *Ovis gmelini musimon* |
| **Cyprian Mouflon** | *Ovis gmelini ophion* |
| **Asiatic/Konya Mouflon** | *Ovis gmelini anatolica* |
| **Armenian Sheep** | *Ovis gmelini gmelini* |
| **Red Sheep** | *Ovis gmelini orientalis* |
| **Esphanan Sheep** | *Ovis gmelini isfahanica* |
| **Shiraz Sheep** | *Ovis gmelini cycloceros* |
| **Laristan/Kerman Sheep** | *Ovis gmelini laristanica* |
| **Transcaspian/ Elburz Urial** | *Ovis vignei arkal* |
| **Afghan Urial** | *Ovis vignei cycloceros* |
| **Blanford Urial** | *Ovis vignei blanfordi* |
| **Punjab Urial** | *Ovis vignei punjabiensis* |
| **Ladakh/Shapoo Urial** | *Ovis vignei vignei* |
| **BHARAL—*nayar/pseudois sheep*** | |
| **Himalayan Bharal** | *Pseudois nayar nayar* |
| **Tibetan Bharal** | *P.n. szechuanensis* |
| **Dwarf Bharal** | *P.n. schaeferi* |
| **Aoudad or Barbary Sheep** | *Ammotragus lervia* |

| CAPRID—Capra and subfamilies | |
|---|---|
| Altai Ibex | *Capra sibirica sibirica* |
| Gobi Ibex | *Capra sibirica hagenbecki* |
| Mid-Asian Ibex (White Backed) | *Capra sibirica alaiana* |
| Western Tien Shan Ibex (Black) | *Capra sibirica formosani* |
| Himalayan Ibex | *Capra sibirica hemalayanus* |
| Alpine Ibex | *Capra ibex* |
| Nubian Ibex | *Capra nubiana* |
| Gredos Ibex | *Capra pyrenaica victoriae* |
| Beceite Ibex | *Capra pyrenaica hispanica* |
| Southeastern Spanish Ibex | *Capra pyrenaica hispanica* |
| Roda Ibex | *Capra pyrenaica hispanica* |
| Bezoar Ibex | *Capra aegagrus aegagrus* |
| Sindh Ibex/ | *Capra aegagrus blythi* |
| Chilton Wild Goat | *Capra aegagrus blythi* |
| Persian Desert Ibex | *Capra aegagrus ssp* |
| Alpine Chamois | *Rupicapra rupicapra rupicapra* |
| Carpathian Chamois | *Rupicapra rupicapra carpatica* |
| Balkan Chamois | *Rupicapra rupicapra balcanica* |
| Caucasian Chamois | *Rupicapra rupicapra caucasica* |

| | |
|---|---|
| Anatolian Chamois | *Rupicapra rupicapra asiatica* |
| Pyrenean Chamois | *Rupicapra pyrenaica pyrenaica* |
| Cantabrian Chamois | *Rupicapra pyrenaica parva* |
| New Zealand Chamois | *Rupicapra rupicapra* |
| Dagestan Tur | *Capra cylindricornis* |
| Kuban Tur | *Capra caucasica dinniki* |
| Mid-Caucasian Tur | *Capra caucasica caucasica* |
| Astor Markhor | *Capra falconeri falconeri* |
| Bukharan Markhor | *Capra falconeri heptneri* |
| Sulaiman Markhor | *Capra falconeri jerdoni* |
| Kashmir Markhor | *Capra falconeri cashmiriensis* |
| Kabul Markhor | *Capra falconeri megaceros* |
| American Mountain Goat | *Oreamnos americanus* |
| Himalayan Tahr | *Hemitragus jemlahicus* |
| Himalayan Serow | *Capricornis antelope thar* |
| Forest Serow | *Capricornis antelope bubalina* |
| Goral (Nepal & East) | *Nemorhaedus hodgsoni* |
| Goral (West Himalayas) | *Nemorhaedus goral* |

# PART V

# SOME FINAL THOUGHTS

As the sun sets on my lifetime occupation, life for me did not become a "twilight zone." As business responsibilities waned, a new era in my life surfaced in the ensuring 15 years to the time of this chronicle. So here is a little reminiscing as well as what I did to "turn the page."

PART V

# SOME FINAL THOUGHTS

# CHAPTER 1

# The Klineburger Family Working Together

Looking back, this amazing story could only have happened once in world history. Each Chapter in this book was a result of what happened before. Each accomplishment was a result of the building blocks set in place by the three brothers on those lean and tough times after purchasing Jonas Brothers of Seattle, Inc. in 1954. Not one of us alone could have built the foundation that made our company world renowned and respected as the preeminent leaders in our field.

We encouraged one another to take off to explore and hunt new territories. In one's absence, the other two gladly took over his responsibilities and wished him Bon Voyage. We must also credit our wives for their contribution, support, and patience in our absence. During those first twenty years, it was amazing that the three brothers, or their wives, never had a serious disagreement!

In the mid-70s when Bert and Gene left the company, my wife Colleene and son Kent stood in to run the company during those

Bert, Gene, and Chris in their later years shown in the Water Hole at the Klineburgers' Seattle operation.

lengthy trips that I took exploring Asia. Therefore, it was with encouragement when Colleene or Kent took off on safari. When I was honored in January 2007 as "The Pioneer of Asian Hunting and Conservation," I was humbled by these quotes from my family.

### Quote by Gene Klineburger

*When Chris was quite young, he took a real liking to trapping for fox and bobcat. After school, he spent all of his spare time in the desert on his trap line, hunting along the way, and spending little time with the other* kids. *A rumor got started that little Chris was "strange." While out in the desert one afternoon, Chris got hungry, built a fire, and commenced barbecuing a freshly killed cottontail under the shade of a mesquite tree. Lo and behold, some family came driving out and came across Chris, gnawing on a rabbit carcass! That did it—they went back to town with their report. Now, Chris was dubbed the "Wild Boy" for sure!*

*After growing up, serving his country and then a short career in engineering, he went to work for Jonas Brothers Taxidermy, the company* my brothers and I purchased from Guy Jonas when he retired in 1954. Ever since then, the "Wild Boy" has been blazing trails, exploring and opening new frontiers to hunting all over the world. And now you know the real story about my brother, the legendary Chris Klineburger.

## Quote by Bert Klineburger

As young men, we were lucky to be in the right place at the right time; Seattle was the hunting crossroads to Alaska and points beyond.

Our company gained prominence as the largest taxidermy establishment in the world and became the international clearinghouse and information center for hunters everywhere. At that time, while most of Asia was closed to hunting, foreign governments began asking for help in developing their hunting and tourism programs.

Our exploratory hunts in Asia started in Iran, and ultimately involved most all the Continent, including China and the former Soviet Union. Working with foreign governments was difficult and frustrating, but Chris never gave up, opening country after country to hunting. He became known as the "Mountain Man," and did more to open Asian hunting than any man in history.

Those who hunt Asia's sheep and ibex follow in the footsteps of one of the greatest of all mountain hunters—Chris Klineburger.

## Quote by Chris' son, Kent Klineburger

Much of what I learned from my father about integrity, tenacity, and the importance of being an honest and spiritual person was taught in the field, around the campfire, or as we quietly counted stars under African skies.

He always spoke with frankness and sincerity. He cared about feelings of others, and never boasted about his own achievements.

My most cherished memories are of hunting and spending time with my hero, my father, Chris Klineburger.

# CHAPTER 2

# Out with the Old—In with the New

It was Alexander the Great that wept when he felt there were no more worlds to conquer. What made me weep wasn't the fact that there seemed to be no more last frontiers of wildlife to conquer, but the closures of programs that I helped to develop in modern times. Looking back along the Klineburger trail, many great wildlife programs in exotic places that we pioneered have faltered. It seemed a case of "one step forward and two steps backward" on the number of destinations around the World that American sportsmen could hunt.

Behind every closure, the reason was political, directly or indirectly. It was never a case of wildlife populations or the local people; it was the leaders and the bureaucrats that have caused the chaos in the world. With most every ethnic nationality, rich or poor, I have climbed, slept, eaten, prayed, strained, cried, laughed, celebrated and mourned, including those of every skin color and religious belief. The common people are the same the world over, wanting peace and freedom, while loving Americans. The political related problems vary from wars, self-serving leaders, terrorist infiltration, ignorant leaders swayed by anti hunters and many other problems by the hierarchy that should be caring about the wildlife.

Other problems with our sustainable wildlife programs stem from bureaucracies like the U.S. Fish and Wildlife Service (Service). Instead of the Service honoring wildlife programs of other countries, in many cases without proper knowledge, they attempted to dictate to them which of their wildlife are endangered. To my knowledge, no foreign country that I have worked with through the years has ever allowed hunting for an endangered species.

Most all of those countries are a signatory to the Convention on International Trade in Endangered Species (CITES). While those countries that are targeted by the Service, are very concerned about wildlife populations and would not allow hunting for endangered species, they do have much-needed hunting for a sustainable wildlife program. For species collected by foreigners, they issue CITES export permits. Those permits should be honored by the Service and allowed into the U.S.A., but in many cases are not (as in the case of argali sheep in China and much of Asia). As a result, my American cliental had been cut off from a great deal of the hunting opportunities in Asia. The losers are not only the Americans, but also the countries that badly need the programs, as well as the wildlife whose existence depends on management that is financed by hunter's dollars.

With that discouraging word and my approaching the age of 70 in the mid 1990s, I convinced myself it was time to retire. After all, my brothers and I were influential in bringing the world's hunting fraternity together. Gene and Bert left the company in the 1970s as Gene was of retirement age and Bert went on to run an African safari program for several years. Bert authored three hunting books on his own: *Big Game Hunting Around the World; This Is the Greatest Hunting Era;* and *International Hunter.* Gene contributed to a vocation that he loved, the antique and classic car fraternity.

I had a feeling of fulfillment and felt "it is time to meditate and give thanks." After all, I had pioneered parts of Africa and most of Asia; went places most foreigners had never gone; founded or was a founding member of most conservation associations; surveyed wildlife populations; named mountains, lakes, and wild sheep; compiled lists of the scientific names of the world's caprinae; taught hunting operators the criteria of outfitting; supplied samples for DNA studies of caprinae; and, most importantly, opened many Asian countries with sportsman financed wildlife programs.

I sold the Travel Section of my company to a New Zealand operator that ignored our successful procedures and went broke before I received payment. Since they had the use of our name, their failure hurt our reputation. So when the subject came up of disposing of the Taxidermy Division, Colleene, Kent, and I reluctantly decided just to close the doors at the end of December 1996.

Son Kent took over a portion of the business that he excelled in, which included museum and trophy room design and restoration of older mounted specimens. He also was one of the few people in the U.S.A. that

The Klineburger Taxidermy showroom was a display area for most of Chris' specimens from around the world, including the most complete collections of the World's caprinae, partly shown here. Once closing the business, Chris donated most of his trophies to various museums.

was knowledgeable and licensed to appraise wildlife for museum donations and for insurance purposes. The trophy room restoration business has kept him and his wife, Molly, busy and traveling all over the U.S.A.

I had life-size mounted specimens of most all the caprinae of the World that I had collected throughout the years that had been prominently displayed in the show room of the business. Knowing we would never have a home large enough to display them, I donated most all of them, along with some other rather rare specimens to museums for permanent display. Klineburger Taxidermy had also done specimens and extensive work in museums.

Colleene and I wanted to further downsize so we sold the High Lonesome Ranch and bought 5 acres on a mountainside overlooking the Cascade Mountains some 30 miles east of Seattle. There we had our home including several outbuildings, including a large building we called our Treasure House, which displays some of our rare trophies and collectables accumulated through the years from all over the World.

Once the business matters were behind us and settled in our new abode, the plan was to find a southern destination where we could winter away from Washington's rather gloomy wet season. No sooner than we were well settled in, Colleene was diagnosed with

We did the Governor Tom Bolack Wildlife Museum in Farmington, New Mexico, which included this huge "Great Barrier Reef," a mountain with the world's caprinae and wings for every continent.

This display in Klineburger's Anchorage Log Cabin Museum contained (from left) spotted seal, ring seal, ugruk, ribbon seal, and fur seal.

At the Stilliguamish Pioneer Museum in Arlington, Washington, we did a man-sharing-nature theme with the Cascade Mountains and it's wildlife on the one side and an old time logging camp (circa 1900) on the other side.

Darwin "Curley" Miller poses in his wildlife museum in Houma, Louisiana that he donated to the State.

After the author donated most of his collections to museums, the remnants are displayed in their Treasure House in Washington. Grace and Chris review photos for the book. Displayed in a loft are Chris' tiger and lion.

🐏 **Also in the loft of the Treasure House are two of Chris' prized possessions, this desert and bighorn sheep.**

esophageal cancer and succumbed within a year. We had a most happy and adventurous life together for 42 years before she passed on May 9, 2002.

The following winter I got on with my life, hooked the travel trailer, and set out alone on the original plan to head south and see what may be in store. I took plenty of time visiting with family and friends all thru the western states, and then went into Mexico's Baja Peninsula. I returned through Arizona with more visits and then to Las Vegas on the way back north to visit for a few days with good old friends, Andy and Yoni Oldfield, Don and Dianne Kirk and

Thornton and Helen Snider. The Oldfields and Kirks put on a welcoming party for me, to which they invited a good friend and neighbor lady, Grace Mathis, who had recently lost her fiancé. A sequence of things happened that kept me in Las Vegas for 7 weeks.

It became very apparent that Grace and I had an awful lot in common and we dated continuously. Neither one of us had been looking for a mate, but the fateful outcome was that we were meant for one another.

Our life together has been nonstop eventful. Even though we winter in Las Vegas and summer in Washington, we never seem to be at either place, always traveling and exploring both familiar and unfamiliar territories, but now usually a little closer to home. Although we have taken extensive trips to Argentina, China, Australia, and Israel, Mexico, Canada, and the western U.S.A. have been regular destinations.

During the bicentennial of the Lewis and Clark expedition, we followed their same trail and were about every place that they were. Being a sort of explorer myself, I have the greatest respect for those great pioneers and what they were able to accomplish in the most difficult conditions. Grace and I have also followed most of the migration routes, including the Oregon Trail, Mormon Trail, California Trail, and the Pony Express.

We don't let any grass grow under our feet when not on the road. We still take in some of the hunting and conservation conventions every year, along with the Weatherby Award banquet. One event every year is attending the Wyoming Governor's One Shot Antelope extravaganza. There in Lander, Wyoming we team up with brother Bert and host a cocktail party all four days of the event, which is the only informal place where everyone can gather and visit on a one-on-one basis. We bring home all the antelope meat possible to donate to charitable events for the needy,

Chris and Grace in the "Mexican Cantina" at their Las Vegas home.

Chris bottling a batch in his wine cellar. He entered his wines in the Washington State Fair in the years 1999 and 2000, receiving 23 ribbons and 2 Best of Shows.

through the Desert Chapter of Safari Club International (SCI) in Las Vegas.

One probably wonders what we do in our spare time, when we might be in one of our abodes. We always seem to be able to work into our schedule to make wine, a hobby I have had for over twenty years, from over 30 products. They are what I call Country Wines, from fruit, berries, leaves and flowers. As I write, we now have apricot and prickly pear cactus wine bulk-aging in Las Vegas and a peach/nectarine blend aging in Washington.

Last year, Grace didn't think I had enough to do to occupy my time, so she signed me up

for a chain saw carving class in North Bend, so I built a special shed on the property where I carve bears, fish, mushrooms, trees, and the like. More quiet hobbies include bringing my coin and stamp collection up to date that I accumulated from around the World in the old days.

Besides receiving numerous awards, the Klineburger organization gave out many awards, honoring those that were outstanding in their field of endeavor, including wildlife officials and sportsmen. One special recognition would go to those whose hunting and conservation accomplishments occurred after age 60. Many sportsmen did not have the time or money to contribute to the sport until retirement when their physical abilities could not compete with those young nimrods. So we developed the Klineburger Senior Hunter Award, which some jokingly called "The Old Man's Weatherby Award."

In my waning years in the hunting circles, as I "rode off into the sunset," my achievements (along with my brothers, Bert and Gene) were not to be forgotten by the leading hunting and conservation organizations. In 1993, I was inducted into the Safari Club International Hunting Hall of Fame. Bert had already received that prestigious award.

Following the safety rules with gloves and chaps, Chris starts on a standing bear.

 Dr. James Conklin inducted the author into the Safari Club International Hunting Hall of Fame
in 1993.

In 1994, I was the keynote speaker on Asian mountain animals at the Northern Wild Sheep and Goat Council Convention whose members are game officials and biologists that control all the North American mountain wildlife.

In the year 2000, The Weatherby Foundation for the first and only time, awarded each Bert and I with a Weatherby Award of Special Recognition, "In honor and appreciation of outstanding achievements in hunting preservation and wildlife conservation."

In 2004 the Foundation for North American Wild Sheep honored me with the International Service Award for "Your efforts on behalf of Wild Sheep Internationally; your pioneer work in Asia has allowed enhanced opportunities for both wild sheep and wild sheep hunters."

«  **Chris presents the Klineburger Senior Hunter Award to John Batten of Racine, WI, the 1979 recipient, who hunted difficult areas around the World in his senior years.**

In the year 2000, the Weatherby Foundation, for the first and only time, presented a Weatherby Award of Special Recognition to both Bert and Chris Klineburger. From left, Andy Oldfield, Weatherby Foundation President, Bert, Chris, and General Charles Yeager, the presenter of the Awards.

Also in 2004 Safari Club International qualified me for these World Hunting Awards: Grand Slam of Wild Sheep; Global Hunting Award; Trophy Animals of Asia; Ibex of the World; Top Ten Award; Goats of the World; Sheep of the World; Hunting Achievement Award; and the Oxen of the World.

In 2007 various wildlife organizations, including SCI, the Weatherby Foundation and Water for Wildlife Foundation honored me as "The Pioneer of Asian Hunting and Conservation" in a banquet in Seattle, at which over $21,000 were raised for future conservation efforts.

In 2008, the Wild Sheep Foundation created a new award, the Mountain Hunter Hall of Fame "To recognize individuals who have shown exemplary conduct in fair chase hunting exploits of wild sheep and goats and demonstrated an ability to be a good ambassador of the hunting fraternity, and who has a strong conservation background." I was the first to receive that prestigious award.

As I entered the 21st Century my time in the "field and stream" was not as exotic as it was in those faraway places with strange sounding names, but just as enjoyable.

☝ In 2008, the Wild Sheep Foundation created a new award program, the Mountain Hunter Hall of Fame. Chris Klineburger was the first to receive that prestigious award.

Here I am with son Kent and an antelope taken during the Governor's One Shot Antelope Hunt in Wyoming.

A mule deer buck taken in my home state of Washington.

« I never pass up a chance to fish. A king salmon on the Kenai River, halibut off Admiralty Island, and dorado in Mexico with son Kent.

Dove shooting in Sonora is a frequent occurrence. From right, Thornton Snider, Chris,
Andy Oldfield, and in the back is Javier Artee,
owner of Alcampo Hunting Services.

The author on the deck of his shed
reminiscing subject matter for his
autobiography.

Chris Klineburger's quote:

*"The essence of life is discovering what is on the other side of the
mountain. We start out with a dream and are propelled by the challenge
of the unknown, the lure and the mystery of faraway places.*

*Upon reaching the destination, we realize that there is no end. Distant
mountains lie before us; it is time to meditate and give thanks.*

*Most of all, we must share with others the delight of God's creation."*

## REFLECTION
# Wyoming Governor's One Shot Antelope Hunt and Water for Wildlife

**T**he legendary One Shot Antelope hunt began in 1940 when the governor of Wyoming challenged the governor of Colorado to a pronghorn antelope hunt, with each governor selecting four other team members. The catch was that only one bullet would be allowed in their high-powered rifles, reflecting back to the pioneer days when a muzzle loader or one arrow from an Indian bow was the only chance for a kill. The historic occasion in Lander, Wyoming was not just for the opening-day hunt, but a four-day affair with much camaraderie, including the involvement of the Shoshone Indians. It was such a wonderful affair that the two governors agreed to do it again the following year with new team members. The past team members wanted to join in the fun again, but were allowed to come only as guests.

World War II interrupted the event from 1942 to 1945, but the hunt resumed in 1946. Other state governors became aware of the hunt and wanted to join in the competition. So as time went by other governors were included, but the teams were reduced to three competitors each, eventually getting up to eight teams. They began running out of governors who could participate, so they allowed other teams of high-profile hunters, including stars of every sort, astronauts, other politicians, armed forces, and more. The team with the best score, i.e., all getting antelope with one shot and earliest in the day, would get high praise and awards and get to dance with the chiefs and the braves, while all other team members would have to dance with the squaws!

It seemed that most all team members from the beginning wanted to return and join in the fun, resulting in the formation of the Past Shooters Club. The Club took over the management formation of the One Shot Hunt in cooperation with Wyoming governors, each of whom has participated in the annual competition. The affair is not open to the public, but only to team members, Past Shooters, and their guests. However, many Wyoming volunteers have come forward to put on the major event, including hunting guides, hosts, cooks, servers, shooting range hosts, and many more locals are welcome at the grand finale banquet. The Shoshone Tribe is also welcome, as their dances and participation are key attractions. The tribal chief and medicine man perform a pageant around the campfire to bless the single bullet of each of the 24 team members as they are introduced and given Indian names.

The One Shot Past Shooters Club formed the One Shot Antelope Hunt Foundation, as these sportsmen wanted to put back more than they have taken. From the sense of fellowship and tradition, a shared vision of the Foundation to preserve, protect, and benefit the wildlife, the Water for Wildlife effort began in 1975. Over the years, the club has raised over $1.3 million, installing over 400 water sources from Kansas to California in the arid West, increasing wildlife populations for everyone to enjoy. The Foundation also created the permanent Evans/Dahl Memorial Museum in Lander, dedicated to the preservation of One Shot Antelope Hunt memorabilia.

⌃ **The International Team at the Wyoming governor's One Shot Antelope Hunt is welcomed by the Shoshone Indians. From left, Chris; Willy LeClair, the tribe medicine man; General Charlie Duke, astronaut; tribal chief Darwin LeClair; and Stan Studer, Texas rancher.**

## REFLECTION
# 3 Shot Honker Hunt

**B**ack in the 1960s Richard Carlsberg of southern California notoriety joined the author on a One Shot Antelope Hunt. Dick became very intrigued about that wonderful concept of bringing together a fine class of hunters.

Dick and his brother, Arthur (Art), grew up in Alturas in Modoc County in the northeast corner of California. One of their first landholdings was a big spread near Alturas, which they developed by putting in a lodge and named it California Pines. Not much went on in Modoc County, but the hunting was good for mule deer, antelope, and a terrific waterfowl flyway, so the lodge was frequented a great deal by hunters.

Dick and his wife Barbara, along with Art and his wife Judy, entertained a lot of fine people at California Pines, usually treating them to some terrific goose and duck hunting. So they came up with the idea to do one big gala affair annually,

The Carlsberg 3 Shot Honker Hunt was a gathering place for stars of every sort. From left, Dick Carlsberg, Bert Klineburger, astronaut Ron Evans, Art Carlsberg, Art's son David, astronaut Rusty Schweikart, actor Slim Pickens, and astronaut Joe Allen.

starting in 1967, throw in some competitiveness, and call it the Carlsberg 3 Shot Honker Hunt. The 4-day event was by invitation only and drew countless people of fame, and remained stag only, so that they could take up to around 50 guests, by doubling the guys in the twin-bedded rooms.

At first, a chartered aircraft from Burbank was used to get the whole lot directly there, but unstable weather conditions soon changed the plan to have the guests arrive in Reno and bus the group from there. This process allowed another bonus event en route, stopping for a barbeque and "clay goose" shootout, firing their magnum goose loads at clay pigeons.

We Klineburgers were honored to be invited to the fabulous gathering on a regular basis. The residents of Alturas loved the Carlsberg families and volunteered their services as guides and helpers to cater to the massive event. In fact, I believe it was the biggest function to ever hit little old Alturas. The hunt was uninterrupted when Arthur met his death in 1978 on a hunt with me in the U.S.S.R.

Dick and his family carried on the traditional hunt that hosted royalty, heads of state, movie stars, astronauts, military leaders and high-profile sportsmen. Dick, like his brother Art, died doing what they loved best, hunting. On October 3, 1994, Dick succumbed to heart failure while hunting grouse in the Western Highlands of Scotland. Dick and Art were two of the greatest hosts ever, but without their presence the Carlsberg 3 Shot Honker Hunt rightfully was discontinued by their surviving widows. It was 25 years of nonstop camaraderie for the finest sportsmen.

☝ **Roy Weatherby and Chris Klineburger in front of the California Pines sign as they gathered for the annual 3 Shot Honker Hunt.**

☝ **Chris and his shooting buddies, along with the guides show off their morning bag at the Carlsbergs'.**

# CHAPTER 3

# Famous People in the Lives of the Klineburgers

*Bert Klineburger*

The Klineburgers became the preeminent leaders in the development of sport hunting and the most knowledgeable source of information about hunting and outfitting worldwide. As a result, they were befriended by people everywhere with common interests, including renowned individuals, such as royalty, heads of state, astronauts, and celebrities of every sort. In this part of the book, we felt it would be of interest to the readers to hear about individuals of notoriety who came in contact with the Klineburgers.

Chris's brother Bert Klineburger tells about many people of fame in the following paragraphs.

## ROYALTIES

### HRH Prince Khalid Bin Sultan of Saudi Arabia

Prince Khalid was the Commander of Joint Forces working in a parallel command with General Norman Schwarzkopf in Gulf War Desert Storm in 1991. He enjoyed sport hunting, and a Washington dignitary, John Freitag, referred our first association with His Highness.

The Prince wanted an African safari, which included extra special security services for his staff and friends. Since I was a representative of Tanganyika Wildlife Safaris, in the Selous Reserve of Tanzania, I was able to arrange that extraordinary and successful safari. From then on, we were his hunt coordinator and did all his taxidermy work in our Seattle studios.

I also accompanied the Prince on a jaguar and puma hunt in Paraguay, outfitted by Rocky McBride of Texas. Chris and I both visited the Prince in Saudi Arabia on occasion and once we sent one of our taxidermists, Rob Frivold, to mount trophies that the U.S. Fish and Wildlife Service refused to permit into the U.S. In addition, brother Gene had to go Nepal to prepare those same skins for the taxidermy work.

### HIH Prince Abdorreza Pahlavi of Iran

Prince Abdorreza was the brother of the Shah of Iran. He was a renowned international big game hunter besides being the head of the

**HRH Khalid bin Sultan and Bert Klineburger with the prince's trophies in Tanzania's Selous Reserve.**

HRH Prince Khalid Bin Sultan (right) watching
Bert and guides skinning his two jaguars in Paraguay.

HRH Prince Abdorreza Pahlavi sitting with Chris and Colleene Klineburger and
Charles Napier at the head table at the Weatherby Foundation Award Banquet.

(L to R) Bert Klineburger, Steve Gose, and the pilot greet Prince Abdorreza where he was to hunt on Steve's Valdina Ranch in Texas.

Ministry of Forestry that oversaw the country's wildlife. The Prince became early friends of ours as we had done most of his taxidermy work and had many visits with him as he passed thru Seattle on his way to hunts in Canada and Alaska. He would always set time aside for us when attending major events like the Weatherby Award Banquet and the Shikar Safari Club meetings as well as welcome us when we visited Tehran.

On one trip thru Seattle, he asked if we would train a couple of Persian taxidermists, so that they could establish a Royal museum and have their own people to do the work. We agreed and the Prince sent the Tajbakhsh brothers Nourala and Hedayet, who we took in like family and trained them in all aspects to do the museum work.

The Prince was responsible for Chris' ability to open the hunting program in Iran to foreigners back in 1965. Our last visit with Prince Abdorreza was at the Weatherby Awards Banquet in Reno in January 2007 shortly before he passed away.

Prince Abdorreza's falcons being shown to Bert, astronauts Bill Pogue and Stu Roosa (behind falconers) along with the Tajbakhsh brothers, Nouri (back center) and Heda (right front).

HRH Prince Abdorreza Pahlavi with Chris at the Weatherby Foundation Awards Banquet in 2007 shortly before the Prince passed away.

## HRH Prince Sultan Mahmud Ghazi of Afghanistan

In the 1960s, Afghanistan was a Kingdom and a very peaceful country just beginning to allow tourism. Dr. Leonard Milton, president of the People-to-People Sports Committee and I, as a director, contacted U.S. Ambassador Neumann in Kabul in relation to conducting a sports mission between America and Afghanistan. Ambassador Neumann directed us to the Director of the Air Authority, an elite member of the Royal lineage, Prince Sultan Mahmud Ghazi. His Highness welcomed us and not only favored developing field sports, but also became very interested in hunting sports. Sultan's brother, Prince Salahidan Ghazi, was a keen hunter and joined in on the negotiations that led to opening Afghanistan to the greatest hunting expeditions of the time, including Marco Polo Sheep and Markhor.

Both Princes became our good friends from the mid 60s until 1979 when the Russians invaded Afghanistan. Salahidan joined Chris on one of his hunts in the Pamirs, while the Princesses entertained our wives during times that we were in the mountains. Sultan was even a guest in our homes in Seattle.

Sultan had left the country by 1979 and we understand Salahidan was murdered by the Taliban.

## HRH Prince Bandar Bin Sultan of Saudi Arabia

For a great length of time, Prince Bandar was the Saudi Ambassador to the U.S.A. His offices in Washington contacted our firm requesting our help in arranging a hunt for Alaska brown bear. His requirements included deluxe accommodations and special security along with plenty of space for a large staff, including four Secret Service agents. I knew just the place at Don Johnson's Bear Lake Lodge on the Alaska Peninsula near Cold Bay. I had hunted with Don there in 1961 so I knew he could handle the Prince's arrangement.

The arrangement was made and Don asked if I could also attend and assist.

Don's son, Warren, put Prince Bandar onto a fine bear that he collected. I personally took the bear to the Klineburger taxidermy facility for processing.

The Prince had a complex in Aspen, Colorado that he used for skiing and vacationing, so he chose that for his trophy display location. When Chris discussed the position for the life-size mounted bear, his Highness requested him to come look at the location. In looking over the buildings, the very low ceilings prevented any kind of a trophy room. Chris suggested adding a side room with high ceilings. The Prince said ok and six months later, he requested Chris to come take a look. He did and was amazed to find a gigantic log-lodge on a hillside overlooking the mountains and valleys. The bear was mounted standing for the entryway.

We assisted the Prince on additional hunts to add specimens of North American game to his private lodge.

Prince Bandar Bin Sultan in the Bear Lake Lodge kitchen where he took over one night and cooked a typical Saudi meal. On right are guide Warren Johnson and his sister on left.

Prince Bandar waves "goodbye" as they board the Twin Otter after a successful hunt at Bear Lake, Alaska.

## HIH Jigmesingye Wangchuck, the King of Bhutan

Bhutan is a tiny kingdom literally clinging on the south slope of the Himalayas that was little known by the outside World in the late 1970s. Through the People-to-People Sports Committee, Leonard Milton and I arranged a mission to Bhutan. Since archery is the main national sport, the sports equipment that we gathered was heavy on archery equipment, much of which was donated by Fred Bear of Bear Archery.

We took the equipment to Bhutan's Capitol, Thimpu, where we met the young King. In a special ceremony, we discussed World sports, including hunting. We were invited to return the following year for an experimental hunt for bharal, takin and Himalayan black bear. We ended up hunting there three times, including once with Stan Studer of Texas.

During our many visits I met most of the government officials including Chief Justice Pij Dorji, Secretary of Planning, Col. Lam Dorji and the Minister of Foreign Affairs, Dowa Tsering. During many meetings with the King and his staff, we arranged for Bhutan to compete in the Summer Olympics in Los Angeles in 1984.

**Dr. Leonard Milton (left) and Bert Klineburger during a visit with HIH King Jigmesingye Wangchuck at his palace in Thimpu, Bhutan.**

⚜ **Bert Klineburger and HIH King Mahendra of Nepal with his mountain goat taken on the Alaska hunt.**

## HIH Mahendra Bir Bikron, the King of Nepal

In 1970, King Mahendra and Queen Ratna arranged a hunting trip in Alaska to hunt all possible game during the month of October. Alaska hunting outfitter Al Burnett was selected to manage the hunt, so Al contracted other guides to assist in this rather complex arrangement. Al was requested to appear in Washington D.C. for protocol instructions where he was told the Alaska trip and the hunt was considered an official visit and government assistance was available to make their Highnesses visit most pleasant and successful. The Klineburgers were requested to assist on an advisory standpoint, as well as selected to do the field care of specimens and the ultimate taxidermy work.

I reset my schedule to be able to spend my time on the majority of the hunt. We made a formal invitation for the Royal party to come to Seattle as our guests after the hunt, which the King gladly accepted. I was present when the entourage arrived in Anchorage on Air Force One, the U.S. President's private jet. Coast Guard aircraft were made available to transport the party from place to place for the various wildlife that was hundreds of miles apart. The hunt was very successful and I had the various specimens' air freighted to Seattle at the completion of each hunt.

Chris had the motorcade, including police escort, all arranged as our commercial airline landed at Sea/Tac Airport. The first was a tour through our taxidermy studios and a cocktail reception. After settling them in their hotel, we all motorcaded to the Space Needle restaurant, where we had it half blocked off for our party of about two-dozen. The Royal party was quite impressed with the beauty of Seattle as the restaurant rotated its hourly 360°. A great friendship resulted with the King and Queen, as well as with many of their staff, including General Sushil Shumshere, the leader of the group.

Chris was able to open Nepal for an ongoing hunting program in the spring of 1974 as a result of our association with the Nepal Royalty. He has distinguished honor of holding Hunting License #1 issued in Nepal.

HIH King Mahendra and Queen Ratna of Nepal (left) in the Klineburger taxidermy studio, while the Klineburgers, Bert, Chris, Brigitte, and Gene (second from right), guide them through.

The 1978 Safari Club International Convention drew the top guns. (From left, Mrs. Carter, NRA Executive Vice President Harlon Carter, Dottie Oldfield, Texas Governor John Connally, and SCI Past president and a founding member Andy Oldfield.)

## American Leaders

Politicians, Armed Forces heroes, and Astronauts are among the many American leaders that had a sensible outlook for wildlife. Most all of them had many things in common: they rejoiced in God's great creation of the outdoors and all the living things in it; they were hunters and fishermen; they were conservationists; and they were proud to have fought for the Right to Bear Arms and not shy about letting the world know that they use them to hunt. They also knew that hunters provided the majority of conservation dollars so they attended and contributed to many major gatherings of sportsmen.

Aside from the many hunter and conservation clubs mentioned in Chapter 20 of Part I of this book, here were some other groups, whose gatherings included many of the "Who's Who" of American leaders: Wyoming Governor's One Shot Antelope Hunt; the Carlsberg's 3 Shot Honker Hunt; The African First Shotters; The Weatherby Foundation Hunting and Conservation Awards; and the Klineburger's Annual Safari parties.

It seemed another thing that most of these American leaders had in common was they befriended the Klineburgers. Our place of business, including the renowned Klineburger Water Hole, was a regular stop for celebrities passing through. We arranged hunts for them, did their taxidermy work, and often accompanied them on expeditions. We shot with them, drank with them, and palled with them at major gatherings as well as hosting them at our private ranches (see Chapter 21, Part I, Safari Island and Ranches).

When Brigitte and I moved to Texas in November 1979, several of our old friends had ranches, many of which were also game farms. They frequently used any excuse to have hunt parties for guests that included dignitaries of sorts. I was invited to a great many of these extraordinary Texas style events with open bar, chuck wagon, and the evening campfire. Brigitte and I fit right in

as the ranches had the extra bonus of my guiding and skinning expertise, our ability to help out in the hosting and they even put up with my strumming my guitar and singing an occasional old west or Mexican song around the campfire. These ranches owned by high profile Texans included Dos Arroyos Ranch owned by Bob and Andy Phillips, Steve Gose's Valdina Ranch, and the Anvil Park Ranch of Stan Studer.

We became friends with a number of VIPs at parties on these ranches, as well as bringing a lot of our renowned friends. Here is some brief information about some of our great American leaders of their field and were an inspiration to the world of hunting.

John Connally, Governor of Texas, visits the Klineburger's in Seattle. Left to right Chris, Bert, the Governor, and Gene.

Bert congratulating Oliver North at the Weatherby Award Banquet in Reno, where Ollie spoke and presented the Award.

Firearms manufacturer Roy "Magnum" Weatherby introduces President Gerald Ford to Bert.

Tom Bass of Colt Firearms presents Ronald Reagan with a Colt Sauer rifle at the Mzuri Safari Foundation Convention in 1975.

General Jimmy Doolittle, Chris Klineburger, and Roy Rogers socializing at Jimmy's home in Los Angeles.

From left, Governors **Pat Brown** of California and **Steve McNichols** of Colorado enjoy camaraderie with Chris at Carlsberg's 3 Shot Honker Hunt.

## Governors

*John Connally* was a powerful American who served as Governor of Texas, Secretary of Navy under J.F.K., and Secretary of Treasury under Kennedy. He was seriously wounded as a passenger when President Kennedy was assassinated. We enjoyed many gatherings with John, including a lengthy visit with us in Seattle.

*Tom Bolack* served as Governor of New Mexico in addition to other state offices. He hunted extensively and collected much of the world's fish and game. In the early 1990s Tom asked brother Chris to come to Farmington and assess what to do with his huge collection of specimens. Chris proceeded to design and build the Governor Tom Bolack Wildlife Museum. Chris also escorted Tom on a hunt in the U.S.S.R.

Texas Governor John Connolly, his wife Nellie, Yuri Bagrov (Russian official as Chris's guest), and Chris together at Game Conservation International Convention in San Antonio.

*Ed Herschler,* a two-term Governor of Wyoming was a regular attendee of the Carlsberg 3 Shot Honker Hunt and many of the hunters conventions, besides hosting the One Shot Antelope Hunt for his eight years of service.

*Governor John Love* of Colorado competed five times in the One Shot Antelope competition and often started the celebration early, where some of us would arrive en route to Lander in Denver where John hosted a pre–One Shot party.

*Governor William Egan* of Alaska, 1959–1966, became a good acquaintance of the Klineburgers as he often stopped for a visit at our "Anchorage Log Cabin Museum." Bill was a down to earth "sourdough" and we could dial him direct to get whatever information we wanted.

*Governor Carroll Campbell* of South Dakota was my hunting partner at the One Shot Antelope Hunt when I was on a team and he was the leader of the South Dakota team. Carroll and I had a great time swapping hunting stories.

*Governor Haley Barber* of Louisiana came forward for the Right to Bear Arms following Hurricane Katrina. The officials began confiscating firearms from citizens after the devastating storm. The governor made them return the firearms to protect themselves from looters, and came up with the slogan "You Loot, We Shoot." It brought looting under control.

*Governor Sarah Palin* of Alaska is a hunter herself and kept our nation's most abundant wildlife populations in balance with use of hunter's dollars.

Chris and I attended the Governors One Shot Antelope Hunt from early on, first as guests of good Past Shooter friends, but later we were team members ourselves, becoming Past Shooters. We enjoyed many wonderful times with g*overnors of many States at the one shot* throughout the years. Here are some that led a team starting from the beginning in 1940: W. Harold Dahl CO; Harold Evans WY; C.J. Bender TX; Joe Bunten WY; John Woodring CO; Drayton Boucher LA; L.C. Hunt WY; Lee Knous CO; Robert D. Blue IA; Ben Laney AR; G.C. Redfield SD; Zack Brinkerhoff WY; William Mashburn OH; Harry Yesness WY; Alex Kerr CA; Dan Thornton CO; Lanny Ross NY; Frank Barrett WY; Lindley Scarlett PA; Ed Dutcher CO; Scott Hayes IL; Lester Bagley WY; Ed Arn KS; Nels Smith WY; J. Bracken Lee UT; J.C. Rogers WY; Larry Skutt CO; Joe Foss SD; Ed Johnson CO; Victor Anderson NE; Milward Simpson WY; Steve McNichols CO; Caleb Boggs DE; T.T. Varney NE; J.J. Hickey WY; Charles Russhorn NY; W.J. Cleveland LA; George Nigh OK; Jack Gage WY; John Anderson KS; John Love CO; John Anderson, Jr. MO; Clifford Hanson WY; Otto Kerner IL; Warren Knowles WI; Tirn Babcock MT; Henry Bellmon OK; Harold Hughes IA; Norberty Tiemann NE; Don Samuelson ID; Stanley Hathaway WY; Claude Kirk FL; Jack Williams AZ; Louie Nunn KY; Frank Farr SD; Harlow Platts CO; Richard Ogilvie IL; David Cargo NM; Warren Knowles WI; Calvin Rampton UT; Daniel Evans WA; Winfield Dunn TN; Thomas Meskill CT; John Vanderhoof CO; Marvin Mandel MD; John Hanes VA; James Foster NM; Richard Kneip SD; Eldon Cooper CO; William Peters NE; James Harris SC; Ed Herschler WY; Ernie Day ID; Jack Schooley CO; Morris Blakely MT; Richard Lamm CO; William Janklow SD; William Clements TX; Allen Olson ND; Martin Schreiber WI; Terry Branstad IA; Mark White TX; Edwin Edwards LA; Mike Sullivan WY; Mike Hayden KS; Tommy Thompson WI; Carroll Campbell SC; George Mickelson SD; George Sinner ND; Norman Bangerter UT; Roy Romer CO; Benjamin Nelson NE; Bruce Sundlun RI; Edward Schafer ND; Jim Geringer WY; William Graves KS; Dave Freudenthal WY;

Governor Dan Evans of Washington State (second from left) and his team members Red Dahl and Boyd Sharp, pose with Bert Klineburger and Roy Rogers during the One Shot Antelope Hunt.

Jeff Crawford CO; Bill Witter, Jr. CO; and Joe Manchin WV.

## Armed Forces

One of the great sportsmen of all time became governor of South Dakota in 1955 after spending two elected terms in the Legislature. It was *General Joe Foss* of World War II fame. In his later years, he rarely missed attending the One Shot Hunt and other major hunter/conservation gatherings. He became the Commissioner of the American Football League and President of the National Rifle Association. He also hosted the ABC American Sportsman TV series from 1964-1967 and then the Outdoorsman series 1967-1974. We arranged many of Joe's hunting trips and enjoyed camaraderie with him throughout the years. Our last visit with him was at the One Shot Hunt in 2002, shortly after of which he passed away. Joe's fame began in WWII as a fighter pilot where he commanded what became Foss's Flying Circus, which was accredited to shooting down 72 Jap aircraft,

26 of which were credited to Joe himself, all in Guadalcanal alone. He became a general and was eventually awarded the Congressional Medal of Honor as a war hero. He then remained in the Air National Guard and served as Director of Operations for the Central Air Defense in the Korean War before going into private life and politics.

*General Charles Yeager* was another hunting pal that fought as a pilot in WWII.

He became an Ace in one single mission in his P-51 Mustang shooting down five German aircraft. In one mission over France, he shot down a German aircraft and then was shot down himself. The French resistance helped him escape thru Spain. After abating a ruling that escaped pilots could not fly again over enemy territory, Eisenhower allowed him to return and he flew another 61 missions over Europe and then another 127 missions in

**Congressional Medal of Honor recipient General Joe Foss and Bert starting their safari in Mozambique.**

the Vietnam War. He also received America's highest honor, the Congressional Medal of Honor. Right after WW II, Chuck was assigned as a Test Pilot and on October 14, 1947 was the first person to cross the speed of sound.

We had many good shoots with Chuck at Carlsberg's Honker Hunt, and the One Shot Hunt and many fine visits at other hunter gatherings. He was a frequent keynote speaker at major hunter's conventions.

*General David Lee "Tex" Hill* of Flying Tiger fame became a good friend of mine after I moved to Texas in 1979. I first met him at a party on Studer's Anvil Park Ranch and bonded with him from then on.

In the beginning of WW II, the only group winning over the Japanese was the Flying Tigers that stopped the advance of the Japanese in the China Arena. Tex was the Squadron leader that destroyed a bridge on the Salween River, as well as wiping out most of the troops and equipment after which the Japanese never advanced further into China. John Wayne played "Tex" in the movie Flying Tigers. Tex was awarded the Distinguished Service Cross and Distinguished Flying Cross.

It seemed that all of the top brass in the armed forces were hunters, so I could go on forever. To keep it short, I will mention just a few other great comrades. *General Norman Schwarzkopf* was the co-leader of Desert Storm in Iraq along with our good friend and client Prince Kahled Bin Sultan. He hunted at the Governors One Shot Hunt, presented the coveted Weatherby Award, and was a

keynote speaker at various hunters' conventions. *General Ollie Crawford* of the U.S. Air Force served two terms as president of the Air Force Association. He shared many war stories along with Tex Hill after hunts at Studer's Anvil Park Ranch. *General Curtis LeMay* was the commander of the notorious 305th Bomb Group on the German front and later transferred to the Pacific's front in charge of Strategic Air Operations whose operation was bombing the Japanese home islands. He was a regular attendee at the One Shot Hunt, Weatherby Awards and hunters' conventions. I personally hunted with him on Studer's ranch.

*General E.R. "Buck" Bedard* having served 37 years in the Marines and receiving the Bronze Star for Valor Device uses hunting as his relaxation. He was chosen as the presenter of the Weatherby Award in 2009. Buck was very active in the Vietnam War and everything involving the military from then on and he is assisting in Iraq as we write. *General Craig Boddington*, also in the U.S. Marines became one of the most active International hunters and the most prolific sports writer of our time. He served as editor of a number of outdoor publications, wrote many books on hunting and firearms, and currently is the firearms editor for Safari Magazine. Craig is a director of the Weatherby Foundation and had served as president. I was proud when speaking at a convention; he referred to me as his mentor.

*General Jimmy Doolittle* needs little introduction. His early fame is when he took off from the Carrier Hornet and led the "Tokyo

Bert Klineburger (left) and friends gather with the One Shot Antelope Hunt team (the ones with "Team" hats on) Pat Bruly, actor James Drury, and General Curtis LeMay.

Raiders" to bomb Japan. That raid was a wake-up call to the Japs, when it appeared we were losing everywhere else in the Pacific. Jimmy went on to do great things all during the War, which brought him the Nation's highest award, The Congressional Medal of Honor. Anyone wanting to know more about Jimmy should read "Thirty seconds Over Tokyo."

Jimmy was a fine, down to earth sort of guy that was always fun to be with, whether shooting or just partying. He was one of "Our Gang," a group of Southern California notables, including the likes of Roy Rogers. One time at a Carlsberg 3 Shot Honker Hunt, we thought it would be fun to have Jimmy bunk together with W.T. "Yoshi" Yoshimoto, a renowned Japanese American hunter. They both thought it was hilarious! He was also a regular at the One Shot Antelope Hunt. We arranged hunting trips for the General and did his taxidermy work.

ⓒ **Chris and General James Doolittle were shooting partners at
Carlsberg's 3 Shot Honker Hunt.**

At the end of their shoot, Chris captured this photo when General James Doolittle seemed to be saying, "It was raining ducks!"

So now, we need to talk about the most renowned General, *Dwight D. Eisenhower*. Nothing needs to be said of Dwight's notoriety as a General and becoming the 34th president of the U.S.A., 1953-1961. As for hunting and sports, he developed the People-to-People Sports (PPS) program that has done great things bringing the common people of the World together with American sportsmen. (See Reflection after Chapter 5 of Part III of this book).

Chris, Gene, and I were early members of PPS and I eventually went on to be the Treasurer and a Director. This association helped us to get our "foot in the door" of a number of foreign countries to develop Sportsmen Financed Wildlife Programs.

While Ike was President, he was to come to Anchorage Alaska for an official visit; officials and City Fathers got together to work out his program. The only two places to visit were Elmendorf Air force Base and Jonas Brothers of Alaska Log Cabin Museum, which was our place of business and the only thing "Alaskan" in town.

Other high profile politicians have been active in recognizing the importance of hunters being the primary source of wildlife conservation. President *George H. Bush* 1989–1993 has made many appearances at hunting gatherings, as has *Spiro Agnew, Dan Quayle*, and *Ronald Reagan*.

President Dwight D. Eisenhower and his entourage as they exit the Klineburger's Anchorage Museum during the President's official visit.

(See copy of Ronny's letter to Chris when still Governor of California). Reagan's mission as President went on to clean up "big government" in Washington, including an attempt to turn the misdirection of the U.S. Fish and Wildlife Service. In 2008, President *George W. Bush* signed his executive Order 13443, titled Facilitation of Hunting Heritage and Wildlife Conservation. It instructs the Departments of Interior and Agriculture to facilitate the expansion and enhancement of hunting opportunities on federal lands.

### Astronauts and Other High Flyers

Astronauts are among the most adventurous sportsmen. They cherish the outdoors and love their hunting and fishing. From early on they connected with the Klineburgers. We shot with many of them at Carlsberg's Honker Hunt and the Governor's One Shot Antelope

At an African First Shooters meeting in New York, Vice President Spiro Agnew receives a custom-made shotgun in appreciation for his conservation effort. From left, General Joe Foss, Spiro Agnew, John King, Dick Griffith, and Bert Klineburger.

hunt. We traveled with a number of them to Africa and beyond. I hunted and traveled Africa with Apollo Astronauts *James Lovell*, *Stu Roosa*, and *Deke Slayton*. Also to Bhutan with Stu Roosa and *Ed White*. Chris escorted *Charlie Duke* and his wife Dottie on their Mozambique safari. Brother Gene joined in when we took Jim Lovell and Deke Slayton to Mozambique in 1972. A number of astronauts came to Seattle to speak at functions of the Klineburgers. *Wally Schirra*, Charlie Duke, and Stu Roosa came at different times as keynote speakers at Klineburgers Safari Parties. Charlie Duke was the presenter at a special banquet in 2007 honoring Chris as the Pioneer of Asian Hunting.

Astronauts and other high-flyers that shot on teams at the Wyoming Governors One Shot Antelope hunt include Donald Slayton, Gordon Cooper, Frank Borman, James McDivitt, R. Cunningham, Bill Anders, Eugene Cernan, Ronald Evans, Jack Lousma, James Lovell, Joe Engle, Jack Swigert, Joe Allen, Stuart Roosa, David

**Walter Schirra, astronaut of all three U.S. Space programs, was the speaker at Klineburger's Seventh Annual Safari Party. Colleene Klineburger seated, while Chris and Gene Klineburger introduce Wally.**

🐧 **Gene and Betty Klineburger visit with old friend astronaut Walt Cunningham of Apollo 7 fame at the Museum of Flight on Boeing Field.**

Scott, Frank Tallman, Vance Brand, Paul Weitz, Henry Hartsfield, Charles Yeager, Marcus Hansen, Virgil Young, Thomas March, Charles Duke, Oliver Crawford and David Lee "Tex" Hill, as well as Cosmonauts Vladimir Shatalov, Valery Kubasov, and Aleksey Leonov.

## Stars

One usually associates "Stars" as motion picture performers, but they come in many different forms. There are singing stars, stars in racing and athletics, trick shooters, magicians, burlesque queens, variety show performers and many more. The Klineburgers associated with stars of every type through their stores, ranches, their participation in hunting and conservation events and hunter gatherings of every sort.

Stars that competed with the Governors at the Wyoming Governors One Shot Antelope Hunts include Roy Rogers, George

🎙 **Astronaut Charlie Duke, speaker at the Klineburger Safari Party, looks on while Chris and Bert Klineburger present their Wildlife Officer of the Year Award (1979) to George Smallwood of the Washington State Game Department.**

Montgomery, Jack Carson, Robert Six, Montie Montana, Rex Allen, John Mahaffey, Tex Ritter, Bob Darch, Merle Travis, Robert Fuller, Wendell Niles, Slim Pickens, Frank Ferguson, John Russell, James Drury, Guy Madison, Rick Jason, Don Bean, Charlie Walker, Mike Lynch, Jimmy Dickens, Ed Banach, Bill Skiles, Pete Henderson, Dale Robertson, Carroll Shelby, Robert Stack, Charlie Daniels, Johnny Rutherford, Parnelli Jones, Jameson Parker, Rick Hacker, James Baker, Jim Abercrombie, Jon Koncak, Roy Clark, Donald Trump, Jr., Sam Snead, Daryl Lamonica, Jay Buhner, Norman Charlton, and David Valle.

Some other high profile "stars" that became close to the Klineburgers include Daryl Lamanico and Mel Renfro (football), as well as Ted Williams (baseball), and golfers Jack Nicklaus and Sam Snead. One odd thing we did for Sam was to make a golf bag from an elephant leg!

Astronauts Jim Lovell and Deke Slayton with Gene Klineburger in Beira, Mozambique as they prepare for their safari.

ô **Bert helped guide astronaut Deke Slayton for his cape buffalo on their Mozambique safari.**

In those early days, we shared good times with sports writer stars and publishers, Jack O'Connor with *Outdoor Life,* Warren Page with *Field & Stream* and Grits Gresham with *Sports Afield.* Other old-time friends were Ed Zern, Gene Hill, and John Jobson. Robert "Bob" Petersen came along with Petersen Publishing and produced a number of sports-related tabloids, including *Guns & Ammo* and *Petersen's Hunting* magazine. As we write, Craig Boddington has come along as a prolific sports writer. (See also Craig Boddington under America's Leaders). Peter Capstick, author of Africa hunting fame came to us for a great amount of data on African countries that he was not familiar with.

Many renowned star business executives were our clientele and hunting partners. Included were Jack Parker, president of General Electric; Bill Spencer, president of Citi Bank; the Larry Potterfield family, founders of Midway Arms Inc., the World's largest supplier of shooting supplies; Dick and Mary Cabela, founders of Cabela's; Bob Chisholm, co-founder of Pizza Hut; Fred Bear of Bear Archery; and Otis Chandler, publisher of the Los Angeles Times. Moreover, we must mention good friend Lowell Thomas, Radio Hall of Fame for news casting, including coverage of WWII. He volunteered to narrate our movie, "The Great Shikar," the story of opening Afghanistan for Marco Polo sheep. To only name a few of foreign business stars, very close to the Klineburgers were Carl Flick, former owner of Mercedes-Benz; Eduardo De Aznar, owner of Caban eros Ranch in Spain, Europe's largest private land ownership; the Sada family of Mexico that controlled the Alpha group and the Vitro Group, the World's largest glass company; and the Zambrano family of CEMEX in México, the world's largest cement company.

Bert on left, along with many friends are pictured with the Apollo Astronaut Team that competed in the One Shot Antelope Hunt. Next to Bert are Gene Cernan, Jack Lousma, Rusty Schweikart, and Ron Evans.

General Tex Hill of Flying Tiger fame and Jim Lovell of Apollo 13 fame and Bert together at the One Shot Antelope Hunt. (Tom Hanks played Jim Lovell in the movie Apollo 13, and John Wayne played the part of Tex Hill in the movie Flying Tigers.)

We must not forget our longtime pal, Roy Weatherby of magnum rifle fame, who also created the most prestigious award honoring hunters for their achievements and conservation efforts, the Weatherby Hunting and Conservation Award. Presenters of the annual award included entertainers Andy Devine, Robert Taylor, Lorne Greene, Cornel Wilde, Roy Rogers, Chuck Connors, Ernest Borgnine, Gene Autry, Robert Stack, Stewart Granger, and Patrick Duffy.

### Foreign Diplomats

In dealing with countries around the world, we usually dealt with high-ranking officials and sometimes the most high. See also a previous chapter on "Royalties," as well as Chris' frequent mention of high officials in this book, especially the Asian section, Part IV. Even though I dealt considerably with hunting worldwide, my main forte was Africa and still is. In fact, when I left our family company in 1975, I lived in Africa for over three years operating a safari company in Central African Republic (CAR). See Part III, Chapter 6 of this book for that story.

I first met President Jean Bedel Bokassa of CAR in the early 1970s when Leonard Milton and I arrived for a People-to-People Sports mission. Surprisingly upon our early morning arrival at the Bangui airport, greeting us was a royal welcome with drums pounding, bare-breasted native girls dancing along the red carpet that led to where Bokassa sat, surrounded by aids handing us Champagne.

That was a preview of what to expect for the next four days, including a flight in his private DC3 for a safari at the Presidential Hunting Lodge, motorcade tour of the city, a

 Bob Hope hams it up in Klineburger's taxidermy studios.

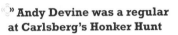 

**Andy Devine was a regular at Carlsberg's Honker Hunt**

**Mae West with Chris Klineburger and Grace Mathis at their Las Vegas home.**

Steve McQueen at Klineburger's Log Cabin Museum in Anchorage.

Hank Williams, Jr., was a big game hunter that never passed a chance to visit Klineburger's taxidermy studio and was a guest at Chris's High Lonesome Ranch.

Hank Jr. hunting antelope on his ranch in Montana

Joe Bowman, known as "The Straight Shooter," taught most of the Western Stars quick-draw techniques. He shot on a team at the One Shot Antelope Hunt and put on a stage show at many hunter gatherings. He has been a frequent guest at Chris' home in Washington and with Chris and Grace in Las Vegas. Here, Nouri Tajbakhsh shows him a cougar head sculpture, while Chris looks on.

Here "The Rifleman," Chuck Connors, gives Colleene Klineburger a hug. Chuck was a guest at Chris's High Lonesome Ranch and other hunting functions.

Burlesque Hall of Famer Tempest Storm at a visit with Chris and Grace at their Las Vegas home. Chris gives an admiring look, while Jim Slemons from Honolulu cuddles in.

Chris and Colleene Klineburger pose with their good friend Foster Brooks, the "Loveable Lush."

Chris and Grace have frequent parties with Bob Markworth (center) and Don Kirk (right). Don is one of the early Las Vegas stars, who reopened the Flamingo Hotel in 1948 and elevated them to Vegas's #1 showplace. Bob is a world famous-archer who performs various variety acts and has been on numerous national TV shows. Here he appears on Ed Sullivan Show (circa 1966) and in 2008 he hunts with the Bushmen in southwestern Africa to experience the ways of the very earliest archers.

Ed Sullivan Show

# BOB MARKWORTH & TYGERR
## INTERNATIONAL VARIETY ATTRACTION

3639 1st Ave. South
Seattle, WA 98134
Phone: (206) 868-1987

Al Unser and Gene Klineburger with Al's polar bear that he took on the Chukchi Sea ice pack just before going back and winning the Indy 500 race in 1971. Al (four-time winner) and his brother Bobby (three-time winner) were hunters and friends of the Klineburgers. Joe Quinn, Safety Director for the Speedway, was also a friend and customer.

Actor Dale Robertson and Colleene Klineburger are being stalked by a dall sheep at a Mzuri Safari Foundation Convention in Reno.

Of all "stars," Roy Rogers was certainly the Klineburgers' favorite. He had always been a hunter and from early on became a taxidermy client of ours. His frequent visits with us led into a lifelong friendship and hunting companion at the One Shot Antelope Hunt, Carlsbergs Honker Hunt and many private hunts, as well as visits in our respective homes.

Roy Rogers and Trigger Junior at Roy's earlier ranch in Thousand Oaks, California. Colleene and Chris Klineburger look on while the trainer, left, brags about the fine mount.

🎵 **A bunch of boys were whooping it up in the Malamute Saloon—oh no, that was Roy Rogers, Bert Klineburger, Wayne Ewing (on harmonica), and Sam Browell looking on.**

late night party attended by all foreign ambassadors and dignitaries and gifts of elephant tusks and diamonds to all members of our party.

He also offered us a hunting concession, which resulted in my organizing a group of sportsmen as partners, who insisted that I manage the hunting operation. So that's when Brigitte and I relocated to Bangui. I had a good relationship with Bokassa during that time and went on to having dealings and

People-to-People missions to Chad, Zaire, and Rwanda.

After our People-to-People mission to Chad, I was able to negotiate with President Francois Tombalbye to hunt various desert wildlife in the north of this arid country where hunting had been closed since the early 1970s. Apollo astronaut Col. Stuart Roosa and I took an exploratory trip, which started with a flight to Abeche that appeared like a scene from a Foreign Legion movie. After

**Roy Rogers at Klineburger Taxidermy with Chris and Colleene Klineburger.**

Roy Rogers was a frequent guest at the ranches the Klineburgers were involved in. Here, from left, Gene, Babo Walker (guide), Roy, and Chris rest after a pheasant shoot at their Quilomene Ranch in Washington.

Roy, Roy Jr. (Dusty), and Chris in the Roy Rogers/Dale Evans Museum in Victorville, CA before it was reestablished in Branson, MO.

Bert and Roy at the Governor's One Shot Antelope Hunt.

« Bert (left) and Chris Klineburger
visit with Roy Rogers in 1998,
just before Roy went to the Happy
Hunting Grounds.

outfitting ourselves we drove north to Biltine and Arada (the last oasis and fuel depot) before going beyond Oum Chalouba to hunt. We were successful in collecting scimitar oryx and dama gazelle before depleting our spare 55-gallon drum of fuel.

Upon our return to N'djamena, President Tombalbye was delighted with our success and agreed to a continued hunting program. He also accepted an invitation to visit us in Seattle. In 1974, he sent the Minister of State for a reconnaissance visit with us. The President himself was to come soon after, but had been assassinated. That put the end to our hunting program. Our hunt will probably go down as the last to ever take place in Chad.

A similar situation happened in Zaire. *President Joseph Desiré Mobutu* allowed me to take exploratory trips to hunt and explore various areas. The only authorization I had was a "To whom it may concern" on his official letterhead stating we had permission to

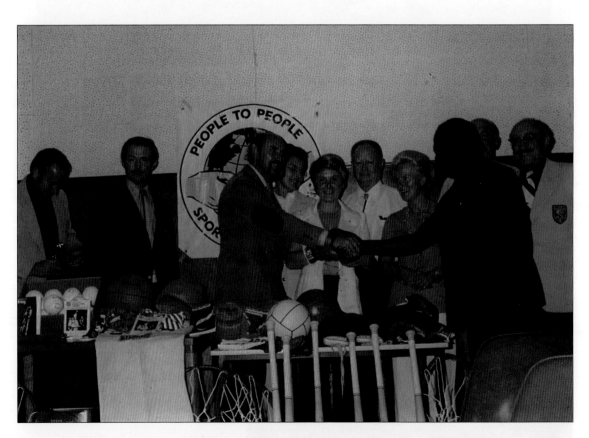

**Bert Klineburger welcoming President Bokassa to the sports equipment presentation, while the secretary of CAR's newly formed Sports Ministry tries on boxing gloves. From left in back, representing People-to-People Sports, astronauts Jim Lovell and Stuart Roosa, Fran and Rusty Gibbons, Joyce and Irwin Wilson, and Leonard Milton.**

On safari in CAR, from left: James Lovell, Leonard Milton, President Jean Bedel Bokassa, Stu Roosa, Erwin Wilson, Brigitte, and Bert Klineburger.

hunt and travel and that all officials were to cooperate with us. We flew to Benïn in the east near Uganda, where we outfitted and began hunting. Being in full camouflage clothing, we were mistaken as terrorists by an army patrol. After being thrown to the ground and rifles to our temples, we finally convinced them to look at the Presidents' letter, which ended up saving our lives.

That behind us, President Mobutu gave us a hunting concession. Good friend Stan Studer of Texas partnered with us and

we went to the business of buying vehicles and equipment, as well as getting the renowned safari operator Adelino Pïres to run the operation, after which hunting was suddenly closed with no explanation. While in the forest areas surveying elephant, we found considerable signs of ivory hunting, which we reported. The closure could very well have been the Zaire government realizing there was a lucrative ivory trade at their disposal and didn't want the interference of hunters.

During a People-to-People mission to Chad, President Francois Tombalbaye greets the committee, from left, Bert Klineburger, Jim Lovell, Joyce Wilson, Fran and Rusty Gibbons, Stuart Roosa, Brigitte Klineburger, and Leonard Milton.

COL. STUART ROOSA    MINISTER OF STATE OF CHAD ABDOULAYE LAMANA    BERT KLINEBURGER

« Astronaut Stuart Roosa came to the Klineburger taxidermy studios in Seattle to help Bert entertain the Minister of State of Chad.

A very successful businessman that I had met in Zaire, *Victor Ngezayo*, introduced *President Major General Juvenal Habyarimana* of Rwanda to us. Leonard Milton and I, representing the People-to-People Sports program went there to investigate their sports needs. The President invited us to his home, along with Victor, at which time the subject of hunting arose. We had much to talk about, as the Klineburgers were the initial partners with Uganda, and Tanzania, their closest neighbors. Victor had told us beforehand that the President was a hunter, so we had a Weatherby rife specially engraved, which we presented to him. To make a long story short, I was able to be awarded hunting rights to Rwanda.

Leonard and I brought our wives on a return trip, when we were shown the mountain gorillas, before doing an exploratory safari. The Minister of Wildlife knew of a possible World record cape buffalo that perhaps would soon succumb to old age. Being a female, which also have horns, they named her "The Princess." We came up with the idea of collecting it and having it mounted full size for display in Rwanda. They agreed and after a lengthy search, we located her. I skinned and measured

**Hedayat Tajbakhsh and Bert Klineburger present a Bear Archery bow and arrows to Prince Abdorreza's son in the Persian's trophy room. Astronaut Ed White looks on.**

the specimen for a life-size mount and sent the skin to Chris in Seattle (See Chris' story "Rwanda," in Part III).

One of our earliest contacts with foreign diplomats was with the *Minister of Home Affairs in India, Vidya Charan Shukla.* Aside from being one of the leading members of Parliament, he was the owner of a tour company, Allwyn Cooper, Ltd, that special-

ized in shikars, hunting tiger, panther, and other wildlife. As a leading Taxidermy business in those early postwar years, we received specimens from India, the only place in Asia open to hunting. When hunters wanted to arrange a hunt to India (or anywhere) we would refer them to the likes of Allwyn Cooper, which positioned us in the "guide referral service," as there were no travel

Victor Ngezayo and Leonard Milton look on while Bert Klineburger presents a custom Weatherby rifle and a copy of his book "This Is The Greatest Hunting Era" to President Juvenal Habyarimana of Rwanda.

agencies handling hunting at that time. This service put us on a friendship course with hunters and outfitters alike, as we were the most knowledgeable source of hunting information worldwide.

Therefore, Vidya Shukla became a pen pal via telex and telegrams, which led to my hunting tiger, panther, gaur and other game with Allwyn Cooper in the early 1960s. Vidya took time off from his minister's post to join me on some of the hunts and became a good friend.

My brothers Chris and Gene also hunted India in the mid-1960s when wildlife thrived and the shikar operators employed scores of people. (See Chris' India hunt in the last Chapter of Part III, Around the World in 80 Days.)

Gene had quite an experience on his shikar, when his shikari, Udiah Singh, informed him of a tiger that had just killed an ox that was pulling a cart, a frequent occurrence in the area. It was the object of shikar operators to always hunt troublesome cats, those killing people and domestic stock. Gene was placed on a trail on which they felt the tiger would use to return to the ox that had been left as bait. Sure enough, the tiger came face-to-face with Gene and a quick shot wounded the cat, then taking 5 days of tracking to finally finish it off.

I took *Bambang Trihatmodjo, the son of President Suharto of Indonesia,* on a hunt on the Alaska Peninsula. I had connections with wealthy Indonesians, as I had helped *Yani Haryanto* and his family buy the large Mount Taylor Ranch in New Mexico. Bambang was attending school in the U.S. and wanted to hunt Alaska, so Yani asked if I would arrange the hunt and escort young Bambang to Alaska. I engaged Denny Thompson and Bill Sims, top outfitters and good friends of the Klineburgers, to carry out the hunt.

We had a great and successful hunt, collecting outstanding trophies of Moose, Caribou and brown bear. Upon return to the "South 48," Yani had left word that we were to continue on to their New Mexico ranch where we collected a fine bull elk for Bambang.

We kept in touch after his return to Indonesia and he encouraged me to come hunt tiger there as his guest. I declined, as the cats there were declared as endangered on the U.S. list. Bambang went on to become a billionaire in his business dealings, so I was happy to be a small part of his life.

Vidya Charan Shukla, Minister of Home Affairs of India (with rifle), organizes beaters on Bert Klineburger's tiger hunt in Madhya Pradesh, the central state of India.

Bambang Trihatmodjo, son of President Suharto of Indonesia, is proud of his brown bear, as is Bert Klineburger and Denny and Jeannie Thompson.

Bert Klineburger and Bambang Trihatmodjo of Indonesia with moose and caribou horns on the Alaska Peninsula.

Steve Gose and Bert Klineburger greet the President of France, Valarie Giscard De Estang, upon arrival in Texas for a hunt on Steve's Valdina Ranch.

**People-to-People Sports entered a team at the Wyoming Governor's One Shot Antelope Hunt. Team members Dasno Jigme Thimley, Bhutan Ambassador to United Nations, Bert Klineburger, and Leonard Milton are welcomed by Willie leClair (Medicine Man) and Chief Darwin Le Clair of the Shoshone Tribe.**

# CHAPTER 4

# Conservation or Preservation

Preservationists often fail to understand the role hunting plays in wildlife conservation. Preservation is the non-sustainable use of a renewable resource and puts little, if any, money into wildlife conservation.

Conservation is the wise sustainable use of a renewable resource. Wildlife worldwide must have an economic value; otherwise, it will be wasted and—at best—used for food. Hunters provide economic value through direct financial and educational support to the people who share the wildlife habitat.

Preservationists claim that hunting is inhumane to animals. However, as they age, animals lose their ability to forge for food, making them weaker and more likely to fall prey to predators or starvation. Furthermore, severe winters wipe out entire herds. In addition to these natural inflictions, the Insurance Institute for Highway Safety estimates 1.5 million deer-vehicle crashes occur in the United States each year (IIHS 2004).

Now, is it humane for an animal to starve, freeze to death, or be eaten by a pack of canines, while still trying to escape? Or, is it better for an animal to enjoy a good, long life that ends quickly at the hands of a conservation-minded sportsman?

The answer is clear: hunting fundamentally must take place in order to humanely conserve suffering wildlife.

Through licenses, excise taxes, private donations, and more, the American sportsmen chronicled here have made significant strides in conserving wildlife and its habitat.

In 1937, a self-imposed excise tax of 11 percent on long guns and ammunition, and, later, a ten percent excise tax on handguns and archery equipment, collected from firearms, ammunition, and archery manufacturers, was passed for the purpose of wildlife management and improvement of its habitat. The law, the Federal Aid in Wildlife Restoration Act, is known better as the Pittman-Robertson Act, named after its principal sponsors. It has raised 5.93 billion dollars since its inception. The funds are prorated to the states depending on each state's number of licensed hunters and its geographic area (see http://wsfrprograms.fws.gov/Subpages/GrantPrograms/WR/WR_AppnFormula.pdf).

Annually, hunting license sales average $725 million (2006 = $753 million; 2007 = $764 million; 2008 = $776 million, according to the U.S. Fish and Wildlife Service), excise taxes average $280 million (2007 final apportionment = $266 million; 2008 = $310 million; 2009 = $336 million, according to the U.S. Fish and Wildlife Service), and private donations average $300 million, totaling over $1.3 billion each year for wildlife conservation.

Nearly $25 billion is spent by hunters annually on sporting equipment and businesses, such as lodges, eateries, automobile service stations, and others that benefit from the rippling cycle. This, in turn, results in increased employment and spending, ultimately having an overall $66 billion economic impact that supports almost 600,000 jobs nationwide (Hunting in America, Association of Fish & Wildlife Agencies 2007).

Nearly 74 percent of wildlife conservation funds in the United States come from sportsmen while only 26 percent comes from other sources.

Here are a few examples of how wildlife has propagated, mostly through sportsmen-backed conservation efforts, through the years, comparing earlier estimates to estimated populations in 2009:

White-tailed deer from 500,000 in 1900 to now 32,000,000.

Ducks/waterfowl from very few in 1901 to now 44,000,000.

Rocky Mountain Elk from 41,000 in 1907 to now 1,000,000.

Wild Turkey from 100,000 in the early 1900s to now 7,000,000.

Pronghorn Antelope from 12,000 in the mid-1900s to now 1,100,000.

(Statistical data provided by the National Shooting Sports Foundation, Inc. www.nssf.org)

*"No one but he who has partaken thereof can understand the keen delight of hunting in lonely lands. For him is the joy of the horse well ridden and the rifle well held; for him the long days of toil and hardship, resolutely endured, and crowned at the end with triumph. In after-years, there shall come forever to his mind the memory of endless prairies shimmering in the bright sun; of vast snow-clad wastes lying desolate under gray skies; of the melancholy marshes; of the rush to mighty rivers; of the breath of the evergreen forest in summers; of the crooning of ice-armored pines at the touch of the winds of winter; of cataracts roaring between hoary mountain masses; of all the innumerable sights and sounds of the wilderness; of its immensity and mystery; and of the silences that brood in its still depths."*

**—Teddy Roosevelt**

# THANKS TO THE READER

One that has traveled with me throughout this chronicle should have a broader view of this world we live in; it is much more than hunting stories, as it gets right to the heart of what the world is all about. On the one side it summarizes nature—the wildlife and the vast and varied terrain—but on the other side, and most importantly, the people that share what all nature provides.

This trek through the world might be compared in a small way to Lewis and Clark's Corps of Discovery, which was to discover the unknown, while hunting wildlife continuously for their three years of traveling. Hunting and establishment of wildlife programs propelled my endeavors, while discovering the unknown. Both efforts involved exploring sustainable use of all the land has to offer.

In addition, both efforts involved fellowship with the people encountered, meeting for the first time as strangers, with only minute hostility, most all wanting peace and goodwill. My experiences were proof of President Eisenhower's theorizing that people the world over want peace and love for one another.

My wholehearted thanks go to you who have patiently read this brief summary of my life and hopefully you enjoyed at least some of the tales. Now, may I one more time remind you . . .

"The essence of life is discovering what is on the other side of the mountain. . . ."

—Chris R. Klineburger